STALIN
TRIUMPH AND TRAGEDY

STALIN
TRIUMPH AND TRAGEDY

DMITRI VOLKOGONOV

Edited and Translated from the Russian by
HAROLD SHUKMAN

An Imprint of Prima Publishing

PRIMA PUBLISHING, FORUM, and colophons are trademarks of Prima Communications, Inc.

First published in Great Britain in 1991 by George Weidenfeld & Nicolson Limited, London.

Originally published in the Soviet Union in 1989 under the title *Triyumf i Tragediya: politicheskii portret I.V. Stalina*, 2 volumes, Novosti, Moscow.

This edition is reprinted by permission of Grove Weidenfeld.

Library of Congress Cataloging-in-Publication Data
Volkogonov, Dmitriĭ Antonovich.
      [Triumf i tragediia. English]
      Stalin: triumph and tragedy / Dmitri Volkogonov.
          p.   cm.
      Originally published: New York: Grove Weidenfeld, 1991.
      Includes bibliographical references and index.
      ISBN 1-55958-216-2
      ISBN 0-7615-0718-3
      1. Stalin, Josef, 1879–1953. 2. Soviet Union—History—1917–
3. Heads of state—Soviet Union—Biography. I. Title.
[DK268.S8V5613 1992]
947.084'2'092—dc20
[B]   92-20674
                                        CIP

96 97 98 99 00 01 AA 10 9 8 7 6 5 4 3 2

Printed in the United States of America

HOW TO ORDER
Single copies may be ordered from Prima Publishing, P.O. Box 1260BK, Rocklin, CA 95677; telephone (916) 632-4400. Quantity discounts are also available. On your letterhead, include information concerning the intended use of the books and the number of books you wish to purchase.

CONTENTS

10 THE CLIMAX OF THE CULT

11 THE RELICS OF STALINISM

Illustrations

Translator's Note

It is virtually impossible to transliterate all Russian names consistently, except by means of a variety of specialized annotations which would require their own glossary. It seems pedantic to insist on Aleksandr or Trotskii (or Trockij or Trotskiy) when Alexander and Trotsky are readily recognizable. Bibliographical references, however, whether within the body of the text or in the end notes, appear as they are commonly found in library catalogues, in order to ensure proper identification. The subject of this book presents a different problem of transliteration. The English form of Stalin's first name is Joseph, and 'Joseph Stalin' is customary. Since, however, he is frequently mentioned or addressed here in the full Russian form of first name and patronymic, it was felt that 'Joseph Vissarionovich' was odd, and that 'Iosif Vissarionovich' had the merit of greater accuracy and also that it conformed more closely to the initials 'I.V.' with which he often signed papers. We have therefore settled on Iosif.

Professional revolutionaries commonly adopted aliases, or 'party nicknames', usually when first signing an illegal publication or following their first arrest and interrogation by the Tsarist secret police. Thus, Vladimir Ulyanov adopted the name Lenin, derived from the name of the river Lena in Siberia where he was exiled, while Leon Bronshtein took the name of one of his prison warders and became Trotsky. Some appear to have adopted names to create an image: e.g. Vyacheslav Skyrabin became Molotov, or 'the Hammer', while Lev Rozenfeld became Kamenev, or 'man of stone', and Iosif Dzhugashvili chose Stalin, or 'man of steel'. Others simply sought anonymity in ordinary Russian names, while Jews, who were disproportionately numerous in the movement, found in a Russian pseudonym the added advantage of ethnic anonymity in the face of the anti-Semitic police force. Where appropriate, we have indicated the real or original name.

Preface

The writing of Soviet history, like the Soviet Union itself, is going through the most profound changes. Virtually every principle and axiom of the last sixty years has been challenged and rejected. Radical Soviet scholars have even begun to peel away the gold leaf on Lenin's halo, and many are saying that the mid-nineteenth-century doctrine of Marxism is irrelevant to today's needs.

The mood for truth-telling was first aroused in 1956, when Khrushchev made his 'secret speech' to the Twentieth Party Congress condemning Stalin for the bloody purges of the 1930s. But it lasted only a brief time, as the self-serving régime of Brezhnev, fearful of undermining its own legitimacy, shut down the debate. No more could be said on the subject (except by dissidents) until the gerontocracy had died off. By 1985, Brezhnev, Andropov and Chernenko had departed the scene and a new generation, personified by the fifty-four-year-old Gorbachev, was on the threshold of power. Men who had been galvanized in 1956 by the belief that the system could be reformed, modernized and made efficient now emerged, bringing out into the open the ideas they had nurtured for thirty years. The Soviet Union entered the period of its perestroika, or reconstruction.

Falteringly, but then with greater assurance, the new régime also introduced 'glasnost', meaning in effect telling the truth, ending the Stalinist practice of manipulating public opinion with lies of all kinds, and being open with the public over matters that the party had hitherto regarded as its own property not to be shared. It began in the spring of 1986 with the disaster at the Chernobyl nuclear power station, which spilled over into the lives of Western Europeans and wrung unaccustomed frankness from the Soviet authorities. Once the chink in the curtain had appeared, once the state had openly admitted its imperfection, Soviet intellectuals began cautiously to test the new climate. Manuscripts that had long lain in drawers were brought out and offered to editors who were as yet far from sure what reaction to expect when they were published. Censorship was still active – and indeed remained at least notionally in being until the summer of 1990 – yet authors who had been encouraged by the spirit of 1956 to write truthfully about 1917 and after began to emerge. Anatoly Rybakov did not know until April 1987 if his novel (written twenty years earlier) about Stalin, *Children of the Arbat*, would be published in the

Soviet Union, but it was, and gradually authentic, unfictionalized memoirs began to appear. In early 1988, beginning with Nikolai Bukharin, the Bolshevik Old Guard that had been exterminated by Stalin as 'enemies of the people' were posthumously rehabilitated and their trials officially denounced as based on false evidence. The names of 'non-persons' could be mentioned without abuse, and the process has continued unabated ever since, culminating in early 1990 in open and 'de-ideologized' debate about Trotsky.

The time has long been ripe for an authoritative, thoroughly documented study of Stalin and his times. Until only the last year or two, most of the revelations were being made not by the professional historians but by journalists and novelists, and indeed the historians, to whom the archives remained – and largely remain – closed, were criticizing themselves for this state of affairs. Dmitri Volkogonov was not, however, a typical member of the intelligentsia: he was a Colonel General with responsibility for the army's political education and its publishing activities. In this position he latterly had unique access to archives, he had talked to long-pensioned-off party bosses and army top brass with personal experience of the Stalin era, of the trials and the purges, of the mood at Staff Headquarters during the war, of Stalin's personal behaviour and his family life.

Among the archival collections which Volkogonov has used in this book, the most important is that of the Communist Party, which is held by the Institute of Marxism-Leninism. Here, for the first time, we are given an insight, among other things, into the debates at the secret Central Committee plenums held throughout the period which, better than almost any other documents, give a flavour of the mood among the leadership. Army archives and NKVD archives provide a unique picture of the mentality and behaviour of senior apparatchiks and military leaders. Interviews with Stalin's aides and their families add enormously to our knowledge of how the dictator lived. It is chilling to read Stalin's laconic comments on the lists of death sentences handed to him by his minions and his total disregard of the most heartrending pleas for mercy sent to him by people as varied as a lonely peasant woman and Lenin's 'favourite' theoretician, Nikolai Bukharin. Volkogonov has gone through Stalin's personal library and made use of the marginal jottings and underlinings which fill the books, in order to throw further light on Stalin's way of thinking. While other Soviet historians are still hammering on the doors of the archives firmly locked against them, it is doubtful if another book, based on so wide a range and rich a collection of documents, will be written on this period.

Born in 1928 in Chita, Eastern Siberia, Volkogonov is the son of an agrarian specialist father and schoolteacher mother. In 1937 his father was arrested and, as was later learned, shot. The rest of the family were then exiled to Krasnoyarsk in Western Siberia. In 1945, Volkogonov joined the army and, despite his politically dubious background, quickly rose in rank, entering the Lenin Military Academy in Moscow in 1961, where he attained a Ph.D. and a professorship. Transferred in 1970 to the propaganda department of the army, he acquired a reputation as a hardliner who advocated the ideological indoctrination of the army and he wrote numerous books on this subject.

At the same time, however, he was gathering material for a book on the Stalin era which would not be limited to laying all the blame on the dictator and his minions. Instead, it would identify as the cause of the Soviet Union's parlous state the lethal combination of Lenin's authoritarian communism, Stalin's ruthless drive for personal omnipotence and his criminal manipulation of internal party rivalries and inertia, and the passive character of the Russians and their love of a strong leader, their ignorance of democracy and absence of individual, personal autonomy.

Like many of the most radical figures in Soviet public life, Volkogonov has admitted publicly that he no longer believes in the dogmas and myths he once blindly accepted. He acknowledges that he did not emerge, like the dissidents he admires, as an open advocate of truth and justice. Also, like many others now in the forefront of the reform movement, he admits to having lived two mental lives, pursuing a successful career in military education, while gathering material on the evils of the past as assiduously as any persecuted dissident. He began writing his book in 1978 and completed the first part of it in 1985.

Such a high degree of disaffection could not continue for long without consequences. In 1985 he was warned that his historical research was incompatible with his work in the Main Political Administration, and that he must choose one or the other. He opted to become director of the army's Institute of Military History, where he completed his book on Stalin. There, too, he assembled full details on the purged officer corps, and collected hitherto unpublished documents for a full-scale study of Trotsky, now complete. He is preparing to embark on a reinterpretation of Lenin.

One of the most striking features of the new Soviet scene has been the emergence of journalists and historians, economists and physicists, philosophers, musicologists and poets as radical politicians, many of them party members who had been inspired in the 1950s and who kept their heads down during the Brezhnev era. Like them, but rather singular among the senior military, Volkogonov, a People's Deputy in the Russian parliament, has openly espoused the political philosophy of liberal democracy, market economics and a new, freely negotiated charter of union for the republics, or their independence if that is what they want. In July 1990 he called for official condemnation of Stalin's crimes, and a month later, the Soviet government issued a decree condemning Stalin for 'violating the basic civil, social and economic rights of the Soviet people and depriving them of freedoms which a democratic society regards as natural and inalienable'.

As for the Communist Party, Volkogonov claims that it lacks the ability to adapt itself to a democratic régime, that it has lost the political initiative to the democratic groups which are more in touch with people's needs. He warned the Twenty-Eighth Party Congress in July 1990 that if it did not reconcile itself to the twin principles of the rule of law and the primacy of democracy, and if it failed to take up the challenge and compete for power on equal terms with other parties, it would suffer the same fate as that of the Communist Parties of Eastern Europe in 1989.

The theme on which Volkogonov has based both this book and his activity as a politician is that of conscience. Failure to exercise conscience led the Bolsheviks to deprive the people of power, to go along with Stalin's blatantly false claim to be serving the cause of socialism and to countenance the most horrendous crimes against society in the history of Russia. The test of conscience today in the Soviet Union is to be able to admit that the country's achievements over the last seventy years, such as they are, could have been accomplished and indeed surpassed by different methods, different politics, different leaders, and that any of these alternatives would have consigned the Communist régime to the utopian fringe.

Harold Shukman
St Antony's College, Oxford
August 1990

Acknowledgements

The author expresses his profound thanks to those colleagues who gave their unstinting help in the preparation of this book, especially A. P. Balashov, F. D. Bobkov, G. A. Volkogonova, I. Ya. Vyrodov, N. N. Yefimov, I. P. Kalinina, Yu. I. Korablev, B. I. Kaptelov, E. I. Katsman, N. G. Fokina, G. G. Chernobrovkin.

Foreword

Stalin was dying. Lying on the dining-room floor of his dacha at Kuntsevo, he had abandoned the attempt to get up, only lifting his left hand from time to time, as if begging for help. His half-closed eyes could not hide his look of desperation as he gazed towards the door. Feebly, his lips mouthed silent words. Several hours had elapsed since the stroke, yet there was nobody with him. Finally, alarmed by the absence of any sign of life within the house, his bodyguards gingerly entered the dining room. They were not empowered to call the doctors at once. One of the most powerful figures in human history could not count on them for this, for it required Beria's personal intervention. When at last Beria was found, he thought Stalin was merely having a sound sleep after a late, heavy supper, and it was only after ten or twelve hours that the terrified physicians were brought to examine the dying leader.

It was a profoundly symbolic, deeply ironic way to die. The leader, in his death agony for many hours, was not able to summon help when he needed it. And this was the man, the demi-god, who with a few words could send millions of people from one end of the country to the other. Now he was a hostage of the bureaucratic 'order' he had himself perfected.

The invisible line between being and non-being can be crossed in one direction only. Even leaders cannot retrace their steps. Can Stalin have known that he faced not merely physical death, but political extinction as well? For his contemporaries his death was a great tragedy. They did not think then that this man regarded the deaths of millions as nothing more than a state secret. His death left his successors the endless task of trying to understand what it was he had created, and of arguing fiercely over the 'enigma' of Stalin himself. His death did not exonerate him. All his actions and crimes were to be submitted to the judgement of history. Myths collapse of themselves, but they can only be fully dispelled by the truth.

Only Stalin knew the whole truth about himself. He liked things to be in black and white, yet he did everything to ensure that his life story would be told in bright colours. I don't know if he was aware of the ancient Roman law of 'the judgement of memory', according to which everything that was not to a given emperor's taste had to be consigned to oblivion by the historians. In any event, that law merely underlined the futility of attempting to regiment human memory. Memory lives (or dies) according to quite different laws. History is always made afresh. It has no rough drafts. Only in the mind can one 'rewind' the past, like a film. Stalin understood this and he exerted himself to ensure that no unnecessary frames were left in the chronicle. People knew about him only what he wanted them to know.

Losing Lenin at the crucial moment, when the historic decision had to be made about what methods should be used to build socialism, the Communist Party entered a phase of fierce internal strife. The Leninist old guard was not sufficiently alert to the danger Stalin posed both to the party and the still insecure state. This led the new political administrators to turn increasingly to punitive, rather than constructive measures. We know now that Stalin would not be the subject of a biography such as this, had he not resorted to force as the chief and decisive instrument for achieving his political, social and economic plans. The change of political direction, which began at the end of the 1920s and became more sharply etched after the Seventeenth Party Congress of 1934, ushered in a period of bitter years, during which only the great charge of social energy generated by the October Revolution, and the party's loyalty to Leninism, kept the people from doubting socialist values and from stopping the process of restructuring the world which Lenin had begun. It is therefore not surprising that assessments of Stalin's personality should undergo major alteration as the historical truth has emerged.

Most people today, when they think of Stalin, remember the tragic year of 1937 with its repressions and its trampling of human values. Yet to be precise, what we think of as 1937 began rather on 1 December 1934, the day Kirov was murdered, and its outlines may have been prefigured earlier, in the late 1920s. With Stalin's knowledge, a monstrous abscess of illegality began to form. There can be no forgiveness for those responsible, but we must also remember that in those years the Dnieper hydroelectric plant and the metallurgical complex of Magnitogorsk were built, and Stakhanov and his like were performing their labours. It was then that the patriotism of the Soviet people grew, reaching its peak in the Great Patriotic War. For these reasons, when we condemn Stalin for his crimes, it is politically and intellectually wrong, and morally dishonest, to deny the achievements of the system and its possibilities in principle. These achievements were made not thanks to but in spite of the Stalinist way of thinking and doing. More could have been accomplished had more democratic methods been applied. In condemning Stalin and his accomplices, we should not mechanically extend our judgement to the millions of ordinary people whose faith in the sincerity of the revolution's ideals remained unshaken.

All his life, Stalin tried (with some success) to turn one of his weaknesses into a virtue. Already during the revolution, when he had to visit a factory or a regiment or attend a street meeting or mix with a crowd, he would experience a sense of insecurity and fear which in time he learned to hide. He did not enjoy speaking before an audience, nor was he good at it. Though his style was simple and clear, without flights of fancy, catchy phrases or platform histrionics, the heavy Georgian accent and monotonous delivery combined to make his speeches unexpressive. It was therefore not surprising that he addressed meetings and demonstrations less than any other member of Lenin's entourage. He preferred drawing up resolutions and instructions, or writing letters and newspaper reports on political events. He was a mediocre writer whose arguments were both fairly consistent and invariably categorical. His newspaper articles are black or white, with no intermediate tones. The Latin clarity of his frank articles was perhaps one of their attractive qualities.

Later on, Stalin became accustomed to the conference platform, but the circumstances were different. His audience now would listen to his quiet, level voice, in a ringing silence waiting to be sundered by their deafening applause. His speeches now were more in the nature of the ritual incantations of a priest. Stalin made it a rule not to come into direct contact with the masses. With rare exceptions, he never visited a factory or collective farm, never travelled to any of the republics, or to the front during the war. His voice would resound from time to time from the pinnacle of the pyramid, while the millions listened in holy terror at its foot. He turned his remoteness into an attribute of the cult. It must always be borne in mind that he was a master at passing off his mistakes, oversights and crimes as achievements, successes, farsightedness, wisdom and constant concern for the people.

My work is based on party documents and materials from numerous holdings: the Central Party Archives, the USSR Supreme Court Archives, the Central State Archives of the Army, the Ministry of Defence Archives, the Armed Forces General Staff Archives, the archives of a number of museums and so on.* On the military aspect of Stalin's activities, I became acquainted with many interesting, original and unpublished documents in the Ministry of Defence. A cursory glance at Stalin's decisions, in army documents and the recollections of his contemporaries, tells us that often he did not believe in what he was advocating. For instance, reading the draft sentence of the Military Collegium of the Supreme Court in the case of Generals D. G. Pavlov, V. E. Klimovskikh, A. T. Grigoryev and A. A. Korobkov, who had been charged with being involved in an 'anti-Soviet conspiracy and the intended collapse of the command of the Western front', Stalin scribbled: 'None of this nonsense.' The words 'anti-Soviet conspiracy', and 'conspiratorial aims' were deleted and in their place was written: 'showed cowardice, lacked authority and efficiency, permitted the breakdown of command'. Although these were still unjust charges, and the sentence issued on 22 June 1941 harsh in the extreme, Stalin no longer felt it was appropriate to indulge in the old game of 'conspirators', in the face of mortal danger to himself and the country.

Gazing at Stalin's orders, written in bold, legible strokes, as a rule in red or

* See Notes.

blue pencil, I have asked myself where the deep springs of his irrationality, harshness and cunning lay. In the copious nourishment of the dogmatic religious education he received in early life? Or in the painful sense of intellectual inadequacy that he felt at the party congresses in London and Stockholm, as he sat and listened to brilliant speeches being made by Lenin, Plekhanov, Axelrod, Dan and Martov? Perhaps his irrationality stemmed from the embitterment caused by the seven arrests and five escapes he endured before October 1917? From the age of nineteen, he did nothing but hide underground, carry out the instructions of party committees, be arrested, change his name, obtain false passports and move from place to place. He was never long in prison, as he would invariably escape and go into hiding. Yet the idea of escaping abroad never occurred to him.

My work on the book was much helped by material from *Pravda* over a thirty-year period, as well as the journals *Bolshevik*, *Politrabotnik* (Political Worker), and many others that were published in the 1920s. Abroad, there is a mass of literature on Stalin. Some of it – for example, the works of Giuseppe Boffa, Louis Aragon and Anna Louise Strong – give a fairly accurate picture. There are also dozens of works published to discredit – with Stalin's 'help' – the very notion of socialism. Without realizing it, Stalin did far more to blacken the name of socialism than anything written by Leonard Schapiro, Isaac Deutscher, Robert Tucker or Robert Conquest. Of special interest is the testimony of foreign statesmen who met Stalin, for example, Franklin D. Roosevelt, Winston Churchill, Charles de Gaulle, Mao Tse-tung, Enver Hoxha and, of course, the memoirs of his daughter, Svetlana Alliluyeva.

I have studied the writings of Stalin's opponents inside the country, such as Trotsky, Zinoviev, Kamenev, Bukharin, Rykov, Tomsky and others, all of them Lenin's comrades-in-arms. None of them would have thought of himself as a protégé of Stalin, unlike Kaganovich, Molotov, Voroshilov, Malenkov, Zhdanov and other new men who rose to take their places. In this respect, Stalin observed the ancient rule of dictators: the people he himself advanced would show more loyalty and would not aspire to the top job.

Trotsky, Zinoviev, Kamenev, Bukharin and the others were more widely known than Stalin at the beginning of the 1920s. During the years of revolution and civil war, Trotsky was incomparably more popular in the party and the country as a whole than Stalin. A recognized leader of the October Revolution, and a theoretician who by 1927 had published twenty-one volumes, Trotsky has gone down in history as the creator of the Red Army. He had considerable talent as a writer and often posed before the mirror of history, as he attempted to justify his ambition to lead the party. He appears to have loved the idea of himself in the revolution more than the revolution itself. Reading his correspondence, I was amazed to find that as early as the civil war period, he was worrying about what history would say of him. Admiring letters to him, notes handed to him during his numerous speeches, lists of diplomats seeking an audience with him, newspaper reports of his actions – everything was carefully filed away and preserved. Trotsky was convinced, and not without reason, that after Lenin's death the leadership might pass to him.

Trotsky aimed most of his critical arrows, whether directly or obliquely, at Stalin, though it is true that most of them were launched after his expulsion from the Soviet Union. His characterization of Stalin as 'our party's most outstanding mediocrity' is well known. On the other hand, Trotsky was apt to make similar remarks about other opponents. He described Zinoviev as a 'bothersome mediocrity', Vandervelde (chairman of the Socialist International who in 1917 wrote on the Russian revolution) as a 'brilliant mediocrity', and Tsereteli (a Menshevik member of the Kerensky government during 1917) as a 'talented and honest mediocrity'. Following his expulsion from the Soviet Union, and to the very end of his life, Trotsky was possessed by a single, abiding and obsessive passion, namely, his hatred for Stalin, as his last and unfinished book, called *Stalin*, shows. Trotsky, it is true, asserts that personal motives played no part in the book: 'Our paths diverged so long ago and so far, and in my eyes he is so much the instrument of historical forces that are alien and hostile to me, that my feelings towards him differ little from those I have towards Hitler or the Mikado. The personal element burned out long ago.'[1] Nevertheless, no one else wrote so caustically and with such a degree of caricature and invective about Stalin. But nor did anyone else do so much to expose Stalin.

On the day Lenin died, Stalin sent the following cable to Trotsky who was in the south: 'Tell Comrade Trotsky that Comrade Lenin died suddenly on 21 January at six hours fifty. Death caused by paralysis of respiratory centre. Funeral Saturday 26 January. Stalin.'[2] In signing the message, Stalin must have been thinking that the hour of pitiless struggle for the leadership was at hand. But did he know that even when he had overcome Trotsky, he would not be rid of him? The methods of an authoritarian bureaucracy, using coercion and 'tightening the screw', which Stalin would apply, were precisely what Trotsky advocated. This may be one of the sources of the impending tragedy. Trotsky's political struggle with Stalin, which went on up to the moment of Trotsky's murder in August 1940, deeply influenced Stalin's outlook, for Stalin always regarded Trotsky as his chief personal enemy.

I have used the testimony of many people who either met Stalin or were in some way drawn into the whirlpool of events caused by his decisions. Much was yielded in conversations with former Central Committee staff, commissars, NKVD people, senior army figures, whom fate brought face to face with the General Secretary and whose lives were all too often changed in the most tragic way by a decision of the 'leader'. Following my articles in *Pravda* and *Literaturnaya Gazeta*, I received some three thousand letters, many from people who had had the most appalling lives.

My book is called *Triumph and Tragedy* to suggest how the triumph of one man became a tragedy for a whole people. In his speech at the Twentieth Party Congress, Khrushchev put the problem in his own way: 'We cannot say that his were the actions of a mad despot. He believed he was acting in the interests of the party and the working masses and in defence of the gains of the revolution. That was the tragedy!' I think Khrushchev's emphasis was misplaced. His evaluation justifies Stalin. In the name of unlimited power Stalin committed monstrous crimes, but Khrushchev did not see this as the tragedy.

Stalin soon became accustomed to using force as an obligatory attribute of limitless power. It seems logical to assume that the punitive machine, which he put into top gear in the late 1930s, seized the imagination not only of lower level functionaries, but of Stalin himself. Possibly the slide into coercion as a universal method went through various stages. First, the struggle against real enemies, and they were real enough; then the liquidation of his personal enemies, who also existed; in the next stage, the machine functioned under its own momentum, and, finally, force was seen as a test of loyalty to the leader and orthodoxy. The shadow of an external threat created a siege mentality in the population which peaked in 1937 and which was the direct result of force taking precedence over law, the displacement of popular power by cult surrogates.

One could show one's orthodoxy, blind faith and allegiance to the leader by making shameless accusations of 'wrecking', 'double-dealing' and 'espionage'. How was it possible even to imagine that every single member of the Politburo, appointed in May 1924 at the Thirteenth Party Congress, with the sole exception of Stalin, would turn out to be an 'enemy'? Stalin liquidated his 'enemies' and the waves rolled on and on. An evil force triumphed. It is hard to explain why he needed to continue 'weeding out' the best people after he had got rid of his rivals. As a matter of fact, earlier than most, some Bolsheviks in the NKVD saw the imminent danger of universal suspicion and repression; still, from among their ranks alone 23,000 people were victims of the rampant lawlessness.

In the final analysis, however, even the worst that history could do could not prevent the people from creating in their own country something that brought them closer to realizing their high ideals. Even in the worst years, belief in humanist values did not die in the hearts of millions of Soviet people. The tragedy lay in the fact that they took Stalin as the symbol and human embodiment of socialism. If lies are repeated often enough, after all, they come to seem like the truth. In the popular mind, deification of the leader justified all the negative effects that accompanied the seeking out of 'enemies', while it also ascribed all successes to the wisdom and will of one man. Stalin, moreover, became adept at using propaganda when promoting his grandiose schemes. Taking big decisions, especially at large meetings, he liked to cite the socialist classics, though in this respect he revealed a typical human weakness. Most people, even the omnipotent, need some ideological prop, either doctrinal authority or the timeless ideas of their great predecessors, even if in this case it was often nothing more than intellectual camouflage. The leader's triumph and the people's tragedy found expression in the dogmatism and bureaucratism of the system, the omnipotence of the apparatus and the brainwashing of millions, but also in the patriotism and internationalism of the Soviet people, in their genuine civic-mindedness and heroic endeavours.

My work was much helped by the memoirs of such famed Soviet army commanders as I. Kh. Bagramyan, A. M. Vasilievsky, A. G. Golovko, A. E. Yeremenko, G. K. Zhukov, I. S. Konev, N. G. Kuznetsov, K. A. Meretskov, K. S. Moskalenko, K. K. Rokossovsky, S. M. Shtemenko, and others. True, these accounts were written at a time when much was still unknown about Stalin and when, after the Twenty-Second Party Congress, Stalinism was to all intents and purposes put out of bounds to full and frank analysis. The military, especially the top echelons, had borne the full brunt of Stalin's cruelty, but, apart from A. V. Gorbatov and a few others who managed in time to describe what they had been through, none was able to reveal everything. The topic was virtually prohibited. There is another side to the problem. When the war began Stalin was compelled against his will to stop the repressions inside the country. The army commanders concerned themselves in their memoirs chiefly with the military aspect and with the rôle Stalin's political authority played in beating Fascism. This no doubt explains why most of the military writers show Stalin in a positive light only and leave out of the picture much of what they had themselves suffered at his hands. And several tens of thousands of military personnel, who on the eve of the war had fallen into the bloody meat-grinder of the purge, perished. We now know that at the beginning of the war, Stalin repeatedly resorted to harsh punishment of many military men, using them as scapegoats for the heavy Soviet losses.

Looking back, one is astounded by the forbearance of the Soviet people, above all of the Russian people. Where does it come from? Two hundred and fifty years of Tatar dominion, or the succession of wars for liberation and freedom? Or having to struggle with the Russian winter and the great expanses of territory? Or was it bred of the wisdom of historical experience, their faith that they were in the right and their loyalty to their historical tradition? Perhaps it was the conviction that they had taken the right course in 1917. Although they did not realize it until later, the people could not but be humiliated by the near-religious rituals which glorified the man who ruled the country. A collection of the paeans of praise, ludicrous hymns of welcome and letters to Stalin calling him 'father', 'the Sun', 'wise leader', 'immortal genius', 'great helmsman', 'unbending commander', would make a worthy monument to this humiliation. The bureaucratic mind excelled in inventing epithets, in disregard of the fact that they were a direct affront to the people's dignity.

Is it totally unrealistic to suggest that, were it not for the political vacuum that followed Lenin's death, the socialist development of society could have been achieved without the distortions caused by Stalin and his accomplices in the 1930s, 1940s and 1950s? The tragedy was not inevitable. Of course, it is easier for us today to speak of the possible alternatives than it was to make the choice back in the 1920s. It is easier to analyse the circumstances than to deal with them. 'The historian is always right to compare his hypotheses with things as they were,' Jean Jaurès wrote. 'He is right to say: "Here are the people's mistakes, and here are the party's," and to imagine how events would have turned out had those mistakes not been made.'[3] Alternatives were available.

From Lenin's death until the beginning of the 1930s, Stalin had the reputation of being one of the harshest and most wilful of the leaders. He did not have the qualities to replace Lenin, but nor did any of the others. Intellectually and morally, he was no match for most of the leaders of the revolution, but in the struggle for succession it was purposefulness, political will and cunning that counted. Despite his 'imperfections', Stalin had something the others lacked, namely his ability to use the party apparatus to the maximum in order to achieve his ends. The apparatus was in his view the ideal instrument of power. And not every Bolshevik had heard of Lenin's warnings about Stalin.

Stalin succeeded temporarily in masking his own negative qualities, after the delegates to the Thirteenth Congress had heard Lenin's view of him, and this helped him to secure the support of the majority of the party. In these circumstances, the chances of the other leaders were not high. Many senior party figures at first simply did not take full account of Stalin and when they did, it was too late.

Stalin, moreover, was a great actor. He acted a host of parts with consummate skill: the modest leader, the fighter for the purity of party ideals, and later the leader and father of the people, great commander, theorist, connoisseur of the arts, prophet. But more than anything, Stalin tried to play the part of the dedicated pupil and comrade-in-arms of the great Lenin. All this gradually brought him popularity in the party and the country as a whole.

The issue is less one of personalities, however, than the democratic potential – however flawed – which Lenin had just begun to build but which was not preserved. Decades later, we are still trying to identify the man who could have been an alternative to Stalin. Most probably, the party's leading core of Leninists ought to have carried out Lenin's 'Testament'. Yet the old guard showed an unaccountable confusion and shortsightedness, instead of expressing the collective idea and collective will. If democratic safety devices for the defence of society had been created, notably in the form of a genuine collective leadership, then the question of finding an outstanding figure as leader would not have been so decisive. If, for instance, the party rules had fixed and held to a precise period of tenure for the General Secretary and other elected posts, then it is possible that there would have been no Stalin cult. As it was, the fate of the country depended too heavily on the historic question of who should stand at the helm.

Despite the fact that, in the formal sense, Stalin's authority was never tested, he virtually abandoned Lenin's notion of socialism. Plutarch's comment comes to mind: 'When destiny raises a base character by acts of great importance, it reveals his lack of substance.'[4] What we call Stalinism provides just such a case. One can argue over the legitimacy of the concept, but one cannot get away from the indisputable fact that a specific social phenomenon stands behind it. It arose because of the deformation of the democratic principles, without which socialism loses both its effectiveness and its appeal.

In my opinion, Stalinism is synonymous with alienation of the working people from power, the installation of a multi-faceted bureaucracy and the inculcation of dogmatic formulas in the public mind. The exercise of autocracy resulted in a specific kind of alienation which in turn gave rise to general apathy, a weakening of the real meaning of socialist values and a dampening of the movement's dynamism. Stalin cast his huge, baneful shadow over every aspect of our lives, and it has not been easy to liberate ourselves from that bureaucratic and dogmatic eclipse.

While it is true that socialist ideals were preserved by the people, it is also true that they have never lost their faith in the 'Russian idea'. The countless attempts to introduce reform have usually been met with a powerful reactionary response. From the Decembrists in 1825 to Bukharin in the 1920s and Khrushchev in the 1950s, the reformers have suffered defeat. It is important to remember this. The fact that Stalin has been knocked off his pedestal does not mean that Stalinism has been eradicated, and one cannot preclude the possibility that some form of equally baneful neo-Stalinism could be restored. This is not a prophecy, merely a warning from history.

1

THE GLOW OF OCTOBER

'There can be no revolution without conscience.'
– Jean Jaurès

CHAPTER 1

A Portrait

By the beginning of 1917 Iosif Vissarionovich Dzhugashvili, or Stalin as he was by then, was thirty-seven. He had been living for several years in Stylaya Kureika in the Turukhansk region on the Arctic Circle. As howling blizzards piled snow up to the roof of his hut, he had plenty of time for thought, time to let his mind wander to the more memorable moments in his life. To December 1905, for instance, when he first met Vladimir Ilyich Lenin at the party conference in Tammerfors. He had attended party congresses in Stockholm and London and observed the art of politics in action, with opponents seeking compromise and standing up for their principles, and noisy debates interspersed with friendly conversation during the breaks. This always amazed him.

His rare trips abroad had left him with the vaguely uneasy feeling of an awkward outsider who couldn't compete in brilliant repartee and witty conversation with the likes of Plekhanov, Axelrod or Martov. Irritated and intellectually frustrated whenever he met such people, it was then that he had begun to harbour his lasting hostility for the émigré life, for foreign parts and for the intelligentsia, who argued endlessly in cheap cafés and smoke-filled rooms in flea-bitten small hotels and held forth on the different schools of philosophy and economic theory.

Stalin's life before October had been punctuated by seven arrests and five escapes from tsarist gaols or internal exile. The future leader did not care to reminisce in public about that time in his life. He would never refer to his part in the armed robberies – 'expropriations' – that he carried out to replenish the Bolshevik Party's coffers, or about the time in Baku he had called for 'unification with the Mensheviks at all costs', or about his first, pitiful literary efforts. Once, he remembered one of his early poems, written when he was a seminary student of sixteen or seventeen. It was one he was particularly fond of and it had even been published in the newspaper *Iveria*. Evoking memories of the Caucasus, his native region, the verses intensified his despair, but also aroused vague hopes. As he recited – to his own surprise – in a near whisper, as if he were praying, his landlady twice poked her head round the door to peep in amazement at her Caucasian lodger. A guttering candle at his elbow, Stalin was sitting with an open book on his lap, gazing at the blank, ice-covered window. He had long ago left behind the naïve poems of his youth, together with everything else considered sentimental by the intelligentsia. Even his mother rarely received a letter from him. After a hard childhood, and a life underground and always on the run, he had become cold, callous and suspicious.

He had learnt to drive away unpleasant thoughts, but the memory of the face of his wife, who had been dead already ten years, ravaged by typhus, always hovered somewhere in the background. He recalled their being secretly married in St David's church in June 1906 by his fellow seminarist Khristofor Tkhinvoleli. The beautiful Yekaterina Svanidze – Kato – her big eyes full of dedication, had gazed lovingly at this husband who would vanish for long periods and then suddenly turn up again. Their life together was brief. Disease deprived Stalin of probably the one human being he had really loved. Photographs of her funeral show him, short and thin, his shock of hair uncombed, standing at the graveside with a look of genuine grief on his face.

The seeds of harshness and callousness that had been planted in him in childhood took firm root. Living the life of a wanted man from the age of nineteen, he had learnt much, not least cunning and thrift, and how to wait. The withdrawal and reserve that were noticeable in him already in his early years, became in time a cold lack of compassion. He nevertheless learnt to wear a mask when he was among people and to give the impression that he was a composed and even affable sort of man.

Why did the young Dzhugashvili become a revolutionary? Was it because he had once upon a time been associated with the few fragments of intellectual life at the Gori Theological School and Tiflis Seminary where he had studied? Was it dissatisfaction with the seclusion of religious life that drew him to people of rebellious turn of mind? Perhaps his eyes were opened to broader issues by 'The ABC of Marxism', a popular pamphlet that came into his hands? No one knows for sure. In any event, had he not made the decisive, if still nebulous, shift from his religious leanings to secular, heretical views at the turn of the century, some little Georgian village would one day have received him as a young Orthodox priest, the spiritual pastor of a human flock. His monotonous life would have been sheltered from the world by the majestic mountains of Georgia and the minor cares of an impoverished parish, a brood of his own children and daydreams about bustling Tiflis. How could he know, as the son of a poor shoemaker, that the whim of fate and force of circumstance would one day make him something infinitely more than a village priest?

Before 1917 no one would have guessed that the underground revolutionary would rise rapidly after 1922 to the peak of power. Shoving aside the solid ranks of Lenin's comrades, he quickly emerged among the leaders and then took the lead. It did not occur to anyone that after Lenin's death this group of famous Bolsheviks would soon begin to melt away and disappear. The higher Stalin rose, the fewer of those who had helped Lenin to light the torch of revolution remained. Before the revolution Stalin was possibly better known to various branches of the police department than he was to other rev- olutionaries. At every contact with Dzhugashvili, the gendarmes would photo- graph him in full face and profile. However slack they may have been at guarding their prisoners, the gendarmes' descriptions of their 'state criminals' were meticulous. Each photograph bore the legend that Dzhugashvili was thin, had thick, black hair, a thin moustache but no beard, the marks of smallpox on his face, an oval head, a straight but not high forehead, arched eyebrows, sunken hazel eyes with a yellow tint, a straight nose, that at 5 feet 4 inches he was of average height, had a pointed chin, soft voice, a birthmark on his left ear, that his left arm was withered, and that the second and third toes of his left foot had grown together. The guardians of state security under Stalin, when he became powerful, would not trouble themselves with such trivialities. Nor would any political prisoner during his time ever manage five escapes, as he had. When it came to trying to discover the fate of Stalin's countless victims, the birthmarks and precise height of 'enemies of the people' wouldn't matter. In criteria and scale, the pictures would be very different.

Stalin's physical traits are perhaps less interesting than the political and moral features he bore in 1917. While he may not have been a villain from childhood, it is nevertheless important to know what sort of childhood he had, if we are to understand his personality as an adult.

Little is known of his childhood, and he himself was not apt to expand on it. His parents, Yekaterina and Vissarion Dzhugashvili, were poor peasants who later on became poor town-dwellers in Gori. Of their three sons, Mikhail and Georgii died before they were a year old, leaving only Iosif, or Soso as he was known. But he, too, almost died at the age of five from the smallpox that would make a regular appearance in his police files as the cause of his facial disfigurement. According to I. Iremashvili, a Georgian Menshevik who knew the family, Stalin's father, the shoemaker, was a heavy drinker who frequently beat his wife and son. Before falling into drunken sleep, he would box the ears of the wilful child who plainly had no love for his father. The undeserved punishment he received hardened him, and he soon learned cunning ways to avoid these encounters. His mother, on the other hand, was dedicated body and soul to her son. It was only thanks to her insistence and enormous effort that a place was found for Soso in the theological school and later in the seminary. The family discord continued and in due course the parents separ- ated, with the father moving to Tiflis where he died alone in a lodging house and was buried at the expense of the state.

Stalin left the family home when he became a professional revolutionary. It appears that after 1903 he may not have seen his mother more than four or five times. She stayed with him in Moscow for the first time the year he became General Secretary and he saw her for the last time in 1935. Her desperate desire, illiterate though she was, to help her son better himself had given Stalin his first chance in life, though he seems never to have reflected on this. At a great age, two years after their last meeting, in July of the terrible year of 1937, Stalin's mother died peacefully.

The German writer, Emil Ludwig, asked Stalin in 1931 what had first pushed him into a revolutionary frame of mind. 'Was it perhaps bad treatment at the hands of your parents?'

'No,' Stalin replied, 'my parents were uneducated people, but they treated me not at all badly.'[1] What we know of Stalin's early years, however, suggests that he was only referring to his mother.

As a pupil in the theological institutions he attended, Stalin revealed considerable abilities and a phenomenal memory. Evincing boundless interest in both the Old and New Testaments, and assimilating religious texts faster than the other boys, he tried to comprehend the notion of the one God as the bearer of absolute good, absolute power and absolute knowledge. Prolonged study of theology as the synthesis of dogma and moral principles, however, soon palled. Without his being aware of it, during his life as a student of theology, certain ways of thinking and behaving took shape in his mind. To ten years of religious study must be added as many years again of prison and exile which befell Koba, as he called himself after a hero in the story *The Patricide* by the Georgian writer A. Kazbegi. Cast out by society, the young revolutionary's feelings of dissatisfaction with his lot were hardened into a condition of permanent bitterness. His personality was undoubtedly affected by the weird mixture of acquired and then rejected religious postulates, and by the rôle of social outcast which combined to create in him an attraction to 'rebellious' activity. Twenty years of seminary and prison cells could not but affect his mind, his feelings and his character.

For instance, he had a strong tendency to systematize, categorize and locate intellectual pigeonholes for any form of knowledge, which suggests a catechistic cast of mind. This in turn created the impression of a man who is organized and logical. Equally, he lacked a self-critical faculty. All his life he believed in postulates, at first Christian postulates and later Marxist postulates. Whatever did not fit the Procrustean bed of his concepts was regarded at first as heresy and then as opportunism. And since he rarely experienced doubt about the truth of the ideas and theories he believed in, he did not see the need to subject them to criticism. In his own mind, he never departed from the classical precepts of Marxism. Perhaps he placed faith above truth, though he would never have admitted as much, even to himself. Faith in one's ideals and values is well and good, but faith should not displace truth. The kind of education he received and the deprivations of his childhood perhaps combined to make it unlikely that he would be capable one day of coping rationally and humanely with the power and responsibility that he would acquire.

Stalin realized at an early age that he had only himself to rely on. His comrades in Baku and Tiflis had often said, 'Koba, you've got a strong will.' He liked what he heard and decided to make that aspect of his character his hallmark by adopting his metallic-sounding name: from 1912 he began to sign himself 'Stalin', or 'man of steel'. He was not the only one who wished to symbolize a hardened personality by an adopted name: L. B. Rozenfeld, for instance, a character far less tough than Dzhugashvili, adopted the name Kamenev, or 'man of stone'. Time would show that stone was no match for steel. Stalin wanted to believe in his own strength of will, his own invulnerability, his own position as a regional leader. Faith, as the cement of dogmatism, remained with him for ever.

His religious education fostered a dogmatic turn of mind that became a permanent feature, even though he himself as leader would frequently criticize dogma, as he understood it in his vulgarizing and simplistic way. He was inclined to canonize Marxist propositions and often came to profoundly wrong conclusions as a result. For instance, by making the meaning of class struggle into an absolute, he arrived in the 1930s at the false formulation that 'the class struggle sharpens as the building of socialism proceeds.' Opportunism, factionalism and alternative ideas were for Stalin synonymous with the class enemy. The ex-seminarist saw the dictatorship of the proletariat as a means of social coercion rather than as a constructive principle.

On the way to the revolution, Stalin assimilated the basic propositions of Marxism, but he showed no creative talent in applying them. The influence of his religious education (and he had had no other) expressed itself not in the content of his views but in his cast of mind. Until the end of his life, he never succeeded in freeing himself from the shackles of dogmatism.

Stalin had virtually no close friends, certainly none with whom he maintained warm relations all his life. Political calculation, emotional sang-froid and moral insensitivity made it impossible for him to form and keep friends. It is therefore surprising to find that at the end of his life he remembered some of his schoolmates from theological school and the seminary. During the war, he suddenly noticed that his assistant, A. N. Poskrebyshev, was keeping large sums of money in his safe. With a mixture of puzzlement and suspicion, and looking not at the money but at Poskrebyshev, he asked where it had come from. 'It's your pay as a deputy. It's been piling up for years now,' Poskrebyshev explained. 'I only use what I need to pay your party dues.' Stalin said nothing, but a few days later he gave orders that substantial sums be sent to Peter Kopanidze, Grigory Glurdzhidze and Mikhail Dzeradze. Stalin himself wrote on the order:

1) To my friend Pete – 40,000,
2) 30,000 rubles to Grisha
3) 30,000 rubles to Dzeradze
9 May 1944, Soso

On the same day, he wrote a brief note in Georgian:

> Grisha!
> Accept this small gift from me.
> 9 May 1944. Yours, Soso[2]

Several similar notes are to be found in Stalin's personal archive. In his seventh decade and in the midst of war, he suddenly started showing philanthropic tendencies. But it was characteristic that the friends he was remembering were those of his distant youth as a theological student. And it was all the more surprising, since Stalin never showed any inclination towards sentimentality or friendly feeling or kindness. There is, however, evidence of another benevolent gesture that he made after the war. He sent the following letter to the settlement of Pchelok in the Parbig district of Tomsk:

> Comrade Solomin, V.G.
> I received your letter of 16 January 1947, sent via Academician Tsipin. I have not forgotten you and the other comrades from Turukhansk, nor will I, I'm sure. I enclose 6000 rubles out of my pay as a deputy. It is not a large amount, but will nevertheless be useful to you.
> I wish you good health. I. Stalin[3]

The Old Bolshevik I. D. Perfilyev, who was exiled during the Soviet period, told me that when Stalin had been exiled together with him in Turukhansk, he had had a relationship with a local woman, and that she had borne a child. Stalin himself never mentioned this, and I have been unable to establish whether he was ever concerned about this woman, or merely contented himself with the note to his friends from Turukhansk.

His coldness was no doubt accentuated by the years he spent as a revolutionary living underground from 1901 to 1917, in and out of prison and exile. Everyone who knew him testified that he had remarkable powers of self-control and imperturbability. He could sleep amid noise, accept his prison sentences with nonchalance and suffer the appalling conditions of the journey into exile under police escort with stoicism. Possibly the only time he was seen to be shaken was when his young wife died of typhus, leaving him with their two-month old baby, Yakov, who was wet-nursed by a tender-hearted woman called Monaselidze.

In Turukhansk, where from the beginning of 1914 he spent his last stretch of exile with Ya. M. Sverdlov and other revolutionaries, Stalin revealed himself as an unsociable, gloomy man. In a number of letters from exile, Sverdlov describes him as 'a great individualist in everyday life'.[4] Stalin was already a member of the party Central Committee when he arrived in exile, joining fellow-members Sverdlov, S. S. Spandaryan and F. I. Goloshchekin, but he kept himself to himself. He seemed to be interested only in hunting and fishing. Once, it is true, he expressed a desire to learn Esperanto from a textbook one of the exiles had brought with him, but he soon got fed up with it. His hermit-like existence was interrupted only by occasional trips to see Suren Spandaryan, who was living in the village of Monastyrskoe. Except for making the odd heckling remark, he generally stayed silent at the meetings organized by the other exiles. He gave the impression that he was either waiting for something to happen or that he was tired of escaping. In any event, his social passivity during the last two or three years before the revolution was marked.

One might have expected that, inspired by the success of the pamphlet he wrote in January 1913 in Vienna, entitled 'Marxism and the National Question', Stalin would have spent his long time in exile writing some more. Even if the published piece owed much to Lenin's editorial hand, he knew that the Bolshevik leader valued it,[5] yet he was not inspired to study the problem at a deeper level. The lack of any creative or social activity during that relatively long period testifies to his mental depression. For four years, with access to a library and ample free time, Stalin made no attempt to undertake any serious activity. On the other hand, he had behaved in precisely the same way during two separate spells of exile, in 1908 and 1910, in Solvychegodsk. It seems that total or partial isolation from the revolutionary centres plunged him into a condition of passive waiting, unless he escaped.

Revolutionaries, whether in exile or prison, customarily read a great deal. Prison for them was something of a university. G. K. Ordzhonikidze recalled that while he was in the Shlisselburg Fortress in St Petersburg he read Adam Smith, Ricardo, Plekhanov, Alexander Bogdanov, William James, Frederick W. Taylor, Klyuchevsky, Kostomarov, Dostoevsky, Ibsen and Bunin.[6] Stalin also read quite a bit, marvelling at the toothless way the tsarist régime struggled with its 'gravediggers': you didn't have to work, you could read to your heart's content and you could even escape, which required only the will to do so. It was possibly then that he came to the conclusion, later proclaimed more than once, that a strong authority needed strong 'punitive organs'.

During the purges of the 1930s, he would support a proposal by Yezhov that the system for holding political prisoners be altered. At Stalin's instigation, the February–March 1937 Central Committee plenum introduced a special point into the decree on Yezhov's report, namely, that 'the prison régime for enemies of Soviet power (Trotskyites, Zinovievites, SRs, etc.) is intolerable. The prisons resemble nothing so much as compulsory rest homes. [The prisoners] are allowed to socialize, they can write letters to each other at will, receive parcels and so on.'[7] Steps were taken, of course. There was to be no question of 'universities' for these unfortunates. Those who landed up in far-flung exile during the Stalin régime had to struggle just to stay alive, and many failed the test. Even the occasional escape was an event and had to be reported to Stalin. For instance, on 30 June 1948 the Minister of Internal Affairs notified Stalin and Beria that on 23 June, at the Ob corrective labour camp under the Northern Railway Construction Authority, a group of thirty-three prisoners disarmed two of their escorts, seizing two rifles and forty rounds of ammunition, and succeeded in escaping along the left bank of the Ob. The situation on 19 June was that four had been killed, twelve recaptured and the rest were being pursued.[8] Stalin ordered a responsible official to travel to the site, organize the recapture of the remainder and submit a report to him when the operation was completed. He did not model his punitive organs on those of the tsar.

As he read the newspapers, which arrived after long delays at the staging-post of Stanok, Stalin could not but be aware that great events were afoot. Yet when the First World War broke out, he ceased all social activity, giving the impression that, though at first he had been preparing to escape, he did not want to break out of exile. He had two reasons. First, it was difficult to support oneself illegally under wartime conditions, and secondly, he had no desire to be conscripted into the army. As it happened, when in February 1917 the draft commission in Krasnoyarsk called him up, he was judged unfit for military service because of his physical deformities, namely, the withered arm and a defective foot.

For four years he was passive, wrote practically nothing, and behaved not at all like a member of the party Central Committee. Spandaryan and Sverdlov became the effective leaders in exile and the other exiles rallied around them. Possibly this period of prolonged mental depression was a time of personal choice for Stalin, a time of reflection. He was nearing forty and his future was still shrouded in mist. He had no qualifications or skills, he had virtually never done a day's work. For thirty years the party and the country were to be ruled by a man who had no skills or profession, unless being a half-baked priest can be considered a profession. Molotov at least completed secondary school, and Malenkov, a university drop-out, showed himself at any early age to be an assiduous apparatchik in the party machine. Stalin, unlike Kaganovich, could not even mend a pair of boots. The space on police forms for 'skill or profession' would either be left blank or filled in as 'clerk'. When he had to complete registration for party congresses and conferences, Stalin was uncomfortable answering questions about the nature of his occupation and his social origin. For instance, on the form for the Eleventh Congress in 1922, where he was a non-voting delegate, in reply to the question: 'To which social category do you belong (worker, peasant, office worker)?' he could not bring himself to write anything.[9]

As a professional revolutionary, Stalin knew less about the life of a worker, peasant or office worker than he did about that of a prisoner or exile. Perhaps in the circumstances this was inevitable, but Stalin had another persistent feature in his personality, namely, that he *appeared to know* a great deal about the workers' lives. But then the time would come when he would 'know and be able to do' everything. The long silence in Turukhansk was perhaps in its way a relatively prolonged period of 'revision'. It was too late to give up his revolutionary career. News of the mounting anti-war mood and a rise in the revolutionary movement in Petrograd gradually restored his confidence in himself and brought him back into fighting form.

The icy polar winds seem literally to have frozen Stalin's intellectual powers for those four years. They were probably the most barren, passive time of his life, even though he had the lively company of other Bolsheviks. And so he waited, taking stock and thinking about his future. What memories were passing through his mind? Party congresses he had attended, prison in Batum, Alliluyev's apartment, the small son he had not seen for so long? Perhaps his activities as an 'expropriator' on Lenin's behalf? During the period immediately following the 1905 revolution, some of the more radical members of the Bolshevik wing of the party regarded it as legitimate to carry out robberies for the good of the cause. The written testimonies of Dan, Martov, Souvarine and other members of the Menshevik wing, indicate that 'the Caucasian militant, Dzhugashvili' had taken part in a number of robberies, if not directly then at least as one of the organizers. In particular, Martov asserted that the particularly audacious attack in 1907 on Cossacks escorting a shipment of money in Tiflis 'would not have succeeded without Stalin'. About 300,000 rubles were stolen. Martov wrote: 'The Caucasian Bolsheviks were involved in various daring enterprises of an expropriatory nature: this is known to Mr Stalin, who was once expelled from the party because of his involvement in expropriations.'[10] Stalin persistently tried to make Martov answer to the charge of slander, laying the emphasis, however, on the suggestion that he had been expelled from the party, and evading the charge of his direct complicity in the robberies.

His years of revolutionary activity, albeit on the provincial level, and the romantic aura of the 'expropriator' who had done time in prison and exile, had given him the reputation of a 'militant' and man of action, which, leaving aside the passive years in exile, he probably deserved.

Lenin undoubtedly played a large part in Stalin's emergence as a Marxist. His first letter to Stalin, who was then in the village of Novaya Uda in Irkutsk province, was written in December 1903. Lenin was very attentive to revolutionaries from the national minority borderlands, and Dzhugashvili had come to his notice through some short pieces that he'd had published in the party press and conversations with comrades. Lenin's letter to Stalin elucidates some basic issues of party organization. Stalin referred to this letter for the first time in public at the end of January 1924, at a Lenin memorial meeting held for Kremlin security guards on the completion of their course. In his thick, unexpressive voice, Stalin talked about his meetings with Lenin:

I first met Lenin in 1903. True, it was not a personal meeting, more of a postal one, through correspondence. It wasn't a long letter, but it was a bold and fearless criticism of the work of our party and it was a remarkably clear and concise exposition of the party's entire plan of work for the immediate future. That simple, bold little note reinforced my belief that in Lenin the party had a mountain eagle. I cannot forgive myself for doing with that letter what the practised underground revolutionary did with many other letters, that is to say I committed it to the flames.[11]

Stalin could not complain that Lenin was inattentive to him. On the eve of the revolution, the party Central Committee, under Lenin's chairmanship, specifically discussed the question of organizing the escape from exile of Sverdlov and Stalin.[12] A little earlier, Lenin had sent 120 Swiss francs to Stalin in Turukhansk.[13] Lenin took note of Stalin's letter from exile in which he discussed the possibility of publishing his articles 'On Cultural–National Autonomy' and 'Marxism and the National Question' as a separate booklet.[14]

Stalin met Lenin several times before 1917. The longest time they spent together was in Cracow. They had met earlier, in Stockholm at the Fourth Congress and in London at the Fifth. Later on Stalin began to cast a new light on those meetings. As early as 1931 he declared: 'Whenever I went abroad to see him – in 1906, 1907, 1912, 1913 ...'[15], making it seem that he had not been going abroad to party meetings, but to see Lenin. This shift of emphasis later enhanced the concept of the 'two leaders' and helped to create the myth that a special relationship between the two men had already existed before the revolution. It is also true that Stalin was characteristically cautious in making such claims.

Skilled in the arts of underground survival, Stalin was quite adept at transforming himself. He was one thing at the Politburo, another when he spoke at congresses, and yet something else again when he was chatting with Stakhanovite model workers. These changes were not always obvious, but they did occur. As people who worked closely with him testified, in his narrow circle he was much harsher than when he was 'on show' to the people. We all have our rôles, some we play better than others, wittingly or unwittingly. But those who occupy high positions in the social hierarchy are literally actors, perhaps because they are so prominently on display and every triviality is noticed. The authority of one man over others depends of course on his power, but also on impressions, on the 'visibility' of his image, on his attractiveness or lack of it as a leader.

The work he had done in Baku, Kutaisi and Tiflis had shown that he possessed not inconsiderable abilities as an organizer. Yet even then perspicacious revolutionaries remarked that Stalin viewed the party organization as an apparatus, a mechanism, a machine for processing orders. Other Caucasian Bolsheviks, such as A. S. Yenukidze, P. A. Dzhaparidze and S. G. Shaumyan, were better known to local workers than Dzhugashvili. He may have been their equal in his Marxist education and practical experience as a revolutionary, but he was plainly lagging behind them in personal popularity.

Along with the end of the Romanov dynasty, exile finally came to a close for Stalin. Few could have predicted then that within a year the centuries-old edifice of tsarism would disintegrate and leave the arena to the struggle of two principles, one the new and revolutionary, the other old and conservative. Stalin, whose 'full-face and profile' were still utterly unknown, would play his part in this conflict.

CHAPTER 2

February: the Prologue

While Kureika's icy fingers were sill clinging to its exiles, unprecedented events were unfolding in European Russia. The war had been reaping its bloody harvest for thirty months. Stalin was far from the muddy, blood-splattered trenches and the stiffened corpses of soldiers transfixed on barbed wire. But from the meagre news that filtered through he knew that industrial production had fallen drastically, that the people were hungry, and that their discontent was rising rapidly. The war brought the crisis of the Romanov empire to a head. A revolutionary outburst was imminent.

The middle classes were hoping a solution would be found, either by some adaptation of the monarchy or the establishment of a democracy along Western lines. The frantic succession of ministers only exacerbated the régime's difficulties. In the three years of war, chairmanship of the Council of Ministers had changed four times, while dozens of other shuffles had taken place among senior state posts. Things at the front were even worse. The War Minister, General A. A. Polivanov, sent the following cable from the front to the palace: 'I put my trust in our impassable expanses, in our quagmires and in the mercy of our benefactor, Nicholas, the protector of Holy Russia.'[16]

Nicholas II, for all his lack of imagination, did manage to manoeuvre quite cleverly, as he sought compromises and made partial concessions in order to save the monarchy. But its hour had come. Three weeks before the collapse of the autocracy, the president of the last Duma and leader of the Octobrist Party, M. V. Rodzianko, told the tsar: 'You have not one reliable or honest man left, Sire: all the best have either been set aside or have gone and those who remain are of poor reputation.' Rodzianko pleaded with Nicholas and begged him 'to grant the people a constitution' to save the throne.[17] But nothing could save it.

The single most significant event of the first act of the February Revolution was the fall of the autocracy. The exiles, including Stalin, who believed that a collapse was possible, did not expect it to happen so suddenly. Recalling the lessons of the 1905 revolution and what he had been reading about the French Revolution, Stalin now knew that their raison d'être as professional revolutionaries was about to be justified by forthcoming events.

One of the characters in the drama, V. V. Shulgin, (who returned from exile in the West to the USSR in 1945, where he lived to the age of almost a hundred), described the details in his memoirs, *Dni* ('The Days'). When, as emissaries of the Provisional Committee, he and A. I. Guchkov arrived at Pskov on 2 March 1917 to receive the tsar's instrument of abdication, they were hoping they could save the monarchy. 'The Emperor,' wrote Shulgin, 'was tranquil, as always. When Guchkov had finished making a speech that was full of contradiction, Nicholas, in a monotone that gave no hint of emotion, coolly announced: "I have decided to abdicate the throne. Until three o'clock today, I thought I would abdicate in favour of my son, Alexis. But then I changed my mind in favour of my brother, Michael." '[18] Michael, however, would soon decline to accept the crown.

While all this was happening, the exiles from Monastyrskoe and Kureika were already in Krasnoyarsk and Kansk, and Stalin and Kamenev were in Achinsk. When they heard that Grand Duke Michael had refused the crown they were ecstatic, and sent a telegram congratulating him on his 'magnanimity and civic-mindedness'. It was signed by Kamenev. Nine years later this fact would resurface at a meeting of the Comintern Executive Committee, when Stalin attempted to exploit Kamenev's 'weakness for the monarchy' to the full. Sounding unusually excited, Stalin said:

The affair took place in Achinsk in 1917 after the February Revolution, where Comrade Kamenev and I were exiles together. We were having a dinner or a meeting, I don't remember precisely, but at that meeting a number of citizens, including Kamenev, sent a telegram to Michael Romanov ... [Kamenev shouted from his seat: 'Admit you're lying, why don't you admit it!'] Shut up, Kamenev. [Kamenev shouted again: 'Admit that you're lying!] Shut up, Kamenev, or it'll be the worse for you. [The chairman, E. Thälmann, calls Kamenev to order.] The telegram to Romanov, as the first citizen of Russia, was sent by a number of merchants plus Comrade Kamenev. I heard about it the next day from Comrade Kamenev himself, who came to me and told me he had done this stupid thing. [Kamenev again shouted from his seat: 'You're lying, I never told you any such thing.'] The telegram was published in all the newspapers, except the Bolshevik ones. That's fact number one.

Now fact number two. We had our party conference in Petrograd in April and the delegates debated whether, in view of the telegram, it was at all permissible to elect Kamenev to the Central Committee. Two closed Bolshevik meetings took place, at which Lenin defended Kamenev, arguing with some difficulty for him to be put up as a Central Committee candidate. Only Lenin could save Kamenev. I defended him, too, at that time.

Now for fact number three. It is perfectly true that *Pravda* supported the repudiation which Comrade Kamenev published, since that was the only way to save him and to defend the party from its enemies' attacks. So you see that Comrade Kamenev is quite capable of lying and of deceiving the Comintern.

Just two more words. As Comrade Kamenev has tried, if somewhat feebly, to deny what is a fact, you will allow me to collect the signatures of those who participated in the April Conference and who insisted on keeping Comrade Kamenev out of the Central Committee because of the telegram. [Trotsky from his seat: 'You'll only be missing Comrade Lenin's signature.'] Comrade Trotsky, you ought to keep quiet! [Trotsky: 'You can't scare me, you can't scare me!'] You're going against the truth and it's the truth you ought to be scared of. [Trotsky: 'You're talking about Stalinist truth, which is rudeness and disloyalty.'] I'm collecting the signatures, as the telegram was signed by Kamenev.[19]

Be that as it may, the Romanov dynasty came to an end. As Shulgin put it: 'Russia was no longer a monarchy, but nor was she a republic. She was a form of state with no name. What had begun with a Jewish pogrom, ended with the destruction of a three-hundred-year-old dynasty.'[20] The 'old-timers' still had a lot left in them, however. They would resurface in due course in the form of the White armies, supported by interventionist forces. In his *Ocherki russkoy smuty* ('A History of Russia's Troubles'), A. I. Denikin recalled that General Krymov of the 3rd Cavalry Corps had proposed 'cleansing Petrograd by force of arms and, of course, the letting of blood'. Denikin regretted with a sigh that they had not taken this advice in time.[21] But the last two days of February 1917 extinguished all remaining hope of halting the revolution. The military commander of the capital lost the last vestige of his authority over the units at which the Bolsheviks had directed their propaganda. On the night of 28 February the ministers of the last tsarist government were being held in the Peter-Paul Fortress as prisoners. The February bourgeois-democratic revolution had triumphed in Russia. It was the prologue to October.

Even before receiving official notice, thousands of political exiles in the remote borderlands were getting ready to travel home to Petrograd, Moscow, Kiev, Odessa, Tiflis, Baku and other revolutionary centres. Stalin and a group of such former exiles got their third class rail tickets and sat gazing eagerly through the window as they sped through the great Siberian wastes, leaving their depression and ennui on the ice-bound banks of the Yenisei.

Stalin gazed at the impoverished villages, as he 'travelled to the revolution'. He knew he would be staying with the Alliluyevs. Through the long years of exile, if he had received regular mail from anyone, it was from Sergei Yakovlevich Alliluyev, his future father-in-law, a Bolshevik who will enter our story, because in July 1917 he would hide Lenin from the Provisional Government.

As they approached the Urals, and at all the stops thereafter, the exiles, of whom there were some on every train, were greeted by noisy welcomes. The 'Marseillaise' was sung, speeches poured forth, and there was a general air of rejoicing. The rhetorical Kamenev and the zealous Sverdlov also made speeches, as did other passengers. Stalin watched the euphoria in silence.

By this time the tide of democracy had risen high. The lower middle classes, leaning now towards the 'progressive' capitalists, now towards the proletariat, were rocking the ship of state with increasing force. A reformist mood was growing. It was felt that, with the collapse of the autocracy, the main thing had already been achieved. 'The gigantic wave of the petty bourgeoisie swept over everything,' Lenin wrote. 'It overwhelmed the conscious proletariat both numerically and ideologically.'[22] The great social pendulum swung back and forth between left and right, symbolizing a unique feature of the Russian Revolution, namely the existence of two centres of power. In one wing of the Tauride Palace (where the old tsarist pseudo-parliament, the State Duma, used to meet), sat the Provisional Committee of the State Duma – the 'plaything of government', in Milyukov's words – its tone dictated by the Kadets (Constitutional Democrats), or 'left' bourgeoisie. In the other wing, headed by the Mensheviks N. S. Chkheidze, M. I. Skobelev, the Socialist Revolutionary A. F. Kerensky, the Petrograd soviet was assembled as the organ of revolutionary power. Its executive committee included Bolsheviks and Mensheviks, because those Mensheviks who enjoyed legal status before February had made good use of their chances. They included among their number many leading intellectuals, propagandists and socialist theoreticians. Lenin was still in exile in Switzerland, while Bubnov, Dzerzhinsky, Muranov, Rudzutak, Ordzhonikidze, Sverdlov, Stalin, Stasova and other party leaders were either still in exile or prison or labour camps.

The Mensheviks in the soviet went along with the Duma members in approving the transfer of state power to the Provisional Government. In unison, Tsereteli and Kerensky chanted the refrain that 'the new revolutionary government would operate under the control of the soviet', and that this was 'the will of history'. Their rabble-rousing revolutionary rhetoric, and their harping on the emotional significance of the moment, turned public opinion in favour of the Provisional Government. Like many others, Stalin was carried along with the current.

Kerensky, who did his utmost in the interests of the bourgeoisie, also wanted to protect the representatives of the dynasty, 'just in case'. In one of his essays, written when he was already on the run, and entitled 'The Departure of Nicholas II to Tobolsk', Kerensky wrote:

Despite all the rumours and insinuations, the Provisional Government ... had decided at the very beginning of March to send the royal family abroad. At the Moscow Soviet on 7 [20] March, in response to heated calls of 'Death to the tsar, execute the tsar!', I myself said: 'This will never happen while we are in power. The Provisional Government has taken upon itself responsibility for the personal safety of the tsar and his family. We will carry out this obligation to the end. The tsar and his family will be sent abroad to England. I will accompany him to Murmansk myself.'[23]

'My announcement,' Kerensky goes on, 'caused an explosion of indignation in the soviets of both capitals, but in the summer, when it became impossible to hold the royal family at Tsarskoe Selo any longer, the Provisional Government received official notice [from the British government] to the effect that, until the end of the war, the entry of the former monarch and his family into British territory was impossible.'[24] It was then that the royal family was despatched to Tobolsk. At the same time, the Provisional Government tried its best to clothe the revolution in the mantle of reconciliation. While maintaining power, as Kerensky said, the bourgeoisie was also determined to 'let the people have their say'.

The revolution had completed its first phase by this time. Awareness was lulled by the dual power. Power ostensibly was in the hands of the Provisional Government together with the old state bureaucracy, while alongside it the Petrograd soviet buzzed with the revolutionary ferment created by the workers' and soldiers' deputies. Two dictatorships were coexisting next to one another. Neither of them had full power, yet nor could either one deprive the other of its authority. However socially ambiguous, the dual power could not slow down the revolutionary rise of the masses. On 2 March 1917, for example, *Izvestiya* published the famous Order No. 1 proclaiming the introduction of democratic principles in the army: elections of soldiers' committees, abolition of ranks and titles, orders to be obeyed only if approved by the soviets, the observance of revolutionary discipline, equal civil rights for soldiers and officers.

Before Lenin's return a special rôle was played by the Russian Bureau of the Central Committee, which in March coopted three new members, among them Stalin. The Bureau confirmed the membership of the editorial board of *Pravda* and Stalin was on it. The reappearance of the proletarian newspaper (suppressed since the beginning of the war) had an enormous impact.

How did Stalin acquit himself in the February and October revolutions? What was his real function? What was he: a leader, an outsider, an extra?

According to the *Short Biography*, 'during this important period Stalin rallied the party for the struggle to turn the bourgeois-democratic revolution into a socialist one. Together with Molotov, he guided the work of the Central Committee and the Bolshevik Petrograd Committee. The Bolsheviks were getting their ideological directions from Stalin's articles.'[25] He is spoken of as the leader of the revolution, as if he had already replaced Lenin. The documents show no basis of truth for such assertions, Stalin gave no 'directions'. After his arrival in Petrograd he was no more than one of many party functionaries. His name is to be found extremely rarely, among a particular group of people who were carrying out the Central Committee's instructions. True, he was a member of important political organs, but during those months he gave little account of himself. Known to practically no one outside a small circle, he was an inconspicuous person, a 'representative of the national minorities'. He was simply unknown. That is the truth.

Trotsky, who did become well known after returning from abroad, when describing this period of Stalin's life in his *The February Revolution*, noted that 'the position in the party became more complicated in the middle of March after the return from exile of Kamenev and Stalin, who gave the rudder of official policy a sharp turn to the right.' Trotsky pointed out that Kamenev had spent several years abroad with Lenin, at the party's theoretical centre, and was a writer and speaker, whereas Stalin, the so-called practical activist who lacked the necessary 'theoretical outlook, as well as broad political interests, to say nothing of foreign languages, was inseparable from Russian soil'. The Kamenev–Stalin faction 'became . . . in effect a behind-the-scenes parliamentary group for "putting pressure" on the bourgeoisie'.[26] Although some of Trotsky's accusations against Stalin – e.g. that he favoured a defensive war policy – are not wholly justified, Trotsky is nevertheless right when he says that Stalin's pre-October thinking lacked vision and that this on occasion led to a narrow, short-sighted concern with practicalities.

Stalin was not caught wholly unawares by the February Revolution. Despite his long depression, his faith in the inevitability of the revolution was implicit. If the truth was not clothed in the mantle of faith, then for him it was an inferior truth. Although such an approach may not be negative as such, it does contain the danger of dogmatic thinking. Faith in a programme, a course, decisions, 'the line', always helped him to remain convinced of the rightness of his actions. He viewed the fall of the monarchy as a revolutionary inevitability and no doubt had expected it to occur in his lifetime, yet he suddenly realized that the cause to which he had devoted his life was not a matter of mere historical chance, but something more.

CHAPTER 3

The Supporting Players

Stalin arrived in Petrograd on 12 March, Old Style.* Appropriately, nobody came to meet him from the train, on which he had travelled together with Kamenev and Muranov. The city was preoccupied with other matters. Carrying his cardboard suitcase, he set off for the Alliluyevs where he was received like one of the family. The same day he met some of the Central Committee and that evening he was elected to its Russian Bureau and the editorial board of *Pravda*. After the silence of Kureika, Stalin found it hard to adjust to the noise and bustle. From the time they arrived, Kamenev, Muranov and Stalin were virtually in charge of the newspaper, and almost at once 'missed the beat' theoretically and politically a number of times, and not by chance. Stalin was not a strong, independent thinker, he had no precise position or clear understanding of the dynamics of the pre-October period. He was used to obeying orders and carrying out the 'line'. In his new situation, he was expected to make his own decisions. His first blunder was to permit the publication of an article by Kamenev called 'The Provisional Government and Revolutionary Social Democracy', in which the author plainly stated that the party must support the Provisional Government, as it was 'genuinely struggling against the remnants of the old régime'. This went blatantly against Lenin's directives.

The very next day, Kamenev, who was well known as a fast writer, published another article, entitled 'Without Secret Diplomacy', in which he virtually espoused the 'revolutionary defencist' position. In so far as the German army carries on the war, he wrote, the revolutionary people 'must stand steadfastly at their posts, meeting bullet with bullet, shell with shell. This is indisputable.'[27] Kamenev's semi-Menshevik views met no objection from Stalin, who himself

---

* The Russian calendar lagged thirteen days behind that of the West until January 1918, when it was brought into line. For this reason, the 'February' Revolution took place in March, New Style, while the 'October' Revolution has since 1918 been commemorated on 7 November.

published an article the day after Kamenev's appeared, called 'On the War'. Despite its being in general anti-war, the article was nevertheless in complete contradiction to Lenin's views. Stalin saw the way out of the imperialist war as 'putting pressure on the Provisional Government to announce its willingness to open peace talks at once'.[28]

(To his credit, during a speech to the Communist faction of the Trade Unions Central Committee in 1924, Stalin publicly admitted his error. He said, concerning his attitude to the Provisional Government over the issue of peace, that his had been 'a gravely erroneous position, for it generated pacifist illusions, provided grist to the mill of defencism and made the revolutionary education of the masses all the harder'.[29] He added that this was the position taken up by the entire party, even though some of its organizations had adopted the proper tone. Later, in the period when he became infallible, such public admissions would, of course, be unthinkable.)

A week after Stalin's article, the Bureau passed a resolution directly in line with his thinking on the question of war and peace. But in Lenin's absence, it was Kamenev's influence on *Pravda* that was decisive. Kamenev was the real hero of the 'interregnum' in the Bolshevik leadership, and he contributed to the growth of the defencist, semi-Menshevik tendencies that burgeoned in March. Stalin lacked the authority to resist him. Even in the absence of Lenin and other prominent Bolsheviks, Stalin failed to behave as a leader when the party, having just emerged from the underground, needed energetic leadership. Sverdlov, Kamenev and Shlyapnikov were all more in evidence than Stalin during that complex moment when political direction and party tactics were being defined.

No doubt, Stalin could not guess that Lenin was going to proclaim a course for socialist revolution when he arrived in Petrograd a month later. He was too involved in the political manoeuvrings which he saw as an end in themselves. Lenin's absence was felt acutely during March. Ultimate goals could not be determined by ordinary intellect and revolutionary zeal, and the returnee from Kureika was not up to raising his sights any higher. A prominent Menshevik intellectual, N. N. Sukhanov (Gimmer) wrote in his memoirs: 'In the political arena, Stalin was nothing more than a vague, grey blur.'[30] The other members of the Bureau, who included P. A. Zalutsky, V. M. Molotov, A. G. Shlyapnikov, M. I. Kalinin and M. S. Olminsky, were equally incapable of consistently carrying out the orders Lenin had laid down in his response to the events of February, 'Letters from Afar'. It seemed that Stalin, Kamenev and some of the others were not fully free of their defencist illusions and faith in the Provisional Government, and that they regarded the bourgeois democratic reforms as virtually the peak of achievement.

Stalin's hesitation was understandable. He did not have his own conception of how the great idea was to be made real. February and October exposed his weaknesses, his shallow theoretical grounding, his low level of initiative, his inability (as yet) to convert a political slogan into a concrete programmatic proposition. No one ever reproached him for not entering the fray or for seeking the easy way, for being afraid of confronting the political enemy. He never lacked will-power, but the perceptive observer would notice that this professional revolutionary was extremely vulnerable in one place, and Stalin knew it.

As we have already remarked, whenever he had to visit a workshop or factory, an army unit or a street meeting, Stalin felt an anxiety which, it is true, he learned in time to conceal. Unlike other revolutionaries, he never felt drawn into the thick of the masses, he did not enjoy and was anyway not good at speaking in front of large crowds. A worker (A. I. Kobzev) who heard Stalin speak at a meeting in Petrograd in April 1917 wrote: 'What he said sounded all right, it was understandable and simple enough, but somehow you couldn't remember his speech afterwards.' It was therefore not surprising that Stalin spoke at meetings and demonstrations less than any other Bolshevik leader.

It became especially hard for him to speak to large crowds once Lenin and Trotsky had returned, in April and May respectively, and when Lunacharsky, Volodarsky, Kamenev, Zinoviev and other brilliant speakers started attending meetings. Trotsky, for instance, chose as his favourite venue the Modern Circus, and always packed it out. He was often carried to the stage over the heads of the audience. An impression was created that Trotsky sometimes paid less attention to the content of his speeches than to the emotional effect he was having on his listeners. As Sukhanov noted in his seven-volume diary of the revolution, published in 1922–23, in the first weeks after his return Trotsky would finish one of his routine speeches at the Modern and dash off to the Obukhov factory, then to the Trubochny factory, then the Putilov, the Baltiisky, then from the Manège to the barracks. It seemed as if he was speaking everywhere simultaneously. Stalin simply could not match up to this Cicero of the revolution. Trotsky became intoxicated with the rise of his own popularity and knew better than anyone how to fire up a crowd. When he heard Trotsky speak, Stalin felt hostility bordering on hatred. Trotsky was the centre of attention and everyone was drawn to him, unlike Stalin, whom Trotsky, especially before October, simply 'did not notice'.

Instead of making public appearances, Stalin wrote on political events for the newspapers. Between March and October he published more than sixty articles and comments in a wide variety of Bolshevik papers. Although he was only an average writer, his arguments were nevertheless consistent and invariably categorical. His writing was of an elementary simplicity, without abstruse terminology or complex definitions or tricks of logic. He laid out simple truths which no one would have remembered decades later but for the fact that they had been written by him.

It was more to Stalin's taste to remain at headquarters, working in the organs of control, such as the Bureau, the Central Committee and the soviet. As early as March, the Bureau had given him the additional job of sitting on the Executive Committee of the Petrograd soviet. The Bureau met almost daily to discuss practical issues and to allocate more and more new tasks to its members. In this way, Stalin maintained contact with the party organizations in the Caucasus and other regions.

By this time, united organizations of Bolsheviks and Mensheviks had been set up in numerous provinces. The Central Committee attacked this practice, as it always had, although it has to be said that its approach on this issue was not wholly commendable. At a time when cooperation might have strengthened the struggle against the autocracy and later against the bourgeoisie, it could perhaps have been viewed as a policy of political compromise for the sake of achieving specific ends. Stalin in particular was zealous in breaking up and liquidating such alliances, even though they could have helped to strengthen Bolshevik influence.

Perhaps, when a conciliatory line threatened ideals, or programme points and concrete achievements, it might be justifiable to destroy the united organizations. But the concentrated efforts that were made against the Mensheviks, and even more so against the Socialist Revolutionaries, did more harm than good. Regrettably, with time this approach became a tradition. When the Fascists of the 1930s were lining us up in their gunsights, we were still looking upon the social democrats as our 'main enemies'.

When Lenin arrived in Russia on 3 April (16 New Style), he was met at nine in the evening at Beloostrov, the first station on Russian soil, by representatives of the Central Committee and the Petrograd Party Committee, as well as by delegations of workers. Among those who were there to greet him were Kamenev, Alexandra Kollontai, Stalin, Maria Ulyanov (Lenin's sister), F. F. Raskolnikov and A. G. Shlyapnikov. They had barely entered the compartment and exchanged a warm welcome when Lenin flabbergasted them, as Raskolnikov recalled, by demanding: 'What are you writing in *Pravda*? We've seen a few issues and we cursed you roundly!'

Lenin's arrival was witnessed by Sukhanov, who quotes Chkheidze's speech of welcome, in which the Menshevik leader said that 'the chief task ... is to defend our revolution from any encroachments, whether from within or without. We hope that you will pursue this aim together with us.' Sukhanov records that Lenin behaved as if all this had nothing whatever to do with him. 'He gazed around, or at the flowers of his bouquet which seemed so out of keeping. And then, turning his back on the welcoming party, replied: "Dear comrades, soldiers, sailors and workers. I am happy to greet in you the victorious Russian revolution, I greet you as the vanguard of the world proletarian army. The hour is near when our comrade Karl Liebknecht will call on the peoples to turn their weapons against their capitalist exploiters. The Russian revolution which you have made has opened a new era. Long live the world socialist revolution!" '[31]

There, at the station, Stalin felt Lenin's internationalism obliterating his own naive doubts and erroneous attitude to the Provisional Government. Stalin himself later recalled that on the evening of 3 April 'many things became much clearer'. Lenin, despite coming from 'afar', understood the significance of the moment better than others. Next day at the Tauride Palace, when Lenin made his ten 'April Theses' public, Stalin was amazed at his intellectual power. The Theses totally demolished his cautious posture and exposed the danger of his passive wait-and-see policy. Stalin's admiration, however, was less a tribute of respect for the leader than appreciation of the impact of the new idea, an assessment not everyone else shared. For Lenin's comrades-in-arms, the party leader was not inviolable. Given the totally unprecedented situation, as well as the novelty of Lenin's ideas, even leading figures in the party were not ready to accept Lenin's programme. They said emigration had cut him off from Russian reality and that he had become an extreme radical. Not until the Seventh Party Conference at the end of April did Lenin win the support of the majority of the Petrograd Committee. Having made his cautious speech in March, Stalin felt Lenin's arguments as a direct reproach to himself. Sukhanov noted in his diary that Lenin's speech caused 'many heads to spin'. At the April 4 (17) meeting, the only one to speak in his defence was Alexandra Kollontai. Many Bolsheviks (and not only Zinoviev and Kamenev, as Soviet historiography has been accustomed to say) could not accept Lenin's viewpoint, and his arguments were subjected to severe criticism.

At the Seventh Party Conference of 24–29 April (which made public the fact that its 151 delegates were representing a party of 80,000 members), Kamenev attacked Lenin for failing to appreciate that present circumstances dictated they form a bloc with the Provisional Government.[32] Others who disagreed with Lenin included Smidovich, Rykov, Pyatakov, Milyutin, Bagdatyev, all of whose speeches would later be classified by Stalin as 'treacherous', 'hostile', 'counter-revolutionary' and included in the catalogue of their 'crimes'. Following Bubnov, who advocated monitoring the Provisional Government 'from above and below', Stalin spoke up in favour of Lenin's Theses. His speech was pale and unconvincing, however, and since arguments are the muscles of ideas, and Stalin lacked arguments, he made little impact on Bubnov's points.

Stalin's report on the national question, by contrast, was more weighty. There, he stated that 'organizing the proletariat of a state according to nationality can only cause the idea of class solidarity to perish'.[33] The surest path for the working class of a multinational state was to create a united party, he said. This was an approach that had been Leninist policy since the beginning of the century. The speech itself was a conscientious, lacklustre effort by a 'hardened practical revolutionary', but as a rule during those heady days, Stalin tried to cling to a 'middle' position, believing it to be the safest thing to do when things were changing at such a rapid rate.

Equally, it emerges from the documents that Stalin was little more than an inconspicuous functionary in the party organization. For instance, in a chronicle compiled in 1924, for the period June to September 1917, while Savinkov is mentioned more than forty times, Skobelev over fifty, and Trotsky more than eighty times, Stalin's name appears a mere nine times. It may be objected that the statistical approach does not tell us everything, yet it does give some idea of an individual's rôle, as seen through the prism of public opinion. Beyond listing his memberships of various committees, in Stalin's case it is hard to find anything very concrete to say about his activities. The chief cause of this may be his lack of revolutionary initiative. He was a good executive, but lacked imagination. In March, even as a Central Committee member and in Lenin's absence, he had shown himself lacking in leadership qualities on a national scale, and had come up with nothing more original than 'we mustn't force events'.

The fact that Stalin remained in the shade during 1917 was the result not only of his social passivity, but also of his rôle as an executive, a rôle for which he had undeniable talent. In the stormy months of 1917, he was incapable of rising above his day-to-day tasks. Working alongside far more lively personalities than himself, it is unlikely that he was consumed with ambition. The secondary rôles that he played, nevertheless, imperceptibly earned him stable political authority among the Bolshevik leaders, and he was re-elected to the Central Committee at the Seventh Conference.

CHAPTER 4

Uprising

Once Lenin had returned, Stalin's rôle became more firmly established as the executor of the leadership's orders. He served a valuable function where secret operations were concerned, forming links with party committees and organizing matters as they arose during the preparations for the armed uprising.

The Central Executive Committee of the Soviets, appointed by the First All-Russian Congress of Soviets which met from 3–24 June, was not a Bolshevik body. It comprised 123 Mensheviks, 119 Socialist Revolutionaries, and 57 Bolsheviks, among them Stalin.[34] Its decisions, like the Committee itself, were conciliatory towards the new government. This emerged clearly after the Provisional Government's violent suppression of a Bolshevik-inspired demonstration in early July. That made it plain that the socialist revolution would not be accomplished by political means. Lenin wrote later that 'our party fulfilled its undoubted obligation by marching shoulder to shoulder with the rightfully indignant masses on 4 July and in trying to introduce into the movement as peaceful and organized a character as possible. For on 4 July a peaceful transfer of power to the soviets was still a possibility.'[35] The SR and Menshevik leadership, however, had already 'slid to the bottom of the revolting, counter-revolutionary pit' – in Lenin's words – by making a deal with the Provisional Government which used troops against the demonstrators. The uneasy coexistence of the two centres of authority had come to an end, and now a new stage had arrived, that of preparing for the seizure of power by the Bolsheviks.

The Provisional Government was preparing a case against Lenin as a German agent. Lenin got wind of his imminent arrest and sought refuge, with Stalin's help, in Alliluyev's apartment where, in early July, members of the Central Committee met, including Nogin, Ordzhonikidze, Stasova and Stalin. The issue at hand was whether Lenin should give himself up to 'justice', as the authorities were demanding. Before this meeting, Lenin had stated: 'If the government orders my arrest and the TsIK [Soviet Central Executive Committee] ratifies the order, I will turn myself in at any place indicated by the TsIK.'[36] Opinions were divided. Some argued that he should turn himself in, if the TsIK would give certain guarantees. But M. I. Liber and N. A. Anisimov, (Menshevik members of the TsIK) declared that there were no guarantees that they could give. In view of the unbridled press comment against Lenin and other Bolshevik leaders, it was plain that reactionaries were expecting the government to make short shrift of them. After prolonged discussion, Lenin was persuaded not to give himself up but to go into hiding outside Petrograd for the time being.[37] At first, Stalin took no position, but then he came out strongly against Lenin's surrender to the court, warning that he risked being assassinated if he gave himself up.

There was ample justification for this view. V. N. Polovtsev, a former member of the Duma, recalls in his memoirs that he was asked by the officer sent to Terioki in Finland to arrest Lenin: 'How should I deliver this gentleman – complete or in pieces?' 'I replied with a grin that when people are arrested, they often try to make a run for it . . .'

Stalin was no doubt aided in his task by his experience in the underground, and the plan to get Lenin out of Petrograd with the help of trusted friends was well thought out.

At this highly dramatic moment, an important event took place in Stalin's personal life: he became acquainted with Alliluyev's daughter, Nadezhda, his future, second wife. Twenty years her senior, he had known the family since the late 1890s when he had first arrived in Baku. As a matter of fact, his daughter, Svetlana Alliluyeva, wrote in her *Twenty Letters to a Friend* that in 1903 Stalin saved his future wife when, as a two-year old, she fell into the sea and he pulled her out. Returning home one day, Nadezhda found the apartment full of people she had never seen before. They began questioning her closely about the situation on the streets. In a state of excitement, the girl reported that she'd heard it said that the people accused of the July uprising were 'secret agents of Wilhelm, that they'd already escaped to Germany by submarine, and that their leader was Lenin'. When she realized that the hero of the rumours was there in the flat, she was terribly embarrassed.

The visitors ceased their questioning and summed up the situation. The proposal that Lenin not give himself up had been the right one, as the government was evidently planning to settle the score. Now Lenin must disguise himself, change his clothes and leave for Sestroretsk and Finland. Alliluyev later recalled: 'We set off in the evening for Primorsky Station. Yemelyanov, a worker and party member since 1904, went in front, followed at a short distance by Vladimir Ilyich and Zinoviev, with Stalin and myself bringing up the rear. The train was already in and the three who were going boarded the rear carriage. Stalin and I waited to make sure it left, and then went back.' Alliluyev's recollections are not entirely accurate. Zinoviev was not among the travellers, as he was already in hiding, and the worker, V. I. Zof, was among those who accompanied the disguised Lenin.

Despite his many tasks, Stalin began to spend a lot of time at the Alliluyevs. A hard, cold man, he was attracted to the pure, naive half-child who was to become his future wife. For her part, Nadezhda watched the 'old conspirator', as he presented himself to her, with interest.

Stalin now became one of the links connecting Lenin to the Central Committee. There is every reason to suppose that Lenin entrusted him with instructions and advice. On the eve of the Sixth Party Congress, for instance, Stalin met Lenin.[38] No record of the meeting was made, but Lenin's imprint was plainly evident in all the chief documents of the congress. Lenin was delighted that the delegates now represented a party of 240,000 members. The party's ranks had multiplied threefold in four months. Lenin saw this as a vindication of the course he had taken. His articles, for instance, 'The Political Situation', 'On Slogans', 'A Reply' formed the basis of the congress decisions. A special resolution was passed, approving the decision that he not give himself up, and his line on the armed uprising was also supported.

On the political scene, with the party now in semi-hiding, it was left to Stalin and Sverdlov to carry out Lenin's instructions. Still virtually unknown to the masses, Stalin's rôle within the organization grew steadily.

On 10 October, returned after his long absence, Lenin attended a meeting of the Central Committee at the apartment of the Menshevik Sukhanov, whose wife was a Bolshevik. Sverdlov presided. Lenin asserted that the political situation 'is now entirely ripe for the transfer of power ... We must discuss the technical side. Everything depends on that.'[39]

The press reported that the capital's supplies of grain were dwindling at an alarming rate. The city council asked the mayor to call on the population to remain calm, while a special session of the council was called to discuss the food situation. Lenin, meanwhile, was calling on all organizations and all workers and soldiers to engage in outright and intensified preparation for an armed uprising. The party Central Committee appointed an operations centre, consisting of Bubnov, Dzerzhinsky, Uritsky, Sverdlov and Stalin, to supervise the organization of the uprising.

On the evening of 24 October, Lenin duly arrived at the Bolshevik headquarters, the Smolny Institute, where the Military Revolutionary Committee was located. That evening a cadet unit turned up to arrest Lenin. They were disarmed by Red Guards and marched off to the Peter-Paul Fortress. A Central Committee meeting took place on the same day. The next day, Kamenev proposed that no Central Committee member be allowed to leave the Smolny without special instructions, adding that, in case the Smolny was destroyed, they should have a stronghold on the battle cruiser *Aurora*. Stalin was not at the meeting.[40] That night, the Military Revolutionary Committee stormed the Winter Palace where the Provisional Government was entrenched.

On 25 October, Red Guards occupied key positions, the Cossack regiments of Petrograd were refusing to act in support of the Provisional Government, and the telephones at staff headquarters and the Winter Palace were cut. That afternoon, a special session of the Petrograd soviet opened under Trotsky's chairmanship. To noisy applause, he announced that the Provisional Government was no more, that prisoners had been freed and that telegrams had been sent to the Army reporting the fall of the old régime.

Organizing the uprising had been the responsibility of the five-man practical centre, including Stalin, and the Military Revolutionary Committee, which did an enormous amount of work recruiting forces for the decisive onslaught. In his historic letter to the Central Committee on 24 October, Lenin had urged the entire leadership that 'this evening or tonight, we must arrest the government, disarming the cadets etc. and overcoming them if there is any resistance. We must not wait! We could lose everything! The government is vacillating. We must finish it off, whatever the cost! To delay the offensive would be death!'[41]

Lenin's call was heeded and the revolution took place. Its first significant measures were ratified at the Second Congress of Soviets which opened on the night of 25 October. During these events, Stalin was simply nowhere to be seen. He was carrying out Lenin's orders, ensuring that instructions were circulated to the committees, and preparing material for publication. His name does not occur in any document relating to those historic days and nights.

At the congress, the Menshevik leader, Martov, attempted to put a motion calling for a peaceful resolution of the crisis. On behalf of the Socialist Revolutionary Central Committee, Gendelman proposed a resolution condemning the seizure of power, but even among the SRs it only secured sixty votes with ninety-three against. The Jewish Bund, the Menshevik-Internationalists and the Poalei-Tsion (Worker Zionists) walked out. Meanwhile, in an atmosphere of tobacco smoke and body heat, so graphically described by John Reed in his *Ten Days that Shook the World*, the Congress continued its work through the night.

Having passed Lenin's decrees on land and peace, the congress appointed the All-Russian Central Executive Committee (VTsiK), sixty-two of whose 101 members were Bolsheviks. The Bolshevik leadership was not, however, united. Kamenev, Zinoviev, Nogin and Milyutin argued that power must be shared with the other parties. A fierce political struggle ensued, with Bubnov, Dzerzhinsky, Stalin, Sverdlov, Stasova, Trotsky, Ioffe, Sokolnikov and Muranov taking Lenin's side.

Power was in the hands of the Bolsheviks, but the makers of the February Revolution would not accept the situation. On 29 October 1917 the Mensheviks addressed the country:

Citizens of Russia! On 25 October the Provisional Council of the Russian Republic was forced at bayonet-point to disperse and suspend its operations for the time being.

With the words 'freedom and socialism' on their lips, those who have seized power are committing violence and exercising arbitrary rule. They have arrested members of the Provisional Government, including the socialist ministers, and incarcerated them in tsarist cells. Blood and anarchy are threatening to overwhelm the revolution, to drown freedom and the republic and to bring in the restoration of the old order. This régime must be seen for the enemy of the people and the revolution that it is.[42]

Within a few days, this and other opposition newspapers would be closed down by the Bolsheviks.

It should be made perfectly clear that the Bolsheviks seized power with the support of the Left Socialist Revolutionaries. Although they differed with the Bolsheviks on a number of issues, the Left SR's were firmly in the mainstream of the revolutionary current. Founded as a separate party in November 1917, like their parent Socialist Revolutionary Party, they expressed the broad interests of the peasantry. They were against the dictatorship of the proletariat and in favour of a wider representation of socialist parties in the Council of People's Commissars, but at the crucial moment they supported the Bolsheviks. In December 1917 they agreed to enter the Soviet government and were given about a third of the portfolios. Among those who accepted posts were I. Z. Steinberg. P. P. Proshyan, A. L. Kolegaev, V. E. Trutovsky, V. A. Karelin, V. A. Algasov, M. N. Brilliantov.

Such socialist pluralism as this undoubtedly provided an exceptional historic opportunity. Lenin realized this when he stated that the union of the Bolsheviks and the Left SRs '*could* be an "honourable coalition", an honourable union, for there is *no* fundamental difference of interest between the hired labourer and the exploited peasant'.[43] Had this union survived, it is possible that many of the tragic features associated with the monopoly of political power would not have arisen. But neither the Left SRs nor the Bolsheviks were fully aware of the historic importance of their alliance and its collapse in the summer of 1918 was the source of future evils. Stalin, incidentally, always regarded the Left SRs as a typical petty bourgeois party which was more drawn towards counter-revolution than revolution. Unfortunately, he was not the only one who thought this way. The opportunity to consolidate revolutionary pluralism was lost in the summer of 1918, with the result that political monopoly, uniformity of thought and the absence of an alternative form of authority were soon turned into a cruel one-man rule.

How did Stalin behave during the critical days of October? What was his real rôle? Why is it that his name appears so rarely in the chronicles, although he was a member of various top bodies?

The propaganda purveyed by the *Short Biography* was aimed at consolidating the idea that there had been only Lenin and Stalin: Lenin and Stalin had inspired and organized the October victory; as Lenin's closest associate, Stalin was directly responsible for preparing all aspects of the uprising; his articles were syndicated throughout the provincial Bolshevik press, he summoned the regional representatives whom he charged with various local tasks, and he directed solely by means of 'summonses' and 'instructions'. But this was the terminology of the 1930s. The authors of the biography found it hard to say anything concrete, precisely because Stalin was neither 'directing' nor 'guiding and instructing' anyone. He was just carrying out Lenin's orders and the decisions of the Military Revolutionary Committee.

When Provisional Government forces closed the party's central organ, *Rabochii Put* , on 24 October, Stalin was there to give support to the Red Guards who defended it. On the same day the paper carried an article by him, entitled 'What Do We Need?', in which he continued to call for the Constituent Assembly to be convened.* This article virtually echoed the ill-famed letter from Kamenev and Zinoviev of 11 October, which they entitled 'On the Current Situation', and in which they opposed the Central Committee's decision to launch the armed uprising. They wrote, 'We are holding a pistol to the bourgeoisie's head and under such a threat they cannot be expected to convene the Assembly.' Stalin was equally capable of raising the subject of the Assembly, and on the eve of the uprising, no less. True, he also said that the 'government of [the liberals] should be replaced by one of the Soviets . . .'[44]

Stalin's first post in the new Soviet government was as Commissar for Nationalities. Yet, despite being one of the team of leaders who were tackling problem after problem in 1917, he never once proposed any important initiative, nor raised any original idea. To be fair, on 28 November 1917 at a meeting of the Council of People's Commissars (Sovnarkom), he did stand alone against the rest, including Lenin, when he voted against handing over leading liberals to revolutionary tribunals as enemies of the people.[45] But, in all, he was a leader of the second or third rank.

Although he was a member of every conceivable revolutionary organ, in practice he had virtually no concrete responsibilities. Yet he missed nothing. He was amazed by Trotsky's energy, by Kamenev's capacity for hard work, by Zinoviev's impulsiveness. On a number of occasions, he heard Plekhanov, for whom he had feelings bordering on respect, and was taken aback at one meeting when Plekhanov declared bitterly: 'Russian history hasn't yet ground the flour to make the wheatcakes of socialism.'

The 'father of Russian Marxism' and one of the founders of the party, Plekhanov went still further. He called Lenin's April Theses 'ravings', condemned the October Revolution and in due course the peace treaty of Brest Litovsk. Swept into the shallows of reformism by the revolutionary flood, and disillusioned by the fact that what was happening did not correspond to his theories, Plekhanov left for Finland. He could not accept the revolution, but

---

*Following the February Revolution, the new government was under pressure to convene a Constituent Assembly which would determine the nature of the new state. Elections, set in motion by the Provisional Government, were eventually held *after* the seizure of power by the Bolsheviks, who received less than one quarter of the seats in the Assembly which they promptly dispersed by force after its first and only session on 18 January 1918.

nor could he fight against it. He was a man of moral political principles.

On 4 June 1918, a joint meeting of the All-Russian Central Executive Committee (VTsIK), the Moscow soviet and the local trade unions, attended by Lenin, observed a minute's silence in memory of Plekhanov, who had died in May. Stalin was amazed. Anyone who had publicly expressed disagreement with his cause was an enemy forever. Similarly, he thought a eulogy by Trotsky and an obituary in *Pravda* by Zinoviev were excessive. Revolution in Stalin's view was a struggle. Either an ally or an enemy. Privately, he regarded these signs of respect for Plekhanov as 'liberalism', a hangover of intellectual sentimentalism, unworthy of revolutionaries. His party comrades would one day have the opportunity to see how consistent Stalin was in his views.

Three years after the armed uprising, on 7 November 1920, a group of participants gathered for an evening of reminiscence. Stalin was invited, but he did not feel like taking part. Many others, however, chose to attend, including Trotsky, Sadovsky, Mekhonoshin, Podvoisky and Kozmin. Lenin was mentioned many times, as were Trotsky, Kamenev, Zinoviev and a host of others. The minutes of the meeting have been preserved, and the name of Stalin is not to be found among them even once. Neither in connection with the Military Revolutionary Committee, nor the work of the Bolsheviks among the silent masses of soldiers and sailors, did it occur to any of those present to recall his name. To them, he had been no more than an insignificant extra.

As the 'autocrat' he became, his insignificance and inconspicuousness were painful for him to confront. In the 1930s he could only bear to hear about the events of October if they were presented in the light of the 'two leaders'. At first, the real heroes of the revolution were subjected to 'silence', 'historical purging' and 're-editing'. In 1937–39 they were done away with physically. By the 1940s, you could count the active leaders of the revolution on the fingers of one hand. Only those who had helped to create the new October biography of the leader remained. The fewer the number of October veterans, the more inflated Stalin's rôle became.

Naturally, Trotsky, who after 1929 made Stalin the chief object of his critical studies, was extremely scathing about Stalin in October. In his *Stalinist School of Falsification* he asserts that in 1917 Stalin was usually silent at meetings and generally followed Lenin's line: 'He showed no initiative whatever. He made not a single independent proposal, and no "Marxist-Historians" of the new kind can alter that fact.'[46]

In 1924, after Lenin had died, Trotsky published a profile of the late leader in which he included the following dialogue: 'Well?' Vladimir Ilyich said to me soon after 25 October, 'if they kill us both, will Sverdlov and Bukharin be able to manage things all right?' 'Perhaps they won't kill us,' I replied with a laugh.

'What the hell!' Lenin exclaimed, and laughed, too.

'After the appearance of this profile', Trotsky later recalled in his book *My Life*, ' ... Stalin, Zinoviev and Kamenev felt deeply offended by what I had written, although they made no attempt to dispute its accuracy. A fact is a fact: Lenin did not mention any of them as his successors, only Sverdlov and Bukharin. No one else's name came into his head.'[47]

One should not, however, take Trotsky's words at face value, knowing how ambitious and power-seeking he was and that he regarded himself as Lenin's only rightful 'heir'. One could argue with equal validity that in 1924 Trotsky was also trying to consolidate his own position and his reputation in the struggle for power.

As for Stalin, he was pathologically sensitive to anything getting into print that might obliterate his more than modest part in October or exaggerate Trotsky's. It was largely this that prompted Stalin's speech in November 1924 at the plenary meeting of the Trade Union Communist fraction, and which was published as a separate brochure by the state publishing house, Gosizdat, only in 1928. In it, Stalin gave the following analysis of Trotsky's part in the October uprising:

It's true that Comrade Trotsky really fought well in the October period. But he was not the only one, there were others who fought well, such as the Left SRs who stood shoulder to shoulder with the Bolsheviks. But one wonders why, when Lenin chose the practical operations centre for the uprising, he didn't include Trotsky, but did appoint Sverdlov, Stalin, Dzerzhinsky, Bubnov and Uritsky? As you see, the centre did not include the 'inspirer', 'the chief figure', 'the sole leader of the uprising', Comrade Trotsky. How are we to reconcile this with the current opinion about Comrade Trotsky's special role?[48]

This is another example of Stalin's juggling with the facts: it was the Military Revolutionary Committeee that conducted the uprising, not the practical centre.

We see here two party leaders within a few years of the revolution each trying to highlight their own parts in the armed uprising while at the same time minimizing the contribution made by the other. Although one cannot properly speak of cabinet leadership during October, Stalin's part, I repeat, was limited to preparing the instructions of the Central Committee and circulating them to the revolutionary organs. There is no evidence of his having taken part in any of the fighting, organization of armed detachments, or visits to units, ships or factories for the purpose of raising the masses. By force of circumstance, he was in the headquarters of the revolution, certainly on centre stage, but as an extra. He had none of the intellectual gifts, moral appeal, fiery enthusiasm or bubbling energy that are so valuable at such times. At the apex of the revolution stood Lenin. Below him stood the figure of Trotsky, lower still were Zinoviev, Kamenev, Sverdlov, Dzerzhinsky and Bukharin. Below them came an entire cohort of Bolsheviks of the Leninist school, and somewhere among these was Stalin.

Although Stalin had been a party member since the 1890s, a member of the Central Committee since 1912, a member of various soviets, committees and editorial boards, and Commissar for Nationalities, all this merely gave him official (i. e. bureaucratic) status. His presence at meetings and conferences merely attested to the fact that he belonged in the upper ranks of the leadership. This enabled him to get to know and to study a wide range of people, and to penetrate deeper into the mechanism of the apparatus and acquire political experience. It also enabled him to gain Lenin's appreciation of him as a reliable political worker who was capable not only of making the kind of decisions and actions which come naturally to a simple executive, but also of making skilful compromises, manoeuvring and identifying the main elements in a wide spectrum of problems. In the Bolshevism of October, Stalin was a centrist who knew how to sit and wait and adapt himself.

CHAPTER 5

Saved by Chance

The October Revolution saw Russia break its banks, and the social floodwater carried everything before it. The chief month of the chief year of Soviet Russia's new history was exceptionally stormy and triumphant for the Bolsheviks. In a matter of a few months, they had changed from a relatively small party into a mighty political force. The honeymoon period was, however, rather short. Problems long postponed emerged by the end of this unforgettable year as threatening, mortal dangers. In seizing power, the Bolsheviks had promised the people land, bread and peace. They began by giving the land, and land raised the hope that there would be bread. But peace did not depend on the Bolsheviks alone. Just as one cannot applaud with one hand, so one cannot make peace with only one side, especially a just, democratic peace without annexations and reparations. But how was one to achieve it, with the Hapsburg and Hohenzollern hordes trampling Russia's western territories?

No one understood the drama of the moment as well as Lenin. Within days of becoming chairman of the Council of People's Commissars (Sovnarkom), he was giving instructions to A. A. Ioffe who was to head a delegation for peace talks with the German high command.

It seemed at first that peace would be achieved quickly, for as early as 2 December 1917 an armistice was signed to last until 1 January 1918. Peace talks began again soon after. Ioffe was supported by Kamenev and a number of other Bolsheviks and Left SRs. But the situation had changed: nationalist forces had gained the upper hand in Berlin and were aiming for the maximum possible gains. They knew that the Russian trenches were already half-deserted and that the Bolshevik delegation was backed by a mere shadow of Russia's former strength. The Germans put forward conditions for peace which would have meant the loss of a wide expanse of Russian territory.

Lenin showed unique foresight and will-power. If we don't sign the treaty, however harsh and unjust, he said, 'the peasant army, unbearably exhausted by the war, after the very first defeats, which will come most likely in weeks, rather than months, will overthrow the socialist workers' government.'[49] The fate of the revolution was at stake. Two diametrically opposed points of view clashed in the Central Committee, where the Left Communists gained a majority against Lenin for the idea of a 'revolutionary war'.

The Lefts, who included Bukharin, Bubnov, Preobrazhensky, Pyatakov, Radek, Osinsky and Lomov, claimed that the Soviet Union could count on the rise of a revolutionary movement in Europe. Pyatakov asserted that, indeed, without such an upsurge, the Russian revolution was doomed. A revolutionary war against German imperialism would prompt the proletariat into a revolutionary assault on their own governments. The revolutionary symptoms, which were to be seen in many European countries, were interpreted by the Left Communists as signs of the start of a continental conflagration which itself would ignite world revolution.

The second phase of the Brest-Litovsk talks was led by Trotsky who, despite a shift in sentiment on the Central Committee in favour of signing a peace treaty, took an unexpected step. On 10 February 1918, he suddenly declared the talks terminated. 'Our soldier-ploughman,' he said, 'must return to the plough, so that by the coming spring, in peaceful conditions, he will have worked the land which the revolution took from the hands of the landowners and put into the hands of the peasant. Our soldier-worker must return to the workshop, not to produce the weapons of destruction, but the tools of creation. We are getting out of the war. We are going to issue a decree for the total demobilization of our armies. In this connection, I convey the following signed statement:

> In the name of the Council of People's Commissars, the government of the Russian Federative Republic hereby brings to the notice of the governments and peoples which are at war with us, as well as of the allied and neutral countries, that, in declining to sign an annexationist treaty, Russia, for its part, declares the state of war with Germany, Austria–Hungary, Turkey and Bulgaria as terminated.
>
> A decree calling for total demobilization of the entire front is being issued simultaneously to Russian troops.
>
> Brest Litovsk
>
> 10 February 1918.
>
> People's Commissar for Foreign Affairs L. Trotsky.
>
> Members of delegation: V. Karelin, A. Ioffe, M. Pokrovsky, A. Bitsenko. Chairman of All-Ukrainian TsIK Medvedev.[50]

Three days later, at a meeting of the All-Russian Central Executive Committee, Trotsky tried to show that his decision to 'revolutionize' the revolutionary movement in the West, and the slogan 'neither peace nor war', would be supported even by the German troops. In fact, this slogan opened up the heartland of Russia to the aggressor and, within a few days, German troops began advancing along the entire front. After fierce debate, the Central Committee voted seven to four to accept Germany's terms.

In the words of Chicherin, Trotsky's successor, Germany offered a predatory peace 'while holding a gun to the brow of revolutionary Russia.' Russia lost Poland, Lithuania, Estonia, Kurland, Kars, Batum, and some Baltic islands. The party still had to defend the treaty at the Seventh Emergency Party Congress and Fourth Extraordinary All-Russian Congress of Soviets, both of which took place a week apart in March.

Stalin was mostly passive over this issue, not because he disagreed with one side or the other, but rather because the question was too complicated for him to follow. For instance, at a Central Committee meeting on 23 February, when Lenin threatened to resign if they did not agree to make peace, Stalin began to vacillate, but not before he had managed to ask whether 'resignation from one's post also means resignation from the party?' Lenin replied in the negative.

The confusion which occasionally affected Stalin was especially in evidence when the idea was voiced that 'the honour of the revolution takes precedence over its demise.' Lomov, for instance, declared, 'Don't let Lenin's resignation frighten you. The revolution is more precious.' Uritsky said that 'this shameful peace will not save the Soviet régime.' In the midst of such varied opinions, Stalin adopted an indecisive position: 'Maybe we don't have to sign the treaty?' To which Lenin replied: 'Stalin is wrong when he says we don't have to sign. We have to sign these terms. If you don't, you're signing a death warrant for the Soviet régime within three weeks. The Soviet régime is not afraid of these terms. I haven't the slightest hesitation. I am not setting an ultimatum for the treaty to be withdrawn. I'm not looking for a "revolutionary phrase".'[51] Lenin parried all the opposing arguments, and as he subjected them to his criticism, Stalin started to feel better and fell into line behind his leader.

At the Party Congress, Lenin was able to demonstrate the vital need for the hard choice that had been made. Stalin managed to overcome his inner divisions and found the strength to follow Lenin to the end. Equally, Trotsky held to his own position, declaring that he did not regard either position as decisive for the régime's survival.

Regardless of the official Soviet version, Lenin's view of Trotsky's position was not one of black and white. Giving the closing speech on the Central Committee's political report on 8 March 1918, he said:

Further, I must deal with Comrade Trotsky's position. Two sides must be discerned in what he has been doing: when he began the negotiations at Brest, and exploited the opportunity for agitation so brilliantly, we were all in agreement with him. He cited part of a conversation he had had with me, but I can add that it had been agreed between us that we would hang on until the Germans issued their ultimatum and then we would surrender. Trotsky's tactics, to the extent that they were aimed at delaying things, were correct; they became incorrect when the state of war was declared at an end and no peace was signed.[52]

Subsequently, however, Soviet writing began to describe Trotsky's position as treacherous. As for Bukharin, he expressed his disagreement plainly:

The prospect being offered by Comrade Lenin is not acceptable to us ... But it seems to me that we at least are offering a way out. That way out, which Comrade Lenin rejects and which we see as necessary, lies in a revolutionary war against German imperialism.[53]

This revolutionary romanticism of the left, however, broke up on the reef of Lenin's more sober pragmatism.

CHAPTER **6**

Civil War

The breathing space afforded by the peace of Brest-Litovsk was brief. Foreign military intervention, raising hopes of revenge among the bourgeoisie and landowners, began as early as March–April 1918. Rebellions and counter-revolutionary outbursts by White officers, Cossacks and nationalists became widespread. Already ruined by four years of war, the country was again engulfed in the flames of conflict. The Republic had no frontiers, only fronts.

The demise of the Soviet régime seemed imminent, especially as it appeared that open season had been declared on its commissars. In Petrograd, the SR Leonid Kanegisser shot and killed Moisei Uritsky; in July, commissar of the Latvian Riflemen, Semyon Nakhimson, was killed; food commissar of the Turkestan Republic, Alexander Pershin, died at the hands of insurgents in Tashkent; in May 1918, Fedor Podtelkov and Mikhail Krivoshlykov, well known Bolsheviks of the Don region, were hanged on Cossack gallows; Lieu-tenant-General Alexander Taube, who had gone over to the Bolsheviks from the tsarist army to become commander of the Siberian headquarters, fell into White hands and was tortured. But the worst blow fell in Moscow, when, after speaking in front of the Mikhelson factory workers, Lenin was shot by the SR Fanny Kaplan.

A bloody boundary now split long-suffering Russia down the middle, as she was lashed by civil strife. In its ferocity and implacability, the civil war in Russia was a reflection of the deep class hatred that had divided the nation into two hostile camps. Prisoners were not taken, as a rule. Whites bayoneted wounded Red Army men as they lay on their stretchers. No quarter was given in the fighting. The fronts were rife with typhoid. Hostages were taken to gullies and shot. Life was cheap. The call to class solidarity was stronger than sympathy, pity, wisdom or reason. It was war conducted not only by the armed forces of the rival classes, but by virtually the greater part of the population. The country was soaked in the blood of compatriots. The chief catalyst of the civil war was foreign armed intervention. 'It is world imperialism,' Lenin remarked, 'that really provoked our civil war and is to blame for its dragging on.'[54] The government declared the Soviet Republic a military camp and created the Revolutionary Military Council of the Republic (Revvoensoviet) under Trotsky's chairmanship.

Stalin became more visible during the civil war, as he carried out the Central Committee's increasingly complex and responsible commissions. By the middle of 1918, as the noose of hunger tightened around the arteries of Russia's political and industrial centres, the town of Tsaritsyn, in the southeast of the country on the Volga, was becoming increasingly important, more because of the food situation than military considerations. On 31 May, Lenin signed Sovnarkom instructions putting Stalin and A. G. Shlyapnikov in overall charge of food in the south and investing them with special powers.[55] Since his return to Petrograd in April 1917, Lenin had had occasion to meet Stalin on many occasions, and by now he had evidently come to see him as a reliable executive. The taciturn Georgian rarely asked questions or raised doubts in public about Central Committee decisions, he would take on any job and generally seemed satisfied with the rôle that had been assigned to him. Just as calmly, he accepted his commission to Tsaritsyn. Before his departure, he was informed that Lenin, in addition to the Sovnarkom's orders, had instructed A. N. Aralov, a responsible staffer of the war commissariat, to select a detachment of 400 men, of whom 100 should be Latvian Rifles, to be despatched with Stalin.[56]

Tsaritsyn was tightly encircled by Cossacks and Stalin was immediately faced with military decisions. He joined the regional military soviet which soon succeeded in reuniting scattered Red units, carrying out mobilization, forming new divisions and special detachments, as well as a column of armoured trains and some workers' auxiliaries. At Stalin's request, Lenin sent an urgent telegram to the head of the local water transport authorities, ordering them to carry out immediately and without question all instructions and dispositions issued by the Sovnarkom's special plenipotentiary, I.V. Stalin.[57]

The situation in Tsaritsyn became more secure when units of the old 5th Army were transferred there from the Donbass under Voroshilov's command. It is noteworthy that Stalin did not transmit his reports via Trotsky, the commander-in-chief and chairman of the Revvoensoviet, to whom he was operationally subordinate, but over his head directly to Lenin, even on trivial matters. Most of Stalin's telegrams are characteristically devoid of generalization, political evaluation or prognosis. They are exclusively pragmatic. As a result of measures taken by the centre and the military soviet, Tsaritsyn was quickly made ready for a siege. The White assault under General Denikin was not successful, despite the support of the former tsarist officer Colonel Nosovich, who had acted as a military expert for the Soviet régime and had now turned traitor. Tsaritsyn, like other locations where Stalin served during the civil war, acquired not merely a legendary name, but virtually a mystical significance in Soviet history.

Stalin revealed dictatorial tendencies at critical moments. In a note to the centre, he wrote: 'I chase and swear at everyone who asks for it and I hope to restore the situation soon. You can rest assured that I will not spare anyone, neither myself nor others, but everyone will get food. If our military "experts" (bootmakers!) hadn't been sleeping and idle, the line would never have broken, and the fact that it was restored is no thanks to them, but in spite of them.'[58] Nosovich's treachery, and that of a number of other former tsarist officers, reinforced Stalin's suspicions of the military experts which he made no effort to hide. He had a large group of them arrested and incarcerated on a specially converted raft, where many of them were shot. He had his followers. It was this that prompted Lenin, when speaking on the military question at the Eighth Party Congress, to condemn guerrilla warfare and to state unequivocally that 'a regular army is our top priority, we have to go over to a regular army with military experts.'[59] Stalin did not protest publicly against this view, but even at the end of the 1930s former membership of the tsarist officer corps was still an aggravating factor for Red Army commanders.

Comprising Stalin, Voroshilov, chairman of the Tsaritsyn soviet S. K. Minin, and front commander P. P. Sytin, the Revvoensoviet of the Southern front did not operate in a friendly atmosphere. Stalin took the view that all decisions should be made collectively, while Sytin, as a commander applying military logic, sought to avoid the endless 'understandings' and 'clarifications' that accompanied decision-making. Stalin informed Moscow that Sytin was not to be trusted. Sytin responded with a written report to the Revvoensoviet of the Republic in which he asserted that Minin, Stalin and Voroshilov were hampering his activity as front commander by demanding the military soviet's approval of even the most trivial issues, and that this greatly complicated operational procedure.[60] Stalin won the day and Sytin was recalled in early November 1918.

The military experts – former tsarist officers – under Stalin had been placed in a position of constant surveillance and assessment. Stalin knew that Trotsky was on their side, and the two of them had already had a series of telegraphic skirmishes, thus laying the foundation for their profound mutual dislike, which developed into hostility and finally hatred.

Stalin did not burden himself with visits to the trenches or sick-bays, assembly points or observation posts. He was always at headquarters, endlessly sending telegrams, summoning commissars and commanders, demanding reports and summaries, issuing threats of court martial and sending off people 'to be looked into'. He frequently resorted to the extreme sanction, giving orders for saboteurs or suspect military experts – people who in his opinion had harmed the cause – to be shot. In his speech to the Eighth Party Congress, Lenin made direct reference to Stalin's executions in Tsaritsyn and to the disagreement between them on the issue.[61] The civil war was a bloody affair, however, and Stalin felt more assured by then than he had in 1917. Like Carrier, the Convention commissar described by Georges Michelet in his history of the French Revolution, he regarded as natural the unbridled outburst of fierce passion and violence in the name of achieving one's ends. Stalin already believed in the omnipotence of violence and its justified use against one's enemies.

His style was disquieting to many perceptive commanders who even then sensed that this man had an iron grip, that it was hard to nudge him into making a spontaneous decision or to exert influence on his plans. For instance, on 19 May 1919 Antonov-Ovseyenko complained to the Central Committee about the unjust attitude shown towards him as commander of the Ukrainian army. Remarking on the feeble support given him by the centre, he wrote that 'Lev* Davidovich [Trotsky] understands this,' and 'as soon as Comrade Stalin piped down, the Ukrainian comrades stopped their intrigues and got down to business.' This indirectly confirmed that Stalin did have an influence on the course of events at the front.

Lacking operational and tactical knowledge, Stalin relied mainly on discipline, proletarian duty, revolutionary consciousness and frequent threats of 'revolutionary retribution'. After Tsaritsyn he felt more self-assured among the other members of the Central Committee and Sovnarkom. He was by now quite well known among party and military leaders. Certainly he revealed no special military talent while he was carrying out Lenin's instructions at the front. His reports contain no assessments of the operational position, no arguments about the disposition of forces, no original strategic ideas. His operational commands were extremely simple, not to say primitive. For example, in October 1919, Ordzhonikidze, who was in the 14th Army's Revvoensoviet, reported that the army was preparing to recapture the town of Kromy and needed reinforcements. Stalin replied:

The point of our last order was to give you the opportunity to reassemble these regiments into a single group in order to destroy Denikin's best regiments. I repeat, to destroy, because what we are talking about is destruction. The capture of Kromy by the enemy is nothing but an episode that can be corrected, whereas our main task is not to use the regiments as individual assault units, but to strike at the enemy in one massive group and in a single and definite direction.[62]

Although it was his browbeating style that predominated in his orders, it was his skills as a military leader that were lauded in the books and doctoral dissertations of the 1930s and later. Voroshilov, for instance, wrote of him as 'the greatest military leader of all time'. But he was not a military leader, he was a political representative of the centre and a member of a number of revolutionary military soviets. Many other members of the Central Committee contributed no less than Stalin to the victory in the civil war.

Nevertheless, Stalin's personal involvement in the civil war was marked not only by his duties as head of two commissariats, Nationalities and State Control,

---

*The Russian form of Leon, plus Trotsky's patronymic. His original name was Leib Davidovich Bronshtein.

but also in the political, propaganda and, be it said, military fields. Lenin frequently used him as an emissary of the Central Committee to carry out an inspection or a check or to obtain exact information. Thus, in June 1918 Lenin cabled Stalin to say that the government's orders relating to the sinking of ships of the Black Sea Fleet must be carried out to the letter, or else those responsible would be declared outlaws. Stalin was advised to send someone who was capable of carrying out the orders to Novorossiisk.[63] Speaking later that month to a conference of trade unions and factory committees, Lenin, in reply to a question about the fate of the Black Sea Fleet, announced: 'People's Commissars Stalin and Shlyapnikov will be back in Moscow soon and will tell you what happened.'[64]

When Lenin briefed Stalin before his trips to the front, he saw in him not only a member of the Central Committee, but also the representative of a multinational country whose fate depended on the union of Russia with the other republics. Preparing his decree for the Politburo on the defence of Azerbaidzhan, for instance, Lenin instructed Stalin 'to round up the maximum number of Communist Muslims from everywhere for work in Azerbaidzhan.'[65]

Stalin performed the part of political leader in every phase of the civil war. When the first attempt was made to liquidate the Soviet régime, on the occasion of General Krasnov's rebellion in the winter of 1917, Stalin took part in organizing the defence of Petrograd and the mobilization of forces, together with Dzerzhinsky, Ordzhonikidze, Podvoisky, Sverdlov and Uritsky. He helped to prepare the garrison for combat, to build defence lines and to create Red Guard units in factories.

Even at that early date, many people became convinced of his energy and inflexibility, as he dictated orders and gave instructions in a voice that would brook no objection. At the same time, party members noted his vindictiveness and unforgiving nature. In December 1918, Stalin and Voroshilov accused A. I. Okulov, a member of the Southern front Revvoensoviet, of disorganization. On Stalin's insistence, Lenin passed the following resolution: 'In view of the extremely sharp relations existing between Voroshilov and Okulov, we regard Okulov's replacement as essential.'[66] After agreeing with Stalin, Lenin said his piece at the Eighth Congress in Okulov's defence: 'Comrade Voroshilov said such monstrous things that one would think Okulov had destroyed the army. That is monstrous. Okulov was carrying out the Central Committee's line. Okulov informed us that guerrilla tactics were still being used.'[67] Stalin clashed again with Okulov in June 1919, this time when the latter demanded that the Petrograd military district come under the command of the Western front. Stalin, who was then the Central Committee and Defence Council's representative in Petrograd, made insistent demands which prompted Lenin to send a telegram ordering that Okulov be recalled 'to prevent the conflict from growing'.[68] Stalin would remember Okulov in the late 1930s.

Lenin probably began using Stalin from the moment the Dukhonin revolt was crushed. On 9 November 1917, with Stalin and Krylenko standing next to him, Lenin was on the direct line to Dukhonin's headquarters. As Supreme Commander of the Russian army following the collapse of the Kerensky government, and a monarchist by conviction, Dukhonin took no heed of the Soviet government's orders. After a brief exchange, Lenin gave a terse command: Dukhonin was to stand down as commander-in-chief, and his place was to be taken by Ensign N. V. Krylenko as Commissar for War. Next day, the new commander-in-chief set out for general headquarters accompanied by a unit of 500 fighters. Despite the efforts of Krylenko and others to prevent it, Dukhonin was lynched.

Lenin and the Revvoensoviet also used Stalin to identify the causes of various defeats and catastrophes at the front. This was made necessary not only by the various kinds of disorganization that were typical of troop activities, but occasionally by the outright treachery of monarchists and White Guards masquerading as fellow travellers. When the 3rd Army suffered a major defeat in the region of Perm in December 1918, thus opening up the threat that the White Admiral Kolchak might unite his forces in the north with units of British, American and French troops, who occupied substantial territory at Murmansk and Archangel, the Central Committee sent a special commission to Vyatka, under Stalin and Dzerzhinsky, charged with the job of discovering the causes of the defeat and taking steps to correct the situation.

The emissaries acted with determination and despatch. A group of individuals, identified as responsible for the defeat, were handed over to a military tribunal. Weak commanders and commissars were removed from their posts. Emphasis was laid on strengthening the political work in the Red Army, on tightening discipline and improving supplies. Always suspicious of the military experts, and armed with real facts of treachery by a number of former tsarist officers, Stalin acted with particular severity and lack of mercy.

As a result of the steps taken, the 3rd Army, together with the 2nd, was able to restore the situation with a counterattack in January. Stalin wrote in his report to the centre that 'the battle-worthiness of the troops has been restored. A serious purge of soviet and party institutions is being carried out in the rear. Revolutionary committees have been set up in Vyatka and district towns. The provincial extraordinary commissions [Chekas] have been purged and replenished with new personnel.'

Stalin's evaluations, as always, were categorical. For instance, the Revvoensoviet of the 3rd Army 'consists of two members, one of whom (Lashevich) does the commanding, while as for the other one (Trifonov), it is impossible to know what his function or rôle is – he does not look after supply, or the political education of the army, and in general does nothing. In fact, the 3rd Army has no Revvoensoviet.'[69]

Without naming Trotsky, Stalin's report speaks transparently of the 'weak leaders' of the Revvoensoviet of the Republic whose work consists in merely issuing 'general dispositions'. Stalin's exaggerated assessments nevertheless called for corrective measures. On his orders, a large group of functionaries were handed over to a military tribunal for trial. On 5 February 1919, the Central Committee, reviewing the reports of its plenipotentiaries, resolved that 'All those arrested by the Stalin–Dzerzhinsky commission in the 3rd Army are to be placed at the disposition of the appropriate institutions.' Stalin got to know Dzerzhinsky better on this trip, and was apparently full of respect for his thoroughness and determination.

On occasion, he showed this determination even in his communications with the centre. In a letter to Lenin of 3 June 1920, he demanded the immediate liquidation of the Crimean front: 'Either we establish a real armistice with Wrangel, and in doing so take the opportunity to withdraw one or two divisions from the Crimean front,' he wrote, 'or we reject any talks with Wrangel, not wait for him to sit it out, but strike him now and, having dealt with him, release our forces for the Polish front. The present position, which gives us no clear answer on the Crimea, is becoming intolerable.'[70] Lenin wrote at once to Trotsky:

> This is obviously Utopian. Won't it cost too many lives? We'd be killing a multitude of our soldiers. This has to be tried and tested ten times. I suggest this reply: Your proposal for an offensive on the Crimea is so serious that we have to take stock and think it over with extreme caution. Await our reply. Signed, Lenin and Trotsky.[71]

Trotsky replied that, in approaching Lenin directly, Stalin had breached the established order: the commander of the Southwestern front, A.I. Yegorov, ought to have made the report. Lenin added a note: 'Possibly this was to make mischief. But the question must be discussed urgently. What extraordinary measures are needed?'[72]

Despite Lenin's efforts to smooth relations between Stalin and Trotsky, they remained cold and guarded. The future General Secretary found Trotsky's rising popularity painful to observe and thought it was undeserved. On his rare visits to Moscow, people in the Revvoensoviet of the Republic showed Stalin a number of telegrams of similar content, for example:

> To Revvoensoviet chairman Trotsky. On the first anniversary of the October revolution ... the citizens of Kochetovka, Zosimov District, Tambov Province, resolved to change the name of the village to your name, calling it Trotskoe. We request your permission to call our village by the name that is dear to us as that of the leader and inspirer of the Red Army. Chairman of Soviet S. Nechaev.

As a matter of fact, the first Soviet Russian towns to be renamed (currently Gatchina and Chapaevsk) were called Trotsk.

Lenin's civil war correspondence with Stalin contains several examples of mutual tetchiness. For instance, in February 1920, when Lenin called for help to be given to the Caucasian front, Stalin replied: 'I don't see why I have to do this. It is entirely the responsibility of the Revvoensoviet of the Republic, who, as far as I know, are all fit, and it is not Stalin's, who is so overburdened with work.'[73] Lenin told him to get on with it, 'and not squabble over departmental responsibility.'[74]

But undertones of Stalin's mischief-making continued to be detected in his reports. On 4 August of the same year, Lenin asked him to send an account of the situation in the south, and to assess the outlook.[75] Stalin felt disheartened. On the one hand, he did not want responsibility for 'the most important political decisions', but nor did he possess the ability to make predictions. He replied: 'I really don't know why you need my opinion and therefore I am not in a position to give you the findings you have asked for, and so I will limit myself to reporting the bare facts without comment.'[76] He was a genuine executor of the centre's orders, but when something more was required of him, his feelings of offence and misunderstanding came out and merged with the mischief-making Lenin had identified.

Along with the various fronts on which Stalin, like many other prominent Bolsheviks, served during the civil war, the Petrograd district was facing a severe situation in the spring of 1919. The White General Yudenich and Allied intervention forces were planning to seize the flagship capital of the revolution immediately. The 7th Army and the Baltic Fleet were charged with the defence of the city. Superior enemy forces were approaching Red (formerly Tsarskoe) Selo and Gatchina. The Red Army command was transferring strong units to Petrograd from other fronts. As a plenipotentiary, Stalin was always either at the Petrograd soviet or at defence headquarters. As usual, his methods were dictatorial, whether he was removing incompetent personnel, or arresting those he thought responsible for the situation, or organizing supplies, or 'shaking up' the local leadership. A conspiracy was discovered in the head-quarters of the Western front and 7th Army. The conspirators were, naturally, shot. Mob rule was gradually giving way to a no-nonsense discipline and revolutionary determination. The organizers of the defence of Petrograd included Remezov, Tomashevich, Pozern, Shatov, Peters and Stalin, who, like Trotsky, was awarded the Order of the Red Banner for his services.

Earlier accounts always had it that, wherever Stalin was sent, the situation improved, but this was far from the truth. Moreover, Stalin usually went with a group and was always carrying out the orders of the centre and Lenin. On the military level, his services were in fact very modest. But already in 1918 the comrades in the centre knew that he was not simply a dedicated executive, but was also a specialist in 'extraordinary', i. e. punitive, measures. And they knew that he was already showing signs of self-congratulation. In a cable to the centre, Stalin reported the destruction of two White-held forts, adding that 'the naval experts are saying [the actions] were against all naval science. I can only bemoan such a so-called science. I consider it my duty to declare that I shall henceforth act as I have done, regardless of my reverence for science.'[77]

When Stalin returned from one of his routine trips, he was given a job in the Central Committee apparatus, running everyday affairs. A number of telegrams from the front show that he had already acquired a degree of real power. For instance, on 15 November 1921, Trotsky cabled him: 'We must settle the question of the Trans-Caucasian national brigades and military depots firmly and once and for all,' and went on to ask about getting three decisions through the Politburo on this issue. This was one of his rare telegrams to Stalin. Each tried his best not to notice the other. Their mutual dislike had begun on first acquaintance, and at heart Stalin continued to regard Trotsky as a Menshevik. He didn't like Trotsky's self-confidence, his eloquence and authority, and his ability to present himself. He didn't like the way Trotsky, as chairman of the Revvoensoviet of the Republic, toured the fronts in a special train accompanied by one, if not two, armoured wagons and a large detachment of smart young Red Army men in leather tunics. Stalin felt provoked by the comfort Trotsky surrounded himself with, and he both envied and despised the eloquent commissar, with his panache and popularity. On the other hand, he did not condemn Trotsky when the latter declared publicly, 'You cannot build an army without repression. You cannot lead the masses to their deaths, unless you have the death penalty in your arsenal of command.'[78] He secretly agreed with this line and resorted to such measures himself in critical situations, and he was not the only one who did so. On 12 May 1920, Berzin, a member of the Revvoensoviet of the Southwestern front, reported that units of the 14th Army had deserted on the Polish front, and that 'the order had been given to shoot every tenth man who had run away.'[79]

The civil war was harsh to its enemies, but also to its own. Nosovich, the former chief of the Northern Caucasus military district, mentioned above as having deserted to the Whites, recalled that Stalin did not hesitate when he was sure he was confronted by an enemy. Thus, in Tsaritsyn, an engineer called Alexeyev, his two sons and a number of former tsarist officers were accused of belonging to a counter-revolutionary organization. Stalin's decision was terse: 'To be shot.' People were summarily executed without any trial. Stalin regarded this as a matter of course, since he deeply believed in the 'universality' and implacability of punitive actions that were capable of yielding the appropriate political 'result'.

A Central Committee meeting of 25 October 1918 discussed, among other things, a letter from Stalin reporting sabotage of the 10th Army's supplies. He insistently demanded that the commander of the front and members of the military soviet be handed over to a military tribunal. The Central Committee, under Sverdlov's chairmanship, resolved, however, 'not to put anyone on trial, but to order an investigation'. Stalin's solicitations were rejected.

On another occasion, when he was a member of the Revvoensoviet of the Southern front, Stalin had a difference of opinion with Smilga, another member, over where to direct the main blow against Denikin's forces. Stalin was sharp, rude and impatient. It was important for him not only to be right, but also to humiliate his opponent. Instead of calmly debating the pros and cons with his comrades, who were after all members of the same organization, he became entrenched in a position which bordered on bitter hostility. Three years later, in one of his last notes, Lenin remarked on Stalin's bitterness when dealing with important matters. And 'bitterness in general,' he commented, 'usually plays the worst part in politics.'[80] When Stalin was faced with disagreement or argument, he would call on the authority of the centre, refer to orders from Moscow, and express doubt as to his opponent's political reliability. Virtually everyone who was ever in conflict with him during the civil war would pay for it dearly two decades later. Stalin had a vicious memory.

Since he was a member of the Revvoensoviet of the Southwestern front for a relatively long time, Stalin soon established a common language with its commander, A. I. Yegorov, a future Marshal of the Soviet Union. A powerful military leader, Yegorov would be repressed with Stalin's knowledge and approval during the bloody purge of 1937. Stalin gave no response to a letter from Yegorov asking for mercy, despite the fact that Yegorov reminded him that during the civil war they had 'more than once eaten from the same mess-tin'. Yet there was an episode in which Stalin did intercede for Yegorov, albeit in the strangest way. A proposal from Trotsky to remove Yegorov from his post as front commander was being debated in Moscow and Stalin was asked for his opinion. On 4 June 1920, he cabled Trotsky:

I object strongly to the replacement of Yegorov by Uborevich who is not yet ready for such a post, or by Kork who is not suitable to be a front commander. It was Yegorov and the commander-in-chief [S. S. Kamenev] together who let the Crimea slip through our fingers, for the commander-in-chief was in Kharkov for two weeks before Wrangel's advance and he left for Moscow without realizing that [Wrangel's] army had disintegrated. If it's so important to punish someone, then punish them both. I don't think we will find anyone better than Yegorov at present. It would therefore be better to replace the commander-in-chief, who fluctuates between extreme optimism and extreme pessimism, gets in everyone's way and confuses the front commander, having nothing positive to offer.[81]

Stalin probably 'defended' Yegorov because the idea of replacing him had come from Trotsky. As for those who had 'let the Crimea slip through our fingers', Stalin was one of them. As early as 1920 we see that Stalin could peremptorily declare that the commander-in-chief, S. S. Kamenev, was 'getting in everyone's way'. Stalin's vital attribute had long been the ability to inflict moral damage. And as his position became more secure, so this quality would become more dangerous and more malicious.

After its early success against Poland, the Red Army suffered serious defeat in 1920, and nearly twenty years later, Stalin would blame Yegorov, Tukhachevsky and the other military leaders for the 'criminal delay that was dictated by their treacherous schemes'. It would never enter his head that, as a member of the military soviet himself, he also bore full responsibility for the successes and failures of the forces at the front.

On 2 August 1920, the Politburo took the decision to carve out a part of the Southwestern front and create an independent Southern front. The military soviet of the front tabled a proposal to transfer the 12th and 14th Armies and the 1st Cavalry Army to the Western front. They were unable to carry out this operation rapidly. On 13 August Stalin and Yegorov reported to Kamenev, the commander-in-chief, that the forces at the front were already overstretched and that altering the armies' basic tasks would be impossible under present circumstances.[82]

When Kamenev sent a new directive to the command of the Southwestern front concerning the transfer of the 12th Army and 1st Cavalry Army, the order was signed by R. I. Berzin, Stalin having refused. Precious time was lost through squabbling and negotiation. The withdrawal of forces towards Lvov began only on 20 August, and they were too late to give any help. Of course, responsibility for this strategic error lay with the Revvoensoviet of the Republic and the commander-in-chief of the front. But, after all, Stalin had concurred with the idea of transferring three armies to the Western front as early as 5 August, and had then slowed things down, with serious consequences. Stalin had made no special effort to see that his own proposal was implemented, even though it had been ratified in Moscow. He was just as guilty of this major failure as were Trotsky, Tukhachevsky, Yegorov and others. But of course Stalin would never dream of admitting his own omission. He was already developing the instincts of infallibility.

Analysing the outcome of the failure, Lenin said that 'when we were approaching Warsaw, our troops were so exhausted that they hadn't sufficient strength to carry their victory further, whereas the Polish troops, buoyed up as they were by a patriotic upsurge in Warsaw and feeling themselves in their own country, found the support and the fresh opportunity to go forward. It turned out that the war gave us the opportunity to go almost as far as the complete devastation of Poland, but at the decisive moment we lacked the strength.'[83] It is most significant that subsequent military chroniclers, while they highlighted Stalin's 'special' contribution to the breakthrough on the Southern, Eastern and Northwestern fronts, never mentioned his rôle in the Polish campaign, because they had nothing positive to say.

Leaving aside all the appalling and unforgivable things that he would do in the future, and assuming that he was not born a scoundrel, one can say that Stalin did make a certain contribution in the civil war. But it was the contribution of an emissary carrying out orders. He made none of the 'decisive input' that would be claimed for him later. At the same time, it should be remembered that, from the first moment of the revolution, Stalin was a member of the highest party bodies: first in the Central Committee, then the Politburo and Orgburo. By degrees, especially as the civil war approached its end, Stalin's position became stronger and he became one of the key figures in the governing nucleus of the party.

Examination of Stalin's activities during this period shows that he was second to many other party leaders. As a theoretician, he was nothing more than a popularizer, and he had no oratorical skill, an important consideration at a time of historic revolutionary convulsions. No one could say of him that he was an 'understanding' or 'good' person. He manifestly lacked the moral qualities that one normally associates with virtue. Yet he had something that his peers lacked, namely a rare degree of purposefulness and the ability to hold obsessively to a concrete idea. These qualities impressed the people he worked with in his numerous appointed tasks. It is plain that as a leader Stalin was formed to a great extent during the years of the civil war. He had a feeling for power, he understood how it worked, both at the centre and in the localities, and he became convinced that the application of pressure at critical moments could bring the desired result.

Many of the party leaders were members of the intelligentsia, or, as Stalin once remarked sarcastically in the late 1920s, 'writers'. He never expanded on this topic, chiefly because Lenin was also an 'intellectual' and 'writer' and 'émigré'. But Lenin's intellect was such that Stalin, having launched the concept of the 'second leader' who was 'always together with Lenin', never uttered a single critical remark about his master. When, however, Lenin criticized Stalin – on the nationalities, the foreign trade monopoly, military and other issues – Stalin, usually in silence, agreed with him. Lenin's psychological power over Stalin was plain to see.

The thin intellectual stratum that was the 'Lenin old guard' failed at the crucial moment by allowing a man with dictatorial, Caesarist tendencies to usurp power in the party and state. They all considered themselves to be Leninists, yet they were incapable of carrying out the last testament of the leader of the revolution. How and why did this happen? Why was no other alternative sought? This question will occupy students of Soviet history for a long time to come. The past is not a shadow theatre. What rules there is not the ephemeral, but the irreversible.

2

THE LEADER'S WARNINGS

'The rarest courage is the courage of thought.'
–Anatole France

CHAPTER 7

Comrades in Arms

Lenin rarely complained about his health and while he was still healthy his comrades were never discussed as possible successors. As soon as the first signs of overstrain and illness appeared in late 1921, however, more and more people began to ponder on those close to him. After his death, his physicians stated in their report that his illness had begun at the end of 1921, though it had probably been developing slowly for some time. In March 1922, the doctors were still unable to find any organic disorder, but in view of his severe headaches and signs of exhaustion, he was advised to rest for several months, and he moved to Gorky. In early May, however, the first symptoms of organic brain disorder appeared. The first attack took the form of general lassitude, loss of speech and a sharp reduction of movement in his right arm and leg. Substantial improvement took place by July, with so much progress in August and September that in October he returned to work, though at a reduced level. In November he gave three long, programmatic speeches.[1]

Aged only fifty-one when his illness began, Lenin was still a young man by present-day standards, but since returning to Petrograd in 1917 he had had practically no rest. His working day lasted fourteen to sixteen hours. According to his secretaries, when he was ill he remarked that he had had only two breaks in all those years, first in Razliv, when he was hiding from the Provisional Government, and the second by courtesy of Fanny Kaplan, who had shot him.

When in late 1921 he became aware of his impending illness, he realized that, once he had left the scene, a split could occur in the party leadership. Perhaps the idea of a political 'testament' occurred to him then. In November 1922, as if anticipating another stroke, he handed back the books he had just read to the librarian, Sh. M. Manucharyants, with the particular request that he leave behind Engels's *Political Testament (from the Unpublished Letters)*. He wrote on the cover, 'Keep on the shelf. 30.11.1922. Lenin'.[2]

Less than a month later, on the night of 26 December, having barely recovered from a serious stroke, Lenin dictated the third part of his 'Letter to the Congress' to L. A. Fotieva. This letter shows how, despite being over-burdened with the problems of the present, Lenin was constantly preoccupied with the future and what would happen when he was no longer there. He was the leader by virtue of having personified the Bolshevik Party before, during and after the revolution, but he had no official status. Who were the people around him? How had they reached the crest of the revolution? What had they achieved in life? How did Stalin appear in the galaxy of Lenin's comrades?

It is always difficult to shift from peace to war, but in the conditions obtaining in Soviet Russia after the civil war, it was no simple matter to go from war to peace. Dislocation, desolation, starvation – the words do not do justice to the degree of the shock, the deformation and the shattered state of society that existed at the beginning of the 1920s. Russia was a vast revolutionary island in a sea of hostile states. The country was convulsed as whole provinces and districts openly rebelled against or passively resisted the new order. The revolution had won, it had survived and consolidated the power of the soviets, but the new régime could still do almost nothing for the workers and peasants. The government's economic policy for the first three years – War Communism, as it was called – meant the nationalization of industry and trade, wages in kind for workers and employees, the forcible extraction of produce from the peasants and compulsory labour service by the middle classes. None of this was successful in making good the promises that had been made by the Bolsheviks: the right to work, to rest, to have social security and education. To escape from the prospect of communism based on poverty, the country needed the sort of bold ideas and energetic measures that only the party could bring about. The party was the spiritual and political axis around which life still revolved. At the beginning of 1921 more than 20,000 cells united over 730,000 Communist Party members, and almost one quarter of them were in the Red Army.

The Central Committee under Lenin's leadership was the brain of the régime. It had only a small number of members. For example, the Tenth Party Congress appointed a Central Committee of twenty-five with fifteen candidate members. Its numbers were only marginally increased, to twenty-seven and nineteen respectively, by the time of the Eleventh Congress, which was Lenin's last. While Lenin was alive, its plenums took place generally twice a month. The core of the membership were Moscow men who bore the full burden of the work in hand, namely, settling questions of economic and military construc-tion, forming close ties with the national elements in the party and determining policy over such issues as the Democratic Centralists* and Workers'

---

* The Democratic Centralists were a faction of the party formed in 1920 and led by former Left Communists V.V. Osinsky, T.V. Sapronov, V.N. Maximovsky. They were for collective as against one-man management of enterprises, opposed central party control in the localities, and demanded freedom of factions and groupings in the party.

Opposition,* and introducing the New Economic Policy (NEP). Some of its members, moreover, belonged to these same factions or platforms, which today would be called 'informal' or 'non-institutionalized'. Everything was strange and new. The party became the guiding force, its power became real. Therefore much depended on the political positions, moral qualities and professionalism of those who operated within the nucleus of the party.

Lenin was the only person to be appointed to the Central Committee at every one of the post-war congresses – the Tenth, Eleventh and Twelfth (though he did not attend the last). His example, experience and theoretical works were uniquely influential in the Central Committee and its governing nucleus, and his absences were keenly felt.

Giving the organizational report to the Twelfth Congress on 17 April 1923, Stalin stated:

Within the Central Committee there is a nucleus of ten to fifteen men who have become so good at handling the political and economic work of our organs that they risk becoming something like high priests of government. This may be a good thing, but maybe it has its dangerous side, too, for these comrades, having accumulated a great deal of experience in governing, could become affected by self-importance, they could become enclosed in themselves and cut off from working with the masses ... If they do not surround themselves with a new generation of future leaders who are closely linked with the work of the localities, then these highly qualified people stand every chance of becoming ossified and cut off from the masses.[3]

Lenin was still alive when Stalin uttered these words, and this part of the speech was suffused with Lenin's notion that the leading core should be renewed constantly. The passage of fifteen years would see these views evolve into something very different, although even in 1937–38 Stalin was still capable of saying good things, while practising their very opposite. In the early 1920s, however, this dualism of word and deed was not so evident. At the congress, he formulated his thoughts on Lenin's comrades and pupils as follows:

The nucleus in the Central Committee, that is so good at governing, is getting old and needs replacing. You know the state of Vladimir Ilyich's health, you know that the other members of the nucleus are also pretty worn out. But as yet there is nobody to replace them, that's the trouble. It is very hard to create party leaders, it takes time, five to ten years or more. It's easier to make war on another country with the help of Budyonny's cavalry than to forge two or three leaders from the ranks who can really become the country's leaders in the future.[4]

---

*The Workers' Opposition was also formed in 1920 by A. G. Shlyapnikov, M. K. Vladimirov, A. M. Kollontai, Yu. Kh. Lutovinov, C. P. Medvedev. They regarded the highest form of working class organization to be, not the party, but the trade unions, and they proposed that the management of the national economy be handed over to them.

While this argument seems reasonable, by present-day standards the average member of the Central Committee was rather young. Lenin, who was barely fifty, was the oldest. The main body of members were in their forties, the age regarded by the ancient Greeks as the acme and crowning glory of life, the age when one's intellectual and physical strengths are supposed to be in harmony.

The inner core of the leadership during the first years after the revolution had vastly different backgrounds, revolutionary experience, education and, of course, personal likes and dislikes. Practically half of Lenin's close comrades had spent years in exile abroad, they had taken part in countless social democratic, socialist, humanitarian and cultural conferences, congresses and meetings. Stalin did not fit into this pattern. His emergence had followed an odd course. His native wit and cunning, and his calculating cautiousness came from a dubious school. Twenty-odd years of religious education and internal exile, and the lack of working class experience or any professional training, had made him into the executor of an idea. Before any of the others in Lenin's entourage, he had seen the importance, sensed the power to be derived from an apparatus. Most of Lenin's colleagues plainly underrated the rôle played by the anonymous structures of authority.

Stalin gradually formed his own attitude to each member of the ruling nucleus. The people he described as 'good at governing' were extremely varied. Stalin himself, as we have noted, lacked self-assurance when confronted by Trotsky's condescension and self-confidence, but he realized later on that his rival was often merely striking a pose or uttering an elegant phrase. During the revolution and civil war, Trotsky's skill as a speaker helped him shine. His popularity spread and he acquired followers, among them people who saw in him not merely the 'second man', but a potential future leader of the party. He revealed himself as a man whose chief talents lay not in organization, but in oratory and a sharp and at times paradoxical mind. It was these qualities that enabled him to lead people, to inspire the troops at the front, and artificially to inflate his own popularity. But when the time for mundane tasks arrived, the leader of the Red Army quickly began to fade. Even some of his good ideas were put forward in such a provocative way that he lost support. Not for him the spade-work. He had to have a slogan and a platform on which to speak and make effective gestures.

Perhaps earlier than most, Stalin spotted Trotsky's strong and weak sides. Taking Trotsky's enormous popularity into account, Stalin at first tried to establish if not friendly, then at least stable relations with him. On one occasion, Stalin turned up unannounced at Trotsky's place in Arkhangelskoe outside Moscow to congratulate him on his birthday. The meeting was not a warm one. Each sensed the other's dislike. On another occasion, with Lenin's assistance, Stalin tried to establish better relations. This emerged in a telegram from Lenin to Trotsky dated 23 October 1918, in which Lenin gave an account of his conversation with Stalin. As a member of the Defence Council, Stalin gave his assessment of the position in Tsaritsyn and expressed the desire to work more closely with the Revvoensoviet of the Republic. Lenin added:

In conveying Stalin's statements to you, Lev Davidovich, I request that you think about them and say, first, whether you agree to discuss them personally with Stalin, for which purpose he would come here, and secondly, whether you consider it possible, in certain concrete circumstances, to set aside the existing friction and work together, which Stalin wants so much to do. As for myself, I believe it is necessary to make every effort to work well together with Stalin.[5]

Nothing came of it, however. Trotsky could not hide his superior attitude. As he himself wrote of Stalin:

Being enormously envious and ambitious, he could not but feel his intellectual and moral inferiority every step of the way ... Only much later did I realize that he had been trying to establish some sort of familiar relations. But I was repelled by the very qualities that would strengthen him ... namely, the narrowness of his interests, his pragmatism, his psychological coarseness and the special cynicism of the provincial who has been liberated from his prejudices by Marxism but who has not replaced them with a philosophical outlook that has been thoroughly thought out and mentally absorbed.[6]

Stalin even spoke highly of Trotsky's rôle in the revolution and civil war in some of his speeches, but that did not improve Trotsky's aloof attitude towards him.

Leading lights in the galaxy were Zinoviev (real name Radomyslsky) and Kamenev (real name Rozenfeld), who are generally treated as a duo. They shared the same views and hardly ever argued with each other. Zinoviev, who had held a prominent position in the party for a very long time, was the dominant one of the pair. His career had its soaring heights and its plunging lows. A member of the party since 1901, he spent many years in exile abroad where he was engaged mainly in writing. During October 1917, both Zinoviev and Kamenev blotted their revolutionary copybooks pretty thoroughly by coming out openly in the press against the armed uprising. Lenin later wrote that 'the episode in October was of course not accidental.'[7]

Zinoviev reached his peak as chairman of the Executive Committee of Comintern, a position he held for seven years. He wrote countless articles which he saw to it were published as separate brochures and even as a special edition of collected works with a silhouette of his head embossed on the cover. He polished many of his better qualities while living in close proximity to Lenin, both when they were abroad and after the revolution. Lunacharsky went particularly far in assessing Zinoviev as one of Lenin's supports, 'one of the four or five men who represented the preponderance of political brains in the party'. According to Lunacharsky, Zinoviev was regarded by everyone as 'Lenin's closest and most trusted assistant'.[8]

Zinoviev possessed superhuman energy, but he was subject to frequent changes of mood, swinging from unbridled optimism to despondency and sinking right down to depression or 'cold' hysteria. He was always having to be cheered up and got going. For a long time he was condescending towards Stalin, even arrogant. In the early 1920s he half-jokingly teased Stalin for the primitive style of his articles, which suffered from tautology and lack of colour. He himself was capable of writing in a light, aphoristic style and some of his articles are extremely rich in content. His article 'On the First Battles for Leninism', for instance, subtly demonstrates the inconsistency of Trotsky's claim to a special position in the party.

As leader of the Petrograd party organization, Zinoviev tried in his time to show firmness and even exhibited dictatorial mannerisms, although when Yudenich was approaching the city Zinoviev simply lost his head. And this was witnessed by Stalin, who had just arrived in Petrograd and who mentally marked him down as a vain and ambitious milksop. Until Lenin died, Stalin tried to maintain something like friendly relations with Zinoviev and Kamenev. When Lenin went into conference with Zinoviev, Kamenev and Stalin in early November 1922, the impression was readily created that the trio were extremely close, friendly and united. This impression could not last very long, however, for each member of the troika had his own ambitious plans. Nobody would have predicted that it would be precisely on Stalin's initiative that Zinoviev would be expelled from the party twice and then reinstated, and that his final expulsion in 1934 would shortly precede his execution. A similar fate faced Kamenev.

Zinoviev was one of the party's best speakers, and gave the Central Committee's political report at the Twelfth and Thirteenth Party Congresses. He was among those who approved the existence of a nucleus in the leadership. Speaking at the Fourteenth Congress in 1925, he said:

Vladimir Ilyich was sick and we had to have our first congress without him. You know that there was discussion about the nucleus that had formed in the Central Committee, and that the Twelfth Congress silently went along with the idea that this nucleus, with the entire support of the Central Committee, of course, would continue to lead the party until Ilyich was back on his feet.[9]

Zinoviev, like Kamenev, was long regarded as one of Stalin's close friends. When he was removed from the Politburo in 1926, he thought his exclusion would not last long. On New Year's Eve that year, he and Kamenev, bearing bottles of brandy and champagne, turned up unannounced at Stalin's apartment. One would have thought the world revolution had taken place. They addressed each other in the familiar form and recalled old times and friends, but they uttered not a word about the affair. 'Koba' was hospitable and gave his old 'pals' a friendly welcome. He spoke simply and sincerely, as if it had not been he who had secured their expulsion from the Politburo the previous October. The duo felt they were floating on air. But Stalin had long ago decided that the services of these people, who knew so much about him, were no longer required.

There would be one more occasion when they would come, or rather be brought, to Stalin together. As former comrades of Lenin and ex-members of the Politburo who had counted with good reason on remaining in high positions after Lenin's death, they had been writing letters to Stalin while in gaol in 1936, when suddenly he reacted. They entered the study of the man they had once so underrated to find, apart from Stalin himself, Voroshilov and Yezhov. Stalin did not respond to their greetings nor invite them to sit down. Pacing up and down, he offered them a deal: their guilt was already established and a new court might impose the extreme sentence. But he remembered their past services. If they would confess to everything at their trial, especially Trotsky's direct leadership of their subversive activities, he would save their lives, or rather, he would try to save them. And then he would do his best to get them released. They had to make up their minds. The case required it. A long silence ensued. Zinoviev, who was the weaker and more compliant of the two, said quietly: 'All right, we agree.' He was used to speaking for Kamenev. Two months later they were shot.

This story was related to me in 1947 in Siberia by a prisoner known as Boris Semyonovich. In the village where I lived with my mother, my brother and my sister, a camp had been hastily built in 1937. Some of the inmates had been given 'unescorted' status, that is, they were allowed on occasion to go outside the zone. Boris Semyonovich was a shoemaker and he came to us two or three times to patch my own and my brother's tarpaulin boots. Until he was arrested in 1938, he had worked in the security force of the very prison where Zinoviev and Kamenev were held. He had accompanied them to their last meeting with Stalin. The night they were taken for execution, each behaved differently. Although they had both written to Stalin many times begging for mercy and were apparently expecting it (he had after all promised), they sensed this was the end. Kamenev walked along the corridor in silence, nervously pressing his palms. Zinoviev became hysterical and had to be carried. In under an hour, two more of the old Central Committee nucleus crossed the fateful threshold. In their time they had done more than anyone to consolidate Stalin's position, and the payment for their services was their lives.

It is worth recalling that Stalin had known Kamenev well from their time together in exile in Turukhansk, where they had first heard news of the February Revolution. Stalin had already then noticed in Kamenev a combination of erudition and a certain impulsiveness, an ability to make definite decisions quickly and just as quickly to reject them. Stalin's attitude to Kamenev was much influenced by the fact that the latter was Lenin's deputy in the Sovnarkom and frequently chaired Central Committee plenums as well as party congresses. As a rule, while Lenin was alive Kamenev also chaired the Politburo.

Although Zinoviev and Kamenev were both good speakers and writers, they lacked 'backbone' and were capable of sudden shifts of attitude at crucial moments for the sake of their personal aims, ambitions and prestige. Whether or not they meant to, unfortunately for them they took their struggle with

Stalin into the orbit of the party apparatus, where, despite all their abilities, their chances of success were very low.

Knowing their weaknesses, Lenin nevertheless relied a great deal on Zinoviev and Kamenev, especially the latter, who carried out many personal commissions for him. It was known that Kamenev was good at smoothing ruffled feathers in internal party relations. While he was less popular than Zinoviev, he was more solid and more of an intellectual. He had his own ideas, he was capable of making quite profound theoretical generalizations, and he was bold and decisive. The speech he made on 21 December 1925 (Stalin's birthday) to the Fourteenth Party Congress deserves to go down in history:

We are against creating a 'leadership' theory, we are against making a 'leader'. We are against having the Secretariat which in practice unites both policy and organization, standing abové the political organ. We are for having the Politburo so organized internally that, while it unites all the politicians of the party, our top body genuinely has full power; and we are for the Secretariat being subordinate to the Politburo and carrying out its instructions. I personally suggest that our General Secretary is not the person to unite the old Bolshevik headquarters staff around him. Precisely because I have said this on countless occasions to Comrade Stalin personally, and I have said it countless times to the group of Leninist comrades, I repeat it at this congress: I have come to the conclusion that Comrade Stalin cannot carry out the rôle of unifier of the Bolshevik staff. I began this part of my speech with the words: we are against the theory of one-man leadership, we are against creating a leader![10]

These were brave words. And, spoken in public at a time when Stalin's one-man rule had barely begun to show itself, they were weighty words of warning, for which alone Kamenev deserves credit. He seems to have assimilated the Bolshevik precept of courageous thinking better than the others. Why else did none of the 'group of Leninist comrades' come out in support of the sober and prophetic remarks of one of the governing nucleus? But it was not only the 'Leninists' who were guilty of a short-sighted understanding of the position, it was Kamenev himself: his unprincipled feints, away from and then back to Trotsky, in the struggle with Stalin created the justified impression that his behaviour was largely motivated by personal ambition. Kamenev was not the man to stop Stalin. Instead of being weakened, Stalin was reinforced, for Kamenev, after all, had attacked the General Secretary from his position as a member of an 'opposition'.

Relations between Trotsky, Zinoviev and Kamenev were complicated. Despite being married to his sister, Kamenev had no close ties with Trotsky. The central issue was the fact that Trotsky and Zinoviev both aimed at leadership of the party, especially when it became clear that Lenin's health was in a critical state. Trotsky published his sensational *Lessons of October* and showed Zinoviev and Kamenev in a most unflattering light. They in turn demanded his expulsion from the Politburo and the party. Stalin was not yet, however, the man he was to become in the late 1920s and 1930s. At the Fourteenth Congress, when the Central Committee limited itself to removing Trotsky from the post of Commissar for War, Stalin said:

We did not agree with Zinoviev and Kamenev because we know that a policy of severance is pregnant with dangers for the party, that the severance method, the blood-letting method – and they demanded blood – is dangerous and contagious: today we sever one person, tomorrow someone else, the next day a third person – what will be left of the party?

The congress greeted this with applause, but two or three minutes later, further on in his closing speech, Stalin would say, commenting on the closure of the Leningrad journal, *Bolshevik*: 'We are not liberals. For us, the interests of the party are higher than formal democracy. Yes, we are capable of prohibiting the publication of a factional organ, and we will prohibit similar things in the future.'[11] These words were greeted with stormy applause. The delegates liked Stalin's firmness and determination, but could they guess that Stalin would soon be ready for the 'severance method', or that so many of them would be mounting the guillotine themselves?

Let us jump ahead a little. Kamenev had already been thrown out of the leading nucleus and was working as director of the Institute of World Literature. During one of Yagoda's routine visits to Stalin, the master said: 'Keep an eye on Kamenev. I think he's tied up with Ryutin.* Lev Borisovich [Kamenev] is not one to give in so easily. I've known him for more than twenty years. He's an enemy.' Yagoda did as he was told. Kamenev was arrested in 1934, tried in 1935 and given five years. He was tried again in the same year and this time given ten years. At the end of 1936, a full stop was put to his case, forever. For the time being, however, Stalin needed Zinoviev and Kamenev in his struggle with Trotsky, whom he saw as his and the party's chief enemy.

Stalin quickly showed himself to be a fairly good administrator. As he carried out his tasks, he paid special attention to the needs of the members of the Politburo and other senior figures in the Central Committee. In his own mind, the people he regarded as most influential were those he privately called the 'writers', that is, the former émigrés. He could not deny that these people possessed a high degree of intellect, theoretical grounding and broad general learning, and this aroused in him a certain resentment, as if to say, 'while we were preparing the revolution, they were over there reading and writing.'

Once he almost expressed himself openly on this. A provincial secretary was being confirmed as a Central Committee representative when it transpired that the comrade could barely read or write. Stalin threw his opinion onto the scales by saying, 'He's never been abroad, where was he supposed to learn? He'll get by.'

---

*In 1932 Mikhail Ryutin circulated a lengthy document calling for a slower pace of industrialization and collectivization, party democracy and the removal of Stalin.

Lenin's assistants included many talented people. Stalin soon took note of the fact that Bukharin, Rykov and Tomsky, although they formed no special group, were very keen to solve the country's economic and industrial problems. They were good economists, or technocrats, as we would say today. Regrettably, in the 1930s and for decades following the Second World War, there was no room in the upper echelons of power for real economists and technocrats. Their places were occupied as a rule by administrators and bureaucrats like Kaganovich and Malenkov. As a matter of fact, under the directive-command system, economists were of no use, since so much was achieved in disregard of economic laws.

Nikolai Ivanovich Bukharin was of course the outstanding figure in this particular trio. His first book, *Political Economy of the Leisure Class*, published before the First World War, penetrated deep into the origins of economic relations. In the first volume of his *Economics*, which appeared in 1920, he set out to reveal the process of transformation of a capitalist into a socialist economy, but, swept up by the struggle and changing circumstances, he never wrote the second volume. In his *Economics* he wrote that 'people did not build capitalism, it built itself. As for socialism, which is an organized system, we are building it. The main thing for us is to find the balance between all the elements of the system.' Since Stalin's understanding of economics was only rudimentary, he took careful notice of Bukharin.

Relations between them at that time were not notably difficult; after all, Bukharin was an easy-going, gentle sort of intellectual. At times it seemed they were close friends. And they even lived in neighbouring apartments in the Kremlin. Stalin soon realized that Bukharin had no ambitious plans. Bukharin found the struggle for the leadership and the friction that arose between various members of the Politburo both incomprehensible and unpleasant and it was a long time before he took a position in the contest between the 'triumvirate' and Trotsky. Trotsky later called Bukharin's interventions in the debate 'a strange sort of peace-making'. What Bukharin valued above all was, first, Lenin's authority, even though he often argued with him fiercely, and, secondly, the collective authority of the Politburo.

Stalin's attitude towards Alexei Ivanovich Rykov was cautious, not merely because he took Lenin's place as chairman of the Sovnarkom, but because Rykov was exceptionally direct and frank. For this reason he was not always on good terms with his colleagues. Smilga, for instance, petitioned the Central Committee to be relieved of his jobs as deputy chairman of the All-Russian Council of National Economy and head of the chief fuel agency (Glavtop) because it was impossible to work with Rykov. When Lenin saw Smilga's letter, he wrote to Stalin to the effect that Smilga ought not to be moved, as party members can and must settle relations between themselves.

Rykov usually told people to their face what he thought, and he wrote the same way. In 1922 he published a piece entitled 'The Country's Economic Situation and Conclusions as to Future Work'. In effect, he was coming out in support of the New Economic Policy and against attempts to solve economic problems by means of the command method. He was involved in GOELRO (the State Commission for the Electrification of Russia), Dneprostroy (Dnieper Power Station), Turksib (Turkestan–Siberian Railway), the growth of the cooperative movement, the first Five-Year Plan, and other important initiatives of the socialist state. It was Rykov who later tried to convince Stalin and his supporters that socialism should improve and develop trade and financial relations, and not limit the economic independence of the direct producers. Alas, the debate was being conducted in different languages.

When at the end of the 1920s Stalin had already acquired great political weight, Rykov once flung at him: 'Your policy doesn't even smell of economics!' The General Secretary remained unperturbed, but he did not forget the jibe.

In fact, he never forgot anything. His icy, computer-like memory kept thousands of names, facts and events firmly locked in its cells. And he did not forget that Lenin valued Rykov highly and that his name figured in the leader's works scarcely less often than Stalin's. As chairman of the Sovnarkom, from 1926 Rykov also chaired the Council of Labour and Defence, and the committee on science and the development of scientific thought. Stalin did not forget that in 1922 Rykov had made a speech at the Moscow soviet in which he said that it was not permissible to resort once again to the methods of War Communism, and severely criticized those who attacked the NEP, calling such attacks 'unusually harmful and dangerous', and demanded an end to coercive methods in the countryside where, in his words, it was essential to maintain 'revolutionary legality'. His first post in the Soviet government had been as Commissar of Internal Affairs, but he had resigned in protest after a few days because the government was composed entirely of Bolsheviks and was not a coalition. Many years later he spoke for the last time at a Central Committee plenum, where he repudiated the monstrous charges against him of espionage, sabotage and terrorism. Stalin smirked maliciously: 'He's always been like that.'

Bukharin and Rykov were particularly concerned about the fate of the Russian peasants, whereas Trotsky – and Stalin, who fundamentally agreed with him – regarded them as 'material for revolutionary transformation'. It was impossible not to see how popular Bukharin and Rykov were. They went around without bodyguards, they were accessible and responsive. The ordinary people always valued these qualities in their leaders. Stalin called it playing to the gallery.

Stalin was equally suspicious of Mikhail Ivanovich Tomsky (real name Yefremov). A participant in three revolutions and a trade union worker, Tomsky knew how to stand up for himself. Stalin tolerated this 'friend of Rykov' until Kaganovich and Shvernik got onto the presidium of the Central Trade Union Council and pushed Rykov out as chairman. When Tomsky committed suicide on 22 August 1936 at his dacha in Boltsevo, Stalin said, 'His suicide confirms his guilt before the party'. In fact, it was an extreme act of protest against Stalin's rule.

A notable position in the leadership was occupied by Felix Edmundovich Dzerzhinsky, dubbed by Bukharin 'the proletarian Jacobin'. He was a very early member of the party and an organizer of the Social Democracy of the Kingdom of Poland and Lithuania at the beginning of the century. In evaluating Dzerzhinsky's rôle later on, Central Committee member and leading light in Comintern Karl Radek remarked:

Our enemies invented an entire legend about the all-seeing eye of the Cheka,* the all-hearing ears of the Cheka, and the ubiquitous Dzerzhinsky. They depicted the Cheka as an enormous army, covering the whole country and penetrating its own camp with its tentacles. They did not understand the source of Dzerzhinsky's strength. It derived from the strength of the Bolshevik party, namely the total trust of the working masses and the poor.[12]

Stalin's relations with Dzerzhinsky were not bad, especially after they had gone together on a number of missions to the front in the civil war. After Dzerzhinsky's premature death, Stalin, who was not one to lavish high praise, said, 'He was consumed by the stormy work he was doing for the proletarian cause.'

Mikhail Vasilyevich Frunze had an appealing personality, though he did not cut an especially striking figure. Stalin, who had been through prison and exile himself, held him in great esteem, for Frunze had twice been sentenced to death in 1907, had spent many weeks in the death cell and then several years doing hard labour. Few people knew in detail how much he had done to achieve victory on the Eastern, Turkestan and Southern fronts. Even Stalin had been impressed by his cool leadership and the high degree of political and military will-power he displayed. During his brief spell as Commissar for Military and Naval Affairs in 1925, Frunze impressed everyone with his intelligence and his original approach to military doctrine, reform of the armed forces and operational techniques in modern warfare.

He suffered from stomach ulcers which he preferred to treat with conservative medicine and generally managed to control the routine pain. A team of physicians, however, recommended that he undergo surgery. According to a number of testimonies, for example, I. K. Gamburg's book *Tak bylo* ('That's How It Was') and Boris Pilnyak's short story 'Povest nepogashchennoy luny' ('A Tale of the Unextinguished Moon'), Stalin and Mikoyan visited Frunze in hospital and insisted that the surgeon, Professor Rozanov, operate. Shortly before the operation, Frunze wrote a note to his wife: 'At this moment I feel completely fit and it's rather silly even to think of surgery, let alone undergo it. Still, both teams are insisting on it.'[13]

---

*Cheka, the initials of the Extraordinary Commission for Combatting Counter-revolution and Sabotage, which was founded in December 1917, with Dzerzhinsky as its head, was the forerunner of the GPU, NKVD and KGB, i. e. the political police.

It is difficult to assess the truth of the rumours that flew after Frunze's death as to whether it was the hand of fate or that of someone else that had struck him down. Many doctors expressed the opinion that the operation, which was simple enough even by the standards of those days, had not been necessary. At Frunze's funeral, Stalin said, 'Maybe it's best when old comrades slip so easily and simply into the grave. Unfortunately, it is far harder for our young comrades to replace them.'[14] Some people thought they detected a hidden meaning in this, but there is no evidence for any categorical assertions. Frunze, had he lived, would undoubtedly have continued to play a major part, and Stalin was aware of it.

One of the most important organizers on the Central Committee was Yakov Mikhailovich Sverdlov, a man totally devoid of personal ambition, as Luna-charsky wrote of him. He was the classic example of the dedicated functionary. 'He had orthodox ideas about everything, he was no more than a reflection of the general will and the general directives. He personally never gave any himself, but merely transmitted them, either from the Central Committee or from Lenin.' When he spoke, according to Lunacharsky, he sounded like the leading article of a party newspaper. But he possessed something very few others had, namely a brilliant grasp of the minute nuances of attitudes in the party, and an outstanding organizational ability. In fact, when it was decided that the Secretariat should have a single head and that the General Secretary of the Central Committee should occupy the position, Sverdlov was already fulfilling that function. Stalin liked the quietly efficient way Sverdlov ran the Central Committee meetings. At one memorable session in March 1918, the agenda included the situation in the Ukraine, a declaration by the Left Com-munists, the evacuation of *Pravda*, supervision of the military, a statement from Krylenko, and the Dybenko affair. The country was seething. Sverdlov reached for the black oilskin exercise book in which he kept the minutes, looked around at those present, who included Lenin, Zinoviev, Artem Sergeyev, Sokolnikov, Dzerzhinsky, Vladimirsky and Stalin, and blandly asked everyone to keep to the point.[15] After his premature death, Lenin said of him that such people could not be replaced and that a whole group of workers would be needed to do so.

Many aspects of character are formed in the process of working with a group of colleagues who are like-minded or even competitors. As one of Lenin's cohort, Stalin was bound to absorb much that was both valuable and lasting from the leader himself and from his entourage. But not all human charac-teristics are capable of being changed. Features that have been formed in one's early years, such as secretiveness, calculation, harshness, suspiciousness, lack of feeling, may with time become more deeply ingrained, rather than smoothed away. Stalin had long ago begun to manifest the quality described by Hegel as 'probabilism', that is, the type of personality that, having committed a morally reprehensible act, mentally attempts to justify it and to represent it to itself as good. That was Stalin. Once he was sure the recognized leader was seriously ill, he gradually began his great game of maximizing his own strength within the leadership. At first, he tried to convince himself that this was necessary 'for the defence of Leninism'. Then everything he did he considered morally justified in the name of 'the building of socialism in one country'. Probabilism finally came to occupy an important place in his armoury of political means. The people had to know, he believed, that everything he did was in the name of the people.

It seems clear that many of the people in Lenin's entourage did not see through Stalin for a long time. Some saw him merely as an executive, some as the fairly effective representative of the national minority elements in the party, while for others he was a typical mediocrity of the sort to be found in the governing circles of any régime or system. Lenin's comrades underrated him, whereas he saw through all of them. Even Lenin's closest comrades, such as Zinoviev, Kamenev, Bukharin, Rykov, Tomsky, Rudzutak and Kosior, would end up as 'enemies of the people' because Stalin so ordained it. After all, he took particular note of the fact that the Red Army was led in the civil war almost exclusively by his 'enemies': Trotsky, Blyukher, Yegorov, Tukhachevsky, Uborevich, Dybenko, Antonov-Ovseyenko, Smilga, Muralov, plus hundreds and thousands of other 'traitors'. Lenin did not see it, but Stalin shrewdly perceived that the 'commanders of industry' almost entirely consisted of 'saboteurs', like Pyatakov, Zelensky, Serebryakov, Lifshits, Grinko, Lebed, Semenov and thousands of others. Only Stalin was able to spot that the Soviet diplomatic service was shot through with 'spies' like Krestinsky, Rakovsky, Sokolnikov, Karakhan, Bogomolov, Raskolnikov. How many 'double-dealers' he saw through and unmasked in virtually every sphere of the state! Could such a person really be a 'mediocrity'? Trotsky was wrong. Robespierre told the Convention on 5 February 1794 that 'the first principle of our policy must be to rule the people with the help of reason and to rule the enemies of the people with the help of terror.'[16] Robespierre's was a dualistic, non-universal system. Stalin's political 'principle' was monistic – everyone was to be ruled by the single method of coercion. I doubt if any one of Lenin's comrades could have dreamed in his worst nightmares that such a monster was being nurtured in their midst, right there within the nucleus of the leadership.

CHAPTER 8

The General Secretary

In the barely six years that Lenin was fated to live after the October Revolution, years packed with accomplishment, hope and disillusion, he managed only to sketch the barest outline of what was to come.

The Eleventh Party Congress was the last he attended. The report on organizational activity was given by Molotov, whose description of the internal state of the party showed how overloaded with the work were the various sections of the Central Committee. 'During the year,' he said, '22,500 party workers passed through the Central Committee, that is, about sixty a day.' He raised the issue of the movement of cadres, keeping proper records and introducing more organization into the work of the Central Committee apparatus, and noted that during the year the number of Central Committee sessions and the number of issues it dealt with increased by 50 per cent, with corresponding increases in the number of conferences and various non-party meetings. Delegates expressed their dissatisfaction with the work of the centre. Osinsky, for instance, rebuked the Politburo for wasting its time on such matters as whether or not to hand the Boyar Palace over to the Commissariat of Land, or a printing works to this or that institution.[17] The congress proposed that improvement in the management of the party and of the country should be handled by three bureaux of the Central Committee, namely, the Politburo, the Orgburo and the Ekonomburo.

The minutes of the early post-revolutionary party congresses are remarkable for their openness and genuine frankness of debate. Criticism flowed naturally, while eulogies, deference and flattery were unknown. No one sought unity for its own sake. There were leaders, but no cults. For example, despite the high value generally placed on Lenin's ideas and arguments, his report to the Eleventh Congress was criticized by many delegates. To the general amusement of the assembly, Ryazanov (real name Goldendakh) said:

Our Central Committee is a special institution. They say the English Parliament can do everything but turn a man into a woman. Our Central Committee is much more powerful: it has turned more than one very revolutionary man into an old woman, and the number of such old women is increasing rapidly. As long as the party and its members don't take part in collective discussion of all the measures that are issued in its name, and as long as these initiatives go on falling on the party members' heads like snow, we will continue to have what Comrade Lenin has called a panic mentality.[18]

Frank discussion of everything affecting party life was regarded as the norm, whereas similar critical remarks made in the 1930s would be condemned as 'wrecking', while unanimous approval, or support and adulation became the rule. The congress minutes of Lenin's day were models of democracy, ideological comradeship and openness of the highest order – within the party.

As early as 1920, the everyday work of the Central Committee apparatus showed that the secretariat needed someone to attend to its own organization. At the Central Committee plenum of 5 April 1920, it was decided that Krestinsky, Preobrazhensky and Serebryakov be appointed secretaries, that the appointment of one executive secretary should not be delayed, and that, in addition to the three secretaries, the Orgburo should include Rykov and Stalin.[19] The minutes of the Central Committee (usually kept in ruled school notebooks) show that the question of appointing a single executive secretary arose much earlier than 1922. After the Eleventh Congress, one of the secretaries was especially singled out, while Stasova, Krestinsky and Molotov had earlier been appointed as executive secretaries. Now, however, the issue was the elevation of this function to the status of General Secretary. Whose idea was this and where did it come from? The evidence shows that it came from Kamenev and Stalin. It follows therefore that Lenin knew about the impending innovation.

In accordance with the intentions expressed at the Eleventh Congress, the plenum of 3 April 1922 chose a Politburo, Orgburo and Secretariat. The plenum also decided to introduce the post of General Secretary and chose Stalin that day. This, added to his membership of the Politburo and Orgburo, meant that he was holding three important party posts at once. At the same time, Molotov and Kuibyshev, who were candidate members of the Politburo, were appointed secretaries. The question is asked today, why it was Stalin who was given the post and not someone else? Who proposed him? What part did Lenin play? Did Stalin's appointment as General Secretary imply that he was also being given special extra powers? The answers to these questions address the history of both the party and country, but they also go to the root of future ills. Let us therefore turn to the dispassionate documents.

The members of the Central Committee attending the plenum were Lenin, Trotsky, Zinoviev, Kamenev, Stalin, Dzerzhinsky, Petrovsky, Kalinin, Voroshilov, Ordzhonikidze, Yaroslavsky, Tomsky, Rykov, A. A. Andreyev, A. P.

Smirnov, Frunze, Chubar, Kuibyshev, Sokolnikov, Molotov and Korotkov, while candidate members included Kirov, Kiselev, Krivov, Pyatakov, Manuilsky, Lebed, Sulimov, Bubnov, Badaev, and Solts, who was a member of the Central Control Commission.

The first question debated by the plenum was the composition of the Central Committee. About its chairman, the plenum resolved 'to confirm the unanimously accepted custom of not having a chairman. The Central Committee's only officials are its secretaries; the chairman is chosen at each session.'

The question was then raised of why, on the list of Central Committee members chosen by the congress, there were notes about appointing Stalin, Molotov and Kuibyshev as secretaries? Kamenev explained, and the plenum took note, that 'with congress's full approval, he had announced during the elections that, because some tickets were marked with the names of candidates for the posts of secretary, the plenum ought not to be inhibited in making its own selection, for this merely indicated the preferences of a particular section of delegates.'[20] These preferences derived above all from Kamenev, Zinoviev and, covertly, Stalin.

Officially, the congress appointed only members of the Central Committee, but the evidence suggests that Kamenev exerted himself to secure the selection of future secretaries. In simple terms, Kamenev wanted 'his own' man to head the Central Committee apparatus. He had excellent relations with Stalin who more than once emphasized his special position as former deputy to Lenin in the Sovnarkom, and he was deferred to as higher than perhaps anyone else in the hierarchy. Many indirect indications suggest that Kamenev was trying to secure the post for Stalin with the latter's knowledge. Stalin liked the work and had spotted the advantages it harboured.

The plenum further decided that 'the post of General Secretary and two secretaries should be established, Comrade Stalin to be General Secretary and Comrades Molotov and Kuibyshev secretaries'. Lenin proposed that secretaries not take upon themselves any work other than their leadership rôle, and instructed Stalin to find deputies and assistants to relieve him of his work in the soviets and the Workers and Peasants Inspectorate.[21]

At the time Stalin was appointed, Lenin's physicians were insisting that he follow a strict regimen. Indeed, it was in April 1922 that they decided he needed a prolonged rest and mountain air, and they proposed a trip to the Caucasus, but the cure had to be postponed and he went on working. He wanted the Central Committee apparatus to avoid becoming bureaucratic and getting into a rut. Following Lenin's suggestion, the Politburo met once a week, but the work had to be dealt with on a daily basis. The Secretariat prepared the papers for Politburo sessions, conveyed its decisions to those carrying them out and executed the orders of its members. While it had no direct involvement in matters of the economy, defence, state administration or education, it played a significant technical part in the general management of the party apparatus. Since the main agencies were run by leading Bolsheviks who did not pay much attention to the technical side, it was decided to make one member of the Politburo responsible for all the work of the Secretariat, with the rank of General Secretary. To reiterate: the concrete proposal of Stalin's candidature was made by Kamenev. He was also in the chair at the plenum that appointed the General Secretary. All the evidence suggests that these questions were gone over preliminarily with Lenin.

Was Stalin qualified for the job? Evidently he was. He had been a member of the party since 1898 and of the Central Committee since 1912, and he was in the Central Committee Bureau, the Orgburo and the Politburo. The only Politburo member to occupy two state posts, that of Commissar for Nationalities and the Workers and Peasants Inspectorate, he was also the Central Committee representative on the board of the Vecheka-OGPU (Unified State Political Administration) and was a member of the Revvoensoviet of the Republic and the Council of Labour and Defence – and this does not exhaust the list of the posts he held when he was made General Secretary.

This all showed indisputably that his contribution to the restructuring of society, his knowledge of the workings of the political and state administration, and his inclination for working in the organization were recognized and acknowledged by many Old Bolsheviks. His elevation to the post of General Secretary did not therefore come as a surprise. Most of the others in the leadership continued to view the post essentially as mundane. All this took place when Lenin was still alive and well. The question of the leadership of the party and state simply did not arise. There was a leader, an indisputable one, and that was Lenin. In his new rôle, Stalin continued to remain little known both to the party and to the country. Within the leadership, however, his positive and negative qualities began to be noticed more plainly.

It will be decades, if ever, before a complete picture of Stalin's character can be drawn. He knew how to hide his feelings. Very few people ever saw him angry. He was capable of making the harshest decisions with complete composure. In time, his entourage would take this as a sign of his great wisdom and perspicacity. Pity was unknown to him, as was filial love or the love of a father for his children and grandchildren. Of the latter, he saw his daughter Svetlana's children and those of his son and first-born, Yakov, only a few times. His private life was completely fenced off. He had nothing but work. Decisions, meetings, orders, speeches.

The world was black and white, and whatever did not correspond to the 'line' was harmful. Half-tones were not recognized. His preferred form of reasoning was binary logic, yes or no. He was categorical and single-minded, and he did not distinguish within the great range of difference between those two poles. His style, in notes, speeches or reports, was terse to the point of being telegraphic. People liked this, they thought he was businesslike, a man who knew his duty, a man without sentimentality. He did not like the word 'humanism'. No one as yet had any idea about all this. In the Central Committee what they saw was that for Stalin there was nothing higher than party discipline, party duty, and the general line.

Throughout 1922 and the beginning of 1923, when his illness finally incapacitated him, Lenin, preoccupied as he was with the organizational and political outcome of many problems, wrote dozens of notes, projects and letters to Stalin. Nine months after Stalin had become General Secretary, and had made a number of bad decisions, Lenin saw that he had not been a good choice and that he must be moved to a different job.

Among Stalin's bad decisions, for instance, was the support he gave in May 1922 to a proposal by Sokolnikov and Bukharin to remove the state monopoly on foreign trade. Lenin was categorically opposed to this move.[22] In September 1922 – Lenin having recovered from his first serious attack – Stalin came out with the idea of 'autonomization', that is, the unification of the national republics by means of their joining the Russian Federation. In effect, this approach did not mean the creation of a Union of Soviet Socialist Republics, but a Russian Soviet Socialist Republic in which the other national entities would have the right of autonomy. Stalin had already got his proposal through a special Central Committee commission formed to deal with the problem. Lenin reacted at once, in a letter addressed to Kamenev but directed at the members of the Politburo:

> Comrade Kamenev. You have no doubt already received the resolution from Comrade Stalin's commission on the entry of the independent republics into the RSFSR ...
>
> In my opinion, this is an issue of the greatest importance. Stalin is somewhat inclined to rush things. You must give this careful thought (you once had the intention of dealing with this and even made a start), and Zinoviev, too.[23]

Probably, nobody visited Lenin during his illness at Gorky as often as Stalin. Sometimes Lenin invited him when he wanted to be brought up to date on current affairs, and often the General Secretary came on his own initiative. Among the myriad questions Lenin raised was the health of Dzerzhinsky and Tsyurupa, and other comrades who were not well at the time. He even discussed Stalin's health, having first talked about it on the telephone with Stalin's physician, V. A. Obukh.

On 26 September 1922, Lenin invited Stalin to Gorky where they had a three-hour conversation,[24] in which Lenin emphasized that the problem of the unification of the republics was of the greatest importance and could not be rushed. He proposed a new basis in principle for the creation of the union state: the voluntary unification of the independent republics, including the RSFSR, into a Union of Soviet Socialist Republics with the full equal rights of all of them preserved. Stalin never publicly differed with Lenin, and generally accepted his arguments quickly, although on the national question he regarded Lenin's position as 'liberal'.[25]

These frequent conversations were not merely Lenin's means of obtaining information, giving advice and making suggestions, but were also an education for the head of the Central Committee apparatus. During their many talks, Lenin no doubt got a good idea of Stalin's strong and weak sides, and the comments he made on him at the end of 1922 and beginning of 1923 were the result of deep analysis and reflection. The national question in particular, and Stalin's way of dealing with it, opened Lenin's eyes to some new political facets of his personality, and also to some moral ones. In his notes entitled 'On the Nationalities Question or "Autonomization"', Lenin described Stalin's idea as a departure from proletarian internationalism. In his summing up, he gave a political and moral assessment of Stalin: 'I believe that a fatal part was played here by Stalin's hastiness and his tendency to resort to administrative methods, as well as by his animosity towards the infamous "social nationalism". Animosity in politics generally plays the worst rôle.'[26]

Ordzhonikidze was also implicated for having used physical force during the commission's trip to the Caucasus. He had been sent as the head of the commission in order to regulate a conflict that had flared up with the leaders of the Communist Party of Georgia. He proved inadequate for the task. When the situation was being explained to him, moreover, he had struck Mdivani, a local central committee member. Lenin wrote that 'no provocation, nor even any insult, can justify this Russian violence and Comrade Dzerzhinsky is irreparably wrong to look on such violence so lightheartedly.'[27] It was the fact that Stalin did not take a stand on principle in this conflict that permitted Lenin to remark publicly that the General Secretary had not only acted hastily and used 'administrative', i. e. coercive methods, but had also exhibited animosity in his handling of political affairs.

The journal kept by Lenin's duty secretaries shows that he returned to this matter repeatedly. L. A. Fotieva's notes, for instance, show that Lenin requested additional material on the incident. Stalin replied with a refusal, on the grounds that the invalid should be spared any unnecessary stress. Lenin, however, insisted. On 5 March 1923, that is five days before suffering the next stroke that would deprive him of speech, he wrote to Trotsky: 'I earnestly request that you take it upon yourself to defend the Georgian affair at the party Central Committee. At present it is being "prosecuted"* by Stalin and Dzerzhinsky and I cannot rely on their impartiality. In fact, quite the contrary!'[28]

The same day, Lenin dictated another letter, this time to Stalin. It appears to be of a personal nature, but only ostensibly so. Its background was that in December 1922 Lenin dictated a series of letters to his wife, Krupskaya, that were of enormous importance for the party's future. During the night of 22 December, apparently after dictating a letter to Trotsky on the foreign trade monopoly, Lenin's condition took a turn for the worse. His right arm and leg became paralysed. Members of the Politburo were informed. The next day, Stalin reprimanded Krupskaya on the telephone in the rudest terms for 'break-

---

* A pun on 'prosecute' and 'persecute', which in Russian are the same word.

ing the sick leader's regimen'. Shaken by Stalin's utter lack of tact and courtesy, Krupskaya wrote to Kamenev that day:

> Lev Borisovich, because I wrote a brief note, dictated by Vladimir Ilyich with the doctors' permission, Stalin allowed himself to make the most abusive attack on me yesterday. I didn't join the party yesterday. In thirty years I have never heard a member use a coarse word. The party and Ilyich are no less dear to me than they are to Stalin. I need all my self-control now. I know better than any doctor what should or shouldn't be said to Ilyich, as I know what disturbs him and what doesn't, and in any case I know better than Stalin.

Krupskaya went on to ask Kamenev to protect her private life from such 'crude interference and unworthy abuse and threats'. And she concluded:

> I do not doubt the unanimity of the Control Commission's decision which gave Stalin the right to threaten me, but I have neither the strength nor the time to waste on such a stupid farce. I'm also human and my nerves are stretched to the limit.
> N. Krupskaya.[29]

In accordance with the Politburo's wishes, Stalin was 'protecting' the leader from disturbances, but it is easy to see that Lenin's isolation from information and his limited influence on the situation in the party entered into Stalin's plans for strengthening his own position during this period.

Kamenev brought the contents of Krupskaya's letter to Stalin's attention. The latter, without any argument, immediately wrote to Krupskaya, apologizing and explaining that his behaviour was solely determined by his concern for Lenin. It is difficult to be sure whether or not he was being sincere. He was entirely pragmatic about moral principles, and he would transgress any one of them if it suited him. Be that as it may, Lenin only heard about the incident from Krupskaya some two months later, on 5 March 1923. He saw the incident as something more than personal. Soon afterwards, he summoned his secretary, M. A. Volodicheva, and dictated a note to Trotsky about the forthcoming Central Committee plenum on the Georgian affair. He told her to read the letter over the telephone and to bring him the reply as soon as possible. He then dictated a letter to Stalin, as follows:

> Respected Comrade Stalin,
> You were offensive enough to call my wife to the telephone and to abuse her. Although she has told you she is prepared to forget what was said, she told Kamenev and Zinoviev what happened. I am not ready to forget so easily what has been done against me, for it goes without saying that anything done against my wife I regard as being done against me. Therefore, please consider whether to take back what you said and to apologize or to break off relations between us.
> With respect
> Lenin, 5 March 1923[30]

Lenin's tone was terse. No one in the party yet knew that in December 1922 he had written his 'Letter to the Congress', giving his assessment of the personal qualities of the party leaders and recommending the removal of Stalin from the post of General Secretary. The letter of 5 March merely adds detail to the political and moral picture he had formed of Stalin. Lenin finally came to the conclusion that while the party had no choice but to tolerate such behaviour among rank and file members, Stalin's moral failings were absolutely impermissible in a leader. Prophetically, he saw in Stalin's character bad omens for the entire issue of the party leadership. On the following day, he dictated the last document in which Stalin figures:

> To Comrades Mdivani, Makharadze and others. Copies to Comrades Trotsky and Kamenev.
> Respected Comrades.
> I am following your cause with all my heart. I am appalled by Ordzhonikidze's rudeness and by the connivance of Stalin and Dzerzhinsky. I am preparing notes and a speech for you.
> With respect.
> Lenin. 6 March 1923[31]

Lenin managed to prepare neither notes nor a speech. Four days later, another stroke made it impossible for him even to dictate. All the evidence – notably his three last notes, dictated on 5 and 6 March – suggests, however, that Stalin's actions over the Georgian affair had convinced Lenin firmly that his Letter to the Congress was well grounded. It was not easy for Lenin to accept the disappointment. The choice he'd made in April 1922 had been a bad one. They had all been at fault, including him. But the fault could be corrected. They could not have such an utterly immoral person at the head of the Central Committee apparatus, a man so potentially dangerous to the cause. If Stalin could be abusive, hypocritical and offensive to someone as close to Lenin as Krupskaya, how would he behave towards the others? Perhaps Lenin's health had declined sharply during the first ten days of March with good cause? The dramatic surge of events at the time, the Georgian affair and the row with Stalin, could have hastened the course of the illness. Lenin's state of mind could have predisposed him to the fatal stroke.

In the end, Stalin's 'autonomization' idea was rejected and it was Lenin's policy on nationality relations that was accepted. At the Congress of Soviets, which opened on 30 December 1922, the formation of the Union of Soviet Socialist Republics was announced. Lenin's letter on the subject – which incidentally did not see the light of day for another thirty years – formed the basis of the report given by Stalin. The report, like the Declaration on the Formation of the USSR which he also proclaimed, was centred on the idea of proletarian internationalism, the commitment of all the nationalities to friendship, class solidarity and dedication to the revolutionary ideals. Reiterating Lenin's ideas without citing him, Stalin proclaimed the special task of the new union to be the liquidation of the national inequality which they had inherited from the past.

Lenin was ill, and yet he could persist in pursuing the most equitable solution of the national question in a vast country embracing more than one hundred nationalities. Stalin could hardly have wanted a different outcome, but he lacked the perspicacity and intelligence to deal with such a difficult problem. Trotsky in his memoirs claims that it was only Lenin's illness that 'prevented him from destroying Stalin politically'. He wrote that Stalin's wilfulness frequently drove Lenin to distraction, resulting in a worsening of his illness. The fact alone that, nine months after Stalin's elevation to the post of General Secretary, Lenin could express the urgent need to remove him from the post, says much. In this respect, his Letter to the Congress, and his other last essays and letters which together are known as his Testament, are of seminal importance for understanding Stalin's political and moral personality.

CHAPTER 9

Letter to the Congress

The fate of Lenin's last writings was dramatic. A substantial part of them was wrapped in a shroud of Stalinist secrecy and kept from the party. It was not until after 1956 and the Twentieth Party Congress that his 'On Granting Legislative Powers to Gosplan', 'On the Nationalities or "Autonomization"', 'Letter to the Congress', and some other jottings finally saw the light of day. His article, 'How to Reorganize Rabkrin (Proposals to the Twelfth Party Congress)' was printed in a single copy for him to see. Then, after a cut version of it was published, a special letter was sent to provincial committees, saying that these were pages from the diary of the sick Lenin who had been permitted to write because his mental idleness had become intolerable to him. This piece of tactlessness was jointly signed by Andreyev, Bukharin, Kuibyshev, Molotov, Rykov, Stalin, Tomsky and Trotsky on 27 January 1923.

Lenin's concerns, which were prompted by the threat of the authoritarianism he had identified, were incomprehensible to Stalin, and to many others. The main thought in Lenin's last writings, however, was fundamentally optimistic: that socialism had a future in Russia. The cardinal issues, like industrialization, the restructuring of agriculture on voluntary cooperative principles, the transformation of culture into the property of all the people, the state administration, all this was seen by him through the prism of making the power of the people real and introducing democracy into all facets of social life. The developments he had in mind also required new people, and that, for Lenin, was now the main thing.

Antonio Gramsci, discussing the origins of Caesarism, once expressed the interesting idea that, when contending forces have exhausted each other, a third force may emerge which then prevails over both sides.[32] In Russia, the issue was probably not so much particular groups of people as social forces, the working class, the peasantry and the party, or rather, as Lenin put it, 'the vast, limitless authority of that thinnest of layers, the party's old guard'.[33]

Socialism could be built only on the foundation of the wise social compromise, proposed by Lenin, of applying the New Economic Policy together with the gradual spread of voluntary cooperative agriculture in the countryside. Any other policy would lead to a clash with the peasantry and the consolidation of totalitarian methods of government. And totalitarianism always has to have its Caesars. Like other leaders, Stalin could not see the point when Lenin said 'our party is a small group of people compared to the population of the country,'[34] and that the NEP* would become the chief condition of the movement towards socialism.

The Bolsheviks were a product of the urban proletariat. The union with the peasantry, even if it was not on equal terms, was meant to derive from the opportunity the peasant had to own the land and to engage in free trade. The peasant would be brought closer to socialism only through voluntary cooperativism, as Lenin foresaw, and the New Economic Policy was intended to cement relations between worker and peasant. Even within the 'thinnest of layers' at the top of the party not everyone understood entirely what he had in mind or the dangers the people would encounter if a different path were taken. A different path was bound to entail coercion and an immediate shift towards authoritarianism and Caesarism.

Being so ill, Lenin made great haste in case he was not given time to reflect on the future. Once, in the autumn of 1922, he had been given a glimmer of hope and been able to return to active service. Maybe he would conquer his illness again?

Bukharin recalled the joy it had given them all to see Lenin back in harness at the Fourth Comintern Congress of 13 November 1922:

Our hearts stood still as we watched Lenin mount the podium, knowing the enormous effort it took. But then he finished. I ran over to him and wrapped him in a coat, as he was wet with exhaustion, his shirt was soaked through, beads of sweat hung on his brow, his eyes looked hollow, but they had a radiant gleam, crying out with life, as if his great soul was singing a song about the work.

Weeping with joy, Clara Zetkin rushed over to Ilyich and began kissing the old man's hands. Embarrassed and shaken, he tried to kiss her hand instead. And no one realized that the illness had eaten up his brain and that the awful, tragic end was near.[35]

Evidently, Lenin knew it. Therefore he insisted and pleaded. On the morning of 24 December, Stalin, Kamenev and Bukharin discussed the situation. They did not have the right to make Lenin keep quiet, but care and attention and maximum tranquillity were essential. They decided he should be allowed to dictate five to ten minutes daily, but not to conduct correspondence and not to expect replies to his notes. Meetings were prohibited. Neither friends nor

---

*The New Economic Policy, introduced by Lenin at the Tenth Party Congress in March 1921, allowed private enterprise in agriculture, trade and mostly small industry, and was aimed at both restoring the national economy and pacifying the peasantry.

domestic servants were to convey to him any news of political life, lest it occupy and disturb him.[36]

During his illness, Lenin had a number of duty secretaries. He dictated notes to the Politburo, requested messages to be conveyed by telephone, asked for facts and figures, materials, documents. The secretaries were N. S. Alliluyeva (Stalin's wife), M. A. Volodicheva, M. I. Glyasser, Sh. M. Manucharyants, L. A. Fotieva and S. A. Flakserman. Volodicheva was on duty on 23 December 1922, when Lenin began dictating his Letter to the Congress. Her notes in the journal are terse:

Dictated for four minutes. Felt ill. Doctors there. Before dictating, said: 'I want to dictate a letter to the Congress. Write!' Dictated fast, but his poor condition obvious.[37]

The Twelfth Congress would be taking place in April, and if he were not well enough to attend, they could read out his letter to the delegates. His phrases were polished and carefully thought out. 'I would strongly advise that a number of changes in our political system be undertaken by Congress.' He clearly had fundamentals in mind: democracy in the party, the power of the people in society and ways to achieve these. Democracy was to be the chief lever and means of accomplishing the new order.

I want to share with you some of the considerations I regard as most important.

At the top of the list I place increasing the number of Central Committee members by several dozen or even up to a hundred. I think the Central Committee would face great dangers if the course of events turned unfavourable to us (and this cannot be ruled out) and we have not carried out this reform.

I think the party has the right to ask for fifty to a hundred Central Committee members from the working class and can get them without excessive effort.

This reform would greatly increase the stability of our party and facilitate its struggle among the hostile states which, in my view, could and will become much sharper in the near future. I think such a reform would increase the stability of our party a thousand times.[38]

As a first step towards realizing Lenin's main idea, that is, to guarantee the genuine democratization of all aspects of life in the party and state, the workers, constituting the main force of the revolution, must be better represented in the Central Committee which itself should be increased in size by two to three times. A completely renewed Central Committee, that both embodied wider representation and was closer to the masses, would make it less likely that conflicts between small groups could spill over and have an excessive effect on the party as a whole. Furthermore, Lenin had warned that the international situation could soon worsen. They must hurry.

It is important to remember that all too frequently Lenin was not fully understood by his comrades. And if he was fully understood, then he was not always fully supported: for example, October 1917, Brest-Litovsk, the New

Economic Policy, the enlargement of the Central Committee by the recruitment of workers. But he had been able to drag the revolutionary caravan along behind him through sheer force of argument and will. He would never know that his direst warnings would go unheeded, that his last wishes, in relation to Stalin, would not be carried out.

To return to the 'Letter'.

I have in mind stability as a safeguard against a split in the near future and I propose here to look at a number of considerations of a personal nature.

I think that such Central Committee members as Stalin and Trotsky are basic to the question of stability from this point of view. In my opinion, relations between them constitute a full half of the danger of a split that can be avoided, and incidentally by increasing the Central Committee membership to fifty or one hundred it could be avoided.[39]

A number of Soviet scholars still persist in giving insufficient political weight to Trotsky, whose relations with Stalin constituted 'a full half of the danger'. Lenin saw that Trotsky was more popular than Stalin, but he also knew how much grip the latter had acquired. The strained relations between these two central figures were in danger of spilling over into a conflict that could split the party.

Having become General Secretary, Comrade Stalin has concentrated unlimited power in his hands, and I am not sure that he will always use that power with sufficient care.[40]

Where did the General Secretary derive his 'unlimited power'? He had responsibility for all current problems, many of them of vital interest to the party. But his main power came from having in his hands the selection and advancement of party members to the centre and the localities. And that embraced thousands of members. At first, most people did not see the political possibilities connected with the distribution of party workers. Stalin, however, noticed the connection very soon and made an identification between the apparatus and the party. Lenin went on:

On the other hand, Comrade Trotsky, as his conflict with the Central Committee over the Commissariat for Communications has already shown, is distinguished not only by his outstanding abilities. He is personally perhaps the most capable man in the present Central Committee, but he has excessive self-confidence and is excessively drawn towards the purely administrative side of the work.[41]

Lenin may have thought, as he prepared to utter these words, that if Trotsky had a firmer revolutionary backbone he could have been a leader of statesmanlike calibre. He might have recalled with a smile Trotsky's speech on the Red Army at the last congress when, instead of winding up with some general conclusions about improving the military structure, he started talking about the 'elementary military–cultural education of the soldiers'. To an animated audience, he had said:

Let us try to see that the soldiers have no lice. This is an enormously important task of education, because what is needed is persistence, tirelessness, firmness, example and repetition in order to liberate the mass of the people from the slovenliness they have grown up with and that has eaten into them. For a soldier with lice is not a soldier, but a half-soldier. As for illiteracy, that is spiritual lousiness. We can probably liquidate it by 1st May and then carry on the work with undiminished pressure.[42]

Lenin liked the expression 'illiteracy is spiritual lousiness'. Trotsky was good at inventing brilliant aphorisms on his feet. In fact, the publicist frequently overcame the politician in him, just as his vanity often overcame his common sense, or his desire to please an audience pushed modesty aside. No, he and Stalin would not learn to get on. They were both too ambitious and plainly poles apart. He went on:

These two qualities of two outstanding leaders in the present Central Committee may lead inadvertently to a split.

I will not dwell on the personal qualities of other members of the Central Committee. I would only say that the October episode involving Zinoviev and Kamenev, while it was not accidental, should not be held against them personally, just as Trotsky's non-Bolshevism should not be held against him.*

Of the younger members of the Central Committee, I want to say a few words about Bukharin and Pyatakov. They are, in my view, the most outstanding forces (of the very youngest forces) and the following should be borne in mind regarding them: Bukharin is not only a most highly valued and important party theoretician, he is also legitimately regarded as the favourite of the entire party, but it is very doubtful if his theoretical outlook can be considered as fully Marxist, as there is something scholastic about him (he has never studied dialectics and has never quite understood it, I think).[43]

Lenin's duty secretary that day wrote in the journal after taking his dictation:

Next day [24 December] during the break from 6 to 8 o'clock, Vladimir Ilyich called me in again. He warned me that what he had dictated yesterday (23rd) and today (24th) was *absolutely* secret. He repeated this several times. He told me to keep *everything* he dictated in a special place with special responsibility and regard it as *categorically* secret.[44]

Unfortunately, Fotieva, who was in charge of the Sovnarkom secretariat and also took Lenin's dictation, ignored his instructions and soon informed Stalin and some other Politburo members about Lenin's December notes, so that his 'Letter' did not come as a surprise for the party leadership.

---

*On the eve of the Bolshevik seizure of power, Zinoviev and Kamenev, believing an armed uprising to be premature, published their objection in the press. Trotsky's 'non-Bolshevism' refers to the fact that it was not until August 1917 that he entered the Bolshevik Party.

Lenin continued dictation the next day, 25 December:

As for Pyatakov, he is a man of outstanding will and outstanding abilities, but he is too much drawn to the administrative side of the work to be relied on in a serious political matter.[45]

On 26 December, Lenin developed his ideas on broadening internal party democracy. He saw this also as a commitment to improving the state administration which 'in effect we inherited from the old régime, since it was impossible to reform it in such a short time, especially with the war and the famine and so on'.[46] He added that the Central Committee should be broadened by bringing in peasants, as well as workers, and he regarded their presence at Politburo sessions as essential.

Along with these ideas, Lenin kept returning to his main preoccupation, namely the question of personalities. Who should be the leader, if he died? He knew that in his absence the post of General Secretary, with its 'unlimited power', would become decisive. As he had been prevented by illness from heading the Central Committee, one of the members of the Politburo had automatically stepped into first place. Stalin, as General Secretary, was responsible for running the day-to-day affairs of the Secretariat, and so it was patently clear that if Lenin did not get better – which he himself evidently thought unlikely, since he was writing his 'Testament' – Stalin would try to reinforce his position as potential leader. But Trotsky might try to do the same. There would be a conflict, there would be a split. His advice and warning must be more specific. A few days later, on 4 January 1923, he added his famous postscript:

Stalin is too rude, and this failing, which is entirely acceptable in relations among us Communists, is not acceptable in a General Secretary. I therefore suggest that the comrades find a means of moving Stalin from this post and giving the job to someone else who is superior to Comrade Stalin in every way, that is, more patient, more loyal, more respectful and attentive to the comrades, less capricious and so on. These considerations may seem like a triviality, but I believe that from the point of view of preventing a split, and in view of what I have said about relations between Stalin and Trotsky, it is not a trivial matter, or it is the kind of triviality which can assume decisive significance.[47]

Stalin as yet had revealed no major political ambition. He seemed to be true to the great idea, though perhaps he understood it differently. But, as a Bolshevik, his political escutcheon was as yet still unblemished. Politics and morality, however, go hand in hand, and when they are out of harmony, intrigue or dictatorship may result. Lenin's postscript reveals his worry about the future, but shows no personal animosity. Lenin was above that. 'Though he was a harsh political opponent and would exploit any device in political struggle, except underhand ones,' Lunacharsky wrote of him, 'in his attitude to his opponents one felt no rancour.'[48]

Lenin saw that Stalin's defects could become a source of much trouble, but Trotsky also gave cause for concern, and not only because of his extreme arrogance on the political level. His having joined the Bolsheviks so late must have had an effect. His left-wing extremism had frequently put him at odds with the Central Committee, while his ambition was so strong that he was even offended to be asked in September 1922 to take the post of deputy chairman of the Sovnarkom – that is, to deputize for Lenin. He had been counting on getting a special position. He barely concealed his own opinion of himself as a genius, and may have believed that, if Lenin's wish to remove Stalin had been carried out, he would have been made the leader of the party.

In proposing the removal of Stalin, Lenin wisely left open the question of who should take his place, for to have named a 'crown prince' would have been tantamount to creating a succession and thus to express doubt that the Central Committee was capable of finding the best candidate. In giving his assessment of the best-known leaders, Lenin was making it plain that not one of them was suitable as the party leader. Not a single one. He was also making it plain, however, that the party should not seek its leader elsewhere. Implicitly, Lenin was saying that the 'old guard' was capable of acting as a collective leadership which, having first created safeguards against one man gaining power, could choose any one of a dozen or more well-known figures to serve as first among equals. In this case, whether or not this or that individual was more talented or less would not be so important. Above all, the democratic system, in accordance with constitutional and party norms, would be working in support of whatever served the interests of the country.

But it would be precisely with the aid of the old guard that Stalin would create his bureaucratic system. To understand why, to everyone's surprise, Stalin emerged at the top of the pyramid, one has to be aware of several factors: Russia's autocratic past and the absence of democratic customs in the new society, the low political culture of the people and the party, the great need for the maturity of the masses which a one-party system imposed, the lack of legal safeguards against the abuse of power, and the peculiar nature of the class structure of the USSR.

In addition, there was Stalin's 'secret of invulnerability', perhaps the most important feature of all. He usurped the right to present, interpret and comment on Lenin's ideas to such an extent that in the end people believed that he belonged alongside the leader, that he was indeed Lenin's comrade-in-arms, his pupil, his successor. The Stalin phenomenon was a social, historical, spiritual, moral and psychological phenomenon. Lenin seems to have sensed that the General Secretary would use his unlimited power to transform the emerging system into a totalitarian bureaucracy, and he realized that Stalin must go no further within the party's governing nucleus. But Lenin's warning can only be properly understood against the background of Stalin's impending triumph.

Two months before the Twelfth Congress, a Central Committee plenum discussed a number of theses on the reorganization of the party's central organs on the basis of Lenin's 'How to Reorganize the Workers and Peasants Inspectorate' and a supplement entitled 'Better Less, but Better'. It was agreed that the organizational issue be made a special item on the congress agenda, as Lenin had suggested. The theses advocated increasing the size of the Central Committee from twenty-seven to forty and urged that the Politburo be regularly accountable to Central Committee plenums. Three representatives of the Central Control Commission should be present at Politburo meetings, where they would see to it that 'nobody's authority, not that of the General Secretary nor of anyone else on the Central Committee, should prevent them from making enquiries, checking documents and generally obtaining essential information and ensuring the strictest regularity of business.'[49]

In addition to this supervision of the elected leading organ, Lenin wanted a special commission which would monitor the work of the Central Committee and Politburo in the periods between Communist forums. The plenum effectively accepted Lenin's arguments and agreed that the Central Control Commission (CCC) should be enlarged and the closest links established between the organs of party and state control. Who could know that the rôle of the CCC would be reduced to recording insignificant party matters and that it would be abolished altogether by Stalin in due course?

Although Stalin had been General Secretary for about a year, outwardly he had made no particular mark. The plenum subjected his report on 'National Factors in Party and State Construction' to serious criticism. Taking his theses merely as a basis, it expressed a number of remarks on matters of principle. It was agreed to show Lenin the theses after they had been worked on. Stalin's text shows that there were many gaps in his knowledge, even though he was regarded as an expert on the subject. The plenum appointed a commission to work on the theses consisting of Stalin, Rakovsky and Rudzutak.[50]

Lenin felt that the victorious revolution required some elaboration, that its arguments needed correction. But Lenin was also a product of the time. He had no doubts about the dictatorship of a class which was a tiny minority compared to the peasantry, and he did not return to the idea of revolutionary pluralism which he had defended at the end of 1917, nor did he condemn the use of force as a revolutionary means for solving social problems. He lived within his time and, although he could see further than many, and saw the danger to *party* democracy in the predominance of one leader, he was unable to foresee the dangers to the society as a whole of relying on the infallibility of a single party. One has the feeling that he did not have the time to say everything. While he did not doubt the orthodoxy of nineteenth-century Marxist dogma, the importance of his last writings cannot be exaggerated.

As often happened, Trotsky took up a position of his own at the plenum. In his opinion, broadening the Central Committee would make it unwieldy and deprive it of 'the necessary stability', and in the last analysis 'threaten to cause extreme harm to the accuracy and correctness of its work'. He proposed that a party council be formed of two or three dozen persons. This organ would give directives to the Central Committee and monitor its work. In effect, Trotsky was proposing dual power and dual centres in the party. The plenum rejected these proposals after only a little debate. As we know, the Twelfth Congress accepted Lenin's proposal and created the Central Control Commission–Workers and Peasants Inspectorate as a unified body. Some of the ideas in his 'Testament', then, began to come into effect during his lifetime, though far from all of them.

The five copies of the Letter that were made were sealed in a number of envelopes: one for Lenin's own secretariat, three for Krupskaya, and the fifth for Lenin himself. Lenin told his secretary, M. A. Volodicheva, to write on the envelopes that they were to be opened only by Lenin, and, after his death, by Krupskaya, but Volodicheva could not bring herself to print the words 'after his death'. Only the first part of the Letter, concerning the enlargement of the Central Committee, was transmitted to Stalin, and this proposal was conveyed to the congress as part of Stalin's report on the organizational activity of the Central Committee, without, however, Lenin's authorship being acknowledged. Lenin was still alive and the sealed envelopes remained sealed. Under Kamenev's chairmanship, the congress elected Lenin unanimously (and him alone!) to the new Central Committee and sent warm greetings to him, to Krupskaya and to Lenin's sister, Maria.[51]

In March 1923 Lenin was devastated by another massive stroke which made it impossible for him to exert any further influence on party affairs, in particular to see that the ideas in his Testament were put into effect. The issue of a future leader now assumed full significance.

CHAPTER 10

Stalin or Trotsky?

It is not absolutely clear to which congress Lenin addressed his 'Letter'. He wrote, 'I would strongly advise that a number of changes be made at this congress'. It would appear that he had the Twelfth Congress in mind, but he did not say so. His health when that congress was in session in April 1923 made it virtually impossible for him, moreover, to insist that his Letter be read to the delegates. A situation had arisen for which he had not taken account. He had left instructions for the envelopes to be opened after his death. It is therefore possible that the Letter was addressed to the Twelfth and also the Thirteenth Congresses. Since the issue of the General Secretary was not raised at the Twelfth, it acquired greater significance after Lenin's stroke in March, when he could no longer communicate.

After March 1923, Stalin, as General Secretary, took a number of steps to strengthen his position. His authority had been somewhat enhanced by the Twelfth Congress, where he was perhaps more visible than any other delegate and where he presented reports on Central Committee organization and the national factors in party and state structures, and had also given the closing speeches on both these items. His reports were written in a strikingly schematic way, characteristic of his personal style. He was fond of pigeonholing his thoughts according to importance. This tended to make an impression, since it enhanced their clarity and precision. Thus, he introduced the term 'drive reins' which united the party and the people. 'The primary, basic drive rein' was, he said, the trade unions, where 'we have no strong opponents now'. The second drive rein was the consumer and agricultural cooperatives, although here, he admitted, 'we are still not strong enough to liberate the primary producers from the influence of forces hostile to us', meaning the kulaks.* The

---

* The word (literally a fist) connotes a well-off peasant in Soviet terms. In fact, any relatively successful peasant became liable to be so labelled.

third 'drive rein' was the youth organizations, where the enemy's attacks were particularly stubborn. He even enumerated and categorized according to their niche a number of other 'reins': the women's movement, schools, the army, the press. He attempted to impart to each of these elements its own rhetorical label: the press was 'the party's tongue'; the army was the 'assembly point of the workers and peasants', and so on.[52] It was typical of Stalin that, while he said practically nothing about the *content* of the work of these 'drive reins', he said a great deal about the hostile forces that 'are resisting us'. Without doubt, the class war was still going on, though by now less overtly, yet Stalin continued to live by struggle, clashes and confrontation with enemies, blatant and ephemeral.

After Lenin's stroke in March, Stalin became more active, he consulted less with Zinoviev and Kamenev, less still with Bukharin and extremely rarely with Trotsky. His political authority inside the party grew slowly but surely and revealed itself above all in his rôle within the Politburo. He achieved this by the gradual isolation of Trotsky, something he could not have achieved without the help of Zinoviev and Kamenev.

In an interview with the author, A. P. Balashov, an Old Bolshevik who had worked in Stalin's Secretariat, described an incident at the Politburo when Zinoviev and Trotsky clashed:

Everyone was on the side of Zinoviev, who flung at Trotsky, 'Can't you see you're surrounded? Your tricks won't work, you're in the minority, on your own.' Trotsky was enraged, and Bukharin tried to calm things down. It was often the case that before a session Stalin would meet Kamenev and Zinoviev and agree a position. In the Secretariat we called these meetings of the troika the 'ring'. In the twenties, Stalin always had two or three assistants. At various times these were Nazaretyan, Kanner, Dvinsky, Mekhlis and Bazhanov. They all knew about Stalin's negative attitude to Trotsky and acted accordingly.

Zinoviev and Kamenev both nourished ambitious plans, especially Zinoviev, and as they feared Trotsky more than they feared Stalin, he got them on to his side without great difficulty. When on 8 October 1923 Trotsky wrote a letter to members of the Central Committee which contained sharp criticism of the party leadership, Stalin, feeling himself to be objectively in the right, attacked his political rival's methods.

Trotsky had the support of a group of Bolsheviks who had signed the so-called 'Platform of 46' and who included such prominent figures as Preobrazhensky, Pyatakov, Kosior, Osinsky, Sapronov and Rafail, among others. Chief among Trotsky's criticisms of the Central Committee was that the 'party has no plan for further movement forward'. He reiterated his ideas about the 'tough concentration of industry' which would involve the closure of several major plants, 'the hardening of policy towards the peasants', and again insisted on the need for the 'militarization of labour'. These points are worth dwelling on.

In his speech at the Ninth Congress in March 1920, Trotsky had proclaimed that 'the working masses cannot be nomads, like the Russians of ancient times. They must be transferred, assigned, commanded just like soldiers. That is the basis of the militarization of labour, and without it, there can be no serious talk of industrializing on new foundations. We cannot do it in conditions of ruin and starvation.'[53] Three years later he still believed that the application of military methods in industry and agriculture had not lost its relevance. As an advocate of 'barracks communism', Trotsky often contradicted himself: he was fond of talking about the absence of democracy in the party, yet he insisted on the application of militarization for the general good during a period of change. Be that as it may, by launching a debate on economic issues in the autumn of 1923, when Lenin was seriously ill, he compromised the policy of the Central Committee on this issue to a certain extent, but more significantly, he compromised Stalin, as General Secretary. And yet Trotsky's authority fell, while Stalin's rose.

A combined plenum of the Central Committee and the Central Control Commission in October 1923 condemned Trotsky. He was supported by only two out of the 114 participants in the meeting. In effect, even before the meeting, Trotsky was isolated in the struggle for leadership of the party. He had been utterly defeated. He then tried to rely on the army, where he still had considerable authority. With the help of his old ally, Antonov-Ovseyenko, who was head of the Political Administration of the Revvoensoviet, he proposed to use the armed forces to demonstrate against the Central Committee's line. But, with few exceptions, the Communists in the army and navy would not support him, either. The Thirteenth Party Conference of January 1924, which debated the issue, not only condemned Trotsky, it also passed a number of measures in the field of economic policy. As a result, Trotsky admitted that his attacks on the Central Committee, and the discussion he had initiated, were undertaken with the aim of his becoming leader of the party. One cannot help noticing, however, that Trotsky started up every discussion at a time least favourable to himself, and virtually knowing in advance that he would be defeated. In overestimating his own intellectual influence, he was underestimating Stalin's grasp and ability to conduct a political struggle using any means.

It was symbolic that, during October 1923, just as Trotsky was setting light to the party's internecine conflict, Lenin was visiting Moscow for the last time. As if sensing that his fears of a split were coming true, he had himself driven to the capital on 18 October, against the advice of his doctors. On the last day, he gazed from the car for the last time at Red Square and the Kremlin domes, the streets of Moscow and the pavilions of the Agricultural Exhibition. Before leaving for Gorky, he took some books from his library in the Kremlin. He met none of his comrades. His silent, half-secret visit had been his private farewell to the capital of this troubled land.

During the revolution and civil war, and for a short time thereafter, Trotsky was second only to Lenin in popularity. The names of the leaders at, for example, Central Committee plenums would appear as follows: Lenin, Trotsky,

Zinoviev, Kamenev, Stalin, Rudzutak, Tomsky, Rykov, Preobrazhensky, Bukharin, Kalinin, Krestinsky, Dzerzhinsky, Radek, Andreyev. But Trotsky's popularity was not reflected in the number of his personal supporters. The situation was paradoxical: Stalin, who was not popular, personified the party line.

It is clear, however, from Trotsky's works that he did not share Lenin's fundamental ideas on everything. For instance, after Lenin's death, he tried to use the idea of socialist democracy as a weapon, while still advocating authoritarian methods. The impression was given that he was closer to Bonapartism, Caesarism and military dictatorship than he was to the idea of the people exercising genuine power. The same age as Stalin (they were born within two weeks of each other in 1879), Trotsky had the much finer, brighter, richer intellect. Eyewitnesses and biographers all agree that his ideas were lively, that his culture was solidly European, that he had boundless energy, was widely read and a brilliant speaker. But he exaggerated the importance of his own personality and towards everyone, except Lenin, was condescending, haughty, authoritarian and categorical, and he seemed intolerant towards the ideas of others. People naturally came to dislike him.

Stalin steadily felt out Trotsky's weak spots and used them to maximum effect in the contest. Trotsky was not particularly fussy about the 'tidiness' of his many speeches and remarks, caring more about the aphorisms he put in to make them all the more paradoxical and striking. Once in conversation with Lenin, he came out with a pithy remark that got back to Stalin: 'The cuckoo will soon be cuckooing the demise of the Soviet Republic.' Another time, talking to delegates at a Comintern congress, he commented that, if a revolution did not break out soon in Europe or Asia, then 'the torch could go out in Russia'. Stalin thus acquired the 'cast-iron' argument he needed to accuse Trotsky of capitulationism and lack of faith. And the more Trotsky tried to justify himself, the more it appeared he was accusing himself. Stalin was already showing himself to be an exceptionally tenacious and skilful fighter, and beating him was no simple matter.

Like many other party leaders, Lenin, while noting Trotsky's great literary and organizational skills, as well as his extreme vanity, also saw the political limitations that were harboured in his leftist understanding of many important Marxist ideas. It is plain now that Lenin was trying to turn Trotsky in the direction he thought desirable and no doubt, had Lenin lived longer, Trotsky's life would have been different.

Later, in emigration, Trotsky would forcefully propagate the notion that Lenin had wanted to draw him into a 'bloc' against Stalin and, with Trotsky's help, remove the General Secretary at the Twelfth Congress. In his book, *My Life*, Trotsky wrote:

Lenin systematically and persistently brought matters to the point where, at the Twelfth Congress, in Stalin's presence, a massive blow would be dealt at bureaucratism, the mutual protection of the bureaucrats, arbitrariness and wilfulness and rudeness.... In effect Lenin managed to declare war on Stalin and his allies, though only those who were directly involved knew about it, not the party.[54]

Why did Trotsky have to make these confessions, sensible though they were to some extent? Above all, in order to show that Lenin had regarded him as his successor. With that aim he commented on Lenin's Letter to the Congress, concluding that 'the indisputable purpose of the Testament was to facilitate the work of leadership for me. Lenin naturally wanted to achieve this with the smallest possible amount of friction.' These words contain the whole meaning of Trotsky's long battle. He could never come to terms with the bitterness of his personal defeat. After all, he had seen himself as the leader.

The dubiousness of Trotsky's version is revealed by what Lenin actually wrote. Lenin had absolutely no need of any sort to form a 'bloc' with Trotsky against Stalin. His authority was indisputable. The fact that on occasion he was not understood by some of the top intellectuals is another question. When he fell ill, there were attempts to explain this misunderstanding as the result of the illness, the difficulty of communication and the fact that he was isolated. But there was no doubt that, had he been well, his one personal, solidly motivated desire, namely to change the General Secretary at a Politburo meeting, would have been met. Lenin may have seen Stalin as unsuitable in his post, but Trotsky's candidacy was hardly more likely. Neither of those two 'outstanding leaders' was meant to take command on the bridge of the gigantic Russian ship of state.

Relations between Stalin and Trotsky were complicated before Lenin's death. Stalin sensed that Trotsky felt beckoned towards the leadership. He thought of his enemy as an 'adventurist' and a 'cheat', echoing what Lenin had said about Trotsky's Menshevik past. With his excellent memory, Stalin strung together all of Trotsky's many mistakes, his zigzags, twists and turns and made a thread for future arguments, unmaskings, criticism, judgements. He did not forget Trotsky's radical left-wing phraseology at Brest-Litovsk, or his order to shoot a large group of political workers on the Eastern front because of the treachery of some military experts, a tragedy only averted by Lenin's intervention, he remembered Trotsky's proposal to send a cavalry corps into India to start the revolution, and he did not forget Trotsky's cuckoo that was going to cuckoo the end of the Soviet régime.

Stalin did not like the fact that, soon after the civil war, Trotsky surrounded himself with a large staff of assistants and secretaries who helped him to run a large archive, maintain correspondence, and prepare papers and materials for endless articles and speeches, often giving him his creative impulse. Stalin believed that Trotsky viewed Russia's countless problems to a great extent through the prism of his own narrowly careerist, egotistical, power-seeking interests, without regard to the difficulties of the social and political situation. Their relations soon became mutually deeply hostile. Trotsky, it should be said, had bad relations not only with Stalin. He had virtually no close allies among the other leaders. Even the short-lived alliance with Zinoviev and Kamenev would be cobbled together on an unprincipled, anti-Stalin platform. Trotsky, moreover, seriously underestimated Stalin, the 'outstanding mediocrity', as he began calling him openly after being expelled from the Politburo.

After Lenin's stroke in March, Stalin privately saw himself as the person responsible for preventing Trotsky from becoming the party leader. Trotsky's defeat in the discussion launched by his supporters greatly reduced his chances, irrespective of what decision the congress might take over Lenin's Letter. Stalin was convinced – and he repeated it in a narrow circle, perhaps as his own justification – that, were Trotsky to become party leader, the gains of the revolution would face mortal peril.

Trotsky not only underrated Stalin's will and intellect, but by his endless attacks, discussions and polemical articles he inevitably raised Stalin's authority, and Stalin was thereby able to come out as the defender of Lenin's heritage, the protector of party unity. The more Trotsky flew at Stalin, the lower his own popularity sank. The issue was less Stalin himself than the publicly perceived fact that Trotsky was in effect attacking the party line, the centre. Thus, Trotsky himself helped to consolidate Stalin's political position. In the eyes of the party, Stalin never seemed to swing to either right or left, but appeared to show flexibility, and at times subtle cunning, by leaning for support against Trotsky on his two future enemies, Zinoviev and Kamenev.

January 1924 was a painfully sad time. On the 19th of that month, Kalinin reported to the Politburo that Lenin's doctors were now definitely optimistic that he would gradually be able to return to work. He was walking, business matters were being read to him. There were definite signs of hope, but they were quickly dashed.

No half-ruined country needs a leadership that is in constant conflict within itself, and yet the Thirteenth Party Conference, which took place in mid-January 1924, enacted precisely that paradox. It debated routine issues of economic policy and gave a political account of the Trotskyist opposition.

In small doses, on 19 and 20 January, Krupskaya read reports of the conference proceedings to Lenin. She later recalled that, when he became agitated on the Saturday, she told him that the resolutions had been passed unanimously. The debate on the opposition was acrimonious. Zinoviev and Kamenev, Trotsky's future allies, demanded his expulsion from the Politburo and Central Committee. Perhaps Lenin saw signs of a potential split here, emanating from the force of a single personality? He must have realized that his warnings had become a grim reality.

His condition worsened sharply during the day on 21 January and he died at 6.50 p.m. The post-mortem confirmed the doctors' opinion that the underlying cause of the illness had been pronounced sclerosis of the brain cells due to the strain of excessive mental effort; and the direct cause of death was a cerebral haemorrhage. Trotsky, who was in the south, was for some unexplained reason not present at the funeral, although he had sufficient time to get there. At the Tiflis railway station on 22 January he cabled a short article to *Pravda* which included the lines:

And so Ilyich is no more. The party has been orphaned. The working class has been orphaned. It is this feeling above all that news of the death of the teacher, the leader, brings.

How will we carry on, will we find the way, won't we lose the way?

Our hearts are torn now by such boundless pain because, by the great grace of history, we were born contemporaries of Lenin, we worked together with him, learned from him.

How will we go forward? With Lenin's torch in our hand . . .[55]

A special Central Committee plenum was held on the night of 22 January and on the 27th Lenin's body was installed in the Mausoleum on Red Square. The Second All-Union Congress of Soviets, which opened on 26 January, passed a resolution that Lenin's memory should be immortalized. A mourning ceremony was held at the Bolshoi Theatre, which was draped in black for the occasion.

At 6.20 in the evening, Chairman of the Central Executive Committee Kalinin called on the members of the Executive Committee presidium and the Central Committee to take their places on the platform. As Soviet sources depicted this occasion until recently, it seemed as if Stalin, making his 'vow', was the only speaker. In fact, many others spoke. Stalin's speech which, as was his custom, he wrote himself, was delivered in the passionate style of a vow, couched in his familiar catechistic form. Everything was categorized. In a hymn to strength and sacrifice of the sort that would become characteristic until the end of his life, he said, 'we would fend off countless blows . . . we would not spare our lives . . . in building a kingdom of labour on earth, not in heaven'.[56] In the name of the party, Stalin swore to cherish the title of member of the party, to protect its unity, to reinforce the dictatorship of the proletariat, to strengthen the union of the workers and peasants and that of the fraternal republics, and to remain faithful to internationalism. Nothing was said about the power of the people, or socialist democracy, or freedom. Possibly they were implied in the promise to strengthen the dictatorship of the proletariat, which after all had its non-violent side. It is more likely, however, that Stalin simply did not feel the need for such subtleties.

A new chapter of history had begun. Lenin's successor as chairman of the Sovnarkom was Rykov, while Kamenev was made chairman of the Soviet of Labour and Defence. Remaining as General Secretary, Stalin began to await the outcome of the Thirteenth Congress, where the dead Lenin's Letter would be read out. But what did he know about the Letter? The testimony is contradictory.

CHAPTER 11

The Roots of the Tragedy

As Lenin had wished, Krupskaya handed his Letter and its Postscript to the Central Committee on 18 May 1924, five days before the opening of the Thirteenth Party Congress, accompanying them with a handwritten note indicating that Lenin had expressed the firm wish that after his death his notes should be brought to the attention of the next party congress.[57] On the basis of a report submitted by the commission deputed to receive Lenin's notes, the plenum which met on the eve of the congress agreed to allow the documents to be read out 'within the delegations and on the understanding that they are not for reproduction.'[58]

Unfortunately, no one in the Politburo could or would fully understand Lenin's ideas. The Thirteenth Congress dealt with many important problems, but they were all related to contemporary matters and not to the future. Lenin's central idea, that of developing the power of the people, was not the congress's main preoccupation. And here perhaps lay the seeds of future misfortunes.

While both the Twelfth and Thirteenth Congresses did in fact broaden the Central Committee, the people they appointed, however worthy. were overwhelmingly former professional revolutionaries, whereas the whole point of Lenin's proposal was that the Central Committee should be broadened by bringing in workers and peasants.

In a one-sided way, Zinoviev discussed the question of socialist democracy, which had given Lenin such concern. He quoted a 'bourgeois engineer' who was now serving the régime as saying that it was not enough to give people the basic necessities, they must also be given 'the rights of man'. As long as we do not have such rights, the engineer had said, we will remain inert. Until it is recognized that 'man is the highest value in the state', people will still have low social and labour initiative. Zinoviev's response to this prevalent mood among the intelligentsia was, however: 'We don't have to waste time on this matter. It is patently obvious that people like this are as likely to see such rights in our republic as they are to see their ears in a mirror'.[59] Zinoviev was not alone on the Central Committee in lacking a deeply humanistic conception of socialism. Their ignorance also harboured the roots of future ills. True, only six and a half years had passed since the revolution, and without the party's authoritarian rule the Soviet Republic would barely have withstood the onslaught of its internal and external enemies. But the neglect of democratic principles was bound to surface, sooner or later.

Lenin's Letter was not dealt with as it should have been at the congress. A selected few acquainted a limited number of delegations with it. Kamenev was particularly active, going from delegation to delegation. The Letter was not discussed by the congress as such. After the 'readings', the commission on Lenin's papers verbally tabled a resolution, prepared in advance, in which Stalin was enjoined to take account of Lenin's critical comments, and that was the end of the matter. Dealing with the Letter in this way meant that its contents were never fully appreciated, and it was therefore not used as the basis for strengthening the democratic norms of party life, or making structural changes in the leading echelon, or bringing forward a new figure for the post of General Secretary. On the other hand, almost a year and a half had elapsed since the Letter was written, and during that time, Stalin had had to declare war on Trotsky who, shortly before Lenin's death, had sharply attacked the party line and the New Economic Policy. In defending the party from these attacks, Stalin was actually defending himself, but he was supported by the majority of the party, and this was bound to make the delegates think that to remove Stalin would also be to acknowledge that Trotsky had been right.

Many delegates could not fathom the stratagems of politics and often mistook the form for the content. It was largely thanks to his memorable speeches that Trotsky retained his popularity for so long. Partly because delegates were subjected to a degree of 'processing' and pressure, but also because of the low level of their political culture, many of them could not understand why this vital document was not being discussed openly by congress, why so much secrecy was necessary and why Lenin's proposals could not be published. Underdeveloped political culture, not only in most of the population but in the party, too, was a major source of future ills.

Meanwhile, the individual consciences of those Bolsheviks of sufficiently high political culture who did realize that Lenin's Testament required close scrutiny, were silenced by the slogan of 'unity'. They did not exercise their consciences, and not for the last time. The raising up of a new leader would take place in conditions where true democracy was continually curtailed and emasculated, the party was turned into a power machine, and the conscience of many who ought to have protested publicly and openly against the usurpation of power by one man was stifled. The fact is, expressing one's conscience demanded intellectual courage, and as a rule craven anxiety turned out to be stronger. Freedom did not have a high priority in the Bolshevik creed.

When Stalin heard about Lenin's Letter, he announced his resignation.[60]

Had it been accepted, things might well have been different. He had made the right decision, as any Bolshevik in his position ought to have done, but it was not a determined act. As a matter of fact, he twice offered his resignation in the 1920s. The second time, after the Fifteenth Congress in December 1927, he behaved more categorically. The Trotskyite–Zinovievite opposition had been defeated and the congress noted this formally. At the first plenum after the congress, Stalin submitted a request to the Central Committee:

I think recent circumstances have forced the party to have me in this post, as someone severe enough to provide the antidote to the opposition. Now the opposition has been defeated and expelled from the party. We have Lenin's instructions moreover and I think it is now time to carry them out. I therefore request the plenum to release me from the post of General Secretary. I assure you, comrades, the party can only gain from this.[61]

By this time, however, his authority had risen and he was seen in the party as the man who had fought for its unity and who had come out against various factionalists. His resignation was again rejected. Stalin had no doubt expected this and staged the resignation as an act to strengthen his position.

To return to the Thirteenth Congress, however, Kamenev and Zinoviev made sure that Lenin's urgings to remove Stalin were not carried out. They persuaded Stalin to withdraw his verbal declaration and together concocted a formula which would permit Stalin to take the late leader's strictures into account. They personally canvassed the major delegations, practically disavowing Lenin's ideas, while whitewashing their future gravedigger. Their main motivation was to prevent Trotsky from getting the top posts which they themselves were seeking. They were less concerned about the fate of the revolution, Lenin's will or the future of the country. The oldest imperative in the world was at work, namely, personal interest, ambition and vanity. Like Trotsky, however, they grossly underestimated Stalin. At the beginning of the 1920s, Zinoviev, for instance, had repeated to a narrow circle, 'Stalin is a good executive, but he always has to be led, and can be. Stalin himself does not have leadership qualities.' Zinoviev and Kamenev apparently expected Stalin to remain as General Secretary solely in order to run the Secretariat, while someone else would play first violin in the Politburo, and that, naturally, would be Zinoviev. Stalin saw what the duo were up to and for the time being gave them the impression that he was compliant. He made sure that none other than Zinoviev should deliver the political report to the congress. Being afraid of Trotsky, the duo did not see Stalin as a danger. For his part, Trotsky was passive at the congress. It seemed he was just waiting to be called. Such was the situation in the leading core of the Central Committee.

Now, decades later, it is possible to see that the people standing in the way of Lenin's wishes were Zinoviev and Kamenev, and of course Stalin who could have done nothing without them. This was the Zinoviev who was apt to boast publicly that for all of ten years, from 1907 to 1917, he had been Lenin's closest pupil, and that nobody had supported Lenin so assiduously at Zimmerwald and Kienthal as he had. For his part, Kamenev was close to the Ulyanov family and did not hide the fact. One way or another, these political twins came to believe in their special rôles after Lenin's death. It was they who with Stalin took the decision not to make Lenin's Letter public. And although at the Fifteenth Congress this document was published in a current bulletin at Ordzhonikidze's suggestion, it still did not reach wide sections of the party or the nation.

As soon as Stalin had beaten Trotsky, he would lose interest in Zinoviev and Kamenev and within a dozen years calmly order their physical destruction. How many times would they return in desperation to the time when, disdaining Lenin's Letter, they themselves gave the dictator and their future executioner a helping hand? To be sure, when Stalin split with them they took a stand on 'principle' and came out against him. As early as the Fourteenth Congress of December 1925, Kamenev, one of the leaders of the 'new opposition', had uttered the true but tardy words: 'I have come to the conviction that Comrade Stalin cannot fulfil the rôle of unifier of the Bolshevik headquarters', but the delegates merely took this as a routine attack by a factionalist. Nothing, however, alters the fact that it was they who, against Lenin's will, had kept Stalin in his post as General Secretary.

In these circumstances, Trotsky, having lost the debate, sought to save face by taking up a flexible position. Zinoviev called his speech to the Thirteenth Congress 'not a congress speech' but 'a parliamentary one'; he was addressing not the delegates but the party as a whole and was attempting 'to say not all that he thinks'. Trotsky's speech was indeed unusual. Its main point was a criticism of bureaucracy in the party apparatus. He bolstered his argument by referring to Lenin and Bukharin, and attacked the leadership of the Central Committee from the position of an innovator and a fighter for the defence of the party's revolutionary traditions. According to Trotsky, it was bureaucratism in the apparatus, and at every level, that spawned factionalism, and while there was more than a grain of reason in this argument, Trotsky was thinking more of himself than of the party. He remained himself; he needed the toga of democracy as a verbal covering for his attacks on the line being taken by the Central Committee. But the party had not forgotten that he was one of the initiators of the very 'barracks communism' that had given rise to bureaucratic degeneration. The Thirteenth Congress made no advance towards the development of democracy as envisaged by Lenin. Many perhaps thought that to remove Stalin would enhance Trotsky's position. And, had he not compromised himself by his October 1923 challenge, his chances of succeeding would have been quite high, even though he did not suit the majority of the old guard. One may therefore say that Stalin retained his post thanks to Trotsky's 'help'.

The democratic foundations of the state and party structures had only been marked out by Lenin. He did not have time to develop them. Take only one facet of democracy: the rotation of leading functionaries. Even if Stalin remained in his post, had his tenure been limited by established procedure, the deformations brought about by his personality cult in the future might not have occurred. It is perfectly understandable that Queen Victoria or Catherine the Great or the Shah of Iran could remain on their thrones for decades, as they were monarchs. But the prolonged presence of Stalin as head of the party and the state, virtually unlimited by anyone or anything, could not but lead to trouble. Lenin's proposals to the Twelfth Congress, contained in his note on the reorganization of the Workers and Peasants Inspectorate, envisaged compulsory renewal of the leading party organs and the limitation of the functions of the Central Committee and the soviets. These first shoots of democracy were left untended and were soon completely engulfed by the more powerful weeds of dogmatism, bureaucracy and mechanical rule by administration. The future cult of 'the great leader' did not arise by accident.

There were no early, outward signs that the usurpation of power was taking place. On the contrary, Stalin fought Trotsky under the banner of a collective struggle against his Bonapartist, dictatorial ways, his claims to individual leadership and his unbridled ambition. Trotsky continued to exploit the political capital he had acquired in the civil war, without realizing how fast it was disappearing. In attacking Trotsky, Stalin proposed another, more progressive and democratic alternative, namely collective leadership, though he was already planning the gradual transformation of the leadership to his own advantage. The first person he had to remove was, naturally enough, Trotsky. Meanwhile, it was important not to force matters. The composition of the Politburo after the Thirteenth Congress was therefore the same, and even Trotsky still kept his place. The only new face was that of the party's rising star, Bukharin. Lenin's description of him as 'the party's favourite' accelerated his advance into the highest reaches. Dzerzhinsky, Sokolnikov and Frunze became candidate members of the Politburo. The Secretariat acquired a new look, with Stalin as General Secretary, Molotov as second secretary and Kaganovich as secretary – a much more secure base of support from Stalin's point of view. He had survived probably the worst moments of his party career. He had not been removed as General Secretary, despite Lenin's wishes, and his position in the leadership had been strengthened.

Lenin's Letter disappeared from the party's view for decades. It was not published in *Leninskii sbornik* ('Lenin Miscellany'), despite Stalin's promise to do so. To be sure, the Letter did surface a few times in the 1920s in connection with the internal party struggle. It was even published in Bulletin No. 30 of the Fifteenth Party Congress (printrun 10,000), stamped 'For VKP(b) members only',* and was distributed to provincial committees, Communist fractions of the trade unions central committee, and part of it was printed in *Pravda* on 2 November 1927. It is therefore not true to say that the party knew nothing

---

*The All-Russian Communist Party (Bolsheviks) (RKP(b) for short) became the All-Union (VKP(b)) etc. at its Fourteenth Congress in 1925.

about it. But omitting to carry out Lenin's will straightaway made it harder to do so later, especially as at first Stalin tried to change his behaviour, at least outwardly. Chiefly, however, it was because in the party's eyes he had become the leader of the Central Committee majority that was in conflict with the oppositionists, even though the opposition as a rule only expressed intellectual differences, different points of view and alternatives. Stalin, however, strove to make the terms 'opposition' and 'faction' synonymous with hostility.

Subsequent generations of party members heard about Lenin's Letter only after the Twentieth Party Congress in 1956. This kind of secrecy was harmful, as it eroded such democratic elements as existed and inevitably created the impression that the truth can be held captive. It is worthy of note that Karl Radek wrote in his 'Results of the Twentieth Congress of the RKP', published in 1923, that some people wanted 'to gain capital' out of Lenin's last letters, saying that 'they contained something secret', which made it impossible to publish them.[62]

In the end it was futile to go on trying to hide the truth, but not before the public's awareness, the political culture and the spiritual values of Soviet society had been hugely damaged. Stalin was innately secretive, and henceforth the rubber stamp of secrecy would appear on all manner of files and even basic documents. Of course, state secrets did exist and will continue to do so, but turning routine correspondence and basic information into secrets became a way of life. No one seems to have thought that imposing excessive secrecy on state and social life would nourish the soil for corruption. In the centre of all the secrets stood Stalin himself, reacting personally to the constant flow of information.

The text of Lenin's Letter was, thanks in part to Trotsky's efforts, published repeatedly in the West. First it was published in the USA with an extensive, anti-Soviet commentary by Trotsky's long-time ally, Max Eastman. Then, in France in the 1930s, Boris Souvarine, a French citizen of Russian origin and a contributor to *L'Humanité*, also analysed it. Trotsky made repeated and strenuous efforts to draw attention to the Letter, but by the end of his life he had only one interpretation of it: Lenin had proposed removing Stalin from his post and recommended that the delegates put Trotsky forward as party leader, as the most capable and clever candidate. He repeated this so often in his books and articles that it is quite likely he came to believe it.

Lenin's ideas, as expressed in his Testament, envisaged a broad spectrum of democratic measures. He proposed that the flow of new blood in the party and state leadership be increased, that the rôle of the trade unions be enhanced, along with that of the soviets, the social organizations, and the security organs, and that the leadership be more responsive to the workers. Even if there was no question of plebiscites, referenda, opinion polls or compulsory monitoring of the leadership, or the strict rotation of party cadres and similar features of democracy, there was an implicit sense of fairness in what he advocated at the end of his life.

The party's neglect of this basic principle was to take its toll on all spheres of life. Nevertheless, to give the political system its due, enormous attention was paid to educating the population and successive generations in the principles of the revolution, socialism and communism. The image of the ideal 'new man' was propagated as a model of the individual of the future. As early as the 1920s, despite the upsurge in bureaucratic tendencies, the ideological side of restructuring society was given primary importance. Simplicity, public modesty, absence of possessiveness in everyday communal living, readiness to respond to society's every call, deep hostility to philistinism and acquisitiveness, and a high level of spirituality that was alien to commercial values: these features of the people of the 1920s, 1930s and 1940s testify that bureaucratism did not kill the best in them. The people kept faith in the idea.

After Lenin's death, Stalin, who did not propose to relinquish the captain's bridge for some mere ministry or other, took his fate into his own hands. But the danger of what was to come was already there, in the centralized system. Lenin's warning went unheeded. The old guard, tied up as they were in internecine struggle, did not accept the rôle of collective leadership. The freedom that had been won clouded their vision of what was to come. As Nikolai Berdyaev wrote: 'The experience of the Russian revolution confirmed an old idea of mine, namely, that freedom is not democratic, but aristocratic. The rising masses are not interested in freedom and they don't need it, nor are they up to bearing the burden of freedom.'[63] A debatable idea, no doubt, but it was true when applied to both the masses and the old guard who were incapable of coping with freedom.

3

CHOICE AND STRUGGLE

'Truth is the daughter of time, not of authority.'

– Francis Bacon

CHAPTER 12

Building Socialism

The birth pangs of the new society were continuing. After the Thirteenth Congress Stalin began to recover the trust he had been on the verge of losing. Before Lenin's death, he could hardly have entertained serious personal ambitions. One can scarcely say with complete certainty that even afterwards he believed that the apparently impossible might be realized.

Many of the books in the library he had begun to assemble in the small apartment he occupied in the Kremlin from 1920 were pre-revolutionary editions. They included the works of Marx, Engels, Plekhanov, Lafargue, Rosa Luxemburg, Lenin, Tolstoy, Garshin, Chekhov, Gorky, Uspensky, as well as the books of lesser known writers. Many contain pencilled notes, underlinings and markings.

Napoleon's *Thoughts* contain thick pencil marks against the paragraph where the emperor recalls: 'It was precisely the evening in Lodi* that I came to believe in myself as an unusual person and became consumed with the ambition to do the great things that until then had been but a fantasy.'[1] Did Stalin believe that clinging to the post of General Secretary against Lenin's will had been his Lodi? It probably was indeed the culminating point of his political career: at the age of forty-five he felt by no means weaker than his colleagues in the Politburo and the Central Committee.

He thought about this more and more during the rare moments of relaxation he took at his dacha at Zabolovo, outside Moscow. At the beginning of the 1920s, there were hundreds of abandoned mansions, villas and suburban houses in the environs of Moscow. Their former owners had either fled abroad, been submerged in the bloodbath of the civil war, or had their 'bourgeois luxury' simply expropriated. Many of these homes had been converted into

---

*A small village where Napoleon scored a brilliant victory during the Italian campaign of 1796–97.

hospitals or orphanages for waifs and strays, or warehouses, or sanatoria for the institutions that were being proliferated endlessly by the state. Not far from Usovo there were a dozen or so villas. The one that had belonged to the oil baron Zabolovo was given to Stalin, while others were allocated to Voroshilov, Shaposhnikov, Mikoyan, Gamarnik and other party, state and military leaders.

Stalin's son, Vasili, was born in 1921 and a few years later came Svetlana. Shortly after she was born, they were joined by Yakov, their father's son by his first marriage. Stalin's wife, Nadezhda Sergeyevna Alliluyeva, who was twenty-two years his junior, went about the task of setting up a simple household with zeal and dedication. They lived modestly on Stalin's salary until she went to work, first, for the journal *Revolution and Culture* then in the Sovnarkom secretariat, and finally to study at the Industrial Academy. One day at dinner Stalin suddenly said to her, 'I've never loved money, because I usually never had any.' Interestingly, the archives contain receipts, which he passed through Stasova, showing that he received advances on his 'next month's salary' for amounts of twenty-five, sixty, seventy-five rubles.

Eventually, they took on a nanny and a housekeeper. As yet he did not have a large staff of security people or messengers, or the dozens of other posts of all kinds that would be created later on. The leaders in those early days avoided the term 'servants', with its bourgeois connotations, and referred instead to their 'service staff'.

Like all the other leaders at that time, Stalin lived in simple circumstances, in keeping with the family budget and party norms. In October 1923, the Central Committee and Central Control Commission distributed a special document to all party committees, listing the measures that had been adopted at the Ninth Party Conference of September 1920. It had stated that it was impermissible to use state resources for improving one's private accommodation, for furnishing a dacha, giving bonuses or rewards in kind to functionaries, and it enjoined the strictest observance of party members' moral conduct. The salaries of 'experts' and functionaries must not be allowed to get too far out of line with those of ordinary workers. To ignore these guidelines, the circular concluded, would be counter to democratism and would lead to 'the demoralization of the party and the lowering of the Communists' authority'. This circular underlined the Leninist principle that 'Communist functionaries do not have the right to personal rates of pay, nor to bonuses, nor overtime payments.'[2] In Lenin's day, there was even an unwritten law that Central Committee members should hand over their royalties from writing to party funds.

Party leaders at that time did not own valuable possessions, and even talking about such things was regarded as a sign of bad taste, philistinism, even an anti-party mentality. Stalin had a natural bent for physical asceticism. When he died, he was found to have owned very few personal items – some uniforms, a pair of embroidered felt boots and a patched, peasant sheepskin coat. He did not love objects, he loved power.

Circumstances permitting, gatherings would sometimes take place on Sundays, often at Stalin's dacha. Bukharin and his wife would come, as would Yenukidze, Mikoyan, Molotov, Voroshilov and Budyonny, often with their wives and children. Budyonny would sing Russian and Ukrainian songs to the accompaniment of an accordion, and they might even dance. Trotsky never visited Stalin at his dacha.

The company would sit around the table for hours discussing the domestic situation and international affairs. Stalin's father-in-law, the Old Bolshevik, S. Ya. Alliluyev, whom he greatly respected, was usually there, repeating stories of 'the old days'. He'd been a member of the party since its foundation and was very proud of the fact. There would be arguments, sometimes quite heated, but everyone was on intimate terms, addressing each other as 'ty', and no one felt the need to be deferential, still less flattering or ingratiating. Stalin was an equal among equals.

Ten years earlier, these people had been the pariahs of their society, and now they were at the head of a gigantic state whose wounds of war and rebellion had barely healed. Many of the questions discussed at these gatherings would later find their way on to the Politburo agenda. For instance, on one occasion, Molotov revealed the amount of money the Treasury was losing because of the quantity of grain being used in the making of illicit liquor. A few days later, on 27 November 1927, an order came from the Politburo, signed by Stalin, to form a permanent commission to combat home-distilled vodka, cocaine and gambling (especially Lotto).[3] Also, following discussion of the causes of Lenin's illness and death, it was decided that certain steps should be taken to improve the medical service for the party leadership. At the Central Committee plenum of 31 January 1924, the decision was taken to select 'a particular comrade to monitor the health and working conditions of the leadership'.[4]

It all started from such 'trivialities'. The élitist thinking of a leadership that preached egalitarianism gave rise to other privileges: various supplements ('envelopes'), personal railway carriages, villas in the south, large 'service staffs'.

They often debated 'how to instil socialism'. The direction had been clear enough at the outset, they thought, but how were they to follow it, at what speed, by what means? All this was far from clear. After his guests had left, Stalin would pace for a long time, thinking of the day to come. He had acquired both responsibility and fear for the future, but he had also gained greater vanity and self-esteem: perhaps this phase of struggle and lack of definition was his Lodi?

The ideal occurs when strength and wisdom are in harmony, and that happens rarely. As a rule, the future belongs to the strong and not, unfortunately, to the wise. Socrates said philosophers must be rulers and rulers must be philosophers. Strength always needs wisdom. Despite the fact that for a long time the Soviet people mistook his cunning and crafty ways for wisdom, Stalin had strength but not wisdom, and when it came to choosing the means of bringing the great ideas into everyday life, this played a tragic part.

The energies of the masses had been released, the question was how to direct them towards the aim, the ideal, the heights, which even Lenin had thought were near. The party press was full of articles by experts giving their advice on how to proceed. It was all so new. At times it seemed a slogan was enough to get things going by themselves.

At the end of 1924, in Kislovodsk, Trotsky wrote his *Lessons of October*, in which he again attempted to belittle the rôle of the other leaders of the revolution with the aim of establishing the 'theoretical' basis of his own claim to be leader. As the journal *Bolshevik* (No. 14, 1924) remarked, he had ceased to be a 'chronicler' and become a prejudiced prosecutor. He tried to show that during the revolution 'the Central Committee was right when it was in accord with Trotsky, and Lenin was wrong when he did not agree with Trotsky.' A revolution, Trotsky wrote, has its tides, and if one misses the tide one may miss the revolution. He evidently knew how to catch the tide at its peak. The revolution took place because Lenin and Trotsky were at its head, despite the majority of the 'Old Bolsheviks'.

Trotsky again argued that the fate of the revolution depended to a decisive extent on the 'sequence in which the revolution in various countries in Europe takes place'.[5] In his *The Permanent Revolution* (a reworking in book form in 1928 of the original article published in 1905), he wrote even more emphatically that the completion of a socialist revolution in one country was unthinkable, that 'the preservation of the proletarian revolution within national limits could only mean a temporary, even if prolonged régime, as the experience of the Soviet Union has shown.' To the question of how to build socialism, Trotsky effectively gave the reply, 'by waiting for the world revolution, by giving it a push'. Trotsky believed that October Revolutions would occur in the world one after the other, and that the Red Army must help other countries in the great upheaval. This may have been blatant leftism, but it was not the 'crime' it was later declared to be. Unlike Stalin, Trotsky had a powerful streak of revolutionary romanticism in him.

On the theory of 'permanent revolution', Trotsky had written: 'Russia cannot of course come to socialism independently. But having opened the era of socialist transformations, she can give a push to the socialist development of Europe and in this way be brought to socialism by the tugboat of the advanced countries.'[6] That had been his view before 1917. He changed his position somewhat after the revolution and elaborated his point of view in the form of a dialogue:

Stalin: 'So, you deny that our revolution can lead to socialism?'
Trotsky: 'I believe, as I always have, that our revolution can and must lead to socialism by assuming an international character.'

Further on he explains: 'The secret of our theoretical contradictions lies in the fact that you lagged far behind the historical process and are now trying to catch up. And as a matter of fact this also explains the secret of your economic mistakes.' The theory of building socialism in one country, according to Trotsky, was incompatible with the theory of permanent revolution. Only super-industrialization at the cost of the peasant sector, as Preobrazhensky wrote in support of Trotsky, could provide the state with the industrial base and the possibility of socialism.

Stalin's knowledge of economics was extremely superficial, but he could see well enough that the country was in a parlous state. The party debates and arguments, which went on for nearly a decade, were not only a struggle about the level and character of the democratic society, but were also a search for the way to develop the economy. Had Stalin been economically more perceptive, he would have been able to see in Lenin's last articles the outlines of a conception of socialism that embodied a link between industrialization and voluntary cooperative farming, a powerful rise in the culture of the broad masses, an improvement in socialist relations and the unconditional development of demo-cratic principles in society. But Stalin had never properly understood Lenin's prophecy that the NEP would tie many of these problems into a single knot: that by linking town and village, by freeing the economic levers, and through trade and the age-old enterprise of the man of business, 'socialist Russia would emerge from the Russia of NEP.'[7]

Stalin was at first interested in the economic views of Bukharin, Pre-obrazhensky, Strumilin and Leontiev, but he found their abstruse terminology hard to follow. Never having been in a factory or known the smell of spring ploughing, and never having mastered the alphabet of economics, he finally conceded the possibility of a 'goods famine' under socialism – still with us today. To be sure, he did make an effort to understand something of economics. For instance, he had O. Ermansky's book *The Scientific Organization of Labour and the Taylor System*. The fact that Lenin had praised Ermansky (a Menshevik, real name Kogan) for being able to expound 'the Taylor system, showing, and this is most important, *its positive and negative sides*',[8] was probably why Stalin read it.

Judging by his written works, however, as well as his notes and utterances, but chiefly by his practical measures, it is plain that Stalin's economic credo was more than simple. The country had to be strong, and not merely strong, but mighty. First, it needed to be totally industrialized. Secondly, the peasants must be brought closer to socialism. The method should be the broadest reliance on the dictatorship of the proletariat, which Stalin understood purely in coercive terms. In 1926, he wrote in *Bolshevik* (No. 9–10, 1926): 'We are attempting to solve bigger and more serious tasks, the solution of which will more surely secure our successful steps towards socialism, but as the *tasks become greater*, the *difficulties* will grow *larger*.' This formula would find a sinister echo later in his dictum: 'The class war sharpens, the faster we progress towards socialism.' In the middle of the 1920s, Stalin had only a dim awareness of the path of socialist construction, but he undoubtedly already had his method in mind: force, command, directives, orders. That is to say, dictatorship.

As he read the endless speeches of prominent party figures about the fate of socialism in the USSR, Stalin felt that the wide spectrum of views was determined not only by their authors' differences of intellectual and theoretical position, but also by the fact that reality had turned out to be much more complicated than the Bolsheviks had anticipated. As Bukharin candidly wrote in 1925:

This is how we used to see the problem: we would gain power, take almost everything into our own hands, immediately introduce a planned economy, give some of the recalcitrant odds and ends what for and subdue the rest, and that would be that. Now we see perfectly clearly that this is not at all how it is done.[9]

Stalin could hardly disagree, but he felt that the biggest danger was represented by Trotsky. He had just been told that Trotsky had declared to a circle of adherents that 'some new grandees in the party could not forgive him for the historic rôle he had played in October'. Coming from Trotsky's lips, a 'grandee' could only mean Stalin, and that was apparently not the worst epithet Trotsky and his friends had reportedly applied to him.

Although his relations with Kamenev and Zinoviev remained outwardly satisfactory, Stalin felt that his straightforward manner and steadily growing influence were not to the taste of the duo. He sensed this particularly acutely after the Thirteenth Congress. In his report on courses for district committee secretaries, Stalin had criticized Kamenev for stating the existence of a 'dictatorship of the party', and he had concluded by saying, to shouts of approval from the delegates, 'We don't have a dictatorship of the party, we have a dictatorship of the proletariat.' It should be noted that Bukharin, who at that time shared the idea of the 'dictatorship of the party', declared at the Central Committee plenum of January 1924:

Our task is to see two dangers: the first arises from the centralization of our apparatus. The second is that of the political democracy that could emerge if democracy goes too far. The opposition, however, sees only the danger of the bureaucracy. It fails to see the danger of political democracy beyond the danger of bureaucracy ... In order to support the dictatorship of the proletariat, we have to support the dictatorship of the party.

To which Radek added: 'We are a dictatorial party in a petty bourgeois country.'[10]

But Stalin, who saw no need to fight with many, criticized only Kamenev. For him, the most important thing was not to rush his fences, but to take everything in its time. Immediately the political tandem struck back. Stalin's criticism of Kamenev was condemned at a Politburo meeting as uncomradely and inaccurate about Kamenev's true position. Stalin at once offered to resign.

This was the second time he had done so as General Secretary, though it would not be the last. Again his offer was turned down, and by none other than Kamenev, supported by Zinoviev. Stalin sensed a growing uncertainty in his opponents. They evidently still feared Trotsky. But yet again Stalin had witnessed the duo changing their views like a weathervane. What good was Zinoviev's book *Leninism?* In effect, he was trying once more to camouflage and justify his and Kamenev's behaviour in October 1917 and their disagreement with Lenin. Stalin had a malicious memory and he would most definitely use these facts in the future.

As soon as he had done with Trotsky, he would remove these 'unprincipled loudmouths'. Even he, who had made a virtue of his rudeness, sometimes felt Zinoviev's assertiveness grating on his nerves. Speaking at a Central Committee plenum of 14 January 1924 on the subject of the 'discussion list', Zinoviev made very outspoken comments on many Central Committee members and other Bolsheviks taking part in the debate, just as if he were a company commander evaluating his subordinates. 'Pyatakov,' he confidently declared, 'is a Bolshevik, but his Bolshevism is still immature. Green and immature.' Of Sapronov he said, 'He stands with both feet on the ground but represents anything but Leninism.' Osinsky 'represents a deviation of a more intellectual kind, having nothing at all in common with Bolshevism'. Nor did he miss the chance to take a sideswipe at Trotsky, which must have pleased Stalin, even though there was no obvious connection: 'Once, when we arrived in Copenhagen for a congress, we were given a copy of the newspaper *Vorwärts*, in which there was an anonymous article saying that Lenin and his group were criminals and expropriators. The author of that article was Trotsky.'[11]

As Stalin sat and listened, it must have crossed his mind that Zinoviev was already thinking of himself as leader. He expressed no view of Zinoviev's speech at the plenum, but two years later he would dismantle Zinoviev's position, brick by brick. In May 1926, in a note to the bureau members of the party delegation to Comintern, Stalin wrote:

Referring to his seventeen years of literary activity, Comrade Zinoviev brags that it is not for Comrades Stalin and Manuilsky to teach him about the need to struggle against the ultra-left tendency. There is no need to prove that Comrade Zinoviev regards himself as a great man, but whether the party thinks so, too, is open to doubt.

From 1898 right up to the February Revolution of 1917, we old illegals managed to spend time and to work in every region of Russia, but we never met Comrade Zinoviev either in the underground, or in prison, or in exile.

We old illegals cannot but know that there is an entire galaxy of old members who entered the party long before Comrade Zinoviev and who built up the party without making any fuss or bragging. What is Comrade Zinoviev's so called literary activity compared with the work all our old illegals did in the underground for twenty years?[12]

By the mid-1920s, Stalin's main opponents would come to realize that this 'outstanding mediocrity' was an exceptional politician, cunning, crafty and wilful. Soon, any party and state leaders who had anything to do with him would also realize it. In examining this period of history, one inevitably feels that the great issues surrounding the historic choice were frequently pushed into second place by the personal ambitions of the leaders, and that the struggle over how to build socialism was severely affected by personal rivalry. The chief contenders were Stalin, Trotsky and Zinoviev. Behind their contest lay concrete issues of politics and economics, attitudes to the peasantry, the way to industrialize, the theory and practice of the international Communist movement. On occasion, the differences over these issues were in fact of secondary importance and agreement could have been based on their common denominator. But personal ambition, rivalry and militant irreconcilability, particularly between Stalin and Trotsky, gave the struggle a dramatic quality which meant that any ideas that differed from his own were regarded by Stalin solely as class-hostile, capitulationist, revisionist, traitorous, and so on.

We should also note that Stalin did not settle straight away on a particular concept of how to build the new society. He did not always understand or perhaps share Lenin's ideas, especially those expressed in the last letters and essays. Stalin frequently returned in his mind to the ideas of War Communism, he was compelled for a while to tolerate the NEP and he realized that, without a close, organic union between the working class and the peasants, it would be impossible to deal with all the problems. The choice he made was marked by a gradual slide towards Caesarism, one-man rule, dictatorship, isolating the people from a say in their own fate. Stalin was no theoretician. His arguments were generally based on quotation, reinforced by the impulse of will. He felt mentally in tune with Trotsky's coercive methods, and in effect he was closer to Trotsky in this respect than he was to any other Bolshevik leader. This inner affinity, embellished by personal dislike, paradoxically sustained the mutual repulsion and tension between these two poles of ambition.

Turning over in his mind Zinoviev's and Kamenev's pearls of wisdom, he sneered, 'And these people are writing about Leninism?' *He* would write about Leninism, but he would write so that everyone would sense his totally opposite understanding of it from that of his temporary fellow-travellers. Meanwhile, he had to attack Trotsky. Stalin prepared himself with special care for the speech he would make at the plenum of the Communist trade union fractions on 19 November 1924. Speaking after Kamenev, he called his speech 'Trotskyism or Leninism?'

The entire speech was devoted to an attack on Trotsky, with a passing reference in defence of Kamenev and Zinoviev, characterizing their October episode as 'accidental': 'The disagreement lasted merely a few days and that was only because in Kamenev and Zinoviev we were faced with Leninists, Bolsheviks.' He then posed rhetorical questions to the audience:

Why were Trotsky's recent written speeches on the party necessary? What is the meaning, the point, the aim of these speeches now, when the party does not want to debate, when the party is overloaded with pressing tasks, when the party needs united work to restore the economy, and not a new fight over old questions? Why does Trotsky have to drag the party backwards to new debates?

Following this tirade, Stalin swept the hall with his gaze and harshly answered himself in a deep, level voice:

The 'motivation', judging by all the facts, is that Trotsky is making another (yet another!) attempt to prepare the ground to substitute Trotskyism for Leninism. Trotsky badly needs to dethrone the party and the cadres that went through the uprising, so that, having dethroned the party, he can proceed to dethrone Leninism.[13]

There was a grain of truth in this. While bestowing flattering epithets on both Lenin and Leninism, Trotsky gradually and repeatedly cast doubt on certain Leninist arguments about the building of socialism. According to him, socialism in Russia was an impossibility without the support of other countries; industrialization could be accomplished only at the expense of the peasantry; the NEP was the first step towards capitulation; the plan for cooperatives was premature; October was simply the continuation of the February Revolution; without the training of the population in 'labour armies' they will not understand the 'advantages of socialism', and so on. Bearing in mind that, in forming the 'new opposition' that would 'lay siege' to Stalin, Zinoviev and Kamenev had already met Trotsky half-way, Stalin's speech, first against Trotsky and then against his new allies, could at this stage qualify as a 'defence of Leninism'. There was very little constructive thinking in what he said, especially bearing in mind that Trotsky was not wrong about everything, notably concerning the danger of bureaucracy. Stalin was still fighting with permitted means, though what he was 'defending' was mostly quotations, minus their intellectual motivation. He wound up at the plenum thus: 'They talk about repressions against the opposition and the possibility of a split. That is nonsense, comrades. Our party is tough and mighty. It won't permit any splits. As for repressions, I am decidedly against them.'[14]

For the time being Stalin displayed generosity by not criticizing Zinoviev and Kamenev and by even protecting them from Trotsky. The founders of the 'new opposition', however, did not accept his olive branch. At a Politburo meeting in early 1925, Kamenev, supported by his confrère, declared that Soviet technological and economic backwardness, compared to the encircling capitalist countries, presented an insurmountable obstacle to the building of socialism. In effect, Zinoviev and Kamenev had formed a bloc with Trotsky, whom they had subjected to devastating criticism a few months earlier on precisely this theme. The 'new opposition's' attack on party policy demanded a rebuttal and the formulation of an all-party directive on further steps to be taken in the sphere of socialist construction. In this respect, the Fourteenth Party Conference at the end of April 1925 was of great importance. Stalin neither gave a report nor took part in the debate at this occasion. The key reports were given by Rykov on cooperatives, by Dzerzhinsky on the metallurgical industry, by Tsyurupa on the agricultural tax, by Molotov on party structure, by Solts on revolutionary legality, and by Zinoviev on the tasks of Comintern. Due to either tradition or inertia, the conference was presided over by Kamenev, just as he chaired the Sovnarkom and the Politburo. But this would be the last time. Neither he nor Zinoviev would ever head such a meeting again. Perhaps the most important item dealt with by the conference was the proposition which declared that, despite Zinoviev's thesis, the victory of socialism was possible in the USSR, even in the context of a slowdown in the world revolution. The victory of socialism would only be considered complete, however, when there were international guarantees against the restoration of capitalism.

The debate on socialist legality was an important one. Solts, who opened the discussion and who had shared exile with Stalin in Turukhansk once upon a time, remarked that after the victory of the revolution 'we felt the need to improve our economy more acutely than the need for revolutionary legality'. Now, however, he said pointedly, 'party members ... must understand that our laws in all their manifestations both confirm and reinforce the edifice we want to build and strengthen, and that in breaking our laws we destroy that edifice.'[15]

A few days after the conference, Stalin made a speech to activists of the Moscow party organization. He entitled one part of his speech 'On the Destiny of Socialism in the Soviet Union'. Again he subjected Trotsky to vitriolic criticism, quoting many of his works and mocking yet again his theory of 'permanent revolution'. Speaking with feeling and conviction, he explained the essence of the complete and final victory of socialism in the USSR. The first signs of his special rôle and place in the party emerged here. Casting modesty aside, he felt able to quote himself at length. As he expounded his (as yet) correct propositions, he was gradually preparing the party for the idea that he had a particular right to postulate the truth.

Stalin tested his views not only in speeches to the Central Committee and in the press, but on very rare occasions also in front of workers. His assistant, Tovstukha, wrote down one such speech that he made in the Stalin workshops of the October Railway on 1 March 1927. Stalin, beating time with his hand, slowly expounded:

We are completing the change-over from a peasant country to an industrial one without help from the outside world. How did other countries make this journey?

England created her industry by robbing her colonies for a period of fully two hundred years. There can be no question of our taking the same path.

Germany took five billion [francs] from defeated France. But that way, too, the way of robbery through victorious wars, is not for us. Our cause is a policy of peace.

There is also a third way, that chosen by tsarist Russia. That was through foreign loans and secret deals at the expense of the workers and peasants. We cannot take that path.

We have our own way, and that is to accumulate our own. We will not get by without mistakes, there will be shortcomings. But the edifice we are building is so grand that these mistakes and shortcomings will not be important in the end.[16]

Next day, the newspaper *Rabochaya Moskva* carried a report:

The applause came like machine-gun fire. The man wearing soldier's khaki and worn-down boots, a pipe in his hand, stopped at the curtain. Long live Stalin! Long live the [Central Committee!] Notes are passed to Stalin. Twirling his black moustache, he studies them diligently. The hall falls silent and Stalin, General Secretary of the party and the man after whom the workshops have been named, begins his conversation with the workers.

Such appearances by Stalin were extremely rare. He much preferred to make his speeches at conferences, in the Kremlin or at Central Committee plenums. And his appearances before the public would become rarer still. The more enigmatic and secretive the leader, the more he provides fuel for legends about himself.

Preparations for the Fourteenth Party Congress (as distinct from the Fourteenth Conference) took place against a background of the first successes in economic and cultural construction. In 1925, gross output of agricultural production was 112 per cent of pre-war levels. This was remarkable. The NEP was beginning to bear fruit. Industrial production, which for five years had lain in total ruin, reached three-quarters of its pre-war level. The first new plants had made their appearance, most notably the power stations. And all this when the best foreign economists had predicted that pre-war levels would not be achieved for fifteen to twenty years.

Substantial results had also been accomplished in the battle against illiteracy. A network of schools had been established, notably in the national republics. Major steps had been taken to create a system of higher education and a series of important measures were adopted to speed up cultural and educational work. The All-Russian Academy of Sciences was transformed into its All-Union equivalent. By this time works of world repute had been produced by the historians M. N. Pokrovsky and V. I. Vernadsky, the geneticist N. I. Vavilov, the agrobiologist V. P. Vilyams (Williams), the chemist N. D. Zelinsky, the geologists A. E. Fersman and I. M. Gubkin, the physicist A. F. Ioffe, and many other pioneers of Soviet science.

The Red Army had been successfully placed on a peacetime footing, and military reforms were carried out at the same time. This work was greatly accelerated after Trotsky was released from his post as Commissar for the Army and Navy at a Central Committee plenum in January 1925 and was replaced by M. V. Frunze.

An episode that took place at that plenum is worth recalling. Zinoviev and

Kamenev took an unexpected step. In place of Trotsky as Commissar for the Army and Navy and chairman of the Revvoensoviet, Kamenev proposed Stalin. This move was open to more than one interpretation. It is possible that Zinoviev and Kamenev, sensing Stalin's growing power, decided to move him to another responsible and respected position which would then enable them to remove him as General Secretary at the forthcoming congress by resurrecting Lenin's Letter. Or perhaps they were hoping to kill two birds with one stone, pushing Trotsky out for good and striking a blow against Stalin at the same time. Alas, if Trotsky played the part of one bird, Stalin was not so compliant. The General Secretary openly showed his surprise and even his irritation at Kamenev's proposal, as many Central Committee members present were able to witness. Kamenev's initiative was defeated by a majority of votes. The matter was discussed in Trotsky's absence, since he had reported sick. This plenum was in general important for Stalin, for it weakened Trotsky's position still further, and in effect declined to give support to Zinoviev and Kamenev. In the 'combinations game', the General Secretary was able to do what his opponents could not do, namely, to weaken both Trotsky and the old duo. The influential trio of Stalin, Zinoviev and Kamenev had effectively fallen apart, for the General Secretary had no further use for it.

The Fourteenth Party Congress was approaching. It would become a major landmark in the debate over the means of industrializing the national economy. Yet in December 1925, when it took place, it was hard to believe that what the newspapers were writing about would come to pass. The Dnieper was still quietly rolling along, no dam as yet harnessing its waters; where the Turkmenistan–Siberian railway was planned to run sandstorms were still piling up great dunes; the site of the famous Stalingrad Tractor Works was still an empty plot of land; no one could even dream that in the course of the Five Year Plan the blast furnaces of Magnitka would rise to tower above the hills nor imagine that the pioneers of rocketry were approaching the era of space flight – at the beginning of the 1930s the first Soviet rocket, the GIRD-X (Group for the study of rocket propulsion, 1932–34) would be launched.

Conditions were decidedly improving. The New Economic Policy gave the Bolsheviks historic opportunities. In effect, this was the first model of 'market socialism' that was capable of sustaining the engine of enterprise in new circumstances. The NEP facilitated the rapid rise of agriculture. Industry was approaching its pre-war levels. Perceptive people saw in the State Commission for Electrification not simply a means to electrify the country but a way of raising the socialist economy to the heights of a new political structure. But this was only the beginning and depended on many difficulties being overcome.

Prices were set by the industrial trusts which had begun to operate on commercial principles. Distortions appeared. For instance, for a piece of soap, a length of cotton cloth or a bucket of paraffin, a peasant had to sell three or four more times as much grain as in 1913. Discontent grew and became a cause for concern. Hopes for the development of concessions were not realized, loans from capitalist states did not materialize and export trade did not even reach 50 per cent of the pre-war level. A million and a half unemployed people crowded the labour exchanges. One out of two adult males could not read or write. There was nothing with which to buy machinery and tools. Virtually no new major constructions were under way. Yet the newspapers were reporting that the country was on the eve of enormous changes. It seemed the young state had no choice: in order to survive in a complex and dangerous world, it must speed up.

It was against this background that the Fourteenth Party Congress took place. The dominant figure at the congress was Stalin, chiefly because he gave the political report and this was the main issue on the agenda. Confirming the position taken by the Fourteenth Conference, the congress passed a resolution stating that 'in general the victory of socialism (not in the sense of its final victory) is definitely possible in one country.' The congress declared the shift to industrialization as the key task in restructuring society, while the delegates recognized that this course would demand maximum pressure and sacrifice. The question of tempo was discussed, though no one had a clear notion of what this meant.

Besides dealing with the chief economic issue, the congress also found itself confronted once again with the fight against the 'new opposition', whose main forces were represented by the Leningrad delegation headed by Zinoviev. And it was Zinoviev who produced the opposition's report. His speech to the congress sounded extremely bland, however, his arguments, and those of his supporters, were weak and unconvincing. They warned, with good grounds, of the danger of bureaucratization of the party, which in their view had already begun. Their arguments, however, bore too personal a character to have the desired effect on the delegates. It was here, as we have noted elsewhere, that Kamenev first stated openly that he had 'come to the conclusion that Comrade Stalin cannot fulfil the rôle of unifier of the Bolshevik general staff'. But as he spoke most of the delegates began chanting 'Stalin! Stalin!' in an ovation to the General Secretary. Stalin felt that his 'defence of Leninism', which he never tired of rehearsing, was gaining large support in the party. It was precisely in this monopoly on 'defending Leninism' and interpreting it, combined with the low level of political culture of many party members, that the secret of his popularity lay. Stalin's authority was gradually and almost unnoticed reaching an all-party level. A decisive rôle was also played by the fact that, since Lenin's death, Stalin had spoken in the name of the 'collective leadership', and advocated bringing about those of Lenin's behests which the masses best understood: restoring the national economy, developing the cooperatives, reviving trade, expanding literacy.

Stalin appeared never to sway towards any opposition, but that impression was only created because he proclaimed all his measures, decisions, criticisms and proposals as purely 'Leninist'. In fact he frequently supported different groupings and made a number of false moves, but he was always able to 'correct' his position rapidly. Like no one else, he learned how to project his position as Leninist. To be sure, on many (though far from all) issues the ideas he defended were indeed Leninist, but it was obvious that his notion of Leninism was acquiring an increasingly autocratic character. Many party members often identified the party line or the work of the Central Committee with a particular individual, and in the absence of Lenin and an obvious leader, Stalin, the 'unifier of the Bolshevik headquarters staff', emerged as the one who gave personal expression to the first successes in the economy, the policy of party unity and the revival of the agricultural sector. It was plain enough to the majority of the delegates that Zinoviev, Kamenev and Trotsky were motivated in their attacks on the Central Committee by their desire to take over the leadership. The defeat of the opposition was unqualified.

This phase of party conflict also found its expression in the organizational question. The Central Committee recalled Zinoviev as chairman of the Comintern Executive Committee and, on the initiative of the Soviet delegation, the post was soon abolished altogether. S. M. Kirov replaced Zinoviev as head of the Leningrad party organization. Kamenev was relieved of his post as deputy chairman of the Sovnarkom and chairman of the Council of Labour and Defence. Both Zinoviev and Kamenev retained their positions in the Politburo, while Voroshilov and Molotov joined it for the first time, thus greatly strengthening Stalin's position.

In his closing speech on the political report, lasting more than an hour, Stalin again subjected Zinoviev, Kamenev, Sokolnikov, Lashevich and their supporters to blistering criticism, and concluded by affirming the party line on the building of socialism and strengthening unity in the party's ranks. On the other hand, it could not have escaped the notice of the perceptive that Stalin was constantly quoting his own speeches and articles and doing so without the least reticence, while those with some political insight – and they were pitifully few – could not but be aware of the unceremonious way he was dishing out criticism. He responded insultingly to a speech by Krupskaya, calling it 'utter rubbish'. He would return later to Krupskaya, declaring, not without a dash of rabble-rousing hypocrisy: 'In what way, then, is Comrade Krupskaya different from any other comrade with responsibility? Do you think the interests of some comrades should be placed above those of the party and its unity? For us Bolsheviks, formal democracy is an empty vessel, and the real interests of the party are everything.' He called Lashevich a schemer, said that Sokolnikov liked to make mischief with his speeches, Kamenev was muddle-headed, Zinoviev was a hysteric, and so forth.[17]

It appears that Stalin was already beginning to slide towards the position where even informal democracy was for him an empty vessel. The unforgivable rudeness towards Krupskaya was of course not merely a lack of political tact towards her person and Lenin's memory, but also covert revenge for the remembered letters, phone calls and conversations in which she had been involved during Lenin's lifetime. Stalin never forgave anyone for anything.

Evidently aware that he might have overstepped the mark in some parts of his closing speech, Stalin resorted to a device he would use again on other occasions. He justified the roughness in his criticism of Zinoviev's article, 'The Philosophy of an Epoch', by saying that it was aimed only at what was hostile and alien, and was due solely to the straightforward nature of his character. He gradually turned this repellent side of his nature into a party virtue, if not a revolutionary quality. But already as early as this, the Fourteenth Congress in 1925, there was lamentably no Communist, whether delegate or member of the Central Committee, who was capable, calmly and with dignity, of assessing Stalin's personality and his slide towards the sort of abusive criticism that would in time come to sound like a judgement.

Stalin did not of course omit Trotsky from his critical survey of the oppositionists. Sensing the mood of the majority, and sweeping aside Kamenev's proposal that the Secretariat be turned simply into a technical organization, he emphasized that he was against 'expelling' certain members of the leadership from the Central Committee. He calculated, given the atmosphere, that it was prudent once again to declare that, if the comrades insisted, he 'was ready to leave his place without a fuss'. 'Expulsion means bloodletting,' he declared to applause, 'and that is a dangerous and infectious way to proceed. Today one person is expelled, tomorrow another, the next day someone else – who will be left in the party?' He spoke like a practised politician, again and again finding support among the delegates, demonstrating his disinterest and his concern for the party's future. As he mocked and criticized the opposition, he displayed his 'magnanimity' by the use of such phrases as 'Well, good luck to them!' Although he had already decided it was time to part company with Zinoviev and Kamenev, he nevertheless demonstrated that he wanted peace: 'We are for unity, we are against expulsions. The policy of expulsion is repellent to us. The party wants unity and it will achieve it, with Kamenev and Zinoviev, if that is what they want, and without them, if they do not.'[18]

It is worth noting that in his closing speech Stalin uttered a number of propositions which, had they been implemented, would have averted the worst time in the party's history. For instance, to the applause and obvious approval of the delegates, he announced:

The plenum decides everything, and it brings its leaders to order when they begin to lose their balance. If one of us oversteps the mark, it will bring us back into line, and that is both essential and needed. The party must not be led from outside the collective. It is silly to think of it, after Ilyich, silly to talk about it.

Collective work, collective leadership, unity in the party, unity in the Central Committee's organs and subordination of the minority to the majority – that's what we need now.[19]

Unfortunately, these laudable propositions were not underpinned by any regulations governing the rotation of the leadership, or the duration of the general secretaryship and other senior posts, and so on. It was precisely about such matters that Lenin had written his theses on improving the apparatus. The Fourteenth Congress was the last one under Stalin at which criticism and self-criticism were integral to the atmosphere of the meeting. Criticism declined steadily thereafter from congress to congress. Only Stalin, or those acting on his orders, would criticize henceforth, with the result that intellectual stagnation, dogmatism and bureaucratic formalism became the norm.

In opting for socialist construction and industrialization, the congress became an important landmark in the country's history, but democratic principles were not similarly laid down for further development. Unseen alongside the great idea, its very negation was born. The struggle between these two principles harboured the origins of the coming triumph of the 'Leader' and the tragedy of the people. Not everyone realized that they would be made to pay for economic strength with their personal freedom. This was no paradox, it was the law of autocracy.

CHAPTER 13

Leninism for the Masses

Finding himself in charge of the core of the Central Committee, Stalin quickly realized that, apart from possessing organizational skills and the 'firm hand' which had become familiar to many in the apparatus, he must also show himself to be a theorist. On the one hand, shifting to a new stage in the struggle to create a new society required theoretical understanding of a wide range of questions. Everything was new, whether in the economic, social or cultural sphere. While the outlines of the concept of socialist construction made it possible to envisage the broad direction in which life must change, Lenin's arguments nevertheless required concrete application to immediate practice.

On the other hand, Stalin knew that the leader of the party, which he very much wanted to be, must have a sound reputation as a Marxist theorist. He knew that his articles would not make a mark on public opinion. Most of them had been written for specific, current purposes and they were just so many boring pieces in the welter of slogans, ideas and appeals that were thrown up by the revolution. To be sure, by the time he was consolidating himself in the top leadership after Lenin's death he had published some theoretical works, for instance, 'Anarchism or Bolshevism?'. One can judge its philosophical level by quoting just one fragment:

The bourgeoisie are gradually losing the ground under their feet and are retreating day by day. However strong and numerous they may be today, in the end they will be defeated. Why? Because they are disintegrating as a class, growing weak and old and becoming a deadweight. This has given rise to the well known dialectical position: everything that exists, that is, everything that grows from day to day, is rational, and everything that disintegrates from day to day is irrational and therefore cannot avoid defeat.[20]

The primitiveness and naivety of these deductions are depressingly obvious, not that this prevented Academician Mitin from describing them as 'a classic feature of the new'.

Other articles by Stalin, such as 'Marxism and the National Question' (1913), 'The October Revolution and the National Question' (1918), 'On the Strategy and Tactics of the Russian Communists' (1923), were similarly relatively unknown. He soon sensed that he had nothing of significance to contribute to Marxist theory, that Lenin, having lifted the curtain on the future, had left his mark in every sphere in which Stalin became involved, and that intellectually he, Stalin, could not hold a candle to the departed leader.

The fierce internecine strife which continued to rock the party effectively compelled Stalin to resort to propagating Lenin's heritage, his ideas and arguments on the broadest front. He was up to the task; his categorical way of thinking could not have been more useful. Telegraphically short sentences, no sophisticated terms and no depth, but clarity, clarity and yet more clarity. His published lectures were popular. Agitators used them in the campaign to abolish the population's political ignorance. In due course, Stalin's *Questions of Leninism* and *The Foundations of Leninism* were canonized and turned into dogmatic phrasebooks by zealous Stalinist propagandists, a purpose for which they were ideally suited. Without the quotations, indeed, these works might consist of little more than punctuation marks. They were published in one edition after another.

The outlook of millions of Soviet people was conditioned by many of the propositions in these works, Leninist ideas which the General Secretary reshaped as he interpreted them. Thus, in defining the essence of the dictatorship of the proletariat, he concentrated almost solely on its coercive aspect and 'cleansed' it of any democratic content. It is impossible today, for instance, to read his 'On the Policy of Liquidating the Kulaks as a Class' without shuddering at the thought of what lay behind it.

Stalin's intellect – a subject to which we shall return – was formed under the influence of dogmatic religious training, the experience of revolutionary struggle and a selective acquaintanceship with the works of the founders of Marxist socialism. It is clear that he did not have a complete understanding of the relationship between theory and practice, objective and subjective factors and the essence of the laws of social development. His assertion that everything in nature and society is programmed by iron inevitability smacks of fatalism: 'The socialist system will follow the capitalist as day follows night.' For him, Marxist theory was like a compass on a ship that is going to reach the other shore in any case, but with the compass it will do so more quickly.

The entire history of the party, as laid out in Stalin's *Short Course*, is nothing more than a chain of victories for some and defeats for others, for spies, double-dealers, enemies, criminals. He laid everything on the schematic Procrustean bed in which everything must be in reality as it is in theory, the theory he happened to be expounding. In Stalin's logic, everything that had happened was to be expected: the growth of the Communist parties, the rout of the 'right deviation', the 'treachery' of the social democrats. Creativity, free will, the play of imagination, intellectual audacity – none of this is to be found there.

Stalin's mind was a prisoner of the schematic approach. Thus, for instance, there were three basic features of the dialectic, four stages of development of the opposition bloc, three basic features of materialism, three characteristics of the Red Army, three fundamental roots of opportunism and so on. Perhaps this was not a bad way to teach, but to catalogue an entire theory in this way and to reduce it to a few features, peculiarities, stages and periods, is to impoverish social studies and foster a dogmatic outlook.

Ritual elements began to appear in Stalin's work at a certain stage. It is difficult to find nuances in his thinking, or transitions, reservations, original ideas or paradoxes. His thinking is uniform, everything that issued from his pen was presented as the development of Marxism–Leninism. His every utterance was a programme, whatever was not in accordance with his directives was suspect, if not hostile. By vulgarizing, simplifying and giving everything a straightforward, categorical quality, Stalin's views acquired a primitive, orthodox character. He probably never doubted that whatever he said was inspired by genius, as his fondness for self-quotation suggests. Despite all this, however, there was one inherent, strong feature in his thinking – one, moreover, which he had in common with Lenin – and that was its practical side. He tried to link every theoretical proposition to concrete needs, not something that could be said of all Marxist theorists. On the other hand, the mechanical, automatic nature of this thinking, bordering as it did on fatalism, often imparted a quality of caricature to his writings.

The debate in the 1920s over how to proceed to the building of the socialist society was accompanied by renewed theoretical activity by the party leaders. *Pravda* and *Bolshevik* regularly carried articles by Trotsky, Zinoviev, Kamenev, Stalin, Kalinin, Yaroslavsky and others. Some were particularly active in this respect. Trotsky, for instance, in the ten years after the revolution, succeeded in publishing twenty-one volumes of his writings. On 4 December 1924 *Pravda* announced that the Leningrad branch of the State Publishing House was about to begin publication of Zinoviev's works in twenty-two volumes. The responsible committee claimed them to be something of a 'workers' encyclopedia'. *Pravda* also announced the publication of a miscellany entitled *October*, consisting of selected articles by Lenin, Bukharin and Stalin. Many works by Bukharin were appearing at the time, such as 'The Contradictions of Contemporary Capitalism', 'On the New Economic Policy and Our Tasks'.

Stalin did his best to keep up, but the greater part of his writings in the 1920s was devoted not so much to popularizing Leninism as to polemicizing with the leaders of the various groupings, oppositions and factions. It was perhaps in the course of his energetic, loud mud-slinging that he became a 'theorist'. Trotsky thought so. In his book *The Stalinist School of Falsification* he remarked that Stalin became a theorist in the fight against Trotskyism. Stalin's mind was sharpened by all the clashes and 'unmaskings'. His speeches at congresses and conferences, at plenary sessions and meetings of the Politburo, were harsh and resolute and mostly implacable, though he did allow himself an occasional expression of liberal 'weakness' when it was tactically prudent to do so. For instance, on 11 October 1926 he reported to the Politburo on 'Measures to Mitigate the Inner Party Struggle', though it is also true that these 'mitigating measures' were formulated as five points which the opposition leaders would have to accept, if they wished to remain members of the Central Committee.

The polemics with his ideological opponents wrought a transformation in Stalin. He learned to use rhetoric and added a personal and offensive dimension to his customary trenchancy, calling people such names as 'chatterer', 'slanderer', 'muddlehead', 'ignoramus', 'empty vessel', 'yes-man'. He revelled in the reputation he had gained as a coarse but implacable fighter for party unity, against factionalism and for the purity of Leninism. In his closing speech to the Fourteenth Congress, where, as we have noted, he attacked Kamenev, Zinoviev and Sokolnikov, he practically appropriated the right, as General Secretary, to be as rude as he liked. To the approving laughter of the delegates, he declared: 'Yes, comrades, I am straightforward and rude, that's true, I can't deny it.'[21]

This outspoken rudeness, as we have seen, was frequently of an insulting kind. Replying, for instance, to the jurist S. Pokrovsky, who had attempted to elucidate Stalin's attitude to the proletarian revolution, the General Secretary opened his letter by calling Pokrovsky 'an impudent narcissist', and ending on the same note: 'You haven't understood a damn thing, not one damn thing about the bourgeois revolution regenerating into the proletarian revolution. The conclusion to be drawn is that one has to have the impudence of an ignoramus and the complacency of a mediocre tightrope walker to be able to turn things on their heads so casually.'[22] He made his judgements with complete assurance: here lies the truth, there delusion. As Rabindranath Tagore put it: 'We slam the door on our mistakes. Truth is confused: how shall she enter now?'

As his authority and political importance grew, so Stalin relied more and more on his own utterances to support his arguments, and they were now presented as truths issuing from the highest level. Yet the more this happened the less Stalin himself was aware of it. Thus, having given a lecture at Sverdlovsk University on the definition of Leninism, he repeated this definition virtually as a perfect and universal truth in his work *Questions of Leninism.* Citing his own utterances, he would add such phrases as, 'All this is correct, that is, it stems entirely from Leninism.' In time it became the rule that he would refer his readers to his own articles and books. In a polemic in 1926 on the possibility of building socialism in the USSR, an idea which he presented as his own, he wrote: 'You should get hold of [Moscow] *Bolshevik* No. 3 and read my article. It would make things easier for you.' He also took the opportunity here to harp on one theme: 'the working class in union with the toiling peasants can finish off the capitalists in our country'; 'the opposition says we are not able to finish off our capitalists and build the socialist society'; 'if we hadn't thought we could finish off our capitalists, we would have seized power for nothing'.[23] The accent on 'finishing off' the remnants of the exploiting classes sounded very obvious in 1926, although it was not then the main task at hand. In time it would mature into a deeply erroneous theory about the class struggle becoming sharper, the closer society moved towards socialism. 'Beating' and 'finishing off' would soon become Stalin's main occupation.

Despite the mediocre, primitive level of the theoretical generalizations that issued from Stalin's pen, he was very fond of giving definitions and formulating interpretations. These included, for instance, the essence of Leninism, of nations, of political strategy and tactics, of deviations, to name a few. Possibly this activity contributed something to the popularization of Leninism, but, inclined as he was to thinking dogmatically, Stalin literally canonized his definitions and was capable of devoting an entire speech to proving that one or another oppositionist had failed to understand a particular question.

Perhaps the most negative aspect of Stalin's theoretical contributions lay in the fact that he threw out the humanistic essence of socialism and gradually replaced it with what one might call 'sacrificial socialism'. With such an outlook, he would in time permit himself to carry out unheard-of mass repressions with a light heart, and to apply force on a broad basis as the main lever in economic life. Stalinism was a blend of bureaucratic and barracks socialism, couched in dogmatic terminology. Today we know that we cannot call a society 'socialist' merely because it practices a high degree of public ownership, or holds the values of the collective as higher than those of the individual, or plans everything from above. Genuine socialism occurs when the centre of attention is man, and where democracy, humanism and social fairness are intrinsic properties. Such an approach has no room for violence, for distancing the people from power, for demigod leaders.

It should be noted that Stalin worked on his articles and speeches himself. Various assistants who were employed in his secretariat at different times have testified that, despite the great load of work he carried, Stalin nevertheless did an enormous amount of reading for himself. A large selection of books, extracts of articles, digests of the local party press, reviews of foreign publications and the most interesting letters were brought to him on a daily basis.

Between 1924 and 1928 Stalin consulted professors from the Industrial and Communist Academies on questions of social science. He felt particularly wanting in philosophy; in history he was on firmer ground and he showed no special desire to expand his knowledge of economics. Through prolonged experience on the job, where he was expected to deal with the most wide-ranging problems, he had developed quite a subtle feel and an extremely practical mind, he was capable of assessing situations rapidly and finding his way through the labyrinth of issues and identifying the key links. Being observant by nature, with an excellent memory for faces, names and facts, the rich experience of mixing with a wide range of the most highly educated people in Lenin's entourage could not but have had an effect and imparted some qualities to him. Though he was no theorist, he was superior to many of his colleagues in his pragmatic approach to theory and in his ability to marry theory and practice to the maximum effect.

Having once set himself a goal, he was capable of the most amazing persistence in sticking to it. This was evident in his written work. He naturally made some amendments in his articles and pamphlets, but basically he went on repeating what he had said before, producing a sort of textbook effect. Having once said that 'Leninism is the theory and tactics of the proletarian revolution in general and the theory and tactics of the dictatorship of the proletariat in particular,' he turned this definition into a dogma. Undoubtedly, at a time when the régime was fighting to survive, it served its purpose by making Lenin's ideals and aims easier to understand. But reducing Lenin's ideas to no more than the dictatorship of the proletariat was the prelude to many defects in the subsequent practice of Soviet statecraft.

It was probably Remarque who said that dictators always begin by simplifying. Stalin was a master of simplification and he was responsible for implanting primitive schema in both theory and the history of the party. Perhaps, given the low level of general and political culture among the workers, this was necessary, but already by the beginning of the 1930s more serious and deeper studies simply could no longer be published. For decades, social science theory sank into stagnation. Dogmatism grew from the soil of simplistic and frequently wrong concepts. Dogmatism is like a ship that has run aground: the waves run, the ship stays put, but the impression of movement persists. Stalin's attitude to ideology was profoundly pragmatic: current ideology must function within the country like cement, not like an explosive. Many of his theoretical arguments became in due course the source of great social misfortunes. Inhabiting a mental environment of unrelieved grey, Stalin's ideas lacked dynamism and shut out creative innovation in politics.

The Central Committee plenum of 14–15 January 1924 affords an example of this effect. The meeting dealt with many issues. Zinoviev reported on the international situation and both he and those who spoke after him were critical of the failure in Germany where, in their view, a revolutionary opportunity had been missed. In his speech, Stalin dwelt on the rôle Radek had played in the events. 'I am against punishing Radek for his mistakes in the German question,' he said. 'He committed a number of them, of which I will single out seven items.' It was one of Stalin's favourite devices to string out an opponent's mistakes on a long tow-rope. According to Radek, Stalin went on, 'The chief enemy in Germany is fascism and he suggests that it is necessary to form a coalition with the social democrats, whereas our conclusion is that what is needed is a battle to the death with the social democrats.'[24] Stalin's political myopia would cost the Communists dear, as well as all future democratic forces. His failure of imagination showed an inability to analyse complex ideas.

Another example of his lack of theoretical vision occurred during the October 1924 plenum of the Central Committee, which debated the question of 'work in the countryside'. Molotov gave the report. Zinoviev, who was just as ignorant of agrarian matters as Stalin and Molotov, made a long speech in which he nonetheless gave a fair account of the general situation:

What we are discussing here is not just the question of work in the countryside, but our attitude to the peasants in general, that is to say, a much more general question that will no doubt be on the agenda for several years to come, since it impinges on the problem of carrying out the dictatorship in present circumstances.[25]

Stalin in his speech listed a number of political and theoretical recommendations in which one can detect the embryos of the great mistakes of the future. The first thing we have to do, he said, 'is to conquer the peasants again'. Secondly, we have to see that 'the field of battle has changed'. Thirdly, 'we have to form cadres in the villages'.[26] The year was 1924, but Stalin was speaking as if it was already 1929.

CHAPTER 14

Intellectual Disarray

The philosopher Evgeny Trubetskoy, a disciple of Vladimir Solovyov, developed the idea in his work, *The Two Beasts*, that Russia was threatened by two extremes, the 'black beast of reaction and the red beast of revolution'. For many cultural figures these 'beasts' were no mere figments of imagination. Artistic and intellectual fluctuations swung wildly, from outright non-acceptance of the very idea of revolution to its ecstatic glorification. Many others, however, did not define their positions at once.

Kipling has some beautiful lines which suggest that the power of the long night breaks when an hour still remains before the dawn. The force of the old order had been broken in Russia, but it was unreasonable to expect all the artists to rise and greet the approaching dawn. The big boulevards and side streets of literature were in ferment. The main questions nagging the intelligentsia were the place of culture in the 'new temple', the problem of artistic freedom, attitudes to the values of the past. Some writers genuinely believed that the only future Russian literature had was its past. Many writers feared that the revolutionary storm threatened not only themselves, but Russian culture as such.

Most of the intelligentsia did not accept the socialist revolution, although equally not all of them became its enemies. Many would probably have been happy to stop at the February Revolution, with some sort of parliament and other features of pluralistic liberalism. Their dismay and intellectual confusion continued for some years, after which two diametrically opposed tendencies emerged: either full acceptance of the ideas of the October Revolution or their complete rejection, with prolonged hesitation and gradual changes of mind along the way. The slim anthology *Smena vekh* ('Changing Landmarks'), published in Prague in June 1921, was a good example of this process. Most of its contributors were of the Constitutional Democratic tendency or had been active in the White camp, and they now called for 'capitulation'.

Klyuchnikov, Potekhin, Bobrishchev-Pushkin and Ustryalov declared that, by an irony of history, the Bolsheviks had become 'the curators of the Russian national cause'. As a matter of fact, Stalin frequently referred in his 1920s' speeches to the Changing Landmarks movement as a sign that the enemy camp was disintegrating. The writers in *Smena Vekh* made it plain that they regarded Bolshevism as utopian, but they recognized that as Russian refugees 'history would give them short shrift.' Their nostalgic thoughts, painted in Slavophile colours, signalled something more important, however, namely that a part of the intelligentsia had become supporters of socialist Russia. Class instincts were stifled by the nebulous attachment they felt for the motherland and they became reconciled, however painfully, to the new realities inside Russia.

Most intellectuals, as we have noted, however, did not accept Bolshevism. One of the most extreme in her rejection of the revolution was the poet Zinaida Gippius. In her *Seraya Knizhka* ('Grey Book') and *Chernyi bloknot* ('Black Notebook'), she roundly condemned the ideas of the revolution which had, in her view, buried the culture of Russia:

> All is in vain: the soul is blinded,
> We are destined for the worms and maggots,
> And not even the ashes remain
> In the land of Russian justice.

Describing the political position taken up by her husband, Dmitri Merezh-kovsky, and herself, she said proudly: 'All right, maybe we are only protecting the whiteness of the émigrés' raiment.' In the Motherland they had seen 'the kingdom of the Antichrist'.

Even Trotsky, who was otherwise quite tolerant towards all this casting about and who thought the intelligentsia's confusion was inevitable, quipped angrily about Gippius's 'whining'. He wrote that her art, which combined mystical and erotic Christianity, had become transformed the instant 'a Red Army man in his hobnailed boots stepped on her dainty toes. Straight away she started up her howling, in which one could hear the voice of a witch obsessed by the idea of the sanctity of property.'[27]

Stalin's range of aesthetic interests was immeasurably narrower than Trotsky's, and he was not particularly excited either by the decadents or the iconoclasts. He can have had little notion of the works of Gippius, Balmont, Belyi, Lossky, Osorgin, Shmelyov and many other intellectuals who left their mark on Russian cultural history. Empirical and devoid of emotional range, Stalin viewed the entire edifice of culture in strictly pragmatic terms: Does it help or doesn't it? Is it in the way? Is it harmful? Aesthetic criteria, if he had any, played no decisive part in his thinking. He would express his credo about literature and art two decades later in his dismally well known verdict on the journals *Zvezda* and *Leningrad*. For him, the arts remained encapsulated in a primitive binary model: 'ours' and 'theirs'.

Although the number of émigrés was extremely high, exceeding perhaps two and a half million people, and consisting in the main of all kinds of intellectuals, it is far from the case that they were all hostile towards the Soviet Union. Moreover, they had different destinies. Quite a few ended up in the slums of Shanghai or the doss-houses of Paris. Others returned home to Russia and of these some even managed to revive their literary careers, while others found that they could not adapt to the new social environment and either fell silent forever, or fell into the Stalinist meat-grinder.

Those who remained in Soviet Russia also reacted variously. Associations quickly arose, among them the Union of Peasant Writers, the Serapion Brothers, Pereval ('The Crossing'), the All-Russian Association of Proletarian Writers, the Association of Artists of Revolutionary Russia, Kuznitsa ('The Smithy'), the Left Front of Art. In chilly clubs and unheated palaces, debates went on about proletarian culture, literature and politics, and whether to employ the values of bourgeois culture. A unique opportunity had arisen to create and consolidate artistic pluralism. The command methods which would signal the withering of the arts were not yet dominant.

At first, Stalin saw nothing dangerous in the new mosaic of literary schools and tendencies, especially as most of the writers were themselves talking about the revolution, the new world, the new man. Even avant-garde, sectarian concerns with radical methods seemed little more than naive and amusing. Like art itself, the pluralism of those early years was spontaneous, and in only a brief period it gave to the cinema, music, literature, painting and sculpture works which have entered the treasure-house of Russia's cultural heritage.

Many writers and artists matured rapidly in the hothouse atmosphere of the revolution, and the debates, quarrels and competition between the various schools were a natural outcome. It was a great pity, to put it mildly, that in only a few years this atmosphere of quest would evaporate in the crucible of bureaucratic style and uniform thought, and that in the ensuing climate a plethora of books of utterly ephemeral interest would emerge. In two issues of the journal *Bolshevik*, P. Ionov wrote an article on proletarian culture in which he claimed that 'pure art', beyond the influence of social storms, economic shocks or class conflict, was an impossibility. Replying, Leopold Averbakh asked: 'Who is going to reform whom?'[28]

A leading article in *Bolshevik*, entitled 'Commanding Cadres and the Cultural Revolution', gave the terse reply that cultural matters should be governed by administrative means, that is by the cadres, or 'builders of socialism'.[29] But as soon as they acquired some education, they started demolishing churches, while autonomous creative associations began to disappear and individuality fell silent. This had been the sad fate, for instance, of the entire group of 'peasant poets' whose brightest spark had been Sergei Yesenin, and it was Bukharin, still the radical, who had a hand in it. Freedom of creativity was becoming increasingly programmed, and hence narrower. And art, devoid of human spirit, was already becoming a surrogate for culture.

Stalin observed the ferment in the literary world closely. He sensed that the cultural revolution, which had evoked enormous changes in social awareness, would inevitably evoke also a heightened interest in cultural values in general, and in creative literature in particular. By the middle of the 1920s, literacy had increased markedly. Improvement in the national republics was especially striking. Compared to 1922, in 1925 the number of literate workers in Georgia grew fifteen times, in Kazakhstan five times, in Kirghizia four times, and the pattern was similar in other regions. The main sources of literacy and culture were the workers' clubs in the cities and the reading huts in the villages. The printing of periodicals was three times what it had been in 1913. The building of libraries began on a massive scale. Film studios were built in Odessa, Yerevan, Tashkent and Baku. More creative literature was being published.

The Politburo repeatedly discussed ways of creating the best conditions for bringing culture to the masses and of strengthening Bolshevik influence on it. In June 1925 the Politburo approved a resolution 'On Party Policy in the Field of Creative Literature', calling for a caring attitude towards the old masters. It also adopted a resolution, proposed by Stalin, which emphasized the need to maintain the pressure in the Changing Landmarks movement. The resolution furthermore pointed out that 'the party must take all measures to root out unauthorized and incompetent interference by the administration in literary matters.'[30]

Stalin's minions kept him informed on the new books and articles being written by proletarian writers. He could not of course read everything himself, but after his library was reorganized many of the cheaply bound books of the period remained in his collection, marked by him in red, blue or ordinary pencil. Most of his comments, as it happens, were in red. Judging by these notes, Stalin seems to have been familiar with Furman's *Chapaev* and *The Rebellion, The Iron Current* by Serafimovich, Vsevolod Ivanov's stories, Gladkov's *Cement*, the works of Gorky, which he loved, and the poetry of Bezymensky, Bedny and Yesenin, among others. He evidently also took note of Platonov's *In Store*, but was apparently irritated by this talented writer, as he once confessed to Fadeyev. Stalin was largely ignorant of the Western classics, being generally suspicious about the West and its 'disintegrating' democracy.

He loved the theatre and the cinema the way the great landowners had loved their serf theatres. He was a frequent visitor at the Bolshoi Theatre in the 1930s and 1940s, and he would regularly watch new films at night in the Kremlin or at his dacha. They provided, as it were, a window on life for him in his seclusion. He did not hide the fact that he had no eye for painting, which was his least favourite art form. He frequently discussed art with such writers as Gorky, Bedny, Fadeyev and of course Lunacharsky, as well as with other members of the Politburo who knew as little about it as he did.

In a number of his public utterances Stalin took the opportunity to voice his views on writers and their work, usually in categorical terms that would brook no reply. For instance, in a letter to Bill-Belotserkovsky, he roundly condemned the director of the Bolshoi, D. Golovanov, for his attack on the practice of mechanically updating the repertoire at the expense of the classics. Stalin described the situation as 'golovanshchina' (i. e. dictatorship by Golovanov) and as 'the expression of an anti-Soviet state of affairs'.[31] Such a judgement in the 1930s would have cost someone his head. In the same letter Stalin commented that Bulgakov's plays were staged so frequently 'because there aren't any of *our own* plays that are good enough to put on. In the land of the blind, the one-eyed man is king.' This was vintage Stalin, entertaining no doubts about his own judgement, confident, and contemptuous of the artist's intellectual processes.

He could also be harsh towards those he normally treated with respect, such as Demyan Bedny, a Bolshevik since 1912 who quickly achieved recognition as a proletarian poet after the revolution. The topicality of his fables, ditties, songs, serials in rhyme, tales and parables brought him enduring popularity among the masses. But then in a number of pieces ('Tearing Apart', 'Get off the Stove', 'Without Pity'), he criticized the inertia and other negative traditions that Soviet society was dragging with it from the past. The propaganda department of the Central Committee regarded this view as anti-patriotic; Bedny was summoned to the Central Committee for a 'chat' and complained about it in a letter to Stalin. The General Secretary's reply came swiftly: 'All of a sudden you're snorting and complaining about millstones ... Maybe you think the Central Committee has no right to criticize you? Maybe its decisions aren't meant to apply to you? Don't you think you've caught the unpleasant disease known as "conceit"?' Stalin concluded that Bedny's criticism amounted to slander of the Russian worker, the Soviet people and the USSR. 'This is the point, not the empty lamentations of a scared intellectual who is jabbering about them wanting to isolate Demyan and that they're not going to print Demyan any more.'[32]

Only a few years earlier, in June 1925, Stalin himself had compiled the Central Committee regulations on the party's policy on literature which condemned any 'hint of literary commands' and 'pretentious, semi-literate, self-satisfied Communist arrogance'. By the end of the decade he had forgotten these wise guidelines. The 'commanding cadres' were operating in the field of culture with increasing energy, and the intellectual ferment and confusion gradually faded away at all levels of the administration.

It had been only three or four years earlier that Stalin had requested that his gratitude be conveyed to Bedny for his 'true, party' verses on Trotsky which were published in *Pravda* on 7 October 1926 under the title 'Everything Comes to an End', and which included the lines:

> Our party has served long enough
> as the target for spent politicians!
> It's time at last
> to put an end to this outrage!

Stalin liked the poem and rang Molotov among others to say so. They all approved Bedny's political satire, and Stalin remarked: 'Fewer people will read what we say about Trotsky than will read these verses,' which was no doubt true. And yet the poet had only to change his tone very slightly and reveal his 'grudge', and Stalin became cold, angry, authoritarian and censorious.

Knowing that the fate of their work depended on Stalin's judgement, writers often wrote asking him for an opinion. His summaries were usually condescending and invariably pointed out their 'weaknesses', though occasionally he found it in himself to give praise. For instance, he wrote to A. Bezymensky: 'I've read both "The Shot" and "A day in our Life". There is nothing "petty bourgeois" or "anti-party" in them. They can both be regarded as models of revolutionary, proletarian art for our time.'[33]

Informed witnesses testify that Stalin closely studied the political personalities of leading writers, poets, scientists and cultural figures. He knew that not all of them accepted the revolution, witness the large-scale emigration that had taken place. He noted a letter to Lunacharsky (Commissar for Education and Culture) from the Russian writer, Vladimir Korolenko, posthumously published in Paris where he had died in 1921. In it, Korolenko expressed his concern that the use of coercion in post-revolutionary Russia would slow down the growth of socialist awareness.[34] Stalin decided the letter was a forgery. He was also disturbed by Zamyatin's article entitled 'I Am Afraid', published in the small Leningrad journal *Dom Iskusstv* ('House of the Arts'). Zamyatin was allowed to leave for France in 1932, never to return, and wrote to Stalin that he could no longer go on writing 'behind bars'. In 1920, he had written, intemperately but accurately:

True literature only exists when it is created by madmen, hermits, heretics, dreamers, rebels and skeptics, and not by reliable clerks just doing their jobs. I am afraid we won't have any genuine literature until the Russian people are no longer looked upon as children whose innocence must be protected. I am afraid we won't have any genuine literature until we have been cured of this new kind of Catholicism which is just as afraid of heresy as the old one was.[35]

The outlook of a number of writers was encapsulated in a book by the Marxist philosopher, and Lenin's one-time rival for leadership of the Bolsheviks, Alexander Bogdanov, in which he asserted that genuinely creative work is only possible when there is no compulsion, and when the social system does not generate faith in fetishes, myths and clichés.[36] Bogdanov was plainly attacking the concept of dictatorship over creative literature. It was too much for Stalin who sensed that people like Bogdanov knew that the endless repetition of the revolutionary myth eventually becomes almost indistinguishable from Biblical precepts. Indeed, many of the myths expounded by Stalin in his *Short Course* would come to be taken on trust without any critical or rational consideration. He would have to 'lay siege' to these 'perspicacious' intellectuals.

Stalin began to think about ways of channelling artistic ideas towards raising the level of the masses, as well as towards resolving the vast array of problems facing the country. But he thought in terms of administrative measures: regulations, expelling those who could not serve the cause, introducing censorship. In fact, he was in agreement with Trotsky on this, although he did not intend to make their common understanding public. In *Literature and Revolution*, Trotsky had stated categorically that there had to be 'harsh censorship' in the land of the victorious proletariat.[37] It was advice Stalin would heed. He would help the artists make the right choice! But how? He would have to think about it. Political censorship would be a major element. He found it hard to comprehend that here too an important part would be played by intellectual conscience, an invariable attribute of democracy.

During Lenin's illness, the GPU, with Stalin's support, had taken an unusual step: one hundred and sixty people – writers, scientists, philosophers, poets, historians – representing the flower of Russian culture, were expelled from the country. On 31 August 1922, *Pravda* carried an article significantly entitled 'The First Warning', in which reasons were given for mounting this intensified struggle against counter-revolutionary elements in the field of culture. The genesis and consolidation of the principle of socialist realism was accompanied by a lack of understanding and spiritual confusion on the part of many cultural workers. Instead of helping artists to understand their place in the revolutionary reconstruction of their country, workers on the 'ideological front' emphasized only the pragmatic aspects of the principle and made it into a directive. The expulsion was undoubtedly meant to serve as a signal. Coercive methods would be applied in the cultural sector.

Stalin's assistants sometimes reported on what Russian émigrés were writing. When he was shown P. Krasnov's multi-volume novel, *From the Double-Headed Eagle to the Red Flag*, which the former White general had published in Paris in 1922, Stalin would not even touch the book, remarking, 'When did the swine manage to write it?' With Stalin's support, however, a number of writers and poets, including A. Kuprin and Alexei Tolstoy, returned to the Soviet Union. When he was informed in 1933 that Ivan Bunin had become the first Russian to receive the Nobel Prize, he commented, 'Well, now he'll never want to come back. What did he say in his speech?' Having read a brief extract from Bunin's speech in Stockholm, where the writer had said that 'the main thing for a writer is to have freedom of thought and freedom of conscience', Stalin said nothing, but became pensive. He couldn't understand: hadn't Bunin been given the chance in the USSR to think and reason in accordance with his intellectual conscience? Surely he, Stalin, was not opposed to freedom of thought if it served the dictatorship of the proletariat? True, he could not recall what Bunin had written, but he had a vague, and not entirely inaccurate notion that 'this gentry writer had prophesied something to do with the mystery of death and the kingdom of God.' He thought no more about Bunin. When some time later he was given a pile of Western journals, one of which – *Sovremennye Zapiski* ('Contemporary Notes') – contained Bunin's story

'The Red General', dedicated to the Russian revolution, Stalin had no time for it.

There was another émigré about whom he was informed, and that was Vladislav Khodasevich, who wrote of 'the drying-up of the creative spring in exile'. But the dead end in which such writers found themselves did not interest him. And he knew his own Soviet poets little better. He heard that the 'kulak poets' N. Klyuev, S. Klychkov and P. Vasiliev had taken the path of hooliganism and counter-revolution, but either Averbakh or someone from the Central Committee's agitprop department had put them in their place. He was in fact altogether uninterested in poetry, despite having written three dozen or so naive verses as a youth. He had never had time to acquire the music and rhythm of poetry, and less opportunity to read any, apart from having once used some of Pushkin's verses, in Tsaritsyn, as the basis for a code to inform Moscow of the number of bread convoys that were on their way.

Stalin was far more concerned with writers in Moscow and Leningrad and elsewhere in the country, than with the exiles. He had conflicting views on, for example, Pilnyak's *Naked Year*, Babel's *Red Cavalry* and the works of Platonov, Kin, Vesely, Tynyanov and Khlebnikov, whereas he took at once to the works of Furmanov, Fedin, Alexei Tolstoy and Leonov. He liked some of the films of Vertov, Kuleshov, Eisenstein, Pudovkin and Emler. He heard that the plays *Oliver Cromwell* by Lunacharsky, *Spring Love* by Trenev, Vsevolod Ivanov's *Armoured Train 14–69*, and Seifullina's *Virineya* were being well received. His wife, Nadezhda, went to see them with colleagues from the Commissariat of Nationalities. It was comforting to know that great directors, like Nemirovich-Danchenko and Konstantin Stanislavsky, were putting on Soviet plays. The revolution in the theatre would strengthen the revolution in the real world.

Stalin had less idea of what was happening in the world of fine art and music. He was scornful of all the experimentation in 'industrial art', as well as the efforts of the avant-garde, the Constructivists, Futurists and Cubists. The people who supported these 'eccentrics', whom he did not understand and doubted if others did, were in his view not committed to a serious cause.

The artists themselves were perpetually engaged in heated argument. Often their squabbles were not about whether to support the revolution, but rather about forms of art, freedom of expression, how 'to read the dials' of the new culture and so on.

The names of countless new unions and associations were scattered throughout the pages of the newspapers like a mosaic. Stalin thought it was time to bring some order to this kaleidoscope. True, he did not put his hand to this matter while he was still busy dealing with successive political oppositions. But he did think that the Commissar for Culture, Lunacharsky, was allowing too much 'licence'.

The party needed unity, it needed a course agreed by the majority. The last congress had achieved much in this respect. It had become increasingly clear to Stalin that, without industrialization and the collectivization of agriculture, the party would not be able to carry out its social programme. While the tsar and the landlords and the bourgeoisie had remained, the burdens of the struggle had been justified. But now ten years had elapsed since the revolution! True, exploitation had been got rid of, the land had been handed over to the peasants and the workers had been given the opportunity to manage the factories. So why was there so much discontent? Why were things not going as fast as everyone would wish? Maybe the opposition was not entirely wrong?

Everyone was talking about the apparatus. *Pravda*, for instance, had just published a report by Lebed on 'Measures for Improving the State Apparatus and for Combatting Bureaucratism'. He had written scathingly:

What are the shortcomings of our state apparatus? Basically, the inflated status and inferior qualifications of its workers, which is also true of the grass-roots organizations of the soviets. A cumbersome structure, duplication of function, bureaucratism and red tape, poor selection of specialists based on inadequate understanding of their qualifications, and finally poor and sometimes utterly non-existent monitoring by the higher organs of the execution of jobs, or of the work of the institutions themselves.[38]

The poet Mayakovsky had been writing in the same vein. The germ of an idea was forming in Stalin's mind that he must get rid of all these tiresome oppositions, and that he must do it by advocating the speeding-up of the great process of restructuring, though as yet he did not know how this would be achieved. Such a programme would make it easier to put pressure on the intelligentsia and to harness them more fully for the cause of industrialization and transforming the agrarian economy. It would also help to reduce the artists' mental confusion. There could be no such thing as neutral art in a class society. The well known old masters must be used to train workers' and peasants' writers. There could be no place for anti-proletarian elements in Soviet culture.

The artists' intellectual uncertainties came to seem to Stalin like nothing less than counter-revolutionary heresy, though not as dangerous, it is true, as that preached by Trotsky. The struggle on that front appeared to have reached its culmination. Before analysing the final phase of the struggle with Trotsky, however, some further remarks on culture, the intelligentsia and Stalin's attitude to them are in order. The key feature of this attitude was a total lack of respect for freedom – freedom of creation, freedom of expression, freedom of understanding. And this was not accidental. Stalin thought it was natural to deny freedom of the mind in the name of force and power.

CHAPTER 15

'Enemy Number One' Defeated

Trotsky liked to travel. He enjoyed holidays and he took care of himself. Indeed, he had several doctors attending him. Even during the worst years following the civil war, he somehow managed to get away to a resort for a little hunting and fishing. In the spring of 1926 he decided to go to Berlin for a medical consultation. The Politburo tried to dissuade him from making the trip on security grounds, but he persisted. His travel documents were made out in the name of Kuzmenko, a member of the Ukrainian board of the Education Commissariat. He and his wife said goodbye to Zinoviev and Kamenev at the station and set off with the former commander of his armoured train, Sermuks.

Trotsky was not the most astute of politicians. In the contest with Stalin he frequently put himself at a disadvantage, for instance by not appearing at Lenin's funeral, or by not turning up for Politburo meetings. And every vacation or hunting trip, as well as his literary activity, took him further away from political affairs. Stalin, meanwhile, used every one of Trotsky's absences to strengthen his own position.

In later years Trotsky would have the time to reflect on his life, and in one of his works he writes that during the trip to Berlin he came to the conclusion that there could be no compromise with Stalin, that one of them would have to give way, and that it would be Stalin. He recalled that Zinoviev and Kamenev were now siding with him, and together they had decided that between the three of them they ought to be able to wrest the initiative from the General Secretary. He thought he could still prevent the descent into Thermidor by making Stalin carry out Lenin's will.

In addition to his public attacks on Trotsky, Stalin was working by stealth to reduce Trotsky's influence. As A. P. Balashov, a member of Stalin's secretariat staff, witnessed, Stalin would often gather his supporters before a Politburo meeting in order to discuss ways of weakening Trotsky. 'We knew,'

Balashov told the author, 'that Stalin was cooking up another anti-Trotsky dish.'

When Stalin discovered that Trotsky was still being described in the Army's political studies programme as 'the leader of the Workers' and Peasants' Red Army', his reaction was swift. He wrote to Frunze on 10 December 1924 proposing an immediate review of these programmes. When Frunze replied a few days later, he attached a report from the chief of the army's political department, Alexinsky, stating that 'Trotsky no longer figures in the political studies programme as a leader of the Red Army.' Stalin also saw to it, in the second half of 1924, that Trotsky's name should no longer be adopted by towns or factories, and that fewer sympathetic notices about him should appear in the press.

In the interval between the Fourteenth and Fifteenth Congresses, Stalin both initiated and presided over a number of meetings – combined sessions of the Central Committee and Central Control Commission, sessions of the Central Committee and Politburo – which debated the activities of the opposition and took appropriate decisions. A variety of approach was adopted towards Trotsky and his supporters: warnings were issued, party penalties exacted, expulsions from the editorial boards of party organs carried out. Wide breaches soon appeared within the opposition's ranks. With the support of other party leaders, Stalin secured Zinoviev's removal from the Politburo in July 1926, followed by Trotsky's in the following October. Kamenev was relieved of his duties as a candidate member. A Central Committee plenum recognized that further work by Zinoviev in Comintern was impossible. A number of other oppositionists were similarly removed from their party and state functions.

In a report to the Fifteenth Party Conference of October–November 1926, entitled 'On the Opposition and the Internal State of the Party', Stalin harshly criticized the opposition trio and their supporters. He expounded the same ideas at the enlarged Seventh Plenum of the Comintern Executive Committee in December of the same year. The draft notes of these speeches show that he had prepared the 'unmasking' of the factionalists with the utmost care. Their weaknesses and 'sins' were enumerated on separate sheets:

1 Trotsky, Zinoviev, Kamenev: they provide no facts, only invention and gossip.
2 Make Trotsky explain with whom he was allied before October, the Left Mensheviks or the Right Mensheviks?
3 Why was Trotsky not a member of the Left Zimmerwald?*
4 Is Stalin really persecuting the half-Menshevik Mdivani? It's gossip.
5 At the IV Congress Kamenev said it had been a mistake to 'open fire on the left'. Is Kamenev a leftist?
6 Trotsky asserts that he had 'anticipated' Lenin's April Theses. He's comparing a fly with a watchtower!

---

*The radical wing of the anti-war socialist movement, dominated by Lenin, during the First World War.

7 Kamenev's telegram to [Grand Duke] Michael Romanov.
8 Zinoviev insisted on accepting Urqhart's crushing terms for the concession.*
9 Zinoviev: 'party dictatorship' etc.

Stalin punctiliously gathered every major and minor misdemeanour – of which there were not a few – and tirelessly cast them onto the bonfire of the struggle. At the December plenum, he gave a speech, entitled 'Once More on the Social Democratic Tendency in our Party', which lasted about five hours. The main brunt of his attack was the question, 'Leninism or Trotskyism?' He marshalled every petty and insignificant mistake the opposition had ever made, but made no attempt to test their views with intellectual argument. For him it was enough to lash them with mere abuse.

Naturally, the opposition had the chance to defend themselves, but they sounded unconvincing. For instance, they took a long time trying to persuade the delegates at one party conference to allow them an hour for their speeches, then asked for another half-hour, then ten more minutes, then fifteen. The proceedings show that, apart from a host of quotations from Marx and Lenin, plus some of their own, they had virtually no line of defence against the charge of factionalism. Even Trotsky, for all his reputation as an orator, could find no satisfactory arguments to justify his numerous attacks on the Central Committee and the party. At the end of an extremely long and confused statement, he merely asserted: 'We do not accept the views that have been ascribed to us.' Yu. M. Larin – (real name Lurie, whose daughter was Bukharin's last wife) – who spoke after him, remarked astutely that they were all present at a moment when 'the revolution is outgrowing some of its leaders.' He added that the opposition's speeches had been 'merely a literary argument about quotations and about various interpretations of various places in various works'. Trotsky, Zinoviev and Kamenev had 'behaved not like political leaders, but like irresponsible men of letters'.[39] Other speakers commented (with unconscious irony, in view of what was to come), that Trotsky and the others wanted to industrialize the country at the expense of the peasantry and without regard for the social consequences.

The fight against Trotsky took place not only in the Central Committee and Central Control Commission, but in Comintern also. Trotsky was a member of the Comintern Executive Committee and when, in May 1927, the Chinese revolution came up for debate, Stalin decided to strike a blow against him there, too. The speech Stalin made at the Tenth Plenum of the Comintern Executive Committee on 24 May 1927 is not widely known and is worth quoting at length:

I will try as far as possible to avoid the personal element in my polemic. The personal attacks made on individual members of the Politburo and the Presidium of the Comintern Executive Committee by Trotsky and Zinoviev do not merit our

* Leslie Urqhart was a British businessman who in 1923 attempted to conclude an agreement for a major Soviet concession on harsh terms which the Sovnarkom would not condone.

attention. It would appear that Comrade Trotsky would like to depict himself as some sort of hero at the Executive Committee's meetings, with the aim of turning the work of the Executive Committee – on the danger of war, the Chinese revolution and so on – into work on the question of Trotsky. I believe that Comrade Trotsky does not deserve such great attention [a voice from the floor: 'Quite right!'] especially as he puts one more in mind of an actor than a hero, and we must on no account confuse heroes and actors. I am not saying that Bukharin and Stalin are not offended by the fact that people like Comrades Trotsky and Zinoviev, whose social democratic deviation was established by the enlarged VII Plenum of the Executive Committee, abuse the Bolsheviks utterly to no purpose. On the contrary, I would find it deeply insulting if semi-Mensheviks of the likes of Comrades Trotsky and Zinoviev were to praise, rather than curse me.[40]

However superficial this speech may have been, it was thrusting and angry and it stuck labels on the oppositionists, demeaning them as practical politicians. The Comintern Executive Committee prepared itself for Trotsky's expulsion and this took place on 27 September of the same year, 1927. Even though he was now totally isolated, Trotsky went on fighting a hopeless battle. After his exile from the Soviet Union and until 1940 he would be possibly the only one who continued to expose, abuse and accuse Stalin, but the longer this went on, and the more angry Trotsky's lone voice became, the plainer it seemed that he was fighting less for the revolution and its ideals than for himself. Until his dying day, he never came to terms with the absurdity that he, the near genius, had been placed beyond the pale by the 'crafty Ossetian'. He would soon come to use Marxist concepts as tools for debunking Stalin, while for his part Stalin never ceased to view Trotsky with the most profound personal hatred and as the embodiment of evil, the symbol of degeneration.

Meanwhile the opposition failed to draw the appropriate lesson and the struggle continued. In the spring of 1927 they sent a new programme to the Central Commitee signed by eighty-three of Trotsky's supporters. After several Central Committee and Central Control Commission meetings, Trotsky and Zinoviev were expelled from the Central Committee in October 1927, and from the party in the following month, a move ratified by the Fifteenth Party Congress when it met in December of the same year. Among twenty-five other active members of the opposition expelled from the party at the same time was Kamenev, although he and Zinoviev would later be reinstated and even make declarations of repentance at the Seventeenth Party Congress.

While it is true that the struggle with the opposition had taken place against an international background of growing tension and a domestic background of the developing industrialization, it is also true that Stalin had provoked the struggle. The endless debates distracted the party's attention from its vitally important tasks, and the party's internal condition was repeatedly discussed inside Comintern, but there too Trotsky and his supporters founded virtually no allies. His aura as the hero of the revolution had faded away. He was seen by the party and the international labour movement as a speechmaker and a leader who never was.

Paradoxical as it may seem, it was Trotsky, more than anyone else, who strengthened Stalin's position. By foisting endless debate about his struggle with Stalin on to the party, Trotsky, despite himself, had reinforced Stalin's authority as the new leader. It was significant that Stalin was the only speaker at the Fifteenth Party Congress to receive a standing ovation, both for his report and for the closing speech. He cannot be accused of having 'stage-managed' or 'scripted' the proceedings; most of the delegates simply saw him as the true emergent leader of the party, an impression strengthened by the unconvincing speeches of the opposition whose nerve had failed. As Trotsky angrily recalled, 'The only concern of Zinoviev and his friends was to capitulate while there was yet time ... They hoped to buy forgiveness, if not to win favour, by a demonstrative break with me ...'[41]

It had become clear to everyone that Trotsky's alliance with his former enemies had been brought about solely in order to concentrate their forces against Stalin, while Stalin, whose ambition and faith in his own destiny had grown steadily stronger, did not miss the golden opportunity that had presented itself. Having begun the battle on the ideological plane, he now set out to complete his destruction of Trotsky politically.

A combined plenum of the Central Committee and Central Control Commission of 23 October 1927 was convened to discuss the agenda of the forthcoming Fifteenth Congress. When the plenum agreed that congress should debate the Trotskyist opposition, shouts came from the floor and notes were handed to the platform to the effect that the Central Committee had concealed Lenin's Testament and not carried out his will. Stalin could no longer remain silent on this matter. His hour-long speech was full of anger and undisguised hatred of Trotsky. Once again he rehearsed all the sins of the rejected leader, going back to 1904. Knowing that Trotsky's main weapon against him was Lenin's warning about his personal shortcomings, Stalin countered along the same lines:

The opposition thinks it can 'explain' its defeat on the personal grounds of Stalin's rudeness, the obduracy of Bukharin and Rykov, and so on. That's too easy. It's mumbo-jumbo, not an explanation ... In the period between 1904 and the February Revolution Trotsky was hobnobbing with the Mensheviks the whole time and carrying on a desperate struggle against Lenin's party. In that time Trotsky was defeated again and again by Lenin's party. Why? Perhaps Stalin's rudeness was to blame? But Stalin was not then secretary of the Central Committee, he was passing his time in those days far from foreign exile, he was carrying on the struggle in the underground, against tsarism, while the struggle between Trotsky and Lenin was being played out abroad, so what has Stalin's rudeness got to do with it?[42]

Stalin launched his attack under the banner of defending Lenin, whom Trotsky in the early days had called – among other things – 'Maximilien Lenin', an allusion to the dictatorial ways of Robespierre. He dealt Trotsky a telling blow by noting that his early pamphlet, 'Our Political Tasks', had been dedicated to the Menshevik P. B. Axelrod. Triumphantly, and to the accompaniment of the audience's jeers, Stalin read out the dedication: 'To my dear teacher, Pavel Borisovich Axelrod':

Well, good riddance to our 'dear teacher', Pavel Borisovich Axelrod! Good riddance! But you'd better hurry, venerable Trotsky, because Pavel Borisovich is pretty decrepit and could die at any moment and you might be too late getting to your 'teacher'.[43]

Recalling the July–August 1927 plenum, Stalin regretted having dissuaded the comrades from expelling Trotsky and Zinoviev from the Central Committee immediately. 'Maybe I was being too kind and made a mistake . . .' Now, by contrast, he was calling for support from 'those comrades who want to expel Trotsky and Zinoviev from the Central Committee'.[44]

As for dealing with Lenin's 'Letter to the Congress', Stalin gave his own interpretation:

It has been shown time and again, and no one is trying to hide anything, that Lenin's Testament was addressed to the Thirteenth Party Congress, that it was read out at the congress, that the congress agreed *unanimously* not to publish it because, by the way, Lenin himself did not want or ask for it to be published.[45]

As our analysis of Lenin's last letters has shown, Stalin was distorting the historical truth. It had never been clear whether Lenin was addressing his letters to the Twelfth or Thirteenth Congress. The Testament was read only to delegations, not to the congress. The congress took no decision, still less unanimously, about not publishing it, and there was only Stalin's word that Lenin himself did not want it to be published.

In the event, feeling his strength growing and sensing that he had virtually the full support of the plenum, he set out to give battle on the ground on which he himself was most vulnerable, lying without hesitation in the process. He exploited the fact that, at the Politburo's (and above all his own) insistence, *Bolshevik* of September 1925 had published a statement by Trotsky concerning the Testament. Giving in to pressure from Stalin on that occasion, Trotsky had written:

Since becoming ill, Vladimir Ilyich had frequently written proposals, letters, etc. to the party's leading bodies and its congresses. All these letters etc. were naturally always delivered to their intended destinations, and were brought to the attention of the delegates to the Twelfth and Thirteenth Congresses and always, naturally, had the appropriate influence on party decisions . . . Vladimir Ilyich left no testament, and the very nature of his relations with the party, as well as the nature of the party itself, exclude the possibility of any such testament, so that any talk about concealing or not carrying out a testament is a malicious invention and is aimed in fact entirely against Vladimir Ilyich's intention.[46]

Could Trotsky have guessed that, in attempting to dissociate himself from rumours circulating in the West to the effect that Lenin's secret papers had reached the West through his hands, he had painted himself completely into a corner? The bell, as it turned out, was tolling for him. In the eyes of the plenum, the leader of the opposition appeared once more as a political intriguer, and Stalin did not miss the chance to finish him off.

Citing the article in *Bolshevik*, Stalin went straight for his target:

That was written by Trotsky and by no one else. What basis can Trotsky, Zinoviev and Kamenev now have for wagging their tongues and claiming that the party and its Central Committee are 'concealing' Lenin's Testament? ...

It is said that in his Testament Lenin suggested that, in view of Stalin's 'rudeness', the congress should consider replacing him as General Secretary with someone else. That is absolutely true. Yes, comrades, I am rude towards those who rudely and treacherously destroy and split the party. I have never hidden this, nor do I now. Maybe a certain gentleness is required towards the splitters. But it is not in me to be like that. At the very first session of the Central Committee plenum following the Thirteenth Congress, I asked the plenum to release me from the duties of General Secretary. The congress itself had debated this question. All the delegates, including Trotsky, Kamenev and Zinoviev, unanimously obliged Stalin to remain at his post. What was I supposed to do? Run away from the job? That is not in my nature, I have never run away from a job, nor did I have the right to do so, as it would have amounted to desertion. A year later, I again asked the plenum to release me, and again I was compelled to remain at my post. What more could I do?

It is significant that the Testament contains not one word, not a hint about Stalin's mistakes. It speaks only of Stalin's rudeness. But rudeness is not, nor can it be, a shortcoming of Stalin's political line or his positions.[47]

Sitting there in the hall, Trotsky felt that this devastating and triumphant tirade by Stalin spelt his political end. As he would write later in Mexico, after Stalin's speech he had a physical sensation that the knife of the guillotine was hanging over him. Like other revolutionaries of the time, Trotsky was well acquainted with the history of the French Revolution. He can hardly have denied himself the grim satisfaction of remembering Robespierre's last words to the Convention: 'The Republic has perished! The kingdom of brigands is at hand!' Naturally, Trotsky saw only himself in Robespierre. But unlike Robespierre, Trotsky could not count on the Parisian sans-culottes. Trotsky was a field marshal without an army. The party was hostile towards him, and was tired of his intrigues. It was all over.

The dialogue going on in the mind of the defeated would-be dictator and party leader must have been self-destructive. How could he, Trotsky, have so underestimated the moustachioed Ossetian? The gloomy thought that he had missed his chance had nagged at him even while Lenin was still alive. But he could not have dreamed that he would be publicly trampled on by someone who had been so little noticed in those days. Later, when he was abroad, Trotsky would read a book by the émigré Essad Bey which seemed to say it all:

Trotsky and Stalin were the two opposing poles of the Communist Party. Neither in personal nor political terms did they converge at any point. Trotsky was a brilliant European, an experienced and conceited journalist, and Stalin was a typical Asiatic, a man without vanity or personal needs, with the cold, dark mind of an eastern conspirator. Two men such as these were bound to hate each other. Stalin had a physical revulsion for Trotsky, just as Trotsky felt deep disgust from one look at Stalin and his pock-marked face.[48]

Trotsky gave his last speech as a party figure at the plenum of October 1927. It was confused but passionate. He later wrote that he had wanted but completely failed to warn the 'blind men' that 'Stalin's triumph would not last long and that the collapse of his régime would come suddenly. The victors of the hour are relying excessively on force. You are expelling us, but you cannot prevent our victory.' Leaning on the rostrum, and trying to shout down the din in the hall, Trotsky rapidly read through his speech, like the 'cribber' he had often called Stalin and other party leaders. The audience was inattentive, interrupting him with cries of 'Slander!', 'Lies!', 'Chatterer!', 'Down with the factionalist!' Trotsky tried to fire off what he had written about the weakening of the revolutionary principle in the party, the domination of the apparatus, the creation of a 'ruling faction' which was leading the country and the party into a state of political reaction. Despite the fact that much of what he said was right, he provided no convincing arguments or clear socialist ideas. His hatred of the Central Committee and of Stalin were plain to see, but this was not echoed among the participants of the plenum, nor among Communists who would read the speech in the documents of the Fifteenth Congress.

On the occasion of the tenth anniversary of the October Revolution, Trotsky's followers decided they would join the celebrations as a procession, forming their own columns and carrying banners with such unexceptionable slogans as 'Down with the kulak, the Nepman and the bureaucrat!' 'Down with opportunism!' 'Carry out Lenin's will!' 'Preserve Bolshevik unity!' Attempts were made to raise portraits of Trotsky and Zinoviev, but Stalin had taken appropriate precautions and the militia scattered Trotsky's groups. Zinoviev, who had gone to Leningrad for the occasion, and Trotsky, who was touring the streets and squares of Moscow in his car, discovered that they had only minimal support. Perhaps Trotsky was remembering the occasion of the Second Congress of Soviets, ten years earlier, when he had dismissed the departing figure of Martov with the words: 'Go to the dustbin of history, where you belong!' The same words were being cast at him now, as he tried to appeal to the crowds on Revolution Square, making their way into Red Square. Stones were thrown at him and the windows of his car were smashed. Stalin was dropping him into the sewer of history.

In ten years, Trotsky's meteoric party career had come to a catastrophic end.

After Trotsky's expulsion from the party, Zinoviev and Kamenev tried to persuade him to repent, to admit that he'd been in the wrong. But Trotsky, whatever would be said or written about him, always viewed himself through the prism of the future, and being extremely ambitious and vain, he took account of the way historians would weigh a temporary success in their overall assessment of him.

Both his families would have to drink the bitter cup to the dregs. His first wife, Alexandra Sokolovskaya, and their two daughters, Zina and Nina, and both their husbands, were his zealous supporters. He had left his first family back in 1902 when his younger daughter was only four months old. At first he wrote to his wife from abroad, but then time and a new family drove Alexandra and her daughters into what he himself called 'the sphere of the irretrievable'. As he was to write in 1929 in *My Life*: 'Life separated us, but nothing could destroy our friendship and our intellectual kinship.' After the revolution both daughters bathed in their father's reflected glory, only to share his ostracism a few years later. The first family's further destiny was sad. For their political unorthodoxy and for belonging to a 'clan of enemies' – or 'socially dangerous elements by origin', as would be written in the 1930s – Stalin would exact a terrible price.

Trotsky's second wife, Natalya Sedova, also began life as a revolutionary. For a time they lived together in St Petersburg under the name Vikentiev. She was with him constantly, sharing the triumph of his rise during the revolution and civil war, as well as his endless wanderings in exile.

Trotsky had two sons from his second marriage. The elder one, Lev, who was always with his father, was an active Trotskyist and died very young in mysterious circumstances in Paris after his father had been banished from the USSR. The younger one, Sergei, left home when his father was living in the Kremlin, announcing that he found politics 'objectionable'. He did not join the Komsomol, but plunged himself into science. Refusing to go into exile with his father, Sergei, as Trotsky's son, was of course doomed. In January 1937 an article appeared in *Pravda* under the title 'Trotsky's son, Sergei Sedov, attempted to poison workers'. Already an exile in Krasnoyarsk, Sergei was declared an 'enemy of the people'. At a meeting in the foundry of a machine-building plant, a foreman, called Lebedev, stated: 'We had working with us as an engineer the son of Trotsky, Sergei Sedov. This worthy offspring of a father who sold himself to Fascism tried to poison a large group of our workers with gas from a generator.' Remarks were made at the meeting about Zinoviev's nephew, Zaks, and their 'protector', the factory manager Subbotin. The fate of people accused in this way was sealed.

All of Trotsky's children perished in the bloody whirlpool into which they had been sucked by their father's fight with Stalin, and this gave the exile an aura of martyrdom in the eyes of the West. Natalya survived both her husband and Stalin and lived to see the Twentieth Congress.

At first, also for the sake of 'history', the General Secretary publicly undertook 'not to touch Trotsky's family', but theirs was a bitter fate. Some of his distant relatives survived intact and are living under different names in Moscow, where they have spoken to the present author, but most of them had endured a harsh life, following the banishment of their famous kinsman.

In the fifteen or so books that he wrote in exile, Trotsky often addressed his own personal fate, especially on the eve of his murder. His *History of the Russian Revolution, What Further? Lenin's Hidden Testament, Their Morals and Ours, Diary in Exile, My Life, The Third International after Lenin*, bear the stamp of tragic egocentrism. He found it hard to accept that he was not being talked about, or written and argued about. Fame, popularity and glory would become more important to him than food. Mensheviks who had once shared his views, now wrote stinging articles about him. David Dallin would write:

Trotsky does everything possible to make sure that, God forbid, people do not begin to forget him. Day and night he writes big books and little articles, he publishes family bulletins and issues variations in all languages on the same themes: Stalin's treachery, his betrayal of the Chinese revolution and Lenin's tender love for Trotsky. But mankind is ungrateful, and in time they will remember Trotsky and talk about him less and less.[49]

The Politburo repeatedly discussed the question of how to deal with Trotsky, whose attacks had shifted from an anti-party to an anti-Soviet mode, and it was decided to move him away from Moscow. First he was made to leave the Kremlin. Zinoviev, Kamenev, Radek and some other leaders were similarly removed. Ioffe committed suicide soon after Trotsky's defeat. Zinoviev and Kamenev decided to repent at the next party congress. 'Lev Davidovich,' they wrote to Trotsky, 'the time has come for us to have the courage to surrender'. They had lost the match decisively and were trying to regain a foothold on the train of history. The decision was soon taken to send Trotsky to Alma-Ata in southern Kazakhstan, the move, according to some sources, being given to Bukharin to handle.

During the departure some of Trotsky's supporters attempted to stage a political protest. Trotsky refused to leave the house and enter the car and had to be carried out bodily, and was similarly manhandled into the train, his elder son shouting meanwhile 'Comrades, see how they are carrying Trotsky away!' His wife described the scene:

There had been a tremendous demonstration at the station. People waited, shouting 'Long live Trotsky!' But Trotsky was nowhere to be seen. Where was he? Around the car reserved for us there was a stormy crowd. Young friends set a large portrait of L.D. on the roof of the car. It was greeted by jubilant 'hurrahs'. The train started, first one jerk, then another; it moved forward a little and then stopped suddenly. The demonstrators had run in front of the engine; they clung to the cars and stopped the train, demanding Trotsky. A rumour had run through the crowd that the GPU agents had conducted L.D. secretly into the car and were preventing him from showing himself to those who had come to see him off. The excitement at the station was indescribable. There were clashes with the police and the agents of the GPU, with casualties on both sides. Arrests were made.[50]

In the Kremlin, Stalin was following events closely, being kept informed on progress by frequent telephone calls during which he muttered: 'No shilly-shallying! No concessions! Trotsky's accomplices are to be cut off! Do it quickly and without delay!' He paced nervously up and down his study, thinking. Some years later, in the 1930s and in the company of his cronies, hearing of Trotsky's most recent speech abroad, he snapped: 'We made two mistakes on that occasion. We should have left him for a time in Alma-Ata, but on no account should we have let him out of the country. And the other one was, how could we have let him take so many documents with him?'

While he was in Alma-Ata, Trotsky continued his political activity. Every month he sent hundreds of letters and telegrams to various addresses. His elder son's notes show that the clandestine correspondence, which Trotsky carried on in Alma-Ata between April and October 1928, amounted to some 800 political letters and 550 telegrams from him, and more than 1000 political letters and 700 telegrams received by him.[51] In addition, letters and other items came and went by courier. He was trying to reactivate the opposition. His rôle as a disgraced leader gave him a certain moral authority. Exile did not change his way of thinking, nor did he feel compelled to stop trying to sow dissension inside the party. To his alert mind, Stalin had come to personify the Thermidorean evil and was the portent of future misfortunes.

A year later, in January 1929, the Politburo decided, after many long discussions of various options, that Trotsky and his wife and son, Lev, should be expelled via Odessa to Constantinople. As the steamer *Ilyich* was approaching Constantinople on 12 February, Trotsky decided to draw the attention of world opinion. His statement to the president of Turkey, Kemal Pasha, read:

Dear Sir,
At the gate of Constantinople, I have the honour to inform you that I have arrived at the Turkish frontier not of my own choice, and that I will cross this frontier only by submitting to force. I request you, Mr President, to accept my appropriate sentiments.
L. Trotsky, 12 February, 1929[52]

He was thus launched on a further ten years of the most energetic struggle against Stalin and, on occasion and even despite himself, against the very state which he himself had helped to create and defend.

The chief cause of his personal drama lay in the fact that, in the last analysis, he had put his personal ambitions first and had pitted them against an utterly unscrupulous opponent. The dénouement was hastened by the personal clash of the 'two outstanding leaders'. Having a powerful and original mind, and given his highly ambitious character, Trotsky gradually moved into the ranks of the irreconcilable enemies of Stalinist socialism. His personal hatred for Stalin often overcame elementary decency even towards the ideals and values he himself had so recently proclaimed.

Having barely arrived in the roadstead of Constantinople that leaden February, Trotsky handed the Western press a collection of six of his essays, entitled *What Happened and How*. In one of these essays, Trotsky made an assertion he had been trying to disguise only six months earlier, namely that the theory of socialism in one country was a reactionary fabrication, 'the main and most criminal undermining of revolutionary internationalism'. It was a theory, he claimed, with an administrative, not a scientific basis.[53] When Stalin saw this in his morning mail two weeks later, he said, in the presence of one of his assistants, 'At last, the swine has stopped pretending.'

Now that he was abroad, Trotsky was constantly preoccupied with preserving his reputation as a revolutionary. He continued publishing his collected works, often resorting to strained interpretation and invention, all with the aim of wounding Stalin as painfully as possible and of presenting himself in the mirror of history as the man whom Lenin had wanted to make his successor, an intention frustrated by Stalin's treachery. It must be said that Trotsky had seen through Stalin sooner than others had, and had not bowed down before him, but in combatting Stalin, Trotsky had also managed to insult the whole nation in the process. In volume twenty of his collected works he permitted himself to make some scathing remarks about the Russian people. In his view, 'not one state official in Russia had ever risen above a third-rate imitation of the Duke of Alba, Metternich or Bismarck', and as for science, philosophy and sociology, 'Russia has given the world precisely nothing'. Only a politician who thinks that he has been called upon to play nothing but leading rôles in history would be capable of making such slavophobic, chauvinistic utterances. Abroad, Trotsky called himself the man for whom the whole planet had become accessible without a visa. As before, he tried to play the part of the 'second genius':

They brought Lenin to the revolution through Germany in a sealed train. Against my will they took me to Constantinople on the steamer *Ilyich*. Therefore, I do not consider my exile to be history's last word.

He was still hoping to return, but fate decided otherwise and he was to remain banished forever.

CHAPTER 16

The Leader's Private Life

Many people who knew and saw Stalin in what might be called the domestic setting – doctors, bodyguards, secretarial staff, writers, military leaders – have told me that, broadly speaking, Stalin's private life and working life were one and the same thing. Days off did not exist for him, and the pattern of his days varied little. It is true that, towards the end of his life, when old age was beginning to slow him down, he did not go in to the Kremlin every day, but would work at his dacha. Politburo meetings took place there occasionally, and there also he received ministers and army men and foreign visitors.

Stalin had developed his habit of doing without time off during the difficult years immediately after the revolution. True, there were occasions when members of the Politburo and others would still be sitting around Stalin's supper table of a Sunday until beyond midnight. But even then the talk, however 'free', would be about the problems facing the country and the party.

The leadership of the 1920s lived rather modestly. At first, Stalin lived in a small apartment he had been given on Lenin's orders. A letter from Lunacharsky of 18 November 1921 requests that Stalin be found something more comfortable. When Lenin saw the letter he sent a note to the head of security, A. Ya. Belenky (real name Khatskelevich): 'This is news to me. Can nothing else be found?'[54] There is also a note from Lenin to A. S. Yenukidze, requesting that the matter of Stalin's apartment be expedited and asking to be informed by telephone when it had been settled. And indeed Stalin was soon rehoused in former servants' quarters in the Kremlin, an inelegant dwelling with some of the original furniture, a worn floor and small windows.

The new master was, however, hardly there, as he would arrive home late at night and leave first thing in the morning. In the early 1920s he began to spend his time at the dacha at Zabolovo, and in the 1930s at Kuntsevo. He was constantly ordering the dacha to be remodelled. In his last years, he had a small wooden house built next to the large villa and he moved into it. As A. N. Shelepin, (at one time head of the KGB and a member of the Politburo in the early 1970s), told me:

When Stalin died and an inventory of his possessions had to be made, it turned out to be a very simple job. There were no antiques or valuable objects of any kind, apart from a government-issue piano. The furniture was cheap and the armchairs had loose covers. There was not even a single good 'real' picture, they were all printed reproductions in plain wooden frames. Hanging in the central position in the sitting room was an enlarged photograph of Lenin and Stalin, taken at Gorky in September 1922 by Lenin's sister, Maria.*

There were two rugs on the floor. Stalin slept under an army blanket. Apart from his marshal's uniform, his clothes consisted of a couple of ordinary suits, one of them in canvas, embroidered felt boots and a peasant's sheepskin.

As we have mentioned elsewhere, this 'asceticism' was merely external, as Stalin also had the use of several villas in the Moscow area and in the south, as well as a large staff of servants. His every whim would be fulfilled instantly, but he did everything possible to underline the 'proletarian' simplicity of his lifestyle. Stalin's dislike of 'Europe' and things foreign was carried into his domestic life, and he was not fond of imported objects, even though he insisted all his life that there was no direct relationship between a man's political or moral outlook and his attitude to lifestyle, valuables and possessions. What was important was to know how to focus on the main thing, and for him that was power, power as an aim, as a means and as an eternal value. The domestic trappings of this power were of little matter. In 1938 he chose another apartment in the Kremlin, in a superb building constructed in the eighteenth century by Kazakov for the Senate. It had beautiful windows, high ceilings and sweeping staircases, rooms for guests, guards, receptions, and it occupied almost the entire first floor, the floor above being allocated to the service staff. But Stalin hardly used it, preferring instead his dacha nearby. He had another dacha further out, which he also did not use.

For his seventieth birthday, Beria gave Stalin a dacha on the banks of a reservoir near Moscow and persuaded his boss to view it. The ageing leader gave in and went out to see the beautiful house hidden among tall pines and spruce. 'What sort of a mousetrap is this?' Stalin snapped at Beria suspiciously. He toured the rooms without taking off his coat, walked around the outside, eyed the people accompanying him, got into his car without a word and drove off. He never went to the place again.

Stalin's way of life was unhealthy. A night-bird since the early 1920s, he hardly ever went for a walk, and smoked heavily, giving it up less than a year before his death, a fact of which he was apparently proud. He would drink only a little dry Georgian wine before dinner. It was not his custom to spend

---

* This has been exposed as a fake.

long hours on what he called the aristocratic pastimes of hunting and fishing. The nineteenth-century thinker Alexander Herzen once wrote to his friend Nikolai Ogarev that the aim of human life was to express all the facets of one's personality by learning to 'live in all dimensions'. Stalin lived in only one dimension, and that was in his work. He was a slave to it. People who worked for him recall that on the rare occasions when he would appear in the grounds, the stooped figure would take one or two turns around the paved path and then come to a halt by a flowerbed or a lilac bush, seemingly gazing in wonder at the miracle of nature, perhaps comparing its eternal order with the state of his own affairs.

He may have just been looking at a file from Voroshilov, containing material on all kinds of subjects: requesting his permission to exempt tractor- and combine-drivers from military service; asking him to review a proposal to build new houses for the army; a report of a speech by the Polish leader Pilsudski; extracts from the Czech press; a report of a letter from the 26th Caucasian regimental commander about a misunderstanding with Moscow's emissary Gostintsev; a letter from Ilyushin about the need to develop airship construction and new air defences, and so on. And how many telegrams had he dictated today! For instance:

To the secretary of the Sasov district, Prosyanye Polyany village, Ryazan.
A telegram has been received from schoolteacher Shirinskaya. This teacher of the Tatar school is to be protected from the unnecessary rudeness and excesses of Kadom district committee secretary Ivanov, who burst into her apartment on the pretext of removing her father's unwanted cupboard, prevented her from working peacefully and making her feel like killing herself.
Please intervene immediately to shield Shirinskaya from any such violations and inform the Central Committee of the result.[55]

File after file of such matters were handed to him every day by his assistant, Tovstukha, although gradually more of it would be dealt with by his secretarial staff. To the end of his life, however, Stalin enjoyed settling such trivial issues, especially if they had to do with job appointments, or overbearing, dissident or particularly obdurate officials.

The more his influence grew in party and state affairs, the more eagerly people brought a wide range of issues to him 'for his personal attention'. Why couldn't the appropriate commissar settle the matter of the tractor drivers and the call-up, or the building of new houses? Surely a secretary could handle the matter of the wretched schoolteacher? The fact is, Stalin got used to the idea that people couldn't manage without him, that he must do everything.

He may have felt that universal centralization, framed by the most complex bureaucratic rituals, was making him a prisoner of the system, and that it could slow down or even prove disastrous to the cause. What did he have People's Commissars for, where was their flexibility? What were the countless All-Union agencies and offices supposed to be doing? He knew perfectly well, but he did not want things to be different. If one-man rule is subdivided, it ceases to be one-man rule. Gradually everything became centred on him, and whether the stream of proposals ran smoothly or became trapped in a web of contradictions depended on his decision, and to some extent that of his entourage.

The cinema and the theatre were the only incursions he would allow into his working life. It had become his habit since the late 1920s to see one or two films a week, usually after midnight. Any film that was being talked about would be screened in the small Kremlin cinema and later in his projection-room at the dacha. He once told a group of agitprop leaders that 'cinema is nothing but an illusion, but its laws are dictated by life.' He saw cinema as an educational tool, which was how he viewed art in general.

It was through his wife that he became acquainted with the theatre. They were often to be seen together at the Moscow theatres, and after her death the theatre became part of his life, especially the Bolshoi. He seems to have seen all its productions several times. As A. T. Rybin, one of his security guards and later manager of the Bolshoi, told me, Stalin went to see *Swan Lake* on the eve of his fatal stroke for perhaps the twentieth or thirtieth time. He was usually alone, taking his seat only after the lights had been dimmed and sitting in a corner at the back of his box. He would sometimes attend a dress rehearsal and would always send his thanks to the dancers. The cinema and the theatre were the only 'lyrical' outlets in his life, which was otherwise wholly dedicated to spreading his personal power and influence throughout the decision-making system.

Personal life means above all family life. Nadezhda Sergeyevna Alliluyeva was twenty-two years younger than Stalin. Practically straight from high school she had become the wife of a party leader. The documents and eye-witness testimony, as well as the memoirs of her daughter, Svetlana, agree that she had a very well balanced character. In due course she became a party member, worked in the Commissariat of Nationalities and studied. She also worked as one of Lenin's duty secretaries at Gorky. When it was decided to transfer the capital from Petrograd to Moscow, Stalin brought his wife's parents with them and they all lived together in the small apartment in the Kremlin.

Nadezhda soon adapted to the atmosphere of endless consultations, meetings, journeys and struggles which comprised her husband's life. Many of the letters, telegrams, orders and directives among Stalin's papers are signed not only by Stalin's secretaries, such as Nazaretyan, Tovstukha, Kanner, Mekhlis and Dvinsky, but also by Nadezhda. Her big schoolgirl's eyes had gazed avidly at her husband's world. She saw that he belonged to his work and to it alone, but she did not at first realize how little time and space he would leave for her. Stalin had no need of company. When she reproached him, which she did frequently, with the charge, 'You're not interested in your family and the children,' he would rudely interrupt her, sometimes using foul language. To some extent, Nadezhda found consolation in her work and study and in meeting other leaders' wives, such as Polina Semenovna Zhemchuzhina (Molotov's wife), Dora Moiseyevna Khazan (Andreyev's), Maria Markovna Kaganovich and Esfir Isayevna Gurvich (Bukharin's second wife). (It is worth noting that, among the Bolshevik leaders of Russian origin, many had Jewish wives, a fact that may be at least partially explained by the fact that Jewish women intellectuals had been relatively numerous and active in the revolutionary movement.)

Two children were born to Stalin and Nadezhda: Vasili in 1922 and Svetlana in 1926. Then Yakov, his son by his first wife, Yekaterina Svanidze, came to live with them. He was only seven years younger than his stepmother who evidently cared for the young man who was so plainly starved of a father's love. As she worked, the children were looked after by a nanny. There were always lots of relatives around, whether in the Kremlin apartment or at the Zubolovo dacha. Apart from Nadezhda's parents, her brothers, Fedor and Pavel, were also frequent visitors, and there was her sister, Anna, and her relatives. Then there were Stalin's relatives by his first wife who also came to visit. After Nadezhda's death in 1932, the noise and bustle faded and finally came to a stop.

Stalin evidently did not wish to take a serious part in his children's upbringing, nor was he able to. He saw them very rarely, perhaps on a Sunday when they were brought out to the dacha, or in the south, in Sochi, Livadia or Mukhalatka, where he liked to spend his vacations before the war. It is not uncommon for the children of famous people to grow up damaged. Stalin's children hardly knew their father, and he had little time for them. According to Svetlana, Vasili once let her into a 'secret' by telling her that 'Father was a Georgian when he was young.'

The fate of Stalin's elder son, Yakov, was the most tragic. His relationship with his father was very bad. Stalin regarded him as a weak character, mistakenly, as it turned out. Stalin was not pleased with Yakov's choice of wives, neither the first nor the second, Yulia Isakovna Meltser. He had two children from these marriages. Svetlana Alliluyeva recalls that, driven to despair by his father's coldness towards him, Yakov even tried to shoot himself, but the bullet passed right through him and he survived, though he was ill for a long time. When Stalin saw him after this extreme expression of their total alienation, he greeted him with a mocking: 'Ha! You missed!'

With his father's permission, Yakov completed his studies at the Moscow Railway Engineering Institute, worked at the power station of the Stalin factory and then announced that he wanted to join the army. On the orders of Stalin's assistants, Yakov Dzhugashvili was registered first for the evening section and then transferred straight into the fourth year course of the first faculty of the Red Army Artillery Academy.

Perusing the personal dossier of Lieutenant Ya. I. Dzhugashvili, one is struck by the questions every officer had to answer when compiling his own curriculum vitae. For a flavour of the psychological atmosphere of the times, a few of the dozens of such questions will suffice:

Have you been a member of the Trotskyist Right, the national-chauvinist or other counter-revolutionary organizations, when and where?'

Have you deviated from the party's general line or had any hesitations? If you have had hesitations, on what issues and for how long did the hesitations last?'

Did you serve in the White army and the army of intervention, in anti-Soviet nationalist units (Constituent Assemblyists, Petliurists, Musavatists, Dashnaks, Georgian Mensheviks, Makhno's, Antonov's or other bands), where, when, as what, how did you end up there, what unit did you serve in, for how long?'

Yakov passed the test, but there were still some people who had not sold out. For instance, Ivanov, Kobrya, Timofeev, Sheremetov and Novikov (no initials appear in the files), all officers at the academy, signed the following testimonial about Stalin's son:

Political development satisfactory. Disciplined, but has not acquired adequate knowledge of the military rules about attitudes to senior officers. Has had no practical training. Little training in infantry tactics. His academic work leaves much to be desired. Received 'satisfactory' and 'good' in state examinations.

Despite his immediate superiors' recommendation that he be made a battalion commander with the rank of captain, the head of the faculty, Sheremetov, was of a different opinion: 'I agree with the testimonial, but I think the rank of captain should only be given after he has served a year as a battery commander.'

All were agreed that Yakov was a decent, honest, shy person who seemed to have been destroyed by his father's hostility. Yakov was ill at ease in the rôle of commander, perhaps feeling that he was skating on thin ice: he had bypassed several courses and his work had not been good. This may have played a fateful part at the critical moment during his active service.

Yakov was at the front from the first days of the Second World War. According to the documents, he fought bravely and did his duty to the end, but his unit was surrounded and he was taken prisoner. There is a rare photograph showing a group of German officers gazing with open curiosity at Captain Ya. Dzhugashvili. The most interesting thing about the photograph is Yakov's expression and his posture: he is staring at his enemies with hatred in his face and clenched fists. The Nazis tried to use the fact of his being a prisoner of war for their own propaganda purposes, scattering leaflets showing the photograph, but it was generally regarded as a forgery.

Rather than suffering over his son's fate, Stalin was afraid Yakov's will would be broken in the prison camp and that he would be made to work for the Germans. In the memoirs of Dolores Ibarruri, published in Barcelona in 1985, a little known fact appears which has yet to be either corroborated or disproved. She writes that in 1942 a special commando group was formed that was to be sent behind enemy lines to liberate Yakov, then in Sachsenhausen. The group included the Spaniard José Parro Moiso who was carrying papers in the name of an officer of the Francoist Blue Division. The operation ended in failure and the group perished.[56] Yakov turned out to have a much stronger character than his father credited him with. He too was afraid that under torture, psychological conditioning and drugs he might crack and become a traitor in his father's and the nation's eyes. The thought was worse than death. Although he did not become a traitor in the circles of Hell he passed through – Hammelburg, Lübeck and Sachsenhausen – his strength was failing. On 14 April 1943 he threw himself on to the barbed wire fence and was shot by a guard.

As with so many other people, Stalin had been wrong about his son. Svetlana Alliluyeva claims that after the victory at Stalingrad, her father said to her, as if *en passant*: 'The Germans proposed exchanging Yasha for one of their own ... As if I would do a trade with them! No, war is war ...'

The fate of his other son was no less tragic. Stalin had been unable to make a man of him. After his mother's death, the boy was virtually brought up by Vlasik, the head of Stalin's security guards. But living as he did in a climate of flattery and permissiveness, he turned out to be spineless, capricious and weak. True, he fought quite well, but not so well as to begin the war as a captain, which he did, nor end up in 1947 as a lieutenant general. The personal dossier of Lieutenant General Vasili Iosifovich Stalin provides eloquent testimony to the cavalier way Stalin's entourage, with his knowledge, made free with rank and favour. Let us take just a few facts from Vasili's thick file: At age twenty V. I. Stalin immediately attains the rank of colonel (Defence Commissar's Order No. 01192 of 19 February 1942). At twenty-four he becomes an Air Force major general (Sovnarkom Order of 2 March 1946) and a year later he is a lieutenant general. While still completely 'green', and only an average pilot, he is made chief of Air Force Inspection. In January 1943 he is made commander of the 32nd fighter air regiment; a year later commander of the 3rd, in February 1945 commander of the 286th fighter division. In 1946 he is made a corps commander, then deputy and later commander of the Air Force. Vasili's meteoric career was not of course due to his special abilities or personal qualities. In the course of the war, as his superior officers' reports witness, he flew twenty-seven sorties and shot down one enemy plane, a Fokker-Wolf 190; he was awarded two Orders of the Red Banner, the Order of Alexander Nevsky, the Order of Suvorov 2nd Class, and various other medals.

Air Force Lieutenant General E. M. Beletsky and Air Force Colonel General N. F. Papivin wrote in their testimonial of him:

He is hot-headed and excitable by nature, lacks self-control; there have been incidents of physical violence against subordinates. In his private life he has behaved in ways unbecoming his post as a divisional commander, there have been incidents of tactless behaviour during parties with flying staff, rudeness towards individual officers, an occasion of irresponsibility when he drove a tractor from the aerodrome to the town of Shiaulyai and was in conflict and a tussle with the NKVD control post. His health is not good, especially his nervous system, he is extremely irritable, a condition which was revealed recently when he did very little personal flying training ... All the above listed shortcomings significantly diminish his authority as a commander and are incompatible with his duties as divisional commander.

Similar remarks occur in other testimonials, all of them concluding that Vasili Stalin should be sent back to the Academy for further study. This was the only means such distinguished generals as S. I. Rudenko and E. Ya. Savitsky could find to spare their subordinates from the attentions of the 'dissolute prince'.

Showered with honours and the blessings of well-wishers seeking their own ends, Vasili had, almost unnoticed, become a fully-fledged alcoholic. One can well imagine the torments suffered by his wives – all four of them – at the hands of this man in steady decline. He was not an especially interesting person, but he was fine proof that the abuser of power corrupts everyone he touches, including his own children. The Caesars, having reached the acme of their power, often left behind them children flawed in body and soul, morally dead while the dictator was still living and revelling in his own immorality.

After the reports of his compromising behaviour had been submitted, Vasili was removed from his post as commander of aviation of the Moscow military district and went rapidly downhill. Only twenty-one days after his father's death, and aged only thirty-six, Lieutenant General V. I. Stalin was discharged from the army and deprived of the right to wear military uniform by Ministry of Defence Order No. 10726. Everyone had despaired of him, and the former pilot ended his life still young, destroyed by alcohol.

A. N. Shelepin, my main source of information about Vasili, told me that Vasili was arrested after his father's death. Some of his former sins, such as abuse of power and so on, were dug up. Vasili's daughter, Nadezhda, insists that there was no trial or investigation, but her father nevertheless was sentenced to eight years. They wanted to keep him out of sight, as he was going around telling everyone that his father had been poisoned. Shelepin continued:

Khrushchev asked me to go to Lefortovo prison where Vasili had been brought from prison in Vladimir. The prisoner was making something on a lathe – 'labour education', they called it. When they brought him to me he threw himself to his knees and sobbed, 'Forgive me, forgive me, I won't let you down again.' I told Khrushchev about the visit. He was silent, and then he said, 'Bring him to me.'

Next day they took Vasili to Khrushchev. Again he fell to his knees and begged and implored and wept. Khrushchev took him in his arms and was in tears himself, and they talked for a long time about Stalin. After that, it was decided to release Vasili immediately. The resolution was prepared and he was let out. The permit insisted that he take his official name Vasiliev.

This was the name Stalin himself had used to sign a number of orders during the war. Shelepin went on:

For all his spinelessness, Vasili resolutely refused to do this. He went home, where he told his daughter he was thinking of becoming the manager of a swimming pool. But his friends soon brought him back to his old ways. A month after his release from prison, and in a drunken condition while driving his car, he was involved in an accident. Cursing him to high heaven, Khrushchev asked, 'What shall we do? If we put him back inside he'll perish, and he'll perish if we don't.'

It was decided that he should be sent away. Kazan was the chosen place, and Vasili went into 'exile' with his current wife. There, in their one-room flat, he had the leisure to look back on his short, hectic life. There also he heard the news that on 31 October 1961 his father's body had been removed from the [Lenin] Mausoleum. Prison, illness, vodka and the heartlessness of his former 'friends' had turned him into a complete invalid.

Vasili's life was an illustration in miniature of the moral sterility of Stalinism. He died on 19 March 1962. On the gravestone it was not Stalin, the name that he had borne all his life, that was engraved, nor the Vasiliev that he had refused to have foisted on him, but Dzhugashvili. He left seven children, four of his own and three adopted.

The dictator, who could order a new canal to be cut in rapid time, or a palace to be built, or who could banish millions to the barbed wire of the camps, had been utterly useless as a father. And it was he who was chiefly responsible for his younger son's unhappy life. No doubt the same charge will be levelled against him by historians when they look at Svetlana's fate. Apparently, while she was still a schoolgirl, Stalin loved her more than he loved his sons. Hard as it is to imagine it, he often wrote her warm notes. For instance:

My little housekeeper, Setanka, greetings!

I have received all your letters. Thank you for the letters! I haven't replied because I'm very busy. How are you passing the time, how's your English, are you well? I'm well and cheerful, as always. It's lonely without you, but what can I do except wait. I kiss my little housekeeper.

The war separated father and daughter, apparently forever. Intimacy and family warmth had gone. Svetlana was growing up and, like all girls of her age, she had her first boyfriend. Alexander Yakovlevich Kapler was a journalist and film director (and a Jew). He was arrested and given five years, and then another five. From camp he wrote to Stalin:

Dear Iosif Vissarionovich,

I was sentenced by a special commission for anti-Soviet utterances. I did not admit this, nor do I now. I have been awarded the Order of Lenin and have earned the Order of Stalin First Class. I was involved in making the films

She Defends the Motherland, Kotovsky and *A Day of War*. I admit only to immodesty. Let me go to the front, I beg of you.

27 January 1944. A. Kapler.

Stalin asked Beria for a report on Kapler and was told: 'Kapler has a sister in France. He has met the American correspondents, Shapiro and Parker. He does not admit his guilt but was unmasked by agency reports. 16 March 1944.'[57] It is not hard to imagine which of these two documents Stalin chose to believe.

Svetlana's first two marriages were unsuccessful, as was her third, when she chose to marry a foreigner. He died in Moscow and when in 1966 she took his body back to India for burial she decided to remain abroad. She was not happy there, either, and returned in 1984 to the USSR, where, again, she could not settle happily, and once again left for the West.

Perhaps Stalin's children would have grown up differently had their mother not died when she did. The evidence suggests that here, too, Stalin was the indirect (or possibly not so indirect) cause of her death. On the night of 8 November 1932 she apparently killed herself. The cause of this tragic act appears to have been a quarrel, hardly noticed by those in the vicinity, which took place during a small celebration. Those present included Molotov and Voroshilov and their wives, and a number of others in the General Secretary's circle. Nadezhda apparently could not take another of Stalin's rude jibes. She went to her room and shot herself. She was found dead next morning when the housekeeper, Karolina Vasilievna Til, came to wake her. A Walther pistol was lying on the floor. Stalin, Molotov and Voroshilov were summoned. There are grounds for thinking that she left a suicide note, but, like many secrets, great and small, it remains unrevealed.

When he heard what had happened, Stalin was shattered. But even here he remained true to his immoral credo: he did not feel at all responsible for his wife's act, but saw it as treachery to himself. The thought seems never to have entered his head that it was his callousness and lack of warmth and attention that had hurt her so profoundly that in a moment of deep psychological disturbance and depression she took this extreme step. He did not attend the civil funeral ceremony, and it was not long before his cronies were trying to arrange another marriage for him with one of their relations. Everything appeared tó be settled, but for reasons known only to Stalin the marriage did not take place. To the end of his days, he would live alone, entrusting his domestic needs to a housekeeper, Valentina Vasilievna Istomina, who took it upon herself to care for him permanently, accompanying him when he took his vacations in the Crimea. When he died, she fell on his breast in the presence of the Politburo, and gave full voice to her grief. He had evidently been closer to her than he was to his comrades-in-arms.

At the very end of his life, Stalin started to show signs of respect for the memory of his wife. Her photograph began appearing in the dining room and study at the dacha, as well as in the Kremlin apartment. Perhaps, like many people, he was taking stock as the end approached. Or was his conscience pricking him in his declining years?

There can be little doubt that Nadezhda had loved Stalin and that she had tried her best to help him in his work. Her family say that during the last years of her life she was in a deep depression. Perhaps Stalin loved her in his own way, but, obsessed as he was by the cause, by his plans, his work and the ecstasy of power, he had no place in his heart for a wife and children and relatives. He had steel strings where there should have been feelings. He could go for weeks without seeing any of his family, though he would want to know how they were. He had grandchildren he had never seen, nor tried to see. Vasili's children by his first wife, Nadezhda and Alexander, for instance, endured many a painful moment because they were ignored by the man of whom it was proclaimed, 'Stalin is thinking of us.'

When the arrest took place of Alexander Semenovich Svanidze, his first wife's brother with whom Stalin was on close terms, it seems not to have occurred to Stalin to wonder how a man he had known all his life, literally since childhood, could turn out to be an 'enemy'. The entire edifice of his morality was shot through with gaping holes. It was impossible to find and touch in him any chords of human feeling. His only concern over the tragedy of his eldest son was that it should not compromise his name. His second son was simply a burden. He had no means other than abuse to try to prevent Vasili from going into a decline. His daughter became utterly distant and alien to him after her two failed marriages. He was indifferent to his grandchildren, and as for his mother, she was hardly spoiled by his attention.

Perhaps these pages in Stalin's political portrait are not the most important, and it is significant that he himself was dismissive of morals and 'moralizing'. For him, politics always took first place, before morality. But in researching the personality of this singularly complex figure, it is precisely here that one of the secrets of his character is revealed. His contempt for normal human values had long been evident. He despised pity, sympathy, mercy. He valued only strong features. His spiritual miserliness, which grew into exceptional harshness and later into pitilessness, cost his wife her life and ruined his children's lives.

Even worse, Stalin found no place for moral values in politics, either. The 'unmasking' of a colleague as 'an enemy of the people' was the most noble behaviour in his eyes. When with Stalin's permission Beria arrested Bronislava Solomonovna, the wife of his closest assistant, Poskrebyshev, the pleas the wretched husband made to his boss to have her freed were, according to her daughter, Galina, invariably met with: 'It doesn't depend on me. I can do nothing. Only the NKVD can sort it out.' The poor woman was charged with the usual ludicrous accusation of espionage. The mother of two children, she was held in prison for three years and then shot. Yet her husband and the father of her children was working twelve or fourteen hours a day at Stalin's side, bringing him papers, preparing enquiries, calling people in, passing on his boss's orders. 'And Beria, who had ordered her arrest,' Galina told me, 'was still visiting us at home. Just as we were visited by other well known people, such as Shaposhnikov, Rokossovsky, Kuznetsov, Khrushchev, Meretskov. Stalin knew my mother personally, and of course he knew that the charge of espionage was groundless. My mother's brother had been travelling abroad to buy medical equipment, which was the basis of the charge, and he too was shot, of course.'

It must be that by arresting the nearest and dearest of the men who worked closest to him, Stalin was testing their loyalty and their devotion. None of them – Kalinin, Molotov, Kaganovich, Poskrebyshev – gave the slightest outward sign that their family life had been shattered by catastrophe. Such submissiveness must have given Stalin considerable satisfaction as he watched them go about their business. Utterly devoid of decent traits, Stalin's monstrous immorality and the cruelty of his actions belong in the realm of the horror film. Incredibly, Poskrebyshev believed him when he said 'It doesn't depend on me.' And no doubt Beria said the same thing when he was visiting Poskrebyshev at home. These people lived in a world of lies, cynicism, cruelty.

We have somehow become used to thinking that humanism and the universal norms of decent behaviour are the province of petty bourgeois moralizing. But morality appeared long before political, legal or even religious awareness. It arose as soon as people began to live together in groups, and without it man would never have become man. 'Before a man can feel like a man, someone has to call to him,' Brecht once remarked. Stalin was a strong personality of the type that strives only for greatness and unlimited power. But a 'reign of terror', as Berdyaev wrote, 'is not only physical action, with arrests, torture, punishment – it is above all mental action'.[58] Stalinist practice gradually deified violence without regard for its moral basis. For Stalin the moral parameters of the revolution and the building of a new world were nothing more than bourgeois moralizing. Nor did he have the least doubts about his own moral rightness. In a book by the nineteenth-century Russian anarchist Bakunin, he underlined the phrase: 'Don't waste time on doubting yourself, because that is the biggest waste of time ever invented by man.' Perhaps Bakunin could allow himself such thoughts, but then he was not the General Secretary of a great party.

4

DICTATORSHIP OR DICTATOR?

'Oh, evil flattery, how sweet the hunt!
The catch is abundant with your snares.'
– Euripides

CHAPTER 17

The Fate of the Peasantry

On 21 December 1929 Stalin turned fifty. The endless glorification, the kneeling at the altar by the multitude of bootlickers, worshipping him as the giver of every blessing, had yet to begin. The thousand-page folios of hallelujahs and tens of thousands of greetings and the leading articles beginning and ending with the utterance of his name, were yet to come.

But already a good half of the 'jubilee' issue of *Pravda* was devoted to Stalin. There was Kaganovich's piece entitled 'Stalin and the Party', Ordzhonikidze on 'The Rock-Hard Bolshevik', Kuibyshev's 'Stalin and the Industrialization of the Country', Voroshilov on 'Stalin and the Red Army', Kalinin's 'The Helmsman of Bolshevism', Mikoyan punning on 'The Steel Soldier of the Bolshevik Party' and so on. The foundations of glorification had been laid. The Central Committee and Central Control Commission sent greetings to the 'best Leninist'. The paper's headlines proclaimed Stalin as 'the true continuer of the cause of Marx and Lenin', 'the organizer and leader of socialist industrialization and collectivization', 'the leader of the party of the proletariat', and so on. The celebrations could not have been better timed to fix public attention on the man who had dealt so decisively with the latest opposition or, as it was by then being called, 'deviation'. Stalin's popularity began to rise rapidly. It was already evident to those with eyes to see that by his fiftieth birthday he had greater confidence and authority.

Molotov and Kaganovich wanted the celebrations to be more elaborate. Stalin was held back not by modesty, but by the memory of Lenin's fiftieth birthday in 1920. More than once he found himself remembering Lenin's words about him, especially when he had to make a choice between fundamentals. One can only make a real choice when one has the ability to put oneself in the position of those who depend on the choice. Stalin did not have that ability, but he did have the capacity to exercise restraint, especially at the beginning of his ascent. The memory of Lenin's fiftieth birthday made him uncomfortable. It had been marked by the Moscow party committee, although Lenin himself was not there. He had wanted to say something unusual and unexpected and of all things he settled on Lenin's ability to admit his mistakes, some of which Stalin chose to enumerate, concluding with: 'Sometimes Comrade Lenin admitted his errors on matters of enormous importance. We were particularly captivated by this simplicity. That's all I want to say, comrades.' By their lukewarm applause the comrades showed what they thought of this most uncelebratory five-minute speech.

Why had Stalin chosen to mark the occasion by pointing out Lenin's mistakes? He could no longer think of a reason. Had he wanted to show that he was no one's puppet, or had he wanted to stand out? Whatever the truth, the memory of that evening made him squirm. When the deputy head of the Central Party Archives, V. Adoratsky, requested his permission to include the speech in an anthology to be called *On Lenin*, Stalin refused. He wrote on Adoratsky's memorandum: 'The speech was noted down *essentially* correctly, although it needs editing. But I'd rather you didn't print it: it's not nice to talk about Ilyich's mistakes.'[1]

The feeling of awkwardness soon faded. By early 1925 he had agreed to Molotov's proposal to perpetuate his name by printing his collected works, including the embarrassing speech. Following this, Kalinin and Yenukidze, President and Secretary of the All-Russian Central Executive Committee respectively, signed an order declaring that the town of Tsaritsyn be renamed Stalingrad; the province of Tsaritsyn be renamed Stalingrad province; the district of Tsaritsyn, Stalingrad district, Tsaritsyn *volost*, Stalingrad *volost*; and the railway station of Tsaritsyn, Stalingrad station.[2]

It was 10 April 1925, barely a year since Lenin had died. Stalin had failed one of his first trials of conscience. Not that he suffered the slightest pangs about giving his 'humble' agreement to the wave of renaming that had begun. In 1927 the newspapers carried 'greetings to the Stalingrad paper *Borba*', signed by him, and this would become the norm. The factories, parks, newspapers, ships and palaces of culture bearing his name would embody his claim to eternity.

Almost all of us Russians have our roots in the peasantry. When sunny childhood memories come to mind, you feel yourself back in the village, with the smell of melting snow, the robins perched on the fence, the ice darkening on the stream, the thin, rust-brown line of the Sayan mountains to the south, the squeak of sleigh-runners along the village street. And the faces of those long departed.

We rarely know who our ancestors were. Who can even remember the names of their great-grandparents? They have vanished into the dim and distant past. If you could reassemble all your past relatives around a long family table, the smoke-dimmed icons on the wall would be gazing down at peasants. Bearded peasants in calico shirts, their hands calloused by endless toil, the kind and gentle eyes of their wives, already old at forty, who had often given birth at the side of a field; and many flaxen-haired infants, at least half of whom would not live beyond childhood. There would inevitably be one or two old campaigners from the Turkish, Japanese or German wars, their St George Medal proudly displayed. These illiterate folk would be guided in their lives by the morals of the village, that is, Russian Orthodoxy, as well as by work, the family and the idea of the Motherland. One member of the group might be able to read and maybe subscribed to the illustrated magazine *Niva*. All we have left of these *muzhiks*, these peasants, is our memories. Yet at the beginning of the 1930s the overwhelming majority of our countrymen inhabited that peasant world. And it was in that world that the real revolution, or more properly, something like a holocaust sanctioned from above, took place.

The first fierce clashes, it is true, occurred in 1917, when the lands that belonged to the gentry, the crown and the monasteries were seized. By the middle of 1918 Committees of the Poor turned their attention to the better-off peasants, the so-called kulaks, and expropriated half their land. Farm machinery and livestock were distributed to the middle-ranking and poor peasants, and the kulaks dwindled in number. The agrarian sector came to be composed of middle-ranking peasants. The New Economic Policy gave the peasants the opportunity to trade after payment of a fixed tax in kind. At the end of 1923, while Lenin was still alive, Soviet agriculture exported just over two million tons of wheat. While the idea of importing grain would have seemed ludicrous, to export it appeared perfectly normal.

Although the production of cereals greatly improved during the period of reconstruction, it was chiefly the supply of grain for domestic consumption that increased, while that for state commercial use lagged, and overall output had a long way to go before reaching pre-war levels. Low prices paid to the peasants and the lack of manufactured goods for sale to the village perpetuated this situation. The creation of producers' cooperatives was only in its first stages. The NEP provided security for the middle-ranking and poor peasants, and naturally also enhanced the position of the kulaks. It should perhaps be pointed out that socialist ideals are not necessarily synonymous with poverty and the rejection of wealth. Marxism condemns only the wealth that is accumulated at the cost of another's labour. The kulaks created most of their wealth by the sweat of their own brows.

Lenin had foreseen that the countryside would present the greatest obstacle to socialist change, but he had faith in propaganda, electricity, tractors and books. He said that in order to secure the peasant's broad participation in cooperatives through NEP 'we need an entire historical epoch. We might reach a happy end of this epoch in a decade or two.'[3] In one of his last writings, he made a significant judgement: 'We can now say that for us the simple growth of the cooperatives is the equivalent ... of the growth of socialism ... In conditions of full cooperativism we would be standing with both feet on socialist soil.'[4] Lenin's plan for the cooperatives was not, unfortunately, at all detailed, especially concerning its practical application.

The lowering of the tax in kind left more of the agricultural surplus, especially grain, in the hands of the middle and better-off peasants, and their purchasing power grew correspondingly. There was, however, a goods famine in the country as a whole and it was therefore natural that the peasants would not be eager to sell their grain when there was little to buy with the proceeds. What they needed was not paper money, but machinery and other industrial goods, all of which were highly priced. Food supplies to the towns therefore began to dry up and by 1927 a grain crisis was looming. The kulaks and middle peasants were holding on to their grain until prices rose and more goods appeared.

The opposition attempted to exploit the difficulties that had arisen between the state and the peasants. For instance, at the Fifteenth Party Congress, Kamenev accused the leadership of underestimating the capitalist element in the countryside, in effect calling for stronger measures against the kulaks. Oppositionists had earlier called on the government to use force to collect the balance of the anticipated 2.5–3 million tons of grain. The Politburo, debating the report that Stalin would make to the Party Congress, had the good sense to reject the proposal. Stalin told the congress:

Those comrades who think you can get rid of the kulaks by administrative means, using the GPU, are wrong. They think you just issue an order, rubber-stamp it and finish. It may be an easy method, but it is far from effective. The kulaks can only be defeated by economic means. And on the basis of Soviet legality. And Soviet legality is not an empty phrase.[5]

But Stalin's manifestly sensible words and his practice were worlds apart. He simply had no knowledge of the agrarian question. Throughout his life he visited an agricultural region only once, and that was in 1928, when he went to Siberia to see to grain deliveries. He never set foot in a village again.

The Fifteenth Congress adopted the policy of collectivizing agriculture and introduced sensible measures to overcome the difficulties the country was experiencing with grain supplies. A. I. Mikoyan, for instance, pointed out that consumer goods had piled up in the cities and never reached the countryside where the demand for them was enormous:

In order to make a serious breakthrough in grain deliveries, we need a real revolution. Such a breakthrough would be achieved by shipping goods to the village from the town, even at the temporary cost of stripping the town markets (for a few months), in order to get the grain out of the peasants. If we don't carry out this revolution, we will face extraordinary difficulties that will be felt throughout our entire economy.[6]

Thus, in order to strengthen the union of the peasantry and working class, the solution to the pressing problems of the village might be found in economic, as well as political means. That had indeed been the basis of Lenin's cooperative plan. It was precisely a system of 'civilized cooperators', he said, that would allow the maximum unity of personal and social interests. The important thing was not to resort only to command methods, with coercion and directives, but rather to observe the economic laws and to apply economic levers effectively. That, however, was not the easiest option to adopt in conditions of rapid social change.

The congress report on the party's work in the village, given by Molotov, who was the Central Committee secretary responsible for rural affairs, was on the whole sensible. In particular, it stressed that 'the progress of the private economy along the socialist path is a slow process, and a long process. It will take quite a few years to move from the individual to a social (collective) economy.' He pointed out that coercion was inadmissible:

Whoever now tells us to apply a policy of ... compulsory extraction of two to four million tons of grain, even if we only take it from 10 per cent of the peasants (that is, not only from the kulaks but also from some of the middle peasants), then that person is an enemy of the workers and peasants, an enemy of the union of workers and peasants, however well intentioned his proposal.

At this, Stalin called out 'Correct!', and went on uttering similar encouraging exclamations as Molotov made his speech.[7]

It seemed the congress had embarked on a path of broad economic cooperative methods, observing the voluntary principle. The resolution it adopted declared openly that experience showed 'the entire correctness of Lenin's cooperative plan, according to which socialist industry would carry the peasant economy of smallholders along the path to socialism precisely by way of the cooperatives'.[8] The congress moreover explicitly condemned efforts to impose command methods in the peasant question. Despite this, soon after the congress Stalin began speaking of the need to 'ratchet up the tempo' of industrialization and collectivization. He very much admired an article by the future Academician S. G. Strumilin, who formulated the credo of the 'directive' economy, which stated that the task was not to study the economy, but to change it; the party was not tied by any laws, nor were there any fortresses the Bolsheviks were not capable of storming; it is human beings who determine the tempo.[9] Stalin frequently quoted and adapted these phrases in his own speeches and articles, as better than any others they reflected precisely his own intentions. Stalin now began a rapid change of course towards extreme measures.

At the end of December 1927 and in early 1928, ominous orders over Stalin's signature began to appear in the villages, demanding that pressure on the kulaks be stepped up and that work should start immediately on collectivizing agriculture. It is possible that this decision was taken because of the difficulties in the grain supply, but the attempt to solve the food problem by artificially forcing the process of nationalization was a major departure from Lenin's cooperative plan.

It would seem that the majority of the party were attracted to Stalin's side by the very grandiose nature of his purpose in making a social revolution in the countryside. The militant left-wing tendency was very much alive and well among the mass of Communists. The idea that all the age-old problems could be dealt with in one fell swoop was more appealing than the balanced, calm approach the situation required.

By nature Stalin was a very cautious person, yet he took the plunge into total collectivization of millions of peasant holdings, knowing that the half-literate peasant masses were not ready for it. His utopian, dogmatic view of the peasant problem was expressed in his intention to turn the agrarian producer into little more than a mindless cog in the agrarian machine. To achieve this, the peasant must be detached from the means of producing and distributing food. In effect Stalin set about changing the social status of the peasant from that of a free producer into that of a worker without rights. And to do this, he made extreme measures a way of life. The Central Committee plenum of July 1928 supported Stalin. The party agreed to incorporate the use of force into the system.

Command-economic methods replaced economic laws and gradually brought about the demise of the NEP, along with the peasant's material interest, his enterprise and his commitment to work. Some of the disgraced left-wingers, who had been associated with Trotsky, were also in favour of 'decisive measures' in the countryside, and supported Stalin. Repentant declarations were submitted by Pyatakov, Krestinsky, Antonov-Ovseyenko, Radek, Preobrazhensky and others and they were readmitted to the party. Pyatakov became the head of the State Bank and later deputy Commissar for Heavy Industry.

The first Five-Year Plan envisaged that 85 per cent of peasant holdings would become cooperatives within five years, up to 20 per cent of them as collective farms. But under pressure from above, it was decided in the Ukraine, Northern Caucasus and the Lower and Middle Volga that this process should be accomplished in one year. Stalin brought about the end of the NEP by the use of draconian measures.

In January 1928 he went to Siberia, where in his speeches to local party and economic group meetings he laid special emphasis on the use of force against the kulaks. His trip took on the character of a tour of the garrisons by the commanding officer. On arriving at each stop, Stalin would summon the local party and soviet workers, listen briefly to what they had to say, and then invariably pronounce the same judgement: 'You're working badly! You're idle and you indulge the kulaks. Take care that there aren't some kulak agents among you. We won't tolerate this sort of outrage for long.'

Following this tirade would come the inevitable concrete recommendations:

Take a look at the kulak farms, you'll see their granaries and barns are full of grain, they have to cover the grain with awnings because there's no more room for it inside. The kulak farms have got something like a thousand tons of surplus grain per farm.

I propose that:

a) you demand that the kulaks hand over their surpluses at once at state prices;

b) if they refuse to submit to the law, you should charge them under Article 107 of the RSFSR Criminal Code and confiscate their grain for the state, 25 per cent of it to be redistributed among the poor and less well-off middle peasants.

You must steadfastly unify the least productive individual peasant holdings into collective farms.[10]

The coercive style became widespread and encouraged. The theoretical and political basis of the slogan, flung about by some of the more zealous administrators, 'For a furious pace of collectivization!', was to be found in Stalin's article 'The Year of the Great Breakthrough'. A certain shift in public opinion in favour of cooperatives – though not necessarily of collective farms, which were merely one form of cooperative – was interpreted by Stalin as readiness on the part of the middle peasants to throw in their lot with collective agriculture. New resolute orders and instructions were issued.

A week after his fiftieth birthday, Stalin gave a speech at a conference of Marxist agrarians in which he stated, before the Central Committee had made its dispositions: 'From a policy of *limiting* the exploitative tendencies of the kulaks, we have gone over to a policy of *liquidating* the kulaks as a class.'[11]

The year 1937 is regarded in the public mind as the peak of coercion and terror in Soviet history. It affected a significant part of the intelligentsia and so it is hardly surprising that so much has been written about it. That year has become the epicentre of public attention. At the end of the 1920s and beginning of the 1930s, however, the iron heel crushed a far greater number of people, among them possibly quite a few who were genuine enemies of the régime, but far more who were utterly innocent: middle peasants bundled together with kulaks, simply stubborn peasants and their families. Cooperation between the smallholdings was perhaps necessary to achieve the economic revolution, but was mass coercion? Of course not. The whole procedure ought to have been conducted on a voluntary basis.

To facilitate the process of 'dekulakization', Stalin had a document drawn up outlining the characteristics of a kulak: he has an annual income per head in excess of 300 rubles, but not less than 1500 per family; he engages in trade; he leases out equipment, machines, farm buildings; he has a mill, a churn and so on. And any one of these items would render a peasant a kulak. As we see, the criteria were not social but were based on material possessions, hardly an adequate basis for determining a class in Marxist terms. In effect, the possibility had been created to include in the kulak category the widest range of social elements. The peasantry as a whole suffered a trauma virtually as bad as anything the twentieth century could provide. The most industrious, most capable, enterprising peasants were hardest hit.

By January 1929 a special Central Committee commission had prepared a draft decree 'On the Tempo of Collectivization and Methods for Helping the State in the Construction of Kolkhozy'. The completion dates, proposed by the commission on Stalin's handwritten advice, were reduced by half. For no logical reason, and without considering the pros and cons of the argument, Stalin insisted that it be done faster and faster and faster. Enquiries, reports and leaflets flew around the offices of the provincial and district secretaries. A wave of commissioners descended on the villages. Some promised 'tractors, kerosene, salt, matches, soap, you'll get them all, the quicker you sign up for the kolkhoz!' Others acted more resolutely: 'Whoever doesn't want to enter the kolkhoz is an enemy of the Soviet régime!' Passions were roused, there were rows, shotguns came out, party representatives and local kolkhoz activists were murdered, countless letters were sent to Moscow with complaints and petitions for justice. The objective need for cooperative farming which had begun to materialize in various voluntary forms was now underpinned by a whole system of harsh administrative, political and judicial measures.

Abuse became a standard fact. The word 'dekulakization' entered the language and covered the treatment of more than a million peasant households, not all of them kulaks. According to some calculations, there were not more than about 900,000 kulak farms in existence at the beginning of collectivization, a mere 3 per cent of all peasant households. Many hundreds of thousands of families had their houses, tools, chattels and valuables confiscated, and were transported to remote areas. It seems unlikely that the exact number of people swept up in this whirlwind of lawlessness will ever be known. Apart from economic measures designed to reduce the kulak's influence in the village, the most pitiless means were also employed to bring about his liquidation. According to some figures, more than 150,000 families were exiled to Siberia and the north in 1929, while in 1930 the figure was 240,000, and in 1931 more than 285,000. But the process had already begun in 1928 and it went on after 1931. My own calculations bring me to a figure of 8.5–9 million men, women, old people and children who were affected by dekulakization, most of them torn root and branch from their native habitat. Many were shot for resisting, many died en route. In some places, whether because of unfettered zeal or personal material interest, the process also swept up many middle peasants. I estimate that one way or another something like 6 to 8 per cent of peasant households were sucked into the vortex.

Naturally, hundreds of thousands of kulaks meekly accepted what was happening, and it might be thought that the harsh measures were only applied to those who openly conducted anti-Soviet resistance. In that case, most kulak households could have been brought into the nationalization, or cooperative process, by fiscal means, such as differential taxation and production obligations. This was not done, however, and the refusal to induce the kulak into the process faced him with a bleak choice: he must either fight or await dispossession and exile. It was the haste and pitilessness with which questions affecting millions of people were dealt with that led to the tragedy.

A conversation about the kulaks which Stalin had with Churchill on 14 August 1942 is instructive. The talks had come to an end and Stalin had invited the British leader to dine with him in his Kremlin apartment. Molotov and an interpreter were present during the long conversation. Churchill reproduces the occasion in his memoirs thus:

'Tell me,' [he asked Stalin,] 'have the stresses of this war been as bad to you personally as carrying through the policy of the Collective Farms?'

This subject immediately roused the Marshal.

'Oh, no,' he said, 'the Collective Farm policy was a terrible struggle.'

'I thought you would have found it bad,' said I, 'because you were not dealing with a few score thousands of aristocrats or big landowners, but with millions of small men.'

'Ten millions,' he said, holding up his hands. 'It was fearful. Four years it lasted. It was absolutely necessary for Russia, if we were to avoid periodic famines, to plough the land with tractors. We must mechanise our agriculture. When we gave tractors to the peasants they were all spoiled in a few months. Only Collective Farms with workshops could handle tractors. We took the greatest trouble explaining it to the peasants. It was no use arguing with them. After you have said all you can to a peasant he says he must go home and consult his wife, and he must consult his herder.' This last was a new expression to me in this connection. 'After he has talked it over with them he always answers that he does not want the Collective Farm and would rather do without the tractors.'

'These were what you call kulaks?'

'Yes,' he said, but he did not repeat the word. After a pause, 'It was all very bad and difficult – but necessary.'

'What happened?'

'Oh, well,' he said, 'many of them agreed to come in with us. Some of them were given land of their own to cultivate in the province of Tomsk or the province of Irkutsk or farther north, but the great bulk were very unpopular and were wiped out by their labourers.'[12]

The figure of ten million fell easily into general circulation, and while my figures are slightly less, they in no way diminish the scale of the human tragedy. It was the first mass terror applied by Stalin in his own country. The years of collectivization were the crucial turning point both for the peasantry and the country as a whole. The possibility of pursuing voluntary cooperatives and development along the market lines of the New Economic Policy was missed. Extreme coercion became the determining factor in shaping the system.

Meanwhile the collectivization went on. Stalin received tens of thousands of letters of complaint, agony, puzzlement, fear and hatred, but the criminal machinery continued to grind men's lives into the dust. It was not until 2 March 1930 that Stalin, who could not but have been aware of the scale of the protest and resistance from the peasants, published his well known article in *Pravda* entitled 'Dizzy with Success'. The second paragraph reads today like a hymn to coercion: 'It is a fact that by 20 February this year already 50 per cent of peasant households in the USSR were collectivized. This means that by 20 February 1930 we have over-fulfilled the Five-Year Plan for collectivization more than two-fold.'

It never seemed to occur to him to consider the human story that lay behind these cold statistics. Nor did he produce the figures for those who had been exiled, dispossessed and liquidated. It is often said that such a gigantic operation could not have been executed painlessly, smoothly and without mistakes. The collectivization, after all, affected four fifths of the entire population. But who gave Stalin the right to take away the freedom of choice from the ordinary man and to make the decision for him? Stalin had forgotten his own words of warning: 'The kulak has to be conquered by economic means and on the basis of Soviet legality!' In a word, it had become the norm for Stalin to regard any decision or argument or situation as a fiction, if it did not correspond to his plan of the moment.

Stalin comes to the conclusion in his article – as if a national referendum had taken place on the subject – that working the land by companies or communes would not serve the contemporary needs of socialist change in the village. Only collective farms could do that. For the 'agrarian' Stalin, who would never set foot in a village again, the collective farm was the only acceptable way to organize agricultural production. As Khrushchev was to tell the Twentieth Party Congress in 1956, Stalin henceforth 'studied agriculture only in the cinema'. That was an exaggeration, but it is hard to imagine any other leader trying to deal with every kind of problem without leaving his study. One of his worst features was his inability to admit his mistakes. Even in this article, those guilty of 'excesses', 'dizziness with success' and 'a bureaucratic obsession with decrees' were only to be found in the provinces.

After his 'Dizzy with Success' article, Stalin was again inundated with letters from peasants, and again had to explain the party's position on collectivization. His generalizations wittingly or unwittingly at times had the effect of discrediting the very idea of restructuring agriculture along the path of cooperatives. For instance, he wrote to some collective farmers: 'Some people think the article "Dizzy with Success" represents the result of Stalin's personal initiative. That's nonsense, of course. It was the result of reconnaissance by the Central Committee.' And further: 'It is hard to stop people when they are on a wild stampede towards the abyss, and to head them off on to the proper path in time.'[13]

It is noteworthy that when he touches on social, economic and cultural questions, Stalin employs military terminology, such as 'reconnaissance', 'front', 'offensive', 'retreat', 'regrouping of forces', 'bringing up the rear', 'calling on reserves', 'total annihilation of the enemy'. Lenin had used similar terms when outlining his tactics for party organization, but Stalin was talking about the 'annihilation of the kulaks as a class'. Summarizing his understanding of the essence and method of transforming the village, he told the Marxist agrarians in December 1929 that, in order to turn the small peasant village into a socialist city, we must 'plant large socialist farms in the country-side, both state farms and collective farms'.[14] In effect, these would serve as the teams for liquidating an entire social group within the peasantry without discussion by a plenum of the Central Committee and without proper con-sideration of all the consequences. Ten years later an editorial in *Bolshevik* would say of Stalin's 'agrarian' speech:

The Bolshevik party under Comrade Stalin's leadership provided an amazing model for solving the peasant question ... Complete collectivization on the basis of the liquidation of the kulaks as a class represented a triumph of the Stalin programme for transforming the peasant economy. This militant programme ... was expounded by Comrade Stalin in a document of the greatest theoretical force, his speech to the conference of Marxist agrarians.[15]

As a result of deliberations by a Politburo commission chaired by Molotov, and under pressure from Stalin, in January 1930 the Central Committee passed a resolution 'On Measures for Liquidating Kulak Farms in Areas of Full Collectivization'. This party directive raised tension in the countryside by closing the collective farms to kulaks, whose position now became desperate. The harshest measures were used against them, including total confiscation of their property and deportation of their families to remote areas. Corres-pondingly, kulak assaults on the Soviet régime rose, at times extending over wide areas. Actions against the better-off section of the peasantry gave rise to a wave of protest, banditry and armed risings against the authorities.

Grain production immediately went into a slide, soon followed by a decline in stock breeding. The peasant's native enterprise was cut down at the root. Labour productivity in the kolkhoz fell below the level of individual farms, with inevitably serious consequences. The mass slaughter of animals began in many regions: compared to 1928, livestock fell to half or a third in number by 1933. To prevent the salting of meat, the sale of salt was sharply reduced. The area of sown land fell. Hundreds of thousands of families were torn from their land and made homeless.

Stalin was informed of what was happening in the countryside but was unmoved. Once, when he felt a pang of doubt about his choice of policy, he recalled the words of the old anarchist rebel Bakunin: 'The will is almighty; nothing is impossible for the will.' The higher aim always justified whatever means were necessary to achieve it. He believed the peasants simply did not know what was in store for them. Those who opposed his policy were in his eyes not puzzled peasants, but politicians who were incapable of seeing the advantages of a forced offensive on the village. It mattered not at all to Stalin that the offensive was being mounted against the man in his tattered smock, illiterate, sustained by his traditions and his cares, and tied by the umbilical cord to his own patch of land. For Stalin the peasant was a means to the higher goal, a goal that was superior to everything.

During this time, especially in early 1928 when Stalin visited Siberia (14 January to 6 February), a muffled conflict was going on inside the Politburo. At first cautiously, then with growing persistence, Bukharin, supported by Rykov and Tomsky, was campaigning against Stalin's policy. This was not a 'right' grouping, as they would soon come to be called, but merely a number of leaders whose approach to the peasant problem was more balanced and moderate.

Without naming names and using Aesopian language, Stalin and Bukharin began criticizing each other. For instance, on 28 May 1929, Stalin made a speech at the Institute of Red Professors, where Bukharin enjoyed considerable popularity, having recently been made the only academician among the leadership. It was precisely in this setting that Stalin chose to cast doubt on Bukharin as 'the defender of the kulaks'. His carefully prepared attacks on Bukharin were camouflaged, but no one was in any doubt as to who was in the firing line. Reading from his text, Stalin said:

Some people see a way out of the situation by returning to kulak farming. They are suggesting that the Soviet régime support itself on two opposing classes, the kulak class and the working class.

The collective farm movement is sometimes said to be in opposition to the cooperative movement, as if the collectives are one thing and the cooperatives another. That is not correct, of course. Some even go so far as to suggest that the collective farms contradict Lenin's plan for cooperatives. It goes without saying that such a contradiction bears no relation to the truth.[16]

Better than anyone else, Bukharin understood that Stalin was forcing the process of collectivization because it would make it easier to extract grain. And Stalin proved to be right in this: if agricultural production was included in the command system, it would be simpler to return virtually to the practices of War Communism. As an example of this, in 1928, the year in which collectivization began, the peasants delivered some 15 per cent of their gross grain output, whereas in 1932 the figure was just above 30 per cent. But at what a price! In the Northern Caucasus, the Ukraine, the Volga and other regions, a vast famine-stricken tract was created. Exact figures for the loss of human life are not known, but they cannot have been much less than those who died in the collectivization itself.

The famine was caused not only by a drought that struck the chief agricultural areas, but also by the collectivization which disorganized peasant farming, by the forced extraction of produce and by the unbalanced nature of the national economy in general. The urban population was increasing annually at the rate of 2–2.5 million. Given the low prices paid by the state, the collective farm sector could not possibly feed the whole country. From the moment collectivization began, the peasant lost all trace of material self-interest. The state moreover continued to export grain. Hard currency was required to buy machinery and equipment abroad and Stalin, who was in a hurry, insisted on this, and his orders had to be carried out. In many areas, especially in the Ukraine, the full quotas of grain continued to be collected. Industrialization was achieved not only by the dedicated labour of the workers, but also by the bitter and incalculable sacrifice of the peasants.

Hunger forced people to steal grain, and so Stalin initiated a new law, on 7 August 1932, on the protection of socialist property. Annotating the draft, he wrote on it: 'Anyone attempting [to appropriate] public property should be regarded as an enemy of the people.'[17] Theft of kolkhoz property was punishable by execution or ten years in a concentration camp. Stalin demanded that this law be carried out unconditionally. By the beginning of 1933 more than 50,000 people, many of them starving, had been sentenced.

On Stalin's instructions nothing could be written about the famine which had spread through a population of 25–30 million people. The Ukraine and Volga region suffered particularly. Despite severe harvest failure, the state's requirements for deliveries of grain and other produce remained the same as before. Moreover, the kolkhozy, which were barely on their feet, received orders to increase their supply of grain, and any shortfall on their part was interpreted as sabotage and as 'undermining the party's policy in the countryside'. As thousands of villages were thrown into confusion, peasants demonstrated passive resistance by, for example, refusing to go to work.

The famine and the lack of rights endured by the collective farms forced them to break the law in various ways, just to provide a minimum for the starving. The situation would be brought to light in the following way. A newspaper would report that 'News is coming in from the Northern Caucasus about self-seeking kulak tendencies being exhibited by some collective and state farms in grain deliveries. In Khuton kolkhoz, despite the fact that the plan has been under-fulfilled to the tune of 1000 centners (10,000 kg), the management took it upon itself to have grain milled for distribution to the kolkhozniks.'

Speaking in February 1933 at the first All-Union congress of 'shock-kolkhozniks' – that is, collective farm workers who had broken production records – Stalin made no mention of the famine, still less of the need to help the starving, only commenting vaguely on 'difficulties and shortages' in the countryside. He outlined the kolkhozniks' task in stark clarity:

We demand only one thing from you, and that is to labour honestly, divide the collective farm's income according to the work done, take care of the tractors and machinery, ensure that the horses are properly looked after, carry out the tasks of your workers' and peasants' state, strengthen the kolkhoz and chuck out any kulaks and their henchmen who have managed to worm their way in.[18]

It was Stalin's way to impose socialism in the village using the might of the state. Certainly grain was needed in order to purchase industrial equipment abroad, to improve supplies to the rapidly growing towns and to create state reserves, but such extreme measures were not required. Command methods now replaced economic methods entirely. It was not only the kulak who was eliminated, but the individual farmer altogether, and all by the use of force. Reporting to the Central Committee in 1934, Stalin was quite unequivocal: 'We must create a situation in which the individual, meaning the private farmer, will have a harder time and have less opportunities than the kolkhoznik. We must give taxes another turn of the screw.'[19]

The pressure was increased not only on the individual farmer, but on the collective farms also, turning them into an element with no rights, rather than masters of their own land. A new kind of peasant was created, one who was alienated from the land and from the fruits of his labour. People were losing the right to look after themselves. In time the perplexity and confusion would give way to apathy, as Bukharin had feared.

In the speech to the Institute of Red Professors, distorting Bukharin's position beyond recognition and calling him 'the defender of the kulaks' who did not understand Lenin's plan for the cooperatives, Stalin was making public his disagreement for the first time. For his part, Bukharin, also without naming names, was attacking the use of command methods in the economy. As chief theoretician in the Politburo, he repeatedly made the point that, without a flourishing rural economy, a successful industrialization programme was impossible. Pressure, forced requisitioning and coercion in the kolkhoz were inadmissible. The outcome of this clash of views was still unclear in early 1928. At first, Stalin's only obvious allies were Molotov and Voroshilov, while Bukharin had the support of Rykov and Tomsky. A third element, consisting of Kuibyshev, Kalinin, Mikoyan and Rudzutak, vacillated and tried to reconcile the two main protagonists. The outcome of the struggle virtually depended on this 'centrist' group. As usual, however, it was Stalin who proved the more skilled and sophisticated in behind-the-scenes manoeuvrings, and as a result the Central Committee and Central Control Commission plenums of April, July and November adopted a tough attitude towards the alternative proposed by Bukharin on the peasant question.

Stalin could not but know that his coercive policy of nationalizing agriculture would lead virtually to a restoration of the principles of War Communism. Instead of a fixed tax on the sale of grain, compulsory deliveries were imposed. And this was to remain the system for decades.

Bukharin by contrast proposed an evolutionary approach to change in the countryside, in the course of which cooperatives, or the socialized sector, would gradually ease out the individual farmer by economic means and by example. Bukharin was not right about everything, especially in determining the long-term outlook both for the changes themselves and the rate of change, envisaging as he did that the process would take many years. The country would not be given so much time. Nevertheless, Bukharin's struggle against the use of coercion against millions of peasants, who were citizens of the Soviet state, was justified on both moral and political grounds.

To repeat: the restructuring of the agrarian economy could have been accomplished entirely without recourse to the terror and the tragedy that, both in scale and consequence, exceeded the repressions of 1937–38. It goes without saying that in both cases the use of force was criminal. The successful 'liquidation of the kulaks as a class' inflated Stalin's confidence in himself as a dictator and he did not hesitate to liquidate all those who either had or might still come out against him.

Stalin's forced 'agrarian revolution' condemned Soviet agriculture to decades of stagnation. The bloody experiment costing millions of lives brought the country no relief. Although nobody could ever say it, the practices of War Communism had been brought back to the village. At endless meetings, Stalin painted a triumphant picture of agriculture. In fact, free trade quickly dried up, as the kolkhozy had no surplus grain to sell. Yet Stalin continued to seek ways of imposing still harsher methods of governing the villages, now cowed into a stunned silence. Endless conferences took place and countless resolutions were passed with the expressed aim of achieving a fundamental improvement in agriculture, and yet the situation only grew worse. Everything conspired to distance the kolkhoznik further from the land, the means of production and distribution and administration. Fear and apathy descended on the village. The kolkhozy lived by commands, no one remembered that they were supposed to be based on the principle of cooperation. The first victim of Stalinism was the peasant.

Thus died the New Economic Policy and with it the moderate line in the Politburo, and thus began the withering away of collective leadership in the party. Stalin's blatant desire to decide every question himself came to prevail.

The enormous appeal of socialism, generated by the October Revolution, began to fade. To this day, the opponents of socialism point to our peasant affairs when they wish to touch us on one of our sorest spots. There's no denying that Stalin supplied ample ammunition and weighty arguments to discredit the once so attractive idea. By taking the unprecedented decision to use force against his own people, Stalin cut the veins of a vast social group that had greatly benefited from the revolution and could have made good use of that benefit.

A new chapter opens in Stalin's biography from the end of 1928. Not only are all his rivals removed from the leadership, but there also began the phase we have become accustomed to call the 'cult of personality'. The removal of Bukharin was an important milestone in this process.

CHAPTER 18

The Drama of Bukharin

No political portrait of Stalin could be complete without some light being thrown also on his entourage, his comrades-in-arms, the unquestioning compromisers, the yes-men and the opponents. Another side of Stalin's character is revealed in the drama of Bukharin which was played out in the 1920s, with the last act of the tragedy coming in the 1930s.

Stalin and Bukharin had been on close terms for a long time, and it seemed it would remain that way for ever. From 1927, at Stalin's insistence Bukharin lived in the Kremlin, and after the death of Stalin's wife they even exchanged apartments, because, Stalin explained, he wished to escape the constant reminder of that fateful night. Nikolai Ivanovich Bukharin, being a sensitive person, cherished his feelings of friendship, decency and sincerity in their relationship. They always addressed each in the familiar 'ty' form. Stalin always called Bukharin 'Nikolai' and Bukharin always addressed the General Secretary by his old revolutionary nickname 'Koba'. In the period 1924 to 1928 Stalin listened attentively to Bukharin's views, frequently asserting in public 'that Lenin rated his theoretical mind highly' and that the party treasured his native abilities. Bukharin regarded this friendship as something of spiritual value, even sacred, and he could not have dismissed it as easily as Stalin did in April 1929 at the Central Committee and Central Control Commission plenum.

Stalin opened his speech at this meeting by referring precisely to his friendship with Bukharin:

Comrades, I will not dwell on personal matters, even though the personal element played quite an impressive part in the speeches of some of Bukharin's group. I will not do this because the personal element is trivial and it is not worth dwelling on trivialities. Bukharin spoke of our personal correspondence. He read several letters from which it was plain that yesterday we were personal friends, and now we are parting company politically. I don't think all these complaints and wailings are worth a brass farthing. We are not a family circle or a côterie of personal friends; we are the political party of the working class.[20]

By virtually paraphrasing Marx's remarks about Danton, Stalin was trying to convince the Politburo and the Central Committee that, even though Bukharin was on the peak of the mountain, he was to a great extent the leader of the Swamp, that is, the waverers. It seemed reasonable to assert that the interests of the cause were above personal relations, but describing their friendship as not being worth a brass farthing was a repulsive thing to do. The naive idealist Bukharin had been given a lesson in Machiavellianism: his friendship and his opinions were for Stalin nothing but a triviality. But this had not always been the case.

A. P. Balashov, who had worked in Stalin's secretariat, told me that when Stalin was handed Politburo voting papers he would often ask, without even raising his head, 'Is Bukharin in favour?' According to Balashov, Stalin took Bukharin's opinion very much into account when he had to make up his mind on a specific issue.

What sort of man was Bukharin? Why, of all of Lenin's comrades-in-arms who were still in leadership posts after his death, was it Bukharin who inspires warm memories tinged with sorrow? Why did Lenin call him the 'party's favourite', and why did Stalin destroy this outstanding figure?

Born in Moscow in 1888, the son of a school teacher, Nikolai Bukharin, like the majority of Bolshevik leaders, was not of proletarian origin. And like them, he was proof that to be a leader one needed to possess some of the accoutrements of world culture. In the main it was only those from the better-off classes who could acquire, develop and apply such qualities in social practice.

As a student in the economics department of the Law Faculty of Moscow University, he engaged in propaganda among workers and students, becoming a member of the Bolshevik Party in 1906. Slightly built and nimble, with a small beard and red hair above a high forehead, he would as often be seen in the industrial quarter across the river as at student meetings. Arrested in 1910, he escaped from Onega, in the province of Archangel, and remained abroad until after the February Revolution.

The six years he spent abroad were an extremely fruitful time for Bukharin. There he met Lenin, who would always regard him not merely with warmth but with great affection, despite the fierce arguments that took place between them. The scholarly Bukharin spent most of his time in libraries, quickly mastering German, French and English. It was while abroad that he wrote his two major works, *The Economic Theory of the Leisure Class* and *Imperialism and World Economy*.

In New York during the First World War, Bukharin got to know Trotsky with whom, despite many theoretical and political differences, he had warm personal relations for almost ten years. It was in New York that news of the February Revolution reached him. The way home was long: arrested in Japan, he was then placed under guard in Vladivostok for engaging in agitation among the soldiers there, and it was May 1917 before he reached Moscow. He soon became editor of *Pravda*, a post he retained for almost twelve years with one brief interval. As editor of the party's main newspaper, he took an active part in deciding party policy and propaganda.

Bukharin was not good at intrigue, dissembling or 'being diplomatic'. For instance, in 1918, during the dramatic weeks when the new state was negotiating the Brest-Litovsk peace with Germany, he became the virtual leader of the opposition to Lenin. For two months he headed various groups of 'leftists' who were against the treaty and in favour of launching a revolutionary war.

His Left Communist sentiments were not a passing fancy. During the civil war he was the personification of a radical left policy, and it was indeed he who was one of the chief proponents of the policy of War Communism. In his *Economy of the Transitional Period* he wrote that elements of coercion and command in the economy were 'the costs of the revolution'. These 'costs' were in effect a 'revolutionary law'. According to Bukharin, the proletarian revolution first destroys the economy and then rebuilds it at a rapid rate.

His views as a theorist of War Communism were more fully expressed in his *ABC of Communism*, a book which he wrote with the collaboration of E. Preobrazhensky, another capable young theorist. In the 1920s Stalin valued this 'catechism' for Communists very highly. The *ABC* described, in encyclopedic form, the basic propositions about revolution, class war, dictatorship of the proletariat, the rôle of the working class, the Communist programme and so on. It had enormous success and was reissued twenty times and was sold abroad. Thanks to this publication, which set forth the chief problems of the revolutionary movement from a radical, left-wing position, Bukharin became as well known as Trotsky, Zinoviev or Kamenev. His reputation abroad was for many years as the 'high priest of Marxist orthodoxy'.

There were good grounds for this. For instance, in his collection of theoretical articles, *Ataka*, published in 1924, he wrote that the impending world revolution would take over one country after another, that this process will not be hampered by 'all these "leagues of nations" and the other nonsense the social-traitors* are singing in tune with'.[21] Bukharin appeared during the revolution and civil war as a revolutionary radical, a romantic perhaps, willing to go to the most extreme lengths. At that time, however, any supra-state, supra-national or universal ideas were dismissed as bourgeois, and not only by orthodox Marxists.

The rapid change of mind that occurred in Bukharin only a few years later was therefore all the more surprising. He made no secret of the fact that the evolution of his thinking was influenced above all by Lenin's last writings. Bukharin analysed the New Economic Policy in great depth. When Lenin was

---

*Communist jargon for the socialist parties, mostly of the west, organized in the Second International.

ill, Bukharin frequently visited him and they passed long hours in private discussing questions of the theory and practice of socialist construction. Although one can only hazard a guess at the content of these conversations and make certain assumptions, the fact is that from 1922–23 Bukharin became a member of the moderate wing of the leadership.

While Trotsky saw the NEP as the first sign of the 'degeneration of Bolshevism', for Bukharin it was the perfect opportunity for socialism to give the economy and society new possibilities, based on the enterprise potential of the old discarded structures. Speaking at a meeting of the Moscow party organization in April 1925, Bukharin stated:

What we must do now is provide the stimuli for petty bourgeois economic activity that will combine with growing private wealth and ensure that our economy becomes stronger ... The greater the capacity of our factories, the greater our output and hence the more the town will guide the village; the working class will all the more gently and at the same time more firmly be able to guide the peasantry towards socialism.[22]

On one occasion, sometime in early 1925, Stalin and Bukharin had a serious conversation on the economy. It boiled down to Stalin's doubts about the NEP and Bukharin's defence of the policy. Bukharin recalled this conversation in his notes. Stalin repeatedly emphasized the point that a prolonged reliance on the NEP would 'stifle the socialist elements and resurrect capitalism'. He did not understand economic laws and relied instead on 'proletarian pressure', 'party directives', 'the agreed line', 'limiting the potential exploiters' and so on. It was a long conversation and even then Bukharin realized that Stalin neither understood nor trusted the NEP and that, like Trotsky, he saw in it a threat to the gains of the revolution. Dejected by what he had heard, Bukharin decided to set forth his own understanding of the NEP in the press. Using the arguments he had expounded in his speech to the Moscow organization, he published a long article in *Bolshevik*, entitled 'On the New Economic Policy and Our Tasks', two fragments of which read as follows:

The point of the New Economic Policy, which Lenin described as the correct economic policy ... is that a whole series of economic factors, which could not fertilize each other hitherto because they were under the lock and key of War Communism, can now fertilize each other and thus encourage economic growth.

NEP means less pressure, more freedom of exchange because such freedom is no longer a threat to us. It means less administrative reaction and more economic struggle, more development of economic exchange. It means fighting against the private trader not by trampling on him and closing down his shop, but by trying to produce goods ourselves and selling them cheaper, better and of higher quality.[23]

Stalin did not single out this article for comment, although it is peppered with his marginal notes. He could not understand how it was possible to give freedom to the private sector. Surely that would undermine the dictatorship? It was his narrow-mindedness and the primitive nature of his economic thinking that in the end pushed him into choosing the command-bureaucratic method of managing the national economy and into rejecting the great opportunities created by the NEP. He listened to Bukharin and he read him, but somewhere deep down irritation was growing at Bukharin's 'economic capitulation'.

After the death of Lenin, Bukharin was promoted from candidate to full member of the Politburo. His authority was based chiefly on his reputation as a new Marxist theorist, his human feeling and his exceptional accessibility. He was the absolute opposite of Stalin in this respect.

For a long time Bukharin remained on the sidelines in the struggle between the factions. Zinoviev scornfully called him 'the peacemaker', after failing to get Bukharin's support against Stalin. Until 1928, Bukharin was loyal to everyone and tried to remain above the fray. For him the main thing was to map out the main trends of the country's social and economic development and the path of its reconstruction. In this he had to come out decisively against the Preobrazhensky Law, the main point of which was that super-industrialization in a country like Russia could only be achieved by 'squeezing' the maximum of resources from the peasantry. To his credit, Preobrazhensky himself was opposed to the use of force against the peasantry, advocating instead the notion that unequal exchange in market relations between industry and agriculture should be imposed on a broad basis.

It was Bukharin's conviction that 'the city should not rob the village', that only a political alliance, combined with an economic alliance, could help to accelerate the development of the industrial and agricultural economies. In other words, the theorist of the NEP was in favour of harmonious relations between town and village, while admittedly allowing a degree of bias in extracting resources from the village in the early phase. That is to say, although industry must develop faster, the means for transferring resources from the rural sector must be moderate:

Some madmen might suggest that we declare a Bartholomew's Night on the peasant bourgeoisie, and they might try to show that it would correspond to the class line and be entirely possible. The trouble is it would be stupid in the extreme. There is absolutely no need for us to do it. We would gain precisely nothing, and we would lose a great deal. We prefer to allow the peasant bourgeoisie to develop their economy, and to take from it much more than we take from the middle peasant.[24]

It is worth stressing that, while Bukharin envisaged the limitation of the 'bourgeois peasant' in the process of putting the agrarian economy on a cooperative basis, he had in mind economic and not administrative methods. In essence this was the application of Lenin's plan for collectivization without coercion, requisitioning, pressure or threats. In 1928 and more especially 1929 and after, however, Stalin was calling Bukharin's ideas a departure from

Leninism and 'the hostile diversionary plans of the right deviation', an opportunistic heresy of 'elements hostile to socialism'.

Bukharin tried to show that there were no longer any major organized hostile political forces left in the Soviet Union who could pose a serious threat to the socialist state. If force were used against the peasantry, he argued, it would have far-reaching and painful consequences. While all this would be proved true in due course, Bukharin omitted two factors. First, a slow rate of collectivization, taking decades, would put the very existence of socialism in Russia under threat; secondly, industrialization would require huge resources, and the village was the only source. The optimum course would seem to have been somewhere in between.

From 1925 to 1927 Stalin and Bukharin were the most influential figures in the party. And it was Bukharin who in effect helped Stalin in his conflict with Trotsky, Kamenev and Zinoviev, even though he tried at the same time to remain loyal to them. With their departure from the Politburo, Stalin's and Bukharin's influence over current and strategic issues rose noticeably. It had not been long before that Stalin turned angrily on the oppositionists who were attacking Bukharin, with, 'So, you want Bukharin's blood? We won't give you his blood, and you'd better know it!' The imagery, no less than the defence itself, was memorable.

These two leading members of the Politburo in a certain sense complemented each other. Whereas Stalin occupied himself with organizational and political issues, Bukharin was concerned with working out and setting forth the theoretical principles underlying party policy. It would be no exaggeration to say that up to the beginning of 1928 Stalin relied heavily on Bukharin in economic matters and that he followed Bukharin's views. It was of course characteristic of Stalin to borrow the ideas of other leaders and make them his own. Just as he took many of Trotsky's slogans on command methods, so similarly he filled out his understanding of the agrarian problem by borrowing from Bukharin. How then are we to explain the fact that in 1928 he began to turn away from Bukharin? Why should he suddenly begin to label the views he had himself held as a 'right deviation'? Why did their personal friendship so rapidly deteriorate into outright hatred?

There appear to be several reasons. First, Stalin was alarmed by the rise in Bukharin's popularity, in the party and the country at large, as a theorist, political figure and leader with charm. Bukharin's authority in the party at that time was hardly less than Stalin's own. Stalin was put on alert by an article by Bukharin, devoted to Lenin, in which he had written:

Because we have no Lenin, we have no united authority. We can only have *collective* authority at present. We have no one who can say: 'I am without sin and I can interpret Lenin's teaching one hundred per cent correctly.' Everyone tries, but anyone who would claim the one hundred per cent would be giving his own personality too great a rôle.[25]

Stalin took this to be aimed at him. After all, in the lectures he gave on the foundations of Leninism at the Sverdlov University, he spoke as the interpreter of Lenin's entire teaching. And, anyway, what was that about there being no united authority? What about the authority of the General Secretary? Stalin was also troubled by the number of Bukharin's followers, among them Astrov, Slepkov, Maretsky, Tseitlin, Zaitsev, Goldenburg and Petrovsky, who were beginning to emerge in the press, the universities and the party apparatus. Slepkov and Astrov had become editors of *Bolshevik*, Maretsky and Tseitlin worked on *Pravda*, Zaitsev was in the Central Control Commission, and so on. Stalin feared that Bukharin's political and ideological influence was mounting in the party and the country.

Another cause lay in the arbitrary and wilful character of the General Secretary. Collectivization – that is, the real revolution in the countryside carried out by force from above – had begun successfully on the whole, better at any rate than Bukharin had supposed. From all the reports he received, Stalin became convinced that, given the proper degree of pressure, the preliminary expectations could be radically revised upwards. In any event, he believed that the policy would solve the grain crisis quickly.

And yet the crisis deepened. Stalin repeatedly told his immediate circle, 'Without a decisive breakthrough in the countryside, we'll have no bread.' Molotov and Kaganovich eagerly agreed with him. Stalin gradually became convinced that the timetable for restructuring the agrarian economy should be shortened by two to three times. Then, when the pressure evoked the muffled but widespread resistance of the peasants, especially of the kulaks, he suddenly saw, in a flash of 'genius', that the solution was to speed up the 'liquidation of the class' by purely administrative, political methods.

The arguments in the Politburo over this question became sharper. Stalin was supported by Molotov, Kaganovich and Voroshilov, while Bukharin had Rykov and Tomsky on his side. Bukharin's supporters were also in favour of collectivization and the 'offensive against the kulak', but without expropriation and coercion. They believed that in the end economic methods of pressure would be effective. Kalinin, Rudzutak, Mikoyan and Kuibyshev were the waverers. Had they understood the situation better, they might well have supported Bukharin and things might have looked very different. After all, Bukharin himself was not against industrialization and collectivization; he was above all against the use of force to settle these historic tasks. And since it was human lives at stake, this was not a trivial issue. In Bukharin's view, all the transformations must in the end serve mankind and socialism, and not the other way round. The moral conscience of the Politburo members who were deciding the optimum and not necessarily most radical course to adopt, was not, unfortunately, as refined as Bukharin's. And so another opportunity to exercise conscience was missed. Even Trotsky, who was watching the conflict from the sidelines, told his helpers that 'the right could bring down Stalin', bearing in mind that they had among their number the heads of the government, the trade unions, and the intellectual leadership. There seemed to be a chance. The unstable balance did not last long, however, although it seemed for a while as if Bukharin's moderate line would prevail. But by then Stalin was an unsurpassed master at getting his own way.

Rykov, who was Lenin's successor as chairman of the Council of People's Commissars, and Tomsky, the virtually perpetual head of the trade unions, did not regard Stalin as the undisputed leader, but they supported Bukharin out of conviction, not personal considerations. Stalin failed to influence their views. Pyatakov once called Rykov and Tomsky 'convinced Nepists', with some accuracy. The problem was that the struggle against Stalin went on behind closed doors and among a narrow circle. Moreover, the risk Bukharin and his supporters faced of being taken for factionalists was not an abstract one. Bukharin, however convinced he may have been of the disastrous nature of Stalin's policy, found no way to create a broader base of support among those who did not accept coercion, dictatorship and 'extraordinary' measures. He attempted to return to peaceful dialogue with Stalin, but Stalin would only accept him on terms of complete surrender. The disgraced leader agonized: 'Sometimes at night I wonder, have we the right to remain silent? Is this not lack of courage?'[26] But he did not dare speak up. Respecting and at the same time despising Stalin, he hoped until his dying day – in vain, as we know – that Stalin would regain his reason, his decency and his tolerance.

Relations between them deteriorated sharply after Bukharin's famous article, 'Remarks of an economist', was published in *Pravda* on 30 September 1928. Persistently, Bukharin asserted the need for and the possibility of fostering the development of industry and agriculture in a crisis-free atmosphere, and by mobilizing every available economic means: 'We have over-centralized everything.' Within a week the Politburo condemned the article and Stalin went over to decisive attack. Prolonged and heated debates in the Politburo produced no compromise. Many of the sessions were not minuted, with only decisions being noted. These show that Stalin was steadily gaining the upper hand. Bukharin was in a minority. Rykov gave way on a number of points and Tomsky wobbled. Stalin began demanding that Bukharin 'cease his line on slowing down collectivization'. In a sharp exchange of fire, Bukharin angrily called Stalin 'a petty Oriental despot'. Stalin did not respond. But he was thinking to himself, 'I don't need him any more.'

The strained relations grew worse. But even before this turn of events, Bukharin, seeing that the position of the moderates was weakening, had taken what would seem to have been an ill-conceived step: he had suddenly called on Kamenev at his apartment on 11 June 1928 and attempted to establish illegal relations with the former opposition which he himself had helped Stalin to destroy. He visited Kamenev on two further occasions. They were alone at their meetings. What these two old comrades of Lenin spoke about we shall probably never know for sure. According to Trotsky, Kamenev noted that Bukharin was both furious and depressed. He kept repeating 'the revolution is ruined', 'Stalin is an intriguer of the very worst kind', and he did not think anything could be done to improve matters. Trotsky's supporters circulated this conversation in an underground pamphlet dated 20 January 1929. There is no way of substantiating its veracity.

Stalin meanwhile had naturally been informed of these contacts and at the April 1929 plenum they would provide one of the most telling arguments against Bukharin. The contacts with Kamenev did the moderates no good, and Bukharin had allowed Stalin to pin the 'factionalist' label on him. At this point Bukharin decided to appeal to public opinion. On the anniversary of Lenin's death, 24 January 1929, he published an article in *Pravda* called 'Lenin's Political Testament', representing the report to be made at the session marking the fifth anniversary of Lenin's death.

The article described Lenin's plan for building socialism, the importance of the NEP, the need for decisions to be taken democratically and so on. Bukharin wrote that Lenin's articles had called for 'industrialization of the country on the basis of savings, on the basis of raising the quality of work together with the organization of the peasants on cooperative lines, that is, the easiest, simplest means of drawing the peasants into socialist construction without using any form of coercion'. This formula was in so many words the essence of Bukharin's views on the questions exercising the party at the time.

But the main point was contained in the title of the article itself, for it reminded Communists (those who knew and those who remembered) that the Testament had called for the removal of Stalin from the post of General Secretary to another position. This was the last straw, especially as Bukharin wrote that 'conscience cannot be set aside in politics, as some people think.'

It should be noted that, for all his intelligence and prophetic view of what was to come, Bukharin saw through Stalin too late. The destruction of the 'Bukharin group' which Stalin had begun was completed by the April and November 1929 Central Committee and Central Control Commission plenums which reviewed the question of the 'right deviation' in the party. Stalin gave a three-hour speech in which he came down heavily on Bukharin for refusing to accept the compromise offered by the Politburo on 7 February 1929, a compromise which would have been tantamount to complete surrender. This, according to Stalin, now meant the party had 'the Central Committee line and another line pursued by the Bukharin group'. Despite their friendly relations before January 1928, Stalin now chose to outline several 'phases of difference' between them, sprinkling his language with such derogatory expressions as 'nonsense', 'rubbish', 'Bukharin's little book', 'un-Marxist approach', 'mumbo-jumbo', 'sham Marxist', 'big talk', 'Bukharin's semi-anarchistic mess'.

With good reason, Bukharin had been regarded as the leading theorist in the party since Lenin had died, and now Stalin was resolved to remove the crown from his head: 'As a theorist, he is not completely Marxist, he is a theorist who needs to study some more if he wants to be a Marxist theorist.'[27] Here Stalin did not miss the chance to quote what Lenin had said about

Bukharin, particularly the second part of his assessment, which stated that 'there is something of the scholastic in him, (he never studied dialectics and I think he never fully understood it).' So, he was a 'theorist without dialectics, a scholastic theorist'. Stalin further enumerated all the disagreements Bukharin had had with Lenin, characterizing them as 'attempts to teach our teacher'. That, he went on sarcastically, was entirely understandable, considering how recently the 'scholastic theorist' had been a 'pupil of Trotsky's ... and was only yesterday seeking an alliance with the Trotskyists against the Leninists, running to them by the back door!'[28] – a reference to Bukharin's visits to Kamenev.

The whole speech was in this vein, lashing out with devastating criticism against Rykov and Tomsky as well as the chief target. Bukharin and Rykov were removed from their posts, although they remained members of the Politburo. The speech was not published until some years later, in Stalin's collected works, but since the plenum resolution was circulated to all local party organizations, the process of castigating 'right-wingers' began to take place everywhere. Material began appearing regularly in *Pravda* and other newspapers, anathematizing the leaders of the 'right'. This was in effect the signal for forced collectivization, with its excesses and its violent smashing of the peasants' ancient way of life. No one was talking about the voluntary principle anymore. Even now, Bukharin continued to say that 20 per cent industrial growth was the limit that the agricultural economy would stand. Stalin had considerably higher expectations.

In November 1929 the party general line on agriculture was confirmed when Stalin wrote that 'the peasants are now joining collective farms not in individual groups, as they used to, but as entire villages, groups of villages, districts and even regions'.[29] Nevertheless, Bukharin was unwilling to 'repent', as he was being asked to do, and on 17 November 1929 he was removed from the Politburo. A week later, however, tormented by pangs of conscience for their own pusillanimity, Bukharin, Rykov and Tomsky wrote a brief letter to the Central Committee, in which they condemned their own position: 'We regard it as our duty to state that the party and its Central Committee have turned out to be right in this dispute. Our views have turned out to be erroneous. Recognizing our errors, we shall conduct a decisive struggle against all deviations from the party's general line and above all against the right deviation.'[30]

Stalin did not like the fact that the statement made no mention of his being in the right, but that did not matter. Bukharin was finished.

It is unlikely that at that time many people could foresee either what was to befall Bukharin or even the defeat of the moderate wing of the leadership in general. On the other hand, critics outside the Soviet Union were somewhat more perceptive. The April 1931 issue of the Menshevik journal, *Sotsialischeskii Vestnik*,* carried an article on the results of the New Economic Policy in which

---

* Founded in Berlin in 1920 by Martov, this central organ of the Menshevik RSDRP transferred in 1933 to Paris and then, from 1940 until 1963, was published in New York.

it was said that Stalin was doing his utmost to 'shatter any dreams about a return to the NEP, and to shatter any dreams of evolution';

The General Secretary has tried more than once to make the Right Communists knuckle under, but for various internal reasons the punishment has not been carried to the limit and the violent end of Rykov, Tomsky and Bukharin has been postponed. The process of ousting them not only from the apparatus but also from the party is not yet over. The supporters of the NEP, who are sensitive to the peasants' needs (even though they are psychologically incapable of breaking with the idea of dictatorship), have already been removed from their posts, but they have yet to be declared enemies of the people. The dictatorship is getting round to them and will deal with them soon enough.[31]

Having 'recanted', Bukharin suffered terribly as a result of his own inconsistency. Why, he agonized, had he been unable to convince the Politburo? He knew he had not been right about everything. A dash for industrialization was no doubt the correct thing to do. Sacrifices could not be avoided, but what form would they take? Surely not human lives. To the end, he could not reconcile himself to the methods of total violence that were used against the peasants: to 'liquidate' or rather to control the kulaks could have been done by purely economic means. The drama of Bukharin had not yet entered its tragic phase. No one in the party then could have envisaged the bloody 1930s. That would all take place nearly ten years after Bukharin had capitulated in November 1929.

CHAPTER 19

Dictatorship and Democracy

By the early 1930s it was plain to those with eyes to see that Lenin's words, 'The apparatus does not belong to us, we belong to it,'[32] had become a reality. The dictatorship of the bureaucracy, the collective bureaucracy, was born. And the bureaucracy gradually spawned an élite, an entire hierarchy of bosses. Rule by decree became virtually the chief means of social intercourse. Everything was decided inside offices. Meetings, sessions, congresses and plenums merely 'approved' or 'supported'. People's power was nothing but a hollow phrase. The wheels of the bureaucratic machine did not turn fast, but they were irreversible. Stalin sat at the main control panel, watching his brainchild through the windows of the Kremlin. The transfer to socialism had become deformed into the transfer to Stalinism.

Stalin had never understood, or wanted to understand, the essence of proletarian democracy, the very meaning of people's power. From his archives we see that democracy for him was nothing more than the freedom to support – and only to support – the decisions of the party. And since Stalin believed that he personified the party, then genuine democracy consisted of agreeing with and approving his arguments, his decisions, his intentions. Not everyone realized at once that, in dealing with Trotsky, Zinoviev, Kamenev and the other leaders who thought differently, it was not their differences with him that he stressed, but their departure from Leninism. Identifying his own views and attitudes with those of Lenin was one of the cleverest devices Stalin used. Not everyone realized at once that it was thanks to this strategy that no one could appear to be right in their arguments with him. For this to be so, it would be first necessary to dethrone Lenin.

Furthermore, Stalin also managed to present his errors on the national question, his negative attitude to the continuation of the NEP, his false conception of class struggle, his flawed understanding of the essence of collectivization and his exaggeration of the rôle of the apparatus, as if they were correct interpretations of Leninism. Once, after a clash on the eve of Bukharin's expulsion from the Politburo, they reportedly had the following exchange:

Stalin, angrily: 'Your lot are not Marxists, you're witch-doctors. Not one of you understood Lenin!'
Bukharin: 'And you're the only one who did?'
Stalin: 'I repeat, you didn't understand Lenin. Have you forgotten how often you attacked him for leftism, opportunism and muddle?'

In almost the same words, Stalin would put pressure on Bukharin at the April plenum of the Central Committee and Central Control Commission in 1929. The source of countless future misfortunes lay in Stalin's usurping the monopoly on interpreting Lenin, and there was no one then who could expose the profound inconsistency of Stalin's dogmatic claim to this exclusive rôle.

Summing up the results of the First Five-Year Plan at the January 1933 plenum, Stalin included a special section on the tasks and results of the struggle against 'the remnants of the hostile classes'. Despite the fact that he was talking about 'remnants', he nevertheless issued a call to 'struggle against them implacably'. And not a word about re-education, or bringing many 'ex-people' and their families into the new life which might the more effectively help to change their outlook and their 'class instincts'. Depicting the social scene, he said:

The remnants of the dying classes – industrialists and their servants, private traders and their stooges, former nobles and priests, kulaks and their henchmen, former White officers and NCOs, former gendarmes and policemen – they have all wormed their way into our factories, our institutions and trading bodies, our railway and river transport enterprises and for the most part into our collective and state farms. They have wormed their way in and hidden themselves there, disguised as 'workers' and 'peasants', and some of them have even managed to worm their way into the party.
What have they brought with them? Of course, they have brought their hatred of the Soviet régime, their feeling of ferocious hostility to the new forms of the economy, way of life, culture ... The only thing left for them to do is to play dirty tricks and do harm to the workers and collective farmers. And they do this any way they can, on the quiet. They set fire to warehouses and break machinery. They organize sabotage. They organize wrecking in the collective and state farms, and some of them, including a number of professors, go so far in their wrecking activities as to inject the livestock in collective and state farms with plague and anthrax, and encourage the spread of meningitis among horses, and so on.[33]

After hearing such a gloomy picture painted of the situation at the beginning of 1933, decent people were dumbfounded. Nothing but enemies, wreckers, remnants of the exploiting classes who were as dangerous now as they had been in the first years of Soviet power. Of course, there were still many people who were hostile to the régime, but they presented nothing like the threat Stalin had drawn. But he had only drawn it in order to be able to say: 'A strong and mighty dictatorship of the proletariat is what we need now to blow the last remnants of the dying classes into dust and to smash their thieving schemes.'[34] And he was banking on further intensification of the punitive, coercive function of the dictatorship of the proletariat.

Stalin made many such speeches in the late 1920s and early 1930s. A public mood gradually developed in which, alongside the revolutionary zeal, enthusiasm and collective optimism, there began to appear the first signs of suspiciousness, distrust towards one's fellows, and a readiness to believe the most outlandish myths about 'enemies of the people'. The utter insanity of 1937–38 could not have occurred had the population not been prepared for it over quite a long time. Millions of people, living in a state that was in fact surrounded by the capitalist world, gradually got used to the idea that, among their friends, comrades and colleagues at work, in the university, in their army unit or cultural group, enemies were hiding and waiting for their time to come. A summons or a slogan or a directive could prompt many of them to 'smash the last remnants of capitalism'. From this it was but a step to terror, or at any rate to readiness for it. For his part, Stalin believed that the use of violence was an organic element in the peaceful construction of socialism. 'Repression,' he told the Sixteenth Party Congress in 1930, 'is a necessary element in the advance.'[35] Stalin could not understand why the people writing in the social democratic press abroad, and Trotsky who was at odds with them, were so vehement in their attacks on the party apparatus and the dictatorship. Surely they knew it was the most important instrument of power? Again and again Stalin persuaded himself that historically the apparatus had been a weapon of the dictatorship. There could be no talk of socialism or democracy without the dictatorship. It was of course the dictatorship of the bureaucrat, not that of the proletariat, that Stalin was consolidating.

He talked a great deal about equality and social interests as the basic premises of socialist democracy. In conversation in 1936 with a group of Central Committee staff who were responsible for school textbooks, he stressed that:

Our democracy must always put general interests in first place. The personal counts for next to nothing compared with the social. As long as there are still idlers and enemies and theft of socialist property, it means there are still people who are alien to socialism, and that means we must keep up the struggle.

'The personal counts for next to nothing ...' and what belongs to everyone belongs to no one. The sense of ownership simply evaporated, as egalitarianism took over. A worker would not be paid thousands for his invention, even if it earned millions, because it would be 'a lot' for one person. Gradually a type of worker came into being who was afraid to 'overwork', who would look on phoney order sheets and daylight robbery with equanimity. 'Well, the state isn't going to miss this,' he would think. 'The personal counts for nothing ...' And it was Stalinist 'democracy' that sustained this attitude. People were motivated mostly by necessity, by fear and other levers of a system at whose apex stood the autocrat.

Stalin did not make speeches against democracy, because he understood democracy as a despot understands it. There were after all Roman emperors who were not above creating obedient parliaments with the appropriate attributes, such as elections, oaths and formal representation. Democracy as an expression of socialist people's power was acceptable to Stalin as long as it reinforced his own personal dictatorship. In conversation with H. G. Wells, Stalin placed power at the centre of his reasoning 'as a lever of change', a lever of the new legality and the new order. He loved nothing more than he loved power, full, unlimited power, consecrated by the 'love' of the multitudes. In this he was successful. No other man in the world has ever accomplished so fantastic a success as he: to exterminate millions of his own countrymen and receive in exchange the whole country's blind adulation. This was nevertheless part of the Stalinist understanding of the relationship between dictatorship and democracy.

In time the notion of 'sacrifice', or 'cost', became for Stalin one of the essential attributes of socialism. When a new project was destined for Northern Siberia, the 'planning order' included an element to cover 'natural losses'. The NKVD even planned 'capacities' for the regions, special reserves of forced labour for 'socialist sites'. From the late 1920s there was no shortage of cheap slave labour. All initiatives for using prisoners were supported by Stalin. He would either mutter to his assistant or scribble 'agreed' on the document, so that an agency's proposal to employ hundreds and thousands of 'enemies' in one region or another would have official approval.

Running ahead of ourselves, it is noteworthy that Beria in his notes to Stalin often stated that the NKVD's construction tasks were so great that they simply had inadequate 'human resources'.[36] Stalin took the point. On 25 August 1938, the Presidium of the USSR Supreme Soviet met to debate the early release of prisoners for good behaviour. Stalin objected:

Can't we arrange things so that people stay on in the camps? If not, we release them, they go back home and pick up again with their old ways. The atmosphere in the camp is different, there it's harder to go wrong. Anyway, we have the voluntary-compulsory [state] loan. So let's have voluntary-compulsory staying-on.[37]

Stalin had made himself clear, and as a result a decree was passed 'On NKVD Camps', according to which 'anyone serving a sentence in the camps of the NKVD of the USSR must serve the full term as fixed by the court.'

To return to the beginning of the 1930s, the result of the withering of democratic principles was that a machine of coercion and a powerful punitive apparatus were created. Dogmatism in the social sciences, in ideology and propaganda spread rapidly. The lack of democracy soon led to the first signs of the rôle of one person being inflated, exaltation of his merits, the portrayal of Stalin as a mythical messiah.

Stalin's own reaction to all this was interesting, as the following excerpt from a conversation with Emil Ludwig on 13 December 1931 shows:

Ludwig: 'On the one hand, people abroad know that the USSR is a country where everything is supposed to be decided collectively, but, on the other hand, they know that everything is decided by one man. Who actually decides?'

Stalin: 'Decisions taken by one person are always or nearly always one-sided decisions. In any collective there are people whose opinions have to be taken into account. Our workers would never tolerate the rule of one person under any circumstances.'

[Ludwig asks how Stalin views the methods of the Jesuits.]

Stalin: 'Their main methods are shadowing, spying, crawling right inside someone's mind, mockery – what good is there in that?'

Ludwig: 'You were repeatedly at risk and in danger. You were persecuted, you took part in battles. Some of your close friends perished. You are still alive. Do you believe in fate?'

Stalin: 'No. I don't. That's just superstitious nonsense and a hangover of mythology. Someone else could be in my place, and someone else should have been ... I don't believe in mysticism.'[38]

Saying one thing and doing another became the norm for Stalin: condemning the leadership cult while reinforcing it, criticizing Jesuit practices while encouraging them in Soviet life, talking about collective leadership while reducing it to one-man rule. The deification of autocrats is invariably founded on total mendacity.

By the early 1930s Stalin had altogether ceased his rare visits to the provinces, to factories and army units. On the one hand, he had little knowledge of production and had no desire to go into such mundane affairs as technology or labour productivity, profitability etc. On the other hand, he was haunted by the perpetual feeling that an attempt was being plotted against his life. After all, he was not short of enemies and Trotsky or one of the other 'ex-people' was capable of going to extremes. His security organs were always telling him so. For instance, Ulrikh reported:

In 16 December [1935], after two weeks' investigation in closed session by the military collegium of the USSR Supreme Court, sentence was passed on a group of spies and terrorists who were preparing to commit a terrorist act [*terakt*] on Red Square on 7 November 1935 on the orders of a German subject. Death sentences were passed on G. I. Sher, V. G. Freiman, S. M. Pevzner, V. O. Levinsky ...[39]

Stalin had no need to read any further. 'They're out to get me,' he thought. But they wouldn't get away with it, he'd pull them up by the roots.

Stalin rarely made a public appearance because in his subtle way he knew that the less he was seen by the population at large, the easier it would be to cultivate the sort of image he wanted to project. The enigmatic, mysterious and enclosed was akin to the sacred, the legendary and superhuman. Therefore, instead of visiting factories, he studied documents carefully, watched film commentaries regularly, heard endless reports and stood cogitating for long periods in front of maps.

He loved gazing at maps, surveying his vast country like a sovereign. This way, however inadequately, he could get some idea of the way the millions were labouring to bring his decrees to life. He would trace the Trans-Sib with his finger or locate Magnitogorsk, the Dnieper hydroelectric dam, the White Sea–Baltic Canal, the Kuznets Basin, and he would let his eye rest on the Kolyma regions which were so far away it would take him several paces to reach them on the map. After one such routine survey of the territory, he suddenly telephoned Voroshilov and asked him if the Red Army studied geography. Did the soldiers know the geography of their own country well? In his mind, looking at a map of the Motherland would give one pride in it, as well as dedication to the cause and the idea. Voroshilov, who was not prepared for this question, gave an incoherent reply and said he would look into it. Next day the political department of the Revolutionary Military Council prepared a memorandum which Voroshilov transmitted to Stalin, as follows:

In reply to your question about the study of geography by the Red Army, I can report that geography is studied by all Red Army men as a compulsory part of special programmes. In addition to the study of geography as part of the programme of general education, it is also taken in political courses. Special attention is paid to the study of maps.

In the current year, the political department of the Revvoensoviet distributed 220,000 maps, 10,000 atlases, 8,000 maps in national republican languages and 10,000 globes, to add to units' existing holdings.[40]

Stalin read the report with satisfaction and gazed from his chair across to the map; as long as the wall was near enough, he could make out the locations of Stalingrad, Stalino, Stalinsk, Stalinabad.

Soon after Lenin's death, the dubious practice had grown of giving the names of party and state figures to towns and regions, factories, educational institutes, theatres and so on. It became the norm for newspapers to carry reports of the early fulfilment of the quarterly plan by the Stalin Chemical Works in Moscow, the Voroshilov Weaving Mill in Tver, the Zinoviev Paper Mills Number 1 and 3 in Leningrad, the Bukharin Glass Factory in Gus-Khrustalnyi, and so on. By the end of the 1920s there was virtually no district where Stalin's name had not been adopted by one administrative, production or cultural body or another. By this means, the people were surreptitiously imbued with the idea of the exceptional rôle that Stalin played in the nation's destiny. The glorification of the Leader could be heard in every routine report or speech by which the local 'leader' would see that some of the glory was reflected on himself.

Pious oaths became an inevitable element of social life under Stalin, and, being so vitally useful to those who mouthed them, they survived for decades after his death. This process did more than deify the leader, it also insulted the entire populace which, while it was the creator of everything in the country, was instead put in the position of being grateful. The impression was inevitably gained that, having given up belief in God in heaven, the people were creating him again on earth.

And it was indeed an act of creation. The most ardent, the loudest voices raised in exaltation were those of Molotov, Voroshilov and Kaganovich, and, however paradoxical it may seem, also Zinoviev, Kamenev, Bukharin and some of the other disgraced Old Bolsheviks. Zinoviev's speeches and articles, castigating himself for his past sins and praising the 'perspicacity and wisdom of the party leader, Comrade Stalin', make for uneasy reading. Even Bukharin could not restrain himself from making some flattering remarks. Who can say whether they had really lost their faith in the cause for which they had fought, or whether the instinct for self-survival took command of their senses?

Alongside the glorification in official literature, an almost imperceptible process began of reviewing history and of creating the notion that there had been two leaders of the October Revolution, namely Lenin and the ubiquitous Stalin, who was always at his shoulder. In the preface of a six-volume collected works of Lenin, its editor, Adoratsky, wrote that Lenin's writings should be read in conjunction with those of Stalin, that Stalin had expounded Lenin's ideas in a concentrated form in his *Foundations of Leninism* and so on.

In August 1931, before the personal cult reached its zenith, there were attempts to immortalize Stalin in works of political biography. There is a letter in Stalin's archive from Yaroslavsky, which includes the following: 'As he was leaving today, Sergo [Ordzhonikidze] rang fo say he'd spoken to you about the book called *Stalin* that I want to write ...' Stalin's customary pencilled remark on the note reads: 'Comrade Yaroslavsky, I'm against it. I think the time has not yet come for biographies.'[41]

It was an eloquent decision. The peasantry had yet to be broken, the forest of factories had just begun to grow, most of Lenin's old guard were still alive and among them were some who knew what Stalin had been only ten years earlier. Panegyrical articles were only just beginning to appear. The main thing was to operate gradually, consistently and irreversibly. It was important to behave in public with modesty and restraint. Only that day he had seen how the applause had exploded with new vigour when he took his seat in the second row on the platform, and not in the front row where he was expected to sit. The audience had stood on tiptoe to get a glimpse of him. The time for biographies would come soon enough.

For the time being, enough had been done to prompt the sending of devoted letters and reports to the Leader. For instance, the Stalin Commune, in the village of Tsasuchey, in the Olovyannikovsk district of Eastern Siberia, reported its intention to sow 320 hectares instead of the proposed 262.5. 'We are for the general line of the party under the leadership of the Bolshevik Central Committee and the best Leninist, Comrade Stalin! We are for the complete fulfilment of the Five-Year Plan in four years and for the liquidation of the kulaks on the basis of full collectivization!'[42]

Such letters were soon being adopted at every meeting of every enterprise, collective or state farm and institute. It was the beginning of the deformation of the public mind which would henceforth be nourished solely by cult myths. The propaganda laid increasing emphasis on faith: everything said or formulated by Stalin was immutable, true and in no need of proof. In other words, Stalin was a demi-god. In the end, these myths, which became the basis of the whole of social life, boiled down to two simple propositions. First, the leader of the party and the nation is a wise man in the highest degree. The force of his intellect is capable of answering all questions about the past, understanding the present and peering into the future: 'Stalin is the Lenin of today.' Secondly, the leader of the party and the nation is the total embodiment of absolute good and he cares for every person. He repudiates evil, ignorance, treachery, cruelty. He is that smiling man with the moustache who is carrying the little girl waving the flag.

CHAPTER 20

The Congress of Victors

The end of the 1920s and beginning of the 1930s marked an important phase in Stalin's rise. His authority had grown markedly, and the former oppositionists, including Bukharin, were seeking ways and means of proving their loyalty to him, as well as their new 'insight' and their 'complete agreement with the party's general line'. For instance, Zinoviev and Kamenev attempted a number of times to re-establish good relations with Stalin and they went to see him at his dacha to make peace.

It is normal to experience a fall from high office as a personal tragedy and these political figures were no exception. Kamenev, although only in his mid-forties, seemed to have given up altogether and became grey and aged before his time. On the telephone or in face-to-face conversation with Stalin he would invariably look for an opportunity to make cautious reference to the time they had spent together, vegetating on the banks of the Kureika river, or to the fact that the three of them – himself, Zinoviev and Stalin – had been Lenin's closest comrades-in-arms, or to the dramatic events surrounding Stalin's ascendancy to the post of General Secretary. Both Zinoviev and Kamenev, but especially the latter, never gave up hope of returning to the upper echelons of the party hierarchy.

Stalin knew exactly what was going on and his response was condescending. On occasion he even gave encouragement to the disgraced comrades. But he was aware that the people to whom he owed his present position to a significant extent were not only unnecessary to him now, but could become a danger later. Zinoviev and Kamenev knew him too well, and he did not like people who knew more about him than was prescribed in official propaganda. As the Seventeenth Party Congress approached at the beginning of the 1930s, all his attention was concentrated on the revolution in agriculture, the upsurge in industry and on ensuring consolidation of his supporters.

The congress that took place in February 1934 became known in Stalinist propaganda as the 'Congress of Victors'. Stalin himself, in his Central Committee report, described the successes achieved by the party and the country as 'great and unusual'. The country had indeed made a great leap forward by 1934. The draft of Stalin's report, which he edited and annotated most carefully, shows on every page and in every paragraph that he sought to inflate these achievements. He believed that the country's enormous sacrifices must show some result. Whole pages of the report were rewritten by him to show the party and the people that his leadership was productive, successful and victorious.

He laid special emphasis on the fact that, in the three years or so since the previous congress, industrial output had doubled. New branches of industry had been created: machine-tool construction, automobiles, tractors, chemicals. Engines, aircraft, combines, synthetic rubber, nitrate, artificial fibres were now being manufactured in the USSR. He announced proudly that thousands of new enterprises had been commissioned, including such gigantic projects as the Dnieper Hydroelectric project, the Magnitogorsk and Kuznets sites, the Urals truck-building plant, the Chelyabinsk tractor plant, the Kramatorsk auto plant and so on. No previous report of his had ever contained so many facts and figures, tables and plans. He had something to tell the congress.

It is customary to see the 1930s as a decade of massive tragedy, but it was also a time of unprecedented enthusiasm, achievement and huge effort by the workers. It is hard now to think that millions of people, mostly sustained by only the barest necessities of life, believed that they were genuinely creating a communist future and that not only their own fate but that of the world proletariat depended on their self-sacrifice. A few extracts from *Pravda* – which Stalin always read in full, unselectively, marking an occasional passage in pencil – are indicative:

A Baku oil-workers' collective report, discussed at 40 meetings by 20,000 oil-workers and supplemented by 53 local reports and 254 workers' letters, says: 'thanks to the efforts of the workers and specialists and under the well-tried leadership of the Leninist party, the Five-Year Plan for oil has been completed in two and a half years.'

Magnitogorsk reported:

a completely new kind of crew has come into being in the construction section of the blast-furnace workshop – a thoroughly self-financing excavator crew. The change to self-financing excavators has produced excellent results. Self-financing excavators have beaten world records for loading trucks.

From Tataria:

The harvesting and delivery of grain is proceeding under the slogan of preparing for the second All-Tatar congress of kolkhozniks and winning the right to include a local representative in the delegation that will take the report to Comrade Stalin.

To occupy first place on the All-Union red board is the most popular slogan in the kolkhozy of Tataria.

This may all seem like the naive, starry-eyed faith in Stalin of millions of simple people who built the foundations of what we have today. One cannot, however, but admire their indomitable enthusiasm, their pride in their accomplishments, and their confidence that the future was in their hands. The unprecedented force of heroic endeavour, the high level of civic-mindedness, and the faith in justice and a better future. even if couched in terms of the personality cult, derived from the huge social energy unleashed by October 1917. These people, these creators, usually described by Stalin as 'the masses', or sometimes as 'cogs', are a part of Soviet history that should not be forgotten.

At the same time, the newspapers were reporting things which today, knowing what we do, cause a shudder. In mid-July 1933 *Pravda* reported that 'Comrades Stalin and Voroshilov arrived in Leningrad and in the company of Comrade Kirov went the same day to see the White Sea–Baltic Canal. After inspecting work on the canal and the hydro-engineering installations, they went via the White Sea port of Soroka to Murmansk.' Two weeks later the government announced the opening of the Stalin White Sea–Baltic Canal and the awards to be made to those who had performed outstanding work in its construction. The Order of Lenin was conferred on eight people: G. G. Yagoda, deputy chairman of the OGPU; L. I. Kogan, head of the White Sea Canal project; M. D. Berman, head of the main board of OGPU corrective labour camps; N. A. Frenkel, assistant head of the project; Ya. D. Rapoport, deputy head of the project; S. G. Firin, head of the White Sea–Baltic corrective labour camp; S. Ya. Zhuk, deputy chief engineer of the project; and K. A. Verzhbitsky, deputy head of construction.[43]

Speaking later at the Seventeenth Congress Kirov would say: 'To build such a canal, in such a short time and in such a place is a really heroic labour, and we must give credit to our Chekists who supervised the work and literally performed miracles.'[44] It would have been truer to say that the miracles had been performed by hundreds of thousands of prisoners. There was no shortage of them. After the dekulakization of more than one million peasant households, and the harsh policy against the 'remnants of the exploiting classes', the OGPU had at its disposal vast human resources to build more than the White Sea Canal. The job descriptions of those who received the Order of Lenin bear eloquent witness to how and by whom the canal, named after Stalin, was built. The idea of using prisoners in the national economy was not new. In the mid-1920s Trotsky, developing his idea of militarizing labour, had counselled that 'elements hostile to the state should be directed on a massive scale to sites constructing the proletarian state.' The advice of one 'outstanding leader' evidently did not pass unnoticed by the other.

It was less easy for Stalin to report achievements in agriculture. To be sure, more than 200,000 collective farms had been created and 5,000 state farms.

But he had to admit that the development of agriculture had gone 'many times more slowly than industry'. He also conceded that 'in point of fact the period under review was for agriculture less a time of rapid rise and powerful takeoff, so much as a time of creating the conditions for such a rise and takeoff in the near future.'[45]

Having in the course of the ten years since Lenin's death routed countless 'oppositions', Stalin found himself in the end 'without work'. He even spoke about it: if at the Sixteenth Congress he still had to finish off the disciples of various groupings, here at this congress there was no one to beat. Although here too, 'in case we should let our guard slip', he contradicted himself and said 'the remnants of the ideology are alive in the minds of some members of the party', and we must be ready to smash them. Stalin rarely 'smashed' ideology, however, only those who espoused an ideology. Having announced that the country was moving towards the creation of a 'classless, socialist society', he drew the immediate conclusion that classlessness could only be achieved 'by means of strengthening the organs of the dictatorship of the proletariat, by means of expanding the class struggle'.[46]

It might appear that, believing as he did in the universal value of coercive methods and seeing the dictatorship of the proletariat above all as a weapon of coercion, Stalin simply did not realize how ruinous such a policy could be. On the contrary, at the 'Congress of Victors' he called for the screw to be tightened still further. As for developing democracy, he understood perfectly well that any increase in people's power would mean a corresponding reduction of his personal authority. He was an authoritarian by nature, a despot with something of the oriental in his distant past. In 1928 Bukharin had called him Genghis Khan.

As General Secretary of the party, he saw to it that, among the 1,225 delegates to the congress, there were a number who had belonged to various factional groups, 'oppositions' or 'deviations'. They had all long before repented and recanted and were seeking ways of placing themselves at Stalin's disposal. They were not all time-servers or people without principles. Many of them had repented sincerely of their often insignificant sins because they had not wanted to remain outside the party and also supported the line on the forced construction of socialism.

Stalin made a special point of encouraging Kaganovich to ensure that among the delegates there were some whose recantation would strengthen the power of the leader still further. Reading their speeches decades later, one can imagine the humiliation these people felt as they castigated themselves, as if in a religious ecstasy, simply to gratify the vanity of one man. Many delegates saw through this. For instance, Kirov said these former oppositionists 'are now trying ... to jump on the bandwagon of the general celebration, attempting to march in step to the same music, to support this general upsurge of ours ... Take Bukharin, for instance. It seems to me he's singing the notes, but the voice is not right. I won't say anything about Comrade Rykov, or Comrade Tomsky.'[47]

What did these former members of the Politburo and pupils of Lenin say at the congress?

Bukharin, the party's ex-favourite and theorist:

By his brilliant application of Marx-Lenin [sic] dialectics, Stalin was entirely correct when he smashed a whole series of theoretical premises of the right deviation which had been formulated above all by myself ... It is the duty of every party member to rally round Comrade Stalin as the personal embodiment of the mind and will of the party, as its leader, its theoretical and practical leader.[48]

It is hard to believe that this could be said by a man whose conscience was absolutely clear.

Rykov, first chairman of the Sovnarkom after Lenin:

I wanted to describe the rôle played by Comrade Stalin in the first years following the death of Vladimir Ilyich ... How as leader and organizer of our victories he emerged at that time. I wanted to describe the way Comrade Stalin immediately emerged from all the rest of the then leadership.[49]

This was a man who had always been admired for being straightforward, incorruptible and having great civic courage.

Tomsky, leader of the trade unions:

It is my duty to declare before the party that it was only because Comrade Stalin was the most consistent, the brightest of Lenin's pupils, only because Comrade Stalin was the most perceptive and saw the farthest, and because he was the one who led the party along the correct Leninist path most steadfastly, because he smashed us with the heaviest hand, because he was best armed theoretically and practically for the struggle against the opposition – that was why the attacks fell on Comrade Stalin.[50]

Tomsky had the reputation as a party member of sticking to his principles to the end.

Zinoviev, having been defeated again and again, was now once more a party member:

We now know that in the struggle which Comrade Stalin conducted on an exclusively high level of principle, on an exclusively high theoretical level, we know that in that struggle there was not the least hint of anything personal.

He described Stalin's report as a 'chef d'oeuvre', and he went on at length and in an ingratiating way about 'the triumph of the leadership, the triumph of him who heads this leadership.'

When I was readmitted to the party, Stalin said to me: 'What damaged you and still damages you in the eyes of the party is not so much your mistakes on principles, as the lack of straightforwardness towards the party which developed in you over a number of years.'

At this point, shouts of 'Quite right, well said!' came from the assembly. Zinoviev went on:

We can now see how the best people among the advanced peasants of the collective farms are striving to come to Moscow, to the Kremlin, striving to see Comrade Stalin, to feel him with their eyes and maybe with their hands, striving to receive their orders from him directly which they then want to carry back to the masses.[51]

Only fear of being cast for ever into the political dustbin could induce Zinoviev to utter such humiliating remarks. In the same way, mocking their own intellectual dignity and their consciences, Kamenev, Radek, Preobrazhensky, Lominadze and others who had been defeated by Stalin in the factional war made their obeisances to him now.

Sitting in the second row, by now his customary place, Stalin watched with outward indifference as Kamenev mounted the rostrum. He recalled the way Kamenev, as chairman of various congresses and Politburo sessions, used to try to steer the debate in the required direction by making impatient remarks. On one occasion, when relations between them were already bad, Kamenev had snapped at Stalin, as he was listing the opposition's mistakes: 'Comrade Stalin! Are you counting sheep: one, two, three? Your arguments are no cleverer than the sheep themselves.' To which Stalin shot back: 'Considering you're one of the sheep yourself ...'

What would Kamenev say now? In the event his recantation was an unseemly entreaty of self-abasement:

This era in which we are living and in which this congress is taking place, is a new era ... it will go down in history, without doubt, as the Stalin era, just as the preceding era went down in history as the Lenin era, and each of us, especially us, has the obligation to resist with all means and all our energy the slightest wavering of this authority ... I want to state from this rostrum that the Kamenev, who from 1925 to 1933 struggled with the party and its leadership, I regard as a political corpse, that I want to go forward, without dragging the old skin after me, if you'll excuse the Biblical expression. Long live our, *our* leader and commander Comrade Stalin![52]

As he listened with undisguised satisfaction to the panegyrics, Stalin recalled that Kamenev, in conversation with Trotsky, had called him a 'ferocious savage', that Zinoviev had dubbed him, among his cronies, a 'bloodthirsty Ossetian', that Bukharin had often wounded him by referring to his lack of foreign languages, that Radek in the first edition of his book *Portraits and Pamphlets* had had nothing to say about him whatsoever, and in 1922 Preobrazhensky, who regarded himself as a great theorist, had called him an 'ignoramus'.

Was this his revenge, then? No, he thought, that would be small-minded. It was enough for the party to know that he had been right on all the thorny issues, in all the debates and at all the turning points. And that it was not he, but his former opponents, who were saying so. Henceforth everyone would know that he not only possessed political will and organizational abilities – that had long been known – but that he also had special wisdom, far-sightedness, a capacity to anticipate and a firm hand. The Congress of Victors? Perhaps the Congress of the Victor would be more appropriate.

Stalin, however. expected to have more than one new title lavished on him. Khrushchev and Zhdanov, for instance, called Stalin a 'leader of genius' for the first time. Zinoviev was the first to utter the formula 'Marx, Engels, Lenin, Stalin'. Kirov called him 'the greatest strategist of the emancipation of the toilers of our country and the whole world'. Voroshilov said that as a 'pupil and friend' of Lenin, Stalin was also his 'arms-bearer' – an absurd contradiction.

Having tired of hearing what a genius he was, how wise, great, far-sighted and iron-hard, Stalin now paid special attention to what the delegates from the army would say, and he found himself disappointed by the general lack of praise in Tukhachevsky's speech. Again the civil war hero was blowing his own trumpet, expounding his own plans for the technical restructuring of the army. He had already been told that his ideas were too fanciful, yet here he was again ... Stalin recalled the long letter Tukhachevsky had written him in 1930, complaining that the Red Army Staff had called his proposals on modernizing the army 'the memorandum of a madman'.[53] Stalin had known then that Tukhachevsky's letter was in fact aimed against him, as General Secretary, and not against Voroshilov, the Commissar for Defence with whom Tukhachevsky's relations were strained. He did not like to hear such independent judgement coming from a military leader who evidently saw far beyond Voroshilov, whose own outlook was frozen by his experience in the civil war. Stalin already knew what Tukhachevsky was going to say because Voroshilov had brought him a copy of the speech on the eve of the congress.

In his own speech Voroshilov contrived to invent yet a new epithet, 'the steel Stalin'.[54] It also pleased Stalin to hear Dolores Ibarruri,* Bela Kun† and other foreign Comintern figures declaring that he was now the leader not only of the Bolsheviks but also of the world proletariat.

It was on the last day of the congress that he suddenly sensed the fragility and transient quality of everything in life. The procedure had been going smoothly, everything seemed like a formality, whether it was choosing members of the Central Committee and the new organs of party and soviet control, or appointing the Politburo, all of which had of course been 'agreed' in advance. The triumphal celebration of the Leader seemed to be moving effortlessly towards its preordained conclusion. The audit commission was winding up its work when the unexpected happened. Kaganovich and the chairman of the commission, Zatonsky, both in a state of high anxiety and

*Known as La Pasionaria, the leader of the Communists in the Spanish Civil War was a refugee in the USSR from 1938 to 1977, and died in Spain in November 1989.

† Communist leader of the failed Hungarian Soviet revolution. A refugee in the USSR from 1920, he took part in the civil war, held Soviet posts and was a leading figure in Comintern. He was arrested in 1938, and died in camp in 1939.

alarm, came running in to see Stalin.

A. I. Mikoyan, a candidate and then full member of the Politburo from 1926 to 1966, described the work of the congress in some detail in his memoirs, and a number of others have similarly noted these events. In *The History of the CPSU* (in Russian), published in 1962, there is a note to the effect that 'the abnormal situation that had arisen within the party caused alarm among a section of the Communists, particularly among the old Leninist groups. Many, especially those who were familiar with Lenin's Testament, felt the time had come to transfer Stalin from the post of General Secretary to some other job.' According to Mikoyan, (who had been informed by the Old Bolsheviks A. Snegov, O. Shatunovskaya and N. Andreasyan, a member of the audit commission), Kaganovich nervously told Stalin the unexpected result of the ballot: out of 1225 delegates, three had voted against Kirov, and nearly 300, almost a quarter, had voted against Stalin. It was unbelievable!

No one can now say exactly how Stalin responded to this news, but according to Mikoyan the decision was quickly taken to let three votes against Stalin and the three that had been cast against Kirov remain, and to destroy all the other ballot papers. It was the practice to issue just as many ballot papers, bearing a single name, as there were posts to be filled. It was in other words an election without a choice, where only a simple majority was required. Even if the 300 votes against him had been taken into account, Stalin would still have been returned to the Central Committee and would no doubt have continued as General Secretary.* But it seemed impossible to calculate the political effect that publishing these results might have. Everyone would at once have seen that Stalin's greatness was ephemeral – that the emperor wore no clothes.

According to the same accounts, a group of Old Bolsheviks, having learned of the result, went to Kirov and proposed that he agree to be put up as General Secretary. He refused and apparently informed Stalin of what had transpired. For all its dramatic nature and its vagueness, the story has a considerable degree of plausibility. First, among the delegates were many former oppositionists who had come out against Stalin personally. Then, there were many who had experienced for themselves for the first time Stalin's casual rudeness and his dictatorial manner. However, the position inside the party was by now such that no one was capable of actually coming out with open criticism of Stalin, still less of proposing his removal to another post. The opportunity to express their conscience did, nevertheless, present itself in the form of the secret ballot. If Mikoyan's charge is ever substantiated, it will explain more fully Stalin's changed attitude to Kirov, who now became a real rival in his eyes. In another chapter we shall witness the tragic fate that would befall the overwhelming majority of the delegates at this Congress of Victors, for after such a vote, Stalin saw in every one of them a potential enemy.

---

* After this congress, the General Secretary no longer put himself up for re-election. To the end of his life, moreover, party and state documents did not list him as General Secretary.

CHAPTER 21

Stalin and Kirov

Speaking at the Seventeenth Congress, A. S. Yenukidze remarked on the fact that Stalin had surrounded himself with a group of people with whom he could discuss any question that might arise,[55] and it was indeed true that Stalin's entourage still included a number of interesting figures, among them Sergei Kirov. Perhaps he did not quite qualify as belonging to the entourage, since he worked in Transcaucasia and then in Leningrad, but he was someone Stalin regarded as close. Enukidze, who was also a close friend of Stalin's, was exaggerating when he also said that Stalin was surrounded 'by the best people in our party'. There were gifted, original and thoroughly decent comrades-in-arms, but there were also yes-men who had never contradicted him and whose chief concern was to anticipate the leader's wishes and carry them out. Alongside Stalin, especially in the late 1930s and 1940s, were also people who cannot be called anything but criminal.

Stalin was not a stupid man. He wanted trusted and loyal friends, but mainly he wanted unquestioning executives who would understand from a hint or a gesture what his intentions were. He tried to convey the impression for public consumption, of course, that relations based on personal loyalty were not worthy of state affairs. For instance, replying to a letter from party member Shatunovsky, he wrote:

You speak about your 'devotion' to me. Maybe the phrase just slipped out. Maybe ... But if it didn't just slip out, I would advise you to discard the 'principle' of devotion to individuals. It is not the Bolshevik way. Be devoted to the working class, to its party, its state. That is what is needed and what is good. But don't get it mixed up with devotion to people, which is just an empty and superfluous fad of intellectuals.[56]

Fine words, but not, alas, in harmony with practice. He was after all a great hypocrite and, as a rule, he surrounded himself with people who would give him no trouble. This applied above all to his assistants. These included Nazaretyan, Bazhanov, Kanner, Maryin, Dvinsky, Tovstukha and Poskrebyshev. It was to the latter two that he was most attached.

Tovstukha could guess Stalin's intentions from the slightest signal. Quite well versed in theory, he could formulate an idea and detect the intellectual flaws in a document. Stalin valued him especially for his dedication to his work. There is a note in the archives from Stalin to Zinoviev, Kamenev and Bukharin, dated 1923, stating that 'Tovstukha doesn't want to take a vacation. The file contains my memorandum about an immediate holiday for Comrade Tovstukha which he did not put to the vote.'[57] And Stalin thereupon admonished Tovstukha for telling Kamenev about the holiday he hadn't had. In the end, the wretched Tovstukha wrote officially to Stalin, with a copy to Kamenev, stating 'that I have never said to Comrade Kamenev, nor to anyone else, that I want to take a holiday and that Comrade Stalin will not let me.'

Half in fun, Kamenev scribbled, 'I confirm that Comrade Tovstukha has never, anywhere or in any shape or form, spoken to me about his holiday, but has said that he could do more work on Lenin if he could start his work in the Central Committee earlier. I request that I not be held responsible for Tovstukha's death.'[58]

For a short time B. Bazhanov worked for Stalin. He came from an intellectual family background and Stalin soon built up respect for him. Bazhanov had the job of taking the minutes at Politburo meetings, but he had difficulty in hiding his own views. He managed to escape to Persia in 1928 and from there to England. For several decades he made a living by publishing commentaries on what he knew and then by making things up when the material ran out.

For many years Stalin kept Lev Zakharovich Mekhlis on his staff and for a while Mekhlis was the leader's assistant. Mekhlis was born in Odessa, started out as a Menshevik, entered the Communist Party in 1918 and got to know Stalin during the civil war. He held a number of important posts in the apparatus and in *Pravda*, was Commissar for State Control and chief of the Main Political Administration of the Red Army. Although he was not without abilities, his way of thinking was frankly that of a policeman, and he was one of those who regularly kept Stalin 'reliably informed' on the other party leaders. He was hardly a man of ideas. He once asked Stalin to autograph his book *On Lenin and Leninism* which had just come out. Stalin scrawled 'To my young friend in work, Comrade Mekhlis, from the Author. 23.5.24'. Mekhlis never so much as opened the book: dried and yellowing, its pages still uncut.

Mekhlis's influence was measured less by the posts he occupied than by Stalin's attitude to him. He was with Stalin very frequently, and would stay with him alone and for long periods. Stalin gave him his trickiest assignments. The archives contain an entire volume of Mekhlis's personal reports from various places. Hundreds of coded messages, telegrams, commentaries on one and the same thing: 'the enemy is trying to take over', 'carelessness everywhere', 'kindness is killing the cause', 'we need harsher methods'. Stalin trusted Mekhlis perhaps more than he trusted the others. Mekhlis knew how to sniff out 'enemies' where it would have seemed absurd to look. In July 1937, when the Red Banner song and dance ensemble were on tour in the east, Mekhlis cabled Stalin in code as follows:

I report: the situation in the Red Banner ensemble is difficult. I have come to the conclusion that a group of spies and terrorists is trying to take over. I fired nineteen people on the spot. I am conducting an investigation. It includes former officers, children of kulaks, anti-Soviet elements. I have brought in the chief of special branch. Should the ensemble be allowed to continue?[59]

It was a peculiar question to ask, since half the group was already under arrest. Such was the man who worked in Stalin's shadow, playing a special, sinister rôle.

But the man who enjoyed the greatest trust and who was probably closest to Stalin was A. N. Poskrebyshev, whom Khrushchev dubbed at the Twentieth Congress 'Stalin's faithful arms-bearer'. A former medical orderly, this son of a bootmaker from Vyatka was already working in the Central Committee apparatus by 1922, and from 1928 was Stalin's assistant in charge of a special section. Already a member of the Central Committee and a deputy in the Supreme Soviet, he was made a major general by Stalin during the war. Poskrebyshev was known for his extraordinary capacity for work and his assiduity. His eldest daughter, Galina Alexandrovna Yegorova, told me that her father worked at least sixteen hours a day. Although shortly before Stalin's death Beria managed to get Poskrebyshev out of the Kremlin, to the end of his days he remained his master's devoted servant. Incidentally, his first wife had been a distant relative of Trotsky's, a fact which in the end played a tragic rôle.

His daughter told me that he bitterly regretted not having kept a diary, but he had calculated that such an indiscretion would needlessly add to the precariousness of his existence.

All the information Stalin received, of whatever character, came through Poskrebyshev, who knew as much as his master about what was happening in the party and country at large. He was the perfect functionary – unthinking, unquestioning and to be found on the job at all times. His rôle in the corridors of power was, however, far more significant than his official status implied, thanks to Stalin's special disposition towards him. Although Poskrebyshev himself was not a cruel man, people behaved ingratiatingly towards him, as so much depended on how and when he would present their case.

Former Commissar of Railways I. V. Kovalev, who throughout the war reported two or three times a day to Stalin on the movement of forces, called Poskrebyshev a 'tough nut' who was always there whenever Stalin summoned him, the balding head bent over a heap of papers. 'He was a man with the memory of a computer. You could get an exact reply to any question. He was a walking encyclopedia.'

These were the people Stalin called his staff, but there were others, among them Malenkov, Kaganovich and Voroshilov, who were distinguished by always being in total agreement with Stalin on everything.

Voroshilov, for instance, tried in everything he did, however trivial, to support the leader. When the prominent army leader I. E. Yakir was arrested and sentenced to be shot, he wrote to Stalin, swearing that he was absolutely innocent of the crimes he'd been charged with. Stalin's response was a laconic scrawl on the file: 'He's a scoundrel and a prostitute,' and Voroshilov added, 'A totally accurate definition.'[60] Yakir was Voroshilov's subordinate, one of the most talented army leaders whom Voroshilov knew personally very well.

While Molotov, Kaganovich and Voroshilov were people close to Stalin who carried out his every wish, there were others who were equally close but who managed to preserve their good name. One such was Sergei Mironovich Kirov, a Bolshevik of Leninist background, utterly dedicated to the cause, and a simple, responsive sort of man. Wherever he worked, he was liked as an approachable and affable leader. When he was sent on Lenin's recommendation to Azerbaidzhan, his party dossier read: 'Stable in all respects ... An energetic worker ... More than persistent in carrying out all assignments. Balanced and has great political tact ... An excellent journalist ... First-class and excellent speaker ...'[61]

The party in Transcaucasia retained good memories of him. Following the Fourteenth Congress, at which the 'new opposition' attempted to use the Leningrad party organization as its base of support, the Central Committee sent Kirov to the second capital to act as secretary of the city and regional committees. According to his biographer, Yu. Pompeyev, one of Kirov's closest friends, Sergo Ordzhonikidze, wrote to the regional committee as follows:

> Dear friends,
> Your row has cost us dear: they've taken Comrade Kirov away from us. It's a great loss for us, but it will give you the strength you need. I have no doubt that everything will be sorted out for you in a couple of months. Kirov is a wonderfully good peasant, but apart from you he knows no one. I'm sure you will surround him with friendly trust. With all my heart, I wish you complete success.
> P.S. Look after our Kirych* properly, chaps, or he'll be roaming around without a roof over his head and nothing to eat.[62]

Stalin had known Kirov since October 1917. It is hard to say why he was drawn to this perpetually smiling, energetic healthy type. They often went on vacations together, their families were close, although as a rule they worked at some distance from each other. In a note to Ordzhonikidze, written in Sochi,

---

* A combination of Kirov and Mironych, his surname and abbreviated patronymic.

Stalin asked about Kirov's state of health, a rarity indeed, since Stalin was not interested in anyone's health but his own:

Dear Sergo,
So, what's Kirov up to there? Taking the Narzan water cure for his stomach ulcer? That stuff can finish you off. Who's the quack who 'prescribes' it?
Greetings to Zina.
Greetings to all from Nadya. Yours, Stalin.
Sochi 30 June 1925.[63]

There was probably no other party figure for whom Stalin showed such care and even affection, as Kirov. He liked this open, uncomplicated man. Wherever Kirov appeared, a crowd would gather round him. He was the life and soul of any party. Against a background of men like the inscrutable Molotov, or the scowling Kaganovich, or a toady like Voroshilov, Kirov was someone with whom it was possible to have a real human relationship.

Stalin gave signed copies of his books to very few people. Kirov, however, received *On Lenin and Leninism* inscribed in words one would have thought their author quite incapable of expressing: 'To S.M. Kirov, my friend and beloved brother, from the author. 23.05.24. Stalin'.

Every dictator has his weaknesses. Maybe Stalin liked Kirov's smile, his open Russian face, his lack of guile, his obsession with work. Once, on a Sunday when they were playing skittles together at Stalin's dacha – Stalin had a kitchen worker called Khorkovsky on his team, and Kirov had General Vlasik – Stalin asked his guest, 'What do you love most, Sergei?'

Kirov looked surprised, but replied, 'A Bolshevik should love his work more than his wife!'

'But what else?'

'Well, ideas, of course,' Kirov said with a straight face.

Stalin waved his arm vaguely but asked no more. He was probably wondering how you could 'love an idea'? Maybe Kirov had said it for effect? But he knew Kirov was not one to dissemble. He also knew that Kirov, like no one else, perhaps, could exert an influence even on him. The Ryutin affair had been a good example. M. N. Ryutin had been the commander of the Irkutsk military district in 1918, in 1920 he was the Irkutsk district party secretary and in the second half of the 1920s secretary of the Krasnaya Presnya district party committee in Moscow, a member of the editorial board of *Krasnaya Zvezda* ('Red Star') and a candidate member of the Central Committee. Then he had got carried away. In 1932, Stalin was told that Ryutin was circulating an extensive document entitled 'To All Members of the [Party]'. It was aimed mainly against Stalin, who was described there as nothing less than a dictator who carried an anti-Leninist muzzle in his hand. Stalin had demanded at the Politburo not merely Ryutin's expulsion from the party, but also the death penalty. It had been the first time he had attempted to settle someone's fate before the outcome of a trial. The Politburo had sat silent. They were faced with what looked like an attempt by Ryutin to create a 'counter-revolutionary organization', but the death penalty? The party leadership was in confusion. At this point Kirov spoke up: 'We mustn't do this. Ryutin is not a hopeless case, he's merely gone astray ... Who the hell knows how many hands wrote that letter ... We'll be misunderstood ...' For some reason, Stalin had agreed at once. Ryutin got ten years and died in 1938. It had not escaped Stalin's notice, however, that Kirov had expressed his opinion boldly and without so much as wondering whether to consult him first.

When P. P. Postyshev, while presiding at the Seventeenth Congress, announced 'Comrade Kirov has the floor,' the hall exploded into an ovation. Everyone stood up, even Stalin. The assembly applauded this other 'party favourite' for a long time. Only Stalin himself was ever given such a reception. Kirov's speech was extremely lively and informative and, like all the other speeches given at this congress, generously sprinkled with laudatory epithets about the General Secretary. Kirov may even have outdone many in this respect. Lamentable though it was, one must also understand that, even though the opportunity to exercise one's conscience is always there, at times, maybe most often, one can use that opportunity only by stepping outside the norms of ordinary behaviour. And always at the limit of a civic act. Neither Kirov nor anyone else was prepared to perform this act openly at the congress where, before the delegates' eyes and with their help, the cult of Stalin's personality was confirmed.

As we have seen, in the relative privacy of the secret ballot, however, the elections for the top party bodies had given Stalin an unpleasant surprise. His triumph was much overshadowed, but he gave no sign of his disappointment. He had the ability to maintain a mask of equanimity in the most critical situations, having long ago learned that this made a bigger impression on people than bustle and ostensible energy and striking the pose of a 'leader'. Having read the signal that a significant number of delegates were not pleased at his becoming the autocratic leader, he maintained an outward calm. After that moment, everything went according to plan. At the Central Committee plenum which took place following the congress, Kirov was elected a member of the Politburo and Orgburo, and a secretary of the Central Committee, remaining as secretary of the Leningrad party organization. Stalin had intended to transfer him from Leningrad to Moscow, but now he changed his mind.

Since the Seventeenth Congress in January 1934, Kirov's workload had increased. His responsibilities as a member of the Central Committee were heavy industry and the timber industry, and he therefore had frequent occasion to be in Moscow. As before, Stalin would telephone him when he was on one of his flying visits and they would meet to discuss the issues of the day. It looked as if things were going on as before between them, and that Kirov was still the 'friend and beloved brother'. It may be that in fact Stalin's attitude had cooled, that their relations became more official and that Stalin reprimanded Kirov on a number of occasions for some trivial mistake or other, but neither the documents nor the people I have interviewed who knew them both at the time support this view. On the other hand, Stalin knew how to keep his feelings and intentions well out of sight.

The news that on 1 December 1934 Kirov had been assassinated in the Smolny Institute in Leningrad came all the more as a shock. It was reported on 3 December that a preliminary investigation had established the killer to be Leonid Vasilyevich Nikolaev, born in 1904 and a former employee of the Leningrad Workers' and Peasants' Inspectorate.[64]

Only two days had elapsed since Kirov and the other delegates from Leningrad had returned from the plenum, where the important and welcome announcement had been made that bread and food rationing was to end. They had excitedly discussed this long-awaited step in the train. The whole population would be so relieved to hear it! They also exchanged opinions on the play they had seen, Bulgakov's *Days of the Turbins*, and they discussed the forthcoming meeting of the Leningrad party group which was set for 1 December. In general, Kirov arrived home feeling enthusiastic and ready to get down to work.

On the day of the meeting with the party group, Kirov finished preparing his report and went to the Smolny. He strolled along the corridor, exchanging greetings and comments with a large number of people, then turned left into a narrow passage leading to his office. An ordinary-looking man was walking towards him. As he reached the door of his office, two shots rang out, and people who rushed to the scene found Kirov lying face down and his killer writhing hysterically with the revolver still in his hand.

Two hours later, Stalin, Molotov, Voroshilov, Yezhov, Yagoda, Zhdanov, Agranov, Zakovsky and some others were on their way to Leningrad by special train. On arrival at the station, Stalin lambasted the Leningrad people who met them in obscene language, and struck Medved, the head of the local NKVD, in the face. Medved and his assistant, Zaporozhets, were soon transferred to work in the Far East and in 1937 they were exterminated. According to some accounts, Stalin himself conducted the first interrogation of Nikolaev in the presence of those who had accompanied him from Moscow. It was at once plain that there were many mysterious aspects of the murder. Khrushchev alluded to this at the Twentieth Congress, when he described the circumstances of Kirov's murder as enigmatic and still to be properly examined. He said that there were reasons for thinking that the killer, Nikolaev, was helped by one of Kirov's bodyguards. A month and a half before the murder, Nikolaev had been arrested for suspicious behaviour but was released without even having his apartment searched. It was also extremely suspicious, Khrushchev continued, that on 2 December a Chekist, who was one of Kirov's bodyguards, was killed when the car that was taking him in for questioning was involved in a crash, from which none of the other passengers sustained any injury. After the murder, the Leningrad NKVD chiefs were given very light sentences and then shot in 1937. Khrushchev surmised that they were shot in order to cover up any trace of the real organizers of the murder. Borisov, the Chekist who died in the accident, was the head of Kirov's bodyguard and according to some sources he had warned Kirov of a possible attempt on his life. In any event, the man who had twice apprehended Nikolaev, who was following Kirov while carrying a weapon and was then released on someone's authority, had been removed.

The archives that I have searched do not provide any further clues for making a more definitive statement on the Kirov affair. What is clear, however, is that the murder was not carried out on the orders of Trotsky, Zinoviev or Kamenev, which was soon put out as the official version. Knowing what we now know about Stalin, it is certain that he had a hand in it. The removal of two or three layers of indirect witnesses bears his hallmark.

Nikolaev's trial was carried out in great haste. Only twenty-seven days after the event the official sentence was published, describing Nikolaev as an active member of a clandestine Trotskyite-Zinovievite terrorist organization. The announcement was signed by the Deputy Procurator of the USSR A. Ya. Vyshinsky, and the special investigator L. P. Sheinin. As was to be expected, all those implicated in the murder, including Nikolaev, were shot.

But why 'as was to be expected'? Because on the very day of the murder, on Stalin's initiative (and without discussion by the Politburo), a government decree was issued, introducing certain amendments to the Criminal Code. Stalin was in such a hurry that there was 'not enough time' even to get it signed by Kalinin, the chairman of the Central Executive Committee – that is, the head of government. The document, embodying a credo of arbitrary rule, was signed by the secretary of the Executive Committee, A. S. Yenukidze. It stated that:

1 The investigating authorities are instructed to expedite cases of those accused of planning or carrying out terrorist acts.
2 Judicial bodies are instructed not to delay carrying out death sentences involved in crimes of this category on the assumption of possible clemency, as the Presidium of the Central Executive Committee considers clemency in such cases to be unacceptable.
3 Agencies of the Commissariat of Internal Affairs are instructed to carry out the death sentence on criminals in the above category as soon as possible after sentence has been pronounced.[65]

A number of cases under review in Moscow and elsewhere were now speeded up under the new regulations. Since Kirov had been murdered in Leningrad and the investigation linked the crime with the Zinovievites, a large group of 'conspirators' was arrested later in the month and put on trial in January 1935. They included Zinoviev and Kamenev, Yevdokimov, Bakaev, Kuklin, Gessen and others. No direct evidence was produced linking any of the accused with the crime. Following the Seventeenth Congress, Zinoviev, despite not having been re-elected to the Central Committee, had come back to life somewhat and had thought the storm had passed and that better times were coming. He had even written and published an article in *Bolshevik*, entitled 'The International Significance of the Last Decade'. It was to be his last. Now, out of the blue, he was arrested. When he read the report of the murder in the newspapers, together with commentaries on the 'Trotskyite-Zinovievite scoundrels', he suffered a total inner collapse. He knew now that the worst was in store. Under NKVD interrogation and again at the hands of the prosecutor, he had to 'confess' that 'in a general way' the former anti-party group could bear 'political responsibility' for what had happened. And that was enough. There was no need for argument or 'judicial proof'. The first rehearsal of the political trials was complete. Zinoviev received ten years, Kamenev five years and the rest received sentences in the same range, the sentences having been approved beforehand by Stalin. Thus continued the drama of two of Lenin's former comrades. Vain, inconsistent, probably insincere in their repentance, and disturbed, all these things they may have been, but they were certainly not criminals.

Kirov's murder marked the approach of a sinister era. The public believed that former revolutionaries were engaging in subversive, terrorist activity, that apparently there were wreckers, thieves and class enemies at large in society. Since there was no objective information or the slightest degree of openness, conditions were ideal for manipulating the minds of millions. Demands for the most decisive action to be taken against the terrorists were made at thousands of meetings. In the 1930s people had not lost faith in the great idea, and it was therefore possible to mobilize them with a slogan or to ignite their minds with a vision. But it was also possible to make them believe in 'spies, enemies, diversionaries and terrorists'. The press constantly raised the tension, 'revealing' and reporting on one new 'enemy centre' or 'conspiracy' or 'tergroup' (terrorist group) after another.

December 1, 1934 at once sharply raised the 'significance', as Stalin would say, of the NKVD's punitive personnel, who began rapidly to grow in number. Their powers were increased. As state organs, they would soon rival the party committees, and eventually overshadow them totally. The newspapers' most popular topic would be 'the need to strengthen awareness', while press propaganda would sow the seeds of suspicion in every mind. Many leaders would now be followed by NKVD agents. Stalin, who, as we have already said, was extremely anxious about a possible attempt on his own life, redoubled his bodyguards and reduced his public appearances to a minimum. Ordinary people gained the impression that there were hidden enemies in every factory, kolkhoz and university institute. Every failure, disaster, breakage or accident would be associated with sabotage. A situation was created in which Stalin could carry out his bloody purge while counting on the support of the misinformed masses.

Even before the murder of Kirov, Stalin had personally seen to the appointment of a number of individuals who would play a significant part in the struggle against the 'enemies of the people', characters who would perform a sinister rôle in the lawlessness of the approaching years. These were above all N. I. Yezhov, a member of the Orgburo, and from early 1935 a Central Committee secretary and one of the organizers of the 1935–36 purge; A. Ya. Vyshinsky, a former Menshevik who had become deputy and then Procurator of the USSR and with whose name the infamous and shameful political trials of 1937–38 were associated.

Orders and circulars and the press all called for the rooting out and unmasking of 'enemies'. And there were not a few of them, as it turned out. Countless reports of the discovery and unmasking of 'enemies' flooded into the centre. For instance:

To Comrade I. V. Stalin, Central Committee VKP(b)

To Comrade V. M. Molotov, Council of People's Commissars

The State Security board of the Administration of the People's Commissariat of Internal Affairs has completed its investigation in the case of a counter-revolutionary terrorist grouping which was preparing to carry out a terrorist act against Comrade Vladimir Ivanov, Central Committee member and Secretary of the Northern Regional Committee and member of the Central Executive Committee.

The accused are the following seven people: N. G. Rakitin, P. V. Zaostrovsky, P. N. Popov, G. N. Levinov, N. I. Ivlev, A. V. Zaostrovsky, N. A. Koposov. Of these only P. N. Popov has admitted complete guilt.

It is proposed that the Rakitin case be heard by the circuit session of the military collegium of the USSR Supreme Court in Archangel according to the Act of 1 December 1934.

We think it essential that the chief accused, Rakitin, P. V. Zaostrovsky and Levinov, be sentenced to be shot, and that the rest be deprived of liberty for varying periods. We request your instructions.

23 January 1935. A. Vyshinsky, V. Ulrikh.

To Central Committee Secretary I. V. Stalin

L. I. Belozir has been sentenced to death. As a member of a counter-revolutionary underground organization of Ukrainian nationalists, she recruited Shcherbin and Tereshchenko who were supposed to carry out a terrorist act on Comrades Postyshev and Balitsky during the October 1934 celebrations in Kiev.

Under interrogation Belozir stubbornly refused to divulge any information whatever and also declared that she would not ask for mercy. In view of this, I request permission to carry out the sentence on Belozir.

Comrades Vyshinsky and V. A. Balitsky consider it permissible to carry out the sentence.

3 February 1935. V. Ulrikh.

To Central Committee Secretary I. V. Stalin

On 9 March of this year in the city of Leningrad the circuit session of the military collegium of the USSR Supreme Court under my chairmanship examined in camera the case of Leonid Nikolaev's accomplices, Milda Draule, Olga Draule and Roman Kuliner.

In reply to my asking her what her purpose was in obtaining permission to attend the Leningrad party meeting on 1 December at which Comrade Kirov was to speak, Milda Draule replied that she 'wanted to help Leonid Nikolaev'. 'How?' 'That would depend on the circumstances.' We had thus established that the accused had intended to aid Nikolaev in carrying out the terrorist act.

All three were sentenced to the extreme penalty, to be shot. The sentence was carried out on the night of 10 March.

I request instructions as to whether a statement should be given to the press.

11 March 1935. V. Ulrikh.[66]

'Justice' was lightning swift: trial on the 9th, execution on the night of the 10th, report to the high priest on the 11th. Ulrikh's report shows how superficial the whole procedure was. It would soon become the norm.

The last 'case' is worth dwelling on. A year or so before the event, a rumour was put into circulation to the effect that Nikolaev's ex-wife, Milda Draule, had been having an affair with Kirov. People who knew Kirov denied this adamantly. Possibly someone wanted to arouse the neurotic Nikolaev against Kirov. When Ya. Agranov and L. Sheinin began their investigation, Nikolaev first stated that his motive for the murder was revenge, but then went on to admit that he had been acting for the clandestine Trotskyite-Zinovievite group. Apparently the name of Draule was employed by the organizers of the crime to make Nikolaev 'more determined'. In any case, both Milda and Olga Draule presented a risk and it was decided to get rid of them, which was duly done.

Stalin kept up the pressure. In the middle of 1935 his interview with H. G. Wells, given a year earlier, was published, and with obvious intent. In it Stalin asserted that the main point of the dictatorship of the proletariat was coercion. To Wells's question, 'Isn't your propaganda old-fashioned, inasmuch as it is the propaganda of coercive methods?', Stalin replied:

Communists do not at all idealize the use of coercion. But they do not wish to be caught unawares, they cannot count on the old world leaving the scene of its own accord, they can see that the old order is defending itself with force, and therefore the Communists say to the workers, 'Be prepared to answer force with force ...' What's the good of a military leader who lulls his army's alertness, an army leader who does not understand that the enemy will not surrender and that he must be finished off?[67]

How he loved that phrase, 'to finish off'. In countless speeches he called for the opposition, or the remnants of the exploiting classes, or the kulaks, the degenerates, the double dealers, spies and terrorists, to be finished off. And finish them off he did, as well as his potential rivals. As long as the resolutions of the Thirteenth Congress, expressing the wishes of those who were familiar with Lenin's Letter, and as long as Lenin's warnings about him were still fresh in Stalin's mind, his attitude to the oppositionists was as towards his ideological enemies. As we have seen, however, party congresses had continued to show a measure of independence. Those who had recanted were usually reinstated in the party fairly quickly, and they were given responsible jobs and began publishing their articles again. For instance, Zinoviev and Kamenev, who had been readmitted into the party in June 1928, openly expressed the hope that 'the party would again require their experience', no doubt with top posts in mind. Bukharin, Rykov and Tomsky were still being dubbed 'accomplices of the kulaks' in the press, and yet at the Sixteenth Congress they were elected on to the Central Committee. Such tolerance was not merely laudable, it represented the remnant of party democracy. Stalin found such endless 'wobbling' of certain people on this score extremely irritating. For him, dictatorship and democracy were incompatible.

He would soon bank on maintaining society in a state of permanent 'civil war'. It was easier to manipulate and govern a people that was on constant alert, watching everyone else. And with the help of his entourage, he would keep society in this state of political tension until the end of his life.

Kirov's murder provided an excellent pretext for intensifying the course domestic policy was taking. Stalin could not forget that a quarter of the delegates at the Seventeenth Congress had voted against him. But how many more were there like them in the country at large? Few would at that time have imagined that, of 1225 delegates at that congress, 1108 would soon be arrested, and that most of them would perish in the cellars and concentration camps of the NKVD. Of 139 members and candidate members of the Central Committee elected at the congress, 98 would be arrested and shot. And most of them were among the most active participants in the October Revolution, as well as the reconstruction of the country after its collapse, and the great leap from the sickle to the modern industrial state. The Leninist 'old guard' was consciously liquidated because they knew too much. Stalin wanted devoted executives, functionaries of a younger generation, people who had not known him in an earlier life.

For this reason, in the middle of 1935 he abolished the Society of Old Bolsheviks and the Society of Ex-Political Prisoners. The archives of these bodies were in the charge of a commission consisting of Yezhov, Shkiryatov and Malenkov. These archives may well have served, in the nightmare years of the late 1930s, to support accusations against many Old Bolsheviks of 'crimes' committed forty years earlier.

This period also marked the beginning of the rise of L. P. Beria, first secretary of the Central Committee of the Georgian Communist Party. In the middle of 1935 the Central Committee of the All-Russian Party published a 'work' by Beria entitled 'On the Question of the History of the Bolshevik Organizations in Transcaucasia'. Printed on good paper and bound in hard covers, a rarity in those days, half the book consisted of quotations from Stalin and unbridled praise of the 'leader'. But, more significantly, it contained an open political denunciation of two prominent Bolsheviks, Yenukidze and Orakhelashvili. Despite the fact that the former was a long-standing personal friend of Stalin's, and a member of the Central Committee and Central Executive Committee, the fate of both of them was sealed. Stalin always believed denunciations, and Beria quickly absorbed this fact. To be sure, Orakhelashvili tried to protest by writing to Stalin and enclosing the draft of a rebuttal for publication in *Pravda*. Stalin's reply amounted to a rejection of the Old Bolshevik's statement:

> To Comrade Orakhelashvili,
>   I have received your letter.
>   1) The Central Committee does not intend (and has no reason) to raise the question of your work in IMEL [the Marx-Engels-Lenin Institute]. You got over-excited and evidently decided to raise it. This was pointless. Stay at the Institute and carry on with your work.
>   2) A letter to *Pravda* ought to be printed, but I don't think the text of your letter is satisfactory. In your place I would take out all its 'polemical beauty', all the 'excursions' into history, plus the 'decisive protest', and I would say simply and briefly that such and such mistakes were made, but that Comrade Beria's criticism of these mistakes is, let's say, too harsh and is not justified by the nature of the mistakes. Or something in this vein.
>   8.viii.89 I. Stalin.[68]

The country and the party were standing on the threshold of terrible events. The man who had sanctified only the coercive aspect of the dictatorship of the proletariat had become the dictator. Plaudits such as the 'beloved leader', 'a military leader of genius', 'wise architect', could not disguise the fact that he was a deep-dyed dictator. The people did not understand this at the time, and decades would have to pass before they did. Meanwhile, 1934 ended on a tragic note. First the 'Congress of Victors', then the preparation for the Terror. Perhaps, in defiance of the historical calendar, 1937 began on 1 December 1934?

5

THE LEADER'S MANTLE

*'False gods must be repudiated, but that
is not all: the reasons for their existence
must be sought beneath their masks.'*
– Alexander Herzen

CHAPTER 22

A Commanding Personality

As the Stalin cult developed in the period following the Seventeenth Congress, the General Secretary took steps to reduce sharply the collective rôle in the decision-making process. He no longer had any need of the opinion of others. Between 1934 and his death in 1953, only two party congresses, one party conference and twenty-two plenary meetings of the Central Committee were held. Thirteen years elapsed between the Eighteenth and Nineteenth Congresses, and the Central Committee did not meet at all in the years 1941, 1942, 1943, 1945, 1946, 1948, 1950 and 1951. The Central Committee was no longer the 'Areopagus of wisdom' it had been in 1931, but had been turned into little more than the party chancery, a handy device for carrying out Stalin's decisions. The party had in effect become an obedient machine for executing the 'commanding personality's' orders. And yet, in 1925, while preparing for the Fourteenth Congress and editing the draft party statutes, Stalin had stressed the special importance of convening regular congresses annually, and had urged that the Central Committee should have at least one plenary meeting every two months.

The growth of bureaucratic tendencies in the party enhanced Stalin's peculiar notion of party unity. As we have seen, in the 1920s party policy was opposed by significant groups of Communists who were far from being 'enemies'. Sometimes these differences arose from a particular evaluation of the situation, and sometimes from the character of individuals. Looking back on all those 'oppositions' and 'groupings', it seems that in essence they were concerned with the following questions: how should democracy be developed in terms of concrete policy, what was to be the relationship between the leader and the party, and what part was to be played by the masses in the revolutionary process? In many cases the oppositionists were simply against authoritarianism and were not willing to accept a one-dimensional position on a given idea, that is, the uniform psychology for which Stalin strove.

There were in those early days many people who did not subscribe to the party programme. As a rule they entertained other ideals or social priorities. At the Tenth Congress of March 1921, against a background of economic chaos and external threat and the proliferation of various oppositional groups in the party, Lenin initiated his notorious resolution banning factions. After his report, the congress agreed that all factional groups be disbanded at once. Facing mounting unrest and working-class discontent with the actions of the party, the resolution made it plain that party unity was particularly needed at that moment, and that complete trust between party members and the friendly avant-garde of the proletariat was essential.[1] While this ruling played a large part in rallying the party, its purpose was not to stifle alternative thinking or to prevent the clash of opinions. It was designed to prevent these differences of opinion from becoming organized as rival groups which would threaten the existence of the party as such.

Stalin often exploited this resolution when he was attacking the various 'oppositions' and 'deviations', and gradually the very terms 'opposition' and 'oppositionist', when uttered by him, acquired the meaning of 'enemy'. In time, any opinion, even the private opinion of another leading party figure, that differed from Stalin's own would be condemned as a 'struggle against the party', or 'hostile activity'. In the struggle for unity, as understood dogmatically by Stalin, he gradually killed off the healthy exchange of opinion, the free expression by Communists of their views, and their criticism of the higher party organs. Unthinking like-mindedness became the norm in party life. Under the banner of creating a monolithic party, Stalin systematically destroyed the democratic principle of internal party exchange. For him unity meant dedication, unquestioning obedience, readiness to support any decision of the higher organs, and by installing these characteristics, Stalin himself encouraged the habit of dogmatic thinking in the party, while he destroyed the creative initiative of the masses.

But departing from the 'orthodox' canon, however trivially, was not condemned on grounds of dogma alone. Speaking at the January 1938 plenum of the Central Committee, Malenkov cited the expulsion from the party of one Kushchev in the Sarachinsk party organization in Kalmykia. The following exchange had taken place during a political education period:

Question: 'Can we build socialism in one country?'

Kushchev replied: 'Socialism can be built in one country, and we are building it.'

'But will we build communism in one country?'

'Yes, we will build communism in one country.'

'What about full communism?'

'Yes, we'll build it.'

'And will we build final communism?'

Kushchev paused to think. 'Without a world revolution, final communism is a bit more doubtful. But I'll have a look at *Questions of Leninism* and see wha. Comrade Stalin has to say about it.'[2]

For expressing doubt, the wretched Kushchev had been expelled from the party and taken off his job. But it was neither the dogmatism, nor the expression of the Stalin cult, demanding such rigorous political uniformity, that concerned Malenkov: it was 'the plotting of enemies' who had become entrenched 'in every factory, collective and state farm'. Kushchev had made the tiniest slip and the 'enemies' had exploited it by expelling him from the party. Such was Malenkov's logic.

Such interpretations distorted any understanding of unity which pre-supposed a synthesis of the collective will and the opportunity to express one's position freely. After all, the Tenth Congress resolution on unity had envisaged that the party would ceaselessly continue to struggle against all forms of bureaucratism, that it would try new methods for broadening demo-cracy and initiative.[3] Now, any Communist who dared to come out with a new proposal or initiative or who disagreed with any aspect of party policy risked being abused or simply assigned to the assembly of 'enemies'. Communists were more and more expected simply to 'support' and 'approve', and less and less to take a real part in the debate of important issues of party and social life. And in the process, the 'leader' was automatically raised higher and higher above the party and turned into the 'predominant personality'.

On Stalin's suggestion, the Seventeenth Congress abolished the Central Control Commission which had supervised the work of the Central Committee and Politburo. Its functions were handed over to the central organs and above all to Stalin himself.

Gradually Stalin's decisions were accepted by everyone as those of the party. From the mid-1930s his directives were being registered as orders from the Central Committee or as general instructions. His power became virtually unbounded. For instance, before and during the war, by which time the 'night watch' had become the norm for party leaders, Stalin quite often invited a number of Politburo members and candidates to dine with him at his dacha at Kuntsevo. They usually included Molotov, Voroshilov, Kaganovich, Beria and Zhdanov. Less frequent guests at these nocturnal occasions were Andreyev, Kalinin, Mikoyan, Shvernik and Voznesensky. Affairs of the party and state and military matters would be discussed and Stalin would sum up. Malenkov, and occasionally Zhdanov, would record the discussion as Politburo minutes. Arguments did not arise. The comrades tried their best to guess Stalin's opinion in advance and to say yes in good time. There were never any disagreements of principle with Stalin and even the autocrat himself was at times irritated by the kowtowing. On the eve of the Eighteenth Congress in 1939, for instance, the report that Stalin was preparing was discussed and everyone around the table chorused their comradely approval. Stalin sat and listened and then suddenly burst out: 'Ha, I gave you the variant I'd thrown out and you all chant your hallelujahs. The speech I'm actually going to give is completely different!'

They all stopped short and an awkward silence descended. But then Beria quickly recovered himself. 'But one can feel your hand in this version. So if you've revised even this version, one can imagine how strong the final report is going to be!'

The Politburo elected at the Seventeenth Congress consisted of Andreyev, Voroshilov, Kaganovich, Kalinin, Kirov, Kosior, Kuibyshev, Molotov, Ordzhonikidze and Stalin. It met fairly regularly, although not always in its full complement. Most issues were settled by a small circle consisting of Stalin, Molotov, Kaganovich and Voroshilov, plus, at a later date, Zhdanov and Beria. In due course, Stalin would create various commissions within the Politburo, the so-called 'fives', 'sevens' or 'nines'. As Khrushchev revealed to the Twentieth Congress, this system was institutionalized by a special decree of the Politburo. Of course, even in Lenin's day the Central Committee had created special commissions to deal with issues that arose, as they must in any more or less complex political context. But however important they may have been, their decisions could only be ratified by a full meeting of the Politburo or Central Committee. Under Stalin, it was of course his opinion that guided the small commissions and thus the party as a whole. He loved to hear the other members of the leadership expounding their views, while he would wait until the end before giving his own, which would usually clinch the matter.

On the numerous documents which he reviewed, Stalin would scrawl simply 'Agreed', 'In favour', 'Maybe', and occasionally he would send a paper to his fellow-members of this or that body to elicit their opinions, however little attention he might pay to them.

For instance, in 1936 Pyatakov wrote to him requesting permission to order the test flight of the stratospheric balloon CO-35-I, 'given favourable weather conditions'. Stalin wrote on the letter, as if seeking advice: 'To Comrade Voroshilov. What do you think?' Voroshilov replied: 'I think permission may be given. 7.4.36.' Further down there appears a very categorical, 'I'm against. I. Stalin.'[4]

Under such circumstances, collegiality was soon turned into the collective automatic approval of whatever the leader wanted, and the foundations of bureaucratic absolutism were thus well and truly laid.

Examining the results of the many referenda that were circulated among the leadership, whether ballots with names or postal votes on various issues, I have not come across a single instance of anyone even indirectly casting doubt on the blatantly mistaken and even criminal proposals submitted by Stalin. More will be said of this later. For now, let us repeat that no one in the Central Committee leadership made any attempt to exercise their conscience when they had the chance, however late in the day. No one wished to object to Stalin in even the most delicate way. Even when they found themselves on the very threshold of oblivion, they would obediently concur with the leader's

opinion, knowing that it would do nothing to mitigate their sentence. And yet the Central Committee was not composed entirely of yes-men who had been promoted by Stalin.

The mutual relationship of the party and its leader, Stalin believed, should be consolidated by mass publications which should be accessible to both the party and the people. Such were the textbook, *History of the All-Russian Communist Party (bolsheviks). Short Course*, published in 1938, and ten years later the *Short Biography of I. V. Stalin*. In *Bolshevik* No. 9, 1937, Stalin published a letter to the compilers of the all-important *Short Course*. The main emphasis in the book, he wrote, should be on the party's struggle against the factions and groupings, the anti-Bolshevik tendencies. Plainly, the history of the party consisted of much more than the struggle with the factions, but in any textbook written on this principle, Stalin would inevitably occupy centre-stage.

Nor did he hesitate to instruct the compilers of the textbook to rely on his own ideas. For instance, he suggested they refer to 'Engels's letter to Bernstein of 1882, which I cite in my report on the social democratic deviation in the party to the Seventh Plenum of the Comintern Executive Committee, together with my commentary on it'. Without the commentaries, he added, 'the struggle against the factions and tendencies in the [party] will seem like a meaningless squabble, and the Bolsheviks appear as incorrigible and indefatigable squabblers and trouble-makers.'[5] The team of authors, acting on the orders of the Central Committee, soon finished the *Short Course* and it remained for a long time the chief, if not the only guide for the political education of the Soviet people. Printed in nearly 43 million copies, it was permeated with examples of Stalin's 'genius', his 'wisdom' and 'foresight'.

The first edition states: 'The Central Committee commission, under the leadership of Comrade Stalin and with his active participation, planned the *Short Course of the History of the [Party]*.' This formula was not to Stalin's liking, and the *Short Biography* of Stalin, carefully edited by him and published later, contained an 'improved' variant: 'In 1938 the *History of the [Party]: Short Course* appeared, written by Comrade Stalin and approved by a commission of the Central Committee of the [Party].'[6]

He was not at all abashed by the fact that a book which so lauded him should also turn out to have been written by him. It merely confirmed the ideological basis of his absolute rôle as leader and his control over the party and the state. Having physically got rid of all of Lenin's most prominent comrades, he now proceeded to erase them from history as well. Apart from Lenin and Stalin, the *Short Course* contains mention of no other concrete individuals as creators of the revolution and socialism. It mentions only 'enemies'.

The book became essential reading for Communists, university students, and the entire state-wide system of political education. It consisted almost entirely of a series of Stalin's 'axioms': there were two leaders of the revolution, Lenin and Stalin; chief credit for the building of socialism in the USSR belonged to

Stalin; after Lenin, there was only one leader, and that was the 'wise', 'far-seeing', 'bold', 'decisive', etc. etc. Stalin. By means of this mass publication the Stalinist version was broadcast to the whole population. Its simple style and primitive arguments made it accessible to everyone as a teaching aid, and it came to occupy a central place in the educational system that had emerged by the middle of the 1930s.

After its publication on 1 October 1938, Stalin called a meeting of Moscow and Leningrad propagandists and told them, among other things, that 'one of the reasons for publishing this book was to eliminate the gap between Marxism and Leninism'. He went on, without a shred of embarrassment: 'Stalin's book *On the Foundations of Leninism* presents the new and particular contribution Lenin made to Marxism. I wouldn't say it includes everything, but it does provide all the essential contributions made to Marxism by Lenin.'[7] This was the highest acclaim the book could be given, and he was giving it to his own work. By this time he had come to see himself both as a uniquely wise leader and a great theorist.

The emperor Tiberius, according to Suetonius, knew his future in advance and had long foreseen the hatred and ignominy that awaited him.[8] Stalin was not troubled by such thoughts. His papers contain ample evidence that he believed himself immortalized in the people's minds. After the Seventeenth Congress, unlike Tiberius, he took steps to secure and consolidate his glory for centuries to come. His autocratic rule was gradually reinforced by a host of cult acts and rites. For instance, Stalin Stipends and Stalin Prizes were introduced. The order, issued in August 1925 by the government with Stalin's participation, for the introduction of the Lenin Prize was simply forgotten and was not revived until September 1956. The national anthem, in which Stalin took a personal hand, reflected his rôle in the destiny of the Fatherland:

> Stalin has raised us in loyalty to the people,
> To labour and to heroic feats he has inspired us.

S. Mikhalkov and El-Registan, the composers of the anthem, submitted the text to Stalin who made amendments which are still to be found in the archives. In place of 'A noble union of free peoples' Stalin inserted 'An indestructible union of free republics'. The second stanza was much revised. The variant submitted to Stalin read:

> The sun of freedom shone through the storm,
> Lenin lit up the path to the future for us,
> We were raised by Stalin, the people's elected,
> To labour and to heroic feats he has inspired us.

After Stalin's pencil had worked them over, the second and third lines looked like this:

The great Lenin lit up our path,
Stalin raised us in loyalty to the people ...

Mikhalkov and El-Registan naturally agreed at once to Stalin's changes, as did Molotov, Voroshilov, Beria, Malenkov and Shcherbakov, who had been assembled by Stalin on the evening of 28 October 1943. Thus, Stalin did more than merely 'approve' the final text. For instance, without explaining why he did not like it, he rejected one proposed verse:

Live for centuries, O land of socialism,
Let our banner bring peace to the world,
Live and be strong glorious Fatherland,
Our great people will defend you.[9]

The anthem contained no mention of the party, despite the required dose of references to its General Secretary. The idea was gradually being inculcated in the minds of the people that Stalin was not only the leader of the party, he was also the leader of the entire nation, an idea publicly expressed in concentrated form in December 1939 by Politburo member Nikita Khrushchev:

All the peoples of the Soviet Union see Stalin as their friend, their father and leader.
Stalin in his simplicity is the people's friend.
Stalin in his love for the people is the father of the people.
Stalin in his wisdom as leader of the peoples' struggle is the leader of the peoples.[10]

In a chapter entitled 'The Leader of the Peoples', Stalin's minstrel Yaroslavsky (real name Gubelman) wrote: 'Beginning in the 1890s, Comrade Stalin travelled the same path as Lenin, always together with Lenin and never diverting from that path.'[11]

Besides the panegyrics, however, the author, perhaps inadvertently, let slip some truths. For instance, in a number of places Yaroslavsky stresses 'Stalin's mercilessness towards enemies'.

Reading such effusions, Stalin increasingly felt that he still had some way to go before reaching the pinnacle of his ascent. No Russian tsar had ever been so lauded. He came in the end to believe in his earthly messianic rôle as the infallible, all-seeing almighty. The more ceremoniously his triumph as leader was celebrated, the deeper roots of the national tragedy took hold in the social soil.

It must be said that these cult rituals, besides bolstering Stalin as the absolute ruler, also performed a certain stabilizing and unifying function, even if it was on the basis of dogma. In the absence of socialist democracy, inculcating faith in the leader and in his wisdom and infallibility soon produced results. Despite the horrifying repressions of the 1930s, state totalitarianism and dictatorship, the foundations of Soviet society remained firm.

CHAPTER 23

Stalin's Mind

Trotsky's description of Stalin as 'an outstanding mediocrity' has been widely accepted as accurate, but is it really plausible? Could someone with so little mental ability have been a member of the party's top bodies from 1912, or deserve Lenin's description as one of the 'outstanding leaders', or emerge from the complex tangle of political contradictions of the 1920s as the victor over people with greater abilities than he had in many respects?

The fact is that his crimes, his cunning, his cruelty and his mercilessness towards those he regarded as his enemies, have come to dominate any assessment of his personality. These traits, however, highlight a man's moral character, not his intelligence. In this sense, Stalin's exceptional intellect – which I believe it to have been – has been framed by attributes that can only be defined as anti-human. Stalin's intellect in the moral sense has been all but nullified by being inextricably linked to manifestations of evil. One could say, in brief, that he had 'an exceptionally evil mind'. Any moral flaw in itself represents a huge gap in the intellect, creating a twilight zone in the mind, devoid of any scintilla of good. One may say that a moral gap in the personality can reduce even a powerful mind to the functions of a calculating machine, a logical mechanism to the level of a rational but pitiless apparatus.

Having frequently suffered from humiliating inadequacy in conversation with his opponents before the revolution, Stalin was determined not to play the part of an extra in future discussions and therefore did his utmost to broaden to the maximum the range of his political and theoretical knowledge. In addition to his enormous workload, he laboured to raise his intellectual level. The archives contain a very interesting document which, despite its length, deserves to be quoted extensively.

In May 1925 Stalin charged Tovstukha with assembling a good personal library for him. Hesitantly, his assistant asked what sort of books he had in mind. Stalin was about to begin dictating a list, when instead he suddenly sat down at his desk and, with Tovstukha looking on and almost without thinking, took ten to fifteen minutes to dash off the following list, writing in an ordinary school exercise book with a pencil:

Note to librarian. My advice (and request):

1 Books should be arranged according to subject, not author: a) philosophy; b) psychology; c) sociology; d) political economy; e) finance; f) industry; g) agriculture; h) cooperatives; i) Russian history; j) history of other countries; k) diplomacy; l) foreign and domestic trade; m) military affairs; n) national question; o) Party, Comintern and other Congresses and Conferences, (with resolutions, without decrees and law codes); p) position of workers; q) position of peasants; r) Komsomol (everything there is in separate editions); s) history of the revolution in other countries; t) 1905; u) February revolution 1917; v) October revolution 1917; w) Lenin and Leninism; x) history of the RKP and Comintern; y) on discussions in RKP (articles and pamphlets); z) trade unions; aa) creative literature; ab) artistic criticism; ac) political journals; ad) scientific journals; ae) various dictionaries; af) memoirs.

2 Books to be removed from the above categories and shelved separately: a) Lenin; b) Marx; c) Engels; d) Kautsky; e) Plekhanov; f) Trotsky; g) Bukharin; h) Zinoviev; i) Kamenev; j) Lafargue; k) Luxemburg; l) Radek.

3 All other books are to be classified by author (except any textbooks, popular magazines, anti-religious pulp literature and so on, which are to be put to one side).[12]

Considering that this was scribbled down with virtually no forethought, and also given the state of the 'book culture' of the time, a certain breadth of vision was clearly at work here. At the top of the pyramid he placed the basic components of Marxism, history and a number of specific areas of knowledge directly connected with political activity and the struggle against the oppositions.

The application of ideas through action and behaviour provides a measure of a given intellect. Stalin's library, and the traces he left on it, therefore provide a certain amount of material in this respect.

Many of the books from the Kremlin, the dacha or the apartment, some of them bearing an *ex libris* label 'Library No. .... I. V. Stalin', contain annotations, markings and marginal comments. Lenin's *Collected Works*, for instance, are covered with underlinings, ticks and exclamation marks in the margins. Stalin evidently returned to certain items several times, for they are marked in red, blue and ordinary pencil. The topics that seem to have interested him most were Lenin's views on the dictatorship of the proletariat, his struggles with the Mensheviks and Socialist Revolutionaries, and his speeches at party congresses.

Of his contemporaries' writings, Stalin referred most frequently to Bukharin and Trotsky. For instance, Bukharin's pamphlet 'The Technique and Economy of Modern Capitalism', published in 1932, is covered with Stalin's red pencil marks, particularly what the author had to say about productive forces and production relations. M. Smolensky's book *Trotsky*, published in Berlin in 1921, is underlined in those places which criticize his arch-enemy: 'Trotsky is prickly and impatient', he has 'an imperious nature which loves to dominate', 'he loves political power', 'Trotsky is a political adventurist of genius'.[13] From whatever source he could, Stalin sought ammunition against his rivals, e. g. Trotsky's 1920 pamphlet 'Terrorism and Communism', Zinoviev's 'War and the Crisis of Socialism', Kamenev's 'N. G. Chernyshevsky', A. Bubnov's 'The Main Stages in the Development of the Communist Party in Russia', I. Narvsky's 'On the History of the Struggle of Bolshevism with Luxemburgism', Jan Sten's 'On the Stabilization of Capitalism' and others. Anything concerned with 'struggle' seems to have caught his attention.

He maintained a lifelong interest in historical literature, above all the lives of emperors and tsars. He made a careful study of I. Bellyarminov's *Course of Russian History*, R. Vipper's *History of the Roman Empire*, Alexei Tolstoy's *Ivan the Terrible*, and a miscellany entitled *The Romanovs*. All the school and university textbooks that were collected for him in the 1930s and 1940s bear the marks of his close examination.[14] He evidently saw in Russian history, as interpreted by him, a means of forming the kind of public opinion that would accept his authoritarian rule.

His assistants drew his attention to whatever they thought might interest him in the serious journals, and during thirty- to forty-minute breaks that he took from working on official business, he would scan articles and leaf through the latest novels. Occasionally, he would be moved to press the bell for an assistant and ask to be connected with a writer or the head of one of the creative unions so that he could communicate his congratulations or comments personally. Sometimes he took up the pen himself. After reading Korneichuk's *In the Ukrainian Steppes* (1940), for instance, he at once wrote the following brief note:

Respected Alexander Yevdokimovich,
I have read your *In the Ukrainian Steppes*. It is a wonderful piece, artistically whole, joyful and merry. I'm only concerned that it is not a bit too merry. There is a danger that too much merriment in a comedy can distract the reader's attention from the content.
Incidentally, I have added a few words on page 68. It makes things clearer.
Greetings!
I. Stalin

He had inserted the following:

1 'the tax would now be taken not on the basis of the number of livestock, but according to the area of kolkhoz land ... '
2 'raise as many kolkhoz cattle as you like, the tax will remain the same ... '[15]

Always on the lookout for practical opportunities, he had seized on Korneichuk's play to clarify a recent ruling of the Central Committee. Nor was he slow in commenting on what did not please him. After reading N. Erdman's play *The Suicide* (1931), he wrote to the producer, Stanislavsky:

Respected Konstantin Sergeyevich,
I don't think much of the play *Suicide*.* My closest comrades think it is empty
and even harmful. I don't say the theatre will not achieve its aim. Kultprop†
(i. e. Comrade Stetsky) will help you with this. There are comrades who know
about artistic matters. I'm a dilettante in such things.
    Greetings
    9.xi.31 I. Stalin[16]

Wishing to pass in artistic circles as a 'liberal', Stalin here flaunts his dilettant-
ism, but in fact his judgements on plays, books, films, music and architecture
were categorical in the extreme. Making utterances on practically everything,
as first person in the state, he indeed became a universal dilettante, and this
in turn worked to enhance his image as the omniscient leader.

Stalin also closely followed the literature that was being published abroad.
Nearly everything about or by Trotsky was translated for him, in one copy. He
also read the émigré editions. In December 1935, when B. Tal, the manager
of the press and publications section of the Central Committee, requested the
Politburo to say which of the following White émigré subscriptions should be
taken out for 1936, *Poslednie novosti, Vozrozhdenie, Sotsialisticheskii vestnik,
Znamya Rossii, Byulleten' ekonomicheskogo kabineta Prokopovicha, Kharbinskoe
vremya, Novoe Russkoe slovo, Sovremennye zapiski, Illustrirovannaya Rossiya‡*
Stalin snapped, 'Order the lot!'[17]

He had a special cupboard in his study in which he kept a great deal of
purely hostile émigré literature, including virtually all of Trotsky's works,
heavily scored with underlinings and comments. Any interview or statement
that Trotsky gave to the Western press was immediately translated and delivered to Stalin.

Whatever else one may say of him, his religious upbringing evidently had a
lasting effect, as witness his attitude to anti-religious literature, which he flatly
described as pulp, and also some of his speeches and writings, for instance, his
dramatic speech on the radio on 3 July 1941, in which he addressed the Soviet
people as 'brothers and sisters', not a formula they had been accustomed to
hearing from him. After the celebration of his fiftieth birthday in 1929, he sent
the following handwritten note of thanks to *Pravda*: 'Your congratulations and
greetings I will bear on behalf of the great party of the working class which
gave birth to me and which raised me in its own image and likeness.'[18]

In a conversation between Stalin and Churchill in Moscow in August 1942,
the discussion turned to Lloyd George, who (like Churchill himself) had been
one of the instigators of the Allied Intervention against the Bolsheviks during
the civil war. Stalin fell silent and sighed, as if summing up all his memories

---

* The name of the play is *The Suicide*, i.e. one who has committed suicide. Stalin calls it *Suicide*,
meaning the act of suicide.
    † The department of culture and propaganda.
    ‡ All these newspapers were published in Berlin, Paris, New York, Prague and Harbin, by émigré
groups ranging from the extreme right to conservative, liberal and socialist.

of those distant times: 'All that is in the past, and the past belongs to God.'[19] No one would want to suggest that religious elements played a central part in Stalin's outlook, but his dogmatic cast of mind strongly suggests a religious origin. He loved formulae, definitions and fixed interpretations. In order to crush or shut up his opponents 'incontrovertibly', he would spend hours looking for the right word or expression in the Marxist classics. Thus, at the April 1929 joint Central Committee and Central Control Commission plenum, he accused Bukharin of 'not knowing his Lenin'.

At a meeting prior to the plenum, Bukharin had argued, quite rationally, that the transfer of excessive resources from agriculture to industry would impose an 'insupportable tribute' upon the peasantry. Stalin at once took note of the phrases 'military feudal exploitation of the peasants' and 'tribute' and spent a long time that evening, in his library with Tovstukha, scouring Lenin's works. After digging, he found what he was looking for – a whole array of 'murderous' arguments, so he thought. At the plenum he declared:

Bukharin has destroyed himself here over the alleged fact that Marxist literature cannot tolerate the word 'tribute'. He was upset and surprised that the Central Committee and Marxists in general can permit themselves to use the word 'tribute'. But what is so surprising, if one can show that this word was granted civil rights long ago in the articles of no less a Marxist than Comrade Lenin? [Pause.] Unless Bukharin thinks Lenin does not satisfy the requirements of a Marxist?

Here Stalin cited 'On "Left-Wing" Infantilism and Petty Bourgeois Mentality', 'On the Tax in Kind', 'Routine Tasks of Soviet Power', where Lenin used the term 'tribute' in a completely different context. A voice from the hall protested: 'But Lenin never applied the concept of "tribute" to the middle peasant'. Stalin calmly replied:

Maybe you think the middle peasant is closer to the party than the working class? Then you're even a fake Marxist. If one can speak of 'tribute' in respect of the working class – the working class our party represents – then why can one not say the same about the middle peasant who is our ally, when all is said and done?[20]

The original question, on the use of the term 'tribute', was thus buried under a typical exchange about 'orthodoxy'.

The endless debates of the 1920s undoubtedly sharpened Stalin's intellect as a polemicist. To be sure, he commonly resorted to the device which trapped his opponents in a corner: he would present himself as Lenin's champion, arguing as if only he knew how to interpret Lenin correctly. In almost any argument, he would quickly find an appropriate quotation or expression of Lenin's, often from a totally different context. He had long ago realised that arming himself with quotations from Lenin would make him virtually invulnerable. Once, while discussing Comintern affairs, Zinoviev, whose relations with Stalin were already bad, snapped at him, 'You use quotations from Lenin like a certificate of your own infallibility. You should look for their meaning!'

Stalin shot back, 'And what's wrong with having a "certificate" of socialism?'

In the end, his rigid thinking, aggressiveness, militancy and rudeness enabled Stalin to gain the upper hand over his opponents. It is strange, but the more subtle and often more cogent arguments made by Trotsky, Zinoviev, Kamenev and Bukharin found no support among the delegates in the hall, while Stalin's crude, often primitive and abusive invectives, tightly bound up with his claim to be 'defending Lenin', the general line of the party, the unity of the Central Committee and so on, were quickly absorbed by the party. Being of pragmatic mind, he did not bother too much, as Trotsky did, with an elegant style, or as Zinoviev did with rhetorical aphorisms, or Kamenev with intellectual rationality, or Bukharin with theoretical argument. Stalin's main weapon was to accuse them of wanting to revise Lenin while he defended him. And this became the official version from the early 1930s.

Stalin's way of thinking was schematic. As we have seen, he liked to have everything properly 'shelved', and he would predigest and popularize ideas almost to the point of primitive pastiche. If his opponents aired their ideas differently, he would castigate them for their 'un-Marxist approach', for 'showing petty-bourgeois tendencies' or 'anarchistic scholasticism'. His reports and speeches were always structured within a strict framework of enumeration, particulars, features, levels, directions, tasks. This is one reason why his works were popular, since they were accessible in their simplicity and people could grasp their meaning. But while this way of thinking may have facilitated the popularization of Stalin's ideas, it severely shackled the people's creative abilities, demanding no deep analysis or understanding of the complexity and interdependence of the world.

Perhaps Stalin had not thought, like Nero, that the study of philosophy 'was a hindrance to a future ruler', but he seems to have been intellectually incapable of achieving even the slightest grasp of that subject. The weakest spot in his intellect was his inability to understand dialectics. He was aware of this, for he spent a long time and devoted much effort trying to enrich his philosophical knowledge. On the recommendation of the directors of the Institute of Red Professors, in 1925 he invited Jan Sten, a leading philosopher among the Old Bolsheviks, to give him private lessons on the dialectic. Sten, who was the deputy head of the Marx-Engels Institute, and later an executive of the Central Committee apparatus, had been a delegate at several party congresses, was a member of the Central Control Commission, and a man of independent judgement. Appointed as Stalin's philosophy tutor, he devised a special programme which included the study of Hegel, Kant, Feuerbach, Fichte and Schelling, as well as Plekhanov, Kautsky and Bradley. Twice a week at a fixed hour he turned up at Stalin's apartment and patiently tried to elucidate to his pupil the Hegelian concepts of substantiation, alienation, the identity of being and thought. He tried in other words to give him an understanding of the real world as the manifestation of an idea. Abstraction irritated Stalin, but he controlled himself and sat listening to Sten's monotonous voice, occasionally losing his patience and interrupting with such questions as, 'What's all this got to do with the class struggle?' or 'Who uses all this rubbish in practice?'

Reminding his pupil that Hegel's philosophy, like that of the other German thinkers, had become one of the sources of Marxism, Sten carried on unperturbed. 'Hegel's philosophy,' he declared, 'is in effect an encyclopedia of idealism. The dialectical method is developed in his metaphysical system with sheer genius. Marx said that Hegel had stood the dialectic on its head and that it was time to put it back on its feet in order to see it rationally.' Visibly irritated, Stalin cut in, 'But what's this got to do with the theory of Marxism?'

Again Sten tried patiently to boil down and explain Hegel's philosophical subtlety to his uncomprehending pupil, but despite his best efforts, Stalin could not master some of the basic notions in Hegel's philosophy, as his own 'philosophical works' show. All he seems to have gained from his lessons was hostility for his teacher. Together with N. Karev, I. K. Luppol and the other philosophers who were pupils of Academician A. M. Deborin, Sten was declared a theoretical 'lickspittle of Trotsky', and in 1937 he was arrested and executed. The same fate seemed to be in store for Deborin, who had been very close to Bukharin in the late 1920s and who in 1930 was labelled by Stalin a 'militant idealist Menshevik'. He was, however, spared, although he was prevented from doing any scientific or public work.

A meeting of the Communist Academy took place in October 1930 to discuss 'differences on the philosophical front'. It was in effect a lengthy condemnation of Deborin for his 'underestimation of the Leninist stage in the development of Marxist philosophy'. Deborin put up a stout defence, but Milyutin, Mitin, Melonov and Yaroslavsky 'established' his guilt, along with that of Sten, Karev and Luppol, for 'underestimating the materialistic dialectic'. Passions in the academy continued to seethe after this meeting. The academics could not accept the use of police methods in their work. Philosophy was probably the first victim of Stalinist 'scientific research'. Stalin made it perfectly clear that there was to be only one leader in the social sciences and that was the rôle of the political leader, i. e. himself.

Two months later, in December 1930, he spoke on 'the philosophical front' at the party bureau of the Institute of Red Professors, whose director was Abram Deborin. His speech is an eloquent example of his philosophical thinking, the level of his rationality and simply of his lack of tact. According to the minutes of the meeting, he said:

We have to turn upside down and dig over the whole pile of manure that has accumulated in philosophy and the natural sciences. Everything written by the Deborin group has to be smashed. Sten and Karev can be chucked out. Sten boasts a lot, but he's just a pupil of Karev's. Sten is a desperate sluggard. All he can do is talk. Karev's got a swelled head and struts about like an inflated bladder. In my view, Deborin is a hopeless case, but he should remain as editor of the journal* so

* *Pod znamenem marksizma* ('Under the Banner of Marxism').

we'll have someone to beat. The editorial board will have two fronts, but we'll have the majority.

Questions began to rain in as soon as Stalin stopped speaking:
'Can one link the struggle over theory with the political deviations?'
Stalin replied: 'Not only can one, but one absolutely must.'
'What about the "leftists"? You've dealt with the "rightists".'
'Formalism is coming out under leftist camouflage,' Stalin replied. 'It is serving up its dishes with leftist sauce. The young have a weakness for leftishness. And these gentlemen are good cooks.'
'What should the Institute concentrate on in the area of philosophy?'
'To beat, that is the main issue,' Stalin replied. 'To beat on all sides and where there hasn't been any beating before. The Deborinites regard Hegel as an icon. Plekhanov has to be unmasked. He always looked down on Lenin. Even Engels was not right about everything. There is a place in his commentary on the Erfurt Programme about growing into socialism. Bukharin tried to use it. It wouldn't be a bad thing if we could implicate Engels somewhere in Bukharin's writings'.[21]

Thus, Stalin, who knew practically nothing about philosophy, 'instructed' the philosophers. The main thing was 'to beat'. As for Marxist philosophy, he explained what it should be in a special section of his *Short Course*. A series of short, sharp phrases divide philosophy up into a number of basic features, like so many soldiers lined up in ranks. Perhaps this 'philosophical alphabet', plus a few other sources, would do for the campaign against illiteracy, but after Stalin's works appeared, philosophy shrivelled up, as no one had the courage to write anything more on the subject. Within a month the Central Committee passed a special resolution about the journal *Pod znamenem marksizma*. Deborin's supporters, who were united around the editors of the journal, were dubbed 'a group of Menshevizing idealists'.

A. P. Balashov told me that Stalin absorbed a colossal amount of information in a day, including reports, telegrams, ciphers and letters, and that on almost every document he wrote his instructions or comments, tersely expressing his attitude and thus issuing a definitive decision on the most varied questions. Having read through a pile of letters and written his customary laconic comments, such as 'Thanks for your support', 'Help this man', 'Rubbish', he would often select one or two and write a substantial reply. For instance, in 1928, a veteran Bolshevik living in Leningrad wrote to ask about the danger of a restoration of capitalism and also whether there were any deviations in the Politburo. Stalin tore a sheet out of a big notepad and, in his large clear hand, wrote:

Comrade Shneer,
    The danger of a restoration of capitalism does exist here. The right deviation underestimates the strength of capitalism. And the left deny the possibility of

building socialism in our country. They propose to carry out their fantastic industrialization plan at the cost of a split with the peasantry.

The Politburo has neither right nor left deviations.

With comradely greetings.

I. Stalin[22]

During the height of Stakhanovism* in the 1930s, the coal miners Stakhanov and Grant submitted a proposal to the government 'on the training of engineers and technicians', which would entail the release of Stakhanovites from work for one or two days of the six-day week in order to study. As it was both new and revolutionary, the idea was discussed in the press and gained a great deal of support. Stalin read the proposal and wrote tersely to Ordzhonikidze, 'This is not a serious matter.'[23]

It is difficult to trace the intellectual qualities that enabled Stalin to deal inventively with problems as they arose. He tried always to act in accordance with a plan, or a dogma or some postulate or preconceived notion. At the same time, he was capable of intuitive thinking and could see the point things would reach several stages ahead. At such times, his mental processes are hidden from view and only the result is visible, whether it be a decision, a generalization, a guess or a suspicion. The intuitive process bypasses logical thinking and produces an immediate 'output' in summary form. Of course, groundless suspicion often arises where there is a deficiency in moral awareness. Such was the case with Stalin. He could turn on one of his comrades and declare, 'You're trying not to look me in the eye!' Pathological suspicion in this case was less a manifestation of intuitive thinking than of the fact that his suppositions lacked a basis in reality, and were rather an expression of a profoundly flawed, paranoid outlook which gave rise to a tendency to see potential enemies everywhere.

Knowledge enables a man to be competent, emotions may ennoble him, and will-power helps him to turn his convictions and initiatives into reality through action. The will is like the muscles of the mind, the motive force of the intellect. A strong will can make an intellect active and purposeful – the sort of intellect that may be found among military leaders. It is not surprising that it was they who were the first to notice that Stalin had a strong intellect.

A separate chapter will be devoted to Stalin as military commander, but for the purposes of describing his intellectual qualities, the testimony of two outstanding war leaders, Marshals G. K. Zhukov and A. M. Vasilievsky, both of whom worked closely with Stalin during the war, merit attention. Zhukov detected in Stalin 'an ability to formulate an idea concisely, a naturally analytical mind, great erudition and a rare memory'. He also had an enclosed, fitful character. Usually calm and rational, he was capable of lapsing into sharp

---

*A fake propaganda campaign, based on the record-breaking performance of a miner called Stakhanov, which was used to raise production by creating artificial working conditions.

irritation. At such times he would lose his objectivity, changing before one's eyes, he would go pale and his glance would become heavy and menacing. [24]

Recalling Stalin's traits, Marshal Vasilevsky singled out his phenomenal memory:

I have never met anyone who could remember as much. He knew by name all the army and front commanders, of whom there were more than one hundred, and he even knew the names of some corps and divisional commanders ... Throughout the war Stalin had the composition of the strategic reserves in his head and could name any formation at any time. [25]

Stalin's ability to grasp the essence of a situation quickly also made a deep impression on Winston Churchill: 'Very few people alive could have comprehended in so few minutes the reasons which we had all so long been wrestling with for months. He saw it all in a flash.' [26]

It seems indisputable that Stalin had considerable intellectual powers, in addition to his highly developed purposefulness and strong will, and that it was more than force of circumstance or mere chance that made of him one of Lenin's comrades-in-arms during the revolution and civil war. He was able to show these qualities at a time when they were most needed, and it was perhaps for that reason they became evident. Perhaps as a result Stalin came to believe in himself, and perhaps he was therefore able to do things that others found impossible. On the other hand, when Zhukov and Vasilevsky wrote about Stalin, there was still much they did not know and, more important, much they could not say.

While Stalin may be said to have had an exceptional intellect, he was far from being a genius. Nor was he at all realistic about his own capabilities, but made categorical judgements in almost every field of knowledge, from politics and economics to linguistics, lecturing film-makers and agronomists alike, and imposing peremptory opinions in military matters as readily as in the writing of history. For the most part, his views were those of an amateur, if not of an outright ignoramus, but the chorus of praise that greeted his every utterance raised those views to the rank of the highest revelation.

For instance, at the initiative of a group of architects (and according to a decision taken as early as 1922), Molotov and Kaganovich submitted a proposal to Stalin for the construction of a Palace of Soviets on the site of the superb cathedral of Christ the Saviour. Stalin quickly approved the plan, showing in full measure his utter lack of appreciation of a major monument of Russian culture. No one thought of asking the population of Moscow, who had contributed the money for the cathedral only fifty years earlier, what they wanted, and the edifice was duly blown up on 5 December 1931. When the explosions rang out, Stalin, in his Kremlin office, trembled and anxiously inquired: 'Where's the bombardment? What are those explosions?' Poskrebyshev explained that, in accordance with the July decision on the site for the Palace of Soviets, which Stalin had approved, the cathedral of Christ the Saviour was being demolished. Stalin relaxed and paid no further attention to the explosions, which went on for another hour, but returned instead to reading local reports on the progress of collectivization. He probably did not even know that the cathedral had been built with pennies contributed by ordinary folk, or that the interiors and sculptures had been done by Vereshchagin, Makovsky, Surkov, Pryanishnikov, Klodt, Ramazanov and other famous masters. The cathedral, built to stand for centuries, was demolished for 'atheistic and architectural reasons'.

The architect of the Palace of Soviets, B. Iofan, wrote of the event:

It was 1931. The cathedral of Christ the Saviour was still standing in the middle of a vast square on the Moscow River. Golden domed, huge and cumbersome, looking like a cake or a samovar, it overwhelmed the surrounding houses and the people in them with its official, cold, lifeless architecture, a reflection of the talentless Russian autocracy and the 'highly placed' builders who had created this temple for landowners and merchants. The proletarian revolution is boldly raising its hand against this cumbersome edifice which symbolizes the power and the taste of the lords of old Moscow.

Iofan ecstatically described the 'comments of genius' that Stalin had made on the plan for the Palace. His 'audacious' suggestions envisaged that the palace would rise to more than 1200 feet, with a figure of Lenin 300 feet tall surmounting it, while the great hall was to have no less than 21,000 seats. Stalin's megalomania was well expressed in his comments on the project. Why is the podium raised so little above the hall? It must be higher! There must be no chandeliers, the illumination must come from reflected light. The chief artistic motifs should express the six parts of the oath that Stalin had taken after Lenin's death. He made it perfectly clear that this was not to be merely a Palace of Soviets, it was to be a monument glorifying him, the leader, for centuries. The whole grandiose civic structure was to express the 'idea of the creativity of the multi-million Soviet democracy ...'[27] Some democracy, when everything from the shape of the building to its facing, the lighting, the height of the pylons, the subjects of its sculpture and mosaics, its very proportions and many other strictly professional matters were determined by one man who in his 'genius' thought it normal that he should be the one to give the final orders!

Politics always took priority when history, culture or art were under discussion. For instance, when Khrushchev announced at the February-March 1937 plenum that 'in reconstructing Moscow, we should not be afraid to remove a tree or a little church or some cathedral or other'[28] he received Stalin's silent approval. Cultural values were of secondary importance, and in any case he was the chief arbiter of what was valuable. The fate of many a work of art hung on his sole decision.

Stalin's mind lacked the embellishment of a single noble feature, a trace of humanitarianism, to say nothing of love of mankind. In July 1946, for instance,

Beria reported that his corrective labour camps contained more than 100,000 prisoners who were completely incapable of further useful work and whose upkeep was costing the state a fortune. Beria recommended that the incurably ill and the mentally disturbed be released forthwith. Stalin agreed, but insisted that especially dangerous criminals and those serving hard labour, however sick, be kept in.[29]

CHAPTER ██ 24

Caesarism

Early in 1937, Lion Feuchtwanger, the German writer, visited Moscow. The result was his *Moscow 1937 (an account of my trip for my friends)*, published in Amsterdam. He did not hide the fact that he had set out as a sympathizer, and his book indeed amounted to little more than a whitewash of the Soviet system. His sympathy for the USSR grew during his stay, but what he could not have missed, and what he devoted the greater part of his book to, was the place occupied by Stalin in the lives of the Soviet people:

The worship and boundless cult with which the population surrounds Stalin is the first thing that strikes the foreigner visiting the Soviet Union. On every corner, at every crossroads, in appropriate and inappropriate places alike, one sees gigantic busts and portraits of Stalin. The speeches one hears, not only the political ones, but even on any scientific or artistic subject, are peppered with glorification of Stalin, and at times this deification takes on tasteless forms.[30]

When Feuchtwanger told Stalin himself about this, the General Secretary merely grinned and shrugged, remarking that 'the workers and peasants are too busy with other matters to cultivate good taste,' and he joked about the hundreds of thousands of portraits of the man with the moustache, enlarged to monstrous size, which gazed back at him from all the processions.[31] Going somewhat further than Stalin in attempting to explain the origins and pre-conditions of this mass idol-worship, Feuchtwanger wrote that worship of the leader

had grown organically with the success of economic construction. The people were grateful to Stalin for their bread and meat, for the order in their lives, for their education and for creating their army which secured this new well-being. The people have to have someone to whom to express their gratitude for the undoubted improvement in their living conditions, and for this purpose they do not select an abstract concept, such as abstract 'communism', but a real man, Stalin ... Their unbounded reverence is consequently not for Stalin the man, but for the representative of the patently successful economic construction ...[32]

This naive explanation so delighted Stalin that he had the book translated into Russian at lightning speed and published in a large print run. It was probably the only book ever printed in the Soviet Union under Stalin which acknowledged the existence of the Stalin cult and offered some explanation of it. In effect, for Feuchtwanger, Stalin personified both the socialist ideals and the reality and therefore, according to him, the people owed Stalin their gratitude.

The leadership cult was humiliating for the people, even insulting. It was Caesarism of the twentieth century, that is, the usurpation of power by one person while maintaining the formal symbols of democracy. How did this practice arise and what were its preconditions?

By identifying the sources of the leadership cult, it is possible to understand how Stalin could have been so popular, despite his cruelty and his contempt for elementary human norms. As we have seen, the main foundation of the cult was the lack of democratic principles in the party and the state. A people which had lived for centuries in the shadow of the tsarist crown could not in a matter of a few years throw off the old habits. The tsar, the dynasty and the tsarist trappings had been destroyed, but the old way of thinking, with its tendency to deify a powerful sovereign figure, lived on.

Nikolai Berdyaev wrote in 1918, in his *The Fate of Russia*:

Russia is a culturally backward country. There is a barbaric darkness there, a dark, chaotic, Asiatic elementalism. Russia's backwardness must be overcome by creative activity and cultural development. The most original Russia will be the coming Russia, the new Russia, and not the old, backward Russia.[33]

It was this backwardness which revealed itself in many of the social processes that got under way after the revolution, when democracy was not in evidence. Even while Lenin was still alive, there was too much glorifying of the leaders, too much recognition of their 'special merits'. The system itself contained no restraining or critical mechanisms of the sort that could have been found only within genuine revolutionary pluralism. Had the Left SRs remained on the scene it is hard to imagine them joining in to praise Stalin.

The first to note the danger of making a leader into an ideological concept was Trotsky, who in 1927 wrote his reminiscences of Lenin under the title 'On Sanctimoniousness':

The deceased Lenin has, it seems, been reborn: there you have the solution to the mystery of the risen Christ. But the danger starts with the bureaucratization of esteem and the automation of attitudes towards Lenin and his teaching. N. K. Krupskaya recently spoke some very good and simple words against both kinds of danger. She said there should not be too many monuments to Lenin, nor should useless and unnecessary institutions be founded in his name.[34]

The eradication of openness in the party and in state functions following the Seventeenth Congress marked the formal end of an era. The 1920s were by comparison a much more congenial time, when everything could be discussed. For instance, it was regarded as normal for *Pravda* to report that at the Fourteenth Congress the resolution on the report by Stalin and Molotov received 559 votes in favour and 65 against, or that there were 1,026,000 registered unemployed in the country on 1 September 1926. People could find out most of what they wanted to know about social, economic, cultural, financial and historical matters.

From the early 1930s the truth began to be doled out in limited doses, with the result that the people had no way of judging the leadership. In time Stalin himself and his entourage and their actions would become fenced off from the people and from public opinion by an impenetrable curtain. The most glaring example was of course the purges and the terror. What was known of them? Publicity applied only to the major figures, the well-known scientists, prominent military men, who had been 'unmasked' as enemies of the people and whose exposure was designed in part to serve as an example. The millions of unfortunates who made up the main mass of victims disappeared unnoticed in the silence of the night, often forever. The monstrous sentence imposed on so many – ten years without right of correspondence – was in itself an act of censorship. What did anyone know about the 'special meetings' held by the NKVD in July 1934? It was believed at the time that their authority did not go beyond exile and prison for five years, but it emerged later that they were sentencing innocent people to be shot or to twenty-five years of hard labour.

The people gradually learned to make do with only a part of the truth. Thus, for instance, on 20 February 1938 they were told that the ice-breakers *Taimyr* and *Murman* had rescued four Soviet explorers from an ice floe in the Greenland Sea, but they knew nothing of the preparations that had just been completed for the trial of Bukharin that was to take place in two weeks' time.

When truth was a luxury, a careless word or act would be seen as an attack on the monopoly of truth as proclaimed by the leader. Speaking at the February-March 1937 plenum, for instance, delegate Mogushevsky detected danger in the work of Minsk Radio:

Minsk Radio has been broadcasting anti-Soviet programmes. On 23 January they broadcast the charges against the Trotskyist centre. After broadcasting the charges and a report on the morning session in court, they broadcast a concert which included Chopin's well known B-minor sonata. This was no coincidence. It was very subtle: they didn't play just the funeral march, as that would have been too obvious, so they broadcast the whole sonata. Not everyone realizes that it includes the march. No, this was no coincidence.[35]

For those who depended on Stalin, showing such 'alertness' for 'enemies of the people' was one way of keeping their jobs, and also their lives. It was under such circumstances, for instance, that Sverdlovsk party secretary Kabakov* found 'wrecking' in a different area. He told the plenum: 'We discovered a stall where they were wrapping up purchases in copies of Tomsky's report.† We looked into it and found that trading organizations had bought a substantial quantity of such literature. Who can say if this literature is only being used as wrapping-paper?'[36]

Stalin would not have been able to don the emperor's toga – even if it was only a modest army tunic – without first having achieved dominion over the minds of the people. He knew he must secure their faith in him as almighty leader and stimulate their enthusiasm by trumpeting their achievements and by blaming their failures, for the most part, on 'the efforts of enemies and wreckers'. And he was successful in this, The people's enthusiasm was not artificial; their efforts were often self-sacrificing. When they demanded the death penalty or harsh punishment for the traitors, they were being sincere. Even Alexei Stakhanov wrote:

When the trials took place in Moscow, first of Zinoviev and Kamenev, and then of Pyatakov and his gang, we immediately demanded that they be shot. Even the women in our settlement, who had never been interested in politics, clenched their fists when they heard what the papers said. The old folk and the young all demanded that the bandits be destroyed.[37]

Generations were growing up with a fundamental belief that everything their great leader did was right, and very few of them had any doubts. Now that nearly all of Stalin's political enemies have been rehabilitated, the history of the party in those years appears in quite a different light. A struggle had been going on for the leadership and for choosing the means to build a new life. Some people chose badly, many had views which were different from those adopted by the party, but few of them were, as Stalin described them, enemies. Yet the slightest hint of suspicion against them grew into gross accusations and a tragic end.

Stalin often dealt with matters without giving a written decision. I must have looked at several thousand items of correspondence addressed to him personally on all manner of subjects: progress reports on the harvest, the deportation of entire peoples, notification that sentences had been carried out, the removal of senior staff, the building of arms factories, decoded cables from intelligence sources, translated articles from the Western press, personal letters to him, and all sorts of schemes and inventions and crazy ideas. I estimate that he read between one hundred and two hundred documents a day, ranging from one page to whole files. In most cases he simply initialled them. Before submitting material, Poskrebyshev would append a square sheet of paper with the draft of a suggested decision and the name of its author. Stalin rarely wrote

---

* Soon to be liquidated.
† Tomsky had already been declared an enemy of the people and killed himself.

long decisions. If he agreed with a plan, he would put his initials on the piece of paper, or simply say 'Agreed' and hand it back to his assistant to be put in a pile.

Occasionally Stalin would indicate to the party and the people that he was against all the glorification and idolatry. Such moves were simply playing to the gallery. There is, for instance, the following letter in the archives:

> To Comrades Andreyev (Detizdat)* and Smirnova.†
> I am decisively against publishing *Tales of Stalin's Childhood*. The book is full of factual errors. But that's not the main thing. The main thing is that the book has the tendency to instil in the minds of the Soviet people (and people in general) a cult of personalities, of leaders and infallible heroes. That is dangerous and harmful. The theory of 'heroes' and the 'crowd' is not a Bolshevik one, but is SR [Socialist Revolutionary] . . . The people make heroes, the Bolsheviks reply.
> I advise you to burn the book.
> 16 February 1938. I. Stalin.[38]

This carefully written note was calculated in fact to enhance the glorification of Stalin, not to stop it. Who would now be able to say that he was not modest? But there was another side to the matter, namely, that he did not like mention being made of his childhood. Such a vast chasm now yawned between it and the peak on which he was perched that to think of it made his head swim. In any case, why did people need to know what he had been once upon a time, when all they needed to know was what he was now?

It pleased him most to hear others remark on his modesty. At the February–March 1937 plenum, Mekhlis said that 'as early as 1930, Comrade Stalin sent me the following letter for *Pravda*. I will allow myself to read it out without his permission':

> Comrade Mekhlis,
> There is a request to publish the enclosed instructive story of a kolkhoz. I have deleted what it says about 'Stalin' as the 'vozhd of the party', the 'leader of the party' and so on. I think such laudatory embellishments can only do harm. The letter should be printed without these epithets.
> With Communist greetings. I. Stalin[39]

Such remarks were intended to create legends about 'the exceptional modesty of Comrade Stalin' who was 'totally devoid of vanity'.

Stalin knew that any degree of decentralization or strengthening of the rôle of the state bodies and raising the importance of the social organizations, was bound sooner or later to lead to an intellectual and political crisis for the very idea of a leadership cult. It was therefore essential for him to keep the public mind shackled in dogmatism by feeding it with his own works. The people

---

* Children's book publishing.
† Author of *Rasskazy o detstve Stalina* (Tales of Stalin's Childhood).

believed Stalin's articles and speeches (which were becoming less frequent), and they gazed at his ubiquitous portrait with hope in their hearts. From childhood they knew that 'Stalin is thinking about us.' This perpetual mental massage did more than condition the minds of the young, it also led to the degeneration of the cadres. Henceforth the only useful worker was one who was willing to agree with the most absurd ideas, arguments and decisions, as long as they bore the name of Stalin. Mikoyan cannot have believed his own words, on the occasion of the twentieth anniversary of the Cheka (OGPU-NKVD) in 1937, when he said: 'Learn the Stalinist style of work from Comrade Yezhov, just as he learned it from Comrade Stalin!'[40] But this was how everyone had to speak, whether they held high or low office or no office at all. Conscience, or the opportunity to exercise it, was stifled. As Yevtushenko wrote in his poem 'Fear':

> The people were gradually tamed,
> And all was placed under seal;
> Taught to shout when they should have been silent,
> They were still when they should have cried out.

CHAPTER ▮ 25 ▮

In the Shadow of the Leader

After the Seventeenth Congress, the Politburo was a vastly altered body, the old guard having been virtually wiped out in the internecine tempest. Stalin had felt uncomfortable with them around, as they knew him in all his different states of mind – firm and hesitant, steadfast and confused, affable and pitiable. They also knew that there had been only one leader in the revolution, Lenin, and that Stalin had played third or fourth fiddle. They knew that in all but will-power Stalin was inferior to many. There was not enough room on the captain's bridge for Trotsky who thought him a mediocrity, or Bukharin who thought him an Asiatic despot, or Rykov who respected no one but Lenin, or Zinoviev and Kamenev who each thought that, as Lenin's closest friend, one of them should have succeeded him. Moreover, they did not see Stalin as their leader. He needed new comrades-in-arms.

Among the survivors, new faces appeared alongside Stalin on the Mausoleum, on assembly platforms or around the Politburo table: A. A. Andreyev, K. Ye. Voroshilov, L. M. Kaganovich, M. I. Kalinin, S. M. Kirov, S. V. Kosior, V. V. Kuibyshev, V. M. Molotov, G. K. Ordzhonikidze, as well as A. I. Mikoyan, G. I. Petrovsky, P. P. Postyshev, Ya. E. Rudzutak, V. Ya. Chubar, and later A. A. Zhdanov and R. I. Eikhe. From this group he quickly singled out a nucleus consisting of Molotov, Kaganovich and Voroshilov. Soon, however, gaps appeared in the ranks: Kirov was murdered, Kuibyshev died in 1935, Ordzhonikidze committed suicide, while Kosior, Postyshev, Rudzutak, Chubar and Eikhe were eliminated in the great purge. Between 1937 and 1939, six Politburo members and one candidate member were present during one of the most harrowing episodes in Russian history, but they were not mere eyewitnesses; they were all, particularly the nucleus of three, closely involved in the events. In Goethe's words, evil followed evil, and lawlessness became the law throughout the empire.

But it was not an empire, it was the first socialist state of workers and peasants, the first in history to take power, and the first to hand it over to a 'great leader'. Yet not one of Stalin's circle had the courage to scream Goethe's words at the leader, or to try to stop the process. What sort of men were they, these people who dwelt in the shadow of the leader?

In Zhukovka, a summer-house settlement outside Moscow, as late as the spring of 1986, one might still have encountered an old man with a high forehead and the inevitable pince-nez, slowly shuffling along, tapping his stick and turning his faded hazel eyes towards the rare passer-by. The worn petersham coat and trodden-down old man's boots spoke of someone who had seen and experienced much. But one would not have guessed that he was going on ninety-seven and that he was none other than the former chairman of the Sovnarkom, former member of the Politburo, former Commissar of Foreign Affairs and one of Stalin's closest accomplices, Vyacheslav Mikhailovich Molotov.

Molotov had been a Central Committee secretary and candidate member of the Politburo under Lenin, and although history has recorded some unpleasant things that Lenin said about him – e. g. that 'under his very nose he was generating the most shameful bureaucratism and the most stupid'[41] – he was one of the last of the Mohicans who had worked with Lenin all those years ago. The poet, F. Chuev, met Molotov frequently and in conversation with me in 1985 described him as 'modest, precise and thrifty. He would see that nothing was wasted, that no lights were left on in an empty room. When he died on 8 November 1986, and his will was opened, an envelope was found to contain his savings book, with 500 rubles for his funeral.'

This was the man who had worked with Trotsky and Bukharin and Rykov. Churchill and Roosevelt knew him, and he had sat for hours in talks with Hitler and Ribbentrop, as one of the architects of the Nazi–Soviet Non-Aggression Pact and the Treaty on Frontiers. Many Soviet citizens remember the dramatic words he, not Stalin, uttered at midday on 22 June 1941: 'Our cause is just. The enemy will be smashed. The victory will be ours.' This episode will be dealt with in greater detail below. For the moment, let us note that Stalin was so stupefied by the catastrophic start of the war that he rejected the pleas of the Politburo that he speak, and instead charged his 'right-hand man' with that task.

For many decades, Molotov was Stalin's shadow, always with him at Politburo meetings, on the Mausoleum, in newspaper reports, at international conferences. Even when *Pravda* published his speeches, they usually printed a large photo of Stalin alongside.

What did he think about in his declining years, living in his Moscow apartment on Granovsky Street or his official villa at Zhukovka? What did he recall to mind? Maybe the Central Committee meeting of December 1930, when Rykov was pushed out of his job as chairman of the Council of Ministers and Stalin himself proposed Molotov as his replacement? On that occasion,

Molotov declared he had 'passed through the school of Bolshevism under the direct supervision of its best teacher, Lenin, and under the supervision of Comrade Stalin. I am proud of this.'

Nothing changed him during the decades after Stalin. Shortly before his own death, he told Chuev that 'if it hadn't been for Stalin, I don't know what would have become of us'. To the end of his life he regarded Stalin as a genius, and he was convinced that Tukhachevsky had been the armed force of the 'rightists', Rykov and Bukharin, who were, he believed, hatching a conspiracy. He claimed that '1937 enabled us to avoid having a fifth column in the war.' He admitted that mistakes had been made, 'that many honest Communists perished, but with gentle methods we could not hold on to what had been won'. Having survived history's most violent storms, the man's mind had, as it were, come to a stop. As an obedient, zealous and sophisticated executor of Stalin's wishes, Molotov bore a huge responsibility for the corruption of legality and for making coercion into an instrument of power.

At the notorious February–March 1937 plenum, Molotov gave a report on the 'lessons of sabotage, diversion and espionage by Japanese–German–Trotskyist agents'. The whole speech amounted to a call for a social pogrom:

Yesterday's hesitations by vacillating Communists have already become acts of sabotage, diversion and spying by agreement with the Fascists and for their advantage. We must answer blow with blow, we must everywhere smash these detachments of scouts and subversives from the Fascist camp. We must hurry to complete this task, and we must not delay or show hesitation.[42]

Molotov showed no hesitation. Nor had his call to complete the task been made into thin air. In June of that year, an informer reported to Stalin that G. I. Lomov, an Old Bolshevik and staff member of the Sovnarkom, was allegedly close to Rykov and Bukharin. Stalin inquired of Molotov, 'What do you think?' The reply came quickly and was to the point: 'I'm for the immediate arrest of that swine Lomov.'[43]

Lomov's fate was sealed: arrest, interrogation, sentence, execution. A party member since 1903, a delegate at the historic April 1917 Party Conference, a member of the Central Executive Committee of the USSR, he was, like so many thousands of other honest Bolsheviks, listed as an 'enemy of the people' by the stroke of a pen. It was Molotov who sanctioned the arrest of Kabakov, first secretary of the Sverdlovsk regional party committee, of Ukhanov, Commissar of Light Industry, of Krutov, chairman of the Far East regional executive committee, and many others. Of the twenty-eight members of the Council of People's Commissars which he chaired, more than half were shot.

He was a harsh man. In March 1948 Rodionov, the chairman of the Council of Ministers of the RSFSR, asked him to help in some way to find accommodation for 2,400 sick and very old exiles. Molotov's response was terse: 'The USSR Ministry of Internal Affairs will accommodate 2,400 invalids and very old exiles in concentration camps.'[44]

Stalin found Molotov very useful. He could grasp the boss's intentions from a hint and his capacity for work was legendary, as Stalin himself often remarked in the presence of other members of the Politburo. On Molotov's fiftieth birthday in 1940, Stalin proposed that the town of Perm change its name to Molotov, although there were many other towns, villages and farms already so named.

By the 1930s, Stalin had got rid of all the theorists. Of course, he himself was the chief 'theorist', but on occasion he condescended to allow one of his aides, usually Molotov, to try their hand. Adoratsky invited Stalin to write an article on the strategy and tactics of Leninism for the *Philosophical Encyclopedia* being prepared by the Communist Academy. Stalin's reply to Adoratsky reads: 'I am terribly busy with practical matters and am quite unable to meet your request. Try asking Molotov, he's on holiday and maybe can find the free time.'[45]

Molotov was of course no theorist, but compared to Kaganovich, Andreyev and Voroshilov and the rest, he was much to be preferred. With Bukharin gone, the only 'interpreter' and 'generator of ideas' was Stalin himself, and it is therefore not surprising that during the 1930s and 1940s social studies had a very thin time, as far as innovations were concerned. They simply could not occur. It is equally unsurprising that in such circumstances, Molotov considered himself something of a theorist.

Behind Molotov's imperturbable, extremely reserved, inscrutable façade of polite official decorum, there resided a strong and malevolent will. Assiduous in his support of Stalin in domestic affairs, Molotov was no less the diligent and resourceful mouthpiece of Soviet foreign policy. Without accomplices like Molotov, Stalinism would not have been possible.

No less zealous than Molotov was Lazar Moiseyevich Kaganovich, another survivor into great old age. In November 1988 he celebrated his ninety-fifth birthday in his apartment on Frunze Embankment in Moscow and probably expects to outdo Molotov by living to a hundred. S. I. Semin, who worked for N. A. Voznesensky after the war, told me about Kaganovich:

He was head of the war-industries commission at the time, and I had to take some papers into him. I was wearing a new pair of boots. Kaganovich took the papers, then his gaze fell on my boots.
'Take them off,' he ordered.
'Why?' I stammered in confusion.
'Get them off, quick!' He wasn't going to explain.
He took the boots in his hands, turning them over and over and stroking the uppers. Finally he threw them down on the floor and said in a satisfied tone, 'That's a good pair of boots you've got there. I should know, I used to be a bootmaker.'

He might have kept his good name if he'd remained a bootmaker, but he made his choice in 1911, when he followed his elder brother into the Bolshevik Party. He met Stalin in Moscow in 1918 when he was working in the All-Russian commission for organizing the Red Army. He was sent to Turkestan in 1920, but when Stalin became General Secretary he was recalled to Moscow and put in charge of the Central Committee section responsible for instructing organizers. With minimum education but a high level of administrative ability, Kaganovich began his rapid rise through the party and service ranks.

Stalin liked Kaganovich for three things: his superhuman capacity for work, his absolute lack of any opinion on political matters – before he even knew the issue at hand, he would say, 'I'm in complete agreement with Comrade Stalin' – and his uncomplaining willingness to carry out instructions, especially those of the boss. On one occasion, after the Eighteenth Party Conference and before a Politburo meeting, Stalin asked him:

'Lazar, did you know that your Mikhail* is hobnobbing with the rightists? There is solid evidence,' Stalin added with a testing look.

'He must be dealt with according to the law,' Lazar forced out, his voice shaking.

After the session he rang his brother and told him of the conversation. This speeded up the process. Mikhail decided not to wait for arrest and shot himself that very day.

It was people such as this that Stalin valued, people who felt they had to keep on proving their loyalty to him, and not through trivialities or mere sycophancy. Kaganovich showed this at that agonizingly long plenum of February-March 1937. The punishment machine was barely ready, only just set up and adjusted for mowing down the ranks of the party, the intelligentsia, the working class, the peasants, the military; yet Kaganovich already surpassed himself. In a two-hour speech, the Commissar for Railways reported on the first 'test' results:

In the political apparatus of the railways commissariat we have unmasked 220 people. In the transport division we have sacked 485 former gendarmes, 220 SRs and Mensheviks, 572 Trotskyists, 1415 White officers, 285 wreckers, 443 spies. They were all linked with the counter-revolutionary movement.[46]

It is not hard to imagine what Kaganovich meant by 'sacking spies and wreckers' on the railways. Stalin must have been pleased with his commissar's 'analysis' when Kaganovich went on heatedly to tell the delegates:

What we're dealing with here is a gang of desperate intelligence agents. Their methods in relation to the railways are especially sophisticated. Serebryakov, Arnoldov and Lifshits exploited the low level of security on access, they organized derailments and hampered the efforts of the Stakhanovite movement. Particular harm was done by Kudrevatykh, Vasiliev, Bratin, Neishtadt, Morshchikhin, Bekker, Kronts and Breis who prevented the locomotive FD from being commissioned. The building of the Moscow–Donbass line was sabotaged. Pyatov sabotaged the building of the Turksib line; Mrachkovsky sabotaged the Karaganda–Petropavlovsk line; Barsky and Eidelman sabotaged the Eikhe–Sokur line.[47]

---

* Kaganovich's brother, a Bolshevik since 1905, was Commissar for the aircraft building industry.

Despite the fact that the newspapers were reporting the overfulfilment of the plan in freight, inventions and the Krivonos movement,* Kaganovich kept up the pressure: 'Shermergorn, the head of railway construction, committed sabotage. Comrade Stalin told us more than once that he was a bad man and an enemy. Comrade Stalin gave us a clear warning and told us to keep an eye on him and check up on him.'

'He was a very suspicious man,' Mikoyan interjected.

'That swine Serebryakov,' Kaganovich continued, 'gave very precise information on the defence industry centres and drew up the sabotage plans'.[48]

The entire speech was in the same vein, naming and cursing whole flocks of wreckers who were apparently fully engaged in blowing up, creating bottlenecks, making flawed plans and disrupting freight:

The scoundrel Yeshmanov was head of the Moscow–Donetsk line from 1934. After he was taken off the job he didn't get any other work and went straight to Comrade Yezhov at the NKVD for a residence permit. He told Arnoldov about the reprimands, everyone talked but no one wanted him. Now he's under the care and control of Comrade Yezhov.[49]

Like the rest of Stalin's circle, the profoundly ignorant Kaganovich tried to acquire some sort of reputation as a theorist. The Central Committee had issued a directive ordering the heads of institutions, enterprises and agencies to conduct Marxist-Leninist studies with their staff. I. V. Kovalev, a former staff member of the commissariat of railways and the commissar himself during the war, told me about this:

Kaganovich gathered a group of managers and opened the seminar. Soon he asked me to speak. I made a point of the fact that the proletariat, because of its position and its ability to act only spontaneously, was capable of developing only trade-union consciousness. Kaganovich gave me a crazed look, and then burst out, 'What rubbish, so what if they have unionist consciousness! The proletariat can develop anything! Proletarian consciousness!'

We all looked at each other. However hard I tried, citing Lenin, to explain the need to introduce scientific theory into the minds of the proletariat, it didn't sink in. Giving me a suspicious look, he soon wound up the meeting and never again undertook such a burdensome chore.

Kaganovich acquired his authority through the 'trouble-shooting' trips he made on Stalin's orders. These visits, e. g. to the party organizations in Chelyabinsk, Ivanovo, Yaroslavl and other provincial centres, resulted in the wholesale removal and investigation of local officials, usually ending in tragedy. Stalin was well pleased with his 'Iron Lazar', as he called him.

Kaganovich acted entirely on his own initiative, guided merely by Stalin's instruction to 'take a good look at the place and be decisive. Don't be soft.' The

---

* P. F. Krivonos, an engine driver at Slavyansk depôt who extracted unprecedented performance from his locomotive, gave his name to a movement of such railway workers, cf. Stakhanov.

documents show that, even before a case was complete, Kaganovich would often personally fix the sentence, or arbitrarily alter the wording of a deposition to reveal a terrorist plot against him, as commissar.

He became head of the Central Committee section that was responsible for appointment to important posts. Stalin soon noticed his zeal, his harshness and commitment. Aged only thirty-three, in 1926 he was made a candidate member of the Politburo. In 1925, on Stalin's recommendation he had been sent to the Ukraine to head the party organization of the republic, where a difficult situation existed. His relations with the head of the Ukrainian council of people's commissars, V. Ya. Chubar, deteriorated, which in due course would have fatal consequences for the latter. Kaganovich's conflicts with the other Ukrainian party leaders continued and in 1928 he returned to Moscow to become first secretary of the Moscow city and provincial party committees. At the Sixteenth Party Congress in 1930 he became a full member of the Politburo.

His influence was especially great in the first half of the 1930s. As railways commissar he was constantly visiting provinces where collectivization was going badly, and soon after one of his descents things would rapidly speed up. Stalin was not concerned about the methods 'Iron Lazar' used. Cruel and extremely crude by nature, Kaganovich was the classic man of the system, the bureaucrat who would wade straight into any job without ceremony. His visit to the Northern Caucasus resulted in an increase of 'dekulakized' peasants being sent to the north. In Moscow he summarily removed anyone who would not carry out an order; through ignorance he banned plays from the stage, as head of the Central Committee commission on the party purge he was merciless. Under the guise of reconstructing Moscow, he was among those responsible for destroying many historic monuments, such as the Cathedral of Christ the Saviour, the Sukharev Tower, the Passion Monastery, the Iversky Gates. In a word, he was an all-round 'success' and to show his appreciation of this stalwart comrade, Stalin made him one of the first recipients of the Order of Lenin when it was created in 1930.

Another of Stalin's closest associates in the 1930s was Kliment Yefremovich Voroshilov. He joined the revolutionary movement early and in 1906 was a delegate at the Fourth Party Congress, where he met Lenin, Stalin and other well known figures. After years of arrests and periods of exile, he was in Petrograd for the February Revolution. He fought on various fronts in the civil war and came to notice during the battle for Tsaritsyn, when his friendship with Stalin was established. His reputation as a civil war hero came largely as a result of Stalin's patronage. To be sure, he had fought with courage, but without much thought. Speaking at the Eighth Congress, Lenin said: 'Comrade Voroshilov says, "We had no military experts and we had 60,000 losses." That is terrible. The masses will learn of the heroism of the Tsaritsyn army, but to say we managed without military experts is hardly to defend the party line.'[50]

During the civil war, Voroshilov served with the First Cavalry, fighting on the northern front, in the Caucasus, the Crimea, against the Anarchist forces of Makhno, and taking part in crushing the Kronstadt uprising in March 1921, when the soldiers and sailors of the Baltic Fleet rebelled against the Bolshevik government which they themselves had helped to power. For all this he was twice decorated with the Order of the Red Banner. A permanent member of the Central Committee following the Tenth Congress of 1921, after the Fourteenth Congress he became a member of the Politburo. On the death of Frunze he became Commissar for Army and Naval Affairs and made a certain contribution to the reorganization of the Red Army. His success in this sphere is partly explained by the fact that at that time in the commissariat, as well as in the military academies and a number of circles, there were many intellectually creative military theorists, both those who had emerged in the revolution and those who had been officers in the old army. Among these were B. M. Shaposhnikov, who wrote *The Brains of the Army*, M. N. Tukhachevsky, the author of *Questions of Modern Strategy*, K. B. Kalinovsky, K. I. Velichko, A. I. Verkhovsky, A. M. Zaionchkovsky, V. F. Novitsky, A. A. Svechin, R. P. Eideman, I. E. Yakir and many more.

Already by the end of the 1920s there were biographies, books and articles about Voroshilov. There was a marksmanship badge called the 'Voroshilov rifleman', and the KV heavy tank was named in his honour, (its replacement, the IS, was named for Stalin). Voroshilov's glory was truly nationwide, yet Stalin paid little attention to it, because in the 1930s Voroshilov was being lauded as the man 'who carries out the will of the leader', or as a 'Red marshal under the guidance of Comrade Stalin', or as a 'Stalin commissar'. Stalin knew him better than anyone; he knew his true worth. It was widely thought that they were real friends, but in a true friendship there can be no debtors, and Voroshilov always regarded himself as being in Stalin's debt, for the glory, the status, the jobs, the rewards and the position.

In the 1930s Voroshilov was an utterly mindless executive with no opinion of his own. He did not have Kaganovich's superhuman capacity for work, nor the intellect and cunning of Molotov, nor the caution and circumspection of Mikoyan, and he was inferior to the other members of the Politburo in many respects. But Stalin valued him for the aura of legend that had formed around the 'leader of the Red Army'. Stalin was sure that at the crucial moment, his commissar would give his support without a thought. And he was not wrong. When Stalin unleashed his purge, Voroshilov stood unflinching by his side as the flames consumed three Marshals of the Soviet Union and hundreds and thousands of Red Army officers. In his speech at the February-March 1937 plenum, Voroshilov named many 'enemies of the people' who had penetrated the Red Army, and he demonstrated this by citing Trotskyist wreckers who were not from among the high-ups. He read out the following letter that he had received in August 1936 from a Major Kuzmichev:

To Defence Commissar K. E. Voroshilov

I am charged with being a member of a counter-revolutionary terrorist group which is planning an attempt on your life. True, between 1926 and 1928 I belonged to a Trotskyist organization. Since 1929 I have tried to make amends. In you I have always seen not only the leader of the Red Army but also an exceedingly responsive man. I hold two Orders of the Red Banner. How can I be included among a gang of Fascist murderers?

No doubt they are going to shoot me. Perhaps in a few years the Trotskyists will explain why they slandered an honest man, and when the real truth is revealed I request that you restore my good name to my family. I apologize for the scribble, but they won't give me any more paper.

At this point Voroshilov swept the hall with his gaze and concluded dramatically, 'And ten days later he confessed that they intended to carry out the terrorist act in the Belaya Tserkov district during manoeuvres.'[51] Voroshilov knew perfectly well how such confessions were obtained. He told the plenum, addressing Stalin of course, that he often 'spoke with Yezhov about people who were being discharged from the army'. Sometimes, he said, 'I defend individuals. True, at the present time one can get oneself into an unpleasant situation: one defends someone who then turns out to a real enemy, a Fascist.' This was evidently what lay behind his attitude to a letter which Yakir wrote on the eve of his execution in June 1937:

To K.E. Voroshilov.

In memory of my many years of honest work in the Red Army I ask you to see that my family are cared for and that they are helped, as they are helpless and guilty of nothing. I have requested the same of N. I. Yezhov.

On 10 June, Voroshilov scrawled on the letter, 'I altogether doubt the honesty of a dishonest man.'[52]

There are several volumes of documents signed or minuted by Voroshilov. One contains letters from officers who managed to write to him before being tried or executed, requesting, begging, crying out for help. There are letters from Goryachev, Krivosheyev, Sidorov, Khakhanyan, Bukshtynovich, Prokofiev, Krasovsky. The following letter from M. G. Yefremov,* who wrote in a similar vein to Stalin and Mikoyan, reads:

Comrades,

Possessing all the evidence to overturn the accusation laid upon me by the Fascists Dybenko and Levandovsky, to my shame I was so confused at the Politburo meeting on 18.iv.38 that I forgot to reveal the proof of my innocence and my loyalty to the party of Lenin and Stalin. Army commander Dybenko said something unbelievable about himself. He must have gone mad after

---

* Yefremov was a senior officer who survived to serve in the Second World War. He was killed in action in 1942.

training, otherwise I cannot understand, as this was in 1934! According to Dybenko, he 'recruited' me, but he says the task was to recruit the officers.

All my brothers are Communists, four of them Red Army officers. My son of seventeen is a Komsomol member. My mother and my sisters and their twelve children live in the 'Path to Socialism' kolkhoz in Orel region. My uncle was hanged in 1905 for his part in a naval mutiny, my father was murdered by kulaks. I myself was a Moscow worker. I fought in the war in China. I was wounded. I have received the Order of Lenin, three Orders of the Red Banner, the Order of the Red Labour Banner. I ask you to end my sufferings and torments soon.

Yours ever,

Mikhail Yefremov.[53]

Like thousands of others, this letter was left unanswered. True, Yefremov, as well as Bukshtynovich and Krasovsky were lucky and survived, but with no thanks to Voroshilov. Neither he nor anyone else was willing to stop the meatgrinder in its work. When replying to inquiries, he would laconically sanction arrests, punishments and executions. I cite below the texts of a number of cables, of which there are literally thousands for 1937 and 1938:

Khabarovsk. Re-Blyukher. Number 88. Put on trial.

Sverdlovsk. Re-Gorbachev. Number 39. Arrest.

Polyarnoe. Re-Commander of Northern Polar flotilla. Number 212. Put on trial and sentence accordingly.

Sverdlovsk. Re-Gailit. Find, arrest and give severest sentence.

Leningrad. Re-Dybenko and Mager. Number 16758. Arrest and put on trial.

Tbilisi. Re-Kuibyshev and Apse. Number 344. Put on trial and shoot.[54]

In April-May 1937, Voroshilov sent Stalin one note after another of the following sort: 'I request that the following who have been expelled from the Red Army be expelled from the War Council of the Defence Commissariat of the USSR: M. N. Tukhachevsky, R. P. Eideman, R. V. Longva, N. A. Yefimov, E. F. Appog.'[55] He then deleted the word 'expelled' and substituted 'discharged', even though he knew where they would be 'discharged'. In the following days he sent Stalin similar notes but with different names: Gorbachev, Kazansky, Kork, Kutyakov, Feldman, Lapin, Yakir, Uborevich, Germanovich, Sangursky, Oshley and many others. He seemed unconcerned that virtually the entire War Council of the Defence Commissariat were 'spies', 'Fascists' and 'Trotskyite-Bukharinite'. The important thing was not to contradict but to uphold Comrade Stalin's line. Since he was more in the public eye than the others, Voroshilov was perhaps the member of the troika least overshadowed by Stalin. This had no effect, however, on his lack of independent judgement or on his actions.

With Beria, these three bear a heavy responsibility for the crimes committed by Stalin, but it is a responsibility that must also be shared by the many who simply voted in favour and said yes to Stalin's 'wise decisions'. The degree of blame varies and history will decide who was more and who less to blame. Andreyev, Zhdanov, Kalinin, Mikoyan, Malenkov, Khrushchev and some other figures in the top echelons of the party and state leadership did nothing to try to limit Stalin's personal rule.

CHAPTER 26

Trotsky's Ghost

Trotsky was no longer present, yet Stalin grew to hate him even more in his absence, and Trotsky's spectre frequently returned to haunt the usurper. Stalin came to curse himself for agreeing to let Trotsky go into exile abroad. He would not admit even to himself that he had feared Trotsky at the time, but he certainly feared the thought of him. The feeling that he would never be able to solve the 'problem' of Leib Davidovich (as he tended to address Trotsky in his mind, using the Yiddish form of Lev) boiled over into violent hatred. On one occasion, he lost control and almost mentioned it publicly. Speaking with Emil Ludwig on the subject of authority, he suddenly declared:

'Trotsky also had great authority, but so what? As soon as he turned his back on the workers, he was forgotten.'

'Completely forgotten?' Ludwig asked.

'They occasionally remember him – with malice.'

'All of them with malice?'

'As far as our workers are concerned, they remember Trotsky with malice, irritation and hatred.'[56]

Possibly many workers did indeed remember Trotsky unkindly, but it was Stalin himself, above all, who remembered him with malice, irritation and hatred. He thought of Trotsky when he had to sit and listen to Molotov, Kaganovich, Khrushchev and Zhdanov. Trotsky was of a different calibre intellectually, with his grasp of organization and his talents as a speaker and writer. In every way he was far superior to this bunch of bureaucrats, but he was also superior to Stalin and Stalin knew it. 'How could I have let such an enemy slip through my fingers?' he almost wailed. On one occasion he confessed to his small circle that this had been one of the biggest mistakes of his life.

Another cause of his mounting hatred derived from the fact – which he could not admit even to himself – that he often found he was following Trotsky's approach in practical policy. He remembered that once, when the Politburo was discussing the NEP, Trotsky had declared that 'the working class will only approach socialism through great sacrifices, by harnessing all their energies and giving their blood and nerves'. He had expounded the same notion in October 1922 at a Komsomol congress, and repeatedly stated that, without 'workers' armies', the 'militarization of labour' and 'total self-denial', the revolution risked never being able to free itself from 'the kingdom of necessity into the kingdom of freedom'. Almost the whole of the fifteenth volume of Trotsky's works is devoted to the 'militarization of labour'. Speaking on 12 January 1920 at a meeting of the Communist trade union fractions, Trotsky had called for 'shock battalions' to be sent to especially important sites, 'so that they can raise efficiency by personal example and repressions'. It was necessary to apply 'coercive methods, necessary to establish military conditions in ... urgent areas. We must apply labour conscription using military methods.'[57] Here was the classic expression of barracks communism, and Trotsky, who was one of its advocates in the early 1920s, never completely abandoned it, though it must be remembered that these ideas were expressed under the conditions of the civil war.

Stalin was always impressed by any idea that meant people would voluntarily 'give their blood and their nerves' for the cause. In exile, Trotsky would often refer to Stalin as an 'imitator', presumably implying his tendency to borrow from others in the field of social methodology. But the main reason Stalin feared the spectre of Trotsky was because Trotsky had created his own organization, the Fourth International, and had placed Stalin on the same level as Hitler, which Stalin found intolerable. The spectre was wreaking a revenge more painful than Stalin himself could have devised. It seemed at times as if the battle he had thought finished, when the *Ilyich* steamed unnoticed out of Odessa with Trotsky on board on 10 February 1929, was just beginning.

It was nevertheless an unequal battle. In one corner, the ascendant leader who had set out to inculcate in the party and the people a feeling of hatred towards Trotsky as a traitor and Fascist accomplice. In the other corner, the vanquished leader who spared no rhetoric to show that Stalin and Hitler deserved each other.

Supported by small groups in the various countries of his exile, Trotsky was able to influence public opinion. His speeches, whether in person or in print, were as always effective. As before, his main target was Stalin, whom he dubbed the 'gravedigger of the revolution'. Trotsky knew a great deal. During the revolution and civil war he was closer to Lenin than Stalin was. More than once Lenin came to his defence, appreciating as he did Trotsky's talents as an organizer and propagandist. Stalin remembered that when their relations had still been tolerable he had fundamentally agreed with many of Trotsky's leftist ideas. For instance, to advance on Warsaw in order to hasten the revolutionary conflagration in Europe, and to organize a campaign in Asia. Trotsky had also believed that Asia was more revolutionary than Europe, and that therefore, if a revolutionary base were created in the southern Urals, a march into Asia to hasten the revolution there was a realistic policy. In such circumstances, the revolution in China and India would definitely succeed. Stalin did not object to this analysis. Trotsky had wanted to speed up time: he was no longer thinking on the Russian scale, but in terms of world revolution. He was in a sense a world-revolution romantic and many of his long-term plans in the 1920s were linked to that end. Stalin realized, however, that to speak publicly of these 'sins' of Trotsky would be to cast a shadow on himself, for he was now the 'heir' to the revolutionary causes of October.

The thought that Trotsky was speaking not only for himself, but for all his silent supporters and the oppositionists inside the USSR, was particularly painful to Stalin. When he read Trotsky's works, such as *The Stalinist School of Falsification*, *An Open Letter to Members of the Bolshevik Party*, or *The Stalinist Thermidor*, the Leader almost lost his self-control. He had been so blind! Can he really have been wrong when he told the Communist trade union fractions in November 1924 that Trotsky had functioned well during the revolutionary upsurge, but that he had lost his bearings and was drifting in defeat?[58] Trotsky had after all suffered total defeat, yet he would not surrender, he was still fighting. Again and again Stalin was tormented by the thought of his mistake: why had he put Trotsky outside the pale? Now he was having to pay for that careless lapse. Trotsky's accomplices were preparing a plot against him, organizing diversionary actions, carrying out espionage, putting together an underground, and here he had been doing nothing for all these years.

In his speech to the February-March 1937 plenum 'on inadequacies in party work and measures for liquidating Trotskyists and other double-dealers', Stalin singled out 'the chief link', which turned out to be 'Contemporary Trotskyism'. Addressing his audience as if they were schoolboys, he asked: 'What is Trotskyism?' And he gave the reply: 'Contemporary Trotskyism is a desperate gang of wreckers. Seven or eight years ago,' he went on, 'it was an erroneous anti-Leninist tendency. But now it is a gang of Fascist wreckers.' He continued:

Kamenev and Zinoviev denied that they had a political platform. They were lying. At their trial in 1937, Pyatakov, Radek and Sokolnikov did not deny the existence of such a platform. The restoration of capitalism, the territorial dismemberment of the Soviet Union (the Ukraine to the Germans, the Maritime provinces to the Japanese); in the event of an attack by our enemies – sabotage and terror. All that is the platform of *Trotskyism*.[59]

In this way, Stalin tied up all his vanquished and potential enemies with the same Trotskyist rope.

It is high time Soviet historians arrived at a more accurate assessment of Trotsky. I have already referred to his intellectual and moral qualities, contradictory and complicated though they were. He had one incurable weakness, namely his conviction that he was a genius, a belief he was barely able to conceal. His ambitions stemmed from this. Those who say that, had Trotsky conquered Stalin, the Soviet Union might still have been ruled by no less of a dictatorship, are not necessarily wrong. But, given Trotsky's high intelligence and culture, it is very doubtful that he was capable of the sort of crimes Stalin committed.

The fact remains that, during the revolution and civil war, Trotsky was second only to Lenin in importance. It is impossible to know how Trotsky would have turned out, had Lenin lived. One thing is certain, and that is that between 1917 and 1924 Trotsky was not hostile to the revolution and socialism. He was, however, Stalin's consistent enemy. The anti-Soviet attacks to which he resorted in his last years were the logical result of his fight with Stalin. Possibly these attacks damaged the Soviet cause, but to his credit Trotsky did not cave in before Stalin's despotism. One of the first to realize that Stalin was preparing a Soviet reactionary terror, he turned out to be right about many things. As Lunacharsky wrote of him:

Trotsky was as a man prickly and overbearing. However, after Trotsky merged with the Bolsheviks, it was only in his attitude to Lenin that Trotsky always showed – and continues to show – a tactful pliancy which is touching. With the modesty of all truly great men he acknowledges Lenin's primacy.[60]

But as I have said elsewhere, Trotsky may well have loved the idea of himself in the revolution more than the revolution itself. His tragedy stemmed less from his fight with Stalinism than his fight with Stalin in the succession struggle, and his disappointed hopes merely reinforced the personal element in his thinking.

How real was the danger from Trotsky in the 1930s? What influence did he have on the political and social processes in the USSR? It is important to clarify these questions, since the 'Trotskyist danger' served as the excuse for the most appalling tragedy in the country's history.

While Stalin was strengthening his personal rule, Trotsky was wandering the world, from the island of Prinkipo in the Sea of Marmara, to France, Norway and finally Mexico. At first, he was hoping for an early return to the USSR, believing that Stalin would not last much longer. Stalin's intellectual shortcomings, his ignorance, rudeness and cunning, were so obvious, Trotsky reasoned, that they were bound to generate growing opposition and multiply his enemies. This was another of Trotsky's mistakes. He believed that, given his widespread popularity, all the elements hostile to Stalin would regroup around him. As he wandered among the brown rocks of Ada on Prinkipo, he recalled that this was where the Byzantine rulers had exiled their enemies, and now it was to house one of the 'architects of the Russian revolution', as he described himself in his diary.

The Western press reacted somewhat cautiously at first to Trotsky's exile. It was rumoured for a while that Stalin had deported him purposely to help raise the workers in capitalist countries. The German and English press even went into some detail, referring to Trotsky as a 'revolutionary detonator', and for this reason he was not readily offered political asylum. Gradually, however, it was realized that, although he continued loudly to condemn Fascism, bourgeois philistinism and imperialist expansion, the main force of his anger was directed above all against Stalin and the Stalinist régime.

With the help of his followers, who made the pilgrimage to Prinkipo from various countries, Trotsky began to establish contact with various groups that were hostile to Comintern, to the Stalinist régime and to Stalin personally, and he soon launched *The Bulletin of the Opposition* in several languages. He even managed, before 1935, to get a small number of issues into the Soviet Union, making it clear that he wanted to establish contact with his former supporters there, as his biographer, Isaac Deutscher, notes. In the third volume of his biography, Deutscher writes, for instance, that via Sobolevicius-Senin (*alias* Jack Soble), a German correspondent in Moscow, Trotsky obtained important Soviet information, including statistics for his books and articles. Sobolevicius and his brother handled Trotsky's correspondence with his supporters in the USSR, including ciphers, letters in special inks, post box numbers, and so on.[61] Despite the relative meagreness of such contacts, up until 1935 Trotsky was able to obtain information about the USSR and to send in his own letters by illegal means.

When he left the USSR, Trotsky took with him about thirty boxes of archives and books, an oversight Stalin later blamed on the security organs which had handled the deportation. The four long years spent on Prinkipo were a time of waiting, and of choosing and determining his further course of action. Gradually it dawned on him that he was not going to be called back to Moscow and he decided that the only way to 'stay afloat' was to carry on the fight against Stalin, though he did not yet have a clear idea of how this was to be done. He still could not fully accept that this was his final exile and that he would never again set foot inside his homeland.

Sitting in the little room which served as his study, its windows facing the sea, Trotsky leafed through the pages of his collected works. Though it is flawed by its author's blatant egotism, the best of them, as he himself recognized, was his *History of the Russian Revolution*, which he wrote after the break with Stalin. Another volume, devoted to portraits of political figures and embracing an extraordinarily wide range, and written as always in an engaging manner, does not include a separate study of Lenin, though he is frequently mentioned.[62] He read again the speech he'd made so long ago at the Seventh Congress: 'The party congress, the highest party institution, has indirectly rejected the policy that I among others was following ... and so I am relinquishing all the posts of any importance which the party has given me.'[63]

There is little mention of Stalin in Trotsky's works to this date, with the possible exception of the volume on culture, where there are indirect references. On democracy and bureaucracy he had written that 'Socialist construction is possible only in conditions of the growth of genuine, revolutionary democracy of the toiling masses. Wherever there is bureaucracy, it will inevitably give rise to *mochalinstvo*.* The main principle of mochalinstvo is obsequiously to oblige. Oblige whom? The boss ...'⁶⁴ He resolved that all that was left for him was to fight Stalin, not so much the system as the man himself.

According to Deutscher, before the final defeat and deportation, Trotsky, together with Zinoviev and even Shlyapnikov, attempted to organize insignificant groupings of his supporters in foreign Communist and labour parties. In France they were led by such men as Albert Rosmer, Boris Souvarine and Pierre Monatte, in Germany there were Arkadi Maslov and Ruth Fischer (former comrades of Zinoviev), in Spain Andrés Nin, in Belgium the ex-Communists Van Overstraaten and Lesoil. Tiny groups of Trotskyists arose in Shanghai, Rome, Stockholm and several other towns and capitals. It was on these fragments that Trotsky hoped to build a new movement of anti-Stalinist persuasion. But he had no serious social base, nor a serious programme. Anti-Stalinism could not have much appeal for a worldwide organization. He therefore began to chew over again his idea of 'permanent revolution' and its variants, showing that 'the doctrine of socialism in one country was a national-socialist distortion of Marxism.' The constant element of his 'programme', however, remained rabid anti-Stalinism, with his personal animosity for the man, the personal injury of his disappointed ambitions, and the personal pain at the loss of his family in Russia barely concealed. Trotsky hoped that his open anti-Stalinism would find a broad echo in Communist parties, but it did not happen.

For Communists of many countries, Soviet achievements in the economy, culture and education were associated with the name of Stalin. The infamous political trials had not yet begun and there was too little known about Stalin for the West to have any significant view of his character. Trotsky's attempt to bring pressure on the Soviet Union and on Stalin and his policy was doomed to failure, while any hope of 'raising' his former supporters inside the USSR against Stalin was even less realistic. Through articles, press releases, speeches and interviews, however, he managed, almost inadvertently, to create the provocative impression that the number of his supporters was growing and that anti-Stalinist forces were consolidating. This was not so, unfortunately, but Stalin, an acutely suspicious man, took many of these airy declarations at face value.

Stalin was consumed with anger, but could do nothing. Several of Trotsky's works were aimed against him, even in their titles alone: *The Stalinist School of Falsification*, *Stalin's Crimes*, and *Stalin*, which Trotsky was prevented from completing by his death. Trotsky's collected works were published in dozens of countries, and it was from these that world opinion formed its image of Stalin, not from books by the likes of Feuchtwanger and Barbusse. The morose Asiatic despot rose from the pages of Trotsky's books, cunning, cruel, fanatical, dull-witted and vengeful. Trotsky laid it on thick, and the mere thought of him

* Mochalin is a character in Griboyedov's *Woe from Wit* who lent his name to toadying careerism.

stoked the fire of Stalin's desire for revenge. In every Trotskyist he saw a fragment of Trotsky, and he demanded they be shown no mercy.

While he was in Norway in 1936, Trotsky wrote his book *The Revolution Betrayed*. In it he appealed to Communists, former opposition members, former Mensheviks, SRs and drop-outs from other parties, to carry out a coup d'état, or what he called a 'political revolution'. His hatred for Stalin and the hopelessness of his own position made a sober assessment of the political situation inside the USSR impossible. The book contained not only an account of the past as seen through Trotsky's lens, but also a long-term prognosis of social development in the USSR. His analysis was flawed, however, because his prediction of a political revolution against Stalin was based solely on his passionate desire for the Leader's defeat. He predicted also that, should Germany unleash a war against the Soviet Union, Stalin could hardly avoid defeat.

Stalin read the translation of *The Revolution Betrayed* in a single night, seething with bile. It was the last straw. For some years he had been nurturing two decisions in his mind, and now he proposed to have them carried out. First, he must at all costs remove Trotsky from the political arena. He knew that any attempt at a disguised murder would be useless, as everyone would assume he had inspired and organized it. Secondly, he was now even more convinced of the need for a determined and final liquidation of all potential enemies inside the country. It is possible that he himself did not know just how far this decision would go. He felt that the time was approaching when he must not hesitate, particularly as Yezhov – often reeking of vodka – was constantly reporting that the former oppositionists had become active.

Stalin recalled the half-forgotten Blyumkin affair. Blyumkin was the Socialist Revolutionary who had assassinated the German ambassador, Count Mirbach, in Moscow in 1918 in order to disrupt the Brest-Litovsk peace talks. He had been sentenced to be shot, but thanks to Trotsky's intercession the sentence had been commuted to 'penance by fighting in defence of the revolution'. Blyumkin had worked for some time on Trotsky's staff, had become close to him and had then gone to work for the GPU. When returning to the USSR from India in 1929 via Constantinople, he visited Trotsky on Prinkipo. According to Deutscher, Trotsky handed him the text of a speech for his followers in Moscow and also some advice on how to struggle against Stalin. Blyumkin was arrested immediately upon his return to the USSR; perhaps he had been followed during the trip to Prinkipo, or perhaps he had carelessly talked to someone about the visit. Most probably the account given by I. A. Sats, Lunacharsky's secretary, is closest to the truth. According to this, Blyumkin delivered a packet which Trotsky had given him for Radek, and also passed on an oral message. When Blyumkin had left, Radek, without opening the packet, called Yagoda and told him about the visit, Yagoda told Stalin and the 'messenger' was arrested at once. Radek was granted a short-lived indulgence. Blyumkin was shot after a short court hearing. Fate was not prepared to smile on him twice.

Perhaps there were some other Blyumkins close by, under instruction from

sif Dzhugashvili as a student at Gori
eological school. 1893.

Yekaterina (Kato) Svanidze, Stalin's first wife.

e of Monastyrskoe, 1915. A group of exiled Central Committee members: Stalin third from left
ck row, L. B. Kamenev to his right, G. I. Petrovsky seated centre, Ya. M. Sverdlov to his right.

Members of the Revvoensoviet of the South-Western front A. I. Yegorov and Stalin, 1920.

Chairman of the Revolutionary Military Council (Revvoensoviet) Trotsky in his armoured train,

Communism: collecting the harvest.

...ПЛОЩАДИ. ПРОДУКТЫ РЕКВИЗИРОВАННЫЕ У МАРОДЕРОВЪ ТЫЛА.

...cow, Assumption (now Revolution) Square. Unloading requisitioned food, 1919.

Famine in the Volga region
1921.

Lenin and Stalin in
Gorky, 1922.

n, Rykov, Kamenev and Zinoviev, early 1920s.

ay 1925, Red Square, Moscow. In front of the temporary wooden Mausoleum: F. Kon, A. S
ukidze, A. I. Sedakyan, R. A. Muklevich, K. Ye. Voroshilov, A. S. Bubnov, I. S. Unshlikht, M. I.
anov, M. N. Tukhachevsky, Yegorov, S. M. Budenny. On the Mausoleum: S. M. Kirov, A. I. Rykov,
Bukharin, F. I. Kalinin, Stalin, V. V. Schmidt, M. P. Tomsky, E. M. Yaroslavsky, P. P. Postyshev, et

Stalin, S. Ordzhonikidze (far right), Kalinin (with hand over mouth) and Voroshilov (talking to Sta on one of Stalin's rare visits to a collective farm.

A woman's lot ... building the coke ovens at Magnitogorsk, 1931.

an, Kirov and
, 1932.

l height, *Pravda*,
ember 1930.

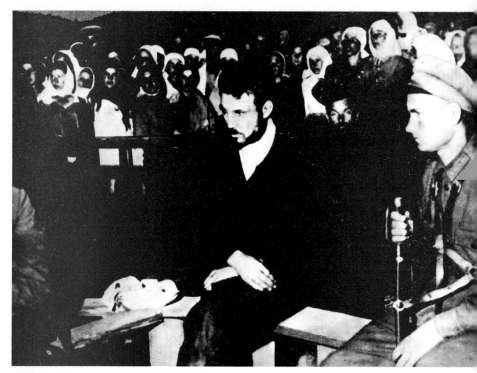

Trial of a kulak, Odessa, 1932.

Kulak victims of terror, 1929.

alin with A. N. Poskrebyshev, 1934.

Voroshilov with future victims of the terror Ya. B. Gamarnik, I. E. Slavin, I. N. Dubov, P. E. Dybenko,
I. Kork, I. A. Khalepsky and I. E. Yakir, during an interval at the Seventeenth Congress.

Voroshilov, Molotov, Stalin and Yezhov at the Moscow–Volga Canal.

The same photograph with Yezhov removed.

...arin in 1920.

...shilov, Stalin and Molotov bearing the ashes of balloonists killed in an accident, late 1930s.

Stalin in Buryat Mongol costume, 1936.

Stalinist elections: Yu. O. Shmidt voting, 19

An obviously faked picture of the platform at a session of the Moscow Soviet, 1935.

...n with his daughter, Svetlana.

...n with his mother, Yekaterina Dzhugashvili, 1935.

Stalin and Voroshilov with their wives.

Stalin and Beria with Stalin's daughter at the dacha.

The family: Stalin with Vasili and Svetlana.

t Stalin and Beria on holiday.

n at his dacha.

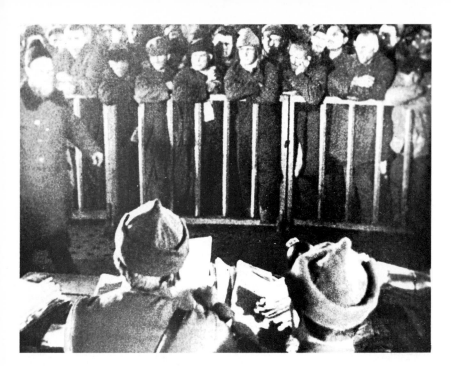

Cases being checked on arrival at a labour camp on the Moscow–Volga Canal.

Prisoners entering a quarantine unit.

ng of the Soviet–German Non-Aggression
August 1939.

Stalin with Poskrebyshev during the signing of
the Pact.

after the signing.

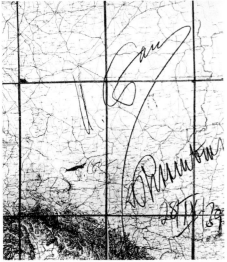

Map of Poland signed by Stalin and
Ribbentrop.

Right Western Belorussians receiving the
news of annexation.

Soviet warplanes destroyed in July
1941.

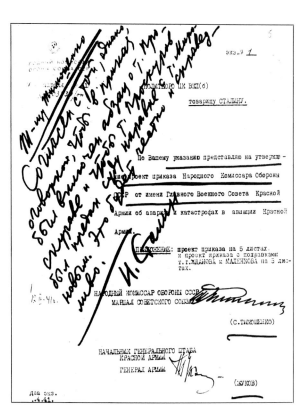

...rt from Timoshenko to Stalin
...t air losses. Stalin adds that two
...d commanders be put on trial.

...ting at enemy planes. Southern front, May 1942.

Soviet POWs, autumn 1941.

Stalin's son, Yakov Dzhugashvili (right), and
Molotov's adopted son, G. Skryabin, as
prisoners of war.

A German camp for Soviet POWs, 1941.

alry attack outside Moscow (3rd Guards Cavalry Division), December 1941.

e village of Khoroshevo near Rzhev. Stalin stayed here during his visit to the front in August 1943.

The Germans reached Moscow, but as POWs, July 1944.

The liberators on foot to Berlin.

n with his children Vasili and Svetlana at
rnaya Rechka, 1947.

A pre-election meeting in the Stalin and Bauman
districts of Moscow to put Stalin forward for the
Supreme Soviet, 15 February 1950.

scow Pioneers bring flowers to Stalin on his seventieth birthday.

The interment. On the Mausoleum: Togliatti, Ibarruri, Chervenkov, Rakosi, Kenny, Duclos, Gottwa
Bulganin, Molotov, Voroshilov, Malenkov, Khrushchev, Cou En-lai, Beria, Yudin, Kaganovich,
Mikoyan, Saburov, Pervukhin, Shvernik.

Trotsky? How many of them were there? Who were they? Who could know the full scale of the threat? How far had Trotsky put out his feelers? Maybe many Trotskyists had been intimidated by Blyumkin's execution, but who could be sure that all of Trotsky's supporters had been terrified into passivity?

In several speeches Stalin proclaimed that Trotskyism was the chief hostile platform on which all the Soviet Union's enemies were grouped. The spectre of Trotsky was blown up out of all proportion as a threat to the state. Stalin saw 'the hand of Trotsky' in every failure or disaster. In the political trials of 1937–38 one of the main charges was that of maintaining direct links with Trotsky, receiving his orders and instructions, and even meeting him either in Berlin or Oslo, and so on. At the February-March and similar plenums in 1937 – there were four such meetings in that year – the words 'Trotsky', 'Trotskyism', 'Trotskyist spies and murderers' were heard more than any others. Whatever the topic under discussion, Trotsky's shade hovered in the hall.[65] For Stalin, Trotsky had become the personification of universal evil.

The real situation was quite different. Even at its height, in the mid-1920s, Trotsky had very few supporters in the party. After his deportation some of them remained loyal, but they amounted to only a few hundred at the most. Some felt that Trotsky had long given up fighting for socialism and was conducting a personal vendetta verging on anti-Sovietism. Others condemned Trotskyism and gave up political life altogether. Those whom Stalin 'forgave' and permitted to return to Moscow – including Rakovsky, Preobrazhensky, Muralov, Sosnovsky, Smirnov, Boguslavsky and Radek – were given third-rate jobs in the economy and education ministries, but none of them was allowed back into the political fold. The overwhelming majority of them recanted publicly in the press, and not one of them represented the least threat to the system or to the internal stability of society.

Stalin knew he had emasculated them all intellectually by forcing them to renounce leftism, to condemn the theory of permanent revolution and to accept Leninism in Stalin's interpretation. But he knew that deep in their hearts they were not reconciled, and that to him was a great danger. Being of an insincere nature himself, he naturally assumed that everyone else harboured the same qualities.

In fact, the threat presented by Trotskyism was not in the least a serious one. After 1935, as his publications and letters show, Trotsky virtually lost contact with the USSR. The newspapers and radio were his chief source of information. As he filtered and strained the information he required, he continued to think he was able to influence the social, political and economic processes in the USSR. Stalin forced himself to believe that this was so, for he needed an excuse once and for all to finish off those who did not share his views, or those who might act in a hostile manner in the future. The thought of Trotsky's predictions drove him to distraction, and the title alone of Trotsky's last book, *Stalin's Crimes* (dashed off in a couple of months following the January 1937 political trial in Moscow of Pyatakov, Radek, Sokolnikov,

Serebryakov and others), was enough to make him rage.

In asserting that the Soviet Union would not withstand a clash with the capitalist countries, Trotsky was in effect claiming that Stalin's position was hopeless. His words rang in Stalin's ears like an ominous augury:

Tomorrow Stalin could become a burden to the ruling group ... Stalin is poised on the eve of accomplishing his tragic mission. The more it seems that he needs no one, the nearer the hour when no one will need him. At that time Stalin will hardly be able to hear the words of gratitude for the work he has done. Stalin will depart the scene, laden down with all his crimes.[66]

In moving to liquidate the remnants of the former opposition, and hence depriving Trotsky of any hope that his prophecies would come true, Stalin was also seeking to deal Trotsky a mortal blow.

In his reading of Trotsky, Stalin saw not only political appeals to incitement. Throughout, Trotsky was saying that Stalin's presence on the Olympus of power was a pure accident, a grimace of history. This wounded the Leader more than anything. In Trotsky's *History of the Russian Revolution* Stalin read:

From the extraordinary significance which Lenin's arrival received, it should only be inferred that leaders are not accidentally created, that they are gradually chosen out and trained up in the course of decades, that they cannot be capriciously replaced, that their mechanical exclusion from the struggle gives the party a living wound, and in many cases may paralyse it for a long period.[67]

The spectre was always there alongside the man in the emperor's mantle, even though the spectre was still a living person and far from Moscow. Perhaps, thinking of the spectre, Stalin also recalled the party congress in London so many years ago when he had first seen Trotsky, with his shock of red hair, his energetic movements, the pince-nez, the eloquent speech, the theatrical gestures. Trotsky had attracted everyone's attention. Several times Trotsky's gaze had come to rest on the sullen Caucasian who still went under the name of Dzhugashvili. Then it was Trotsky who had played the lead and Stalin who had been the silent spectre. Could the young revolutionary have imagined then that this mysterious member of a combat group in the Caucasus would become his companion and enemy to the end of his life, a life which would be cut off, to Stalin's great joy, on 21 August 1940?

CHAPTER 27

A Popular Victor

However artificial the means employed to achieve it, Stalin's popularity was genuine among the masses, whose opinion of him and the nation's affairs was based on appearances, usually because they had neither the opportunity nor the inclination to delve deeper into what was going on. It was a time when uniformity of thought was being imposed by every available means. From kindergarten age, children were being taught to chant rhymes to the health of the great leader. Nobody could afford not to love Stalin, yet the question still arises of why he was so popular?

One reason may be that, despite the enormous moral failure and physical sacrifice, society as a whole did not become degraded, and quite a few achievements were accomplished in the economic, social and cultural spheres. No doubt, given a leader of higher moral calibre, the achievements would have been greater, but the fact remains that the pathological nature of the Stalin cult did not fully retard the development of society.

Major changes were wrought in industrial development. The statistics, though exaggerated, indicate that Lenin's electrification plan for industry was fulfilled. By 1935 average gross output from heavy industry exceeded the pre-war level by 5.6 times.[68] Having lived through the industrial breakdown caused by the First World War and civil war, the people could not but be amazed at the huge energy and creative drive unleashed by the October Revolution. They could proudly tell themselves, 'We can do a lot! Let's complete the Five-Year Plan in four!' As if to confirm Stalin's words, 'Life has become better, life has become more joyful!', by the end of the 1930s hundreds of new factories and plants, roads, towns, palaces of culture, rest homes, hospitals, schools and laboratories had appeared, transforming the landscape.

Things were substantially worse in the countryside where the criminal acts of dekulakization damaged the agrarian sector for decades. If before collectivization there were 25 million small households, of which 35 per cent were poor peasants, 60 per cent were middle peasants and 5 per cent were kulaks, then by the middle of the 1930s, 90 per cent of households had been collectivized. They did not, however, yield a decisive increase in output. Between 1909 and 1940, grain production rose by only some 19 per cent, meat production by 15 per cent, milk by as little as 14 per cent, while wool production fell by 20 per cent.[69]

The use of coercion as a basic instrument of collectivization not only gave rise to prolonged social tension, but was historically 'avenged' by the chronic backwardness in this sphere. Stalin's boasts about achievements in agriculture were all empty. Technology, specialists, education and culture may all have come to the collective farm, but it proved far from easy to replace the age-old structures with new ones.

The statistics for education are more impressive. There were nearly seven times more specialists who had had higher education than in 1913, while those with secondary education increased by almost twenty-eight times.[70] Illiteracy fell dramatically. Press, radio and the cinema had a direct influence on a population that was giving all its energies to the building of the socialist society.

Most of the people felt that this was only the beginning, that tomorrow or the day after new horizons would open up to an improvement in living and working conditions and social security. When food rationing was ended, both industrial goods and food were more plentiful in the shops, and although, compared to the present, life was harder and more crowded, with more short-ages, the general atmosphere was one of optimism. The media proclaimed that all present and future successes were linked with the 'wise guidance of the leader'. From their first years, infants were taught that 'Stalin is thinking about every one of us', 'if it were not for Stalin, we wouldn't be an industrial power, we wouldn't have a roof over our heads and a guaranteed crust of bread'. Thus, despite the criminality, the people went on building, creating, striving. Paradoxically, at a time when thousands upon thousands of innocent men and women were perishing in Stalin's meatgrinder, those who were spared this bitter fate were startling the country and often the world with their achievements.

In June 1937, almost at the same time as Tukhachevsky and the other military leaders were being summarily tried, *Pravda* was reporting that V. Chkalov, G. Baidukov and A. Belyakov had made the first non-stop flight from Moscow to North America via the North Pole in their ANT-25. In March 1937 *Pravda* reported that Alexei Stakhanov had established a new labour record by digging 102 tonnes of coal in six hours at the Stalin Central mine, that is, sixteen times the norm for a faceworker in his section! In one shift he had overfulfilled his section's shift target by eighty-three tonnes.[71] But even this had to be somehow linked to Stalin. In his book, *The Story of My Life*, Stakhanov wrote:

When I remember it all, when I collect all my thoughts together, every time I want to say just one thing: thank you, Comrade Stalin! Comrade Stalin gave me, an ordinary worker, more support than I could ever have imagined. I am now used to the expression, 'the Stakhanovite movement', I often see my name in the papers, and hear it spoken at meetings. Frankly, at first I couldn't understand it all. But now I think it's right to call our movement Stalinist, because it was the working class, which is on the move into the Stalinist campaign for technological advance, that created my record and those of my comrades. It was Comrade Stalin who made our movement a broad one.[72]

Pioneers of labour, innovators, enthusiasts and patriots were advertised not for themselves but inevitably through the prism of the leadership, and of Stalin's participation and concern for each of them, and every such success enhanced the leader's popularity, sometimes in the most unlikely ways. I received a letter from S. E. Plost, a party member whose father, a political officer in the Red Army, had named him Stali by the popular request of his students in the Lenin Military-Political Academy. His father was arrested on 15 May 1937 as an 'enemy of the people' and shot on 4 November the same year. Stali Plost had survived to bear the name of the despot who had murdered his father.

The campaign to unmask and destroy 'enemies' was also tied to Stalin's authority and popularity. The press constantly whipped up the idea that the 'Trotskyite-Zinovievite wreckers' were planning terrorist acts against the party and state leadership and that above all 'they wanted to kill Comrade Stalin', also that 'Comrade Stalin, who was in constant peril, would concern himself with anyone who had made mistakes and who wants to improve himself.' At the February–March 1937 plenum, Molotov read out one of the leader's letters as an example of 'Comrade Stalin's solicitous attitude to the cadres':

> To town committee secretary Comrade Golyshev, Perm.
> The Central Committee has received information concerning the persecution and slander of the manager of the motor factory, Poberezhsky, on account of his past sins as a Trotskyist. In view of the fact that both Poberezhsky and his fellow workers are now working conscientiously and have the full trust of the Central Committee, we request that Comrade Poberezhsky and his fellow workers be protected against such slander and that an atmosphere of complete trust be created around him.
> Inform the Central Committee at once of measures taken.[73]

'That's the way to treat former Trotskyist comrades who are now working honestly in their jobs,' Molotov concluded. Even at the height of the repressions, Stalin strove to bolster his image as a just and caring person. The population for its part willingly accepted the calls for sharpened alertness and the need for fierce struggle against 'enemies of the people', and they responded eagerly to the evidence of 'exposure', unaware of any mystification or falsification.

Stalin was punctilious about detail, if it affected his public image. His simple manner of dress and speech made a big impression. According to Feuchtwanger:

Stalin is definitely not a great speaker. He speaks slowly and without any brilliance, in a slightly muffled voice, and with difficulty. He develops his arguments slowly, appealing to people's common sense so that they will grasp them not quickly but firmly. When Stalin raises his index finger and grins his attractive, cunning grin, he does not create a distance between himself and his audience, as other speakers do.[74]

Stalin prepared meticulously for his rare public appearances. Tovstukha, and later Poskrebyshev, would be instructed to find a dozen interesting quotations from the Marxist classics, literature and folklore. As Antonov, one of Voroshilov's staff, reported: 'Stalin's speech-researchers help him to choose statistics for the appropriate subject. The information is often ordered from the appropriate commissariat. Comrade Stalin selects what he wants from the material. The researchers do not provide any text.'[75]

Stalin always adopted a liturgical tone in his speeches. He was fond of the catechistic form, question and answer, question and explanation. He frequently used refrain or conscious repetition for its hypnotic effect, as he thought. And indeed, this restrained, carefully rehearsed style made an impact. Above all, it convinced people of his wisdom, and nothing makes leaders more popular than the people's belief in their intellectual qualities.

No photograph of Stalin could be published without his, and later Poskrebyshev's, approval. Stalin liked to be shown in soldier's uniform as the personification of 'proletarian sternness', holding a child on his lap as 'the father of the people', in his Generalissimo's uniform as the 'great war leader and victor'. All the official photographs are monotonously unexpressive, whereas those that were unposed and spontaneous, with N. S. Vlasik or Nadezhda Alliluyeva, for instance, while they are the most interesting, are mostly of too poor quality to reproduce.

In consolidating his personal rule, Stalin created an entire hierarchy of leaders throughout the country. One could establish an unofficial table of ranks just by looking at newspapers of the 1930s. Of course at the top of the pyramid was 'Lenin's best pupil'. It would be reported that at meetings the audience stood to welcome the leader. Applause would grow into an ovation. There would be some obligatory 'hurrah!'s. The autocrat would not be allowed to speak for long before genuine ecstasy exploded. The mood would be one of exultation, real idol-worship, and the epithets of praise would know no bounds.

The newspapers also wrote about Molotov, Kaganovich and Voroshilov in terms such as 'Stalin's glorious comrade-in-arms', the 'steadfast Bolshevik-Leninist', the 'Stalinist commissar', 'leader of the Stalinist school' and so on. Lower-ranking bosses, such as regional party secretaries or heads of important agencies, were referred to as 'balanced', 'true Bolsheviks', 'outstanding Chekists', 'dedicated leaders'. But while these people stood significantly lower down the ladder, they were in charge of whole republics, regions or commissariats, and until 1934 were referred to as leaders on the regional scale. Those still further down were working to carry out the plans 'of genius' for industrialization and collectivization, or organizing subscriptions for the air force, arranging meetings and processions, taking part in the dekulakization and covering the boards of honour with their portraits. Any who survived to the end of the decade would rise to the next level. There would be many vacancies. This table of ranks represented one of the foundations of the Stalinist system: less people power meant more bosses.

Stalin knew that the population, especially the peasantry, harboured hidden 'tsarist' traditions. Being downtrodden and ignorant for centuries could not but leave deep marks, an irrational faith in the omnipotence of any ruler, especially one in the capital. The peasants' predisposition to cult worship was not confined to Stalin, but applied to any authority.

Simple folk often wrote to Stalin. Replies were written by one of his secretaries who ordered local bosses to deal with petitioners' requests. Often, Stalin replied in his own hand. Photocopies of such replies are to be found by the dozen in the archives. For example:

> To the Klimkin family. Leningrad.
> Dear Comrades!
> Because of excessive work, I am late in replying, for which I apologize. I have already seen to your request. Vouchers for 100 rubles have been sent to the central committee of the International Relief Organization for Fighters of the Revolution (MOPR), and 300 rubles for the 'Flame of the Revolution' kolkhoz in the district of Khoper, a pioneer of mass collectivization.
> I enclose a photo which the kiddies asked for.
> Greetings! 7.04.30. I. Stalin.[76]

Such letters were later made the object of massive propaganda campaigns at every level as examples of 'the leader's simplicity and concern for the people'.

It is clear that Stalin was not only preoccupied with what today would be called problems of management, but also with the 'technique of one-man rule'. He made a careful study of V. Vorovsky's *On the Nature of Absolutism*, M. Alexandrov's *The State, the Bureaucracy and Absolutism in the History of Russia*, Yu. Kazmin's *The Fate of the Ruler* and similar works. His approach to historical literature was evidently not that of the disinterested reader. He was looking for analogies, studying 'recipes' on the technique of power and its psychological subtleties. He learned, for instance, that his speeches at important meetings in the Kremlin made a big impact on the minds and emotions of his audiences. In the course of 1935, he spoke in the Kremlin to a meeting of railway builders (30 July), to women shock-workers from sugar-beet collectives (10 November), to outstanding combine operators (1 December), men and women kolkhozniks from Tadzhikistan and Turkmenistan (4 December), tractor drivers (20 December) and so on. Every such meeting was publicized in the press and shown on cinema newsreels. As his popularity grew, however, Stalin decided it would be politic to reduce the frequency of such appearances: the less he appeared, the more significant the appearances would become, and his seclusion would enhance the official legends, myths and embellished clichés about him.

A country that has lived for centuries under an autocrat cannot shed its psychological skin by incantations alone. It needs time. Stalin therefore laid special emphasis on creating faith in the leader, on his care and concern about people and his fairness. He blamed all his mistakes and crimes on wreckers and bunglers, on the stupidity of clerks and on local leaders who either did not understand or garbled his instructions. This line worked without a hitch. Even today there are people who claim that Stalin's tragedy was that 'he trusted Yezhov', and later Beria, that 'there was much he did not know', that 'he did not know the extent of the repression'. These are all echoes of the subtle brainwashing campaign Stalin ran for many years. Externally, its essence was simple: all victories and successes were due to Stalin; all excesses, abuses and defeats arose from his orders not being carried out properly.

Stalin's popularity is also explained by the low political culture of the broad masses, which I have mentioned. As soon as he realized that he might become the long-term leader – the first sign came in 1927 and was confirmed at the Seventeenth Congress in 1934 – Stalin set about making this an attractive proposition for the people. Films and books began to appear which dealt with the subject of strong personalities, dictators, 'progressive' tsars. Alongside genuinely revolutionary art, works were produced which rendered the rôle of the individual absolute. He personally consulted Sergei Eisenstein and Nikolai Cherkasov about the image of Ivan the Terrible in the film of that name.

Stalin's entourage did much to enhance his popularity, praising him to win his good graces. Being suspicious, Stalin saw meaning or intent in every careless word or gesture. He even scrupulously analysed the bland, safe articles of adulation – identical but for their titles – that were written to celebrate his sixtieth and seventieth birthdays. He went through piles of books and magazines containing references to him. His vanity was insatiable, though he could hide it in public to bolster the myth of his 'extraordinary modesty'. For the purposes of propaganda, and no doubt to curry favour, his entourage vied with each other in the search for epithets, elevated comparisons, historical analogies. They lost all measure of common sense. In 1939, with the meatgrinder still in operation, Stalin's assistants, Poskrebyshev and Dvinsky, wrote of him as a man endowed with the highest humanitarian qualities. The article, entitled 'Teacher and Friend of Mankind', includes such lines as:

Stalin entered the revolution with the image of Lenin in his mind and heart. He thinks of Lenin all the time. Even when his thoughts are immersed in problems requiring his decision, his hand will mechanically, automatically doodle the words 'Lenin ... teacher ... friend ...' How often after a day's work we have carried away pages covered over their length and breadth with these words.[77]

Such sugary confections, the authors believed, would influence not so much the minds as the feelings of the people. The evidence shows that during meetings Stalin was doodling anything but 'Lenin ... teacher ... friend' on his notepad. The Stalin archives contain everything from documents of historical importance to insignificant notes, from his congress reports to such scribbled messages as 'Comrades Andreyev, Molotov, Voroshilov: time to stop. Wind up the speeches. The plenum must end by four. I. S.' As he listened distractedly to the speeches at a Politburo meeting, he doodled on the cover of a brochure entitled 'The Rightist Danger in our Party':

Stalin. Acknowledge. Teacher. On rightist danger. On rightist danger in our party. Mukhalatka. Private meeting. Tokyo. Teacher. Sokolnikov. Workers' publishing house 'Priboi'. Fire. Discussion. Molotov.[78]

Stalin's doodling at the end of the 1920s tells us only one thing, and that is that what Poskrebyshev and Dvinsky had to say about his subliminal thoughts, and much else besides, was nonsense.

On the other hand, Stalin's popularity was a form, however twisted, of social self-defence. Anyone not wanting to attract suspicion would have to avoid any 'slip of the tongue' in his public references to the leader. The most unintentional and insignificant aspersion cast on Stalin's rôle as leader would end in tragedy. The sociologist A. Fedorov told me that in the late 1940s, at a Motor-Tractor Station near Vitebsk, the following event took place. The office had just been newly whitewashed and the time came to rehang the portraits. A young tractor driver came in and carelessly knocked over a picture of Stalin that had been leaning against the wall, and as he struggled to keep his balance he accidentally stepped on the leader's face. An awkward silence descended on the people in the room, and then the manager gave the tractor driver an earful. Three days later the unfortunate young man was picked up and was not seen again until after the Twentieth Congress.

Embedded within the popularity was a hidden, permanent layer of fear. It was not felt by everyone all the time, and those who had suffered and knew about the repressions continued to praise Stalin while suppressing their knowledge of what was happening. Stalin's popularity was thus sustained both by the manipulation of public opinion on the basis of the people's achievements, and by the often uncertain fear of real punishment for the least criticism of him. As a natural consequence of the suspicion and spy-mania that was implanted in the public mind, informing on all and sundry became the norm.

It would be wrong, however, to assume that all Soviet citizens loved Stalin fanatically and that he was popular with everyone. There was a substantial layer of pre-revolutionary Communists in the party, known as the Leninist old guard. They knew party history and the contribution made by the various leaders to the October Revolution, though not according to Stalin's *Short Course*, and most of them heard of Stalin only after the revolution and civil war, when, as we have seen, he was not in the front rank. His attitude towards them was therefore all the more 'partial'. He knew that, though they said nothing, their image of him was different from the one he wanted to project. These people with a revolutionary past were in the way.

Stalin saw that, despite forward progress, much was not being achieved. Agriculture was in a mess, although 1936 had seen a good harvest. As before, the country was facing serious economic and social difficulties. Despite the time that had elapsed since the revolution, and the slogan 'life is better, more joyful', Stalin was still calling for belt-tightening for the sake of tomorrow. The standard of living had not risen greatly. If Stalin were to say that this was the fault of wreckers, the people – naturally not eager to blame themselves – would surely believe him, especially as there were so many former oppositionists and people with damaged reputations to fit the bill. Everyone could see evidence of wrecking in the economy and the administration.

Molotov, Kaganovich, Yezhov and the fast-rising Malenkov quickly grasped the direction of Stalin's thinking, as well as his utterances. Hunched in his soldier's greatcoat, as if cringing from the gaze of his potential enemies, Stalin seemed to indicate that only their complete eradication would make his position incontrovertibly secure. Decisive action was needed. A massive blow against his hidden enemies would, in his view, both justify the disasters and mistakes of his economic policy and get rid of his ill-wishers. After the war, Molotov added that, in exterminating his enemies, Stalin had been looking far ahead: he had exterminated those who in a war with Fascism might take Hitler's side.

To Stalin, it seemed that his hour had come. Henceforth, no one would be able to threaten his personal rule. The tragedy was at hand. The decision ripened and was finally taken when he was in Sochi, far from Moscow. On 25 September 1936, he sent a telegram to Molotov, Kaganovich and other members of the Politburo in Moscow. It was signed by himself and Zhdanov, who at the Seventeenth Congress had become a Central Committee secretary and quickly entered Stalin's confidence. The telegram read:

We regard it as absolutely necessary and urgent that Comrade Yezhov be appointed People's Commissar for Internal Affairs. Yagoda has shown himself to be utterly incapable of unmasking the Trotskyite-Zinovievite bloc. The OGPU is lagging four years behind on this matter. This has been noticed by all party workers and most representatives of the NKVD.[79]

The monstrous, terrible signal had been given. Who could have imagined how many 'spies and wreckers and terrorists' would be discovered. It was almost as if they were not living among us, but we among them! Stalin had been much encouraged by the great public support for the state's charges in the recent trial of Zinoviev and Kamenev. Before the trial had even taken place and the circumstances of the case had been published, the press and radio were joyfully chanting 'Destroy the vipers', 'Death to the enemies', 'No mercy for the double-dealers'. Stalin felt he had achieved much: in removing the truth from the people, he had turned them into a crowd for which he would take responsibility himself. Among all his other crimes, this was perhaps one of the worst.

6

THE EPICENTRE OF THE TRAGEDY

'To understand everything
Does not mean to forgive everything.'
– Erich Kästner

CHAPTER 28

Enemies of the People

It was New Year, 1937. The usual hubbub of celebration was in swing in towns and villages all over the vast country. In clubs and congested apartments, the people were decorating their fir trees. The men had supplied themselves with a bottle or two of vodka and, in the large towns, acquired some decent wine for the women. In the last year or two the windows and counters of the grocery stores had been a joy to behold. The New Year issue of *Pravda*, for instance, ran a small notice under the heading 'Holiday Shopping', which reported that:

Muscovites were yesterday buying large quantities of a wide assortment of wines, from Soviet champagne to muscat, as well as hundreds of kinds of sausage and processed fish, cakes, pies and fruit. Thousands of errand-boys from 'Gastronom', 'Groceries' and other food shops were delivering purchases to their customers for the New Year's celebrations.

In commissariats and party bureaux the finishing touches were being put to the annual report. And there was something to report. During the last year, the Kharkov Machine-Building Plant had been commissioned, the Kama Cellulose Combine had been ceremonially opened, building had started on the Solikamsk magnesium factory, the Konakar hydroelectric station in Armenia had started up, the Murmansk Fish Combine had started working, alongside hundreds of other enterprises of all sizes. All this was impressive, in quantity, if not in quality. Even the defence industry commissariat, which had only been formed in 1936 and had not fulfilled its plan on a number of lines, sent in a report which began, 'The defence industry will be the best in the country'. Stalin was pleased with the reports he got from commissars Kaganovich, Mikoyan and Lyubimov: rail transport, light and local industry and trade were at last yielding a small surplus. It was as well for people to know that Stalin did not waste his words. He had decreed that 1936 was to be a shock-work year: the means of production had been planned to rise by 22 per cent and consumer goods by 23 per cent. On his orders, *Pravda* had published a leading article under the heading 'A Plan to Raise the Well-being of the People', in which it stated that the words of the great leader, 'life is better, life is more joyful', would be forever true.[1]

The country's pulse was beating stronger and faster. People still lived poorly, dressed simply, life was ascetic and severe, yet the country as a whole was striving towards the future. It was regarded as bad taste to speak of an individual's interests; everyone was swallowed up by the general cause. The state's goals excluded the question of the full and harmonious development of the person, yet the socialist values of the entire system of relations depended on the will and reason of one individual, and it was obligatory to worship at his ideological altar. An editorial in *Pravda* of 1 January 1937 was headed 'The Great Helmsman leads us', and closed with the following panegyric: 'The Soviet ship of state is well rigged and well armed. It is not worried about storms. It steers its course. It is brilliantly designed for struggle with hostile elements in time of war and proletarian revolution. It is steered by a genius, the helmsman Stalin.' The piece was accompanied by a huge portrait of Stalin, raised above a sea of people. Someone in the crowd is carrying a portrait of Lenin.

The newspapers at the beginning of 1937 conveyed more than the often tense atmosphere of the workers' lives: they also warned about the threat of danger from outside. They printed Mikhail Koltsov's reports from Spain, details of the sinking by the Fascists of the Soviet ship *Komsomol*, the award of the title Hero of the Soviet Union to a group of Red Army officers 'for the exemplary execution of special and most difficult government missions'. Everyone knew they were 'Spanish' heroes.

At the beginning of December 1936, the Extraordinary Eighteenth Congress of Soviets adopted a new Soviet Constitution which proclaimed wider basic democratic rights and freedoms, including freedom of conscience, speech, press, assembly and meeting, inviolability of the person, and privacy of correspondence.

Stalin had the ability to transform himself in an instant. In the silence of his study, one Stalin signed lists of names of people to be arrested and shot and also approved plans for inhuman sentences; while, on the rostrum, sweeping his arm in a decapitating movement, another Stalin declared that the new Constitution 'is not limited by the fixing of formal civil rights, but it shifts the centre of gravity to the question of guarantees for those rights'.[2] Only a few months earlier, at his last meeting with Zinoviev and Kamenev, he had, according to some reports, declared:

Our principles do not permit us to shed the blood of old party members, however weighty their sins. The leaders of our party forget neither their rights nor their responsibilities. The trial, in which you must help the state, is not directed against you, but against Trotsky. All this is needed by the Soviet régime.[3]

Stalin could have brought to mind at least a dozen letters from Zinoviev begging for mercy. He could have recalled the letter Yagoda handed him on 17 December 1934 when Zinoviev was subjected to search and arrest. Zinoviev had written, among other things:

I am guilty of nothing, nothing, nothing before the party, before the Central Committee and before you personally. I swear to you by everything that is sacred to a Bolshevik, I swear to you on Lenin's memory.
I cannot even imagine what could have aroused suspicion against me. I beg you to believe my word of honour. I am shaken to the depths of my soul.[4]

Stalin's reply had been to order the hastening of Zinoviev's trial and precisely one month later, on 16 January 1935, his old party comrade would be given ten years, and as a preliminary he would have to confess to his nonexistent crimes, as well as to name all the people he could recall as 'former participants in the anti-party struggle'. Stalin never did anything by halves. A year later Kamenev and Zinoviev were again in the dock and again were forced to drink the bitter cup to the dregs. What Stalin remembered was not the sentence, but the humiliation Zinoviev must have felt at having to beg for mercy. Stalin was the sort of sadist who does not derive complete satisfaction from the death of his victim. He required total moral capitulation. He would have recalled Zinoviev's letter of 14 April 1935:

I have reached the point where I sit and stare at your portrait in the newspapers and those of the other Politburo members and think: my dear ones, look into my heart, surely you can see that I am no longer your enemy, that I am yours, body and soul, that I have understood everything and am ready to do anything to deserve your forgiveness and your leniency.[5]

Could Stalin have thought, as he sat alongside Zinoviev in the Politburo for seven years (from 1919 to 1926), that this man's life, like that of millions of others, would come to mean nothing to him? Could Zinoviev, as he discussed Russian affairs with Lenin in Geneva on the eve of the revolution, or in his blackest moments, have dreamed that one day an unknown internal exile, a fellow party comrade no less, would pitilessly decide whether he was to live or die in a cellar on 25 August 1936?

'Guarantees'? Stalin's assurances that the people's rights would be guaranteed under the new Constitution were worthless. Did the authors of the Constitution understand this? Those who had worked on it included Akulov, Bubnov, Bukharin, Gamarnik, Yegorov, Krylenko, Tukhachevsky, Eideman, Uborevich, Yakir and other prominent party, military and social figures. When they created the Fundamental Law of the state, proclaiming socialist people power on paper, they did not know that, despite their being enshrined in the document, all these rights and guarantees would be pitilessly destroyed. Under Stalin's rule the Constitution provided no protection. Virtually at this moment, USSR Procurator A. Ya. Vyshinsky was putting the finishing touches to the enormously long prosecution speech he would deliver with such feeling at the second show trial of 'Trotskyist conspirators' on 28 January 1937.

As they wished each other a Happy New Year, Soviet citizens could not imagine how bloody that new year was going to be. However paradoxical it may seem, it was to be nearly another twenty years before they would learn about it, and then far from everything. In the meantime, they had to express their indignation and curse the 'Fascist degenerates', 'spies' and 'terrorists'. Stalin had already given a warning to the people when in January 1933 he had said that under certain circumstances 'the shattered groups of the old revolutionary parties, the SRs, Mensheviks, bourgeois nationalists of the centre and the periphery, could have survived and may stir again, as could the remnants of the counter-revolutionary Trotskyists and right deviationists.'[6] And now it seems they had stirred! Against the background of success, the disasters – of which there were plenty – did indeed appear as 'sabotage'. And had not Stalin said that the hidden enemies were only biding their time? The greater the Soviet people's success, the stronger the resistance. That was what he had meant by the sharpening of the class struggle, drawing the bow of resistance to the limit!

On the eve of the Seventeenth Party Congress, a book about the construction (by slave labour) of the White Sea Canal was published. Thirty-six Soviet writers, under the editorship of Gorky, Averbakh and Firin, contributed panegyrics for the first attempt ever to re-educate 'enemies of the people into their friends'. It was, they wrote, 'a uniquely successful effort at the mass transformation of former enemies of the proletariat ... and Soviet society into qualified representatives of the working class and even into enthusiasts of nationally significant labour'. 'It is immeasurably more difficult,' they wrote, 'to rework human raw material, than it is wood, stone or metal.' Engineers, academics, teachers and thousands of other intellectuals were thus changed into 'comrades-in-arms of the proletariat'. Their only crime had been to think differently from Stalin who, as the authors wrote, was endowed with:

a brilliantly organized will, the penetrating mind of a great theorist, the courage of a talented leader, the intuition of a genuine revolutionary who has a subtle understanding of the qualities of others and who, while cultivating the best of these qualities, struggles pitilessly against those qualities which would prevent them developing to their maximum limit.[7]

But it was not a matter of certain 'qualities' that hindered Stalin. It was people. Many, many people. All of these 'un-finished-off' people were (potentially) preventing him from consolidating himself in the rôle of the sole, unlimited and universally loved leader. He had not forgotten that Bukharin and the rest had been his party comrades: it was their misfortune that *they* had not forgotten, knowing as much about him as they did. He had read somewhere, possibly in Cosimo de Medici, that 'There is a precept which says we should forgive our enemies. But there is not a precept about forgiving your former friends.' Stalin was not thinking of forgiving either category.

Who first used the frightening term 'enemy of the people'? We have already seen that, in his Siberian exile, Stalin had been impressed by what he read about the French Revolution, especially the decisiveness of Robespierre, who at the critical moment acquired a law to simplify the legal process against 'enemies of the revolution'. Unlike Robespierre, however, Stalin was mortally afraid of attempts on his own life. Therefore, the charges against countless unfortunates were underpinned by the notorious Article 58 on 'terrorist acts aimed against representatives of the Soviet régime'. If one were to believe the court proceedings of the time, one would think that thousands upon thousands of Soviet citizens were thinking of nothing other than how to get rid of the leader and his entourage.

While the term 'enemy of the people' was in use before 1934, it was from that time on that Stalin gave it definite content. In a 'secret letter' from the Central Committee to the party organizations in the regions and republics, dated 29 July 1936, and plainly of Stalin's authorship, it was emphasized that an enemy of the people usually appeared 'tame and inoffensive', that he did everything possible to 'crawl stealthily into socialism', that he did not accept socialism, and that the more hopeless his position became, the more willingly 'he would seize on extreme measures'.[8]

A. A. Yepishev, who worked in the ministry of state security from 1951 to 1953, told me that Beria was fond of quoting the idea, which he attributed to Stalin, that 'an enemy of the people is not only one who makes sabotage, but one who doubts the rightness of the party line. And there are a lot of them among us, and we must liquidate them.' Yepishev, who was otherwise not expansive about himself, said frankly:

I managed with great difficulty to escape from Beria's den. After my repeated requests to be allowed to get back to party work, Beria scoffed maliciously and said, 'You don't want to work with me? Well, do as you like.'

A few days later I was sent to Odessa, where I was again appointed first secretary of the regional party committee, but the local MVD chief soon came and suggested I should stay at home the next day. I knew that meant I would be arrested at any moment. And those who had worked with Beria and who had doubts he regarded as worse than enemies of the people. I was saved by a miracle: Beria himself was arrested at this very moment.

An enemy of the people, then, was anyone who did not fit Stalin's pattern, and it had nothing in common with the same concept applied in the French Revolution, from which he had ostensibly borrowed it. Robespierre, in establishing the revolutionary-democratic dictatorship, saw enemies in 'the tyrannical aristocracy and those who had acquired their wealth by unjust means', whereas for Stalin, an enemy was anyone who did not or might not share his outlook. No one in fact opposed Stalin's personal rule, but he sensed that many,

paranoia

especially the Lenin old guard, secretly did not approve of his brand of socialism. This was enough for him to arrive eventually at his terrible decision. With the help of his ideological apparatus, Stalin gradually created an atmosphere of suspicion in the country, preparing the people for the impending bloody purge.

The overwhelming majority of Soviet citizens indisputably believed that it was a struggle to the death with people who still wanted to restore capitalism. As early as January 1937, the newspapers were carrying articles under such headings as 'Spies and Murderers', 'Traders of the Motherland', 'Trotskyist, Wrecker, Diversionary, Spy', 'Lowest of the Low', 'Trotskyist Gang of Capitalist Restorers'. This constant massage of the public mind produced results, and the people became indignant when they heard about the baseness of those who had managed to stay out of sight for so long.

How had it come about? Why were Stalin and his henchmen able to convince the party and the people that they were surrounded by enemies? How did the spy and sabotage mania come to be? To a great extent the February-March 1937 Central Committee plenum provides an answer.

Many reports were delivered at the plenum, which lasted two weeks. Central Committee Secretary A. A. Zhdanov began with his report on the work of the party organizations in preparation for elections to the Supreme Soviet under a new electoral system, and on the restructuring of the party's political work. Zhdanov, who by now was enjoying the leader's special favour, expressed a number of what seemed like sensible ideas. For instance, he underlined the fact that the 'new electoral system meant much greater openness [glasnost] in the activity of the soviet organizations'. He properly raised the question of the internal party democracy as an important condition for the party's moral well-being. But at that point he quoted Stalin to the effect that, although 'we are struck by the cultural work of the dictatorship', the repressive organs are as much needed today as they were during the civil war. We must be aware, he went on, that 'while our people slumber and are only getting going, our enemies are already active.' The situation in the party, he added, was not simple. The party ranks were thinning; many enemies had emerged in it. 'The dangerous practice of cooptation has taken root and gone very far. This practice infringes the legitimate right of party members to take part in the election of their leading organs.'

He then introduced some interesting figures. Up to 59 per cent of members and candidate members of district and town committee bureaux had been coopted. In Kiev, for instance, on 19 October 1934 fourteen people were coopted on to the town committee in one go; many of them had turned out to be enemies of the people. In Kharkov, out of 158 members and thirty-four candidates elected to the town committee at the Fourth town party conference, sixty-one had been coopted, and only fifty-nine remained of the total. And the town committee bureau had been entirely coopted, with one exception. On 4 April 1936, Zhdanov continued, the Lenin district committee in Kharkov had debated the 'expulsion of an entire group of people'. Even the activist group had been invited. Why? So that there should be ten people at the district committee meeting where twelve people were to be expelled! So, ten people swallowed up twelve others! This raised a laugh among the delegates.[9]

Zhdanov went on for a long time with similar examples. They were not merely symptomatic of the party's anti-democratic practices. The party was dominated by a situation in which illegality was the rule, as was a permissive attitude towards the widespread use of coercion. Stalin and his crew had already created a moral climate which permitted the shift from administrative solutions to outright force against potential opponents.

By the time of the plenum, Stalin had already carried out a 'reconnaissance in force' by dealing with Zinoviev, Kamenev and other Bolsheviks. These people had been in the way, they knew too much about him. They knew, for instance, about the meetings in his study when he set Zinoviev and Kamenev against Trotsky; they knew about his endless intrigues, his doctoring of old party documents (for instance, he had arranged for a note to be circulated by Vladimir Sorin and Yelena Stasova calling for changes in the minutes of a Central Committee meeting of 23 February 1918 on the Brest-Litovsk peace);[10] they knew about Frunze's mysterious illness and death and so on. Zinoviev and Kamenev were in prison, but Stalin was longing to despatch them into final oblivion.

On 15 August 1936, at Stalin's personal intervention, Zinoviev and Kamenev were again put on trial. The trial had not even begun, nor the charges been read out, but the papers and the radio were baying for no quarter to be shown to the 'enemies of the people'. Stalin's vengeance knew no compromise; his former comrades were sentenced to death and shot. Their letters to him, begging for mercy, went unanswered. He hoped that with Kamenev would die his words to the Fourteenth Congress, 'I have come to the conclusion that Comrade Stalin cannot fulfil the rôle of unifier of the Bolshevik headquarters staff', and that Zinoviev would take with him his assessment of Stalin as a 'bloody Ossetian ... who has no idea of the meaning of conscience'. Whatever else they could have been accused of, neither Kamenev nor Zinoviev were enemies of socialism or of the people. Stalin did not like to confine himself to only one rank of disarmed enemies, and therefore, as with hundreds and thousands of others, the families of Kamenev and Zinoviev were either exiled or also killed off. Kamenev's wife, his two sons (one of them still a minor), his brother and his brother's wife, all perished.

The reports given at the plenum by Molotov, Kaganovich and Yezhov were devoted in effect to only one issue: 'The Lessons of sabotage, diversions and espionage by Japanese-German-Trotskyite agents'. They lacked any rational analysis or real comprehension of the situation for the simple reason that the subject itself was a mirage, an apparition. Many strong words and oaths were uttered, and the first 'results' were reported.

Opening his report, Molotov said he was standing in for Sergo Ordzhonikidze who, on 18 February, a week before the opening, had shot himself. The government bulletin stated he had died of a heart attack. According to many people who knew the family well, Ordzhonikidze was sickened by the spy-mania and witch-hunts, and he had had several sharp exchanges with Stalin. In response, Stalin sent Ordzhonikidze reports received by the NKVD on him, clearly hinting that there was no smoke without fire. Ordzhonikidze must have felt that Stalin was demanding his complete subservience, if he was not to share the tragic fate of the others. To cap it all, Stalin had asked him to make a report to the Seventeenth Congress on 'Sabotage in Heavy Industry'. Out of his mouth, Ordzhonikidze was expected to incriminate many leaders of industry, to take a direct part in the arbitrary rule which no true Bolshevik could accept. He seized the chance to exercise his conscience, though hardly in the most effective way, even if in the circumstances it was the most honourable. On the very day of his suicide, Yezhov's people sent Ordzhonikidze a report on his brother, Papuli. Several other relatives of his had been arrested, as he was literally pushed towards his fateful decision.

Stalin arrived at Ordzhonikidze's apartment and gave instructions that a 'substantiated' account of the suicide be issued to the papers. According to the relatives, Stalin got hold of Ordzhonikidze's suicide note, the contents of which we shall probably never know. In hounding Ordzhonikidze, Stalin had picked on the one member of his entourage who did not share his approach to terror. (It became the norm for Stalin to hound a man to death and then to carry his coffin or his ashes and to make a funeral oration and comfort the relatives.) Ordzhonikidze's funeral delayed the opening of the plenum. He was not the only one to exit as he did: there were also Tomsky, Gamarnik, Sabinin and Lyubchenko, to name but a few.

Molotov littered his report with figures and a multitude of names of 'enemies of the people' who had entrenched themselves in heavy industry. The whole gang, he said, was led by Pyatakov. In trying to prove that 'sabotage' was widespread in the economy, and also that there was an active struggle being mounted against it, Molotov introduced some sinister statistics about the number of people who worked in the administrations of the following com-missariats and who had been sentenced by 1 March 1937: Heavy Industry – 585, Education – 228, Light Industry – 141, Railways – 137, Land – 102[11], and so on, through twenty-one agencies. Throughout the report, Molotov laid special emphasis on the notion that all these wreckers had operated under instruction of the 'Trotskyite centre'. He explained the strategy of sabotage by reference to Trotsky's slogan: 'Sensitive blows must be delivered to sensitive places.'

Even if one accepted the facts about wrecking, Molotov ought to have known that enormous industrial undertakings were often being operated at breakneck speed, by 'cavalry charge'. The undeveloped technology, the low productive and technical culture and discipline, and the incompetence could not but lead to breakdowns of all kinds, including fire and damage. All this, however, was to be explained by the 'actions of Trotskyite wreckers'.

Kaganovich's report on the situation on the railways was in the same vein and also listed names, Not wishing to be outdone by Molotov, he also reported that the railways commissariat was not sitting on its hands and was losing no time in hunting down the enemy. It is not hard to imagine the means he used to 'unmask' and 'let go' (in his words) thousands of individuals. The most amazing thing was how so many utterly varied types of 'enemies' were working on the railways in apparently friendly cooperation. There were former gendarmes, SRs, Mensheviks, Trotskyists, White officers, wreckers and spies.

Yezhov followed the pattern set by Molotov and Kaganovich, revealing that there were enemies literally everywhere. A physical and moral pygmy of a man, on the eve of the plenum Yezhov was honoured with the new title of General Commissar of State Security, a title only Beria would also bear. Yezhov's report was blatantly aimed at intensifying the campaign of informing on 'internal enemies':

In the space of several months I cannot recall a single occasion when someone, whether an industrial boss or the head of a commissariat, rang me on his own initiative to say: 'Comrade Yezhov. there's something fishy about so-and-so, something isn't right there, deal with this man.' It just didn't happen. Usually, when one raised the question of arresting a wrecker or a Trotskyite, some comrades would, on the contrary, come to his defence.[12]

In a special memorandum, adopted by the plenum on Yezhov's report, it was noted that the Commissar for Internal Affairs was lagging at least four years behind in the struggle against enemies. In other words, Stalin felt the purge ought to have started on the eve of the Seventeenth Party Congress. The NKVD was charged with 'carrying out the task of unmasking and smashing the Trotskyists and other agents to the end, in order to crush the least manifestation of their anti-Soviet activity'.[13] But this was merely the prelude. Participants in the plenum, mostly men of common sense, were more alarmed by the way Molotov, Kaganovich and Yezhov produced the investigative facts than they were convinced of the existence of widespread sabotage. Theoretical and political background was lacking. The opening speakers had laid out the landscape in which the enemies were operating, but what these enemies were actually doing and why was unclear. One can only guess now at the thoughts passing through the delegates' heads. It was all of three years since the 'Congress of Victors', and the twentieth year of Soviet power, and yet again they were being confronted by the almost universal 'danger of the restoration of capitalism'. Having largely freed the Central Committee of the Leninist old guard, Stalin was once more resorting to extreme measures.

A precise programme was required. The leader formulated it. A theoretical basis was needed for the terror against 'enemies'. Stalin created it. The people had to be raised up to liquidate the 'Trotskyists and other double-dealers'. Stalin framed this task also. Judging by the careful formulations, the precise structure of the report which he gave as the closing speech, and the resolution which he composed by hand, it is clear that Stalin viewed the imminent bloody purge as of the utmost importance.

His report was entitled 'On the Inadequacies of Party Work and Measures for Liquidating the Trotskyite and other Double-Dealers'. The frequent underlining, insertions and marginal notes in his clear hand testify that it was carefully composed. He did not stoop to fishing for individual hostile functionaries, in the fearless style of Molotov, Kaganovich or Yezhov. As the main speaker, he set everything out on its proper shelf. He first defined the notion of 'political security' and then moved on to the consequences of capitalist encirclement, pointing out that it represented a real threat which had constantly to be borne in mind in the building of socialism, and linking it with the 'Trotskyite danger'. The Trotskyites themselves he characterized as a 'gang of desperate and unprincipled wreckers, diversionaries, spies and killers, operating under the orders of foreign intelligence services'. He virtually declared Trotskyism the main danger to socialism, and came to the following far-reaching conclusion:

The further we move forward, the more success we have, the more embittered will the remnants of the destroyed exploiter classes become, the sooner they will resort to extreme forms of struggle, the more they will blacken the Soviet state, the more they will seize on the most desperate means as the last resort of the doomed.[14]

Since the end of the 1920s, and again in 1934 and 1936, Stalin had been preaching that the class struggle would sharpen as socialism advanced. It is a concept that is at once paradoxical in tone and irrational in content. But Stalin was a pragmatist. He had to find a theoretical basis for the process of total purge that he was preparing. No one, besides himself, was capable of this task, and he was the one who *needed* it. In 1934 he had asserted that the exploiting classes had been liquidated in the USSR, and now, three years later, he was suddenly showing that the struggle was 'sharpening'. He told the plenum that this was possible because former oppositionists had camouflaged themselves and were carrying on clandestine subversive activity, consolidating their forces, and biding their time. He listed 'six rotten theories' that were preventing the party from finally smashing the Trotskyists: it should not be thought that overfulfilling the plan would defeat the wreckers; or that the Stakhanovite movement by itself would liquidate sabotage; it was wrong to think, as some did, that the Trotskyists were not marshalling their forces, and so on and so forth.

If most of the other speakers concentrated on concrete facts of sabotage, Stalin, as ever, forced everything into a rigid framework. In his closing speech on 5 March, he declared that 'there are seven points on which the plenum is not clear.' Among these points he made a number of correct judgements, e. g. that several former Trotskyites had taken up correct positions and 'should not be discredited'. He also made a number of 'leader-like' utterances, e. g. that one should occasionally hearken to the voice of the 'ordinary people', and issued some rallying cries, e. g. 'we will in the future smash our enemies, as we do now and as we have done in the past'. Resorting to his favoured form of the simple aphorism which everyone could understand, he declared: 'To win a battle, you need several armies. To lose it, only a few spies. To build a big railway bridge, you need thousands of people. It only takes a few men to blow it up.'[15]

The resolution adopted on Stalin's report contained twenty-seven categorical points, to which he put the finishing touches with his own pencil. They included:

condemn the practice of underrating the propaganda front;
condemn the practice of turning plenums into window-dressing occasions;
condemn the practice of cooptation and making elections an empty formality;
condemn the practice of grouping [artelnost] in the distribution of party forces;
condemn the practice of a callous attitude to the fate of individual party members.[16]

Unfortunately, the apparent good sense in these postulates was to play no part in the treatment of party members, nor prevent further damage to the foundations of the party. For instance, two days before agreeing to 'condemn callousness', the fate of Bukharin and Rykov had been determined, and one month earlier Pyatakov, Radek, Sokolnikov and others had been condemned. The gap between word and deed had long been immaterial to Stalin. In practice, what was intended for general consumption was more or less respectable, fairly democratic in tone and lawful in contemporary terms. What he told his narrow circle was to be kept strictly secret. This was particularly so in the case of the fate of Bukharin and Rykov.

The plenum adopted a resolution on the case of Bukharin and Rykov, who were still candidate members of the Central Committee up to this time. The decree was drafted by a commission of thirty-six members, headed by Mikoyan and including Andreyev, Stalin, Molotov, Kaganovich, Voroshilov, Kalinin, Yezhov, Shkiryatov, Krupskaya (Lenin's widow), Kosior, Yaroslavsky, Zhdanov, Khrushchev, Yakir, Beria, Eikhe, Bagirov, Budenny, Chubar, Kosarev, Postyshev and Gamarnik.[17]

Before the commission met, Bukharin composed a long and impassioned memorandum repudiating every charge. He also wrote several letters to Stalin in which he tried to convince him that the 'evidence' was inspired by a group of arrested 'enemies of the people', that he had nothing to do with terrorism, espionage or any similar activity. He also managed to call Stalin two or three times on the internal telephone which he still had in his apartment. Stalin reassured him: 'Nikolai, don't panic. We'll sort things out ... We don't believe you're an enemy. But as you've been implicated by Sokolnikov, Astrov, Kulikov and other double-dealers, who have admitted to being wreckers, we have to look into it calmly. Don't worry!'

'How can it even be thought that I am an accomplice of terrorist groups?' Bukharin exploded.

'Take it easy, Nikolai, take it easy. We'll sort it out.' Stalin puffed on his pipe.

The commission paid no attention to the explanations given by Bukharin and Rykov. Its main 'arguments' were as before: the participants in a 'parallel Trotskyite centre' have stated that Bukharin and Rykov and future 'lone operators' knew about the wrecking and terrorist activities of the 'centre' and assisted in it. Bukharin was in despair while Rykov remained composed, realizing that they faced the same fate as Zinoviev and Kamenev, who had recently been shot, and of Pyatakov, Muralov, Drobnis, Shestov and the other 'base traitors' who had followed soon after. Bukharin went on hunger strike against the monstrously unjust accusations.

On the evening of 26 February and again on the morning of the 27th, Bukharin telephoned Poskrebyshev and reported that he and Rykov wished to appear before the commission which had already begun its work, but which, despite their still being candidate members of the Central Committee, did not invite them to all its sessions. Apart from Uborevich and Akulov, no one shook hands with them. The plenum commission on the case of Bukharin and Rykov opened. Even before Yezhov began his report, Stalin called out:

'Bukharin is on hunger strike. Who is your ultimatum aimed at, Nikolai, the Central Committee?'

'You're about to throw me out of the party ...'

'Ask the Central Committee for its forgiveness.'

As had happened before, Bukharin lost his self-control. He thought he detected a glimmer of hope in Stalin's words. But he also knew that the review of his case involved material collected by the NKVD in its investigation, and his explanation, both written and oral, would be interpreted merely as an attempt 'to lead the party into delusion'. We can only guess at what Bukharin and Rykov felt as they faced a wall of incomprehension and programmed hostility. The members of the commission had before them facts which were based on 'evidence' and 'testimony' obtained by impermissible means from already condemned men.

When Mikoyan, the chairman of the commission, suggested that he make a clean breast of it and admit his participation in anti-Soviet activity, Bukharin gave a sharp response without rising:

'I'm not Zinoviev or Kamenev and I won't lie about myself.'

'If you won't confess', Mikoyan answered malevolently, 'you're just proving that you're a Fascist hireling. They're already writing in their newspapers that our trials are a provocation. We're arresting you – confess!'

Bukharin went on: 'There are people in the NKVD who are committing unprecedented arbitrary acts under cover of party authority.'

'Yes, and we're going to send you in there,' Stalin interjected. 'Just you wait and see.'

Possibly only Stalin, Yezhov and the immediate circle knew the charges were false. Bukharin and Rykov had always lived their lives openly, they could not possibly be enemies. Stalin sensed the hesitation in the other members of the commission when they saw Bukharin's written submission, and he therefore sought to wind up the debate by tabling a prepared decision. A resolution by Yezhov was put to the vote by roll-call. It called for 'the expulsion of Bukharin and Rykov as candidate members of the Central Committee, for their trial by military tribunal with the extreme penalty of death by firing squad'. Postyshev said he was 'in favour of expulsion and trial, but not shooting', and Antipov, Khrushchev, Nikolaev and Shkiryatov took the same view. Budenny, Manuilsky, Shvernik and Kosarev were 'for expulsion, trial and shooting'.

Stalin realized that there was not going to be a unanimous decision and so made his carefully calculated move. 'I propose,' he declared, 'that Bukharin and Rykov be expelled from the party, that they not be put on trial, but that the case be handed over to the NKVD for investigation.' He knew this was just as monstrous as expulsion, trial and shooting, but he wanted to appear the humanitarian peacemaker. Possibly his proposal gave Bukharin and Rykov a faint new glimmer of hope. Naturally, after what Stalin had said, the rest of the commission made mitigating speeches. Krupskaya, Vareikis, Molotov and Voroshilov supported Stalin's proposal. Kosior, Petrovsky and Litvinov reiterated Postyshev's formula of trial without shooting. The historical record shows, however, that even after Stalin's proposal, Kosarev and Yakir, who were next in line as the victims of lawlessness, voted for expulsion, trial and shooting. As we can see, several members of the commission had decided the sentence even before the trial, while others gave an opinion that apparently did not envisage a dreadful end. As chairman, Mikoyan did not express his opinion. It was decided, after the roll-call, to vote again, and Stalin's proposal got unanimous support:

1 Bukharin and Rykov are to be expelled as candidate members of the Central Committee; they are not to be put on trial, but their case is to be handed over to the NKVD;
2 A commission, consisting of Comrades Stalin, Molotov, Voroshilov, Kaganovich, Mikoyan and Yezhov, will prepare a draft resolution based on this decision.[18]

The resolution adopted on the Bukharin–Rykov case had Stalin's notes and amendments all over it. It was in effect a political instruction and a methodological key for the approach to similar cases. The plenum not only approved Stalin's theses on the sharpening of the class struggle, but also provided an example of how to respond to 'hostile' acts. The resolution contained three points, summarized as follows:

1 On the basis of investigative evidence, the Central Committee plenum has established that Comrades Bukharin and Rykov, at a minimum, knew about the criminal, terrorist, espionage and diversionary activity of the Trotskyite centre, but concealed it, thereby committing a criminal act.
2 On the basis of NKVD investigative evidence and face to face confrontation, the Central Committee plenum has established, at a minimum, that Comrades Bukharin and Rykov knew about the organization of criminal terrorist groups by their pupils

and followers, Slepkov, Tseitlin, Astrov, Maretsky, Nesterov, Rodin, Kulikov, Kotov, Uglanov, Zaitsev, Kuzmin, Sapozhnikov and others, and not only did nothing to prevent it, but encouraged them.

3 The Central Committee plenum has established that Comrade Bukharin's memorandum to the Central Committee, in which he attempts to repudiate the testimony of the above named Trotskyites and right terrorists, amounts to a slanderous document.

Taking the foregoing into account and bearing in mind the fact that, even during Lenin's lifetime Bukharin conducted a struggle against the party and against Lenin himself (as did Rykov), everything that has happened was neither accidental nor unexpected, and therefore [the rest is in Stalin's hand] Bukharin and Rykov are to be expelled as candidate members of the Central Committee and from the ranks of the [party]. Their case is to be handed over to the NKVD.[19]

Bukharin and Rykov had barely left the room, following the commission hearing, when they were arrested. But they were too well known by the people and party alike to be got rid of straight away. A trial would have to be held, and to make sure the accused were ready for it, time was required. A long, thirteen-month interval now ensued between the plenum and the last act of the tragedy.

The plenum's decisions gave the whole process a powerful shove. Already in March 1937, in the republics and regions, party committees met to hear Stalin's instructions, and also to report the first results of their being carried out. Zhdanov's report in Leningrad on 15 March 1937 serves as a good example:

As it turns out, Bukharin and Rykov were no different from the Zinovievites and Trotskyites. They're all one gang of bandits. I can recall no behaviour more shameful, more foul or more disgusting than that of Bukharin and Rykov. It took us four days to get the truth out of them, but we waited in vain for them to show a spark or a hint of a humane attitude to the party. As they said, we were not their judges.

Zhdanov proceeded to debase Bukharin even further to the Leningrad communists by telling them that Bukharin's hunger strike had been a play-acting ploy. 'At midnight he ate a bigger meal than usual, and then at ten in the morning he announced his hunger strike.'[20]

Zhdanov had some facts to report about the 'work' that had already been done in Leningrad to expose 'enemies'. 'Eight groups of wreckers had been discovered on the Kirov and October railways, ten groups in factories, and in the NKVD, the anti-aircraft defence and the party apparatus.' 'Nests of enemies' were soon found in the Vyborg district (thirteen people), in the Vasilievsky district (twelve) and the Kirov district (twelve). In all, 223 party workers. 'You can imagine the mess in the party apparatus!' he expostulated.

To the accompaniment of a roar of indignation, Zhdanov painted a lurid picture of enemy domination of the city which was the cradle of the revolution: 'Between 1933 and 1936, 183 people graduated from the Institute of Red

Professors. thirty-two of them had already been arrested. Of the remaining 130 now in Leningrad, fifty-five have been declared enemies of the people.'[21] Similar scenes of noisy outrage took place all over the country, while puzzlement, suffering and fear were silent and unexpressed.

CHAPTER 29

Political Farce

Following the trial of Zinoviev and Kamenev, the trial began in Moscow on 23 January 1937 of the so-called seventeen, consisting of Pyatakov and sixteen others. Its aim was to show that Trotsky had used the defendants to organize wrecking and to prepare for the restoration of capitalism in the USSR. The trial was so well staged that Pyatakov, despite his strong will, eloquently described a meeting he had had with Trotsky in Oslo (where he had never been), and said that Trotsky:

in his directive had posed two possible variants for our coming to power. The first would be before the war and the second would be during the war. Trotsky saw the first variant as the result of a concentrated terrorist blow. What he had in mind was the simultaneous execution of terrorist acts against a number of party and state leaders, above all of course against Stalin and his closest assistants. The second variant, which Trotsky regarded as more likely, would come in military defeat.[22]

Stalin had defeated Zinoviev and Kamenev by exhaustion and deception. He took Pyatakov and his 'partners' by torture.

One other trial was especially depressing. That was the so-called 'trial of the twenty-one', where Bukharin, Rykov, Krestinsky, Rakovsky, Rozengolts and others were the victims. Stalin was using the courts to get rid of the last of his opponents physically, but the main political target was, as ever, Trotsky. The duel between them continued. In the few pages of the summing-up against Pyatakov and the others, Trotsky's name was mentioned no less than fifty-one times. The trial documents of Bukharin and his co-defendants show a similar picture. When the trial opened, Trotsky, in Mexico, let it be known that the accused did indeed share his views, but that they were being tried only for their ideas. In almost every issue of his *Bulletin* he published pieces on Rakovsky, Krestinsky and Rozengolts, demonstrating their 'incompatibility' with Stalin, and underlining his own solidarity with them. He published regular protests against the persecution of his 'supporters'. This defence of the 'enemies of the people' suited Stalin perfectly and provided 'supplementary' arguments.

Stalin sensed the approach of war. He could not escape the feeling that he was looking at the outside world through Trotsky's eyes. Though he was afraid to admit it even to himself, he knew, when he read Trotsky's pieces, that its author was not prophesying ill in vain. In *The Revolution Betrayed*, for instance, Trotsky wrote:

Can we expect the Soviet Union to emerge from the approaching war without defeat? To this frank question we will give an equally frank reply: if the war remains only a war, then defeat for the Soviet Union is inevitable. In the technological, economic and military sense, imperialism is incomparably stronger.[23]

This sounded like a sentence of doom not only for socialism, but also for Stalin. Stalin, however, would not give in so easily. Before the war began, he must get rid of all possible accomplices of Fascism. While preparing for war, he must be free of any potential fifth column. Hitler must not find local support in the Soviet Union. According to F. Chuev, shortly before Molotov died he confirmed that on the eve of the war Stalin set out to deprive any possible Soviet collaborators of support in society at large.

On another level, Stalin needed an explanation for the still relatively low standard of living and the countless shortcomings in the country's economy. 'Wrecking and sabotages' provided the answer. Obedient functionaries soon got the message and their daily reports contained the appropriate information. For instance, on 19 October 1937 the following reports were submitted:

In the village of Tabory, Urals, for disrupting the kolkhoz, five men were sentenced to be shot.

Minsk. For the wilful contamination of flour, five men were sentenced to be shot.

Saratov. A Trotskyite-rightist group released a large quantity of oil into the Volga. Nine men were sentenced to be shot, including Professor N. A. Orlov of Saratov University.

Leningrad. On the orders of Gestapo agents, systematic breakages were inflicted on the Leningrad regional energy board and workers were injured. Ten men were sentenced to be shot ...[24]

The list of similar reports is long. Above the signature, V. Ulrikh, would appear the laconic note, 'All the sentences have been carried out.' Often, in one corner, a scribbled note, signed by Poskrebyshev, appears: 'Comrade Stalin has been informed.'

Such mass tragedies became the norm following the great show trials of January 1937 and March 1938. Stalin was now sure that everyone in the country knew just who was hindering forward progress, who was selling the Motherland out to the enemy, who was organizing attempts to assassinate Stalin and his entourage, and who was carrying out Trotsky's orders. The political trials served as a detonator for an explosion of mass terror against not only Stalin's potential enemies, but also, and in the overwhelming majority of cases, against accidental victims, especially administrators, both in factories and institutions that had suffered some misfortune, such as a fire, an explosion, a collapse or a crash. At some point in 1937, the repression got out of control. In many commissariats and other agencies informing became a means of survival. All this was the result of the first great political trials.

Stalin agreed to the extermination of people with a startling and chilling absence of feeling. Enormously long lists of individuals and groups were sent to him. I found only one document in the Stalin archive which suggests a degree of mercy on his part:

> To Comrade I.V. Stalin.
> The Procurator's office has been approached by the wife of A. S. Kuklin, who was sentenced on 18 January 1936 to ten years' imprisonment. Kuklin is being held in Butyrki Prison. According to a medical report of 7 January this year, Kuklin is suffering from a malignant oesophageal tumour. His condition is recognized as hopeless.
> I request your instructions.
> 22 March 1936. A. Vyshinsky.

Below, Vyshinsky has written: 'Comrade Ulrikh is instructed by Comrade Stalin to effect an immediate release.'[25]

On the other hand, he sanctioned the execution of his former assistant, A. Nazaretyan; Lenin's former secretary, N. Gorbunov; his own friend and former secretary of the Central Executive Committee, A. Yenukidze; A. Kosarev, whom he himself had described as 'a real leader of youth'; his own philosophy 'tutor', Jan Sten; A. Solts, who had been with him in the pre-revolutionary underground; Semen Uritsky, an intelligence officer whom Stalin had greatly valued; L. Karakhan, former Deputy Commissar for Foreign Affairs whom Stalin had held up as an example to others; Ya. Agranov, a Chekist and former friend; A. Bubnov with whom he had carried out Lenin's orders during the civil war; I. Vareikis, 'a tough Bolshevik', in Stalin's own words; and he agreed to the arrest of G. Broido, his former deputy in the commissariat for nationalities.

As he scanned the endless lists of executed and arrested individuals, Stalin recognized all the regional and republican party chiefs who had been to see him, the scientists, with many of whom he had personal contacts, and dozens of writers and other cultural figures whose fate has only become definitively known in the last year or so. There were lists of Comintern personnel, and countless army men, thousands of them. Thousands of names, thousands of lives, thousands of people who had glorified him and been ready to carry out his every order. Many of them managed to write him a farewell letter, and he read quite a few of them. But it changed nothing. He knew neither pity nor sympathy, neither the call of comradeship nor a sense of honour. He had only to scribble a word on the page or mutter 'Agreed' to Poskrebyshev and that was enough to send all these people into oblivion. And soon, Vyshinsky and Ulrikh and Yezhov would have the punitive machinery working so smoothly that Stalin would only need to acquaint himself with impersonal statistics.

On the eve of the trials Stalin evidently had several meetings with Vyshinsky and Ulrikh. These meetings, which were no doubt for the purpose of instruction, were not minuted and there is no trace of them in the archives. Stalin liked Ulrikh, an army lawyer, perhaps for his laconic style, the terse brevity of his reports on the bloody harvest which arrived on Stalin's desk in great numbers in 1937 and 1938. Some bear no more than Stalin's initials, others only Poskrebyshev's flourish.

The steady stream of reports, growing into an avalanche, would have broken anyone else's morale, terrified and shaken him to the core of his being. Yet at the height of the repressions Stalin went to the theatre as usual, watched movies at the dacha, received his commissars, edited decrees and other documents, arranged midnight suppers, dictated letters, commented on articles in *Pravda* and *Bolshevik*. Even if he believed that the terror was cutting down real enemies of the people, one still marvels at his absolute lack of feeling and his cruelty. He would watch as Ulrikh signed hundreds and hundreds of death sentences with utter nonchalance, a judge who was free of sentiment, Stalin's ideal and a vital component part of the guillotine.

[handwritten margin note: lack of feeling]

Stocky, thick-set and bespectacled, Vyshinsky was quite a different type. Stalin admired the Procurator General's eloquence, the accusatory tirades with which he literally paralysed his victims in the dock. Most of them could only find the words to agree with him in the end. Stalin awarded him the Order of Lenin for ardour at the trial of Bukharin. His closing speech on that occasion, 11 March 1938, must have made a special impression:

The whole country, from the youngest to the oldest, are waiting for and demanding one thing: that the traitors and spies who sold out our motherland to the enemy be shot like vile dogs!

The people demand one thing: that the accursed vermin be squashed!

Time will pass. The hated traitors' graves will become overgrown with weeds and thistles, covered with the eternal contempt of honest Soviet people, of the entire Soviet people.

While over our happy land, bright and clear as ever, our sun will shine its rays. We, our people, will as before stride along our path now cleansed of the last trace of the scum and vileness of the past, led by our beloved leader and teacher, the great Stalin.[26]

The leader and teacher was well pleased by such enthusiasm and Vyshinsky went on to become deputy chairman of the Council of Ministers,* then Minister of Foreign Affairs, winner of the Stalin Prize and other tokens of Stalin's favour.

No less than Stalin himself, Vyshinsky understood the importance of the

---

* People's Commissars were renamed as Ministers in 1946.

political farce he was expected to play. The last trial, in March 1938, saw the completion of the process of public brainwashing. The charges were the same as before: carrying out Trotsky's orders, spying and sabotage actions, preparing the country for its forthcoming defeat, dismemberment of the Union, attempts on Stalin and other top leaders.

To ensure their success, the trials had a long 'rehearsal time'. Bukharin's trial took a year to prepare. Several months were spent in trying to break the accused. The investigators had a wide range of means to obtain the desired confession which, contrary to legal norms, would serve as the main evidence of guilt. Some witnesses lasted as long as three months, others only a few days. Then would come the humiliating rehearsals. Once broken, the accused were forced to learn the proper version, to make prepared statements 'unmasking' named people. After countless repeats of this shameful pretence, the 'directors' would be informed that this or that 'actor' was ready for his 'premiere'. There were occasional hitches.

For instance, in the summing-up which the clerk of the court read on 2 March 1938, it said that the accused N. N. Krestinsky 'entered into treacherous contact with German intelligence in 1921', that he came to an agreement with Generals Seekt and Hasse on collaboration with the Reichswehr for 250,000 Marks a year for Trotskyite work. When the president of the court asked Krestinsky if he was guilty, Krestinsky, quite contrary to his earlier evidence, began to repudiate everything. There was commotion in the corridors. The court adjourned. Stalin was told. He exploded angrily, 'They prepared the good-for-nothing badly,' and let it be known he would not stand for it again. Steps were taken and by the same evening Krestinsky had returned to 'normal'.

Krestinsky: 'I completely confirm the testimony I gave at the preliminary inquiry.'
Vyshinsky: 'In that case, what is the meaning of your statement yesterday, which can only be seen as a Trotskyite provocation to the trial?'
Krestinsky: 'Yesterday, under the influence of a momentary sharp sense of false shame, caused by being in the dock and the depressing effect of hearing the charges read out, and aggravated by my ill health, I was not in a condition to tell the truth, not in a condition to say that I was guilty.'
Vyshinsky: 'Is this an automatic response?'
Krestinsky: 'I request that the court minute my statement that I completely and entirely acknowledge that I am guilty of all the serious charges levelled against me personally, and I hold myself completely responsible for the treason and treachery committed by me.'[27]

Apart from a few such misfires, the trial went smoothly. The accused agreed with the procurator, accepted the monstrous charges in a friendly spirit, readily adding a detail here and there to their own evil deeds. It must have been a unique occasion of collaboration between the court and the accused. Almost nobody rebutted anything. Almost all of them accused only themselves.

Bukharin's case is particularly painful to contemplate. Six months before his arrest, he had written to Stalin and to the other members of the Politburo. The trial of Zinoviev and Kamenev and their fourteen 'accomplices' was about to take place. During this trial, in which the accused would point the finger at Bukharin, Rykov and Tomsky, the prosecutor, Vyshinsky, would announce that investigations were under way on the 'Bukharin case'. When Bukharin got back from Central Asia, where he had been on vacation, he learned about the 'case' that had been opened on him. The former 'favourite of the party' was in despair. He at once sat down and penned a letter to Stalin. It has proved impossible to find that letter, but he wrote similar letters to the other members of the Politburo and Vyshinsky and two such letters, addressed to Voroshilov, have been found and they give a sense of the way the Bukharin drama grew into a tragedy:

Dear Kliment Yefremovich,
You* have no doubt already received my letter to the members of the Politburo and Vyshinsky: I wrote it last night in Comrade STALIN'S secretariat and requested that it be circulated: it contains everything of importance connected with Kamenev's monstrously base accusations. (As I write I am experiencing a sense of half-reality: is it a dream, a mirage, a madhouse, a hallucination? No, it is reality.) I wanted to ask anyone in the world: do all of you believe it? Really?

So, I wrote an article about Kirov. Incidentally, when I was (deservedly) in disgrace and was ill in Leningrad, he came to see me, sat with me a whole day, wrapped me up, gave me his own railway carriage and sent me back to Moscow with such tender care that I will remember it to my dying day. So, what was I supposed to have written insincerely about Sergei [Kirov]? Ask yourself honestly. If I wrote insincerely I should have been arrested and exterminated at once: because we don't need such scoundrels. If you think I was 'insincere' yet you leave me at large, then you are cowards who do not deserve respect...

True, I would have thought – as long as I still have a brain in my head – that it was stupid from the international point of view to broaden the basis of swinishness (which would have meant meeting the wishes of that scoundrel Kamenev halfway! All he wanted was to try to prove that they weren't acting alone). But I won't talk about that, or you'll think once more that I'm using high policy as an excuse for leniency.

But I do want the truth: and the truth is on my side. I have sinned much against the party in my time and I have suffered much on account of it. But I declare again and again that in all the recent years I have defended the policy of the party and the leadership of KOBA with great inner conviction, even though I never indulged in toadyism.

It was good to be flying above the clouds the day before yesterday: 8 degrees of frost, diamond clear, breathing the peaceful vastness.

Maybe what I have written doesn't make sense. Don't be angry. Maybe it's

---

* Bukharin is using the familiar form.

not very pleasant for you to receive a letter from me at such a moment, God knows, anything is possible.

But 'just in case', I want to assure you, (as you have always had such a good attitude towards me), that *your conscience should be absolutely calm*; I have not let you down: I am genuinely not guilty of anything and sooner or later it will come out, however much they try to blacken my name.

Poor Tomsky! Maybe he did 'become involved', I don't know. I don't rule it out. He lived alone. Maybe if I'd gone to see him he wouldn't have been so gloomy and wouldn't have got involved. Human life is so complicated! But that's all poetry, and this is politics, not a poetic matter, but a rather severe one.

I'm terribly glad the dogs [Zinoviev and Kamenev] were shot. Trotsky was destroyed by the trial and that will soon become absolutely clear. If I'm still alive when the war breaks out, I'm going to apply to fight (not a pretty word), and you'll do me a last favour and get me into the army even as a private (even if I'm hit by a poisoned Kamenev bullet).

I advise you sometime to read the drama about the French Revolution by Romain Rolland.

Forgive this confused letter: a thousand thoughts are rushing around inside my head like wild horses and I have no strong reins.

I embrace you because I am clean.

Nik. Bukharin. 1. IX. 36

Having read the letter, Voroshilov decided he must at once send it on to Stalin and also answer Bukharin, making sure that Stalin and the other leaders knew what was in this answer. At any rate, he took care to establish a political alibi by involving his assistants. Two documents were quickly composed:

> Top secret. PERSONAL.
> To Comrades STALIN
> MOLOTOV
> KAGANOVICH
> ORDZHONIKIDZE
> ANDREYEV
> CHUBAR
> YEZHOV

Further to N. BUKHARIN's letter, sent to you on 1.IX.36, reference No. 2389 ss, I enclose herewith on Comrade K.YE. VOROSHILOV's orders Comrade VOROSHILOV's reply to BUKHARIN and a copy of N. BUKHARIN's reply.

ENCLOSED: 3 pages.

Adjutant to Commissar for Defence of USSR
divisional commander Khmelnitskii

4.IX.36

Voroshilov's reply to his former comrade was in the spirit of the morality then prevailing in the entourage of the autocrat.

To Comrade BUKHARIN

I return your letter in which you permit yourself to make vile attacks on the party leadership. If you were hoping by your letter to convince me of your complete innocence, all you have convinced me of is that henceforth I should distance myself from you as far as possible, regardless of the outcome of your case. And if you do not repudiate in writing your foul epithets against the party leadership, I shall even regard you as a scoundrel.

K. Voroshilov

3.IX.36*

One can imagine the shock Bukharin must have felt on receiving this letter, although in his heart he knew that the blade of Stalin's guillotine had long been poised above his head. He might well have recalled Robespierre's words to the Convention on 8 Thermidor, the eve of his execution: 'They have come to tyranny with the aid of scoundrels, what will those who fight against them come to? Their graves and immortality.' Did Bukharin fight? Having read Voroshilov's murderous letter, Bukharin found the strength in himself to reply to the Stalinist commissar.

Comrade VOROSHILOV

I have received your *appalling* letter.

My letter ended with 'I embrace you'.

Your letter ends with 'scoundrel'.

What is there to write after that?

Every man has, or rather should have, his personal pride. But I want to remove one political misunderstanding. I wrote you a letter of a *personal* nature (which I now much regret) when I was in a grave psychological condition; being persecuted, I simply wrote to a big man; I was going out of my mind thinking only of what might happen or that anyone should believe I was guilty.

And so I cried out, and wrote: 'If you think me "insincere" (for instance, that I had written my Kirov articles "insincerely"), yet you leave me free, then you are cowards etc.' And further: '*And if you yourself don't believe* what Kamenev cooked up ... etc.' Well, then, according to you does it mean I think you're a coward or that I'm calling the leadership cowards? On the contrary: what *I mean is that, since everyone* knows that you are not cowards, it means you don't believe that I wrote insincere articles. Surely that much is clear from my letter!

But if my letter was so confused that it could be taken as an attack, then – not out of a Judas-like fear, but genuinely – thrice, in writing or however you like, I take back all these phrases, even though I did not mean what you thought.

* Voroshilov addresses Bukharin in the familiar form throughout the letter.

I regard the party leadership as wonderful. And in my letter to you, despite the possibility of both of us making mistakes, I wrote: 'There have been times in history when *wonderful* people and *superlative* politicians have also made mistakes of an honest kind'. Wasn't that in my letter? That is actually how I feel about the leadership. I admitted this ages ago and am not tired of repeating it now. I dare to think that I have proved this by my activity in all the recent years.

In any case, I ask you to remove this misunderstanding. I apologize very much for my last letter, and I won't burden you with any more. I am in an extremely nervous condition. That's what made me write the letter. In fact, I have to be as calm as possible while I wait for the outcome of the investigation which I'm sure will prove my total uninvolvement with the bandits. Because there lies the truth.

Goodbye

BUKHARIN 3.IX.36[28]

Bukharin had said 'goodbye', but once more Stalin had relaxed his grip on the suffocating victim's throat. *Pravda* of 10 September 1936 reported that in the absence of incriminating evidence the case was closed. But it was only a breathing spell, and now the time for Bukharin to perform to the prepared script had arrived.

At his trial, Bukharin, however pitiful his pleas to Voroshilov had been, strove to rise to the occasion in his own terms. Realizing that he was doomed, he tried, sometimes directly, sometimes by using Aesopian language, sometimes in the form of tragic satire, to cast doubt on the charges. Perhaps, in saying farewell to his life, he was addressing the future. In this, the most tragic moment of his life, he was able to preserve his presence of mind and his sharp intellect. It was his last attempt to exercise his conscience:

I regard myself ... both politically and juridically responsible for sabotage, although I personally do not remember ever having given orders to commit sabotage.

Citizen Procurator asserts that in common with Rykov I am one of the most important organizers of espionage. What is the evidence? It is Sharangovich's testimony which I had not heard mentioned before the prosecution's summing up.

I categorically deny that I had any part in the murders of Kirov, Menzhinsky, Kuibyshev, Gorky or Maxim Peshkov.* According to Yagoda's testimony, Kirov was murdered on the orders of the 'Right-Trotskyite Bloc'. I did not know about it.

The stark logic of the struggle was accompanied by the degeneration of our psychology, the degeneration of ourselves, the degeneration of people.[29]

Every day Stalin was given progress reports on the trial by Yezhov, Vyshinsky or someone else. He would clear up points of detail and give advice. He was the first to be shown the film of the trial and photographs of the court with

---

* Gorky's adopted son.

the accused. On his orders, the 'show' was widely publicized in the press and on radio. Foreign journalists and even diplomats were invited to attend. They were all struck by the fact that the criminals 'confessed' in ideal terms. Expertise was not needed, nor supplementary investigation, forensic argument or dialogue between the prosecution and the defence. The procurator gave a solo performance and the rest just performed an obbligato. Even Feuchtwanger, however tendentious his book *Moscow 1937*, had to admit:

If a director had been given this trial to stage, he would have needed quite a few years and quite a few rehearsals to get such team-work out of the accused; they were so conscientious and keen not to allow the slightest inaccuracy about each other, and they showed their concern with such restraint. In short, the hypnotists and poisoners and clerks of the court who had prepared the accused, in addition to all their other exceptional qualities, must also be outstanding directors and psychologists. [30]

Feuchtwanger was partly right: the organizers of the farce, especially the director-in-chief, were masters of their craft, but, apart from the intimidation and acts of violence during the investigation, there was another reason why the accused made no complaint. They had been told for weeks and months that their confession was necessary to the party and the people. Only 'a confession will help us finally to unmask the criminals'. This meant both confessing and slandering others. It seems that many accused acted on this motive, though it emerged differently in each final speech. Accused G. F. Grinko said: 'I accept as proper the severest sentence, the highest degree of punishment.' Accused N. N. Krestinsky said: 'My crimes before the Motherland and the revolution are immense, and I accept your severest sentence as entirely deserved.' Accused A. I. Rykov: 'I want all those who have not been unmasked or disarmed to do this immediately and openly. I would like to serve as an example to them of the inevitability of disarmament.' Accused N. I. Bukharin: 'I stand with bended knee before the country, before the party, before the entire people.' [31]

It must have satisfied Stalin to know that, though they were facing death, the enemies of the people and the party did not rebel but said what was required. He saw their 'clean breast' as a victory for himself, not suspecting that it also contained the seeds of his own inevitable moral defeat. But he also knew that Bukharin had resisted for three months after his arrest. They had threatened him and put pressure on him, but the disgraced academician, even while in prison, tried in a series of letters to convince Stalin, as he had at the February-March plenum, that 'there is a conspiracy and enemies of the people do exist, but the main ones are to be found inside the NKVD.'

Stalin did not react to these signals. Perhaps, as he contemplated the icy silence that greeted his letters to Stalin, Bukharin was thinking of the opportunity he had so recently had to escape his fate. He had spent from February until April 1936 abroad with a small delegation to buy up archive material of

Marx and Engels. Even then, he had known what his fate was likely to be, but, like Robespierre. he felt he could only achieve immortality in his own motherland.*

Some time earlier, Stalin had sent the following Central Committee instruction to local NKVD authorities:

The Central Committee ... authorizes the use of physical coercion by the NKVD, beginning in 1937. It is well known that all bourgeois intelligence services use physical coercion of the most disgusting kind against representatives of the socialist proletariat. The question therefore arises why socialist organs should be more humane towards the rabid agents of the bourgeoisie and sworn enemies of the working class and collective farms? The Central Committee believes physical coercion should be used as an exception and henceforth should be used against known and revealed enemies of the people, but should be regarded in such cases as a permissible and correct method.[32]

This 'exception' became the rule and was used the moment an accused showed the first sign of resistance in 'conversation' with the investigators.

As Bukharin was still saying nothing and the 'investigation' was plainly going to drag on and on, Stalin ordered Yezhov to use 'all means'. We have seen, from the letters he wrote to Voroshilov (and Stalin) in September 1936, that Bukharin's emotional state had become precarious as the terror advanced. Now, when threats were made against his young wife and infant son, he caved in completely. He signed whatever monstrous invention the investigators chose to concoct, labelling himself a 'Trotskyite', 'leader of the bloc', 'conspirator', 'traitor', 'organizer of sabotage', and so on. It is painful to read his words:

I confess that I am guilty of the most heinous crime there can be, treachery to the socialist Motherland, and of organizing kulak uprisings, preparing terrorist acts, belonging to a subversive anti-Soviet organization. I further confess that I am guilty of plotting a 'palace coup' ...[33]

To be sure, Stalin was well pleased, yet, reading some of the reports of the questioning, he must also have sensed the concealed mockery of the accused, as they replied to the organizers of the 'show' with deathbed irony:

Vyshinsky: 'Accused Bukharin, is it or is it not a fact that your group of accomplices in the Northern Caucasus had links with White émigré Cossack circles abroad? Rykov has spoken about it, Slepkov has spoken about it.'

Bukharin: 'If Rykov has spoken about it, I have no grounds to disbelieve him.'

Vyshinsky: 'As a conspirator and leader, was this fact known to you?'

Bukharin: 'From the point of view of mathematical probability, one can say with very great probability that it is a fact.'

Vyshinsky: 'Let me ask Rykov again: was this fact known to Bukharin?'

---

* Boris Nicolaevsky in *Power and the Soviet Elite* (New York, 1965) describes his meetings with Bukharin on this trip. Bukharin even had his pregnant wife with him, but when it was suggested he remain abroad, he is reported to have replied. 'I don't think I should be able to live without Russia. We are all accustomed to things there and to the tenseness of life.'

Rykov: 'I personally reckon with mathematical probability that he must have known about it.'[34]

Stalin caught the sarcasm: they're asked about links with White émigrés and they talk about 'mathematical probability'! After each session in court, the defendants were reminded that not only their own fate but that of their nearest and dearest depended on the fullness and accuracy of their testimony.

Stalin was determined to avoid any slip-ups in the trial of the twenty-one; Bukharin and his accomplices must be fully 'ripe'. This trial, moreover, was to be a summing-up of the first stage of the mass purge and terror. He saw the trial not merely as a judicial act, crowning the extermination of his most dangerous enemies, but also as a nationwide lesson in class alertness, irreconcilability and hatred for anyone who might resist him and hence resist socialism. He therefore ordered that the trial be broadcast in the press and radio, and that meetings be arranged to demand 'the extermination of the Fascist vermin'.

He knew that the show trials would enhance his power further, since the people and the party could not fail to draw the lesson that any opposition was hopeless. He used these trials to install a system of mutual social control, by which everyone watched everyone else and only he remained beyond surveillance and informers. Even the people in his immediate circle could not feel safe, as the fate of Kosior, Postyshev, Rudzutak, Chubar and many others eloquently testified.

On the other hand, the trials were so arranged that Stalin could remain in the shadows. He made very few public pronouncements on the trials and for most of the population his true rôle was unknown. This created the illusion that the enemies and spies were being tried by the people themselves. Had the whole nation in fact been responsible for running the trials, it is certain that the result would have been the same. The country had not yet cooled down from the class conflict of the revolution and civil war and collectivization. Any report of a 'terakt' aroused the most heated outrage. Fascism was testing its strength in Spain, Germany was becoming militarized, anti-Comintern pacts were being cobbled together, the capitalist world was looking at 'Bolshevik Russia' through its gunsights.

As *Vechernyaya Moskva* of 15 March 1938 wrote:

History has not known such evil deeds as the crimes committed by the gang of the anti-Soviet 'Right-Trotskyite Bloc'. The espionage, sabotage and wrecking by the bandit-in-chief Trotsky and his henchmen, Bukharin, Rykov and others, arouse a feeling of rage, hatred and scorn, not only in the Soviet people but in all progressive mankind.

They tried to kill our dear leader, Comrade Stalin. In 1918 they shot at Comrade Lenin. They cut off the ardent life of Sergei Mironovich Kirov, they murdered Kuibyshev, Menzhinsky and Gorky. They betrayed our motherland.

The glorious Soviet intelligence service, headed by Stalinist Commissar Nikolai Ivanovich Yezhov, has smashed the vipers' nests of these vermin.

Thus the nation was turned into a lynch-mob. Thus the manipulation of public opinion created the phenomenon of unity around a false idea. Thus Stalin brainwashed the millions.

The wreckers were seen as enemies by everyone, and it could not have been otherwise. On 13 March, the day the trial ended, the 200,000th ZIS came off the assembly line of the Stalin Automobile Works in Moscow, the quarterly plan was fulfilled on time in the Karaganda coalfields, Muscovites and visitors to the city were able to ride for the first time on the completed Pokrovsky circle line of the L. M. Kaganovich Metro. The best kolkhozes of Tula region were beginning to instal running water. Every republic and region, every factory and farm wanted to please the leader with its new achievements. The climate was electric, as new towns and roads were built and the people felt that life was beginning to improve. More and more records were being made and broken, while these 'enemies' had planned to destroy everything the nation held dear.

The manipulation was made easier by the lack of openness and genuine information. Without an impression of the first twenty years of the Soviet régime, the mental climate of the 1930s and the imperatives that dictated the behaviour of the people, it is impossible to understand the social drama and tragic convulsions that gripped the country.

It is not only today that people throw up their hands and ask why all the accused confessed to nonexistent crimes. This was one of the biggest mysteries for the Western press at the time, and Stalin, who measured the mood not only at home but also abroad, reacted immediately. On his orders, an article was hurriedly published in *Pravda* under the title 'Why Do They Confess?' It stated that when Vyshinsky had asked the accused if any pressure had been used on them to make them confess, they had categorically denied the suggestion. They confirmed that the investigation had been carried out in a totally correct way, and that there was no question of direct or indirect coercion being applied. The accused Muralov, for instance, stated that during his imprisonment he had been treated throughout 'in a civilized and cultivated manner'. They had conspired. There was evidence. The charges were based strictly on the facts. The accused were oppressed by the weight of the incontrovertible evidence.[35] As he waited for international opinion to form, Stalin anticipated the worst. Naturally everyone was puzzled by the willingness of the accused not to defend themselves and to second the charges in a friendly tone, but without any background knowledge the Western press never rose above abstract condemnation of 'anti-democratism'. Stalin was infuriated by Trotsky, who published almost daily commentaries and refutations in the Western press and then announced that he intended to stage his own 'counter-trial'.

Trotsky's scathing article in *Bulletin of the Opposition*, No. 65, 1938, drove

Stalin crazy. With characteristic sarcasm and perspicacity, Trotsky pinpointed the phoney nature of the trials:

In this criminal activity the people's commissars, marshals, ambassadors and secretaries invariably receive their orders from one agency, not their official leader but an exile. Trotsky has only to blink an eye and it is enough for the veterans of the revolution to become agents for Hitler and the Mikado. On Trotsky's 'instructions', issued through the best correspondent of TASS, the leaders of industry, agriculture and transport destroy the country's productive resources. On the orders of 'Public Enemy No. 1', whether from Norway or Mexico, the railwaymen destroy military transports in the Far East, while highly respected doctors poison their patients in the Kremlin. This is the amazing picture drawn by Vyshinsky, but here a difficulty arises. Under a totalitarian régime it is the apparatus that implements the dictatorship. But if my hirelings are occupying all the key posts in the apparatus, how is it that Stalin is in the Kremlin and I'm in exile?

Stalin cursed Yezhov for his 'cretinous' fabrication of the cases and, yet again, wondered whether it was not time to wind up the whole campaign. He decided that, while there were still people who might, even if only mentally, see Trotsky as an alternative, he must go on.

The political trials had yet another aim. With their aid, Stalin wanted to show that all the former oppositionists – Trotskyites, Bukharinites, Zinovievites, Mensheviks, Dashnaks, SRs, Anarchists, Bundists – had been anti-socialists, and that they had infected Soviet citizens who were working abroad, such as diplomats, cultural figures, industrial managers, scientists, even those who were doing their internationalist duty in Spain. Many émigrés who had returned home, and foreign Communists working in the Comintern or its organizations in Moscow, were also termed 'enemies of the people', along with anyone who had been expelled from the party earlier, or who had a grudge against the régime or had expressed political doubt. The relatives of the repressed were automatically considered 'enemies'. The NKVD itself constituted a large group of victims, some of them destroyed because they tried to sabotage the criminal fabrications. while others fell into the category of 'enemies' through excessive zeal. Its leaders were also an endangered species precisely because they knew too much. Thus, Yagoda, Frinovsky and Berman, among many others, were accused of committing excesses, distortions and 'wrecking activities in the organs of the NKVD'. Equally, it became dangerous to have known Lenin, or to have fought against tsarism and, therefore, if only instinctively, to know the value of freedom and democracy. And of course there were people who knew more about Iosif Dzhugashvili than was good for them.

Suspicion increased the momentum of violence. V. Zakharov, M. Motsiev and other railway workers at Arzamas can hardly have understood Trotsky's ideas, yet it was these ideas, combined with the 'intention to commit terrorist sabotage', that led to their being sentenced to death on 31 October 1937. As Ulrikh reported to Stalin, 'all the accused fully confessed their guilt.'

A feature of the trials was Stalin's desire not merely to destroy his opponents, real and imagined, but first to drag them through the mud of amorality, betrayal and treason. All the trials are an unprecedented example of self-abasement, self-slander, self-condemnation. This often took on a ludicrous appearance, as the accused insistently claimed to be traitors, spies and murderers. Kamenev, for instance, simply stated that 'we served Fascism, we organized counter-revolution against socialism.' Promises of leniency, threats of repression against their families and systematic physical torture broke these people and forced them to play their humiliating parts according to the scenario written by the 'high priests of justice'. Stalin stayed in the wings, while his assistants, Vyshinsky and Ulrikh, cynically staged the show.

When those brothers in misfortune, Bukharin and Rykov, were expelled as candidate members of the Central Committee, Stalin gave them a faint glimmer of hope by telling them that 'the NKVD would sort things out.' Facing the military collegium of the Supreme Court of the USSR a year later – 'on the other side of the barrier,' as Bukharin was to put it – they felt that the cup of evil cunning was full to the brim, and they were being forced to drink it to the dregs.

CHAPTER 30

The Cadres on Trial

On 4 May 1935, in the Kremlin, Stalin addressed a Red Army graduation class. The young officers and political workers, in their creaking new shoulder-belts, new collar tabs and shoulder bars, concentrated their gaze on the short, stocky figure. Few gestures accompanied the soft voice that echoed in the absolute silence of the Kremlin hall. Stalin spoke slowly, glancing only occasionally at the text which he held before him:

I recall an occasion in Siberia, where I was once exiled. It was spring, when the water was high. Thirty or so men had gone off to collect driftwood that had been brought down by the great river. They returned to the village towards evening, but they were minus one man. When we asked what had happened to him, they just said, 'He stayed there.' I said, 'What do you mean, he stayed there?' They replied casually, 'He probably drowned. What of it?' And one of them dashed off somewhere, muttering something about feeding the mare. When I remonstrated that they cared more for animals than people, one of them said, to the general approval of the rest, 'Why should we be sorry for people: we can make more people any time. But you try making a mare . . .'

The audience stirred. Holding up a crooked index finger to mark the paradoxical nature of the reply, Stalin went on:

The indifferent attitude towards people and cadres shown by some of our leaders, and their inability to appreciate people, is a hangover of that same attitude towards people that I have just mentioned.

And so, comrades, if we want to overcome the famine of people in the regions, and if we want our country to have enough cadres capable of moving technology forward and setting it in motion, we must first of all learn to appreciate people, appreciate the cadres, appreciate every worker who is capable of doing good to the cause. We must, finally, understand that the most valuable capital in the world, the most valuable and the most decisive capital is people, cadres. We must understand that, given our present circumstances, 'the cadres determine everything'.[36]

Thus, as early as 1935, Stalin was aware of the shortage of personnel, but the decimation of the cadres was yet to come. Large gaps would soon appear in the top ranks of the party, state and economic administration, in the professional army and the technical and creative intelligentsia, as well as in organizations in the republics and provinces. Hundreds of thousands would be cut down as if by a terrible plague. Early in 1939, Stalin ordered the chief board of Red Army cadres to produce details on the officer corps of the army and navy. He studied the tables for some time in silence: almost 85 per cent of the officers were under 35 years of age. Slowly he leafed through the pages. Perhaps he was thinking of the marshals and all the other officers he had despatched. He had seen many of them here in the Kremlin. Maybe he was recalling Voroshilov's speech of 26 November 1938? The commissar, as if reporting a great achievement, had said: 'In the course of purging the Red Army in 1937–1938, we got rid of more than 40,000 men ... In ten months in 1938, more than 100,000 new officers were created.'[37] Only ten remained of the fifty-plus members of the old War Council. Whatever thoughts he may have had as he contemplated the yawning gaps, Stalin decided to increase the number of military academies and schools. Such gaps were not, however, confined to the military.

Former Commissar of Communications I. V. Kovalev told me:

In 1937 I was appointed head of the Western railway. I arrived in Minsk and went to the administration office. It was empty. There was no one to hand over the job to me. My predecessor, Rusakov, had been arrested and shot. I called for his deputies. There weren't any. They'd been arrested. I looked for anyone, but there was only a strange and terrible silence. It was if a tornado had passed through. I was amazed that the trains were still running and wondered if anyone was controlling this enormous operation. I went to the apartment of an acquaintance who worked in the railway administration. To my surprise I found him at home with his wife, who was in tears.

'Why aren't you at work?' I asked, before even greeting him.

'I'm waiting. They said they'd come for me today. See, I've got some clean shirts packed. Nasedkin of the NKVD is purging every second man. He's probably paralysing the railway.'

Having got the picture and recovered my composure, I phoned Stalin in Moscow – after all, if the railway didn't work as it was supposed to, I'd be the next on the list. Poskrebyshev answered. I told him of the situation. Somehow the rampage was rapidly brought to a halt. Anyway, there was no one left to put in gaol.

This was the pattern all over the country, as extracts from the October 1937 plenum illustrate. During the debate on Molotov's report on the election campaign (which was incidentally more about enemies of the people than elections), the secretary of the Krasnoyarsk regional party committee, Sobolev, said:

We are now unmasking and destroying enemies: Bukharinites, Rykovites, Trotskyites, Kolchakites, saboteurs, we are crushing all the swine in our region. They are making totally open attacks on us. I have in mind their favourite form of sabotage which is fire-raising.

Peskarev from Kursk region drew a similar picture, but from a different angle:

Since scoundrels, wreckers and enemies of the people had long been active in the leadership of our regional procuracy and court, it turned out that they had shifted the weight of punitive policy on to totally innocent people; in three years, 18,000 kolkhoz and village activists were condemned, often just because a horse had gone lame or they were late for work.[38]

I do not have official figures for the number of victims in 1937–38. It is unlikely that they exist as yet. The most accurate figures come from the commissariat of defence. On the basis of existing material, such as lists of delegates, party statistics, local reports, court records, and various statements by Stalin, Molotov and Beria, among others, one can make a cautious estimate that between 4.5 and 5.5 million people were arrested, of whom 800–900,000 were sentenced to death. Countless more died in concentration camps. The press has published various figures, but until all the relevant archives have been fully opened and a thorough study has been made, no amount of extrapolation or guesswork will provide a reliable figure. The documents I have seen testify that after the war the number of concentration camps and corrective labour colonies was not reduced, but rather increased, and that the number of inmates remained more or less constant over several years. Therefore the number of prisoners in, say, 1948 or 1949 may give an indication of the numbers in 1937–38. For instance, on 18 February 1948, V. Abakumov and S. N. Kruglov wrote to Stalin: 'In accordance with your instructions we enclose a draft plan for organizing the camps and strict régime prisons for holding particularly dangerous state criminals.'[39] Kruglov followed this up on 7 March 1948 with another report stating that 'on 1 January 1948 there were 2,199,535 prisoners in camps and colonies. Twenty-seven new camps have been built.'[40]

One must then add the prison population, for which there are no figures, but which I estimate not to have exceeded 30 per cent of the camp and exile-colony population. A report from Kruglov to Stalin, dated 23 January 1950, adds that: 'On 1 January 1950 there were 2,550,275 prisoners, 22.7 per cent of them for counter-revolutionary activity. 366,489 are serving more than ten years. Two new strict régime camps have been built for spies, saboteurs, terrorists, Trotskyites, Rights, Mensheviks, SRs, Anarchists, nationalists, White émigrés. Average living space for prisoners is 1.8 square metres.'[41]

These figures, I repeat, do not include the prison population. The camps, moreover, were considerably overloaded at that time by Soviet citizens who had served in the Nazi police, or who had been sentenced for nationalist uprisings against the Soviet régime in the Western territories at the end of the war, as well as those deported from liberated areas and arrested for no other reason.* Thus, if we include the prison population, the number of inmates was around three to four million, and not only in 1948 and 1949. It is unlikely that the numbers in 1937–38 can have been much greater than they were 1948–49. Nor can what Kruglov euphemistically called 'living space' have greatly increased in those bitter years. Camp inmates 'lived' in three-tier bunks. It is also important to note that the Gulag population was constantly being replenished by daily arrivals, that many were unable to stand the conditions and died, and that a percentage was also being regularly released. It is unlikely, however, that the punitive machine could have contained more than four or five million people in a given year, but until the official figures are published, one can only speculate.

The chief personal responsibility for these horrific facts rests of course on Stalin. He personally gave Yezhov instructions on the direction and scale of the repressions, frequently indicating individuals for 'checking'. In order to avoid using the term 'death penalty' in written or telephone communication, he would refer to 'punishment of the first category'. The documents show that he was directly responsible for the arrest and execution of, among many others, R. Eikhe, Ya. Rudzutak, R. Chubar, S. Kosior and P. Postyshev. Among the dozens of other Central Committee personnel he suggested be 'checked' were A. Stetsky, head of the agitation and propaganda section, B. Tal, head of the press section, Ya. Yakovlev, head of the rural section, K. Bauman, head of the science section, and F. Zaitsev, an official in the Control Commission. Being 'checked' led to being shot.

When the situation reached mass proportions, Stalin approved death sentences by the list, but in 1938, having tired of this procedure, he gave courts and tribunals the right to decide for themselves. At the Twentieth Congress Khrushchev said that in 1937–38 Yezhov sent Stalin 383 lists with thousands of names of party, state, Komsomol, army and economic personnel. All the sentences were confirmed by Stalin. It is unlikely that Stalin limited himself only to these lists. There must have been many more. As the stamps and signatures of other leaders appeared on them, many of these lists vanished after the Twentieth Congress. In April 1988, A. N. Shelepin told me that a whole series of lists bearing Khrushchev's signature was removed on Khrushchev's orders from the archives by I. A. Serov, the then Deputy Minister of State Security. They were handed over to Khrushchev who, although he had taken the brave step of exposing Stalin's crimes, wished nevertheless to dissociate himself from them.

Stalin had also been most concerned that his name should not appear as having sanctioned the 'highest degree of punishment'. There are many letters to him, as well as to Voroshilov and Molotov and others, begging for mercy.

---

* These categories are dealt with in greater detail in a later chapter.

All the writers of these letters perished. Since they were often read without being initialled or signed, Stalin must have preferred to give his decision orally, and sometimes not to review a case at all, since the fate of those who appealed to him was sealed anyway. It was this concealment of his rôle that led to the legend, still alive today, that 'he did not know' about the repressions. Only ignorance of the real situation can explain the naivety of D. A. Lazurkina, an Old Bolshevik, who told the Twenty-Second Congress in 1961 that during all the years she spent in prison and labour camp she never blamed Stalin: 'All the time I defended Stalin, whom the other prisoners and inmates and exiles cursed. I said to them, "No, it's not possible that Stalin would allow what is happening in the party. It is not possible".'[42]

Stalin and his henchmen turned violence into a way of life. As Khrushchev put it, 'The arbitrary rule of one man encouraged and permitted the emergence of arbitrary rule by others. The mass arrests and exile of many thousands of people, without trial or normal investigation, created a climate of insecurity and widespread fear.'

Several Central Committee plenums took place during 1937, at which, apart from elections to the Supreme Soviet, or errors committed in expulsions of party members, or measures to improve the work of the Machine and Tractor Stations and so on, delegates invariably discussed the membership of the Central Committee. This meant that the purge of the highest organ was continuous. For instance, at the October plenum twenty-four members and candidate members were removed, including Zelensky, Lebed, Nosov, Pyatnitsky, Khataevich, Ikramov, Krinitsky, Vareikis, Grinko, Lyubchenko, Yeremin, Deribas, Demchenko, Serebrovsky, Rozengolts, Ptukha and Shubrikov. Now classified as 'enemies of the people', these were all Bolsheviks of long standing and the backbone of the party cadres.[43] The pattern was the same for all the plenums. For instance, the following resolution was passed at the December plenum:

On the basis of incontrovertible evidence the plenum considers it necessary to expel from the Central Committee and arrest as enemies of the people: Bauman, Bubnov, Bulin, Mezhlauk, Rukhimovich and Chernov, who turned out to be German spies and agents of the Tsarist okhranka [secret police]; Mikhailov, linked by counter-revolutionary activity with Yakovlev, and Ryndin, linked by counter-revolutionary work with Rykov and Sulimov.

A note in Stalin's hand appears further down: 'All these people have admitted their guilt.'[44]

More than half of the Central Committee were 'spies' and 'agents of the Tsarist secret police'! Twenty years after the collapse of the Romanov dynasty, and its police department was still functioning as if nothing had happened! I have searched the yellowing lists that were circulated to members of the Central Committee for their votes, but have yet to find one negative vote, one objection, or any expression of doubt. Only 'in favour', 'I agree', 'definitely agree', 'a sound decision', 'a necessary measure', and so on. Conscience was clamped silent by lies and fear.

By the end of 1938 there were virtually no candidates left to fill the yawning gaps. Of 139 members and candidate members of the Central Committee elected at the Seventeenth Congress, ninety-eight, i. e. 70 per cent, were arrested and executed in 1937–38. Indeed, this was the fate not only of the Central Committee but of the delegates in general. And 80 per cent of those entitled to vote had been Bolsheviks since before 1921. Stalin could not forget that nearly 300 delegates had voted against him. Who were they? The dictator saw an enemy in every one.

The republics and regions were soon drained of their human resources. Many oblast committees simply lost their first secretaries; all party secretaries found themselves, as Kaganovich put it, 'residing' with Yezhov. Only Stalin was in possession of the general statistics. Whatever he made of them, he was nothing if not consistent, and, having made up his mind on this course, he would see it through to the bitter end.

According to I. D. Perfilyev, an Old Bolshevik who had spent many years in concentration camp and who told me the story, once, in Molotov's company, while discussing a routine list with Yezhov, Stalin muttered to no one in particular: 'Who's going to remember all this riff-raff in ten or twenty years time? No one. Who remembers the names now of the boyars Ivan the Terrible got rid of? No one ... The people had to know he was getting rid of all his enemies. In the end, they all got what they deserved.'

'The people understand, Iosif Vissarionovich, they understand and they support you,' Molotov replied automatically. They both knew that the people were keeping silent. The cries of support were the voices of ignorance, lawlessness and intimidation.

Stalin's precept about 'learning to appreciate people, learning to value the cadres' was the height of blasphemy. Yezhov, appointed a candidate member of the Politburo in October 1937, proposed that the NKVD begin preparing lists of people who had ever been investigated by a military tribunal. The following report by Ulrikh shows how such cases were treated and how many were 'uncovered':

To State Security Commissar, First Class, Comrade Beria, L.P.

During the period 1 October 1936 to 30 September 1938, the military collegium of the Supreme Court of the USSR and the circuit collegia of sixty towns sentenced:

30,514 to be shot
5,643 to prison

36,157 total
15 October 1938. V. Ulrikh[45]

In those two years, Yezhov, and later Beria, sent Stalin countless lists of 'spies', together with suggested sentences (mostly shooting) before the court even met. They would first receive a report from Ulrikh, of which the following is an example:

In September 1938 the military collegium of the Supreme Court of the USSR, in Moscow, Leningrad, Kiev, Kharkov, Khabarovsk and other cities, sentenced:

1803 to be shot

<u>389 to prison</u>

2,192 total[45a]

There would be another 3,588 for the month of October, but that only applied to the military tribunals. The ordinary courts were also working.

Khrushchev had no moral right to say, as he did at the Twentieth Congress, that 'We cannot regard Stalin's acts as the behaviour of a mad despot. He believed it was necessary to act this way in the interests of the party and the toiling masses, in the name of defending our revolutionary conquests. That was the tragedy!' This is completely wrong. Stalin could not but know that the terror he unleashed would proceed on the basis of the total violation of socialist legality. He could not but know that the political trials were phoney from start to finish. It is quite possible that he genuinely wanted a flourishing society and the well-being of its members, and undoubtedly he wanted a strong state. But he did not want to have to ask the members of that society how they wished to achieve the socialist ideals.

Despite his determination to reach the goals he had set himself, he did sometimes falter when the extent of the repressions suddenly came home to him. This explains the debate at the January 1938 plenum on mistakes committed by party organizations over the expulsion of members. It was Stalin who raised the issue. Hearing reports from Malenkov, Bagirov, Postyshev, Kosior, Ignatiev, Zimin, Kaganovich, Ugarov, Kosarev, he could not but be amazed at the extent of the terror, the lawlessness and the virtual destruction of the cadres. Postyshev reported that, on arriving in Kuibyshev, he had found all the party bodies paralysed by the purge. He had found no less than thirty district committees where only two or three members remained, which meant these bodies had ceased to function. At once Stalin, Beria, Yezhov, Malenkov and Molotov blamed Postyshev!

The documents suggest that the decision to 'drown' Postyshev had been taken before the plenum. Nearly all the speakers stressed his mistakes. To the accompaniment of approving comments from Stalin, Kaganovich, the chief critic, said, among other things:

I know Postyshev well. The Central Committee sent me to Kiev last year when we discovered Comrade Postyshev had made the biggest mistakes in the leadership of the Kiev and Ukrainian party organizations. Postyshev revealed himself in Kiev as a worker who violated the party's orders in practice, which was why the Central

312 The Epicentre of the Tragedy

Committee took him out of Kiev. Postyshev's blindness towards enemies of the people borders on the criminal. He couldn't see enemies even when the sparrows were twittering it to him from the rooftops ... Watching you in the corridors and hearing you speak at this plenum, I say that you are not being straight with the Central Committee.

'I have been straight all my life,' Postyshev attempted to protest. Kaganovich continued:

What Postyshev has said here at the plenum is a repetition of conversations that were hostile to the party. He doesn't seem to see that in the last year we have promoted more than 100,000 new people. This is a great Stalinist victory.[46]

Speaking of the 'great Stalinist victory', Kaganovich inadvertently had let slip the scale of renewals caused by leaders having been put out of action.

Speeches by Yaroslavsky, Kosarev and Ugarov escalated the criticism of Postyshev into outright accusation and condemnation. He had plainly been chosen as the victim on this occasion. Kaganovich succeeded in transferring his own personal enmity for Postyshev to the rest of the leadership, but subsequent events at the plenum showed that the scenario had been prepared in advance by Stalin. It was left to Ignatov, second secretary of the Kuibyshev regional committee, to deliver the coup de grâce by stating baldly that what Postyshev had done was 'anti-party'. Kaganovich at once rounded on Postyshev:

'You're not being straight with the Central Committee at this moment. You're taking a hostile line. Postyshev is finished as a political leader.'

'I totally and fully acknowledge that the speech I made here today,' Postyshev said, rising from his seat, 'was incorrect and anti-party. Even as I was saying it, I couldn't understand what I was doing. I ask the plenum to forgive me. Not only have I never been with the enemies, I have always fought against them.'

Only Stalin could save Postyshev now. But having waited for the total humiliation of an Old Bolshevik who had tried to exercise his own judgement, Stalin now determined his fate:

We have formed the opinion here in the Presidium of the Central Committee or, if you prefer, the Politburo, that after all that has happened measures must be taken in regard to Comrade Postyshev. In our opinion, he should be removed from candidate membership of the Politburo but remain a member of the Central Committee.[47]

A vote was taken and it was of course unanimous. Postyshev remained at liberty for just one month. On Stalin's orders, the party Control Commission drafted a decree on him in February that was passed by the Politburo. Its main contents were approved and edited by Stalin himself. Postyshev was charged with the following transgressions:

1 The dissolution of thirty-five district party committees.*
2 Provocation against soviets. (Thirty-four deputies had been removed at one session of the town soviet.)
3 Recruiting cadres to work in the fields, dismantling public buildings, wrecking by setting fire to the harvest.
4 While working in Kuibyshev, Postyshev hindered the NKVD in the unmasking of enemies by aiming blows against honest communists.
5 Postyshev's assistants, both in the Ukraine and Kuibyshev, have turned out to be enemies (spies).
6 Postyshev knew of the existence of a counter-revolutionary Right-Trotskyite organization in the territory.
  All the above actions of P. P. Postyshev are to be seen as anti-party and designed to benefit enemies of the people. P. P. Postyshev is to be expelled from the [party].[48]

All the remaining forty-nine Central Committee and candidate members voted for this resolution in writing, but there is no ballot paper in Stalin's name. As always, he took care to leave no trace.

Postyshev was arrested and shot. Stalin's 'concern for the cadres' was graphically illustrated by the case of this Old Bolshevik who did not suit the leader's book. Stalin needed to hear only one item of information, one conversation, a single phrase, and he would make up his mind about an individual. According to Perfilyev, after 'checking' on Postyshev, Molotov had reported to Stalin:

'Postyshev is politically dangerous.'

'Why keep him, then?' Stalin asked.

Not everyone noticed, or perhaps more accurately, paid due attention to Kosarev's skirmish with Mekhlis at the January plenum. In his speech Kosarev effectively criticized the political administration of the Red Army, which Mekhlis ran, for its weak organization of work among the Komsomol: 'There are 500,000 members of youth organizations in the army, yet only a few thousand of them are enrolled in the party each year.'

Mekhlis at once parried with the jaundiced reply: 'The Komsomol Central Committee does not deal with Komsomols in the army. I suggested to Beloborodov† that he enter the army to run the army Komsomols, but he declined. They only want to do it from the Central Committee.'[49]

This exchange no doubt sharpened the hostility between the two men and could well have been responsible for Kosarev's subsequent fate.

In debating the errors committed on the personnel front, the plenum was taking the now well-worn path of blaming all errors and excesses on unseen 'enemies'. This was indeed the conclusion drawn by the plenum itself: 'It is time to unmask all party organizations and their leaders and to destroy once and for all the camouflaged enemy who has infiltrated our ranks.'[50] Stalin's

---

*In fact, they had simply ceased to function, since 3,500 Kuibyshev communists had been expelled from the party over five months in 1937.
† Secretary of the Komsomol Central Committee.

directive, issued at the February–March 1937 plenum, still prevailed: excesses and mistakes in the struggle against the enemies of the people were caused by as yet unmasked Trotskyists and other wreckers. As we see, then, the glimmer of a sensible approach to the mayhem of 1937–38 was weak indeed. According to Stalin's way of thinking, the only fault in the system of violence lay in its executors.

Instead of discovering the causes of the excesses in the criminal treatment of communists, new impetus was imparted to the search for 'enemies'. When the Kiev regional secretary of the Ukrainian Communist Party, Kudryavtsev, spoke at party meetings, he would ask, 'Haven't you made any written denunciations on anyone?' As a result of such calls for vigilance, denunciations were sent in on almost half the members of that party. One of the first victims was Kudryavtsev himself.

The destruction of the cadres, and the wave of denunciation and informing that accompanied it, meant that many unscrupulous people, apart from taking the opportunity to settle an old score, got themselves promoted and often made good careers in the party, in state jobs and in the army. The January 1938 plenum passed a resolution stating that 'some careerist-communists who want to distinguish themselves and to benefit from the expulsions and repression of party members are protecting themselves against possible accusation of inadequate vigilance by engaging in indiscriminate repression against party members.'[51] This perfectly correct recognition of the danger to the party posed by such careerists and informers was not, however, linked to the general party line on repressions, and here lay another deep source of the distortions and the tragedy.

One lie leads to another; lies have the tendency to snowball. In arbitrarily 'sharpening' the class war, Stalin unleashed a wave of lying against which society was defenceless. The lying of Yezhov's security organs coupled with the lying of the courts and the procuracy, the lying of the press and the countless speeches in support of the 'just sentences', created a unique situation. Where could one find the causes of the mayhem? Nowhere. To whom could one turn for help? There was no one. Expose the real scoundrels? It was not allowed.

Let us take a typical example. There is an enormous number of denunciations of all kinds in the Beria archive. I will cite one, without naming the author who may have grown-up children and grandchildren. (It is pertinent here to say that, in naming the many names that I do in this book, I have tried to avoid causing anyone pain, but history would not be history if we had to put everything in coded form.) Here is the denunciation:

Comrade Malenkov.

    I am the deputy commander of a unit of NKVD internal troops. A meeting took place today in connection with the award to Comrade Stalin of the Victory Medal. But only officers were invited to the meeting. The troops were not invited. This was strange. General Brovkin conducted the meeting. Three or four people made speeches and with that the meeting was closed. Afterwards we were told that the unit was going to collect the harvest and that the chief of the political section, Kuznetsov, was being transferred to another job somewhere else.

An occasion as politically important as a meeting dedicated to the award of the Victory Medal to Comrade Stalin had been effaced, wiped away, cheapened.

Malenkov added a note to Beria: 'The addressee's reaction was the "natural" one.'[52]

The February–March 1937 plenum not only resolved that 'the commissariat of the interior should complete its work of unmasking and smashing the Trotskyites and other agents, and crush the smallest manifestation of their anti-Soviet activity', it also stipulated that the NKVD cadres be strengthened.[53] In those days, this could only mean carrying out the leader's will blindly and fanatically. Anyone with a conscience could not survive in the NKVD. Men such as Abakumov, Kruglov, Merkulov, Yezhov, Beria, Kobulov, Mamulov and Rukhadze, among other upstarts, did not hold their own in the NKVD through merit, but precisely because they had none.

CHAPTER 31

The Tukhachevsky 'Plot'

Stalin loved everything about the army. The armed forces were his special concern. He was fond of looking at himself in a large mirror when wearing his marshal's uniform; a carefully pressed tunic with gold shoulder-boards was his idea of aesthetic perfection. He would recall his civil war years with pride: with the exception of Trotsky, he had probably been on more fronts than anyone.

He personally knew nearly all the officers from corps commander up, most of the marshals and army commanders since the civil war, and from the middle of the 1930s all the top Red Army appointments were made by him. When interviewing a candidate he would listen to his brief report, looking him straight in the eye, remain silent and then chat for seven to ten minutes. He was interested in personal experience, knowledge of the battlefield, views on restructuring the army in the light of technical progress. He would ask unexpected questions, such as, 'Are Fortified Districts needed in the present circumstances?' or 'What do you think of the new field staff?' At the end of the conversation, he would give the nervous officer a limp handshake, wish him luck in his new job and hope he would always be steadfast in carrying out the party line. He would then again look hard into the man's eyes: he had to know if he was loyal to him personally.

Stalin spent many hours with commissars, designers, scientists and constructors who were concerned with military hardware. He usually inspected new models himself and was present at tests. He called meetings on various military matters, rarely making speeches but turning the course of the debate by his questions and comments. In 1939, for instance, he spent an entire day with the Red Army service staff discussing the design and quality of battle dress and regular uniform for officers and men.

This concern was not of course motivated solely by his love of military affairs. Like any leader, Stalin knew that a country's place in the world, its political régime and its international authority, depend to a great extent not only on its economic power, but also on its military might. All of his speeches at this period express alarm at the rise of Fascism and the growing imperialist threat in the West and the East. Without exaggeration, one can say that his main priorities at this time were the Red Army and the NKVD. And it was precisely through the NKVD that from the end of 1936 Stalin began receiving worrying news.

The first signals of an impending collision between Stalin and the military were picked up in Germany. The chief of Red Army intelligence, corps commander S. Uritsky, reported to Stalin and Voroshilov on 9 April 1937 that rumours were circulating in Berlin about the existence of opposition to the Soviet leadership among the generals. He added reassuringly that nobody believed them, and cited as proof the utterances of a certain Arthur Just in the newspaper *Deutsche Algemeine Zeitung* to the effect that 'today Stalin's dictatorship enjoys total support. It would be utterly strange to shake the foundations of the army at this time. Nothing at present is more important to Stalin than the unconditional reliability of the Red Army.'[54] It would seem that Stalin was thinking along the same lines, but similar rumours of a generals' conspiracy were beginning to come in from other sources and so he decided 'to shake the foundations' of the Army in order to test its 'unconditional reliability'.

First Yezhov sent Stalin a note from the White émigré organization Russkii Obshchevoinskii Soyuz (Russian General Military Union) in Paris, which stated that a coup d'état was being prepared in the USSR by a group of senior officers. The group was allegedly led by Marshal M. N. Tukhachevsky. Stalin passed on the note to Ordzhonikidze and Voroshilov 'to acquaint you' with its content. There is no trace of their reaction. It is most likely that the manifestly fake nature of the note impressed neither them nor the ever-suspicious Stalin, who tended to rely on any piece of paper or file coming from the NKVD. A digression is called for.

According to A. I. Rybin, who was working at that time in a section of the NKVD and later became one of Stalin's bodyguards, when Stalin was given an oral report on M. Ye. Koltsov's 'contacts' with 'foreign intelligence agencies', he paid little attention. He had recently had a conversation with the writer and was left with a good impression of him. Yet only a month later, when he was shown a file containing denunciations by two of Koltsov's close acquaintances, he ordered that action be taken. He could not believe that anyone would deceive or try to mislead him in writing. Yezhov and later Beria exploited this tendency to trust anything on paper. The most absurd and fantastic denunciations found fertile ground in Stalin's mind.

Many people who saw Stalin at close quarters at the height of his rule have told me of his extraordinarily suspicious attitude, which extended even to his immediate circle, his assistants and relations. According to A. N. Shelepin,

Stalin got Beria to check up on his security staff. Beria played on this by periodically 'finding' a 'spy' or a 'terrorist' among Stalin's personnel. Every now and then he would report on some suspicious signals or facts he had received. For instance, he once ordered the arrest of the cleaning man, Fedoseyev, and his wife for plotting a 'terakt'. Even the gardenias outside the windows had to be kept cut at a height of less than two feet, in case someone tried to hide behind them. No one ever knew if that night Stalin would sleep on the divan in his study or the bed in a small room, and so the beds were always kept made up in both places. No one but Beria dared to enter Stalin's rooms without being called.

As he drove out to the dacha in his armoured limousine accompanied by other cars, Stalin knew that every such trip entailed a whole operation for his security. Next to the chauffeur, Mitrokhin, would sit the bodyguards, either Tukov or Starostin (in the 1940s). If Stalin ever detected a glance he didn't like from any of them, they never worked for him again. It is noteworthy that, contrary to the myths fabricated by Beria and his circle, about attempts on Stalin's life, there is no recorded evidence to this effect.

Khrushchev referred to Stalin's pathological suspicion extending even to the members of the Politburo. He probably trusted only Vlasik and Poskrebyshev, and perhaps Valya Istomina, his 'maid', the young woman who moved into his house soon after the death of his wife, Nadezhda Alliluyeva. She cared for him until the end of his life and tried as far as possible to provide for his creature comforts. Despite his calloused nature, he more than once remarked on her simple and sincere concern for him. But maniacal suspiciousness was nevertheless a dominant feature of his personality.

Therefore, information sent to him by President Beneš of Czechoslovakia sharply increased his doubts about Tukhachevsky. Various sources – including Winston Churchill – claim that Stalin was hooked on a document fabricated in Berlin about a plot by Tukhachevsky and the generals. The German counter-intelligence service, headed by Admiral Canaris, had copied Tukhachevsky's signature which he had put on a document in Berlin back in 1926 about cooperating with a German firm on aviation technology.

The object of this fabrication was to convey the idea that Tukhachevsky was in secret contact with some German generals in order to overthrow Stalin by force. A fire on the night of 1 March 1937 and the theft of documents was staged in Berlin to explain their turning up in Prague.

Beneš no doubt acted with the best of intentions in sending the documents to Moscow, where Stalin, although alerted, did no more than pass them on to Yezhov for the time being. A tail was put on Tukhachevsky and further 'materials' were assembled. Events then probably developed much as B. A. Viktorov, former deputy Chief Military Procurator, has related to me. He headed a special group of military prosecutors and investigators that was assembled after the Twentieth Congress to rehabilitate those unjustly condemned by Stalin.

Among many interesting items, Viktorov recalled the case of an investigator called Radzivilovsky who was sentenced in 1937 for violating legality, and whose testimony included the following:

I was working in the NKVD administration of Moscow region. Frinovsky [an assistant of Yezhov] called me in and wanted to know if I was handling the cases of any important military men. I told him I was working on a former brigade commander called Medvedev. Frinovsky told me I must 'develop a line about an important, deep-seated plot in the Red Army, and that Yezhov's rôle and service to the Central Committee in unmasking it must appear enormous'. I set about my task. Naturally not at once but eventually I got the necessary evidence of a Red Army plot out of Medvedev. Yezhov was informed of the testimony. He personally interrogated Medvedev who told him and Frinovsky that his testimony was fabricated. Yezhov gave orders that all means were to be used to make Medvedev revert to his original story. The notes of Medvedev's testimony, obtained by physical torture, were reported to the highest instance.

Tukhachevsky and the other 'conspirators' were arrested soon after this. Literally the day before, Stalin had been told that Trotsky had announced in the latest issue of *Bulletin of the Opposition* that 'dissatisfaction among the military with Stalin's dictatorship places their possible revolt on the agenda'. Before taking action against the extremely popular Tukhachevsky, Stalin wanted to hear what Molotov, Voroshilov and Yezhov had to say. Molotov believed the story (and incidentally continued to do so until the end of his days), while Voroshilov revealed his long-standing dislike of Tukhachevsky, and Yezhov showed he was hoping to advance himself through the case. All three were for arresting the conspirators. On 24 May the following document, signed by Stalin, was circulated to members of the Central Committee requiring their vote:

On the basis of facts which expose Central Committee member Rudzutak and candidate member Tukhachevsky as participating in an anti-Soviet Trotskyite-Right [sic!] conspiratorial bloc and espionage work against the USSR for Fascist Germany, the Politburo of the Central Committee puts to the vote the proposal to expel Rudzutak and Tukhachevsky from the party and to hand their case to the commissariat of internal affairs.[55]

The vote was unanimously in favour. No one had any doubts, no one came to the victims' defence. Military leaders who had known Tukhachevsky well since civil war days blindly took the word of provocateurs on trust, without even attempting to hear what the marshal had to say. The momentum of lawlessness was already very strong. No one had the slightest desire to know what lay behind the words 'on the basis of facts which expose ...' Some members went even further than Stalin's resolution. For instance, Budenny wrote on the voting slip 'Definitely yes. These scoundrels must be punished.' Mekhlis as usual underlined his 'yes' several times. Neither Voroshilov, nor Yegorov, who had both served with Tukhachevsky, nor Khrushchev and

Mikoyan, who were later to condemn this act of lawlessness, found the courage to abstain from writing the fateful 'yes'. For unexplained reasons, Stalin as usual left his voting slip blank.

Stalin had known Tukhachevsky since the civil war, he knew how well he had commanded the Fifth Army, and he remembered the Revvoensoviet's order of 28 December 1919: 'Fifth Army Commander Comrade M. N. Tukhachevsky is awarded the Honorary Gold Weapon for personal bravery, broad initiative, energy, efficiency and knowledge of the job, all shown in the victorious actions of the glorious Red Army in the East in the taking of Omsk.'[56]

As he listened to Yezhov's reports on the interrogations of M. N. Tukhachevsky, I. E. Yakir, I. P. Uborevich, A. I. Kork, P. E. Eideman, B. M. Feldman, V. M. Primakov and V. K. Putna, Stalin mused about the youngest of these senior officers, five of them Marshals of the Soviet Union. On the one hand, Stalin had always recognized Tukhachevsky's high professional training, the originality of his strategic thinking and his undoubted talent as a theorist. On the other hand, since the civil war Stalin had retained a lingering mistrust of the 'bourgeois specialists' and had come to dislike the marshal for the independence and boldness of his judgement, and he knew of the strained relations between Tukhachevsky and Voroshilov. He recalled a note from Gamarnik, chief of the political section of the Red Army, reporting that Tukhachevsky was proposing the withdrawal of the heads of the district political administration, which both Gamarnik and Stalin regarded as 'absolutely incorrect and harmful in time of war or peace'.[57] On that occasion Stalin had supported Gamarnik. He also knew that Voroshilov took a jaundiced view of Tukhachevsky's theories[58] because they made him more aware that through his own lack of education he was clinging to outmoded notions of military organization. Therefore Tukhachevsky's position, as first deputy to a commissar who was immeasurably his intellectual inferior, could scarcely have been permanent in any event. Voroshilov was unlikely to appreciate Tukhachevsky for what he was worth, and the latter's removal to a lower rank came in due course when he was appointed commander of the Volga military district. This appointment did not last long.

It was plain to Stalin, too, that Tukhachevsky was superior to Voroshilov in every way. But that often happened. A boss doesn't have to be cleverer than his subordinates. The important thing was the 'line', and that was something Voroshilov could deliver, whereas Tukhachevsky ... It was hard to believe everything Yezhov was reporting, but even Trotsky had dropped hints in his book *The Revolution Betrayed*. In a recent interview in Oslo, the 'citizen without a visa' had said, 'Not everyone in the Red Army is dedicated to Stalin. They still remember me.' And Trotsky and Tukhachevsky knew each other ... As he read the reports, Stalin forced himself to believe that the story of a conspiracy was not only true, but was also a real threat. In any case, Yezhov reported that the 'conspirators have confessed'.

Stalin ordered a closed trial to be arranged without delay. They should all be shot. He nodded towards his desk where a copy of *Bolshevik* lay open at an article by Tukhachevsky 'On the New Red Army Field Staff'. Events had moved so fast that the editor had not had time to exclude it from the issue. In early June 1937, before the trial, the Defence Council (all of whom would themselves be shot within six months) heard Yezhov and Voroshilov report on the exposure of 'a foul counter-revolutionary military-Fascist organization'. The plotters had been operating for a long time, the report said, and their activities were closely linked with German military circles. Furthermore, they had planned to assassinate the leaders of the party and state and to seize power with the help of Fascist Germany. Tukhachevsky's fate was sealed. On 11 June 1937, less than two weeks after his arrest, the closed trial took place and was only mentioned in the press the same day. The sentence was reported the following day.

The trial was conducted at extreme speed and with extreme lack of justice. It opened at nine in the morning and the sentence was passed soon after lunch. The bench consisted of military lawyer V. V. Ulrikh, army marshals S. M. Budenny and V. K. Blyukher, army commanders first class B. M. Shaposhnikov and I. P. Belov, army commanders second class Ya. I. Alksnis, P. Ye. Dybenko, N. D. Kashirin and division commander Ye. I. Goryachev. The accused were denied defence counsel or the right of appeal, as laid down in the law of 1 December 1934.

Tukhachevsky, Yakir, Uborevich, Putna, Primakov, Kork, Eideman and Feldman sat opposite their old army comrades. They all knew each other well. No one in the court can have believed that here were plotters and spies. The defendants must surely have felt a faint glimmer of hope that their judges, who had served with them for twenty-five years under the same flag, would hearken, if not to the voice of justice, at least to a sense of esprit de corps.

Ya. B. Gamarnik was also meant to have been in court, as either a defendant or a member of the bench. His daughter, V. Ya. Kochneva, described his last day to me:

My father fell ill at the end of May, either because he sensed things were coming to a head or because he had an attack of diabetes. According to my mother – I was only twelve – he knew that Tukhachevsky had been arrested on 27 May and that Uborevich, Yakir and the rest had been arrested on the 29th, on the train.

Blyukher came to see my father on the 30th. They were old friends from their Far East days. They talked for a long time. Then my father told my mother that he had been asked to sit in judgement on Tukhachevsky. 'But how can I?' he cried. 'I know they're not enemies. Blyukher said if I don't, I could be arrested myself.'

Blyukher came again briefly on the 31st. Then some other people came and put a seal on father's safe. They told him he had been removed from his post and that his assistants, Osepian and Bulin, had been arrested. He was ordered to stay in the house. As soon as the NKVD people left we heard a shot in his study. When mother and I rushed in it was all over.

I think that shot was a reply to Stalin's proposal that father sit in judgement on his army friends. A reply to lawlessness. He had nothing else to reply with. Mother was arrested and given eight years imprisonment as 'the wife of an enemy of the people', and then another ten years in camp for 'aiding an enemy of the people'. I never saw her again and apparently she died in camp in 1943. I was sent to a children's home. When I reached sixteen in 1941 I was given six years as 'a socially dangerous element'. Then my terms of exile began ...

Such was the typical story of thousands and thousands of families of the innocently repressed.

The trial was taken at lightning speed. Everything had been arranged beforehand. Ulrikh connected the 'plot' mainly with the defendants' contacts with the German military. As we have seen, in 1926 Tukhachevsky had headed a Soviet military delegation to Berlin. Yakir had been on military courses in Germany in 1929. Kork had been the military attaché there. Many others had met German representatives at diplomatic receptions, manoeuvres and various talks. All of them, with the exception of Primakov, vigorously denied any 'spy link' with Germany. For instance, Tukhachevsky told the court that 'the meetings and conversations with representatives of the German military were purely official. They all took place before Hitler came to power.'

The defendants confessed to a degree of 'wrecking', not as a premeditated act, but through shortcomings and omissions in military training, in the construction of military sites, and in matters of mobilization. One of the main charges of wrecking was based on Tukhachevsky's call for the rapid formation of tank and mechanized units at the expense of the cavalry. Here Ulrikh sided energetically with Budenny, the civil war commander of the Red Cavalry. Since the defendants refused to confirm the findings of the preliminary investigation, the president of the court repeatedly asked, 'Do you confirm the testimony given by you to the NKVD?', a question which compelled them to adhere to the version that had been fabricated before the trial. As has now been established, all the defendants were subjected to physical torture.

A final charge was that, in order 'to ensure the success of the plot, the accused had intended to get rid of Voroshilov.' To this, Tukhachevsky, Kork and Uborevich replied that, together with Gamarnik, they had wanted to raise with the government the question of removing Voroshilov as commissar, since he was incompetent. This was taken by the court as proof of 'conspiratorial activity'. But the defendants vigorously denied any notion of spying for Nazi Germany or preparing a counter-revolutionary coup. In their final statements they swore devotion to the Motherland, the people, the army, and particularly stressed their loyalty to 'Comrade Stalin'. They asked the court to be lenient towards the mistakes and shortcomings they may have committed in their work.

Primakov's last words introduced a dissonant note into the proceedings. He fully confirmed the official charges and stated that 'all the conspirators were united by the banner of Trotsky and dedication to Fascism.' He said he had given the investigators the names of seventy people whom he personally knew to be involved in the military-Fascist conspiracy. According to him, the leaders of the plot had a 'second motherland': Putna, Uborevich and Eideman had close relatives in Lithuania, Yakir had family in Bessarabia, and Eideman had his in America. After months of torture, Primakov said whatever the investigators had told him to say. Where the rest had been arrested only two weeks earlier, Primakov, a hero of the civil war, had been in the Lubyanka for more than a year and was a broken man.

Only investigators of a certain kind were then in the employ of the NKVD: heartless cynics and sadists. Army General A. V. Gorbatov, who had passed through the circles of the Stalinist hell, recalled:

I found out by accident that my monster-investigator was called Stolbunsky. I don't know where he is now. If he's alive, I'd like him to read these lines and to feel my contempt for him, though I think he knew it even then. I can still hear him whispering malevolently, as they carried me out, exhausted and covered in blood, 'You'll sign, you'll sign.' I survived this torment for a second round of questioning, but when the third round began I just wanted to die.

The investigator in the Tukhachevsky case who particularly excelled was Ushakov (real name Ushiminsky). He was responsible for special cases. In his deposition to the rehabilitation commission after the Twentieth Congress, he wrote:

Feldman was the first to be arrested. He categorically denied any part in any plot, especially against Voroshilov. I got hold of his personal file and having read it came to the conclusion that Feldman was linked by friendship with Tukhachevsky, Yakir and a number of other leading generals. I summoned Feldman to my room, locked the door, and by the evening of 19 May he had signed a statement about a plot involving Tukhachevsky, Yakir, Eideman and the others. Then I was given Tukhachevsky to interrogate, and he confessed on the following day. Taking hardly any sleep, I dragged out of them more and more facts and more and more names of plotters. Even on the day of the trial, I managed to get some additional testimony out of Tukhachevsky which implicated Apanasenko and others in the conspiracy.[59]

Vyshinsky himself took part in one session of Tukhachevsky's interrogation, forcing him to put his signature to the words, 'I confess my guilt. I have no complaints.' In fact, nearly all of the accused wrote letters of complaint and appeals for mercy to Stalin, Molotov and Voroshilov.

Tukhachevsky's comrades also underwent the 'vigorous' treatment, the intimidation, the threats to their families, the physical torture. Throughout the interrogations, the victims were told that they could save their lives only by confessing.

Before the sentences were pronounced, Ulrikh and Yezhov kept Stalin informed of progress and the behaviour of the accused. Ulrikh obsequiously laid the draft sentences on Stalin's desk. Without even glancing at them, Stalin pronounced, 'Agreed'. Then, after a short silence, he asked:

'What were Tukhachevsky's last words?'

'The snake said he was dedicated to the motherland and to Comrade Stalin. He asked for clemency,' Yezhov answered hastily. 'But it was obvious he was not being straight, he hadn't laid down his arms.'

'What about the court? How did the members of the bench behave?'

'Only Budenny took an active part, the rest were silent for the most part. Alksnis, Blyukher and maybe Belov asked one or two questions.'

Stalin had had doubts about the members of the court right from the start, and he decided at once to keep an eye on them. Apart from Budenny and Shaposhnikov, all of them would be arrested very soon, Kashirin and his two brothers literally within days.

The appeals for clemency went unanswered. Stalin did not like 'soft-heartedness'. On the night of 12 June 1937 all the accused were shot, including Primakov and despite the promise of his life in exchange for his 'pure-hearted admissions'. 'No Mercy for Spies and Traitors to the Motherland' was the title of an article in *Bolshevik* on the trial of 'Tukhachevsky and Co.', whom it described as 'playing the same rôle as Franco, the despised enemy of the Spanish people'.[60]

The massacre of the military cadres was only the beginning. The NKVD was working at full tilt. Its every phone call, telegram or report prompted another round-up, more victims, more misery. Two of Mekhlis's telegrams are illustrative:

Commissariat of Defence, Shchadenko, Red Army Political Administration, Kuznetsov.

Chief of staff Lukin is an extremely doubtful person, he's mixed up with enemies and has links with Yakir. Brigade Commander Fedorov should have enough material on him. My report on Antonyuk has quite a lot on Lukin. You won't be making a mistake if you lift Lukin right now.

27 July Mekhlis

To Comrade Stalin

I have fired 215 political workers of whom a substantial number have been arrested. But I am far from finishing the purge of the political apparatus, especially the lower ranks. I don't think I should leave Khabarovsk before at least making a start at sorting out the Communist cadres.[61]

With Stalin's approval, Mekhlis and those like him forged the defeats of 1941 which were to bring millions of new victims. The lists of military commanders and political workers who perished read like an unbelievably terrible and endless obituary. Meanwhile the tragedy continued. Brigade commander Medvedev, who under torture gave the required testimony against Tukhachevsky, was shot. Like Yagoda before him, Yezhov set about sweeping away the traces. Most of the members of the Special Court which had sentenced Tukhachevsky and the rest were themselves despatched. A letter to Stalin from Dybenko is noteworthy:

Dear Comrade Stalin,

It seems the Politburo and government have decided I am an enemy of our Motherland and our party. Politically isolated, I am a living corpse. But why, for what? How could I know that those Americans who came to Central Asia with official representatives of the NKVD and OGPU were special intelligence agents? On the way to Samarkand I was not alone with them for a second. Anyway, I don't even speak American.

About the Kerensky provocation published in the White Guard press stating that I am a German agent, is it possible that White Guardist Kerensky can take his revenge on me after twenty years of honest, devoted work in the party? This is simply monstrous.

Two notes in Yezhov's possession, written by staff of the Hotel National, contain a grain of truth – when acquaintances came to visit me in the hotel I would drink with them. But there were no drunken orgies.

I am supposed to have taken a room next to representatives of the embassy. That's just one more of a whole host of provocations.

I am supposed to have kulak tendencies in regard to agricultural reconstruction. This nonsense can only have been spread about by Comrades Gorkin, Yusupov and Yevdokimov with whom I worked for the last nine years.

Comrade Stalin, I beg you to look again at all these facts and to remove the badge of shame from me, as I do not deserve it.

P. Dybenko[62]

A few days later army commander Dybenko, a party member since 1912, chairman of Tsentrobalt*, was arrested, 'tried' and shot. Stalin merely noted on Dybenko's letter 'For Voroshilov'. Neither Stalin nor Voroshilov, however, had any desire to bother with the fate of an Old Bolshevik.

Convinced if not of the existence then at least of the possibility of a 'military-Fascist' conspiracy, Stalin was already wondering who, in the absence of Tukhachevsky, could be leading it. He had just read a report from Germany sent to him by deputy chief of military intelligence Alexandrovsky. It contained an evaluation of the Red Army leadership by German military officials. They thought for some reason that Blyukher came of Russified German stock and that he was the most influential and authoritative of Soviet military leaders. They thought Yegorov an extremely 'strong commander' with 'an analytical mind'. Stalin did not need such people. He preferred the compliant Voroshilov and Budenny with their ordinary minds.

As he paced the garden paths at the Kuntsevo dacha, Stalin may well have recalled that, soon after he had put through the decree of 20 February 1932 depriving Trotsky and the rest who left with him of their Soviet citizenship,

---

* Central Committee of the Baltic Fleet in 1917–18, i. e. the Bolshevik revolutionary organization of the sailors.

Trotsky had replied with an open letter to the Presidium of the Central Executive Committee, saying that 'the opposition stepped across the decree of 20 February as a worker steps across a puddle on his way to the factory,' and it ended with a call to 'get rid of Stalin!' Shortly after this he declared in a speech that 'even at the highest level, and in the army leadership, too, there are people who are dissatisfied with Stalin and who support my appeal to get rid of him. They are not few in number.'

Now, without Tukhachevsky, there were four influential military men left, four marshals. Stalin had no doubts about Voroshilov. His whole life was based on a mythical past and depended on Stalin. Budenny was an earnest veteran and nothing more. Still, Yezhov reported that Budenny's wife had contacts with foreigners of some sort. He'd better look into it. But neither of them was capable of coming out against Stalin. But Blyukher and Yegorov, both of whom he had known since the civil war, had changed markedly. They were different. The Germans had commented on them in particular. And Voroshilov had not been satisfied with Yegorov as chief of the General Staff. Yezhov should run a check on a letter about Yegorov that Stalin had received. It read:

> In my opinion, a number of most important questions of Red Army organization and operational-strategic deployment of our armed forces have been decided wrongly and possibly in a way to cause wreckage. This could entail major failure and numerous extra losses in the first phase of war.
>
> I request you, Comrade Stalin, to check up on the activity of Marshal Yegorov as head of the General Staff, as he in fact bears responsibility for the errors committed in training for the operational-strategic deployment of our armed forces and their organizational structure.
>
> I do not know Comrade Yegorov's political past or present, but his practical activity as head of the General Staff arouses doubt.
>
> 7 November 1937
> Party member since 1912, Ya. Zhigur[63]

Yan Matisovich Zhigur was a brigade commander working in a department of the Red Army General Staff Academy. Many an honest man went off the rails because of the repeated calls for vigilance and the mayhem of lawlessness which became the norm in those nightmare years. A former ensign in the tsarist army, Zhigur had accepted the revolution and taken part in the civil war. He was twice wounded, won the Order of the Red Banner, but his letter to Stalin did not save him. He was immediately arrested and shot.

Nevertheless, Stalin told Poskrebyshev to tell Yezhov to check up on Yegorov and within a couple of months Yezhov had done his work, in the course of which one of Yegorov's former colleagues, later to become an important military leader, was compelled to write a letter. The marshal's comrade-in arms wrote:

In November 1917, at the congress of the First Army in Stokmozgof, I heard a speech by the then Right SR Lieutenant Colonel A. I. Yegorov in which he called

Comrade Lenin an adventurist and emissary of the Germans. His speech boiled down to saying that the soldiers should not trust Lenin.[64]

Although Yegorov's fate was already sealed, this letter 'confirmed' that he was a 'wrecker'. When the results of the investigation were discussed by a small group including Molotov and Voroshilov, it was decided that Yegorov be removed from the Central Committee and that his case be handed over to the NKVD, especially in the light of yet another compromising fact that came to light and that was linked with his wife.

On 28 February–2 March 1938 the members of the Central Committee were circulated with the following resolution signed by Stalin:

In view of the fact, established during eye to eye confrontation between Comrade Yegorov and the arrested conspirators, Belov, Gryaznov, Grinko, Sedyakin, that Comrade Yegorov is politically more stained than had been thought before this occasion, and taking into account that his wife, née Tseshkovskaya, with whom he is at one, has turned out to be a long-serving Polish spy, as shown by her own testimony, the Central Committee recognizes the necessity of removing Comrade Yegorov as a candidate member of the Central Committee.[65]

Again the vote was unanimous, again Stalin's voting slip was left blank.

There was still one 'doubtful' marshal left, Vasily Konstantinovich Blyukher, perhaps the most distinguished military leader of the pre-war period. He was the first to be awarded the Order of the Red Banner, of which he had four; he received the first Order of the Red Star; and one of his two Orders of Lenin was also among the first to be conferred.

Stalin had not been pleased with Blyukher during the Mongolian campaign in July-August 1938, when the Japanese seized Soviet border territory above Lake Khasan. Voroshilov had issued an order to destroy the enemy, but Blyukher, as commander of the Separate Red Banner Far Eastern Army, refused to rush headlong to carry it out, deciding instead to prepare carefully. He was summoned to the direct line to speak to Stalin. They had a brief but colourful exchange:

Stalin: 'So, Blyukher, tell me why you have ignored the Commissar of Defence's order to carry out aerial bombardment of all our territory occupied by the Japanese, including the Zaozernaya Heights?'

Blyukher: 'Reporting. The air force is ready to take off. The take-off was delayed only because of unfavourable weather conditions. This very minute I have ordered [Air Force commander] Rychagov to get the planes into the air regardless of anything, and to go into the attack. The planes are now taking off, but I'm afraid it's inevitable that we'll be hitting our own units as well as Korean settlements.'

Stalin: 'Tell me honestly, Comrade Blyukher, do you really want to fight the Japanese? If you don't, then tell me straight out, like a good Communist, but if you do want to, then I think you ought to get to the site without delay. I don't understand your concern about hitting Korean settlements, and also your fear that the air force won't be able to do its duty because of the fog. Who said you mustn't hit the Korean population during armed confrontation with the Japanese? Why worry about Koreans when our people are shooting at the Japanese? What's a bit of fog to Soviet aviation when it really wants to defend the honour of the Soviet motherland? I'm waiting for your answer.'

Blyukher: 'The air force have been ordered to take off and the first group of fighters will do so at 1120 hours. Rychagov promises to have the attack under way at 1300 hours. I will be flying out to Voroshilov [the place] with Mazepov and Bryandinsky [Air Force staffers], unless he leaves before us. We are accepting your orders and will carry them out with Bolshevik exactitude.'[66]

Mekhlis, who had been sent out to the Far East, had stirred up the leadership in Moscow with reports of the allegedly indecisive command of the Far Eastern Army, thus compromising Blyukher.

Stalin soon summoned Blyukher to Moscow, although he had no intention of talking to him. The marshal was off the job for a time and then on 22 October 1938 was arrested. The arrest order was signed by Yezhov, who within a few weeks would himself be joining the thousands he had consigned to oblivion.

Blyukher was thrown into the meatgrinder just at the moment it was slowing down. It looked at first as if he might survive. An instruction issued in November 1938 by the Council of Ministers and the Central Committee referred to crude violations of legality in the investigative process, but Beria, who was already in charge of the Blyukher case, ignored it. Blyukher was interrogated for several days, but he bravely resisted and denied being part of any 'Trotskyite-Fascist plot'. Perhaps, as he was being tortured, he recalled taking part in the kangaroo court against Tukhachevsky? He had missed the chance then to exercise his conscience to mitigate the fate of the first Soviet marshal, and now he was on the receiving end.

According to B. A. Viktorov, who also conducted this interrogation, Blyukher was last seen on 5 and 6 November, unrecognizable after having been viciously beaten. His face was a bloody pulp and one eye had been knocked out. Beria's inquisitors had probably been keen to get their grisly business over with before the big public holiday of 7 November. On 9 November, Blyukher died in Beria's dungeons as a result of the torture. He died, but he had not yielded; he had signed no monstrous lies.

The list of officers who perished is endless; they were the flower of the officer corps, with civil war experience, and most of them were relatively young. The blow to the Soviet armed forces was immense. Who would have thought that the seeds of provocation, scattered by the Gestapo, the White émigrés and inadvertently by Trotsky, would have found such fertile ground! Nearly all the defence commissar's deputies had been destroyed, most of the members of the War Council, nearly all the commanders of the military districts and the army commanders. According to available figures, in 1937–38 as many as 45 per cent of the command and political staff of the army and navy, from brigade

commander up, had perished. As Voroshilov himself reported to the War
Council at the end of November 1938, the Red Army had been 'cleansed of
more then 40,000 men ... Enormous changes have been made in the army
leadership: only ten of the original War Council membership remains.' It is not
hard to imagine the situation in the military districts.

In their report to Moscow at the beginning of March 1938, the commander
of the Kiev military district, S. K. Timoshenko, and member of the War Council,
N. S. Khrushchev, described it as a great success that about 3,000 'enemies'
had been purged from the troops of the district, of whom more than 1,000
had been arrested. Practically all corps and divisional commanders had been
replaced. 'As a result f liquidating the Trotskyite-Bukharinite elements, the
strength of the district forces has grown.'[67]

Silence and paralysis of will were not the only responses to the army purge.
Countless reports were coming in from political departments describing the
doubt, confusion and outright disbelief being expressed in the units. For
example:

Lieutenant Shkrobat, non-Party, 101st Artillery Regiment: 'I cannot believe
Stalin that Yakir and Tukhachevsky are enemies of the people.'

Red Army man Zubrov: 'Under Nicholas they couldn't hang enough people,
now they can't shoot enough. But they still won't manage to shoot everyone.'

Trushinsky, artillery school instructor: 'Maybe Stalin himself is a Trotskyist?'

Naval commander Kirillov: 'I don't believe that Bukharin and the others are
enemies of the people and socialism. They just wanted to change the party
leadership.'[68]

Such reports were usually accompanied by a note to the effect that they had
been 'copied to the NKVD for investigation'. While it is the case that many
who saw what was happening said and did nothing, there were some who
voiced their protest to the authorities. For instance, brigade commander S. P.
Kolosov wrote to defence commissar Voroshilov:

Two commanders meet in a tram. 'So, how're things? It's like a Tatar
massacre with us. They've arrested so-and-so and so-and-so ...' The other
one says, 'I'm afraid to open my mouth. Whatever you say, if you say
something wrong, you're an enemy of the people. Cowardice has become the
norm.'

Find out how many you discharged from the Red Army in 1937 and you'll
learn the bitter truth for yourself.

You can call me a scaremonger-Trotskyite-enemy-of-the-people etc. etc. I
am not an enemy, but I think we're heading up a blind alley.

5 December 1937 Kolosov[69]

Kolosov's fate is unknown to me, but his letter shows that not everyone
remained silent. Many people were aware that the army had been bled white
on the eve of a testing time, but Stalin's urge to preserve his power at any price,
even though the threat to it was purely imaginary, outweighed fundamental
concern for the country's security.

CHAPTER 32

The Stalinist Monster

The violence reached its peak at the beginning of 1938. Stalin was receiving more and more reports of the catastrophic situation in factories, on the railways, in the commissariats. The repression was proceeding under its own momentum. Arrests generated 'accomplices'; the chance for careerists to move up the ladder produced more and more denunciations, often in an act of revenge by relatives. The situation was getting out of control. In the summer of 1938 Stalin decided it was time to get rid of his functionaries and to blame them for the 'excesses' and 'abuses' and for 'exceeding their authority'. He accused the executors of his policy of every kind of sin, thinkable and unthinkable. Yezhov, whom he began to watch more closely once he had made him a candidate member of the Politburo, turned out to be a total nonentity. By this time, unfortunately, the press had created the image of him as a 'talented Chekist', 'most loyal pupil of Stalin', 'a man who can see through people'. Writing in *Pravda*, even Mikhail Koltsov could describe this degenerate as 'a wonderful unyielding Bolshevik who without getting up from his desk day and night is unravelling and cutting the threads of the Fascist conspiracy'.

Stalin quickly discovered that Yezhov was an alcoholic, utterly devoid of political flexibility and perception. He was not bothered by Yezhov's total cynicism, or his malevolence and cruelty – Yezhov often conducted interrogations himself – but he would not have weak-willed people working for him, and alcoholism was for him the hallmark of a weak will. The people around Stalin whom he appreciated, such as Molotov, Kaganovich, Zhdanov, Voroshilov, Andreyev, Khrushchev, Poskrebyshev and Mekhlis, apart from absolute loyalty to him also had to have a strong will in order to show that loyalty. To test this, and without being prompted by Yezhov or Beria who would not have dared, Stalin arrested some relatives of almost all of them. Had any of them tried to defend their families, they would have been showing intolerable political weakness. Political will meant being ready to sacrifice everything in the name of loyalty to Stalin.

So, requiring a scapegoat, Stalin picked Yezhov for the part. By September-October 1938, although Yezhov was still nominally in charge, Beria was in fact running the NKVD, as reports from Ulrikh dated October 1938 and addressed to 'Commissar of Internal Affairs Beria' suggest. Yezhov, fired as commissar on 7 December 1938, surfaced once more as Commissar of Water Transport. On 21 January 1939 he was sitting alongside Stalin for the fifteenth anniversary of Lenin's death, but after that he virtually evaporated.

He was no longer in any leading body of the party by the Eighteenth Congress in March 1939. He was arrested during a meeting at the commissariat for water transport. Two men hurriedly entered the room and stood at the door. Yezhov knew at once the end had come. He fell to his knees and begged for mercy. He was given a few weeks. It is known that he was shot but – like many thousands of his victims – when and where and on the basis of what accusations has not been established.

With Stalin's blessing, Beria was firmly in the saddle by the end of 1938. His first job was to get rid of Yezhov's staff. Such vicious men as Frinovsky, Zakovsky and Berman, who had been doing their grisly jobs since Yagoda's time, were condemned and shot, and replaced by Beria's equally vicious bunch, including Merkulov, Kobulov, Goglidze, Tsanava, Rukhadze and Kruglov.

Why did Stalin pick Lavrenti Pavlovich Beria? Had he known him well before? How did Beria become so trusted by Stalin so soon? How could such an opportunist reach the highest rungs of the ladder in so short a time, becoming a member of the Politburo, first deputy chairman of the Council of Ministers, a Marshal of the Soviet Union, a Hero of Socialist Labour?

Stalin first met him around 1929–30 while taking the cure at Tskhaltubo. Beria, as head of the Transcaucasian GPU, was responsible for ensuring Stalin's local security. They had several conversations and Beria revealed an intuitive grasp of Stalin's desires. At the beginning of his career, Beria exploited the acquaintance his wife, Nina Gegechkori, and her brother, a revolutionary, had with Sergo Ordzhonikidze. This may have helped him at first, but Ordzhonikidze soon saw through him and was extremely hostile to his promotion. Beria came up against the serious opposition of several other Old Bolsheviks. For instance, Tite Illarionovich Lordkipanidze, commissar for internal affairs for Trans-caucasia and an NKVD man since it had been the Cheka in Lenin's day, tried to open Moscow's eyes to this werewolf. Stalin, however, removed Lord-kipanidze from his post and in 1937 Beria got rid of him altogether. Beria's path to the top was strewn with such victims.

Beria impressed Stalin with his grasp and authority, his decisiveness and excellent knowledge of the situation in the Caucasian republics. It was possibly the secretary of the Transcaucasian regional party committee, L. Kartvelishvili, who had told Stalin about Beria having had links with various local nationalist movements in the civil war. Stalin was also warned about Beria's out and out careerism, but he regarded these as positive assets, for such people could always be kept on a hook. Take Vyshinsky, who, being then a Menshevik, had signed the order to arrest Lenin, issued by the Provisional Government under Kerensky in 1917. See how willing he was now! Or Mekhlis, another former Menshevik – no one was more dedicated to Stalin.

In October 1931 Stalin had arranged for Beria to be transferred to party work, as second secretary of the regional party committee, and had proposed him as first secretary only two or three months later. True, he had to transfer Kartvelishvili, Orakhelashvili, Yakovlev and Davdaryani out of the region, as they had objected to Beria's candidacy. In only a few years, Stalin saw, Beria had introduced 'order' in the Caucasus. He liked the fact that, at all the plenums of 1937–38, Beria's effective remarks and comments were in line with his own thinking and speeches, especially at the February-March 1938 plenum: 'How could you take on Vardanin when we had kicked him out of Transcaucasia?' he had hurled at Yevdokimov, secretary of the Aral-Black Sea party organ-ization. 'Why did you promote Asilov,' he went on, 'when we had already expelled him from the party?' And further, 'In carrying out Comrade Stalin's instructions on work with the cadres, we unmasked seven members of the Georgian Central Committee, two members of the Tbilisi city committee. In 1936 alone we arrested 1,050 Trotskyite-Zinovievites.'[70] His appointment as commissar came three weeks after an instruction of the Central Committee and Sovnarkom of 17 November 1938, 'On Arrests, the Directorate of Public Prosecutions and the Conduct of Interrogations'.

Following the Eighteenth Party Congress a number of wrongly condemned people were rehabilitated, but it was merely a cosmetic operation when com-pared to the total numbers: however much responsibility was put on Yezhov, to have admitted that mass acts of lawlessness had taken place would have cast a shadow on Stalin himself. And this could not be allowed to happen. Justice was done first of all to people connected with defence. Stalin knew the army had been weakened on the eve of war, and so he ordered the release of some of the officers who had not yet been broken by the NKVD, as well as a number of scientists and designers.

The madness of 1937–38 had slowed down, but the security organs were not idle. More than 23,000 NKVD men perished at the end of the 1930s, among them many who had tried and failed to put a brake on the fly-wheel of violence.

It is clear that such men as Yagoda, Yezhov, Beria, Vyshinsky and Ulrikh set an example of abuse, criminality and moral degeneracy. As for attempts to open Stalin's eyes to the true nature of his henchmen, he already knew it, as it was he who sanctioned their worst excesses. With Molotov at his side, Stalin approved some four hundred lists of names to be processed by the military tribunals alone. With a simple 'In favour' and his signature he consigned hundreds of people to oblivion at a time.

The late Marshal K. S. Moskalenko, who took part in the arrest and trial of

Beria, told me that when that degenerate was sentenced on 23 December 1953, he fell to his knees in tears, writhing and begging for mercy in the Special Office of the Supreme Court of the USSR which took place in the headquarters building of the Moscow Military District.

There is undocumented testimony that Beria intended to usurp power as Stalin grew older. Stalin may have known this, as their relations grew noticeably cooler in the last year and a half of his life. Among the many witnesses who have told me about this, most interesting was the testimony of M. S. Vlasik, wife of Lieutenant General N. S. Vlasik, former chief of the Main Administration of the Ministry of State Security (the KGB). For more than twenty-five years, Vlasik had been Stalin's chief of personal security; he knew much and was trusted by the boss. Beria hated him, but Stalin would not allow him to be touched. A few months before Stalin died, however, Beria managed to compromise Vlasik, as well as Poskrebyshev, and to have them removed from Stalin's entourage. Vlasik was arrested and given ten years' prison and exile. When he returned after Stalin's death, he said he was totally convinced that Beria had 'helped' Stalin to die after first removing his physicians. Vlasik put this in the memoirs he dictated to his wife shortly before his own death.

Whether or not Stalin died naturally, the system at that time was such that the replacement of one dictator by another was a real possibility. The leadership, however, finally found the courage and the perspicacity to render the monster harmless. An important part in this was played by the realization that Beria might well set about getting rid of most of them. His only close relations were with Malenkov. As Marshal Moskalenko told me, Beria's trial took place in the office of a member of the Moscow Military District, while Malenkov, Khrushchev, Molotov, Voroshilov, Bulganin, Kaganovich, Mikoyan, Shvernik and some others sat in the Kremlin and listened to it on a specially installed link.

Stalin had turned a deaf ear to warnings about Beria's evil character; this murderer suited his purposes. At one of the 1937 plenums, the Commissar of Health, Kaminsky, tried to reveal Beria's true face and was arrested and shot soon after the meeting. Kedrov, an Old Bolshevik, made a similar attempt with the same result, the charge against him being fabricated after his execution. The man whose job called for his utmost dedication to the law and nothing but the law, was in fact the very embodiment of lawlessness and arbitrary rule. Nothing was sacred to Beria. He worshipped only violence. He often gratified his sadistic needs by conducting interrogations himself, many of them ending in tragedy. Yet he apparently loved music and was said to have a unique collection of classical records; a Rachmaninov prelude would bring tears to his eyes. Stalin, who was apparently an ascetic and puritan, could not but know that Beria was also a disgusting pervert. Beria's chief of personal security, Colonel Nadoraya, would bring him any young girl who took his fancy, and the slightest resistance would bring tragic consequences for both the girl and her family.

Ye. P. Pitovranov, who had worked in the NKVD since before the war and who after it became chief of administration and deputy commissar, told me that he had survived only because he was imprisoned for being 'soft on enemies of the people'. According to him, Beria was not only absolutely immoral, he was also absolutely apolitical. Pitovranov thought Beria did not understand Marxism at all and knew none of Lenin's works. Politics meant nothing; only power over other people mattered to him. It was hard to understand how he stayed on top for as long as he did, given how much Stalin had on him. Perhaps with Beria, Stalin felt a special 'chemistry' that would not be so easy to find in a replacement?

For his part, Beria liked to demonstrate his special relationship with Stalin in front of the other members of the entourage, often exchanging remarks in Georgian which only aggravated their paranoid fear of the monster. What could the two be saying? Was it about one of them?

During the war Stalin gave Beria's ministry the task of rebuilding bridges, laying railway branch lines, sinking mine-shafts, all of it done, of course, by slave labour in record time. Beria's 'wartime action' consisted of two trips to the Caucasus as a member of the State Defence Committee. The first time was in August 1942, the second in March 1943. The documents show that even then, in Stalin's name he was getting rid of people who were of no use to him, ordering executions and putting fear into the military. He was accompanied by Kobulov, Mamulov, Milshtein, Piyashev, Tsanava, Rukhadze, Vlodzimirsky and Karanadze. He created an atmosphere of tension, nervousness, suspiciousness and mutual denunciation at the various headquarters. Feeble protests to Stalin from local commanders were ignored in Moscow. Beria's very presence paralysed the generals' ability to think creatively, as no one wished to be his next victim. When he left with his large retinue, everyone heaved a sigh of relief.

Beria was powerful not merely because he operated the punitive machinery, but also because he controlled the vast system of the Gulag. When the Americans dropped the atom bombs on Hiroshima and Nagasaki, Stalin ordered that Soviet atomic research be speeded up and entrusted Beria with the general management of the work. With the help of his obedient underlings, and with Stalin's approval, he set up scientific and technical laboratories inside the prison camps. The fact that the Soviet atom bomb was invented in a very short time was not of course due to Beria. The unfettered mind working in normal conditions would no doubt have solved the problem a great deal faster.

Beria's cruelty knew no bounds. Thousands of appeals went unheeded. One example is the following letter written to him in February 1944:

From prisoner Alexandra Ivanovna Gerasimova, Temnikov Corrective Labour Camp.
    I was sentenced in 1937 to eight years. I am answering for my husband V. I. Gerasimov [former deputy commissar of internal affairs of Azerbaidzhan

who had been shot]. I don't know what he was guilty of to this day. I lived with him for twelve years and knew him to be an honest, hardworking man who was dedicated to the party and the country. I feel I am myself absolutely innocent. I have never committed any crime even in my thoughts. I had worked from the age of sixteen up to my arrest.

The day of my arrest I left my two babies with my mother who is entirely without means of support. The children are growing up. They need a mother and a mother's help.

I beg you to look into my case and to give me the right to live with my children, to work and bring them up. I have been living all these years in the camps and I have kept the belief that truth and justice would conquer lies and injustice in our country. That belief gave me the strength to survive being parted from my babies.

Attached to the letter is a note from detective Lyubimov of the Azerbaidzhan NKVD who had handled the 'case': 'She confessed nothing. A special session in 1939 left the sentence in force.'[71] Beria simply confirmed the sentence without taking further action.

CHAPTER 33

Guilt Without Forgiveness

Neither orally nor in writing did Stalin ever call publicly for the repressions of 1937–38 to be intensified. Even the speech he gave at the February-March 1937 plenum, published in abridged form in *Pravda*, amounted only to a call for greater vigilance against the danger of Trotskyism and so on. This, and the other speeches at the same plenum, created an oppressive atmosphere when they were published, but Stalin as it were directed the proceedings from backstage. His signature can be found on many dossiers of arrested 'enemies of the people'. For instance, he edited the resolution on Yezhov's report to the February-March 1937 plenum, including the following points:

b We note the poor state of investigative work. Investigations often depend on the criminal and his goodwill as to whether or not he will give exhaustive testimony.

c The system that has been created for enemies of the Soviet régime is intolerable. Their accommodation often resembles compulsory nursing homes more than prison (they write letters, receive parcels and so on).[72]

The NKVD was ordered to deal with such shortcomings at once, and it is not hard to imagine how they accomplished this.

Even after the 1938 instruction which led to a certain cooling off, Stalin ordered that any cases still open should be completed. Instead of a calm and rational review, followed by the release of the innocent, with apologies, the last waves of arrests swept more and more people into the prisons and camps. In a major report to Stalin dated 16 March 1939, Ulrikh wrote:

From 24 February to 14 March 1939 the military collegium of the Supreme Court of the USSR in Moscow held closed trials of 436 persons. 413 were sentenced to be shot. Sentences were on the basis of the Law of 1 December 1934.

The following confessed their complete guilt: S. V. Kosior, V. Ya. Chubar, P. P. Postyshev, A. V. Kosarev, P. A. Vershkov, A. I. Yegorov, I. F. Fedko, L. M. Khakhanyan, A. V. Bakulin, B. D. Berman, N. D. Berman, A. L. Gilinsky, K. V. Gei,

P. A. Smirnov [former Navy Commissar], M. P. Smirnov [former Trade Commissar] and others.

In court some of the accused denied the testimony given during the preliminary investigation, but they were completely exposed by other evidence.[73]

The memorandum states that A. I. Yegorov confessed and was sentenced. This was false. Yegorov did not confess and he died under interrogation.

Stalin recalled that, in July 1938 following the canvassing of members and candidates of the Central Committee, Vlas Yakovlevich Chubar was removed as a candidate member of the Politburo, which he had been since the Fifteenth Congress. He had written a long analytical memorandum to Stalin about improving the defence industry. Stalin had read it carefully, noting the business-like tone of its arguments and proposals, but the end of the letter was not to his liking. Chubar wrote:

I was preparing to report all these considerations, but again things got out of hand, and again through no fault of my own. It is offensive and painful to admit that, because of the torrent of slander and intrigue created by enemies of the people, I have had to leave the job, but, wherever you choose to send me to work I will always and everywhere struggle honestly and in good conscience for the cause, for the flourishing of the USSR and for Communism.[74]

Stalin evidently thought Chubar was up to something and passed the letter on to Yezhov. When he read Ulrikh's report on the execution of Chubar and the others, he calmly put it aside and turned his attention to a request from M. Mitin and P. Pospelov that they be permitted to write a *Short Biography of I. V. Stalin*.

E. P. Pitovranov confirmed that it was hopeless trying to move Stalin to pity:

When I was imprisoned for being 'soft on enemies of the people', I told myself it was all over. No senior member of the NKVD, once arrested, ever came out of Lefortovo alive. I shared a cell with L. Sheinin, the investigator who later became a writer. As I sat waiting day after day for the axe to fall, I also struggled painfully to think of a way out. And, as it happens, I succeeded. I asked for a sheet of paper and wrote a letter to Stalin. As the head of one of the main NKVD offices I had met him several times at receptions. I asked for nothing, neither leniency nor mercy. I only wrote that I had some important ideas for improving our intelligence service. I managed to get the head of the prison to come to my cell and I said to him: 'They know about this letter "up there", so if you don't make sure it gets into the right hands, it'll be the worse for you.'

I learned later that Stalin was told about the letter. He rang my office and asked them why I was inside. They told him. After a pause, he snapped 'Put him back on the job. He seems to be a clever man.' A few days later I was suddenly released. It had only taken a few words from Stalin, but I knew I had succeeded in playing on the psychology of the dictator: I hadn't begged for mercy, like the rest, and I had put forward some new ideas.

But what had worked for Pitovranov had not worked for Chubar, nor for many others. For instance, Eikhe wrote to Stalin:

I come now to the most humiliating time in my life, my genuinely serious guilt before the party and before you. I am guilty of confessing to counter-revolutionary activity. But this was the position: I couldn't take the torture being inflicted on me by Ushakov and Nikolaev, especially the former. He knew my broken ribs hadn't healed and he used this knowledge to inflict appalling pain during the interrogation, and I was forced to betray myself and others.

I ask you, I beg you to look again at my case not to spare me but to expose the whole rotten provocation which like a snake has ensnared so many people because of my weakness and criminal slander. I have never betrayed you or the party. I know I shall perish because of a rotten, mean provocation fabricated against me by enemies of the party and the people.[75]

The letter echoed with the agony of inescapable death, but also of faint hope. Reading Eikhe's letter, Stalin knew that it was he, the first man in the party and state, who had released the snake of provocation. He did not even consult other members of the Politburo. Once he had given the order for Eikhe's arrest, the die had been cast. He never changed his mind.

Stalin was also shown Rudzutak's statement at his trial – a trial, be it noted, that lasted all of twenty minutes:

My only request to the court is that it notify the Central Committee that there still exists in the NKVD a centre which cleverly fabricates cases and forces innocent people to confess to crimes which they did not commit; the accused are not given the chance to prove that they had no part in the crimes that are mentioned in confessions that have been obtained under torture. The methods used are such that people have to lie and slander the innocent.[76]

Rudzutak requested a meeting with Stalin, who replied with crude abuse. He did not forget that Rudzutak had visited him in May 1937, on the eve of his arrest. He had paid no attention to what Rudzutak had to say, but instead tried to detect whether Yezhov's warning that Rudzutak had been recruited by foreign intelligence at the Genoa conference of 1922 had any validity.

That evening, when signing the Soviet government's welcome to the North Pole expedition, Stalin spotted Rudzutak's signature among the others and, after only a moment's hesitation, ran his pencil through it. The next day, 24 May 1937, he dictated the text of a memorandum to be circulated to Central Committee members. It stated that the NKVD had incontrovertible proof that Tukhachevsky and Rudzutak were German-Fascist spies. Tukhachevsky had two weeks to live, Rudzutak about a year.

Countless documents attest to Stalin's monstrous lack of pity. On a note from Yezhov attached to lists of people awaiting trial by military collegium for capital crimes, Stalin scribbled briefly, 'Shoot all 138 of them', and Molotov added his signature. Or on Yezhov's request for the execution by shooting of four lists of 313 and 208 male and fifteen female enemies of the people, and 200 military personnel, Stalin wrote, 'In favour,' and both he and Molotov signed.[77] On 12 December 1938 Stalin and Molotov sanctioned the shooting of 3,167 people.[78]

The impact of all this inhumanity on the lives of ordinary people has been well described elsewhere, in both Western and Soviet publications. I have received countless letters from Soviet citizens describing their suffering. I will cite just two, the first from Vera Ivanovna Deryuchina, who is nearly ninety, from Belaya Tserkva:

When they came for my husband, who was a miner, a Stakhanovite who had done four shifts, I thought it must be a mistake. They said, 'Don't howl, you silly fool. Your husband will be back in an hour.' But it was twelve years before he came back. And he was crippled. And what I went through with small children and an aged mother, I couldn't describe. They threw us out of the apartment. Everywhere they branded us the family of an enemy of the people. We would all have perished if it hadn't been for good people. Mention my story somewhere in a corner of your book.

And another from a Muscovite, Stepan Ivanovich Semenov, who spent fifteen years in the camps. Two of his brothers were shot and his wife died in prison. He is now an old man without children or grandchildren. He wrote:

The worst thing is when you have no one waiting for you, when no one needs you. I and my brothers might have had children and grandchildren, families. The accursed Tamerlaine smashed and trampled everything. He took the future away from citizens who were not yet born. He didn't allow them to be born because he killed their mothers and fathers. I'm living out my life alone and I still can't understand how it was we didn't see that our 'leader' was a monster, how the people could let it happen?

We all remember Stalin from the photographs, the statues and monuments in which he was often depicted with one arm raised, pointing out the way, with a warm smile and a twinkle in his eyes. Few could imagine the depth of pathological cruelty, the lack of pity, the cunning that lurked behind the façade. Besides the political and other leaders and the anonymous millions who suffered at his hands, his own relatives did not escape his insanity. One of the most careful researchers of the life of Stalin, V. V. Nefedov, has discovered much about the fate of the tyrant's family. On his first wife's side – that is, Ekaterina Semenovna Svanidze – the following suffered:

1 Alexander Semenovich Svanidze, Ekaterina's brother. A party member since 1904, he was commissar of finance in Georgia and then until 1937 worked in the USSR commissariat of finance. One of Stalin's closest friends, he was accused of espionage and shot.
2 Maria Anisimovna Svanidze, Alexander's wife. An opera singer, she was arrested in 1937 and given ten years' prison. She died in camp.

3 Ivan Alexandrovich Svanidze, son of Alexander. Arrested as a 'son of an enemy of the people', he returned from exile in 1956.
4 Maria Semenovna Svanidze, Ekaterina's sister. She was A. S. Yenukidze's personal secretary 1927–34. Arrested in 1937, she died in prison.
5 Iyulia Isaakovna (Meltser) Dzhugashvili, the wife of Stalin's son, Yakov, she was arrested and released in 1943.

On his second wife's side, that is Nadezhda Sergeyevna Alliluyeva:

1 Anna Sergeyevna (Alliluyeva) Redens, Nadezhda's sister, was arrested in 1948, given ten years for 'espionage' and released in 1954.
2 Stanislav Frantsevich Redens, Anna's husband, was commissar for internal affairs of Transcaucasia and Kazakhstan, a delegate at the Fifteenth, Sixteenth and Seventeenth Party Congresses, a member of Central Control Commission and Central Revision Commission. He was arrested as an 'enemy of the people' in 1938 and shot in 1941.
3 Ksenia Alexandrovna Alliluyeva, the wife of Nadezhda's brother, Pavel, was arrested in 1947 and released in 1954.
4 Evgenia Alexandrovna Alliluyeva, the wife of Nadezhda's uncle, P. Ya. Alliluyev, was sentenced to ten years in 1948 for 'espionage' and released in 1954.
5 Ivan Pavlovich Alliluyev (Altaisky), the son of P. Ya. Alliluyev. A party member since 1920, and editor of the journal *Sotsialisticheskoe zemledelie* ('Socialist Agriculture'), he was arrested in 1938 and sentenced to five years. He was released in 1940 with the help of S. Ya. Alliluyev, Stalin's father-in-law.

The notes of Ivan Alliluyev have survived. He was sentenced for 'membership of a counter-revolutionary organization' and served time in the 'Sorok-lager'. He describes his fellow inmates: brigade commander Kholodkov, head of a Moscow military district administration called Lapidus, a naive lad called Zhilu who had become 'an enemy of the people' because he had once sat next to Kosarev on the platform of a Komsomol meeting in the Ukraine. It later emerged that Stalin's aged father-in-law decided to help Ivan, but couldn't get up enough nerve to ask Stalin, so approached Beria and Kobulov instead, and, probably for the only time, Beria was merciful.

Stalin showed no partiality in his cruelty: everyone was dealt with equally and he showed no interest in people once they had been 'exposed'. Possibly with one exception. When he was informed that Alexander Svanidze, his wife's brother, had been sentenced to death as a German spy, he snapped, 'Let him ask for forgiveness.' Before the execution, Alexander was told what Stalin had said, to which he replied, 'What is there to be forgiven for? I haven't committed any crime.' He was duly shot. When Stalin heard how his childhood friend and brother-in-law had died, he said, 'See how obstinate he was; he'd rather die than ask for forgiveness.'

7

ON THE THRESHOLD OF WAR

'The greatest mistake is to imagine we never err.'
– Thomas Carlyle

CHAPTER 34

Political Manoeuvring

It was a dark winter's night in 1939. Labouring Moscow was asleep. The only dim lights to be seen came through the shuttered windows of commissariat buildings, the General Staff or the vast monolith of the Lubyanka. Politburo members, commissars and military leaders were burning the midnight oil, as usual. The custom of working late had come about gradually. Stalin already had the habit of not going home until midnight, but as the international situation worsened he would stay on at the office until two or three in the morning, or even later. As for the NKVD, the night was virtually their normal working time.

Stalin was going over the speech he was to make at the Eighteenth Party Congress which the January plenum had decided should take place on 10 March 1939. The original draft of the speech, compiled by the Central Committee apparatus, was now unrecognizable. Stalin rewrote dozens of pages anew. He wanted to convey two main ideas. First, that the world was on the eve of new convulsions. The system of post-war treaties was going to be destroyed. The clouds of a new world war were lowering on the horizon; 'a new imperialist war has become a fact', as he put it. Secondly, he wanted to emphasise the successes of socialism. In his view, the country had become stronger by smashing the 'capitulationists and wreckers'. After reading several pages of statistics, he wrote:

We have overtaken the main capitalist countries in production technology and the rate of industrial development. That is very good. But it is not enough. We must also overtake them in the economic sense. We can do it and we must do it. We must build new factories. We must forge new cadres for industry. But that takes time, and a lot of it. We cannot overtake the main capitalist countries economically in two or three years. It will take more time.[1]

He then called in Poskrebyshev and asked for the list of delegates of the last congress and the names of those who had been elected to the Central Committee. Opening the thin file, he found that perhaps more than half the names were well known to him, some from his days at the commissariat for nationalities, others from the collectivization and so on. He knew practically all the army delegates. He looked further down the list and underlined the names of former members and candidate members of the Politburo: Rudzutak, Kosior, Chubar, Postyshev. He was glad to be rid of them, with all their urgings to look into the NKVD and 'its nest of provocateurs'.

He noticed as he leafed through the files that most of the names were followed by the pencilled initials 'vn', inserted by Poskrebyshev, sometimes with a date. He realized that the date indicated when sentence, usually death, had been carried out, and gradually it dawned on him that 'vn' meant 'enemy of the people'.* He wondered who was left, but felt reassured when he recalled that three out of ten delegates at the Seventeenth Congress had voted against him.

Next day he said to Malenkov, 'I think we're well and truly rid of the opposition millstone. We need new forces, new people in the party.' That was an understatement. Since the Seventeenth Congress the party had shrunk by 330,000 members. Now it needed a new, young Stalinist generation of replacements. In 1939 more than one million applications to join would be accepted. It was becoming a Stalinist party.

Returning to his report, he added two paragraphs:

Some people in the western media are claiming that the purge of spies, murderers and wreckers from Soviet institutions – of the likes of Trotsky, Zinoviev, Kamenev, Yakir, Tukhachevsky, Rozengolts, Bukharin and other scum – has 'shaken' the Soviet system and brought disintegration. Such cheap gossip merits only our contempt.

In 1937 Tukhachevsky, Yakir, Uborevich and other scum were executed. Then elections to the Supreme Soviet of the USSR were held. The Soviet government received 98.6 per cent of all the votes. At the beginning of 1938 Rozengolts, Rykov, Bukharin and other scum were executed. Then the elections for the Supreme Soviets of the Union republics took place. The Soviet government received 99.4 per cent of votes. So, where are the signs of this 'disintegration' and why didn't they show in the election results?[2]

Despite the obviously weakened state of the party and the liquidation of its intellectual element, along with the technical and military cadres, Stalin continued to claim, as he said at the Eighteenth Congress, that the 'liquidation of the Trotskyites and other double dealers' would be justified in the long run.

From early 1939, in any case, he devoted his main concern to foreign affairs. With good reason, he did not regard the Second World War as having begun on 1 September 1939 with Hitler's invasion of Poland. Japan had already been fighting in Korea; Italy had invaded Ethiopia and Albania, the Germans and

* 'vrag naroda' in Russian.

Italians had intervened against Republican Spain, Germany had annexed Austria and, literally on the day the Eighteenth Congress opened, occupied Czechoslovakia. The conflagration was taking hold on all sides. Stalin asked why so many states were systematically making concessions to the aggressors, and answered his own question: 'The main reason is because most of the non-aggressive countries, above all England and France, do not subscribe to collective security and collective resistance to the aggressors, and have moved from a position of non-intervention to one of "neutrality".'[3]

Hearing the news, during the Eighteenth Congress, that Germany had seized the Lithuanian province of Memel, and that President Hacha of Czechoslovakia had signed the Berlin Pact which signalled the liquidation of Czechoslovak statehood, Stalin ordered foreign commissar Litvinov to send a note to Berlin via Schulenburg, the German ambassador to Moscow, condemning the German actions in strong terms and bringing to the German leaders' attention the fact that 'the Soviet government cannot recognize the inclusion of the Czech lands in the German empire, nor that of Slovakia in any form.'[4]

In conditions of a world conflict it was essential to have a strategy that would allow the USSR to continue its plans for developing the country socially and economically while also guaranteeing it a secure defence. According to Stalin, the advocates of non-intervention were 'playing a big and dangerous game'. The USSR was compelled to take part in these political manoeuvres with no definite aim in sight. The question usually discussed, on several occasions with Litvinov present, was what line to take. The honeymoon period of the popular fronts in Europe was over. The continent seemed to go quiet in anticipation of Hitler's hordes. Franco triumphed in Spain and the Marxist parties, many of them either smashed or in hiding, looked expectantly to Moscow. But Comintern's influence had dwindled, thanks to Stalin.

By identifying the policy of the party with that of Comintern and imposing his diktat on the international body of communists, Stalin had discredited that body. Comintern and its sister organizations, the Communist Youth International, the Trade Union International and the International Labour Relief Committee, were decimated by the criminal repressions of 1937–38. The leaders of the communist parties of Austria, Hungary, Germany, Latvia, Lithuania, Poland, Romania, Finland, Estonia and Yugoslavia, who had been banned in their own countries and had sought asylum in Moscow, were particularly hard hit. The list of victims is long, but some of them must be mentioned: the German leaders H. Remmele, H. Eberlein, H. Neumann; the Poles E. Pruchniak, J. Lenski, M. Koszutska; the Greek general secretary A. Kontas; the Iranian A. Sultan-Zade; the Yugoslavs M. Gorkič, V. Ćopić, M. Filippović; the Finns E. Hülling, A. Shotman and G. Rovio; Lenin's Swiss friend Fritz Platten; the Hungarians Bela Kun and L. Gavro; the Bulgarian P. Avramov.

Stalin was especially cynical in his treatment of the Polish Communist Party, whose leadership he virtually wiped out entirely. The last member of the Politburo of the Polish party, Bielewski, was arrested in September 1937. While the archives appear to contain no documentary proof, it seems from secondary evidence that when Stalin was shown the draft of the Comintern decree abolishing the Polish party because 'agents of Polish Fascism were at work in it', his response was most eloquent: 'It should have been done two years ago. It should be abolished but I don't think there's any need to mention it to the press.' The decree was in fact not even discussed by a full session of the Comintern Executive Committee, only six of whose nineteen members were balloted.

By making the Comintern organization an arm of his own apparatus, Stalin brought about a sharp increase in its repressive methods which in turn greatly weakened its hold over the masses and thus palpably enhanced the rise of Fascism. As for social democracy, Stalin placed it on the same level as Fascism. At any rate, he blamed the decline of the revolutionary wave in the West on the 'reformism' and 'betrayal' of the social democrats. This was another mistake which was to have serious consequences and stemmed from deep roots. We must return briefly to the 1920s.

In January 1924, just before Lenin's death, a Central Committee plenum took place at which, among other things, Zinoviev's report on the international situation was discussed. In criticizing Radek for mistakes over the 'German question', Stalin formulated the profoundly fallacious idea, which gradually became embedded in Comintern thinking, that social democracy was the main enemy of the labour and Communist movement, that it provided a base for Fascism and must be fought to the death.[5] He clung to this idea and thus, instead of uniting the working class for the struggle against Hitler, Stalin turned the Communist Party against the social democrats and weakened the resistance to Fascism, which was the real threat to the labour and the Communist movement.

To return to 1939, Stalin took notice perhaps only of the views on international affairs of Molotov among those of his entourage. Only Molotov, he thought, had the right combination of flexibility and staunchness and it was with Molotov that he formulated the positions to be put forward at the Eighteenth Congress. Just a few hours before the congress opened Stalin redrafted four points which expressed two closely related ideas.

First, that the search for peaceful ways to avert or at least delay the outbreak of war should be continued, essentially through applying the Soviet plan for collective security in Europe. A broad anti-Soviet front should not be allowed to form. Maximum vigilance should be observed and enemy provocations averted.

Secondly, all necessary and even extreme measures should be taken to prepare the country's defence, above all the battle-readiness of the Red Army and Navy. (Questions of strengthening defence further would be discussed at the Eighteenth Party Conference in February 1941.)

Stalin was preoccupied with the question of improving the country's foreign policy agencies by maximizing diplomatic opportunities. Litvinov, who had ideas of his own, was not to Stalin's taste, and soon after the May Day festivities of 1939, Beria turned his attention to Litvinov. Signs of an imminent arrest appeared: a vacuum was created around him, he was not invited to important meetings, the NKVD paid nocturnal 'visits' to his assistants and relations, and he was removed from the Central Committee, The worst seemed at hand. His files were sealed in the commissariat. The NKVD scrutinized the notes he made in his diplomatic diaries. Among them was one of his latest reports to Stalin, which read:

I enclose an account of my conversation today with the English ambassador and a translation of the English draft declaration ... It only calls for a consultative meeting, i. e. the very thing we are proposing. The impression is that a new pact of the four, excluding Germany and Italy, will have some political importance. I don't think Beck* will agree to sign even this declaration.[6]

Litvinov was hoping to form an anti-Fascist alliance with the Western democracies. In a letter of March 1939 to Ya. Z. Surits, the Soviet pleni-potentiary to France, he reported that 'we have given our direct agreement to the direct proposal for a declaration by the four ... We have decided for ourselves not to sign it without Poland.' Poland's reply, he concluded, was, however, 'sufficiently definite for us to see it was negative'.[7] Besides offering the best protection against a world war, Litvinov also believed that an alliance between the USSR and the Western democracies would protect the small states that were about to be swallowed up by Nazi Germany. After receiving Baltrushaitis, the Lithuanian envoy to Moscow, Litvinov wrote in his diary that the envoy had brought him a copy of the German–Lithuanian agreement on Memel and reported on the details. Ribbentrop had been extremely rude to the Lithuanian foreign minister, Ju. Urbshis, handing him the draft and demanding an immediate signature. When Urbshis protested, Ribbentrop declared that the city of 'Kovno [Kaunas] would be razed to the ground if the agreement was not signed at once, and the Germans had everything ready to carry this out. Ribbentrop finally agreed to let Urbshis go to Kovno on condition he return immediately with the treaty signed.'[8]

Since Litvinov was of Jewish origin – his original name was Vallakh – it must have been obvious to Stalin that his Foreign Commissar could have absolutely no trust in Hitler and that he would continue to insist on an alliance with the Western democracies. In these circumstances, Stalin could not trust him and indeed he told Beria to keep an eye on the commissar but, perhaps on a tyrant's whim, ordered that nothing worse was to be done. Since there is no documentary evidence, Stalin must have given oral instructions that Lit-vinov be demoted and replaced by Molotov, a 'true' Russian. In Berlin Litvinov's removal was indeed interpreted as a 'good sign'. The Soviet temporary envoy to Berlin, G. A. Astakhov, reported to Moscow that the Germans now saw a

* Colonel Jozef Beck, Polish foreign minister.

chance to improve relations with the USSR: 'The preconditions for this were strengthened by Litvinov's departure.'[9] Stalin thought that by putting the notional second man in the state into that post he was showing the world the importance the USSR attached to foreign affairs. Perhaps, also, the Russian Molotov was more palatable to Hitler than the Jewish Litvinov, and vice versa. The documents are, however, silent about this assumption.

In 1938, when Hitler was preparing to swallow up Czechoslovakia, Stalin ordered Litvinov on several occasions (in March, April, May, June and August) to seek ways and means of publicizing the Soviet Union's readiness to defend that country. On 20 September Moscow replied positively to a request from Prague as to whether the USSR was able and willing to defend Czechoslovakia from impending invasion.[10] The defence commissar signed an order for troops to regroup in the Kiev military district, while in the Belorussian special military district operational troop movements were carried out in order to effect an appropriate regrouping. The fortified districts and anti-aircraft defence were placed on combat readiness. At the end of September Chief of General Staff B. M. Shaposhnikov sent a telegram to the Western military districts: 'Red Army men and junior officers who have served their allotted time in the Army are not to be discharged until specially notified.'[11] Partial mobilization was introduced in a number of districts. More than seventy divisions were placed on combat readiness. Then the Munich agreement was signed and Stalin realized that the fear of the 'Communist contagion' was greater than the voice of reason. And he was right.

Under British and French pressure, the Czech government capitulated to Hitler, France virtually reneging on her agreement with the Czechs. In these circumstances, Stalin reasoned, it was crucially important not to allow the imperialist states to form a bloc against the Soviet Union. First Litvinov, then Molotov, was instructed to explore ways of disrupting the imperialist deal against the USSR. Stalin was very worried about what was contained in the Munich deal, the Anglo-German declaration of non-aggression signed in September 1938 and the similar Franco-German agreement signed in December. These understandings in effect gave Hitler a free hand in the east and could form the basis of an anti-Soviet alliance. Stalin knew that if this happened it would be hard to imagine a worse position for the country.

Even before the Eighteenth Congress Stalin had ordered his foreign commissar to approach Britain and France with a proposal to begin tripartite talks to seek ways of curtailing further Nazi aggression. With the intention of putting pressure on Hitler, Britain and France agreed, but their real intentions emerged very soon. Numerous sources indicate that London and Paris wanted above all to direct Hitler's aggression eastwards, and they listened reluctantly to the Soviet proposal for a 'defensive rampart'. Litvinov wrote to I. M. Maisky, the Soviet envoy in London: 'Hitler is giving the appearance for the time being that he doesn't understand the British and French hints about freedom of movement in the east, but maybe he will understand if Britain and France add something more than hints to their proposals.'[12]

The diaries of Molotov and his assistant, V. P. Potemkin, both of whom had frequent meetings with the British and French ambassadors, William Seeds and P. Naggiar respectively, show that in general terms these diplomats did not rule out the possibility of a military alliance with the USSR, but they plainly declined to discuss concrete issues. They repeatedly asked if Litvinov's departure as foreign commissar signalled a change in Soviet foreign policy.[13] During a conversation on 11 May 1939, G. Pailliard, the French temporary chargé d'affaires, asked Molotov:

'Will Soviet policy be the same as it was under Litvinov?'

'Yes,' Molotov replied. 'Changes occur more often in the French and British governments without causing special difficulties.'

'May we assume that the article in *Izvestiya*, entitled "On the International Situation", expresses the government's opinion?'

'It is the opinion of the newspaper. *Izvestiya* is the organ of the soviets of workers' deputies which are local organs. *Izvestiya* should not be regarded as official.'[14] Such was Molotov's cynicism.

Officially he did not depart from Litvinov's line, but acute observers knew that Germany now had a better chance of preventing an alliance from being formed between the USSR and the Western democracies, and indeed Germany did everything to exploit it. On the eve of the tripartite talks, Schulenburg obtained a meeting with Molotov and told him in rather sharp terms that the USSR and Germany had no political differences and that there was every possibility of reconciling their mutual interests peacefully. Molotov, as yet uncertain as to how the tripartite talks would go, replied evasively that 'the Soviet government is favourable towards the German government's attempts to improve relations.'[15] The British and French missions then arrived in Moscow and Stalin approved the line the Soviet delegation was to take in the talks.

At the beginning of August 1939, Beria's team prepared exhaustive dossiers on the members of the British and French military missions, including Drax, Barnett, Heywood, Doumenc, Valin and Vuillaume. It turned out that Drax had recently been made naval adjutant to the king and held the tsarist Order of St Stanislav; Doumenc would become a member of the French supreme defence council in November and was a specialist on the mechanization of the army, but had never dabbled in politics.[16] Stalin was not interested in such information, but he quickly saw that, apart from a few generals, most of the delegates were relatively junior officers. He told Molotov and Beria:

'They're not being serious. These people can't have the proper authority. London and Paris are playing poker again, but we would like to know if they are capable of carrying out European manoeuvres.'

'Still, I think the talks should go ahead,' Molotov said, looking him in the eye.

'Well, if they must, they must,' Stalin concluded blandly.

As the talks between the three military delegations* progressed, the real picture soon emerged. The Western powers did not want to extend their guarantees to the Baltic states. Moreover, they were facilitating the rapprochement of the latter with Germany. While the talks were in progress, Hitler was imposing his conditions on Latvia and Estonia. Under Admiral Horthy, Hungary began taking a hostile line towards the USSR. The Polish government's policy remained virtually unchanged. In talks with Hitler in January 1939, Colonel Beck had stated that 'Poland attributes no significance to the so-called systems of security' which were now bankrupt. Ribbentrop replied that Berlin hoped that 'Poland will take up an even more pronounced anti-Soviet position, otherwise we are not likely to have common interests'.[17] It is now known that King Carol II of Romania, during a secret visit to Germany, told Hitler that 'Romania is predisposed against Russia but cannot say so openly because we are neighbours. However, Romania will never allow the passage of Russian troops, although it is often asserted that she is supposed to have promised Russia to allow her troops in. That is not the case.'[18]

As head of the Soviet delegation, Voroshilov had his orders, approved by Stalin on 4 August, headed 'Considerations for the Talks with Britain and France', naming Germany as the main aggressor and itemizing five situations 'in which our forces might move'. The defence and foreign commissariats had worked out precisely how many tanks, artillery, aircraft and divisions the USSR, Britain and France would have to deploy, 'depending on the scenario', and they envisaged the direction of the main strikes, the order of coordinating military action and so on. The USSR was prepared to deploy 120 infantry divisions:

In the event of an attack on us by the chief aggressor we must demand the deployment by Britain and France of 86 infantry regiments, their decisive advance by the sixteenth day of mobilization, the most active participation in the Polish war and equally the unrestricted passage of our troops and rolling stock through the territory of the Vilna† corridor and Galicia. The scenario in which the chief aggressor might attack the USSR would involve the use by Germany of Finnish, Estonian and Latvian, and possibly Romanian territory.[19]

It became clear early in the talks, however, that the Western missions had come to Moscow mainly to air their general views and to inform London and Paris about 'Moscow's large-scale plans', not in order to hammer out a concrete and workable agreement.

Stalin nevertheless felt the need to approach Britain and France once again with a definite proposal for a five- or ten-year agreement on mutual assistance, including military obligations. In essence it meant that, in case of aggression against any of the signatories, the others were obliged to render assistance.

---

* The Soviet side comprised K. Ye. Voroshilov, N. G. Kuznetsov, A. D. Loktyonov, I. V. Smorodinov, B. M. Shaposhnikov.
† Vilna is the Russian form of Wilno in Polish and Vilnius in Lithuanian.

The USSR defined precisely the countries between the Baltic and Black Sea it had in mind. London and Paris gave no answer. Stalin sent messages to hurry them up, but the Western representatives had no authority to take such important decisions. As Stalin learned, his negotiating partners were, moreover, simultaneously continuing their secret efforts to reach an acceptable understanding with Hitler. It was clear that Britain and France were simply playing for time while seeking the most favourable outcome from their own point of view and without regard for Soviet interests. In effect, the Western powers offered no concrete ideas for joint action against Germany. Their intention was plainly to let the USSR play the chief part in resisting possible German aggression without giving guarantees that they would share a proportion of the burden.

Stalin lost patience. As a rule he got where he wanted by taking small, sure steps, but now he behaved like a chess-player who is running out of time. He put the lid on the tripartite talks when on the morning of 20 August Voroshilov showed him a note from Admiral Drax who, like his French counterpart, had been asked for an early reply to the Soviet proposals. Drax wrote:

Dear Marshal Voroshilov,

It is with regret that I have to inform you that the British and French delegations have up to this time received no reply in respect of the political question which you asked us to transmit to our governments.

In view of the fact that I must preside at the next session, I suggest we meet at 10 a.m. on 23 August, or earlier if a reply is received before then.

Yours sincerely

Drax, Admiral, Head of British Delegation.[20]

'Enough of these games,' Stalin snapped irritably. At that moment he can hardly have thought a meeting would take place on 23 August. But it did, though with totally different participants. Meetings with members of the Politburo, military men and diplomats were taking place every day in Stalin's commodious Kremlin office. By the end of the summer of 1939 it had become plain to the Soviet leadership that, with Nazi Germany to the west and militaristic Japan to the east, it had no one on whom to rely. The argument Stalin had put forward at the Eighteenth Congress seemed justified: anti-communism and the lack of a desire by Britain and France to pursue a policy of collective security had opened the sluice gates for aggression by the anti-Comintern pact. London and Paris were blinded to the real danger by their self-interest and hatred of socialism. Short-sighted politicians were saying, let Hitler make his anti-communist crusade in the east. He seemed to them the lesser evil.

The Soviet Union faced an extremely limited choice, but Stalin realized that it must be made, however negative the reaction in other countries. As a pragmatist, he cast ideological principles aside and, once he was sure the Anglo-French-Soviet talks would not produce results, he resorted to the German option which was being offered so assiduously by Berlin. He thought there was now no other choice. The alternative was to place the USSR in confrontation with the broad anti-Soviet front, which would be far worse. He had no time to think of what successive generations would say. The war was at hand and he had to postpone its outbreak at any cost.

After discussing with the Politburo the steps to be taken to activate contact with Berlin and what instructions were to be sent to the Soviet envoy there, he ordered Dvinsky, Poskrebyshev's assistant, to find him all the available literature on Hitler and on Fascism and its social origins. He wanted a better understanding of the phenomenon of National Socialism, of which he had said at the Seventeenth Congress, 'however hard one looks, it is impossible to find an atom of socialism in it.'[21] That evening he spent a long time on Hitler's *Mein Kampf*, underlining the passages where the author wrote of the eternal German drive to the south, her new interest in the east and the settling of new lands: 'And when we speak of new lands in Europe, we can only think of Russia and her borderlands ... The future goal of our foreign policy must be neither a western nor an eastern orientation, but an eastern policy in the sense of acquiring the territory we need for our German nation.' Stalin knew, reading these lines, that Hitler would stop at nothing. The question was, when would he start?

Stalin also read Conrad Heyden's book *The History of German Fascism* and underlined the blatantly antisemitic remarks Hitler had made as early as 1922 about the powerful position the Jews had allegedly acquired for themselves in Germany. Stalin knew he would be fighting this degenerate one day. So, the first man in the socialist state, in whom all political power and might was vested, was dealing here with a leader who personified an extremist, militaristic state. Was it to be a clash of two dictators, or their alliance? Was Trotsky right to say that Stalin was like Hitler? He read further in Heyden's book and took particular note of the author's claim that 'Hitler does not know what he is promising, his promises cannot be regarded as those of a reliable partner. He breaks them when it is in his interest to do so ...'[22] And this was the man who was offering him a non-aggression pact? Motivated, as Hitler claimed to be, by the 'call of Providence', he would regard a pact with Stalin as a pact with the devil, with no holds barred.

Among the other material Dvinsky had brought were reports from Berlin. Soviet intelligence reported that in the summer of 1939 German land forces amounted to 3.7 million men, almost half of them mechanized, 3,195 tanks, more than 26,000 guns and mortars, almost 400,000 air force personnel, more than 4,000 planes, about 160,000 naval personnel and 107 warships. It was undoubtedly the most powerful force in the capitalist world. Thousands of anti-Fascists had been executed, while about a million Germans languished in prisons and concentration camps – not a number to impress Stalin, however.

Stalin's earlier derisive comments on the coming war now sounded hollow and naive. In 1934, to the accompaniment of thunderous applause, he had said that the war would be:

most dangerous for the bourgeoisie also because it would be fought not only at the fronts but also in the enemy's rear. The bourgeoisie should not doubt that the countless worker friends of the USSR in Europe and Asia will strike at the rear of their oppressors who started the criminal war against the fatherland of the workers of all lands.[23]

Turning from intelligence reports, he opened a book called *Germany Arms* by the English writer Dorothy Woodman and was especially struck by a chapter on the ideological preparation for war. The sheer scale of the ideological conditioning of the German people and army was a revelation. The appeals and slogans were addressed less to reason and intellect than to instinct and nationalistic sentiment. The rituals and blind fanaticism of a whole hierarchy of Führers were designed to dim the masses' awareness and to train mindless and cruel functionaries. The Fascist ideologues had created an atmosphere of psychological exultation, nationalistic hysteria and political psychosis, and were using them for their own ends. Stalin knew it would be dangerous to compromise with such people. But without an agreement with Britain and France he was simply not ready to grapple with Hitler.

Stalin was ripe for a decision. He could either make a treaty with Britain and France, or a pact with Hitler or, least welcome, remain in isolation. The first option was the most desirable, as it would make the USSR part of an anti-Fascist coalition, having both enormous material potential and moral advantage. But lacking time, he could not wait any longer, especially as London and Paris were not keen on a rapprochement with the USSR. Stalin's mistake was to exaggerate the possibility that England and France would form a bloc with Nazi Germany.

A peculiar situation had arisen in August. The tripartite military talks were making no progress. Simultaneously, Moscow was desperately making contact with Berlin. Few people knew that secret Anglo-German talks were also going on in London. The German ambassador, Dirksen, and the prime minister's representative, H. Wilson, were trying to 'build bridges'. Stalin read Astakhov's dispatch from Berlin on 12 August: 'The conflict with Poland is escalating at a growing rate, decisive events may occur at the shortest notice ... The press is behaving perfectly correctly towards us. By contrast, the mockery of Britain surpasses the limits of common decency.'[24] Next day Astakhov reported that 'the German government has taken up our offer to hold talks to improve relations and wishes to enter them as soon as possible.'[25]

On 15 August Schulenburg handed Molotov his note, which read: 'The German government takes the view that, between the Baltic and the Black Sea there is no question that cannot be settled to the complete satisfaction of both countries. This includes the question of the Baltic Sea, the Baltic states, Poland, the South-East and so on.'[26] On 17 August Molotov received Schulenburg, who declared that talks should begin with Ribbentrop that week. Speaking on Stalin's behalf, as he made clear, Molotov stated that 'before talks could begin about improving political relations, the talks on a credit-trade agreement must be concluded.'[27]

On 19 August Schulenburg returned to see Molotov and reported that 'there is fear in Berlin of a conflict between Germany and Poland. Future events do not depend on Germany.' He insisted that Ribbentrop be invited immediately to Moscow to conclude the non-aggression treaty. Molotov agreed to a visit on 26–27 August.[28] The credit agreement was signed with lightning speed. Hitler was pushing hard and 26 August was too far off for him. That was when he was planning to attack Poland. Uncharacteristically Stalin conceded point after point to Berlin. Hitler finally lost patience and sent his famous telegram on 20 August, of which the following are extracts:

To Mr. Stalin,
Moscow
20 August 1939
1. I sincerely welcome the signing of the new German–Soviet trade agreement as a first step towards restructuring German–Soviet relations.
2. Concluding a pact of non-aggression with the Soviet Union means for me the consolidation of German policy for the long term ...
3. I accept the draft pact on non-aggression which your foreign minister Molotov has transmitted, but I regard it as urgently necessary to elucidate a number of questions connected with it in the quickest possible way ...
5. The tension between Germany and Poland has become insupportable. Poland's behaviour towards a great power is such that a crisis may occur any day ...
6. I think that if it is the intention of both states to act together in the new relations, it would be wise not to lose any time. Therefore I again propose that you receive my foreign minister on Tuesday 22 August or at the latest on Wednesday 23 August ...
I would be pleased to receive your immediate reply.
Adolf Hitler[29]

The Führer had taken the initiative into his own hands. The tone of an ultimatum was blatant. Stalin read the telegram several times, underlining in blue pencil the phrase 'a crisis may occur any day' and the closing sentence.

CHAPTER 35

A Dramatic Turn of Events

Stalin and Molotov sat looking at the message for a long time, listened again to Voroshilov's thoughts on the talks with the British and French, and tried to verify reports of Berlin's contacts with Paris and London which threatened to create a broad anti-Soviet alliance. They weighed all the pros and cons and came to a final decision. Stalin got up, paced up and down a few times, looked at Molotov and began to dictate:

To Chancellor of Germany A. Hitler.
21 August 1939
    Thank you for your letter. I hope the German–Soviet agreement of non-aggression will be a turning point towards serious improvement of political relations between our countries.
    The people of our countries need peaceful relations. The German government's agreement to sign a non-aggression pact will create the basis for the liquidation of political tension and the establishment of peace and cooperation between our countries.
    The Soviet government has instructed me to inform you that it agrees to Mr Ribbentrop's visiting Moscow on 23 August.
    I. Stalin.[30]

Ribbentrop flew to Moscow on 23 August and that very day the Non-Aggression Pact was signed. It was intended to last for ten years (Ribbentrop had proposed twenty-five as recently as 19 August). During the discussion, Ribbentrop insisted on inserting in the preamble a note on 'the friendly character of Soviet–German relations'. When Molotov reported this to Stalin, he rejected it: 'The Soviet government could not honestly assure the Soviet people that there were friendly relations with Germany, given that for six years the Nazi government has been pouring bucketloads of mud on the Soviet government.'[31] A month later Stalin would concede this point, too.

Simultaneously, the Soviet-Anglo-French talks were broken off. Voroshilov told the press that 'the talks with Britain and France were not broken off because of the non-aggression pact with Germany, but, on the contrary, the USSR signed the non-aggression pact with Germany because the military talks with England and France had reached an impasse.'[32] The last meeting of the tripartite delegations had taken place on the afternoon of 21 August, just when Schulenburg was handing the German note to Molotov. The head of the French delegation, General J. Doumenc, reported to the French premier Daladier:

The arranged session took place in the morning. A second session took place in the afternoon. During these two sessions we exchanged polite remarks about the hold-up over the political problem of passage [through Poland]. A new meeting, the date of which has not been fixed, will take place only if we are able to reply in the affirmative.[33]

The Polish government, however, would not consent to the passage of Soviet troops in the event of war, not that their decision could have changed anything, for the clock of world politics was ticking fast. Stalin gained two years. Hitler moved closer to the next stage of his plans. News of Ribbentrop's flight to Moscow, according to Maisky in London, 'has evoked ... the greatest concern in political and governmental circles. Two feelings were aroused: amazement, confusion, annoyance, fear [sic!]. The mood today was one of near panic.'[34]

Following the unexpected agreement with Hitler, Stalin went still further. He agreed to a number of supplementary treaties, known as the 'secret protocols', which gave a distinctly negative character to an otherwise forced and perhaps necessary step. Stalin's understanding with Hitler over the fate of the Polish lands appears especially cynical, for it was tantamount to the liquidation of an independent state. The originals of these protocols, it appears, have been seen by no one, and what have been circulating for years have most likely been copies of what Ribbentrop brought to Moscow. There can be no doubt, however, that an agreement, whether documentary or oral, concerning the frontiers of Soviet and German 'state interests', did exist. We shall return to this question below.

Looking back, the Non-Aggression Pact appears extremely tarnished, and morally an alliance with the Western democracies would have been immeasurably preferable. But neither Britain nor France was ready for such an alliance. From the point of view of state interest the Soviet Union had no other acceptable choice. A refusal to take any step would hardly have stopped Germany. The Wehrmacht and the nation were tuned to such a degree of readiness that the invasion of Poland was a foregone conclusion. Assistance to Poland was hampered not only by Warsaw's attitude, but also by the Soviet Union's unpreparedness. Rejection of the pact could have led to the formation of a broad anti-Soviet alliance and threaten the very existence of socialism.

In any case, Britain and France had both signed similar pacts with Germany in 1938 and were conducting secret talks with Hitler in the summer of 1939 with the aim of creating an anti-Soviet bloc. It is commonly suggested that the pact triggered the start of the Second World War, while it is commonly forgotten that by then the Western powers had already sacrificed Austria, Czechoslovakia and Memel to Hitler, and that Britain and France had done nothing to save the Spanish Republic.

Nor is it remembered that Poland, another of Hitler's victims, also signed a pact of non-aggression with him. Hitler had planned his attack on Poland as early as 11 April 1939, long before Molotov and Ribbentrop scratched their signatures on The Pact. Hitler indeed had discussed the seizure of Poland at a meeting even earlier, on 22 January 1939, and his designs on Poland were known to everyone. The Soviet leadership, and Stalin above all, had known about Hitler's planned attack on Poland early in 1939. In June 1939 a Soviet intelligence agent met Doctor Kleist, the head of Ribbentrop's eastern section, and was told that:

the Führer will not allow the outcome of the Russian talks to affect his intention to solve the Polish question in a radical way. The German–Polish conflict will be settled by Berlin whether the talks are successful or unsuccessful ... Germany's military action against Poland is planned for the end of August, or beginning of September.[35]

The date of the intended attack was known in Washington, London and Paris, but there it was hoped that Hitler's seizure of Poland would simply accelerate his invasion of the USSR.

Stalin could not have forgotten that in Munich in September 1938 representatives of England, France, Germany and Italy had gathered without a thought for the Soviet Union. The pragmatic arrangement with Hitler on that occasion meant more than the betrayal of Czechoslovakia. On 4 October, a few days after the shameful deal, the French ambassador to Moscow, R. Coulondre, frankly assessed the essence of the agreement by saying: 'After the neutralization of Czechoslovakia, Germany will open the way to the east.' On the very day of the agreement, 30 September, Chamberlain and Hitler signed their Declaration on non-aggression and consultations.

Stalin evidently knew the moral and ideological flaws in the pact he had now signed. Trotsky gloated in Mexico: 'Stalin and Hitler have reached out their hands to each other. Stalinism and Fascism are in alliance.' Many Communist Parties were distressed by the pact and found it hard to accept any sort of agreement with the Fascists. To many Soviet citizens it also seemed that Stalin and the Western democracies were not as wise as they should be.

But Hitler's war machine was already ticking over and required only a touch. Many European and American newspapers had been saying just this. On 24 August 1939 President Roosevelt appealed to Hitler and the Polish president Mosticki to come to the conference table, and King Leopold III of the Belgians had made a similar appeal the day before. On 26 August Daladier called Berlin to come to reason and start talks with Warsaw. The Pope made two similar appeals. Stalin said nothing. In the absence of other options, he had staked everything on Hitler. In the meantime, he could do nothing but prepare and wait for the inevitable attack.

Stalin had not yet left for the dacha when, at 2 a.m. on 1 September, he was brought a cipher from Berlin which reported that on the evening of 31 August allegedly Polish troops had broken into the German radio station in the town of Gleiwitz in Upper Silesia, killing a number of German staff, and had broadcast a text in Polish summoning the population to war. He realized at once that this was Hitler's pretext for war and sent instructions to the Soviet embassy in Berlin to report on further developments. The reply came that Berlin radio was playing martial music and that there was no other official information. Stalin believed that the blow would be struck at any moment.

Poskrebyshev awoke him early in the morning with the news that German troops had entered Poland. Stalin recalled the recent conversation Molotov had had with the Polish ambassador, W. Grzibowski, who said: 'Poland regards it as impossible to sign a pact with the USSR because of the practical impossibility of assisting the Soviet Union from the Polish side.'[36] Stalin and Molotov had decided that the Polish government simply did not wish to tie its hands by any agreement with the USSR on guarantees for Poland's security.

Among the dispatches Poskrebyshev brought him, Stalin read: 'This morning, 4 September, Hitler left for the eastern front. He crossed the former border of the Polish corridor and stopped near Kulm.' In a week, he thought, Hitler's troops could be close to the Soviet border. A new strategic situation had emerged. Border troops had already been given orders to raise their battle readiness. In accordance with existing plans and Soviet–German understandings, Soviet troops were to be ready to invade eastern Poland.

Despite the bravery of the Poles, it was an uneven battle. Hitler threw in sixty-two divisions, including eleven tank and mechanized divisions deploying 3,000 tanks and 2,000 aircraft. It was clear that Hitler did not expect the Polish campaign to take more than a couple of weeks. Britain and France were in no condition to help. On 17 September 1939 prime minister Molotov spoke on the radio:

No one knows the present whereabouts of the Polish government.* The Polish population has been abandoned to its fate by its unfortunate leaders ... The Soviet government regards it as its sacred duty to proffer help to its Ukrainian and Belorussian brothers in Poland ... The Soviet government has instructed the Red Army command to order its troops to cross the border and to take under its protection the life and property of the population of the western Ukraine and western Belorussia.[37]

Stalin had a note of similar content delivered to the Polish ambassador in

---

*That very evening the Polish government left the country and the supreme army command left the next day.

Moscow. With hindsight and from the Soviet point of view, this step was largely justified: the territory entered by Soviet troops was indeed inhabited by Ukrainians and Belorussians.

Units of the Belorussian and Kiev special military districts met no resistance in crossing the Polish frontier. Stalin read dispatches from Timoshenko, Vatutin, Purkaev, Gordov, Khrushchev and others. One from Mekhlis drew his special attention:

The Ukrainian population is meeting our army like true liberators ... The population is greeting our troops and officers, they bring out apples, pies, drinking water and try to thrust them into our soldiers' hands. As a rule, even advance units are being met by entire populations coming out on to the streets. Many weep with joy.[37a]

Timoshenko and Borisov reported that meeting up with German forces was not always smooth. At Lvov 'our troops were met by German weapons at point blank. As a result, two armoured cars were burnt out, a third was knocked out, three men were killed and five were wounded. Our armoured cars destroyed two German guns, killing one officer and three soldiers.'[38]

Two days after the German invasion of Poland, the Soviet envoy to Germany, A. Shkvartsev, presented his credentials to Hitler and then reported to Stalin:

I read the speech I had written in Moscow which you approved. Hitler replied: 'The German people are happy that a Soviet–German treaty of non-aggression has been signed. This pact will serve the cause of cooperation between the two peoples. As a result of the war, the situation that has existed since the Versailles agreement of 1920 will be liquidated. With this revision, Russia and Germany will re-establish the frontiers as they were before the war.[39]

Stalin underlined the last lines in thick red pencil. In attempting to avoid getting into the war, he had become a participant in the 'revision'.

The painful subject now arises of the deportation of a large number of Polish citizens to the USSR after Poland's defeat. The Western and Polish media have given inaccurate figures on these deportations. Working on the Molotov papers, I came across a document which had been prepared for Beria by Deputy Commissar for Internal Affairs Chernyshev. The document, which was destined to figure in a report to Stalin, reads as follows:

During the period from 1939 to June 1941, 494,310 former Polish citizens arrived in the Soviet Union. Those who left over the same period were:
42,492 former prisoners of war who were handed over to the Germans;
42,400 who were released and sent to the Ukraine and Belorussia.

The words 'former Polish citizens' and 'former prisoners of war handed over to the Germans' give one pause for thought. If the Soviet Union was not at war, where did these 'prisoners of war' come from? The same document states that:

at the moment of concluding the treaty of friendship between the government of the USSR and that of W. Sikorski (30 July 1941), there were 389,382 men being held in prisons, camps and places of exile. Of these, in accordance with the Decree of the Presidium of the Supreme Soviet of the USSR of 12 August 1941, 339,041 were amnestied. In 1942 119,865 men were evacuated to Iran (with Anders' army of 76,110 servicemen and 43,755 civilians). There are at present 218,000 Poles in the USSR.[40]

This memorandum for Stalin was signed on 2 November 1945. A number of other documents testify to the return to Poland of virtually all the Poles. For instance, Beria wrote to Molotov on 24 November 1945:

> On 20 October the NKVD camps held 27,010 Polish citizens, arrested and interned in 1944–45 on Polish territory in the course of mopping up in the rear of the active Red Army.
>
> In accordance with Comrade Stalin's instructions, 12,289 of these are to be released and returned to Poland. The rest by the end of this year. A certain number of those arrested for spying and sabotage will be detained.[41]

In 1943, near the railway station of Katyn, in the forest near the village of Kozy Gory, a vast burial ground of several thousand Polish officers was discovered. The Nazis at once declared that this was the work of 'Soviet hands', while a special commission in Moscow stated that it was simply another example of Nazi brutality. A series of documents have been found in a special section of the Main Soviet Archives which make it plain that Katyn was in fact the work of Beria's agency, though no single document has yet been found bearing his signature or that of any of his henchmen actually ordering the massacre. The order must either have been destroyed after the act or have been given orally. The fact is, the trail to Golgotha has been found.

The evidence is contained in documents of the NKVD department dealing with prisoners of war, headed at the time by Captain P. K. Suprunenko. Following the events of September 1939, Beria issued Order No. 0308 on the formation of this special department. Officers of the Polish army were being held in three camps: 6,287 men at Ostashkov, 4,404 at Kozelsk and 3,891 at Starobelsk. During April/May 1940, 15,131 Poles were removed from these camps, but they never arrived anywhere. It is, however, known that in 1941 the Germans captured no camps containing Polish prisoners; no trace of these men was found in other camps, nor were any new camps built for Polish officers. On the other hand, another document, signed on 21 May 1940 by Colonel Stepanov, deputy head of the special staff section responsible for escort troops, speaks of 'the successful completion of the appropriate measures for emptying the NKVD camp at Kozelsk'.

None of the documents I have seen on Polish citizens, who were on Soviet territory at Stalin's will, contain accurate figures of those who were either killed or died. But we are jumping ahead.

As Stalin watched the build-up of the threat of Germany's eastward expansion during the following months, he took a number of decisions aimed at the political consolidation of the country's western flanks. While he had been vacillating between reaching an understanding with the Western powers and doing a deal with the devil, Stalin had also had national and territorial considerations in mind. He taken part in the civil war, and had been implicated in the Red Army's defeat at the hands of the Poles because he had refused to transfer the 12th Army and First Cavalry from the Southwestern front. This episode had rankled and he had even eradicated some of the documentary evidence. In 1925 a member of his secretariat, Brezanovsky, cabled the Kiev archives to despatch 'the Stalin archives' he had sorted and collected.[42] These were duly despatched for the period of six months allowed by the regulations. Six months later the Kiev Central Archives began bombarding Brezanovsky with requests for their return. On 24 December 1925, Brezanovsky cabled: 'The administration of the Central Committee Secretariat hereby notifies you that no materials have been received by the Central Committee Archives.'[43] Brezanovsky was correct: the archives had been given directly to Stalin and, as also happened with other files in the Stalin papers, no further trace of them has been found to this day.

The Riga peace treaty of 1921, which ended the Soviet–Polish war, ceded Western Ukrainian and Belorussian territory to Poland and established the frontier to the east of the so-called Curzon Line. Since Ribbentrop touched the old wound cautiously several times, it is clear the failure of the talks with England and France had another dimension. Stalin was calculating on recovering the lands lost by the Soviet Union after the civil war.

Based on the Kiev and Belorussian special military districts, two fronts were created, consisting of the 3rd, 4th, 5th, 6th, 10th, 11th and 12th Armies. The troops were allowed to use their weapons only if attacked. Only isolated armed clashes took place. There was in fact no resistance. The ethnic majority, being Ukrainians and Belorussians, sincerely welcomed the arrival of the Soviet forces.

By 25 September, in the course of a week, Soviet troops had advanced 250–350 kilometres and come out on the line of the Western Bug and the San, as had been envisaged in the secret Soviet–German understandings, which we shall examine in greater detail below. In November 1939 these territories officially became parts of the Ukrainian and Belorussian Soviet Socialist Republics. In June 1940 the Soviet government succeeded in recovering Bessarabia and the northern Bukovina by peaceful means, and by agreement with the Romanian government the frontier was re-established along the rivers Prut and Danube. The Moldavian Soviet Republic had been formed.

Stalin believed that Hitler would not go back on the understanding they had reached on the Baltic states. Utterly cynical in his attitude to both the populations and governments of the region, which naively trusted him, Stalin manipulated their trust by claiming that, since the Soviet régimes that had been established there in 1917–18 had been overthrown, it was proper to talk of their 're-establishment'. In late September/early October, Stalin ordered Molotov to propose to Lithuania, Latvia and Estonia that they sign a treaty of mutual assistance. After brief hesitation, some internal struggle and consultation with Berlin, the Baltic governments signed treaties permitting the entry of Red Army units. At the request of the Baltic governments, the number of Soviet troops was less than the armies of Lithuania, Latvia and Estonia. The Soviet military contingents were to remain in their quarters and not interfere in the internal life of these countries, although Stalin was perfectly aware that the presence of the Red Army was bound to affect the political climate.

Hundreds of documents relating to these events are preserved in the Central State Archives of the Soviet Army. Responsibility for dealing with the number and place of deployment of Soviet troops, aerodromes and naval bases, railways, payment for accommodation, land, communication lines and so on, in accordance with the protocols and supplementary secret agreements, Stalin placed in the hands of Molotov and his deputy Foreign Commissar Potemkin, deputy Defence Commissar Loktyonov, deputy Foreign Trade Commissar Stepanov, and deputy Army and Navy Commissar Levchenko, and a number of other officials whose job it was to negotiate all financial, diplomatic, military and organizational matters with local representatives.

Despite some inevitable friction, the sides on the whole followed the spirit and the letter of the treaties. Sometimes the Baltic partners went further. For instance, when the Soviet–Finnish war broke out, the military attaché in Riga, Colonel Vasiliev, reported to Moscow: 'On 1 December General Hartmanis declared: "If because of the circumstances of the war you need any landing strips for your air force, you can use all our existing aerodromes, including Riga airport".'[44] The Lithuanian government informed Moscow that 'a committee has been formed for securing food products and forage for the armed forces [of the Red Army] in Lithuania.'[45] During the visit to Moscow in early December 1939 of the commander-in-chief of the Estonian army, General Johan Laidoner – a former lieutenant colonel on the tsarist General Staff – an impression was gained that friendly relations were developing between both states and their armies.[46]

When Hitler took Paris in June 1940, Stalin felt that if he did not at once invade England he was bound to turn his gaze to the east, and Stalin, aware of being unprepared and making sporadic efforts to make up for lost time, now took a new step. In the middle of June 1940, Moscow requested permission from the governments of Lithuania, Latvia and Estonia to deploy additional contingents of troops on their territory. He used the tone of an ultimatum. Encouraged by his recent success, he was now riding roughshod, as witness the fact that he sent Zhdanov, Vyshinsky and Dekanozov to the region. In October 1940, Pozdnyakov, who had accompanied Dekanozov, reported to Stalin and the Politburo: 'The political composition of the main Lithuanian body is still unfavourable, that is, class differentiation has not yet taken place in this body, that is, the hostile element has not been knocked out of the saddle and conducts anti-Soviet work by rallying the troops on national lines.'[47] It is easy to imagine how Dekanozov and the others proposed to knock the hostile element out of the saddle. Such are the bitter pages that fill the criminal chronicle of Stalinism.

While the moral aspect of the annexation of the Baltic states was distinctly negative, the act itself was a positive one, given the threats looming over both the USSR and the Baltic states. But as usual Stalin used force and coercion, and the presence of Soviet troops was the main factor in bringing about the political goal of 'reunification'. Dekanozov nevertheless reported to Stalin and Molotov in early July 1940:

A large meeting and demonstration took place in Vilna on 7 July. Some 80,000 people took part. The main slogans were 'Long live the 13th Soviet republic!', 'Proletarians of all lands, unite!', 'Long live Comrade Stalin!' and so on. The meeting passed a vote of greeting to the Soviet Union and the Red Army. A concert was given by the band of the Lithuanian Army, attended by the president and several members of the government and general staff ... A visit to Lithuania by Soviet performers would be appropriate. I request an urgent order to send Mikhailov, Lemeshev, Nortsov, Shpiller, Davydova, Ruslanova, Kozolupova* and a ballet company with Lepeshinskaya.[48]

It is reasonable to suggest that, had Soviet troops not been there, the Germans would have marched into the Baltic states before June 1941, since they already had a plan to 'Germanize' part of the population and liquidate the rest, as a 1940 memorandum by Rosenberg shows. The overwhelming majority of the Baltic population were favourable to their countries' incorporation into the Soviet Union in August 1940. Stalin took part personally both in the talks and in working out the detailed arrangements, with the result that, while the will of the Baltic nations was expressed, the whole process was blackened by a number of typically Stalinist actions. Stalin was concentrating his entire effort on strengthening the military-strategic position of the USSR and was not particular about the methods used to do so.

Encouraged by the success of his measures on the western borders, he now turned his attention to the northwest. He was worried by the proximity of the Finnish border to Leningrad and Finland's obvious inclination towards Germany. Talks were conducted with the aim of compelling the Finns to move their border further from Leningrad for appropriate territorial compensation, but the Finnish foreign minister, V. Tanner, was under instruction from the country's head of state, Field Marshal C. Mannerheim, a former general in the tsarist army, not to yield to the Russians. In this matter, the usually cautious Stalin lost his sense of reality and decided to resort to political and even military pressure to achieve what he could not get by diplomacy. At the end of November mutual recriminations started up over unprovoked exchanges of fire, notably

---

* All leading singers and musicians.

in the vicinity of the Soviet village of Mainilo. Molotov handed the Finnish envoy, A. S. Irne-Koskinen, a note which contained a demand, amounting to an ultimatum, 'for the immediate withdrawal of your forces 20 to 25 kilometres away from the frontier on the Karelian peninsula.' Two days later the envoy replied that his government was 'ready to enter talks on the mutual withdrawal of forces to a certain distance from the frontier'. Finland had taken up the challenge and, being equally unyielding, announced mobilization. On 28 November 1939 the USSR renounced the 1932 Soviet–Finnish treaty of non-aggression. Neither Moscow nor Helsinki had exhausted all means to avoid war, to put it mildly.

Stalin had imagined that he had only to declare his ultimatum, and even more to begin military action, for the Finnish government to concede all his demands. He was encouraged in this by the optimistic reports of the Leningrad military district council and by Beria's reports. On 5 October, for instance, Beria informed Stalin and Voroshilov of intelligence received from London:

The British envoy to Finland has twice reported that Field Marshal Mannerheim asked him to convey to the British government that in the immediate future Finland expects Soviet demands similar to those made on Estonia, that is, access to naval bases and aerodromes on the Finnish islands. According to his statement, Finland will have to satisfy the Soviet demands.[49]

Stalin was confident the Finns would soon capitulate. Military action began on 30 November and continued for almost four months. A warning by Shaposhnikov about the danger of underestimating the Finns proved fully justified. Stalin meanwhile committed yet another major political blunder: he authorized the formation in Moscow of a 'government of the Finnish Democratic Republic' headed by the Finnish Communist Otto Kuusinen. On 2 December Kuusinen and Molotov signed a treaty of mutual aid and friendship between the Soviet Union and the 'Finnish Democratic Republic'.[50] Typically Stalinist in style, these decisions and the inglorious war led to the USSR's international isolation. On 14 December she was expelled from the League of Nations. The statement by TASS on this event bears the plain stamp of Stalin's hand: 'In the opinion of Soviet circles this absurd decision by the League of Nations provokes an ironic smile and will scandalize only its pathetic authors.'[51]

But it was no smiling matter. The forces of the Leningrad military district were tied down in heavy, long-drawn-out battles. The Finns had built brilliant defences and resisted the attack with some success. Finally, Stalin understood the position and at a meeting of the Chief War Council called for 'decisive steps to be taken'. Two armies under the command of K. A. Meretskov and V. D. Grendal were deployed on the Karelian peninsula. S. K. Timoshenko was given command of the front, A. A. Zhdanov was appointed a member of the War Council, and I. V. Smorodinov was made chief of staff. Stalin's part in what the Finns call the Winter War was as a member of the Chief War Council. The volumes of documents on this inglorious campaign show plainly that the Soviet political and military leadership simply lost their heads, and things got to the point where Moscow was issuing direct tactical orders to the forces and bypassing the headquarters command.[52]

After a month's preparation to break through the Mannerheim Line, Soviet forces went into action on 11 February 1940. Superior strength told in the end. An order to Soviet forces on 9 February 1940, signed by Timoshenko, Zhdanov and Smorodinov, spoke of the 'everlasting glory' that would cover the Red Army in this campaign.[53] But there was to be no everlasting glory. The Mannerheim Line was broken at a very high price to the Soviet Union. A peace treaty was signed at the beginning of March 1940.

Stalin was distinctly put out. The entire world had seen the Red Army's low level of preparedness. As soon as the war was over, he decided to replace Voroshilov, first hearing his report at the Chief War Council and a plenum of the Central Committee. Voroshilov's lengthy report, which bears the marks of Stalin's notes and amendments, was entitled 'The Lessons of the War with Finland'. Among other things, he said:

I have to say that neither I, as defence commissar, nor the General Staff, nor the Leningrad Military District Command, had any idea of the peculiarities and difficulties involved in this war ... The Finnish army, well organized, armed and trained for local conditions and tasks, turned out to be highly manoeuvrable, staunch in defence and well disciplined.

From the start of military action the centre established a Headquarters of the Chief War Council consisting of Comrades Stalin, Voroshilov, chief of staff Comrade Shaposhnikov and naval commissar Comrade Kuznetsov (who attended only for naval questions). A permanent and active participant in the Headquarters was Chairman of the Sovnarkom Comrade Molotov, though he was not a member of Headquarters. The Headquarters, or more accurately its active member Comrade Stalin, virtually conducted all operations and all the organizational work of the front.

Voroshilov went on for many pages to describe the inadequacies of Red Army intelligence, poor technical supply, cumbersome communications organization, poor winter clothing and food for the troops and so on:

Many top commanders were not up to the task. Headquarters had to remove many senior officers and staff chiefs, not merely because their leadership was not doing any good, but because it was doing positive harm. The Red Army sustained its relatively rapid victory above all because, from the outbreak of the war to its victorious end, the virtual conduct of the war was taken on by Comrade Stalin ...[54]

In his closing speech, Stalin correctly stated that it was time 'to renounce the cult of the civil war which only reinforces our backwardness'. He complained that there were still too many participants of the civil war in the leadership who were holding back the younger and more inventive 'engineers of war'.[55] While it was true that the cult of the civil war was a hindrance, it was not true that the old guard held sway: they had all (except Voroshilov) been killed off in the purge. Be that as it may, Stalin now knew just what sort of war leader Voroshilov made. The Red Army had been shown up as having major shortcomings. Hitler was both amazed and delighted. His strategies had been based on sound calculation. A victory at great cost was tantamount to a moral defeat. Stalin and Hitler both understood this and each drew his own conclusions. Stalin, however, had less time for reflection. An unfamiliar lack of self-assurance had come over him. From this moment he was obsessed with the sole idea that, if Hitler were not provoked, he would not attack. When Soviet border defence forces shot down a German plane that had violated Soviet airspace, Stalin personally gave orders to send an apology. Belligerent Germany in fact had a non-belligerent ally in the USSR and Berlin quickly took note of this. In large-scale manoeuvres, Stalin trained as the defensive side. Hitler meanwhile was almost ready to start his eastern campaign.

Even though today we rightly condemn Stalin, we should also recognize that, given the situation at the time, many of the measures he took to delay the war and strengthen the USSR's western defences were to a large extent forced on him. He believed too much in Hitler's word and committed a number of other mistakes he preferred not to remember later, despite telling Red Army commanders in the Kremlin on 24 June 1945 that 'Our government made many mistakes.' To be more precise, it made mistakes not only in the course of the war but before it, too. Perhaps its biggest and most serious mistake was to sign the German–Soviet treaty on friendship and borders on 28 September 1939. According to this treaty the borders and spheres of interest of both states were defined, with a map attached. The border was different from the one agreed in the 'secret protocols' of the pact of 23 August 1939. It lay along the line of the Narev, Bug and San rivers.

The 'friendship' between the socialist state and the Fascist state was noted in the Molotov–Ribbentrop Moscow talks of 27–28 September 1939, with Stalin taking a direct part, as he had in those of August. There is evidence to suggest that Stalin was aware even before the war that he had made an error. In striving to avert or at least postpone war, he had crossed the last ideologically justified boundary, and this would have far-reaching consequences.

CHAPTER 36

Stalin and the Army

On the eve of the war, the army basked in the country's affection. National heroes were made in the Mongolian campaigns, in Spain and in the Finnish war, and there was no shortage of candidates for the military academies. Military service was regarded as an honourable career. The political and military leadership had no qualms about the discipline and political consciousness of servicemen who believed in Stalin and the party, even though the wounds inflicted by the purges had not fully healed. The Finnish war, however, despite its being presented as a victory, made the people wonder how an army as mighty as that depicted in the press could have taken as long as four months to subdue the forces of a small country like Finland. Stalin felt the shame of the Winter War more than most, but of course did not blame himself. In March 1940 he made it plain that someone else would have to answer for it. Voroshilov was that man.

Although no military man himself, Stalin gradually came to see that Voroshilov was not capable of running the army. He had not managed the headquarters well during the campaign at Khalkin Gol or in the Finnish war. According to Zhukov, after Khalkin Gol when he was appointed to command the Kiev military district, out of the blue Stalin said of Voroshilov: 'He boasted and assured me that we'd hit them three times every time they hit us. "Everything's fine, everything's just fine, Comrade Stalin, everything's ready" – and then, what?'[56]

Voroshilov was removed as defence commissar in May 1940, although he was made deputy chairman of the Council of Ministers and chairman of the Defence Committee of the USSR. His place as defence commissar was taken by S. K. Timoshenko, who was also made a Marshal of the Soviet Union. The new commissar's first major decision, ratified by a decree of the Sovnarkom of 6 June 1940, was to create mechanized corps of two tank divisions and one motorized division. Only six months earlier the tank corps administration had been dismantled. Stalin had no opinion of his own on these matters, relying instead on Generals D. G. Pavlov and G. I. Kulikov, who both automatically fell back on their experience in Spain, or on chief of staff Shaposhnikov and his deputy Smorodinov, who both advocated the importance of these formations.

At the end of the 1930s, realizing that the army was too steeped in civil war lore, Stalin appointed Zhdanov and N. A. Voznesensky to head a commission on the state of the army and navy. They came to the sobering conclusion that the 'commissariat has not yet solved the problems of the operational use of forces in modern warfare,' and that the situation was aggravated by the large numbers of young, inexperienced cadres. This of course was largely the result of the mass repressions of 1937–38 which had struck above all at the senior officers, the political administration and the central organization of the commissariat. The figures show that from May 1937 to September 1938, 36,761 men were purged in the army and more than 3,000 in the navy,[57] some of them, it is true, being merely discharged from the service. As a result of the repressions, all military district commanders were removed, 90 per cent of district chiefs of staff and deputies, 80 per cent of corps and divisional commanders, 90 per cent of staff officers and chiefs of staff. A sharp fall in the intellectual quality of officers resulted. By the beginning of 1941 only 7.1 per cent of commanding officers had a higher military education, 55.9 per cent had secondary education, 24.6 per cent had been through accelerated courses, and 12 per cent of officers and political personnel had had no military education at all.[58]

Vyshinsky and Ulrikh had proposed that the purge procedure could be simplified if the Special Conference of the NKVD were given the right to strip an officer of his rank, which previously would only have followed from a court sentence. In April 1938 Ulrikh had demonstrated the need 'to sanction the removal of the military collegium from the Supreme Court and to reorganize it as the Military Tribunal of the USSR'.[59] Stalin was living in a world in which new 'enemies' had to be found every day and his paranoia was transmitted to his entourage, his henchmen and the country at large. Military districts and academies received orders such as that sent to the Red Army political administration in Moscow:

Appoint a commission to investigate and review the teaching staff of the Lenin Academy. If any of the Tolmachev grouping are still there, remove them down to the last one.
5 July 1938 Mekhlis[60]

Although the repressions had subsided by early 1939, on 14 June Ulrikh reported to Stalin and Molotov that a 'large number of cases were pending against members of Right-Trotskyite, bourgeois nationalist and espionage organizations: Moscow military district 800 cases; Northern Caucasus district 700; Kharkov district 500; Siberian district 400. For the sake of secrecy, we suggest the defendants not be allowed to attend their trials. I await your orders.'[61] There is no indication on this document of Stalin's response, but given the huge deficiency of officers in the face of looming war, it is possible that he rejected it as an example of 'mistakes and slander'. From this moment the thinning out of the army and navy began to slow down. Nevertheless, the situation in some military districts was simply catastrophic, and in the army as a whole the officer corps was the weakest element. By the summer of 1941, about 75 per cent of officers and 70 per cent of political officers had been in their posts less than one year. The backbone of the army lacked the necessary experience of command.

Stalin was aware that the serious shortage of officers was exacerbated by inadequate professional training for modern warfare. The speech he gave on 5 May 1941 in the Kremlin to Red Army graduates echoed these thoughts. It was a speech of rare frankness and revealed many state secrets. For instance, to bolster the young officers' confidence, he spoke of the fundamental restructuring of the army and its sharp increase in size. In early 1941, he told them, the army had 300 divisions of which one third were mechanized. He did not tell them, however, that more than a quarter of the total number were only about to be formed and as many again had only just been formed.

As always, he emphasized the army's offensive rôle: 'The Red Army is a modern army, and the modern army is an offensive army.' This was a major error, for it neglected the crucial importance of strategic defence and defensive operations. The USSR's official military doctrine was defensive, but Stalin and the leaders who parroted his views were always proclaiming that the best defence was attack. Regulations, orders, directives, the commissar's speeches and now Stalin himself expressed a single idea: 'The war would be fought on the enemy's territory and victory must be won at the cost of little bloodshed.'

Why was Germany beating its enemies? Was she invincible? At this point in his speech Stalin explained the Wehrmacht's triumph in western Europe very frankly: 'The Germans were able to detach Britain's and France's allies.' Clearly, the only ally in these circumstances was the Soviet Union. 'The German army is not invincible. It is marching now under the banner of expansion, its self-confidence and arrogance are growing. But that augurs the worst.' False ideas became part of Soviet military thinking, so that in an operational review of the Red Army General Staff it was stated that Germany was victorious in 1940 'as a result of circumstances that were too favourable to her' and 'not without the intervention of fortunate accidents'.[62] A draft project on political propaganda for the Red Army stated that 'the German army has lost its taste for further improvement of military technique. A significant part of the German army is tired of the war.'[63]

Some of Stalin's points, however, were sound, even though the army would not have time to put them into full effect. The Red Army academies, he said, were behind the times and were training for 'yesterday's war'. The experience of Khalkin Gol was not significant, he said, because the Japanese did not have a modern army. It was war in the west, the Finnish war, that should serve as a lesson in modern warfare. Shortly before the graduation period, Stalin had convened the Chief Military Council at which speeches were given, by, among others, G. K. Zhukov, K. A. Meretskov, I. V. Tyulenev, D. G. Pavlov, G. M. Shtern, P. V. Rychagov and A. K. Smirnov. Special emphasis was laid on raising battle readiness, carrying out offensive operations, the concentration of forces and means of achieving strategic success. The problem of the opening phase of the war as such was not dealt with. All the more interesting, therefore, was a speech by chief of staff P. S. Klenov who commented that the 'first phase of the war was of the greatest importance, since the enemy would apply all his force to prevent us from carrying it out in an organized fashion.'[64]

Stalin noted Meretskov's comment that the Red Army's regulations were behind the times,[65] and he ordered an immediate review, although this would not be completed by the outbreak of the war. But neither Stalin nor the defence commissar noted that, apart from Tyulenev, no one raised the question of modern defensive operations.[66] They had all learned offensive strategy, and those military intellectuals who had understood their subject more broadly, and with a more modern, flexible approach, had all been killed off by Stalin.

Despite the Pact, then, Stalin saw storm clouds on the western horizon. At the same time, he mistakenly believed that Hitler would not attack in the east until he had won in the west: he would never engage in a war on two fronts, and Stalin laid stress on this notion in his speeches at the time, notably that of 5 May 1941 in the Kremlin. He was, however, also amazed by the ease with which the Wehrmacht had been able to crush the western armies, but he was not sure that the Red Army would learn the appropriate lessons quickly enough. He studied the analyses of the German forces' operations which had been prepared for him by the General Staff, and in conversations with Timoshenko he stressed the need to intensify training.

There was much he did not know, however. For instance, he did not know the German assessment of the Red Army in early 1941. It emerged only after the war that, when Hitler learned of the purges in 1937–38, he ordered an intelligence report on the state of the Red Army officer corps. Six months before the war, on the basis of information from Colonel Krebs, the German military attaché in Moscow, and other sources, Hitler concluded that the Red Army was quantitatively and qualitatively weak: 'It makes a worse impression than it did in 1933. Russia needs years to recover its previous level ...'[67]

It would be hard to find a precedent in history when one of the sides on the eve of a mortal conflict had so damaged itself. Zhukov recalled that during a large-scale war game in December 1940, he was given command of the 'Blues', that is the German side, while Army General Pavlov, commander-in-chief of the Western special military district, commanded the 'Reds'. It so happened, Zhukov recalled, that he developed his operations precisely along the lines that the real battles would take in six months' time. He claimed that his tactics were dictated by the configuration of the borders, the terrain and circumstances. He deduced that the Nazis would make the same calculations. Even though the umpires artificially slowed the progress of the 'Blues', in eight days they advanced to the district of Baranovichi. When in January 1941 Zhukov reported on the exercise to the Chief War Council he drew attention to the unfavourable system of fortified districts along the new border, suggesting they be moved back 100 kilometres. This was criticism of a decision that had been taken by Stalin. Stalin, meanwhile, listened attentively but was puzzled why the 'Blues' were so strong, why had such strong German forces been deployed by the rules of our own game? Zhukov replied that this corresponded to the Germans' real capabilities and was based on a real assessment of the forces they could deploy against us in the opening phase of the war, thereby gaining great superiority by their first strike.

Stalin found Zhukov's report comprehensive, and he admired the bold way Zhukov argued his case, and soon, in February 1941, he appointed him chief of the General Staff, one of his best decisions in this area, as future events would show.

Having completed the diplomatic moves we have described, Stalin remained in two minds. On the one hand, the treaties were more favourable to the Germans, for they had helped Hitler to avoid fighting on two fronts and he could therefore be assumed to observe their conditions. On the other hand, being an opportunist by nature, Hitler would not necessarily follow normal logic. His entire impulsive strategy was based on the calculation of short-term factors, such as surprise, cunning, unpredictability. Stalin therefore intently followed each of Hitler's military and political steps, and the course of the Blitzkrieg in the west. He also ordered Timoshenko to see for himself the real battle-readiness of the troops.

In the course of 1940 Timoshenko visited all the western military districts, put a number of units on alert and observed some training courses and manoeuvres. All his visits were reported in the press, as were those of other military leaders. These tours of inspection revealed many serious shortcomings. Military and political officers, lacking experience, were proving slow to master the new elements of combat training. The basic components of combat force were below par, and this applied equally to the air force.[68]

In the two years leading up to the war, Stalin plainly attempted to effect a major rise in both the size and quality of all the Soviet armed forces, but his effort was based on the fallacious premise that he would be able to avert or at least postpone the war. As the author Konstantin Simonov recalled from a conversation with Zhukov, 'Stalin was convinced he had twisted Hitler round his little finger with the Pact. As things turned out, it was the other way round.' Zhukov said that 'most of the people around him supported Stalin in the political judgements he made before the war, especially the notion that, as long as we did not rise to any provocation, or make any false step, then Hitler would not break the Pact and attack us.'[69] This line was most ardently advocated by Molotov who, after his trip to Berlin in November 1940, continued to insist that Hitler would not attack the USSR.

CHAPTER 37

The Defence Arsenal

In mid-November 1940 *Izvestiya* reported that, 'in the context of the friendly relations that exist between our two countries, and an atmosphere of mutual trust', an exchange of opinions took place between V. M. Molotov and Chancellor A. Hitler, foreign minister J. Ribbentrop, Field Marshal Goering, and Hitler's (party) deputy, R. Hess.' In fact, there was no such 'mutual trust'. Molotov arrived in Berlin on 12 November looking apprehensive, and the tension and distrust between the 'friends' mounted by the hour.

In his cavernous office, Hitler eyed his Soviet visitor intently and got down to his favourite topic straightaway: the Axis powers were on the eve of triumph, the British Empire would soon go under the hammer, and it was time to decide what sort of world would follow the proclamation of the New Order. Germany had an interest in this and so, he hoped, had Russia. Molotov listened without interrupting as the Führer talked of dividing up the world into spheres of influence. But when Hitler dried up and turned to the Soviet representative for a reaction, Molotov coldly remarked that he saw no sense in discussing such notions. Hitler bridled visibly, but Molotov was not intimidated and began to put a number of awkward questions: why was there a German military mission in Romania, why was Germany sending troops to Finland? Hitler lost interest in the talks at once and suggested adjourning until the next day. The sides were plainly speaking different languages and both realized that the agreements of the previous year were dead. They had served their purpose: for Germany, to bluff the USSR and leave her own hands free; for the USSR, to gain time. Sensing the Germans' distrust, Molotov returned to his hotel, the Bellevue, and tried to console himself with the thought that Hitler would not commit Germany's error of the First World War by fighting on two fronts. For their part, according to reports from Beria, the Western governments were of the belief that a Soviet–German military alliance was on the cards.[70] Stalin, nevertheless, however, had growing doubts about German policy. He did not yet know that, while Molotov was in Berlin, General F. Halder, chief of staff land forces, was reporting to Field Marshal Brauchitsch, commander-in-chief land forces, on the latest version of Order No. 21, or Operation Barbarossa, for the invasion of the USSR. Hitler did not intend to be trapped like Napoleon by the Russian winter, and therefore he set the date of the invasion for 15 May 1941.[71] The campaign was planned to take eight weeks.

Despite continuing to hold, with Molotov, to the myth that Hitler would stick to the Pact and avoid fighting on two fronts, Stalin set about intensifying the country's defences. The potential was there. The country now had one of the mightiest industrial bases in the world, however low its quality, and it was managed by strong commissars such as I. F. Tevosyan, V. A. Malyshev, A. I. Shakhurin, I. A. Likhachev, D. F. Ustinov and B. L. Vannikov.

Industrial leaders had been found who could work together with the party organizations to achieve the impossible at critical moments, to produce military hardware at fantastically short notice. Stalin knew all his commissars and many factory managers personally and frequently called them in for consultation. Vannikov recalled that Stalin himself took a direct hand in the defence industry before the war, although the Politburo member nominally responsible was N. A. Voznesensky (whose significant rôle in the war has been largely neglected.) Not being an expert, Stalin in his dealings with the designers tended to rely more on 'pressure' and even threats than science. Vannikov recalled Stalin saying, 'Designers always keep something in reserve, they never show you all the possibilities; you have to press them harder.' And Stalin knew how to press. Ustinov recalled in his memoirs that an entire artillery system was created in the unprecedentedly short time of eighteen days.[72] Stalin's involvement in defence matters, however, often had a damaging effect. For instance, on the eve of the war, Marshal Kulik, who was then chief of the Main Artillery Administration, together with Zhdanov proposed the calibre of tank weapons be increased from 45mm and 75mm to 107mm. Stalin agreed at once, recalling guns of that calibre from the civil war. He was thinking, however, of field guns, whereas what was being proposed required far heavier armour. Armaments commissar Vannikov and factory managers Elyan and Fradkin protested timidly to Stalin, Zhdanov and Kulik, but in vain. The engineering arguments did not convince Stalin. A meeting was convened and, as Vannikov recalled, the conversation took an ominous turn. Stalin snapped at those present: 'Vannikov doesn't want to make 107mm guns for the tanks.' Zhdanov supported him with: 'Vannikov is against everything, it's his way of working.' It was pointless, and dangerous, to argue.

Stalin signed Zhdanov's order and literally on the eve of the war production of smaller-calibre tank-guns was halted. It was a serious mistake, and the war soon made it necessary to rescind the order and return to producing the old guns. But time had been lost. A month after the outbreak of the war, Stalin found his scapegoats, Zhdanov and Kulik, whom he roundly cursed at the Politburo, incapable as he was of admitting it was his own mistake.

The Eighteenth Party Conference of February 1941 was devoted almost entirely to defence matters. The report by Central Committee secretary Malenkov, who had been moving up rapidly, was on 'The Tasks of the Party Organizations in the Field of Industry and Transport' and it dealt with the conversion of industry to war production. Stalin proposed that in 1941 industrial output should increase by 17–18 per cent. That did not seem unrealistic. In 1940, for instance, defence output had increased by 27 per cent compared to 1939. It is easy to forget, when we think of the horrors of Stalinism, that there was also the amazing socialist phenomenon of labour zeal and achievement. True, people were often motivated by fear, but they nevertheless gave material reality to plans which today would be regarded as fantasies. The nation was prepared to sacrifice much if it was for the salvation of the Motherland. And these are not empty words. If the budget allocation for defence in the period 1928 to 1933 was only 5.4 per cent of gross national product, by 1941 it had risen to 43.4 per cent,[73] which called for some very serious belt-tightening. Failure to carry out Stalin's orders could have disastrous consequences, and everyone knew it. But threats alone were not responsible. The people knew a war was coming and that they would have to perform the impossible. By the time of Hitler's invasion, 2,700 airplanes of new type and 4,300 tanks, nearly half of them a new model, had been built.[74]

The rise in output was everywhere accompanied by severe discipline, with especially harsh administrative and judicial measures being applied to those disrupting production. The level of absenteeism fell dramatically, but Stalin repeatedly told Poskrebyshev more effort was needed: 'Tell the commissars the struggle for discipline has only begun!'

At the same time, Mekhlis, now Commissar of State Control, conducted Stalin's campaign to exact greater effort from the party leaders. At the Eighteenth Party Conference, for instance, six members of the Central Committee, including M. M. Litvinov and Ye. A. Shchadenko, were demoted to candidate membership; fifteen people lost their positions as candidate members, among them Molotov's wife, Polina Zhemchuzhina; nine people were removed from the Central Revision Commission. The reason given was that 'they had not carried out their duties.' Commissars M. M. Kaganovich, M. F. Denisov, I. P. Sergeev, Z. A. Shashkov, A. A. Ishkov and V. V. Bogatyrev were all warned in a special ruling 'that if they did not pull themselves together, if they did not fulfil the commissions given to them by the party and government, they would be removed from the leading party organs and their posts'. This warning was to prove fatal for some. Meanwhile, the vacated posts were mainly taken by military men, including Zhukov, A. I. Zaporozhets, I. V. Tyulenev, M. P. Kirponosov, I. S. Yumashev and I. P. Apanasenko, among others. Stalin himself was now working sixteen and seventeen hours a day and the yellow glint in his eyes became dimmed by lack of sleep and overwork.

He knew that only by the total mobilization of the country's resources could the approaching test be withstood, though he hoped it would not come too soon. In May 1941 the Central Committee decreed, 'with the aim of fully coordinating the actions of the Soviet and party bodies and the absolute guarantee of unity in their work', that Stalin be appointed Chairman of Sovnarkom, while retaining his position as General Secretary.

His decisions always demanded sacrifice. For example, in order to overcome the lag in the aviation industry, the Politburo in September 1939 ordered the construction of nine new aircraft factories to be accomplished in 1940–41, and the same number to be rebuilt. The aircraft industry began working at a furious pace. Every day its commissar reported to Stalin on the number of planes and engines built. People had to remain in their laboratories and workshops for days on end. Production leapt, although new models did not become available until the second half of 1940.

Such forced output, however, also took its toll. The quality of aircraft was often inferior, with a discouraging increase in breakdowns and crashes. Stalin naturally accused air force personnel of sabotage and, after reading the latest list of disasters, he demanded a report from the Defence Commissar. On 12 April, Timoshenko and Zhukov reported:

The Red Army Chief Defence Council has examined the matter of breakdowns and crashes in the air force and established that, far from declining, the number is growing due to lack of discipline on the part of aircrews and command staff which leads to violation of the elementary rules of flying. This lack of discipline is causing the average daily loss of two or three airplanes, amounting to 600–900 a year. In the incomplete first quarter of 1941 alone there were 71 breakdowns and 156 crashes, killing 141 aircrew and destroying 138 aircraft.

The memorandum called for the chief of air force administration Rychagov to be removed and for a number of commanding officers to be court-martialled. Stalin approved this proposal, adding: 'I agree, with the single proviso that Comrade Proskurov be included in the paragraph and that Comrade Proskurov also be tried along with Comrade Mironov [both senior Air Force staff]. That would be the honest and just thing to do.'[75]

There were also difficulties in the production of tanks, artillery and ammunition. The designers M. I. Koshkin, A. A. Morozov and H. A. Kucherenko created the excellent medium-weight T-34 tank in a very short time, but together with the heavy KV only about 2,000 were produced by the time war came. Rocket weapons had been invented by Soviet scientists in principle before the war began, but production in significant numbers only began during the war itself, when the Katyusha, a weapon capable of launching sixteen shells within ten seconds, provided highly effective firepower for the Soviet forces.

Production of new weapons had barely begun on the eve of the war. In his book on the war economy, published in 1948, N. A. Voznesensky wrote: 'The war found the Soviet war industry in the process of mastering the new technology, and the mass production of modern military hardware was not yet organized.'[76] In March 1941 Stalin was told that there were sufficient parts properly to supply only 30 per cent of all the tank and armoured units of the army,[77] and that it would take another three or four years to do the whole job. The position was no better with aircraft, of which only 10 to 20 per cent of the new models had been built, and indeed the picture as a whole was much the same across the board. As Timoshenko and Zhukov reported one month before the war began: 'Fulfillment of the plan for the supply of the military technology the Red Army needs so acutely is extremely unsatisfactory.' Stalin, the Politburo and the commissars sought a solution and found it in raising the effort of the Soviet people to the limit. Production was switched backwards and forwards from one weapon to another, for instance from artillery to aircraft- and tank-weapons, despite criticism of this approach. Given the circumstances, it is, however, understandable that such methods were adopted.

Stalin was also worried about agriculture. Labour efficiency in the agrarian sector was extremely low compared to industry, and the usual explanation given to Stalin was that the kolkhozniks spent more time on their kitchen gardens, or the private plot around the homestead, than on the collective. A. A. Andreyev was ordered to study the problem and the report he gave to a plenum at the end of May 1939 was entitled 'On Measures for Protecting Public Collective Farm Lands from being Squandered for the Benefit of the Collective Farmers' Private Plots'. The burden of Andreyev's report was that harsh methods should be imposed to limit the size of the private plot, and that an absolute minimum of collective labour-days* be earned by each member of the artel.† Once again, then, it was force and threats, rather than economic measures, that were to be used to solve a problem.

The plenum was chaired by Molotov. No minutes were taken, but various excerpts, exchanges and notes survive in the archives which show that Stalin and the other leaders were relying on directives and coercion to manage agriculture. Andreyev reported that in the Kiev oblast 5.8 per cent of artel members did not work in the kolkhoz, and 18 per cent of kolkhozniks earned only about fifty labour-days, while Shcherbakov reported that in the Nogin district of Moscow oblast 32 per cent of families did not do collective labour at all.[78] The tense silence of the auditorium was broken by the voice of Stalin:

'Who are these people who don't work on the kolkhoz, have they been identified?'

Andreyev: 'It has not proved possible to identify them, Comrade Stalin. Some are seasonal labourers, others are spongers who feed off the kolkhoz.'

Stalin: 'Are there any who haven't earned any labour-days at all?'

Andreyev: 'Yes, not a single labour-day. They live entirely by their private plot.'

Stalin: 'Can they work or are they invalids?'

Andreyev: 'They are very old seasonal labourers. But they have a dis-

---

* A labour-day was a variable unit of work, equivalent in purpose to factory piece-rates.
† An artel is a working group or association of workers or peasants.

organizing effect, their behaviour disrupts the kolkhozniks who work honestly.'

For the rest of the plenum, the participants discussed only ways of 'compelling', 'obliging', 'limiting', 'forcing' the peasant to produce more. Bagirov from Baku proposed nationalizing all kitchen gardens, to which Stalin replied:

'That needs to be thought about. You should submit detailed plans.'

'Shall we table a resolution?'

'Yes.'

Zhdanov at once composed a resolution requesting Bagirov to submit his proposals on nationalizing kitchen gardens. He also tabled an amendment proposed by Stalin that 'collective farm managers who allowed kolkhozniks and outsiders to mow grass in the forest on an individual basis should be sacked from the kolkhoz and sent for trial for breaking the law.' As a result, large areas of grassland remained uncut and kolkhozniks were forbidden to cut grass even in ravines and forests. There was only one objection, from Kulikov – initials were generally not noted at that time – who said: 'I have to make the following comment: here on page 3 it shows the tax in kind private farmers have to make in grain. Krasnoyarsk region has to give 15 per cent of its grain in July. Where will they get grain in July? What reserves have they got?' Even Stalin seems to have had second thoughts. 'If we publish this thing in the name of the Central Committee and Sovnarkom,' he asked, 'won't it cause confusion for the kolkhozniks?'

'No, on the contrary, they'll pull themselves together,' came some uncertain voices from the hall. 'The people have been waiting for this a long time.'

In the last months before the war, as we have said, the pulse of labour beat faster. The newspapers and radio carried stories about the war, about the Battle of Britain, the temporary banning of ballroom dancing in Germany, the conversion of Poland into a General Government, and the economic achievements of the USSR. They broadcast Stalin's instruction to Gosplan to formulate a general economic plan for the next fifteen years in order to achieve the basic aim of 'overtaking the main capitalist countries in the per capita production of pig-iron, steel, fuel, hydroelectricity, machinery and consumer goods'.[79]

CHAPTER 38

The Murder of the Exile

In the midst of the all-out effort to raise the Soviet Union's defence potential, Stalin suddenly received the long awaited news from abroad that Trotsky had been killed. The hunt for the exile had been going on for several years, but Trotsky had been well protected by his followers and the police. Stalin had created a special unit to deal with the 'problem', and had several times expressed his deep dissatisfaction to Beria over his agents' indecisiveness and lack of resourcefulness. And now it had been done. The duel was over. Yet Stalin felt no particular joy. Had it happened in 1937–38 it would have been a different matter, for then he had seen the shadow of Trotsky behind every major enemy, Trotsky's hand had seemed to be in everything, and his predictions had appeared to be coming true. Trotsky had been the chief defendant in the dock at all the big trials, but after the insanity of those years Stalin had somehow submerged his hatred. Trotsky's potential supporters having been put down, Trotsky himself had come to appear less dangerous. The shadow of war was far darker and more threatening than the citizen without a visa.

Stalin ordered that the information be confirmed and on 22 August 1940 a brief announcement appeared in *Pravda*:

New York, 21 August (TASS). According to US newspapers, on 20 August an attempt was made on the life of Trotsky, who has been living in Mexico. The assassin called himself Jacques Mortan Vandendraish and belonged to the close circle of Trotsky's followers.

On 24 August *Pravda* reported that Trotsky had been buried. The man who had plotted the murders of Kirov, Kuibyshev and Gorky had now been killed himself and by his own people. Stalin read the article carefully. So much emphasis on spies. Had he been struggling only with a spy all these years? And why make it so clear who had killed him? As if the murder had taken place in

Moscow and we knew all about it. Everything could so easily be spoilt by just a few ill-chosen words.

Gradually, however, the significance of the news sank in and Stalin relished the thought that his most dangerous, clever and persistent enemy was no more, and he felt the triumph of the victor. All the old enemies had been got rid of. Only he remained of the original nucleus.

Soon after the news of Trotsky's murder, Beria, with Stalin's knowledge, gave the order for the 'liquidation of the active Trotskyites in the camps', and on the eve of the war another wave of terror swept barely noticed through the penal system. Pechora, Vorkuta, Kolyma and Solovki became the silent witnesses of a bloody vengeance carried out 'in pursuit' of the murdered leader of the Fourth International.

The titles alone of Trotsky's articles had been enough to put Stalin in a rage: 'Stalin, Hitler's Quartermaster', 'The Heavenly Twins, Hitler and Stalin'. As he read them, Stalin could literally hear Trotsky's voice reciting: 'The USSR is on the edge of an abyss. All of Stalin's trump cards will count for little against the resources and might that Hitler possesses and that he will use against the Soviet Union.'

In predicting catastrophe for Stalin, Trotsky had expressed the hope that the 'workers' state had the chance to survive'. He did not wish for the defeat of the USSR, only that Stalin should perish, and he expected the war to bring this about. Stalin recalled the way the decision had been taken to exile Trotsky abroad. The Politburo had raised the matter several times. In unofficial discussion, Kirov, Rykov, Tomsky, Kuibyshev, Mikoyan and Petrovsky had taken a cautious view: perhaps Trotsky had changed his mind? What if he confesses? Perhaps we could give him a second-rank job? After all, he is still extremely popular. But Stalin would not have any sort of reconciliation. He knew that, as long as Trotsky was still alive and in the USSR, he, Stalin, would not feel comfortable. After the sort of exchange of opinion that was at that time still possible, it was decided to sound out Trotsky himself. A man was sent from Moscow to Alma-Ata. A telegram came back a week or two later: Trotsky was not aware either of his guilt or of any cause for reconciliation with Stalin. The General Secretary read the telegram and gazed around at his comrades: he'd told them so! He had been certain that Trotsky was a still-armed enemy. No one now opposed the decision to send him out of the country.

According to Trotsky's record of this event, published posthumously in his *Diaries in Exile*, he told the emissary that he did not want reconciliation and Stalin was incapable of reconciliation, so therefore the affair was bound to end in bloodshed. When this was reported back to the Politburo, Stalin must have said foreign exile was the only solution. When later he heard that Trotsky was working on a book entitled simply *Stalin*, he anticipated a particularly venomous piece of work. But 1938 passed without a sign of it, and then 1939 and now it was 1940, so maybe it wasn't going to appear at all? Even so, he pressed Beria to get on with the job.

Stalin could not, however, know that, having set himself to become the biographer of his mortal enemy, Trotsky had condemned himself to creative failure. His *Stalin* is his weakest book, conveying nothing but bile and anger and revenge. By an act of iron will, he managed to write seven chapters, in the centre of which stood Cain in the masks of Soso, Koba, the revolutionary, the powerful leader of the party and the people. Even without reading it – and unique among Trotsky's published works, Stalin never did – one can guess at its contents, knowing the relationship of the author and the subject. It is written in the blackest ink of hatred. Napoleon once remarked that everything has a limit, even hatred. In overstepping that limit, something is lost, whether it be truth, reason or tranquillity.

In this unfinished book, Trotsky lost his talent as a publicist, writer and, most important, objective historian. Much of what he wrote about Stalin is true, but there is too much supposition and guesswork, all intended to show how Cain became Super-Cain. According to him, Stalin was born a villain; from childhood he was a moral monster. There is no need to prove the scientific weakness of such an approach. No one can be regarded as a born criminal. One cannot look at Stalin in the same light in 1918, in 1924, or in 1937. It is the same person, and yet it is not. In the ten years after he succeeded Lenin, he changed markedly. Yet that is the difficulty of creating his political portrait: while apparently struggling for the ideals of socialism – however twistedly understood – he committed crime after crime.

In his efforts to dethrone the leader of the new International, Stalin of course was aided and abetted by Comintern. Even during the period of reaction following the collapse of the Popular Fronts, there were many people who still thought of the USSR as the sole bulwark against Fascism and the approaching war. Soviet propaganda abroad, carried out via numerous and varied channels, broadcast the idea that Trotsky was an accomplice of capitalism, that he was its spy and an organizer of diversionary acts against the USSR. Pumped out in various forms, this idea had its effect. Wherever Trotsky might be, whether in France, Norway or Mexico, he confronted numerous intellectual and political enemies. These were not only members of Communist Parties, trade unions or progressive organizations, they were also some of his own followers who had become frustrated by the futility of his programme.

The Confederation of Mexican Workers and the Mexican Communist Party, under its leader Lombardo Toledano, protested fiercely against Trotsky's coming to Mexico, and throughout his stay there various organizations campaigned to have him thrown out. Fearing assassination, Trotsky sharply curtailed his excursions into the mountains or the city, and he accepted very few visitors. Gradually, many of his family and friends disappeared or abandoned him. Those who remained close included Alfred and Margarita Rosmer who had known Trotsky and his wife, Natalia Sedova, since the First World War. Once, in conversation with the Rosmers, Trotsky claimed that Stalin had poisoned Lenin. Lacking proper evidence, he was creating new and more horrific masks for the portrait he was painting. He claimed that, hearing about Lenin's Letter to the Congress, Stalin had decided to hasten events. But even the Rosmers were doubtful. Trotsky argued that, since Stalin had murdered all of Lenin's comrades-in-arms, why couldn't he have killed the leader himself?

The Trotskyist organizations in Mexico, helped by the Mexican government, managed to find Trotsky a large house in the village of Coyacan. It was turned into a veritable fortress, with iron gates, an elaborate alarm system and a high concrete wall with a watch-tower. At least ten police and special agents were on duty round the clock. Trotsky even wore a bullet-proof vest when he left the grounds. From his fastness, he made statements and gave interviews predicting the early demise of Stalin and a likely German victory over the USSR. The last two years of his life were dedicated to ideological warfare against his former homeland. In April 1940 he wrote an appeal entitled 'Letter to the Soviet Workers: You Are Being Deceived'. It was virtually a call to remove Stalin. Four months before his death, Trotsky wrote:

The October Revolution was made in the interests of the workers, not the new parasites. But because of the delay of the world revolution, the fatigue and to a great extent the backwardness of the Russian workers, especially the peasants, a new anti-people, coercive and parasitical caste, led by Stalin, looms over the Soviet republic.

Trotsky then loses his sense of reality and calls on the people to rise against the 'new caste'. For this, 'a new party is needed, a bold and honest revolutionary organization of the leading workers. The Fourth International sets itself the task of creating such a party in the USSR.' And the appeal ends with reiteration of Trotsky's constant priorities:

> Down with Cain Stalin and his camarilla!
> Down with the predatory bureaucracy!
> Long live the USSR, fortress of the workers!
> Long live the world socialist revolution!
> 25 April 1940. With fraternal greetings.[80]

After reading this, Stalin called in Beria and warned him that he was thoroughly fed up with all this and that he was beginning to doubt whether the NKVD really wanted to do the job. Beria held a number of meetings and the effort to liquidate Trotsky was redoubled. It appears the decision was made to exploit to the full the dissatisfaction felt by a number of public bodies over the Trotskyists' activities, notably during the civil war in Spain. As the Mexican Communist painter David Alfaro Siqueiros wrote in his book *They Called Me the Dashing Colonel*, even while they were still in Spain he and his friends decided that 'come what may, Trotsky's headquarters in Mexico must be destroyed, even if meant using force'.[81]

The war of words between Trotsky and the Communist organizations of various countries was music to Berlin's ears, though it gave no outward sign of its deep satisfaction. In a number of documents, Comintern roundly condemned the Fourth International and its leader 'for playing into the hands of the forces of war'. It was against this background that two attempts were made on Trotsky's life, the second one successful. The first was carried out on 24 May 1940 by a group disguised as policemen and led by Siqueiros. They sprayed Trotsky's bedroom with bullets, but the target and his wife managed to shelter in a corner of the room and no one was hurt. They now knew, however, that their pursuers meant business. Trotsky had neither the strength nor the desire to run away. He would not hide or be silent. The Mexican police could not find the perpetrators and there were even stories printed in US and Mexican papers that the whole drama had been staged by Trotsky himself to compromise the Mexican Communist Party and Stalin. When the police inspector asked him if he had any idea who might have been responsible, Trotsky replied, 'Of course,' and whispered in the inspector's ear, 'the author of the attack is Iosif Stalin.'

The real killer, however, was right there. 'Jacques Mornard' was a friend of the American Trotskyist Sylvia Agelof, who was one of Trotsky's secretaries. He had been a regular visitor to his target's house since 1939, though he met Trotsky himself for the first time only in May 1940. He had contacts in business circles where he passed as a Canadian called Frank Jacson. Somehow he gained Trotsky's confidence and they had several conversations, usually about 'strong personalities'. Trotsky's wife later recalled that they had wondered whether he wasn't some sort of Fascist. In fact, 'Jacson' was Ramon del Rio Mercader, a Spaniard in the service of Stalin.

In mid-August, 'Jacson' asked Trotsky to correct an article of his. Trotsky made some comments. On the evening of Tuesday, 20 August, 'Jacson' returned with the corrected article and went into Trotsky's study to show it to him. Trotsky was poring over a manuscript. 'Jacson' entered the room and, as he later demonstrated, placed his raincoat on a chair, retrieved an ice-pick from under it and, with his eyes closed, struck Trotsky in the head with full force. The victim, as 'Jacson' told the court at his trial, 'gave a terrible, piercing cry. I will hear it to the end of my life.' Trotsky's death agony lasted nearly twenty-four hours.

A letter was found on 'Jacson' in which he described himself as a 'disillusioned follower of Trotsky who had come to Mexico with a different purpose'. The idea of 'killing the criminal' had matured while he was there. The letter explained that he could not forgive Trotsky for 'conspiring with the leaders of capitalist countries'. The press was soon asking who this man really was. Who had guided his hand? And they just as soon chorused the reply: it was Stalin, the NKVD and the Communists. 'Jacson'-Mercader, however, as he sat out his twenty years in Mexican prison, questioned by doctors and psychiatrists, never departed from his original story.

He had in fact been the tool of an operation to be carried out by a large group of people under the direction of an NKVD man called Eitingon. The final choice of hit-man fell on the former lieutenant in the Spanish Republican Army, Ramon Mercader, who was twenty-seven at the time. He had not only had battlefield experience, but was convinced that the Anarchist and Trotskyist uprising against the Republican government in May 1937 had had Trotsky's blessing. Mercader was still 'hot' from the war and saw the murder of Trotsky as a noble revolutionary act.

After Trotsky's murder Beria was promoted, becoming General Commissar of State Security seven months later. He handed over the administration to V. N. Merkulov, while retaining the post of Commissar of Internal Affairs, to which was added the deputy chairmanship of the Sovnarkom.

Stalin could hardly wait to know what Trotsky's last will and testament contained when it was published. Most of it had been written on 27 February 1940 and mainly concerned his wife's material well-being, but he also found room in it to say something about Stalin:

This is not the place for me yet again to refute the stupid and base slander of Stalin and his agencies: there is no stain on my revolutionary honour. Neither directly nor indirectly have I ever entered into any backdoor agreements, nor even had talks with the enemies of the working class. Thousands of Stalin's opponents perished as victims of such false accusations.[82]

CHAPTER 39

Secret Diplomacy

For Stalin, diplomacy meant seeking the decisions and, if need be, the compromises that would secure favourable external conditions for bringing about the grandiose plans he had announced at the last congress. As leader, he could say he was aiming the country towards catching up and overtaking the developed capitalist countries, but he needed time and he needed peace, peace at any price. For this reason he replaced Litvinov, whom he regarded as too much of an anti-Fascist, with Molotov as foreign commissar. All avenues had to be explored to save the USSR from war. He was not fond of the classic forms of diplomacy, with visits, congresses, international conferences and summit meetings, preferring instead confidential correspondence, special emissaries and private talks, participating himself if the occasion required to be given special importance. But it was crucial that only a very small circle of people should be engaged in diplomacy as an arm of the country's foreign policy. The Foreign Commissariat and Interior Commissariat had to keep him supplied with the necessary facts and information about the real situation, the hidden springs and trends, so that he could make his decisions. Especially valuing secrecy, he had long forgotten the first decree of the Soviet state, namely, on 'Peace', which had condemned secret diplomacy; between December 1917 and February 1918, while Trotsky was Foreign Commissar, the government had published more than one hundred secret documents from the archives of the tsarist foreign ministry.

Stalin had often thought of trying to involve the USA in the mounting world crisis, but he established no constructive contact with the US president until the war. Strongly distrustful of the transatlantic colossus, he was equally doubtful that there was much the US could do in Europe. When on 15 April 1939 Roosevelt wrote to Hitler and Mussolini – his so-called 'Saturday surprise' – offering to act as an honest broker to settle all outstanding issues, and appealing to the Fascist leaders to give a ten- or fifteen-year undertaking not to attack thirty listed countries in Europe and the Middle East.[83] Stalin was at once surprised and sceptical. Discussing this with Molotov, he said, 'Only an idealist could imagine these proposals would even be discussed. Hitler has got the bit between his teeth and it won't be easy to stop him now.'

'Still, it is a noble step,' Molotov replied, 'even if the world is not ready to recognize it.'

It was decided the USSR should publish its view of Roosevelt's initiative and to this end a telegram was at once sent over M. I. Kalinin's signature – Kalinin, as head of state, of course having taken part only formally in the discussion:

Mr President
It is my pleasant duty to express my deep sympathy and heartfelt congratulations for the noble appeal you have made to the governments of Germany and Italy. You may be assured that your initiative will find the warmest response in the hearts of the peoples of the Soviet Socialist Union who are sincerely concerned with preserving the peace of the whole world.
16 iv.39 Kalinin[84]

When Soviet envoy to the USA K. A. Umansky was received by the President on 30 June 1939, however, Roosevelt limited himself to expressing a general desire that the Anglo-French-Soviet talks should succeed. Umansky cabled Moscow that the President 'was not prepared to use his considerable moral and material power to exert influence on British and French policy'.[85] Foreign policy was occasionally debated by the Politburo, but always after it had first been mapped out by Stalin and Molotov. They sometimes called in specialists from the foreign and internal commissariats, as well as military intelligence, to advise on specific issues, but policy was made by Stalin with the advice and suggestions of Molotov, whose opinions did not always coincide with those of his master.

Interviewed by the writer Konstantin Simonov, Zhukov mentioned that he had been present in Stalin's study during discussion of a number of important matters with his immediate circle: 'I witnessed argument and wrangling and stubborn resistance over some issues, especially from Molotov, and the situation got to the point where Stalin had to raise his voice and was even beside himself, while Molotov merely stood up with a smile and stuck to his point of view.'[86] Stalin was impressed by what Molotov told him of his meetings with Hitler. Stalin himself had only met Ribbentrop. He frequently referred to the Nazi leaders as 'crooks'. According to F. Haus, head of the German foreign ministry legal department, even during the talks on concluding the Pact, Stalin could not restrain himself from muttering sarcastically to the German delegation something akin to 'deception'. And, during the signing itself, Stalin said, 'Of course, we are not forgetting that your ultimate aim is to attack us.' In the discussions he had with Molotov about the likelihood of their being able to delay the war, Stalin frequently turned to the subject of Hitler himself, knowing full well how much depended in a totalitarian state on the will of the dictator.

In his dealings with the Germans, Stalin barely concealed his Machiavellianism. When the Pact had been signed, as Molotov told Chuev, Stalin raised his champagne glass and declared without irony: 'Let's drink to the new anti-Comintern Stalin! Let's drink to the health of the leader of the German people, Hitler!'

Ribbentrop at once rushed to the telephone in Molotov's office, where the talks had taken place, and reported to Hitler that the Pact had been concluded and what Stalin had said. As an overjoyed Ribbentrop immediately told Stalin, Hitler had replied: 'Oh, my great foreign minister! You don't know how much you have accomplished! Convey my congratulations to Herr Stalin, the leader of the Soviet people.' When he heard this, Stalin turned to Molotov and gave him a barely perceptible wink.

The Pact might not have been signed on 23 August, for on that day, the two giant Condor transport planes bringing the Ribbentrop delegation to Moscow were fired on in the region of Velikie Luki. No prior orders had been given to the anti-aircraft units covering their flight path, and it was only by a stroke of luck that they were not brought down. This has been confirmed in an interview with the author by M. A. Liokumovich, who was serving in the unit that opened fire. Naturally, that very day a large group of NKVD men flew out of Moscow to investigate the incident and find the perpetrator of the 'provocation'.

The second major action Stalin embarked on was to move the Soviet border further west, a subject we have discussed elsewhere and to some aspects of which we now return. The decision to take over Western Ukraine and Belorussia, in the face of the advancing German armies, was in my view justified, and it was broadly in accord with the desire of the local working class population. But, regrettably, Stalin's action, violating the 1921 Riga Treaty, was conditioned by his agreement with Hitler on future borders and territorial 're-arrangement'. In the absence of the originals, we may cite a number of documents which plainly confirm that an understanding had been reached.

On 10 September 1939 Beria sent a note to Molotov: 'In connection with forthcoming changes in the deployment of NKVD border troops of the Kiev and Belorussian military districts, the line of the Soviet state border is extended from 1,412 to 2,012 kilometres, or by 600 kilometres.' Beria proposed that a new Western military district be formed with five border units.[87] When Soviet troops entered the Western Ukraine and Belorussia, the dividing line between them and German forces was established according to a secret map which must have been agreed by the sides during the talks in August. This is borne out by the following document:

From the German military attaché in Moscow, General Köstring, to Red Army General Staff:

1 I request that Chief of Red Army General Staff Shaposhnikov be informed that at 2230 hours I received my government's reply that, following talks,

the town of Drogobych was handed over without difficulty to units of the Red Army today, 24.9.39, at 1800 hours.

2 It was agreed at the same time that the town of Sambor would be handed over on the morning of 26.9. I repeat again that no difficulties arose during the talks. I am very glad that things have gone so well.

3 It is my duty to report that, according to our airmen, large oil tanks have been burning in Drogobych for ten days. Local rumours are circulating that they were set alight by the Germans and I would ask you not to believe this, as this material was needed by us, too.

4 Concerning railway wagons, the Red Army General Staff knows that we have acted according to the protocol.

That is all I wanted to convey quickly. Köstring.

Received by adjutant to Red Army Chief of Staff, regimental commissar Moskvin.[88]

Other similar documents establish plainly that Stalin had found it necessary to agree on these and other 'details', such as the handing over to Hitler of a number of groups of German and Austrian anti-Fascists who had been arrested in the 1930s and were now either in prison or under investigation. During the August meetings between Molotov and Schulenburg, the German ambassador several times raised the matter of 'German citizens arrested in the USSR', and handing them over to the Reich.[89] After the signing of the Pact, and more so that of the secret protocols, Hitler had no difficulty in getting what he wanted.[90]

Britain's refusal at the tripartite talks to give broader guarantees of security to the Baltic states left no one in any doubt that they would be an easy prey for Hitler. As the result of talks on 28 September 1939 a mutual aid agreement was signed with Estonia, on 5 October with Latvia, and on 10 October with Lithuania, to which Vilna and the Vilna region were attached. Stalin took part in all the talks and ceremonies associated with the Baltic treaties, demonstrating the importance accorded these agreements by the USSR. Another significant step was the Soviet note to Romania of 26 June 1940 demanding the return of Bessarabia, whose seizure by force the USSR had never recognized.

But Stalin would not have been Stalin if the steps he took had not also caused misery and pain. In all the annexed territories in the Western Ukraine, Belorussia, the Baltic and Moldavia (Bessarabia), he at once set about 'sifting out hostile elements': kulaks, bourgeoisie, traders, former White Guards, Ukrainian nationalists, in general, all 'suspicious' categories. Many of them took the well known road to Siberia.

Economic, trade and border agreements were intended to underpin the Soviet–German understanding on neutrality, and, considering Stalin's suspicious nature, it is surprising that he was not alerted by some of Berlin's actions. For instance, in January 1941, the Germans refused to sign the so-called 'Economic Agreement' for a long period, then wanted it limited to 1941. He was also informed that, on the eve of the signing of the treaty establishing the Soviet–German border from the River Igorek to the Baltic Sea, the German officials had willingly made concessions and had not quibbled over every hillock, which would have been normal for border negotiations. As *Pravda* noted, the 'treaty on borders was worked out in an extremely short time, such as never happens in world practice'. Stalin and the other Soviet leaders ought to have realized that the Germans were not concerned about where the borders ran because they regarded them as purely temporary. The Oldenburg Plan, which accompanied Operation Barbarossa, envisaged the frontier of the future empire as being far to the east. Hitler did not conceive his ideas about German 'Lebensraum' in the abstract, but Stalin lacked the statesmanship and wisdom to give proper value to these and other notions. Instead, he was a prisoner of his own false calculations about the timing of the German invasion.

During this pre-war period, there was one final diplomatic action for which Stalin was responsible, and that was the treaty of neutrality signed with Japan. At the end of March 1941, the Japanese foreign minister, I. Matsuoka, arrived in Moscow. The first round of talks produced no result, since the Japanese insisted that the USSR sell them northern Sakhalin. Stalin, who took part in the talks, sat silent as the Japanese minister spoke, and then parried the demand with a single phrase: 'Are you joking?' It seemed the talks would be broken off. Matsuoka bade his Soviet hosts a cold farewell and departed for Berlin, returning again on 8 April for further talks. A treaty seemed unlikely, as the Japanese continued to make unacceptable demands. On this occasion, however, Stalin's firmness paid off, for on the day Matsuoka was due to leave, he received new instructions from Tokyo, the Japanese demands were withdrawn and the treaty on neutrality was signed that evening. The USSR's strategic position in the Far East was markedly improved by this act. The Japanese also undertook to respect the territorial integrity and inviolability of the Mongolian People's Republic. The treaty was not, however, without difficulty for the Soviet side. The Chinese government had been openly opposed to the treaty. As early as 27 August, following the signing of the Soviet–German Pact, the Chinese ambassador to Moscow, Sung Fo, requested a meeting with deputy foreign commissar S.A. Lozovsky, at which the Chinese stated frankly: 'We are worried about two matters: 1) the rumours about a non-aggression pact between the Soviet Union and Japan, and 2) rumours of an agreement between Japan and Britain. From the point of view of China's national interests, neither of these is helpful. If the USSR concludes a non-aggression pact with Japan it would inevitably lead to a lessening of her aid to China.'

Lozovsky replied: 'As far as a non-aggression pact between Japan and the USSR is concerned, we know nothing of this. There was an occasion when the USSR proposed such a pact, but Japan declined. The question is not now on the agenda.'[91]

Such had been the position eighteen months before, but now Stalin was eager to reduce the pressure on his eastern flank.

For the last five years relations between Japan and the USSR had been rife with conflict, friction, the frequent and sharp exchange of notes and major armed clashes. The most serious of these – involving a million troops! – took place in Mongolia at Khalkin Gol and Lake Khasan and were no doubt the reason the Japanese decided finally to sign the treaty. Stalin knew that he was untying Japan's hands to carry out the Tanaka Plan of 1927 for the conquest of the Pacific, but he had no choice while Hitler was the greater threat.

Matsuoka departed for home the same evening, and only minutes before the train was due to leave, Stalin, accompanied by a large retinue of security guards, arrived at the station to say a personal farewell, throwing the Japanese minister into total confusion. As he shook hands with the departing guests, Stalin reiterated the importance he attached to the treaty they had just signed, as well as the Declaration on the mutual respect of the territorial integrity and inviolability of Manchukuo and the Mongolian People's Republic. He also took the opportunity to thank the German diplomats accompanying Matsuoka.

Stalin was in two minds: he knew that war was inevitable yet he refused to believe it was imminent. He therefore repeated over and over that 'we must not be provoked.' The Germans, meanwhile, realizing that Stalin's sole purpose was to gain time, became more brazen. For instance, from the beginning of 1941 German planes began violating Soviet borders by the dozen and penetrating deeper and deeper into Soviet airspace. Even if they were forced down, both crews and aircraft were immediately returned to the Germans. When just before the war a Soviet border unit shot down a German reconnaissance aircraft, killing two airmen, Stalin ordered the punishment of those responsible, while a telegram was sent to the Soviet envoy in Berlin, Skornyakov, saying 'Go at once to Goering and express regret for the incident.'[92]

When Mussolini found he could not establish himself in the Balkans without help, he turned to the Führer, who agreed on condition the Italian army be placed fully under German military leadership. As Hitler's forces began concentrating for the invasion of Greece and Yugoslavia, the latter proposed a treaty of friendship and non-aggression with the USSR. Stalin had already told Berlin as early as 17 January 1941 that the USSR regarded the eastern part of the Balkan peninsula as a zone of Soviet security and that it could not be indifferent to events in the area. As a further signal to Hitler that the USSR did not want the war to spread to the Balkans, Stalin signed the USSR–Yugoslav Pact on 5 April 1941. Hitler, however, chose to humiliate Stalin by totally ignoring both signals, and within days of the treaty having been signed, German forces invaded Yugoslavia.

It had been clear since the middle of 1940 to both Hitler and Stalin that relations between them were deteriorating. Hitler invited Stalin to visit Berlin, but Moscow decided Molotov should go instead. On the eve of Molotov's departure, in November 1940, he and Stalin, with Beria in attendance, spent the long night trying to fathom what Hitler might want and what they might do to keep the Pact going for at least another couple of years.

Molotov was met at the station in Berlin by Ribbentrop, Keitel, Ley, Himmler and other Nazi top brass whose presence made it plain that Hitler thought this a most significant visit. With England's inevitable defeat, as they believed, they wanted to allay the fears of their powerful neighbour and put them off their guard.

As we have seen, during the negotiations Hitler and Ribbentrop spent more than two hours trying to divert Molotov with talk of 'spheres of influence', 'the imminent demise of the British Empire' and so on. Molotov demonstratively showed no interest in Germany's global plans and insisted on getting replies to certain concrete questions, such as why there were German troops in Finland, when would German troops be withdrawn from Bulgaria and Romania, why had Hungary joined the Tripartite Pact [of Germany, Italy and Japan]? Hitler was disappointed. Nothing he said would deflect Molotov, while the latter made it plain that Moscow was presently concerned only by her relations with Germany. As Hitler accompanied Molotov out of the Great Hall in the new Chancellery, he took him by the arm and said: 'I know that history will remember Stalin. But it will also remember me.' Molotov replied with his customary lack of feeling: 'Yes, of course it will.'

A matter of weeks later, on 18 December, Hitler signed the plan for Operation Barbarossa, which envisaged that 'the basic strength of Russia's land forces deployed in western Russia, must be destroyed by bold operations employing the deep and rapid movement of tank spearheads. The retreat and dispersal of battle-worthy enemy troops over a wide expanse of Russian territory must be prevented.'[93] But Molotov sensed none of this and continued to believe that although there would be war, it was not going to come immediately.

Stalin had been very careful to observe the terms of the Non-Aggression Pact with Germany and on the first anniversary of its signing the Soviet press devoted considerable space to it. The Germans for their part barely marked the occasion. A month later, however, on 27 September, they signed the Tripartite Pact with Japan and Italy, giving Germany and Italy a free hand to create 'the new order in Europe', while Japan would be free to do the same in the Far East. Next day, when the Soviet–German treaty on friendship and borders was a year old, the Germans celebrated it. Reading the embassy reports from Berlin, Stalin was amazed at Hitler's audacity.

Discussing the latest developments with Molotov, Stalin, who by now ought to have seen reality staring him in the face, persisted in his belief that the war, though inevitable, was still two or three years away. Instead of consulting with his military leadership and his diplomats, he had relied on his own judgement, knowing no doubt that they would in any case only try to agree with him. The bureaucracy he had so assiduously cultivated was only capable of approving his decisions. He was now reaping the harvest of his one-man rule. Zhukov recalled how, once during a conversation, Stalin had snapped at two senior members of his, Stalin's, secretariat: 'What's the point of talking to you? Whatever I say, you reply, "Yes, Comrade Stalin, of course, Comrade Stalin, you have taken a wise decision, Comrade Stalin."' Apart from Molotov, Voznesensky and Zhdanov, who, if they did not actually disagree with Stalin, at least offered some debate, all the other members of the Politburo did no more than obediently agree with him. For Stalin these top party officials were nothing more than functionaries, executors of his orders. No one doubted Stalin's judgement. Even when his decisions on the eve of the war were plainly at odds with reality, no one allowed himself to think the leader could be wrong. They simply thought they had not fully understood what was in his mind. Zhukov recalled the enormous faith he had had in Stalin's political wisdom and in his ability to postpone the outbreak of war.[94]

In the last two months before the war, Stalin received several reports from a variety of intelligence, diplomatic and other sources, warning of Hitler's impending attack on the USSR. The British and US governments also sent warnings. In April 1941, Churchill, who was now prime minister, sent a report that the Germans were moving large numbers of their forces to the east. Stalin dismissed this as another attempt by the English to push the USSR into war with Hitler. Later, in Moscow in 1942, he told Churchill that he had needed no such warnings, as he knew perfectly well Hitler was going to attack. He had merely been hoping to gain a further six months or so.[95] Similar warnings accumulated, however, to a point where Stalin felt it prudent to test them out in Berlin itself. On 14 June 1941 he ordered TASS to publish a statement dismissing rumours of German troop concentrations on the USSR's borders as nonsense and clumsy propaganda put out by forces hostile to Germany and the USSR:

Germany is observing the terms of the non-aggression Pact as scrupulously as the USSR, and therefore rumours of Germany's intention to violate the Pact and attack the USSR are groundless, while the recent transfer of German forces from the Balkans to the eastern and northeastern areas of Germany must be assumed to be linked to other motives unconnected with Soviet–German relations

This strange statement was explained by a senior Soviet official after the war as having been a normal diplomatic sounding, but it was read by millions of Soviet citizens and the entire armed forces, and it had a profoundly disorienting effect. Such a 'sounding' ought to have been carried out secretly and its results ought to have been made known at least to the senior army command, the defence commissariat and the military districts. It was everywhere understood in the same way, according to L. M. Sandalov, a staff officer during the war:

Coming from an authoritative state body, such a statement was bound to dull the forces' vigilance. The officers were convinced there were some unknown circumstances which made our government feel unconcerned and secure about our borders. Officers stopped sleeping at the barracks. The soldiers started undressing for bed.[96]

While Berlin ignored the statement, the Soviet people, trained to take everything on trust, were further convinced that war was unlikely. As time was running out, and German troops were obviously on the move eastward, Stalin relied still more on diplomacy, sending notes, publishing the TASS statement, and above all putting off the urgent decision to place the troops on full battle-readiness.

Moscow waited for Berlin's response with mounting unease. The Soviet embassy in Berlin, however, reported that the Germans were totally refusing to respond. A note reporting an airspace violation was sent to Berlin, again without evoking a response. In Moscow Molotov called in the German ambassador to explain the incident, and also to evince a reply to the TASS statement, while at the same time in Berlin the Soviet ambassador tried to see Ribbentrop. All was in vain. While Stalin was waiting for German assurances about the Pact, on 21 June Hitler wrote to Mussolini to say that he expected complete success in his eastern campaign:

> Whatever happens, Duce, our position will not be worsened by this step, it can only be improved ...
>
> I feel freer in myself, now that I have taken the decision. I found cooperation with the Soviet Union, despite the sincere attempt to seek détente, very burdensome. For it seemed to me like a break with my past, my outlook and my former obligations. I'm happy to have shed that moral burden.

CHAPTER 40

Fatal Omissions

A month before the German attack, Stalin, speaking to a close circle, said, 'The conflict is inevitable, perhaps in May next year.' By the early summer of 1941, acknowledging the explosiveness of the situation, he approved the premature release of military cadets, and young officers and political workers were posted, mostly without leave, straight to units which were below full strength. After much hesitation, Stalin also decided to call up about 800,000 reservists, bringing up to strength twenty-one divisions in the frontier military districts. Unfortunately, this was done only two or three weeks before the attack.

On 19 June troops were ordered to begin camouflaging aerodromes, transport depôts, bases and fuel dumps, and to disperse aircraft around airfields. The order came hopelessly late, and even then Stalin was reluctant in case 'all these measures provoke the German forces'. Timoshenko and Zhukov had to ask him two or three times to approve their operational orders. While agreeing with the military, he clung to the idea that Hitler would not risk a war on two fronts, and did not appreciate that in fact there was no real second front in the middle of 1941.

The nature of Stalin's miscalculations lay not only in his wrong assessments, his wrong predictions or even the ill will of the aggressor, though these were of course all present. His unforgivable mistakes stemmed from his personal rule. It is hard to blame the commissars or the Chief War Council, when their boss's image was that of the infallible and wise leader. The memory of the political trials was fresh in all their minds, and any 'misunderstanding' or 'objection' or sign of 'political immaturity' could and still did have serious consequences.

To please Stalin, everyone talked about the 'invincibility of the Red Army', the 'strengthening of proletarian attitudes in Germany', and how the internal difficulties of capitalism would cause it to 'explode from within'. The press and radio and even the academic experts were saying similar things. For instance,

Ye. Varga, a leading economic adviser to Stalin at that time (later to fall from grace), said during a lecture at the Lenin Military-Political Academy on 17 April:

The question arises, will there be victors and vanquished in this war, or will it go on so long that neither side will be able to defeat the other? The interests of the USSR demand the preservation of peace until a revolutionary crisis ripens in the capitalist countries. If such a situation should arise, the bourgeois régimes will be weakened and the proletariat will take power, and the Soviet Union must and will. go to the help of the proletarian revolutions in other countries.[97]

Such views were widespread at the time and were inherited from the civil war. On the other hand, even at that time, there were more sober and courageous minds at work. For instance, in 1940 a group at the above academy prepared a thirty-five-page paper on 'Military Ideology' which was shown to Stalin. Alongside the orthodox views of the time, a number of heretical questions were raised. The authors frankly confronted the causes for the USSR's failures in the Soviet–Finnish war: the low cultural level of the officers, false propaganda about the invincibility of the Red Army, 'incorrect presentation of the Red Army's international tasks', 'the deeply rooted and harmful prejudice that, inevitably and practically to a man, the population of countries at war with the USSR will supposedly rise up and go over to the side of the Red Army'. Talk of 'invincibility leads to arrogance, superficiality and neglect of military science; in the field of technology it leads to backwardness, and in the field of military theory it leads to the one-sided development of notions of battle to the detriment of others'. The study of foreign war theory, according to this memorandum, had been thoroughly suppressed, while the best traditions of the Russian army had not been popularized. The experience of Khalkin Gol and Lake Khasan was unknown to the military leadership: 'material on these battles is kept under wraps at General Staff.' Stalin's comment amounted to nothing more than 'File it'.[98] The fate of its authors is not known.

In my opinion, Stalin's biggest mistake was to sign the treaty on friendship and borders with Hitler on 28 September 1939. It was enough – and there was justification – to sign the Non-Aggression Pact of a month before, minus the secret protocols. In Comintern resolutions and those of the Eighteenth Party Congress, Nazism was properly defined as a terroristic, militaristic, dictatorial régime and the most dangerous phalanx of world imperialism. To Soviet minds, it was the embodiment of the class enemy in concentrated form. And now, out of the blue, we were their best friends! It is difficult to explain Stalin's cynical shift to a policy of whitewashing Fascism. One can understand the attempt to underpin the Non-Aggression Pact by trade agreements and economic ties. But to disavow all one's previous anti-Fascist ideological premises was going too far. Germany's expansionist plans were not properly understood by Stalin. For instance, the 'Statement of the Soviet and German governments' declares that 'the mutual agreement expresses the view that the liquidation of the war between Germany, on the one hand, and England and France on the other, would correspond to the interests of all peoples.'[99] The peoples themselves, however, could justifiably have asked how this was possible. Were they to reconcile themselves to Hitler's seizure of most of Europe? How could Poland, lying in ruins, approve the 'mutual agreement' signed by Molotov and Ribbentrop?

In his desperate search for ways to avoid war, Stalin went too far, for the concessions he made added nothing to the Pact itself except Nazi brazenness and Soviet confusion. It is true that Stalin was enormously influenced in his German policy by Molotov, many of whose statements befuddled both the Soviet public and our friends abroad. For instance, the speech he made – approved by Stalin – at the Supreme Soviet on 31 October 1939, includes the following:

Germany is in the position of a state that is striving for a rapid end to the war and for peace, while Britain and France, who yesterday were clamouring against aggression, are now for continuing the war and against the conclusion of peace ... Ruling circles in England and France have recently tried to present themselves as fighters for the democratic rights of the peoples against Hitlerism, the British government declaring that its war aim is neither more nor less than the 'annihilation of Hitlerism' ... It is not only meaningless, it is criminal to fight such a war as a war 'to annihilate Hitlerism' under the false flag of fighting for 'democracy' ... Our relations with Germany have improved fundamentally. This has come through strengthening our friendly relations, developing our practical collaboration and through our political support of Germany as she strives for peace.[100]

Apart from the fact that such a political and ideological change of course created havoc in the public mind, it revealed an utter lack of principle. Stalin, who sent millions to their deaths and the camps on the faintest suspicion of their ideological 'impurity', was startlingly lacking in fastidiousness when it came to fraternizing with Nazism. While many members of Comintern could not understand the reasons for his sudden ideological shift, there was nothing they could do to change Comintern's official line. Up to June 1941, Comintern was at odds with the European Communist and Labour Parties over their assessment of the anti-Fascist character of their countries' struggle. As in the late 1920s and early 1930s, Comintern's sharpest arrows were reserved for attacks on the social democrats as the 'accomplices of militarism'. The slogan 'End the war!' came to have no meaning. How could one end the war when Hitler held half of Europe? Moscow provided no answer. The word Fascist disappeared from the Soviet leadership's vocabulary. Berlin was happy. In his speech to the Reichstag on 1 September 1939, Hitler could justifiably say, 'The Pact has been ratified in Berlin and Moscow ... I can join with every word Foreign Commissar Molotov has said on this subject.'[101]

Propagandists in the country at large, and the Red Army in particular, were placed in an impossible position. For instance, as chief of army propaganda,

Mekhlis issued an order to the political agencies and party organizations stating:

Political instruction of young soldiers must include the 'law on universal military service', Comrade Voroshilov's speech at the fourth session of the Supreme Soviet, the military oath, the law on punishment for treason, the rules and regulations, Comrade Molotov's report 'on the ratification of the Soviet–German Treaty of Non-Aggression'.[102]

Mekhlis entered this last phrase by hand. When he had submitted the draft to Stalin the day before, the leader had snapped: 'Don't irritate the Germans. *Krasnaya Zvezda** is always writing about Fascists and Fascism. Stop it. The situation is changing. We don't have to shout about it. Everything in its time. Hitler shouldn't get the idea that all we're doing is preparing for war with him.'[103]

Stalin was confident that Mekhlis would find a way of stifling anti-Fascist commentary in the press and at the same time give the order to inject mistrust of the Nazis into the army's political instruction. Reports received by the army propaganda administration, after the Soviet–German understandings were reached, contained quite a few concrete examples of the distorted way instructors were seeing things:

Military Engineer second class Nechaev: 'With the ratification of the Pact ... we must no longer call rifle practice "firing at Fascism". There is to be no agitation or propaganda against Fascism, as our government has no differences with Fascism.'

Military-engineering academy instructor Karatun: 'We have no idea now what to write or how to write, we were brought up anti-Fascist, but now it's the opposite.'

First Lieutenant Gromov, Kiev military district: 'If you think about it, Germany seems to have fooled everyone. Germany will now deal with the small countries, but because of the Non-Aggression Pact we won't be able to do anything about it.'[104]

It is now difficult to establish precisely who suggested introducing the word 'friendship' into the title of the treaty. If it was the Soviet side, it testifies to political mindlessness. If it was the Germans, it was a calculated assault on the social awareness of the entire nation. In either case, Stalin was not on top of the situation and it is doubtful that Molotov was right when he later said that Stalin had 'guessed what Hitler was up to in time'.

The way the plan for the country's defence and deployment of the armed forces was prepared represents another serious omission. Soon after the signing of the Pact, the General Staff received Stalin's personal instruction to set about preparing this plan. Under Shaposhnikov's leadership, the chief planner was the future Marshal, then Colonel, A. M. Vasilievsky, whose basic idea was that

---

* The Red Army newspaper, 'Red Star'.

the army must be ready to fight on two fronts, in Europe against Germany and in the Far East against Japan, 'the western theatre being the main area of operations'. The enemy was expected to concentrate his main force in the Western and Northwestern sectors, and the Red Army should therefore group its main force in those areas.[105] The plan was turned down, however, by the Defence Commissar, who thought it had not taken sufficient account of what Soviet forces could do to destroy the enemy.

The revised defence plan was ready for review by August 1940. It had been prepared under the leadership of Chief of Staff K. A. Meretskov, with Vasilievsky again in charge of the planning and again maintaining that Soviet forces must concentrate on the Western sector. The plan was submitted to Stalin on 5 October. He listened carefully to the defence commissar and the chief of staff, looked at the map a few times, paced the room in silence for a while, and finally pronounced:

I don't fully understand the General Staff's insistence on concentrating our forces on the western front. They say Hitler will try to send his main attacking force in the direction of Moscow by the shortest route. But I think the most important thing for the Germans is the grain in the Ukraine and the coal of the Donbass. Now that Hitler has established himself in the Balkans, it's all the more likely he'll launch his main attack from the southwest. I want the General Staff to think again and submit a new plan in ten days time.[106]

While defining the defence plan, the General Staff was simultaneously working on a position paper, entitled 'Views on the Principles of the Strategic Deployment of the Armed Forces in the West and East in 1940–1941'. Here, Germany was identified as the chief danger and the main task was defined as creating a sound border defence with field fortifications to prevent the enemy from entering Soviet territory, thus allowing time for total mobilization. Then strong counterattacks should be mounted to push the enemy back and to carry the battle on to his ground.

Shortly before war broke out, Stalin, characteristically, ordered a copy of the Red Army's field manual to be brought to him. The book bears all the marks of his having read it thoroughly. His remarks at the Chief Defence Council, however, and at meetings with senior military figures, suggest that, rather than military and strategic doctrine, he relied on common sense tinged with caution. He came to the war as a confident politician, not as a military thinker.

The defence plan was resubmitted to him on 14 October 1940. His proposals had naturally been incorporated, meaning that the basic orientation of the forces was shifted to the southwest.[107] Military intelligence, meanwhile, was perfectly aware that the Wehrmacht's main attacking force, consisting of three of their four tank armies, was routed to Smolensk and Moscow. Yet none of the army chiefs had the nerve or the arguments to persuade Stalin. The top posts in the General Staff, moreover, were now occupied by men promoted from the Kiev special military district: S. K. Timoshenko as defence commissar, G. K. Zhukov, who became Chief of General Staff in February 1941, N. F. Vatutin, Zhukov's first deputy, S. K. Kozhevnikov, head of the political section of the General Staff. All naturally considered the southwest of primary importance – and of course they also knew Stalin's thinking. A document on deployment for 1940, prepared by the new chief of the Kiev special military district, M. A. Purkaev, stated baldly that the sharpest attacks of the German army must be expected in the southwest.[108]

Stalin's approval of the plan was accompanied by Zhukov's becoming Chief of General Staff. In the space of six months, three men had held that post. In August 1940, Shaposhnikov had been replaced by Meretskov, who now handed over to Zhukov.

By nature a strong-willed, resolute man, Zhukov believed that, since Hitler would make the first strike, the Germans would gain a decisive advantage. He discussed his thoughts and doubts with Timoshenko, and on 15 May 1941 he sent the following handwritten note to Stalin:

> As Germany is now fully mobilized, and with her rear organized, she has the ability to surprise us with a sudden attack. To avert this, I think it essential that we deprive the German command of the initiative by forestalling their forces during deployment, by attacking them at the moment they are at the deployment stage and have not had time to organize a front or coordinate their forces.

Zhukov concluded by stating that the Red Army's first and last aims were the destruction of the enemy's main force on the Central and Northern sectors.[109]

Thus, five weeks before the catastrophe, Zhukov was proposing a radical change to Stalin, namely that the Soviet Union launch an attack on the Germans. There are no visible signs on Zhukov's memorandum of how Stalin reacted. On the contrary, in early June he ordered the reinforcement of the Southwestern sector with a further twenty-five divisions. In late April 1941, the NKVD intelligence sources had reported that 'the German invasion of the Soviet Union has been finally decided and will occur very soon. The operational plan of attack envisages a lightning strike on the Ukraine and further advance to the East.'[110]

This was an attempt by the Germans to disorient the Soviet leadership. As Zhukov wrote much later: 'We now know about the warnings of an impending attack on the Soviet Union and the concentration of enemy forces on our borders. But at that time, as documents captured from the Germans would show, Stalin was receiving reports of a very different kind.'[111] Stalin, however, did not acquaint his General Staff with all the information that ended up on his desk. For instance, as we have said elsewhere, he dismissed Churchill's warning telegram as a provocation and it only came to the notice of the General Staff long after its arrival in Moscow.

Similarly, I was told by Academician B. N. Ponomarev, an old Comintern hand and party secretary, that at some point in the spring of 1941, probably in late May, two Austrian communists arrived in Moscow from 'over there'. They were alarmed by the huge military preparations going on in Germany on the Soviet Union's western borders, and the endless columns of tanks, artillery and trucks moving eastwards day and night. Ponomarev passed this on to Georgi Dimitrov* who went to Stalin. Dimitrov told Ponomarev next day: 'Stalin took the Austrian news calmly and said he'd had many such signals, but he saw no grounds for particular disquiet. Yesterday, for instance, the Politburo had gone over its vacation schedule and most of the members and candidate members were taking the opportunity to go on their summer holiday. 'The first to go to the south [on vacation] will be A. A. Zhdanov, and he after all is a member of the war council of the frontier district. And on that note,' Dimitrov said, 'Stalin considered the matter closed.'

Ponomarev's puzzlement as to why Stalin could or would not see the danger has been expressed by many others. Zhukov probably put it best when he said that all of Stalin's actions and thoughts on the eve of the war were subordinated to the single effort to avoid war, and this generated in him the certain belief that it would not occur. But the chief of military intelligence, F. I. Golikov, must surely have informed Stalin that by the beginning of March 1941 the Wehrmacht would number eight million men, 12,000 tanks, 52,000 guns and about 20,000 aircraft? It was obvious that Germany could not keep such vast forces inactive for long. And Stalin must have known that the main force of that army was now concentrated on his western border.

On the other hand, Stalin was receiving reports of a different kind, for instance, about the German people's unwillingness to fight, desertion in the German army, a defeatist mood, and that the troops in the east were talking pacifism and saying that, if Germany got herself into a war with Russia, she would be defeated, and similar sentiments.[112] Whether such views really existed or were a subtle form of disinformation, they suited Stalin's mood.

Zhukov told Simonov that, in early 1941, when the flow of reports of German troop concentrations in Poland increased markedly, Stalin wrote a personal letter to Hitler to say he was surprised by these events, for they created the impression that Hitler was preparing to fight the USSR. Hitler replied with a personal and, as he stressed, confidential letter, saying that the information was correct and that large troop units were indeed concentrated in Poland. Being sure that this would not go further than Stalin, he wanted to explain, however, that his troops in Poland were not being aimed against the Soviet Union and that he intended to observe the Pact strictly on his honour as head of state. He found an argument that, according to Zhukov, Stalin must have believed, namely that the British were carrying out heavy bombing of western and central Germany and, since they could observe the territory from the air at will, he was compelled to move large numbers of troops to the east. At the

---

* Bulgarian Communist and Comintern leader.

same time, Köstring, the German military attaché in Moscow, was telling Soviet officials that German forces were being given leave – 'let them have a rest.'[113]

In the Defence Commissar's directive 'On the results of battle training inspection for the winter period of 1941 and orders for the summer period', signed by Timoshenko and Zhukov on 17 May 1941, absolutely no mention is made of tasks for the western military districts, nor for raising vigilance or battle-readiness or steadfastness in defence or preparing to repel mass air attacks and invasion by large numbers of tanks. It contained routine remarks about 'inadequacies in the individual training of the soldier' and the 'complete absence of operational orders'.[114]

Military intelligence meanwhile continued to send in alarming reports. At the end of May 1941 Colonel Bondarev of Kiev reported the incessant arrival of new tank, artillery and infantry units in eastern Poland: 'The concentration of forces on the Soviet border is continuing. The preparation for war is going on at a forced pace.'[115] In the Western sector, Colonel Blokhin of military intelligence reported that 'especially since 25 May, German preparations against the USSR have been intensified,' and that a German agent had stated during interrogation that he was supposed to return with his information to the town of Ciechanow not later than 5 June, because he'd been told military operations against the USSR were an early possibility.[116] The defence commissar sent several missions to inspect the tank units in the frontier districts and the results were collated in a report dated 17 June. But it contained only such routine criticisms as: 1) training is intermittent and uncoordinated, 2) gunnery instruction is running two or three months behind schedule, 3) coordination between different categories of troops within units is bad, 4) the mechanized regiments are training as if they were rifle regiments and have no conception of their proper rôle, 5) wireless operators are inadequately trained; and so on for seventeen items.[117]

The chief of army political propaganda, A. I. Zaporozhets, made a tour of the fortifications along the new western border and his report to Stalin was hardly reassuring: 'The majority of fortified districts on our western borders are not battle-worthy. The completed long-term gun emplacements have no guns. The fortified districts do not have the necessary number of permanent and specially constructed barracks.'[118] Stalin passed the report on to Timoshenko with the suggestion that the builders be told to work harder.

Zhukov said later that Stalin resisted all attempts by the military leadership to put the troops on alert on the western frontier. His fear of 'provoking' Hitler had become 'maniacal'. One can understand the desire not to give Hitler an excuse to attack, but he can hardly have imagined that Hitler would attack if provoked, if invasion of the USSR did not already figure in his plans. Hitler meanwhile consulted his own military leaders who told him the transport of German troops by rail to the east would be completed by 19 June, and that by the evening of 21 June the first strike aircraft would fly at low level to new aerodromes on the Soviet border east of the Vistula. Hitler changed one detail in the plan, namely, he set zero hour at 3.00 instead of 3.30 a.m. on 22 June. Reports came in during the night of 20/21 June of frontier barbed wire having been removed and of large numbers of German aircraft violating the border.[119]

It is perhaps easier to understand the drama of those last hours if we recall that an important feature of Stalin's psychological make-up was that of great cautiousness. Naturally in ordinary everyday affairs the question of audacity did not arise, but in major affairs he was extremely circumspect. For instance, in October 1917, his initiative was minimal because he did not fully comprehend what was happening. In 1934, he did not exploit the murder of Kirov in the way he intended straight away, but waited until 1937–38 to 'root out the enemies of the people', which, in his own words, ought to have been done four years earlier. He had patience and could wait for the public mind to reach the required condition, drop by drop. Bukharin had indeed called him 'the great giver of doses'.

His hyper-cautiousness in dealing with Hitler, however, was counter-productive, for Hitler outwitted him. Stalin's behaviour was dictated not only by a realization of the consequences of a 'premature' war, but also by a deep inner insecurity. The USSR faced the capitalist world alone. Any false step could lead to irreparable results. Berlin took note of Stalin's obsessive avoidance of 'provocations' and concluded that the USSR was weak. When Stalin ordered both the troops in the Western sector and border units not to use weapons against German planes which violated the border, the Germans at once deduced that caution had become indecisiveness.

On the eve of the war, Colonel General M. P. Kirponos, commander of the Kiev district, reported several cases of German deserters coming over. They divulged that the Germans were going to attack that night. Timoshenko telephoned Stalin at once. After a pause, Stalin ordered him to come with Zhukov and Vatutin. Zhukov recalled later that, when they arrived, the entire Politburo was already assembled, Stalin was pacing up and down, as usual, and on their entry, turned to the company and said, 'Well, what now?' There was complete silence. Finally the voice of Timoshenko broke the tension: 'We must immediately order all troops in the frontier districts on to full battle alert.' Stalin snapped, 'Read this.' Zhukov read the draft of a General Staff order which stressed the need for decisive action in accordance with the plan to repel the enemy. Stalin broke in:

It would be premature to issue that order now. It might still be possible to settle the situation by peaceful means. We should issue a brief order saying that an attack might begin if provoked by German action. The border units must not allow themselves to be provoked into anything that might cause difficulties.[120]

As the military were leaving to issue their orders, Stalin muttered, as if to himself: 'I think Hitler is trying to provoke us. He surely hasn't decided to make war?'

The Politburo dispersed at 3 a.m. It was the shortest night of the year. Stalin gazed through his limousine windows at the empty streets, unaware that German aircraft were already on their way to bomb Soviet towns and aerodromes, and he had hardly laid his head on the pillow when there was a cautious knock on the door. He went outside and was told by the duty officer, 'General Zhukov is asking to speak to you on the telephone on a matter that cannot wait!' Stalin picked up the phone and listened as Zhukov briefly recounted the attacks by enemy aircraft on Kiev, Minsk, Sevastopol, Vilna and elsewhere. Zhukov then said, 'Did you understand what I said, Comrade Stalin?' The dictator said nothing. Again Zhukov asked, 'Comrade Stalin, do you understand?' Stalin finally understood. It was four o'clock on the morning of 22 June 1941.

8

A CATASTROPHIC BEGINNING

'A nation pays for the errors of its statesmen.'
– Nikolai Berdyaev

CHAPTER 41

A Paralysing Shock

Stalin finally mumbled: 'Come to the Kremlin with Timoshenko. Tell Poskrebyshev to summon all the members of the Politburo.' He returned to the Kremlin and went up to his office by the entrance reserved for him alone. As he passed the pale-faced Poskrebyshev, he snapped 'Get the others here, now!'

Silent and somewhat cautious, the members of the Politburo filed in, followed by Timoshenko and Zhukov. Without any word of greeting, Stalin said to no one in particular, 'Get the German consul on the phone.' Molotov left the room. A tense silence fell. Around the table sat Andreyev, Voroshilov, Kaganovich, Mikoyan, Kalinin, Shvernik, Beria, Malenkov, Voznesensky and Shcherbakov. When he returned, Molotov felt all eyes were on him. He went to his place and stammered out: 'The ambassador reported that the German government has declared war on us.' He glanced at a piece of paper in his hand. 'The formal reason is the standard one: "Nationalist Germany has decided to forestall an attack by the Russians."'

The silence seemed almost tangible. Stalin sat down and looked at Molotov with angry eyes, as if he were remembering his confident prediction six months earlier that Hitler would never wage a war on two fronts, and that the USSR had plenty of time to strengthen its western defences. 'Plenty of time ...' Stalin felt betrayed. The others were waiting for him to speak and give them their orders.

Timoshenko broke the silence: 'Comrade Stalin, may I get a report of the situation?'

'Yes.'

The first deputy Chief of Staff, Major General N. F. Vatutin, entered the room. His brief report contained little new information: after a storm of artillery fire and air attacks on a number of targets in the Northwest and Western sectors, large numbers of German forces had invaded Soviet territory. The border units which took the main brunt of the attack had sustained heavy losses, but had not deserted their posts. The enemy was maintaining constant bombing of Soviet aerodromes. The General Staff had no further news.

Stalin had never had so great a shock in his life. His confusion was obvious, as was his anger at having been so misled, and his fear before the unknown. The Politburo members remained with him in his office all day, waiting for news from the border. They left the room only to make a phone call, have a cup of tea or stretch their legs. They said little, hoping that the failures were only temporary. No one doubted that Hitler would receive a resounding rebuff.

Malenkov had a file containing a draft decree from the chief administration of political propaganda in the Red Army, which Zaporozhets had given to him in the middle of June. (Zaporozhets was replaced on the second day of the war by Mekhlis.) Malenkov had given the draft to Stalin on 20 June. It had been in preparation since Stalin's speech to the military graduates on 5 May 1941, when he said that war was inevitable and that we must prepare unconditionally to destroy Fascism. The salient points of the decree, which Stalin did not have time to approve by the time the war broke out, were that the present situation was rife with surprises, and that revolutionary determination and constant readiness to go over to the attack were essential. All propaganda must focus on training the political, moral and fighting capability of servicemen to fight a just, offensive and all-embracing war.[1]

Apart from Malenkov, only Zhdanov had seen the draft. It had been drawn up in the spirit of the deployment plan that Zhukov had given to Stalin in May. That had also spoken of the need 'to forestall the enemy and smash his main force in former Poland and East Prussia'.[2] The General Staff and Main Political Administration believed that defence need only be short-term, since the troops were being trained to attack. For this reason, the idea that the first day or two of the war was a catastrophe did not arise in the minds of the party and military leadership.

The decree was late by a day. Stalin did not understand, and no one would tell him – Timoshenko was very much afraid of him – that preparing for war entailed some very strict scheduling. The time needed to put a division on alert and to deploy it varied between four and twenty-four hours. The Western military district, for instance, required between four and twenty-three hours.[3] The defence decree was issued by the General Staff at 0020 hours on 22 June 1941. It was received by the military districts by 0120 hours. It took the local commanders another hour or hour and a half to make their dispositions, and this meant the troops had less than an hour to carry out their orders.

Many divisions only went on to the alert when they came under air and artillery attack. Some units and companies were forced to take on German tank columns before reaching their appointed destinations. The penetration achieved by German mobile units of up to fifty or sixty kilometres in the first day was totally unexpected. Soviet second-line forces approaching the border found themselves under attack by German aircraft which had air supremacy from the outset. Soviet troops passed an endless stream of refugees. All communication was lost. The commanders did not know the situation, and meanwhile Stalin waited for reassuring news.

When on the morning of 22 June the question arose of who should tell the nation about the German attack, everyone naturally turned to Stalin. Almost without hesitating to reflect, he refused unequivocally. It has been generally accepted that Stalin acted in this way because, as Mikoyan, for example, recalled, he was in a depressed state and 'did not know what to say to the people, for he had after all taught them to think there would be no war, and that if it did start, then the enemy would be beaten on his own territory, and now he would have had to admit that we were suffering defeat in the first hours'.[4]

I believe things were somewhat different. The matter of addressing the nation was decided early in the morning when no one in Moscow yet knew that 'we were suffering defeat'. Everyone knew there was going to be a war, yet it came so suddenly. Stalin did not have a clear idea of what was happening on the border. Most likely, he did not want to address the nation until he had clarified the situation. On the 22nd he received no news of victories and so was in a state of alarm and confusion, but he was confident that in two or three weeks he would repay Hitler for violating their agreement, and then he would appear before the nation. The paralysing shock only struck him after four or five days, when he finally understood that the invasion was a mortal threat to him, and not only to the country. This is borne out by two orders approved by him at 7.15 a. m. and 9.15 p. m. of 22 June and signed by Timoshenko, Malenkov and Zhukov.

In the morning, after it had been agreed that Molotov would address the people, and also that mobilization should be declared in all fourteen military districts, Stalin, still unaware of the scale of the catastrophe, demanded that the military 'destroy the invading enemy with crushing blows'. Timoshenko at once set about composing the document known to history as Order No. 2 of the Chief War Council, addressed to all the military districts along the western and southwestern frontier, with a copy to the Naval Commissar:

On 22 June 1941 at 0400 hours the German air force carried out totally unprovoked bombing raids on our aerodromes and towns along the western frontier. Simultaneously, German forces opened artillery fire at various places and crossed our border.

In view of the brazenness of Germany's attack on the Soviet Union, I order that:

1. The forces use all their strength and means to come down on the enemy's forces and destroy them where they have violated the Soviet border. Until further orders, ground troops are not to cross the border.

2. Reconnaissance and combat aircraft are to pinpoint the sites where the enemy has concentrated his aircraft and ground forces. Bombers and dive-bombers must utterly destroy the enemy's aircraft on the ground and his main groupings of ground forces. Bombing attacks are to be carried out up to a depth of 100–150 kilometres of German territory. Koenigsberg and Memel are to be bombed. Finnish

and Romanian territory is not to be bombed until further orders.
22. 6. 41 07.15. Timoshenko, Zhukov, Malenkov.[5]

This directive hardly resembles a military document, but rather bears the stamp of Stalin's hand. It was an act of political will, of determination to punish the perfidious neighbour, and reveals little sign of an intention to extinguish the fires of war quickly. It is otherwise hard to explain why ground troops were not to cross the border until further orders. Issuing the order to destroy the enemy's main groupings, Stalin did not yet know that in the first day the forces of the Western district alone would lose 738 aircraft, of which 528 would be destroyed on the ground. The picture was similar in the other districts. In the first hours of the war, the Germans achieved total air supremacy, destroying in one day 1,200 Soviet aircraft.

Stalin pressed his military men for hard information, but nowhere was there good news to be had. The situation on the Northwestern front was disastrous. The commander of the 8th Army of the Baltic military district, P. P. Sobennikov, recalled that there was no precise plan for defending the border. The troops were engaged mainly on construction work in the fortified districts or on aerodromes. Units were below strength. Permanent buildings were not ready. By morning virtually all the aircraft of the Baltic military district had been destroyed on the ground, and there were only four or five left to support the 8th Army. He added bitterly that from the outset:

conflicting orders started coming in to erect barriers, lay mines and so on, then another order would cancel this, only to be followed by another saying it had to be done at once. I personally received an order from Chief of Staff Lieutenant General P. S. Klenov, on the night of 22 June, telling me most categorically that by dawn I must withdraw my troops from the border. One could sense the extreme nervousness, the lack of agreement and the fear of provoking war. Like the troops, the staffs were also below strength. They had inadequate communications and transport. They were not battle-worthy.[6]

Stalin meanwhile was waiting nervously, lifting his head expectantly each time someone entered the room. All that first day only a single glass of tea passed his lips. He thought the commanders were sluggish, lacking determination, failing to understand the directive that had been sent out that morning. A firm believer in getting things done by pressuring and threatening those in command, the lack of action had a depressing effect on him. He finally lost patience and, breaking off a discussion with Molotov, Zhdanov and Malenkov on a proposal from Timoshenko to create a Headquarters Chief of Command, suddenly got up, began pacing and, according to Zhukov, ordered that senior Staff headquarters people be despatched urgently to the Southwestern and Western fronts. 'That very day, at once,' Shaposhnikov and Kulik were to fly out to join Pavlov, while Zhukov was to join Kirponos. He returned to the table and, glaring threateningly at the others, repeated, 'Immediately!'

Convinced that urgent and energetic new impulses from the centre were what was needed, Stalin ordered Vatutin to formulate another order, issued that day by the Chief War Council (by next day the headquarters under Timoshenko would be in place), and which emerged, heavily edited by Stalin, as Order No. 3. It directed that between 23 and 24 June, Soviet forces must destroy the enemy in the Suvalki sector of the Northwestern and Western fronts by 'concentric concentrated blows', and by similar tactics Soviet armoured corps and all the air force of the Southwestern sector and troops of the 5th and 6th Armies must encircle and destroy the enemy in the Vladimir-Volynia and Brody sector, and they must capture Lublin by 24 June. 'From the Baltic to the Hungarian border, I permit the crossing of the border and action in disregard of the border.'[7]

At ten o'clock that night, Vatutin reported that Red Army infantry had beaten back attacks over most of the border with heavy enemy losses.[8] Everyone came to life and spirits lifted. Stalin and his entourage still did not know that German forces had penetrated deep into Soviet territory. Their illusions only began to be dissipated on the morning of 23 June, when attempts to contact field staff headquarters failed and they had a growing sense that the command was losing control of the troops. This indeed became the case on the Western front within the day. General Pavlov sent two telegrams, one to the commander of the Tenth Army, asking who was responsible for the failure of the armoured corps to attack: 'Without delay, activate action, don't panic, but lead. The enemy must be struck in an organized way, not just charged at without leadership. You have to know each division, where it is, when and what it's doing and what it has achieved.'[9] Pavlov's second order, signed together with Ponomarenko and Klimovskikh, was to the commanders of 3rd, 4th, 10th and 13th Armies, and was the last he was to give. He would face the firing squad within a month:

> Not later than 2100 hours tonight, 25 June, prepare units for retreat. Tanks in the vanguard, cavalry and strong anti-tank defence in the rearguard.
> The retreat is to be carried out swiftly by day and night under the cover of a firm rearguard. The withdrawal is to take place over a wide front. The first jump should be 60 kilometres in a day or more. Give the troops permission to fend for themselves by taking whatever they need from local resources and to use any methods to do so.[10]

Pavlov appears to have been unaware that the Germans had already either captured or destroyed the fuel and transport the army needed for an orderly retreat, with the result that the retreat was carried out in appalling conditions and at the complete mercy of the German air force and lightning encircling manoeuvres by German mechanized units.

Towards the last days of June, the scale of the fatal threat finally sank in on Stalin and for a while he simply lost control of himself and went into deep psychological shock. Between 28 and 30 June, according to eyewitnesses, Stalin was so depressed and shaken that he ceased to be a leader. On 29 June, as he was leaving the defence commissariat with Molotov, Voroshilov, Zhdanov and Beria, he burst out loudly: 'Lenin left us a great inheritance and we, his heirs, have fucked it all up!' Molotov looked at him amazed, but, like the others, said nothing.[11]

The shock was deep but not long-lasting. Before it struck, he had attempted to do something, issued some orders and tried to inspire the government agencies to show energy. On 23 June, during a discussion on the creation of a Chief of Staff Headquarters, he surprised everyone by suddenly interrupting the debate to propose: 'An Institute of permanent advisers is to be created in association with Headquarters consisting of Comrades Marshal Kulik, Marshal Shaposhnikov, Meretskov, Air Force chief Zhigarev, Vatutin, Anti-Aircraft chief Voronov, Mikoyan, Kaganovich, Voznesensky, Zhdanov, Malenkov, Mekhlis.'[12]

Malenkov and Timoshenko, who had prepared the document on the new headquarters, exchanged glances, but of course said nothing, and Stalin's order was sent out to the military districts over Poskrebyshev's signature. The Institute, however, died a quiet death in two weeks, without ever actually functioning.

Another oversight of Stalin and the General Staff on the eve of the war was the failure to elaborate the setting up of a special body to lead the country during wartime, namely the State Defence Committee, and a supreme organ of military leadership, namely the Headquarters Supreme High Command. These were only brought into being after the war had begun. And we have already noted that the General Staff had been weakened by the rapid succession of its chiefs. These failings exacted a heavy price.

There was still no good news. German tanks were approaching Minsk.

'What was that you said, what's happening at Minsk? Have you got this right? How do you know this?'

'No, Comrade Stalin, I'm not getting mixed up,' Vatutin murmured in reply. 'The Western front has virtually collapsed.'

In fact, most of the fronts were in utter chaos. Orders were sent, for instance, expecting troops to go into the attack after marching in retreat for 300 kilometres. Where units made successful counterattacks, as often as not they petered out for lack of fuel. If a commander lacked the resources for carrying out an impossible order, he might be threatened by his superior with execution, and the order itself was as likely as not to be rescinded in any case. In the air, the Germans had total freedom of action, for Soviet aircraft were nowhere to be seen.[13]

Stalin felt the people's eyes on him. He had so often proclaimed the invincibility of the Red Army, and now it seemed to him the situation was hopeless. When Vatutin showed him on the map that the 8th and 11th Armies were retreating in diverging directions, he saw clearly that the colossal gap between the Western and Northwestern fronts had reached 130 kilometres. The main forces of the Western front were either encircled or destroyed. The Southwestern front, by contrast, seemed to be holding up reasonably well. Why had he not listened to the experts and built up the defences of the Western front? In every one of his European campaigns, Hitler had made straight for the capital in order to effect the most rapid capitulation of the country. Why hadn't his strategists pointed this out?

In this nervous state, he behaved in an unsettled way, dividing his time between the nearby dacha and the Kremlin, but in general making himself scarce. Timoshenko, now also Chief of Staff, felt distinctly uncomfortable. Everyone knew that Stalin still held all power and authority, but he was acting impulsively and his state of depression was obvious. This naturally was transmitted to the military leadership to a certain extent and some of their orders bore the mark of desperation, ordering, for instance, rifle regiments to destroy enemy tank formations that had run out of fuel,[14] or giving detailed instructions for the deployment of tank units, instead of leaving it to the local commander to decide.[15]

Stalin went to the nearby dacha that night and lay down without undressing. Unable to sleep, he got up and went into the dining room where as always the light above Lenin's portrait was on. The dark oak panels suited his gloomy mood. Wandering from room to room, eyeing the phones that were installed in three different places, expecting at any moment to be rung up with more terrible news, he opened the door to the duty officer's room and found Major General V. A. Rumyantsev. The general leapt to attention to await the leader's orders. Stalin's gaze passed unseeing over the figure, then he closed the door quietly and went back to his room.

Mikoyan left interesting memoirs of this time. He recalled that Molotov, Malenkov, Voroshilov, Beria, Voznesensky and he resolved to propose to Stalin that they create a State Defence Committee which would take over all state power. It would be headed by Stalin:

We decided to go and see him. He was at the nearby dacha.

Molotov said that Stalin was in such a state of prostration that he wasn't interested in anything, he'd lost all initiative and was in a bad way. Voznesensky, appalled to hear this, said, 'You go on ahead, Vyacheslav, and we'll be behind you.' The idea was that, if Stalin was going to continue to behave in this way, then Molotov ought to lead us and we would follow him. We were sure we could organize the defence and put up a proper fight. None of us were downcast in mood.

We got to Stalin's dacha. We found him in an armchair in the small dining room. He looked up and said, 'What have you come for?' He had the strangest look on his face, and the question itself was pretty strange, too. After all, he should have called us in.

On our behalf, Molotov said power had to be concentrated in order to ensure rapid decision-making and somehow get the country back on its feet, and Stalin should head the new authority. Stalin looked surprised but made no objection and said, 'Fine.'[16]

The Headquarters and Staff now set about trying to establish a new line of defence to replace the Western front which the Germans had swept away. Stalin's mood made a rapid shift from apathy to nervous agitation and on 29 June he twice turned up unexpectedly in the defence commissariat and subjected the military leadership to coarse abuse. His face grey with fatigue, and with bags under his eyes, he at last grasped the scale of the danger hanging over the country. If something extraordinary was not done, if all forces were not mobilized, in a few weeks the Germans could be in Moscow. His first steps to take control not only of himself but also of the situation were perhaps typical of him: he began sacking his military leaders.

On 30 June the State Defence Committee was formally created with him as its head. His first step was to get rid of General Pavlov as commander of the Western front and to put Timoshenko in his place. The same day, Colonel General F. I. Kuznetsov, commander of the Northwestern front, gave the order to withdraw from the Western Dvina river and take the fortified districts of Ostrov, Pskov and Sebezh. As soon as Stalin heard this, he ordered Kuznetsov's dismissal and told his replacement, Major General P. P. Sobennikov, to restore the previous position above the Dvina. The troops who were then in disorderly retreat, however, were in no condition either to advance or defend themselves. Sensing the Soviet disorder, the Germans struck at the meeting point of the 8th and 27th Armies and broke through.

Stalin was shattered by the news that Minsk had fallen. He went to the dacha and stayed there the whole day without returning to the Kremlin. Molotov and Beria went to see him but there is no record of their conversation.

I once asked Marshal K. S. Moskalenko, for whom I was working in the mid-1970s, why he had omitted in his memoirs any mention of the meeting Stalin, Molotov and Beria had had with the Bulgarian ambassador, Ivan Stamenov, in July 1941. He replied that the time had not yet come for such revelations, and anyway there was no hard evidence. I then asked him whether he thought what Beria had said about it was reliable. He replied: 'Everything he said on this matter hardly justifies it. Anyway, given Stalin's position at the time, it is hard to think of anything that would have helped him.'

What happened was that, on 2 July 1957, a meeting took place of the party group of the defence ministry to discuss a Central Committee letter about 'the anti-party group of Malenkov, Kaganovich, Molotov and others'. Zhukov read the report and a number of senior military men also spoke, including I. S. Konev, R. Ya. Malinovsky, F. F. Kuznetsov, M. I. Nedelin, I. Kh. Bagramyan, K. A. Vershinin, F. I. Golikov, K. A. Meretskov and A. S. Zheltov. When it was Moskalenko's turn, he said:

When Procurator General Rudenko and I were dealing with the Beria case, we found that he said that, as early as 1941, Stalin, Beria and Molotov discussed in private the question of surrendering to Fascist Germany, agreeing to hand over to Hitler the Soviet Baltic republics, Moldavia, a large part of the Ukraine and Belorussia. They tried to make contact with Hitler through the Bulgarian ambassador. No Russian tsar had ever done such a thing. It is interesting that the Bulgarian ambassador was of higher calibre than these leaders and told them that Hitler would never beat the Russians and that Stalin shouldn't worry about it.[17]

Telling me this, Moskalenko added that, according to Beria, Stalin had said nothing during the meeting with the Bulgarian. Only Molotov spoke, asking the ambassador to contact Berlin. According to Beria, Molotov described the offer of territory in exchange for an end to the fighting as 'a possible second Brest Litovsk Treaty', and said that, if Lenin could have the courage to make such a step, we had the same intention now. The ambassador, however, declined to act as mediator, adding, 'Even if you retreat to the Urals, you'll still win in the end.' Moskalenko concluded that it was difficult to know how much of this was true. 'We knew that Stalin had been in a state of collapse in the first days of the war. There was little sense in Beria making it all up, especially as the former Bulgarian ambassador confirmed the facts in conversation with us.'

The people were waiting for Stalin to speak. They still believed in him. They put their hopes in him. Possibly it was this that brought him out of his state of mental collapse. He decided to speak on the radio on 3 July, but it was hard to find the words to explain what had happened, the defeats, the collapse of the Soviet–German treaties. The margins of his speech contain such jottings as 'why?', 'the destruction of the enemy is inevitable', 'what must be done?' It has an unusual appearance for a speech by the first man in the land. It contained the main ideas formulated on 29 June by the Central Committee and Sovnarkom.

In it, Stalin tried to explain, or rather justify, why German forces had captured Lithuania, Latvia, part of the Ukraine, Belorussia and Estonia. It all boiled down to a single phrase: 'The fact is, Germany's forces, as of a country already at war, were fully mobilized, and 170 divisions, which had been kept on the Soviet border and were thrown against us, were fully prepared and were only awaiting the signal to attack, whereas Soviet troops had to be mobilized and moved to the frontiers.' He then lied about the Germans' best divisions having been smashed. Naturally, when he mentioned the Soviet–German Pact he said nothing about the shameful treaty on 'friendship and borders'. But his voice acquired more confidence when he said it was necessary 'to put all our work on a war footing'. This was when he first described the war as 'patriotic', acknowledged the need 'to form partisan units', and 'to organize merciless battle using all manner of disorganizers of the rear, deserters, panic-mongers', and when he first publicly expressed the hope of uniting the efforts of the people of Europe and America in the struggle against Hitler's armies. He ended his speech by declaring that 'the State Defence Committee is getting down to work and it calls on the entire people to rally around the party of Lenin and Stalin.'[18]

The speech had a powerful effect, giving as it did simple answers to many questions which were tormenting the people. Paradoxically, the chief cause for the catastrophic beginning of the war, namely Stalin's personal rule, now came to embody the hopes of the people. The faith was working.

CHAPTER 42

A Cruel Time

On 10 July the Staff Headquarters was transformed into the Headquarters High Command and on 8 August this became the Headquarters of the Supreme High Command under Stalin. From that day until the end of the war Stalin was the Supreme Commander. Since 30 June he had headed the State Defence Committee and on 19 July he became Commissar for Defence. Working sixteen to eighteen hours a day, going without sleep, he became still more harsh and intolerant and often vicious. Every day he signed orders for military, political, ideological and economic policy, and it has to be said that this high degree of concentration of power in one set of hands had its positive as well as its negative side. Centralization made it possible in extreme circumstances to consolidate effort. On the other hand, the persistence of the autocracy severely weakened the possibility for independent thinking and initiative at all levels.

In effect, only two or three people worked in direct contact with Stalin. Of Politburo members, apart from Stalin, a prominent part was played by Voznesensky, Zhdanov and Khrushchev. Voznesensky was active in dealing with the country's economic problems. Zhdanov and Khrushchev, as members of war councils, were active conduits of Stalin's purpose. As for Voroshilov, after the first débâcle, he lost Stalin's 'operational' confidence. It was Kalinin's responsibility to formulate Stalin's intentions as orders and to take part in propaganda. Mikoyan and Kaganovich dealt with transport and food-supply, but, though they were both members of war councils at the front, they were hardly involved in military affairs, if one discounts Kaganovich's brief spell on the Southern front.

The real executor of Stalin's wishes in the Central Committee was Malenkov. On several occasions he visited the front, notably Stalingrad, on Stalin's orders, but because he was utterly lacking in military competence he left no trace whatsoever on the military sphere. From 30 June 1941 until the end of the war, Molotov was deputy chairman of the State Defence Committee and was mainly concerned with international affairs. Beria's responsibilities included 'cleaning up' the rear, organizing camps for German prisoners of war, and the war industries which functioned in the prisons and concentration camps. He went to the Northern Caucasus front twice on Stalin's orders. Andreyev looked after agriculture and supplies to the front. Because Stalin's rôle loomed so large, the Central Committee was virtually squeezed out of the picture during the war, its work being effectively taken over by its own apparatus, while the part played by the grass-roots party organizations at the front and in the rear was enormous. Only one plenum took place during the war, in January 1944. In October 1941 members were summoned to Moscow for a plenum and waited two days for it to begin, but Stalin and Malenkov had no time to convene it. In any case, Stalin saw no point in delimiting the functions of the top bodies, since he ran them all, whether it be the Central Committee, the Sovnarkom, Supreme High Command, the State Defence Committee, Head-quarters Staff or defence commissariat, and he signed documents using all and any of these titles.

Until the battle of Stalingrad, his orders tended to be somewhat impulsive and erratic, superficial and incompetent. Often they were also punitive, especially following a defeat. On 10 July, for instance, when it became clear that the Northwestern front could not be held, and he received reports that diversionary groups had been active in the rear, Stalin reacted at once:

The Headquarters High Command and the State Defence Committee are totally dissatisfied with the work of the headquarters staff Northwestern front.

First, the officers who did not carry out orders, abandoning their positions like traitors and leaving the defensive ridge without orders, have not yet been punished. Given such a liberal attitude towards cowards, defence efforts will come to nothing.

Attacking units have done nothing so far, we see no results of their work and, as a result of the lack of action by divisional, corps, army and front commanders, parts of the Northwestern front are constantly rolling back. It is time to put a stop to this shameful state of affairs. The commander and a member of the war council, and the prosecutor and head of the 3rd department [i.e. the NKVD] are to go at once to forward units and deal with the cowards and traitors on the spot.[19]

Nothing had been done before the war to prepare an air-raid shelter for the Headquarters Staff, although both Timoshenko and Zhukov had pressed for it. Neither in the Kremlin nor at his dachas did Stalin have any shelters. In the early months of the war, therefore, he often spent time in a house on Kirov Street next door to some General Staff offices. The Kirov Metro station, which had been separated off from the main network, made an excellent bomb-shelter. In the winter of 1941 a shelter was built for Stalin at the nearby dacha and equipped for direct contact with the fronts.

From the maps prepared by General Staff, Stalin could see clearly the three directions in which Hitler was developing his advance: in the northwest towards Leningrad, in the west towards Moscow and in the southwest towards

Kiev. Possibly Stalin's first major decision of the war was to create three Command HQs, one for each sector, and by 10 July these were in place: northwestern command was under Voroshilov, with Zhdanov a member of the war council; Western command was under Timoshenko, with N. A. Bulganin a member of the War Council; the Southwestern command was under S. M. Budenny, with Khrushchev a member of the War Council. The idea of these separate commands was a good one, but they themselves found it hard to function effectively because Stalin was unwilling to invest them with adequate powers. Orders went to the forces over their heads and the command staffs were ignored. Moreover, since their creation had not been properly planned, they lacked personnel and basic technical support, and they soon became objects of Stalin's abuse for 'passivity and lack of will'.

The Northern front gave little cause for concern, as action did not begin there until the end of June. The situation on the Northwestern front was another matter. In just over two weeks Soviet forces had retreated nearly 450 kilometres, abandoning the Baltic republics and failing to exploit the rivers Neman and Western Dvina as valuable defence boundaries. The new commander, Sobennikov, had not lived up to expectations and Stalin would remove him within six weeks.

But it was the Western front that gave real cause for alarm. By 10 July Soviet troops had fallen back almost 500 kilometres. With forty-four divisions at his disposal, Pavlov had not even been able to hold the enemy attack. Stalin was determined to put the investigation and trial of the Western command in hand right away.

Soviet losses were colossal. Something like thirty divisions had been virtually wiped out, while seventy had lost more than half of their numbers; nearly 3,500 planes had been destroyed, together with more than half the fuel and ammunition dumps. And this after only three weeks of war! Of course, the Germans, too, had paid a price, namely about 150,000 officers and men, more than 950 aircraft and several hundred tanks. However, it would later emerge that the figures for Soviet losses had been artificially reduced, while those of the Germans had been inflated. After two weeks of battle, the following statistics were given to Stalin:

Aircraft lost: enemy minimum	1,664
our losses	889
Tanks lost: enemy	2,625
ours	901
Enemy's human losses: killed	1,312,000

In the fierce fighting on various sectors, moreover, the enemy bore huge losses, but since our troops were retreating it was impossible to count the losses. Many uncounted losses were inflicted on diversionary parachutists.

There are 30,004 prisoners, plus many uncounted parachutists. Our numbers of missing and taken prisoner up to 29.6 are about 15,000.

Five enemy submarines have been sunk in the Baltic and one in the Black Sea. Two enemy off-shore gunships destroyed.[20]

Such reports made it impossible to know the real position, the relationship of forces, the exact number of aircraft, tanks and men available. These statistics were, however, intentionally distorted by people accustomed by Stalin's cult to lie to him, yet he took them as hard facts and would never have imagined that he was being deceived. Nevertheless, the German strength declined markedly after the force of the first strike, and Hitler's armies had not succeeded in achieving his main aim, namely, the destruction of the Red Army.

The army was fighting. It was retreating, but it was fighting. As he studied the maps, Stalin gradually came to the conclusion that this was going to be a long war and that, if the USSR could survive the first phase, there was a chance of winning. As early as 5 July, when he ordered the General Staff to award decorations for those who had showed special bravery, including the first wartime awards of Hero of the Soviet Union, he told the propaganda department to spread the word about Soviet heroism. 'Remember Lenin's call: "The Socialist Fatherland is in danger!" Let the people know that it is possible and necessary to smash the Fascist swine!'

Besides military affairs, Stalin also spent several hours a day on economic matters. On 4 July, Voznesensky and Mikoyan submitted a draft war-economy plan to the State Defence Committee which Stalin signed almost without reading it. Voznesensky managed hurriedly to report that on 30 June the Sovnarkom had approved a general economic mobilization plan which envisaged placing the economy on a war footing in the shortest possible time. Shvernik, who was in charge of the evacuation council, had just reported that so far only factories close to the border had been moved, but that the military débâcle now dictated a more thoroughgoing approach. In practice, by January 1942, 1,523 factories, of which 1,360 were in defence manufacture, would be transferred eastwards in toto and put into operation, an outstanding achievement of cardinal significance. In the agricultural sector, we now know that in November 1941 the decision was taken to create several thousand political sections in Machine and Tractor Stations and state farms. The huge losses of territory and the flood of farm labour into the army imposed a greatly increased burden on agriculture to feed both the army and the country.

As the man in the centre of all this effort, Stalin took the war to mean the absolute confirmation of his absolute dictatorship. Former Transport Commissar I. V. Kovalev gave me the following account of that period:

I remember being invited, as head of the military transport administration, to a meeting in the Kremlin. I saw railway chiefs there, military men and Central Committee staffers. Kaganovich was there and Beria, who was in charge of transport for a while. Stalin entered the room. We all rose. Without any preamble he said, 'The State Defence Committee has taken the decision to create a Transport Committee. I propose Comrade Stalin as head of the Committee.' That's exactly how he put it. I remember something else he said at that meeting, all those years ago: 'Transport is a matter of life and death. The front is in the hands of transport. Remember, failure to carry out the State Defence Committee's orders means the military tribunal.' He said this quietly but deliberately, and a chill ran down my spine.

In the course of the war, I had to report to Stalin dozens, if not hundreds of times on the movement of trains to different sectors of the front. Sometimes, if there was a special freight, I would have to keep him informed every two hours. On one occasion a train was 'lost'. I said it was at a particular station, but it turned out not to be there. Stalin could barely contain his anger: 'If you don't find it, general, you'll be going to the front as a private.'* As I left, looking as white as a sheet, Poskrebyshev added, 'See you don't slip up. The boss is at the end of his tether.'

When I went to the Kremlin, Molotov, Beria and Malenkov would usually be in Stalin's office. I used to feel they were in the way. They never asked questions, but just sat there and listened, sometimes jotting down a note. And all the time, Stalin would be busy issuing instructions, talking on the phone, signing papers, calling in Poskrebyshev and giving him orders, and those three would just go on sitting there, sitting and looking either at Stalin or at whoever came in. I witnessed this scene dozens and dozens of times. It was as if Stalin needed them, either to deal with anything that came up, or as witnesses for history. As a rule Kaganovich would not be present. He worked eighteen hours a day, that one, cursing and threatening everyone and sparing no one, including himself. But I never saw him sitting in Stalin's office, like the other three. When Stalin spoke on the phone, he would utter only a few sentences and put down the receiver. He was laconic and expected everyone else to be the same. It was no good giving him only an approximate report: he would at once drop his voice ominously and say, 'Don't you know? What are you doing, then?'

In spite of having gone to see him so many times, every time I would be in a state of agitation. I was always waiting for him to ask a question to which I wouldn't have an answer. He was an incredibly cold person. Instead of saying 'hello', he would just nod. I would make my report and if there were no questions I'd leave quickly with a sigh of relief. As soon as possible. Poskrebyshev told me to do this. One felt oppressed by Stalin's power, but also by his phenomenal memory and the fact that he knew so much. He made one feel even less important than one was.

In the early months of the war, Stalin spent a lot of time on petty detail, such as the distribution of mines and rifles, getting the civilian population to dig anti-tank ditches, going over press releases for the Informburo. On one occasion, it turned out that a General Staff document, addressed to the armed forces, had sat unnoticed in the coding department for eight hours and fifteen minutes. When Stalin heard about this, he at once ordered that Colonel I. F. Ivanov and First Lieutenant B. S. Krasnov be punished and kicked out of the

---

* This was no idle threat. Major General N. A. Moskvin was stripped of his rank on Stalin's orders and sent to the front as a private. (TsAMO, f. 33, op. 11 454, d. 179, l. 1.)

General Staff, and that the coding department be put in proper shape right away.[21] Meanwhile, there were decisions of crucial importance to be made in the appalling days of that hot August. But it was simply Stalin's habit, which had developed over the years, to decide and do everything himself, and for everyone else. The situation at the front, however, would soon bring about a change in the style and methods of the Supremo's working habits.

As he gave or withheld his approval of the General Staff's proposals, he constantly sought ways to make a greater impact on their actions. For instance, when he heard that there were no weapons to supply reinforcements, he ordered headquarters to send the following instruction to the forces:

Every commander, political officer and private is to have it explained to him that the loss of weapons on the field of battle is a major violation of the military oath and guilty parties must be made to answer according to the laws of wartime. Civilian teams engaged in the collection of weapons are to be reinforced by a number of service personnel and charged with retrieving any weapon abandoned on the field of battle.[22]

Always, his response to a harsh situation was to make things harsher. For instance, Zhdanov and Zhukov, in reporting the situation in Leningrad, mentioned the fact that, when attacking Soviet positions, the Germans had pushed women and children and old men and women ahead of them, placing the defenders in an even harder position. The women and children screamed, 'Don't shoot! We're your own people! We're your own people!' The Soviet forces did not know what to do. Stalin's immediate reaction was entirely in character:

They are saying the German swine who are advancing on Leningrad are driving old folk and women and children in front of them. They are saying there are Bolsheviks in Leningrad who find it impossible to use their weapons against such deputies. I think that if there are such people among the Bolsheviks, then they should be destroyed first, because they're more dangerous than the German Fascists. My advice is, don't be sentimental, smash the enemy and his willing or unwilling accomplices in the teeth. Hit the Germans and their delegates, whoever they might be, with everything you've got, cut the enemy down, never mind if they are willing or unwilling enemies. Dictated at 0400 hours 21.9.41 by Comrade Stalin. Signed B. Shaposhnikov.[23]

Stalin's thinking in the early months of the war was plainly still influenced by the civil war – if not the war of 1812! In September 1941, for instance, after a conversation with Budenny, he showed a sudden renewed interest in the cavalry. At that moment the General Staff was completing its work on the lessons of the first two months of the war, to be sent to the commanders of the fronts and the armies, when Stalin ordered the addition of a further point:

Point four. Our army somewhat underestimates the importance of cavalry. In the present situation at the front, when the enemy's rear is extended over several hundred kilometres in wooded terrain and is totally unable to protect itself against major diversionary action by us, raids by Red Cavalry units could play a decisive part in disorganizing the administration and supply of enemy forces. If units of our cavalry, who are only hanging around doing nothing at and near the front, could be thrown against the enemy's rear, the enemy would be placed in a critical position, while our forces would gain considerable relief. The General Staff believes that such raids could be carried out by a few dozen light cavalry divisions of the attacking variety, each numbering some three thousand men with light transport, and without overloading the rear services.[24]

Not so devoid of common sense in itself, this idea was of course hopelessly outdated, but the situation was so desperate that Stalin was seeking panaceas in almost any method.

Pavlov was still on Stalin's mind. Before becoming commander-in-chief of the Western front, he had made quite a good impression. True, he hadn't had much experience and his rise after Spain had been rapid. But why had his headquarters been so remiss? Stalin conveniently forgot that in mid-June Pavlov had sent two or three urgent coded despatches requesting permission to move troops to field positions, suggesting partial mobilization and urging the need to strengthen the district with communications and new tanks. Still, the question nagged at Stalin: how could Pavlov have lost everything so miserably? He called Poskrebyshev and asked, 'Who, apart from Pavlov, has been sent to the military tribunal? When's the trial? Where's the draft sentence? Get me Ulrikh!' Poskrebyshev brought in a thin file and laid it on the desk. It was labelled '(Draft) Sentence':

In the name of the USSR, the military collegium of the Supreme court of the USSR consisting of:
chairman, military advocate V. V. Ulrikh, members, divisional military advocates A. A. Orlov and D. Ya. Kandybin, secretary, military advocate A.S. Mazur.

In a closed session in Moscow on ... July 1941 the following cases were tried:
1. Pavlov, Dmitri Grigoryevich, born 1897, former commander Western front, army general;
2. Klimovskikh, Vladimir Yefimovich, born 1895, former chief of staff Western front, major general. Both accused of crimes under Articles 63–2 and 76 of the Belorussian Criminal Code.
3. Grigoryev, Andrei Terentyevich, born 1889, former chief of communications Western front, major general;
4. Korobkov, Alexander Andreyevich, born 1897, former commander Fourth Army, major general. Both accused of crimes under Article 180, para. b. of the Belorussian Criminal Code.

The file went on to state that it had been established by preliminary investigation that:

the accused, Pavlov and Klimovskikh, were participants in an anti-Soviet military conspiracy and that they had used their positions to carry out enemy work by not training the personnel under their command for military action, that with their conspiratorial aims in mind they had weakened the preparedness for mobilization of the troops in the military district, they had disrupted the administration of the forces and surrendered weapons to the enemy without a fight, thus causing great damage to the fighting capacity of the Red Army.

Stalin skipped most of the document, which continued in this vein, but read the last section:

Thus the guilt of Pavlov and Klimovskikh ... and that of Grigoryev and Korobkov ... has been established. As a result of the above and in accordance with Articles 319 and 320 of the Criminal Procedure Code of the RSFSR, the military collegium of the Supreme court of the USSR sentences:

1. Pavlov, Dmitri Grigoryevich
2. Klimovskikh, Vladimir Yefimovich
3. Grigoryev, Alexander Terentyevich

to be stripped of their military ranks, Pavlov as a general of the army and the rest as major generals, and to subject all four to the highest form of punishment, namely to be shot, and all their personal property to be confiscated. The sentence is final and not subject to appeal.[25]

Stalin turned to Poskrebyshev and said: 'I approve the sentence, but tell Ulrikh to get rid of all that rubbish about "conspiratorial activity". The case shouldn't drag out. No appeal. And then inform the fronts, so they know that defeatists will be punished without mercy.'

Everything was decided before the trial, so that when it took place on 22 July, only the formalities needed to be gone through. The accused asked to be sent to the front in any capacity; they would show their loyalty to the fatherland and their military duty by giving their blood. They asked the court to believe that everything that had happened was the result of extremely unfavourable circumstances. They did not deny their guilt. They would atone for it in battle. Ulrikh yawned and said, 'Get on with it!' They were shot that night. (The sentence would be overturned by the General Staff fifteen years too late, on 5 November 1956.)[26] Korobkov was especially unlucky. According to Colonel General L. M. Sandalov's report to General V. V. Kurasov, although Korobkov's army had sustained terrible losses, it was still functioning and had not, like many other commands, lost contact with front staff headquarters. At the end of June 1941 it was decided that one commanding officer from the Western front should be 'allocated' to stand trial for the disaster, and since Korobkov's whereabouts were known, his fate was sealed.[27]

Pavlov and the others had all risen fast because of the decimation of the officer corps in 1937–38, and no doubt lacked the proper training and experience, but they were utterly devoted to their country. There were many such cases. Kirponos and Kuznetsov, like Pavlov, had meteoric careers and, like him, their patriotism was inadequately underpinned by qualities of leadership. It was Stalin who bore responsibility for the catastrophic start of the war but, typically, he had to have scapegoats and hence exacerbate the already cruel nature of the war by his own cruelty.

Many men of Korobkov's calibre could have risen to the top but did not. Many died in battle; many others, having exhausted all possibility of carrying on fighting and wishing neither to be taken prisoner nor face Stalin's justice, committed suicide. There are numerous cases reported in the documents.[28]

The story of some other generals was no less tragic. In August 1941 the security organs reported to Stalin that two generals, commander of the 28th Army Lieutenant General V. Ya. Kachalov, and commander of the 12th Army Major General P. G. Ponedelin, had surrendered voluntarily and were working for the Germans. Stalin ordered them to be tried. Not all orders were carried out at once: if they had been, the Germans might not have reached the gates of Moscow in the autumn! But this order was carried out immediately, and the two generals were tried *in absentia* in October 1941 and sentenced to be shot, 'deprived of all their personal property and stripped of their Soviet decorations'.[29]

It never occurred to the miserably cynical informers that Kachalov had been killed on 4 August 1941 by a direct hit from a shell, but until 1956 his family had to bear the stigma of being relatives of 'a traitor to the Fatherland'. The fate of Major General Ponedelin was even worse. Encircled in August 1941, he was seriously wounded and taken prisoner whilst unconscious. Four long and bitter years in Hitler's camps did not break him. He was a support to his less robust comrades and refused to collaborate with the Nazis. After release and repatriation in 1945, he was arrested and given five years in Soviet camps, even though he had been sentenced to death *in absentia* in 1941. He made a personal appeal to Stalin and on 25 August 1950 was again sentenced to death. This time the sentence was carried out.

Of the millions of Soviet troops who fell into enemy hands, those who managed to escape and get back to Soviet lines were immediately put into 'special camps for checking'. There are many reports signed by Beria about the way these camps functioned. After being 'checked', some servicemen were sent to newly formed detachments, others were executed on the spot, and others were sent for long terms to the concentration camps.[30] While the case of Pavlov is perhaps the best known, the fact is that Stalin sanctioned the arrest of a large group of other generals at the same time, some of whom eventually got back to the front, while others ended up in the camps or were shot.[31]

Nor were Stalin's suspicions of his generals confined to the opening phase of the war. In August 1942, for instance, he cabled Vasilievsky and Malenkov in Stalingrad:

I am amazed that the enemy has made precisely the same kind of breakthrough deep behind our lines on the Stalingrad front as he did last year on the Bryansk front ... It is noteworthy that the commander of the Bryansk front then was the same Zakharov and that Comrade Yeremenko's aide was the same Rukhle.

That's worth thinking about. Either Yeremenko doesn't understand the idea of a second echelon where the forward divisions are not under fire, or we are dealing here with someone harbouring ill will and giving the Germans exact details of our weak spots.[32]

Major General I. I. Rukhle was arrested at once, but fate was kind on this occasion and he survived. Stalin could not break the habit of resorting to harsh and cruel measures, but everyone at that time believed that harsh measures were justified by the harsh times.

CHAPTER ◼ 43

Disasters and Hopes

At the beginning of August 1941 Shaposhnikov was summoned to the dacha at midnight to give Stalin an account of the situation on all fronts. What emerged sounded to Stalin like the gloomiest of lectures, matching the bitter taste of wormwood – he told Poskrebyshev – he had had in his mouth since the war began. Referring to the map that had been spread out on Stalin's desk, Shaposhnikov began:

'We can say that we have utterly lost the first phase of the war. Battles are already taking place on the distant approaches to Leningrad, in the Smolensk district and the defensive area centred on Kiev. Our resistance is still not strong. We have to deploy our troops along the front more or less without knowing where the enemy might strike with concentrated force tomorrow. The enemy has all the strategic initiative. The problem is exacerbated by the absence of second-line troops and powerful reserves in many sectors. In the air, the enemy has complete supremacy, though he has lost many aircraft.* Of the 212 divisions of the active army, only ninety have 80 per cent or more of their full complement. The defence of the approaches to Leningrad is acquiring some 'elasticity' and the dynamism of the German advance may come to nothing. It looks as if we should move the entire Baltic fleet to Kronstadt.† Heavy losses are inevitable.

'The engagement at Smolensk enabled us to stop the enemy on the most dangerous, i.e. western thrust. According to our calculations about sixty German divisions took part, amounting to something like half a million men. As you know, Comrade Stalin, in order to consolidate the front the 19th, 20th, 21st and 22nd Armies were moved there as early as the beginning of July. But

---

* By 30 September 1941 the Soviet air force lost 96.4 per cent of the aircraft it had when war broke out. (TsAMO, f. 35, op. 11 285, d. 9, l. 324.)
† An island fortress some twenty miles off Leningrad.

there is still a tangible lack of troops and often divisions are being made up of only one line. Our attempt to mount a counterattack using the 29th, 30th, 24th and 28th Armies was only partly successful, in that it allowed the 20th and 16th Armies to break through the encirclement and fall back behind the line. Our counterattack broke the enemy's attack.'

'What part did the Central front play in this engagement?' Stalin interrupted.

'There are grounds for thinking that the main thrust of the German grouping will be moved there,' Shaposhnikov replied. 'But a single line front, having twenty-four incomplete divisions in all, gives serious cause for concern. We might well have to form another front grouping there.'

From all this, Stalin drew the conclusion that the Red Army was capable of stopping the enemy, even where he had concentrated his main force. Shaposhnikov continued:

'We were not able to hold the old frontier ... The Germans have in effect cut the front in two, separating the 5th Army from the 6th, 12th and 26th, and by tomorrow the 6th and 12th will have been cut off.'

'I'm worried about the Dnieper and Kiev. We've got to do something,' Stalin said.

'Orders have already been given to form a strong line of defence on the east bank of the Dnieper.'

'Can we get in touch now with Southwestern headquarters?' Stalin asked.

'If Kirponos and Khrushchev are not out with the troops, we can make contact.'

A few minutes later, Kirponos and Khrushchev were on the line and there ensued a long conversation in which Stalin urged that the line must be held at all costs, and gave advice on how to rally the troops, temporarily using cavalry as infantry for the purpose. Khrushchev and Kirponos replied that they were doing everything possible to stop the Germans crossing the river and taking Kiev, and they asked for urgent reinforcements. Some of their divisions had been reduced to a couple of thousand men.[33]

The defence of Kiev was a failure. The 6th and 12th Armies fought on, encircled, until 7 August and then ceased to exist. A great number were taken prisoner. Seeing that the troops of the Southern front were threatened with capture, Budenny asked Stalin for permission to get the troops across the river Ingul. Stalin was furious and forbade it, indicating instead another line of defence.[34] He ordered the transfer to the Southwestern sector of nineteen rifle and five cavalry divisions, but though they were formed they were neither well-knit nor trained. Nor were they properly armed. They did not perform well in battle. In the ensuing chaos, many of them panicked and left their positions without waiting for the order to do so.

When Stalin was told that a defensive or recently occupied position had been abandoned, he either flew into a rage or sank into apathy. Contrary to his usual rule of not jumping to conclusions or judging people too soon, he now did both simultaneously. On one occasion, it was I. V. Tyulenev, commander of the Southern front and well known to Stalin from the old days, who caught it. Stalin sent a telegram to Budenny:

> Front commander Tyulenev has turned out to be lacking in substance. He doesn't know how to advance, nor does he know how to withdraw his troops. He has lost two armies in the way one wouldn't even lose two regiments. I suggest you go at once to Tyulenev, see how things are for yourself and report at once on the defence plan. It seems to me Tyulenev is demoralized and not capable of commanding the front.
>
> Dictated by telephone at 0550 hours, 12.8.41.[35]

Despite Stalin's harsh commands, the situation on the Southern front grew worse, reaching a crisis at the end of August. Stalin tried to contact one commander after another, not always with success. On one occasion, having just been informed of yet another unsanctioned retreat, he dictated Order No. 270 of 16 August 1941. In sheer desperation, he was resorting to his usual punitive approach. This little-known order is a model of Stalin's personal directive style. It mentions commanders, political officers and ordinary servicemen who got themselves out of difficult situations with honour, but goes on:

> On the other hand, Lieutenant General Kachalov, commanding 28th Army, showed cowardice and gave himself up, whereas his headquarters and units got out of the encirclement; Major General Ponedelin surrendered, as did Major General Kirillov of the 13th rifle corps. These are shameful facts. Cowards and deserters must be destroyed.
>
> I order that:
>
> 1) anyone who removes his insignia during battle and surrenders should be regarded as a malicious deserter, whose family is to be arrested as the family of a breaker of the oath and betrayer of the Motherland. Such deserters are to be shot on the spot.
>
> 2) those falling into encirclement are to fight to the last and try to reach their own lines. And those who prefer to surrender are to be destroyed by any available means, while their families are to be deprived of all state allowances and assistance.
>
> 3) bold and brave people are to be promoted more actively.
>
> This order is to be read to all companies, squadrons, batteries.[36]

Having dictated and signed this impulsive text without hesitating, Stalin left it as it was, unedited, but ordered that the names of Molotov, Budenny, Voroshilov, Timoshenko, Shaposhnikov and Zhukov be appended, even though some of them were not even present.

At the end of August, Stalin received a letter from the writer Vladimir Stavsky, who had just spent ten days at the front near Yelnya. Part of the letter reads:

> Dear Comrade Stalin,
>
> Several of our units are working marvellously and dealing crushing blows to the Fascists. After the dashing and energetic Comrade Major Utvenko took over the 19th division, the regiments destroyed the 88th infantry regiment

and repelled many German counterattacks ... The units are undergoing battle training, accumulating battle experience, studying the enemy's tactics and beating the Germans.

But here, in the 24th Army, things have gone too far. According to the command staff and political section, 480–600 men have been shot for desertion, panicking and other crimes. Eighty men have been nominated for decoration. The day before yesterday and today army commander Comrade Rakutin and head of political section Comrade Abramov dealt correctly with this situation.[37]

Stalin's only comment on this letter was to mark the note on executions for Mekhlis's attention.

Meanwhile one of the greatest tragedies of the war was approaching. On 8 August 1941 Stalin was again on the line to Kirponos:

Stalin: 'It has come to our attention that the front has decided to give up Kiev to the enemy without a thought, allegedly for lack of troops able to defend the city. Is this true?'

Kirponos: 'Hello, Comrade Stalin. You have been misinformed. The war council and I are doing everything possible not to surrender the city under any circumstances. All our thinking and energy are aimed at not losing Kiev to the enemy.'

Stalin: 'Very good. I send you greetings and wish you success. That is all.'[38]

On 15 September the Germans' first and second tank groups closed the circle in the district of Lokhvitsa, thus surrounding the main force of the Southwestern front. The 5th, 26th, 37th and part of the 21st and 28th Armies were trapped inside the ring. Four days earlier, as the noose was tightening around the dwindling units, Stalin and Kirponos had their last conversation:

'Priluki. Hello. Kirponos, Burmistenko and Tupikov on the line.'

'Moscow. Hello, Stalin, Shaposhnikov and Timoshenko here. Your proposal to withdraw the troops to the ridge of the river you know the name of [the Psyol] seems dangerous to me. You might recall that when you recently withdrew troops from the Berdichev-Novgorod-Volynsky district you had a much better ridge on the river Dnieper, yet even so you lost two armies and the enemy regrouped on the eastern bank of the Dnieper. The conclusion follows that:

1 you must immediately regroup your strength, even at the cost of the Kiev fortified district and other forces, and in coordination with Yeremenko carry out desperate attacks on the enemy's Konotop group.
2 you must immediately organize a defensive ridge on the river Psyol or somewhere along that line, forming a front to the north and west with a large artillery group and then withdraw five to six divisions behind the ridge.
3 Only when this has been done, that is, after forming a fist against the enemy's Konotop group and forming a defensive ridge on the Psyol, only after all this has been done, should you begin the evacuation of Kiev.

Kiev must not be abandoned nor its bridges blown up without permission of Staff HQ. That is all. Goodbye.'

Kirponos: 'Your orders are clear. That is all. Goodbye.'[39]

It was to be Kirponos's last goodbye. As long as the encirclement was incomplete, it was possible to break free of the noose. On 17 September at 0500 hours, the War Council requested Stalin's consent to this once more, and again he forbade a breakout and sanctioned only the withdrawal of the 37th Army under the command of A. A. Vlasov to the east bank of the Dnieper. The position became critical. Despite Stalin's orders, by nightfall on 17 September the War Council decided to extract the troops from encirclement. But time had been lost. The front headquarters had moreover lost contact with the armies. The scattered units and companies fought fierce battles for ten days in an effort to break out to the east. This helped somewhat, but Headquarters Staff, not being in control of the situation, was still sending Kirponos reassuring telegrams as late as 22 and 23 September. For instance:

> More determination and calm. Success is assured. There are only trivial enemy forces ranged against you. Mass your artillery at the breakthrough points. All our aviation is working for you. Our troops are attacking Romny. I repeat, more determination and calm. Report more often.[40]

It was an appalling catastrophe. 452,720 men were encircled, including about 60,000 officers.[41] The enemy acquired a large amount of weapons and equipment. Kirponos, his chief of staff, Tupikov, and War Council member Burmistenko perished in the last battles, along with thousands of other servicemen. Even had Kirponos managed to break out, it is unlikely Stalin would have forgiven him. In fact, Stalin and the Staff were mainly responsible for the tragedy, although it is also true that the front headquarters were not fully capable of handling the forces which, under better leadership, might have avoided their sad fate. Too often, bravery was not backed by ability, organization and competence. The defeat at Kiev sharply tipped the balance in the enemy's favour along the entire front.

Showing no sign of emotion, Stalin merely told Shaposhnikov to 'Plug the hole quickly. Quickly!' Shaposhnikov said, 'I think what's needed in this difficult situation is a firm hand and an experienced head. Probably the best candidate for the job is Timoshenko.' Stalin agreed. 'And Khrushchev should be appointed to the War Council, with Major General A. P. Pokrovsky as chief of staff.' 'Let it be so,' Stalin said.

The losses in the first year of the war were truly monumental, even allowing for the fact that the figures were cooked. At Kiev alone nearly half a million men had gone missing in action, one way or another. One day, Stalin wrote a note to Shaposhnikov asking for details about Soviet losses in the vicinity of Vitebsk.[42] Normally never giving a thought to his family, suddenly his son, Yakov, was on his mind. In the middle of August, Zhdanov, who was on the war council of the Northwestern front, sent Stalin a specially sealed envelope.

It contained a broadsheet with a photograph of Yakov in conversation with two German officers, with the following text:

This is Stalin's elder son, Yakov Dzhugashvili, battery commander of the 14th Howitzer artillery regiment of the 14th armoured division, who surrendered near Vitebsk on 16 July along with thousands of other officers and men. On Stalin's orders, Timoshenko and your political commissars are telling you that Bolsheviks don't surrender. But Red Army men are going over to the Germans all the time. To frighten you, the commissars tell you the Germans treat their prisoners badly. The example of Stalin's own son shows this is a lie. He gave himself up because any further resistance to the German Army is useless.[43]

Yakov's fate concerned Stalin only from one point of view. He felt it would have been better had his son perished in battle, rather than be taken prisoner and possibly used by the Nazis, being a weak person, to broadcast their propaganda against his own father and his country. The thought was unbearable. That evening, when they were alone, Molotov told him that the head of the Swedish Red Cross, Count Bernadotte, had sent an oral message via the Swedish embassy, asking if Stalin would empower him or someone else to try to secure Yakov's release. Stalin pondered for a minute or two and then looked at Molotov and began speaking about a totally different subject. Molotov never raised the subject again.

Stalin expected to be given precise information about what was happening, yet when his commanders gave him the facts straight his reaction was often to accuse them of alarmism. During the Kiev crisis, for instance, Tupikov reported that 'The situation at the front is becoming more difficult by the minute. It's the beginning of the catastrophe you know about, and is only a matter of a couple of days.'[44] Stalin cabled back that Tupikov's message showed panic.[45] Commanders henceforth became cautious of telling Stalin the truth if it was unpleasant. A conversation of 4 September 1941 between Zhukov and Major General K. I. Rakutin, commander of the 24th Army, is typical of the period. Zhukov upbraided Rakutin for throwing his tanks into battle 'mindlessly' and losing them, and also for making false reports.

Rakutin: 'I'll go out this morning to investigate the matter, as I only got the report just now ...'

Zhukov: 'You're a general, not a detective. Send me a written report that I can present to the government. Has Shepelovo been occupied or is that also eyewash?'

Rakutin: 'Shepelovo has not been occupied. I'll look into it myself tomorrow and report to you. I won't lie.'

Zhukov: 'The main thing is, stop the lying coming out of your headquarters, and deal properly with the situation, or you won't look good yourself.'[46]

Rakutin had been let down by subordinates who had reported a nonexistent success. This often happened, as people lied for fear of being punished. Rakutin did look into the matter, but he perished in battle only a month later, anyway.

In the middle of September 1941, Shaposhnikov remarked to Stalin that, if all the divisions had fought as well as the best units, the enemy would have been stopped long before. Stalin, who was desperate to raise the troops' morale, thereupon ordered the General Staff to come up with a way of distinguishing the best units in order to stimulate and set an example to the rest of the army. The result was Order No. 308 of 18 September, creating the Soviet Guards and renaming the 100th, 127th, 153rd and 161st rifle divisions as Guards Divisions for their bravery, discipline and organization, increasing their officers' pay by a half, and doubling that of other ranks.[47]

In March 1942 Stalin called a meeting to discuss proposals from headquarters staff Southwestern front. It was attended by Voroshilov, Timoshenko, Shaposhnikov, Zhukov and Vasilievsky. Timoshenko proposed carrying out a broad attack in the south, using the forces of the three fronts and emerging on the Nikolaev-Cherkassy-Kiev-Gomel ridge. Shaposhnikov objected that there were insufficient reserves and that it would be wiser to maintain active defence along the whole front, paying special attention to the central sector. Stalin remarked: 'We can't just sit doing nothing and wait for the enemy to make the first strike.' Zhukov's idea was to attack on the Western sector and maintain active defence along the rest of the front. Timoshenko dug his heels in and Voroshilov supported him, but Vasilievsky was opposed. Opinions were divided and they waited for Stalin to speak. The time had come for him to make a genuine strategic choice, but he opted for a half-hearted compromise: the forces of the Southwestern sector would carry out a single, local attack against the enemy group at Kharkov as a step towards the ultimate liberation of the Donbass. No one objected. They rarely did at General Staff Headquarters.

Stalin assumed that an attack in converging directions – from the district south of Volchansk and the Barvenkovo bridgehead – would place the enemy in a hopeless position. What he did not know was that the Germans were preparing to attack Soviet forces in the Barvenkovo salient. Stalin's plan was therefore fraught with risk.

The Kharkov offensive began on 12 May and opened well. The troops advanced fifty kilometres in three days, when out of the blue the Germans launched a powerful strike from the south against the flank of the advancing Soviet troops. A series of contradictory orders ensued. By 18 May Timoshenko was apparently asking Stalin to halt the offensive (no documentary record of their conversations has been found). Stalin refused: 'We'll send them two rifle divisions and two tank brigades. The Southern front must hold up. The Germans will soon be played out.'

Later, at the Twentieth Party Congress, Khrushchev blamed Stalin directly for the catastrophe at Kharkov. He recalled that he had called the Kremlin from the front. Malenkov picked up the phone and Khrushchev demanded to speak to Stalin who, standing only a few paces away, told Malenkov to take the call. Khrushchev told him to ask Stalin to call off the offensive, to which Stalin replied, 'Leave things as they are!'

Zhukov gives a different account of events, laying the blame on the leadership of the Southern and Southwestern fronts. He writes in his memoirs that General Staff was aware of the impending danger sooner than the front. As early as 18 May, he claims, General Staff was in favour of calling a halt to the offensive. 'That evening there was a conversation with Khrushchev at the front, who took the same line as the Southwestern staff headquarters, namely that the danger from the enemy group at Kramatorsk was exaggerated and that there was no need to halt the offensive.' It was this report that Stalin relied on, ignoring the worries of the General Staff. Zhukov dismisses Khrushchev's claim to have sent alarming reports: 'I can testify to this, as I personally took part in the conversations with the Supreme Commander.'[48] Zhukov repeatedly asserts that Stalin relied on the reports from Khrushchev and Timoshenko at the front and failed to give proper weight to the General Staff's more sober analysis.

As Kleist's tank army intensified its efforts and widened the gap in the front, Stalin realized that in a day or two Soviet troops would find themselves in the Barenkovo 'mousetrap', and he therefore finally gave the order to stand firm on the Barenkovo salient. But it was too late. The 6th and 57th Armies, and General L. V. Bobkin's army group, advancing on Krasnograd, fell into the encirclement and were virtually wiped out. Whether Stalin understood the causes of this, another great tragedy of the war, or was aware of his own fallibility as a strategist and tactician, is hard to say. Nevertheless, it is the case that both he and the General Staff were learning the bloody lessons of war.

Following appalling defeats in the Crimea and at Kharkov, Stalin decided it was time to step up partisan activity. At the end of May 1942 he signed Order No. 1837 creating a central partisan headquarters staff to be attached to the General Staff. Partisan headquarters were to be attached to the war councils of the Southwestern, Bryansk, Western, Kalinin, Leningrad and Karelian fronts. The military and political importance of the movement was demonstrated by the fact that its central headquarters staff was to include P. K. Ponomarenko of the Central Committee, V. T. Sergienko of the NKVD, and G. F. Korneyev of the intelligence branch of the Defence Committee.

Once it appeared that the Southern front had been more or less stabilized, Stalin felt it was to time intervene again. At 2 a.m. on 26 June 1942, having heard Vasilievsky's routine report, Stalin stopped him from leaving and said:

'Wait a minute, I want to say something about the Kharkov defeat again. Today, when I asked the Southwestern staff if the enemy had been halted at Kupyansk, and how the building of the defences on the river Oskol was going, I could get nothing sensible out of them. When are people going to learn how to fight? Headquarters should surely have learnt something from the Kharkov defeat. When are they going to start obeying General Staff orders? They have to be reminded of this. Those who deserve it should be punished, and meanwhile I'd like to send a personal letter to the leadership there. What do you think?'

'I think it would be useful,' Vasilievsky replied, and Stalin proceeded to dictate the following letter in the name of the Defence Committee, none of whose members he had of course taken the trouble to consult:

> We here in Moscow, the members of the State Defence Committee and the General Staff, have decided to remove Comrade Bagramyan as chief of staff Southwestern front. The General Staff finds Comrade Bagramyan unsatisfactory not merely as a chief of staff who has been called on to strengthen the contacts and leadership of the armies, but also as a simple provider of information whose responsibility it is to inform the General Staff honestly and truthfully about the situation at the front. Comrade Bagramyan has moreover proved incapable of learning from the catastrophe that took place on the Southwestern front. In the course of some three weeks, the Southwestern front, thanks to his negligent attitude, not only lost the half-won Kharkov operation, but also managed to give the enemy another eighteen or twenty divisions.

Stalin paused and asked: 'The general who was defeated together with Samsonov in 1914, the one with the German name, what was it?'
'Rennenkampf,' Vasilievsky replied.
'Yes, that's it. Right, let's continue.'

> This catastrophe is as fatal in its consequences as the one suffered by Rennenkampf and Samsonov in East Prussia. After all that has happened, Comrade Bagramyan could have learnt something had he wanted to. Unfortunately there is still no sign of this. Now, as before the catastrophe, General Staff's contact with the armies is unsatisfactory, our information is of poor quality.
>   We are sending Comrade Bodin, deputy chief of General Staff, to serve as your temporary chief of staff. He knows your front and can perform a great service. Comrade Bagramyan is appointed chief of staff 28th Army. If Comrade Bagramyan serves well in this position, I will raise the question of giving him the chance to move up further.
>   Obviously, Comrade Bagramyan is not the whole problem. There is also the question of errors committed by the war council, above all by Comrades Timoshenko and Khrushchev. If we were to tell the country the full scale of the catastrophe suffered and still being suffered by the front, with the loss of eighteen or twenty divisions, I am afraid the people would deal with you very harshly. Good luck.
>   26 July 1942, 0200. Stalin.[49]

The year had begun so well. The counterattack outside Moscow from 5 December 1941 to 7 January 1942 had been the first major Soviet offensive, coordinating all three fronts. The country had rejoiced. The enemy had been thrown back between 100 and 250 kilometres. It had looked like the turning point. Then there had been a successful landing in the Crimea, success at Tikhvin, the encirclement of a large enemy group at Demyansk. But, as

Suetonius wrote, 'No victory brings as much as one defeat can take away'. And there had been more than one defeat ...

Stalin was shaken by these defeats, but less so than by the threat that had hung over the capital in October 1941, when he was tormented by alarming presentiments. The Defence Committee had declared a state of siege. In those dark days, the enemy struck blow after blow and Stalin felt that only a miracle would save him. But it was the people who saved him, the people who found the strength to stand firm.

On 17 or 18 October 1941 Stalin convened a morning meeting in the Kremlin with Molotov, Malenkov, Mikoyan, Beria, Voznesensky, Shcherbakov, Kaganovich, Vasilievsky and Artemiev. Once everyone had settled down, Stalin started listing the arrangements for the evacuation of all important state and party figures and the laying of explosives at all important buildings in the event of the capture of Moscow. Anti-tank and anti-infantry defences were to be built on all approach roads. A plan was made for the evacuation of the government to Kuibyshev and the General Staff to Arzamas. Stalin said he was still hoping for a good outcome, as divisions would soon be arriving from Siberia and the Far East.[50]

'We won't surrender Moscow!' 'We will retreat no further!' These were the slogans voiced by Soviet citizens when, after the first panic, a calm determination returned by mid-October to the streets of Moscow. A number of anti-aircraft batteries were installed around Stalin's nearby dacha and the security was strengthened. On one occasion, as he stepped from his car arriving home in the early hours, he witnessed an air raid on Moscow. With the deafening crack of anti-aircraft guns in his ears, the sweeping searchlight beams above his head and the overpowering drone of countless aircraft in the sky, Stalin stood frozen by the car. Could he have imagined four months earlier that his dacha would be less than a day's drive for the German tanks? Something fell on to the drive nearby. Vlasik bent down and found a piece of warm shell shrapnel and handed it to Stalin. The security chief tried to persuade Stalin to go inside (a shelter would be built later), but he remained there for several minutes, as if sensing for the first time the immediacy of the war's deadly breath. And it was then that, also for the first time, he felt the desire to visit the front.

At the end of October, a column of several cars left Moscow by the Volo-kolamsk highway, turning on to a country road after some miles. Stalin wanted to watch a salvo being fired but his security chief would not allow the column to go further. They waited. Stalin listened to an officer from the Western front, watched the crimson flashes on the horizon for a long time and then turned away. As they drove back, a heavy armoured car sprayed Stalin's limousine with mud. His chauffeur, A. Krivchenkov, was in despair, and Beria insisted that Stalin transfer to another vehicle. By dawn the excursion to the 'front' was over.

Once, in mid-October, as Stalin was preparing to leave for the dacha, Beria informed him somewhat nervously that he should not go, explaining in Georgian, when Stalin shot him an irritated look, that the dacha had been mined and was ready to be blown up. Stalin was angry, but quickly simmered down. Beria also told him that a special train was ready for him at one of Moscow's stations, as well as four airplanes, including his personal Douglas DC-3. Stalin said nothing. He pondered, but something deep down told him that, as long as the army and the people knew that he, Stalin, was still in Moscow, they would feel more assured, and so, after long deliberation, he decided to stay there until the bitter end. He knew the evacuation of the capital was in full swing and that military objectives were being mined. Beria suggested that if they had to leave they ought to blow up the Metro, as well.

Stalin was not certain that Leningrad would hold out, either. On 25 October 1941, he cabled Fedyuninsky, Zhdanov and Kuznetsov that it seemed they were not yet aware of the critical situation of the forces of the Leningrad front:

> Moscow is in a critical position and can provide no fresh reserves. Either you must break through in the next two or three days and give our troops an outlet to the east, if Leningrad cannot be held, or you'll be taken prisoner. We demand swift and decisive action. Concentrate eight or nine divisions and break through to the east. This is essential whether Leningrad is held or surrendered. For us the army is more important. We demand decisive action.

This was repeated in a later message from Vasilievsky to Lieutenant General M. S. Khozin, commander of the 54th Army, who was appointed commander of the Leningrad front four days later: 'I would ask you take into account that in this case we are talking not so much about saving Leningrad as of saving and bringing out the army.'[51]

In his radio speech on 9 November 1941, of which Stalin was shown the transcript of an intercept, Hitler said the German army had advanced on Leningrad only far enough to take up their encirclement of the city, while 'the enemy will die of starvation. If a sufficient force threatens to lift our siege, I will give the order to take the city by storm. But the city is firmly encircled, and it and its inhabitants are all in our hands.'[52]

Stalin's reaction to the news of the tragedy in Leningrad, where hundreds of thousands did indeed die of hunger, was noteworthy. General Fedyuninsky told me of a conversation he and a group of Leningrad leaders had with Stalin after the blockade had been lifted. He told Stalin the city had become a ghost of itself. Corpses had remained on the streets because there was no one to pick them up. The worst thing, Fedyuninsky said, was that a man who is dying of hunger retains his consciousness to the end. Even fear disappears. 'It's as if he is watching the approach of his own death. The Leningrad siege was one of the greatest tragedies in human history.' Stalin replied: 'Death was cutting down not only Leningraders. People were also dying at the front and in the occupied territories. I agree that death is appalling when there is no way out of the situation, and the starvation was just such a situation. There was nothing more we could do for Leningrad. Moscow itself was hanging by a thread. Death and war are inseparable. Leningrad was not the only place to suffer from that swine Hitler.'

But Moscow held out, and the Germans' second major onslaught on the city collapsed. Stalin soon gave Zhukov the order to prepare the counter-offensive and, when the Germans were literally in the suburbs of Moscow and dropping on their feet from exhaustion, the order was given, and this time it was successful. The Nazis suffered their first major defeat of the Second World War. It seemed the turning point had come. It was now possible to restore the people's faith in the possibility of victory and dispel the fatalistic climate of failure by exploding the myth of German invincibility. In some respects Stalin showed himself to be quite the psychologist. He knew he must not leave Moscow, that the Informburo must not issue panic bulletins and that the papers must write about the exploits and successes of the armed forces. On the eve of the 1941 anniversary of the revolution, he asked Molotov and Beria: 'How are we going to have the military parade? Maybe two or three hours earlier?' The others thought they must have misheard. A parade, with the Germans literally just outside Moscow? As if unaware of their doubts, Stalin continued:

'The anti-aircraft defences around Moscow must be reinforced. The main military leaders are at the front. Budenny will take the parade and General Artemiev will be in command. If there's an air raid during the parade and there are dead and wounded, they must be quickly removed and the parade allowed to go on. A newsreel should be made of it and distributed throughout the country in large numbers. The newspapers should give the parade wide coverage. I will read a report at the ceremonial meeting and make a speech at the parade. What do you think?'

Molotov pondered. 'But what about the risk? There would be a risk, though I admit the political response here and abroad would be enormous.'

'So, it's decided! Make the appropriate arrangements,' Stalin said to Beria, 'but no one, apart from Artemiev and Budenny and a few trusted individuals, is to know about the parade until the last minute.'

It was undoubtedly a bold and far-sighted move, reflecting the sure hand with which Stalin influenced public opinion and guided the people's mental state, and this at a time when many were doubtful about the outcome of the war. The Nazis had found numerous accomplices in the occupied territories, and Stalin knew that Soviet failures were undermining faith. He regarded the mass surrender as treachery, although he never admitted in public that there were so many Soviet prisoners of war in German hands. When he spoke at the ceremonial meeting of the Moscow soviet, at the Mayakovsky Metro on 6 November 1941, he declared that 'in the four months of the war we have lost 350,000 killed and 378,000 missing in action.'[53] Stalin was by now a master at manipulating and indeed inventing facts for propaganda. He knew that there were several times more 'missing in action', but it was not the catastrophic beginning of the war that he saw in these figures, it was the political defects in the training of people, the inadequacy of the punitive organs, enemy influence, survivals of the class war. In this respect he was neither a subtle psychologist, nor a sober politician, nor the 'wise father of the nation'. In this he was the Stalin of 1929–33, 1937–38. A man's inner core changes slowly. In Stalin's case, the fear of enemy encirclement remained with him all his life. Otherwise, he simply would not have been Stalin.

CHAPTER 44

Captivity and General Vlasov

The Nazi invasion brought many misfortunes, among them captivity. A man faced with the choice of life or death in war will usually choose life, even if it means the loss of liberty and his sense of social dignity. In the last war, captivity was almost tantamount to death, for the overwhelming majority of Soviet prisoners of war in fact died in German camps. In May 1918 the Soviet government had informed the International Red Cross and the governments of the world that the conventions on war victims, like 'all other international conventions and agreements concerning the Red Cross and recognized by Russia before October 1917, are recognized and will be observed by the Russian Soviet government'. The new Geneva Convention on prisoners of war of 1929 was not, however, ratified by the Soviet Union.[54]

Millions of Soviet soldiers fell into German hands in the first eighteen months of the war. Accurate figures of Soviet losses and prisoners have still not been published in the USSR. They reached fantastic levels. I will produce my own calculations in a later chapter.

On several occasions in the early months of the war Stalin wanted to know the scale of the losses. The General Staff and the personnel section of the defence commissariat provided reports but plainly had little idea of the real position. The archives contain graphs showing how many were killed and wounded, how many sick and how many missing, how many horses were out of action, how many weapons, aircraft and tanks were lost. But there is no table showing how many were taken prisoner. One report states that in June and July 1941 on all fronts 72,776 men were missing.[55] The number doubles if we add the figures for August and September, but we also know that in the Kiev district alone 452,720 men were encircled and that most of them were taken prisoner. There are some unofficial calculations which are more accurate. For instance, the chief procurator of the Red Army, V. I. Nosov, reported to Mekhlis on 24 September 1941 that, out of the 7,000 combat troops of the

299th rifle division of the 50th Army fighting on the Bryansk-Roslavl highway, less than 500 men remained. About 500 had been killed, 1,500 wounded, and 4,000 had gone missing.[56]

Stalin himself indirectly acknowledged the existence of large numbers of 'missing' soldiers in a telegram to Timoshenko, Khrushchev and Bodin:

> The General Staff finds it intolerable and impermissible that for several days now the war council has sent no news about the fate of the 28th and 57th Armies and the 22nd tanks corps. From other sources the General Staff is aware that the staffs of these armies have withdrawn beyond the Don, but neither these staffs nor the war council has told the General Staff where the forces have gone and what has happened to them, whether they are still fighting or have been taken prisoner. There were some fourteen divisions in these armies and the General Staff wants to know where they have got to?[57]

In November 1941, Hitler claimed that Germany's success in the war was evident from the fact that she had already taken 3.6 million prisoners, 'and I forbid any English blockhead to say this has not been proved. When a German military institution calculates something, it always gets its sums right.'[58] There are various estimates of Soviet prisoner-of-war figures current in Western studies, some of them based on Wehrmacht statistics of June 1941 to April 1945, which put the number at 5.16 million.[59] I believe this figure will be shown to be too high when all the facts are known. But based on what we already know, in the first eighteen months of the war, about three million men, or 65 per cent of Soviet armed forces, were indeed taken prisoner.

What was Stalin's attitude to prisoners of war? Apart from his official prohibition on surrender, he also suspected anyone so doing as a probable traitor. Any soldier who had been a prisoner was, in his eyes, not to be trusted. Any soldier who had retreated from encirclement would either be transferred to a mine-laying unit or be sent to one of the special concentration camps where the NKVD could 'check' him. In August 1942, Stalin sanctioned the construction of three such camps.[60]

Stalin was particularly interested in the fate of missing generals, and he issued special instructions to find out what had happened to Kachalov, Ponedelin, Vlasov, Yefremov, Potapov, Rakutin, Samokhin and Lukin. We have already discussed Kachalov and Ponedelin. When Yefremov and Vlasov disappeared, Stalin ordered Beria to investigate, and there is a telegram from Zhdanov to General Sazonov asking him to inform the General Staff immediately of what he knew about Vlasov.[61]

They did not find Vlasov himself but he soon made his position known, as we shall discuss below. As for Yefremov, his whereabouts were discovered by accident. A woman from the village of Slobodka in the Temkinsk district of Smolensk reported at the end of April 1943 that she had seen some soldiers 'burying a general'. This was reported to higher authority where it was suspected the general had surrendered. As a result, the grave was dug up, his corpse identified, his wound confirmed as incapacitating, and a report was submitted to Stalin effectively rehabilitating Yefremov for having shot himself to avoid inevitable capture.

Many generals went missing in action in 1941–42, most of them killed while breaking out of encirclement. Those who survived either rotted or died in German camps. Some, like Major General P. V. Sysoev, who was taken prisoner in July 1941, managed to escape in 1943, only to spend three years in a Soviet camp being 'checked'. Some in this category were executed for treachery. Very few, like Rikhter, Malyshkin and Zhilenkov, actually went over to the German side.

One would imagine that Stalin, having 'cleaned up' the whole of society in 1937–39, could hope that no one would collaborate with the occupiers. As we have seen, decades later Molotov actually claimed that Stalin had 'destroyed the fifth column' before the war. This was of course not so. First of all, the people Stalin liquidated had not been enemies. The Quislings and Lavals were not all in the West: the Soviet Union provided many collaborators and traitors of its own. Only twenty-odd years had elapsed since the revolution and there were still many people who felt aggrieved by the régime. Many others were motivated by fear of the Nazis or the desire to adapt and survive, while yet others, especially in 1941, believed that the Germans had come for good. Finally there were weak, venal or just plain criminal types who were prepared to commit treason. For instance, Beria reported to Malenkov in December 1941 that one A. I. Ulyanov had been taken prisoner as a simple private and sent back by the Germans with the rank of captain, twice decorated as a Hero of the Soviet Union. He had soon been exposed.[62]

These were isolated cases, but there were also a number of organized forms of collaboration, of which the most blatant case was that of Lieutenant General A. A. Vlasov, commander of the 2nd Assault Army on the Volkhov front. When Stalin was told in June 1942 that this force had been cut off in the district of Masnoy Bor, he took the news calmly. How many other armies were cut off! But since the battle of Moscow, he felt more confident that the outcome of the war no longer hung on a defeat here or a victory there: the Allied cause was on the road to victory. He also knew that, in Vlasov, who was second in command of the front, the 2nd Assault Army had an experienced leader, one moreover whom Stalin himself only three months earlier had promoted to Lieutenant General as one of the best senior officers at the front.

A few days later Stalin asked Vasilievsky how the situation had arisen and what had happened since. Vasilievsky reminded him that on 21 May he had ordered the Volkhov group on the Leningrad front to strike the enemy from the west, while the 59th Army were to strike from the east, thus wiping out the enemy in the Priyutin-Spasskaya Polist salient. The combined force of the 59th Army and 2nd Assault Army, and the right flank of the 52nd Army, would then secure a bridgehead on the west bank of the river Volkhov and close the Leningrad railway and highway to prevent enemy forces from reuniting with their Novgorod and Chudov groupings and restoring the Novgorod-Leningrad line.[63]

'So, how could you allow the 2nd Assault Army to become encircled?' Stalin asked.

'When major enemy forces were threatening the 2nd Assault Army from the north, I repeatedly asked Khozin to send reinforcements to the Volkhov ridge.'

'What did Khozin do?' Stalin asked sternly.

'The front gave the order only on 25 May, much too late. In three or four days, the army's supply lines were cut and they were encircled.' Vasilievsky explained that he had cabled Khozin to act with greater determination and speed in moving his forces.[64]

Stalin then asked if contact had been made with Vlasov.

'No,' Vasilievsky replied. 'His last report was sometime in early June.'

'Perhaps the Volkhov operational group should form a separate front?' Stalin suggested.

Vasilievsky agreed: 'There are six armies in that group. They ought to be capable of rescuing the 2nd Assault Army.'

'Remove Khozin and appoint Govorov commander-in-chief Leningrad front. The commander of the new, Volkhov, front should be Meretskov. If you have no objections, write the orders,' Stalin concluded.*

Other events soon diverted Stalin's attention from Vlasov, although, when German radio began broadcasting rumours that 'one of the biggest Soviet armies' had been encircled, Stalin ordered Sovinformburo to prepare the draft of a special communiqué, which read:

On 28 June the German information bureau broadcast a report from Hitler's headquarters about the destruction of the 2nd Assault Army, the 52nd and 59th Armies of the Volkhov front, alleging that they were encircled by German Fascist troops on the west bank of the river Volkhov. But in fact, the 59th and 52nd Armies attacked from the east and the 2nd Assault Army attacked from the west, cutting communication between enemy units which were mostly destroyed, only a few of them being thrown back into a position from which they could escape. Therefore there can be no talk of the 2nd Assault Army having been destroyed.

Stalin took one look at this draft and handed it back to Poskrebyshev with the words: 'Better say nothing.' A few hours later on 29 June 1942, however, Sovinformburo was instructed by Stalin to broadcast a different communiqué:

The Nazi scribes are quoting astronomical figures of 30,000 supposed prisoners of war and saying that even more than this were killed. Needless to say, this is a typical Nazi lie. According to incomplete figures, at least 30,000 Germans were

---

*Khozin was also reported for entertaining female personnel in his apartment – he claimed they were watching films – and for being too fond of his drink. (TsPA IML, f. 77, op. 3, d. 133, l. 1–4.)

killed alone ... Parts of the 2nd Assault Army withdrew to a prepared ridge. We lost 10,000 killed and about 10,000 missing.

The symmetry of these figures looked suspicious even then, and now we know that thousands and thousands of Soviet troops were swallowed up in the marshes during this badly planned operation and are still listed as 'missing'.

Some time a few weeks later, Beria, who with Molotov was still at Stalin's dacha late one night, took a paper out of his ever-present leather file and laid it before Stalin.

'What's this?'

'Take a look. See where the missing commander of the 2nd Assault Army has turned up,' Beria replied.

Stalin scanned the document which was 'An Address of the Russian Committee to Soldiers and Officers of the Red Army, to all the Russian People and Other Nations of the Soviet Union':

> The Russian Committee has the following aims: to overthrow Stalin and his clique, to conclude an honourable peace with Germany, to create a New Russia. We call on you to come over to the Russian Liberation Army which is fighting in alliance with Germany.
>
> Chairman of the Russian Committee Lieutenant General Vlasov.
> Secretary of the Russian Committee Lieutenant General Malyshkin.[65]

There were permits for crossing the lines, 'An open letter from Vlasov about why I have taken the path of struggle against Bolshevism', and similar publications.

Stalin pushed the papers away and asked Beria: 'Could they be forgeries? What is known about Vlasov? Is there confirmation?'

Beria replied, 'Yes, there is. Vlasov is working for the Germans.'

'How is it we missed him before the war?' Molotov interrupted.

For reply, Beria produced Vlasov's personal dossier from his file. Stalin read that Vlasov had been born in the province of Nizhni Novgorod (Gorky) in a middle (i. e. neither rich nor poor) peasant family. He had no relatives, apart from a wife and an elderly father. Beria had underlined the note that Vlasov had completed church school and studied for two years in a theological seminary before 1917. He had fought in the civil war and all his subsequent service had been successful: the 99th rifle division under his command had been one of the best in the Kiev district. Before that he had been on special assignment in China. He had commanded the 4th mechanized corps which had fought well at Przemysl and Lvov, and had been promoted to command the 37th Army defending Kiev. He had done well there and was given the 20th Army and finally the 2nd Assault Army. On 20 April 1942, Stalin himself had signed the order appointing Vlasov as 'combined' – a rare term in military usage – commander of the 2nd Assault Army and deputy commander-in-chief Volkhov front.[66] He had been awarded the Order of Lenin and the Red Banner. He had an unblemished record. His party report for 1938 stated that 'He is doing much to liquidate remnants of sabotage in the units.' His referees were such well known officers as Kirponos, Muzychenko, Parusinov and Golikov. The only comment in a testimonial dated 19 November 1940 referred to a desire 'to pay attention to the use and maintenance of the horses'. Throughout there were such remarks as 'Dedicated to the cause of the party of Lenin–Stalin and the socialist Motherland'. In a testimonial of 24 January 1942, General Zhukov wrote that Vlasov was well trained operationally, had organizational skills, and was fully capable of leading an army. To earn Zhukov's comment 'fully capable' was no mean feat in that harsh time.

Stalin did not believe that Vlasov would be able to do anything very important for the Germans, but he did realize that, following the announcement of the creation of the Russian Liberation Army, further such national organizations could be expected to come into existence, and he was right. In 1942, the German authorities began scouring the camps for defectors who were willing not merely to serve in Vlasov's army, but also in various national legions: Georgian, Armenian, Turkestani, Caucasian, Baltic and others. Much effort was put into this scheme, but little came of it. Some prisoners of war joined these legions as a means of survival and a possible way to rejoin their own forces, and there were of course some who fell for the nationalist propaganda. Some 'legionaries' even tried to cross the lines in German-issue uniform, not realizing what was in store for them. For instance, on 3 October 1942, Bergenov, Khasanov and Tulebaev, three soldiers of the Turkestani Legion, while searching for partisans for four days, came across Soviet units and told them that a large part of their battalion wanted to get back to their own units. On 8 October, Tsulaya and Kabakadze turned up in a defence zone of the 2nd Guards rifle division and asked for help in getting a detachment of the Georgian Legion back across the lines.[67]

The Germans were especially optimistic about the legions they had formed in the Baltic republics, whose populations had lived under Soviet rule for only a year before the war. The German command, however, only used them as auxiliaries, for guarding sites and roads, and occasionally on punitive expeditions. After the war, these legionaries were tried and exiled. The Baltic governments asked the Soviet authorities to grant an amnesty. On 16 March 1946, V. T. Latsis, the prime minister of the Latvian SSR, and Ya. E. Kalberzin, the Latvian party first secretary, wrote to Moscow:

> During the temporary occupation of the Latvian SSR, the German aggressors forcibly mobilized the entire labour force, some of whom they deported to Germany for forced labour, while others were conscripted into so-called legions of the German army. These people were subsequently exiled for six years to the northern regions.
>
> We ask that those who only served in the legions be allowed to return to the Latvian SSR.[68]

Stalin would normally have handed such communications to Molotov and Beria, but his position on people who had gone over to the Germans was invariable. After the liberation of the Northern Caucasus, Beria reported that:

the NKVD thinks it would be wise to deport from Stavropol, Kislovodsk, Pyatigorsk, Mineralnye Vody and Essentuki the families of bandits, active accomplices of the Germans, traitors to the Motherland and those who went over to the Germans voluntarily, and to resettle them permanently in the Tadzhik SSR as special settlers. The number involved is 735 families, or 2,238 people. I request your orders.[69]

Stalin gave his approval. He was kept informed about the legions by the NKVD. He realized that while these units represented no great force, they could be politically significant. His attitude to them, as shown by the documents, was uniformly irreconcilable, even though they were relatively few in number.

For instance, Kobulov reported to Beria that, in the districts of the Northern Caucasus, during the previous week there had been six incidents. Eight bandits had been killed, including two German parachutists, forty-six bandits had been arrested and thirty-seven weapons captured. The Red Army had lost eight men. The head of the Kayakent gang, Ilyasov-Nadzhmuddin, had been killed and S. Kh. Temirkanov's gang wiped out.[70] Similarly, Beria sent the following report from Kobulov to Stalin on 20 July 1944:

As a result of combing the forest in the district of Kazburun in the Kabardin Autonomous SSR on 12 July, a German parachutist was captured, by name Kh. Kh. Fadzaev (a former member of the Komsomol, an Ossetian, who worked for the German police in the village of Urukh, joined the German army in 1943, and has the rank of sergeant-major). Several more parachutists are being held. Of eight parachutists, two are still being searched for. The rest are either dead or under arrest.[71]

Similar reports came in from the Crimea and elsewhere. Instead of dealing with individual criminals and traitors, however, Stalin and Beria acted on plans drawn up by Serov, Kobulov, Momulov, Tsanava and other masters of such matters, and had entire nations deported from the Northern Caucasus, from Kalmykia and from the Crimea to the east. The documents show that there were a good many turncoats, but how many more heroes came from these peoples who had served with distinction in the Red Army! The Chechens and Ingushes alone produced thirty-six Heroes of the Soviet Union.

In the course of 1944, on Stalin's orders, hundreds of thousands of Chechens, Ingushes, Balkars, Karachays, Crimean Tatars, Kalmyks and Meskhetian Turks were deported. One of the few scholarly studies of this subject is that of the historian Dr Kh. M. Ibragimbeili.[72] Meanwhile, Beria reported to Stalin that 26,359 Kalmyk families, consisting of 93,139 people, had been deported to the Altai and Krasnoyarsk regions, and Omsk and Novosibirsk oblasts.[73]

Stalin followed these developments as assiduously as he did the position at the front. Here, however, he faced no resistance, for the deportees were mainly old folk and women and children, and Beria even reported that 'during the operation of eviction and transportation there were no incidents'. Stalin was pleased and ordered Beria 'to put forward those who have carried out the deportation order in an exemplary manner'. Beria was quick to act and replied:

In accordance with your instructions I submit a draft decree of the Presidium of the Supreme Soviet of the USSR on decorations and medals for the most outstanding participants in the operation involving the deportation of the Chechens and Ingushes. 19,000 members of the NKVD, NKGB and Smersh* took part, plus up to 100,000 officers and men of the NKVD forces, of whom a substantial number also took part in the deportation of the Karachays and Kalmyks and will be involved in the forthcoming deportation of the Balkars. As a result of these three operations, some 650,000 Chechens, Ingushes, Kalmyks and Karachays have been deported to the eastern regions of the USSR.[74]

Stalin had gone so far as to accuse entire nations of treachery, and over 100,000 troops had been employed to deport old men, women and children. Had he followed this logic to its conclusion, after the formation of the Russian Liberation Army he ought to have deported all the Russians and Ukrainians – in fact, all the nations of the USSR!

The Vlasov movement came into being for a number of reasons: the major defeats, feelings of national and social grievance among some representatives (and their children) of the old privileged classes, fear of Stalin's retribution for falling into enemy hands. The more the Red Army succeeded in pushing the enemy back, the fewer the numbers of Soviet prisoners of war joining the Germans, and by the end of 1942 and in 1943 the number dwindled to practically none. Speaking to agitators who worked among non-Russian troops, the head of the political administration of the Red Army, A. S. Shcherbakov, remarked that in August 1942 on the Leningrad front there were twenty-two cases of men going over to the Germans, while in January 1943 there were only two. Thereafter there were none.[75]

In his book on Vlasov, *Die Geschichte der Wlassow Armee*, Joachim Hoffmann states, apparently on the basis of the Vlasov archives, that by May 1943 the Wehrmacht had ninety Russian battalions and almost as many national legions at its disposal.[76] These figures are grossly inflated, and the attempt to portray the Vlasov movement as a viable alternative to Bolshevism is unconvincing in the extreme. Vlasov's formations were not composed of 'ideological fighters', so much as a mixed bag of criminals and nationalists, but mainly of people who had found themselves in a hopeless situation and were possessed by the single idea that here lay a way to survive. Vlasov's resort to such White émigrés as Ataman P. N. Krasnov, General A. G. Shkuro, General Sultan-Girei Kluch and others, is eloquent testimony to the movement's ideological poverty.

It was mainly Soviet military success that undermined the Vlasov movement, dispelling as it did the depression, the panic and the apathy that had provided

---

* A special section of the security police, Smersh – an acronym of the Russian for 'Death to Spies' – was concerned with political surveillance in the armed forces and the occupied territories.

a rich soil for defections. Stalin, however, chose to explain the Vlasov movement as evidence that not all the 'enemies of the people' had been exposed before the war. Strict supervision was to be maintained over returnees from captivity, special measures were to be introduced at the front, with punitive action against anyone overheard voicing their doubt about their commanders' abilities. Checking the liberated territories and keeping an eye on the rear of the Red Army was in the hands of the NKVD and, as his regular reports to Stalin show, Beria did his job on a grand scale. For instance:

In 1943, the troops of the NKVD who are responsible for security in the rear of the Active Red Army, in the process of cleaning up the territory liberated from the enemy, arrested 931,549 people for checking. Of these, 582,515 were servicemen, and 349,034 were civilians.

Of the total number, 80,296 have been unmasked and detained (as spies, traitors, members of punitive squads, deserters, bandits and similar criminal elements).[77]

Beria and his crew did not limit their work to the Soviet side of the line, but also tried to find out what was happening in the prisoner-of-war units formed by the Germans. Beria, who usually reported to Stalin alone or in the company of Molotov, on one occasion showed Stalin the notes taken during the interrogation of Major General A. E. Budykho, who had escaped from a German prisoner-of-war camp and joined a group of partisans. He was now languishing in a Soviet concentration camp at Oranienburg, where most of the inmates were officers who had been German prisoners of war. Budykho provided a detailed account, describing the arrival in the camp of Vlasov's personal representative, General Zhilenkov, and other officials of the Russian Liberation Army.

Zhilenkov had been secretary of a Moscow district party committee before the war and had risen rapidly through the ranks, thanks to the purge of the party organizations. As a member of the war council of the 32nd Army on the Western front, he had been encircled and taken prisoner. As a time-server with no principles and suddenly finding himself among senior party officers, he soon became a collaborator. The same was true of another of Vlasov's aides, Lieutenant General Malyshkin, chief of staff 19th Army. He had been arrested in 1938 and released at the beginning of the war. When Beria reported on a number of generals who had been condemned and then released, Stalin wanted to know who had petitioned on Malyshkin's behalf. He begrudged the time wasted on having to hear about all the traitors he had overlooked in the 1930s.

In February and May 1943 trials were held *in absentia*, at which Vlasov and others were condemned to death. The sentences were carried out in August 1946, after the condemned men had been captured by Soviet forces and repatriated.

In the end, Stalin must have thought that all the Vlasovs put together would make no difference. The country had come through the worst. It would be hard to find a worse beginning to a war than that of June 1941. All the leading political and military authorities had thought the USSR might survive at most three months. But the Soviet people had proved them wrong. However, the fact of unbelievable resistance and staunchness would be ascribed to the 'wise leadership' of Stalin, the very person most directly responsible for the catastrophe.

THE SUPREME COMMANDER

'In the eyes of the people, the general who wins a battle has made no mistakes.'

– Voltaire

CHAPTER 45

Headquarters

Stalin was not the military leader of genius depicted in countless books, films, poems, monographs and stories. Nor did he have the great powers of prognostication ascribed to him. Given his dogmatic cast of mind, it would be surprising if he had. Most significantly, though strong-willed and inflexible, he had no professional military skills. He came to strategic wisdom only through blood-spattered trial and error. His civil war background was plainly inadequate for the post of Supreme Commander-in-Chief and in fact his reputation as a war leader was sustained by the collective capabilities of the General Staff and the outstanding talents of some of the personalities who worked closely with him during the war. These were above all Shaposhnikov, Zhukov, Vasilievsky and Antonov. Lacking real military experience, Stalin, especially during the first eighteen months of the war, had no conception of the working of the military machine, no sense of operational time or real distances or what troops could or could not accomplish. Hence, many of his orders were not carried out, because they were either unrealistic or hasty and half-baked.

For instance, on 28 August 1941, he ordered the air force of two fronts to smash some tank formations with the use of not less than 450 aircraft, and the operation was to begin at dawn the next day.[1] Even in terms of intelligence, let alone logistics, this order shows a total absence of awareness of what was required to get such a force airborne. As Supremo, it was as if he thought he had only to give the order and the system would go into action, with no notion of how the system worked. Gradually, however, he did learn, and by the time of Stalingrad, according to Zhukov, 'he had a good grasp of the broad strategic issues.'[2] A good grasp is not, however, the same as strategic knowledge. This was the collective contribution of the General Staff and its rôle cannot be exaggerated.

On the eve of the war, Zhukov and Timoshenko had raised with Stalin the question of creating one or two specially equipped control points for running the armed forces. Stalin dismissed the suggestion. In May 1941 for the second or third time they proposed the formation of a General Staff Headquarters which, among other things, would institute training throughout the country for the purpose of putting the economy on a war footing. Stalin agreed in principle that the idea of a supreme command headquarters was a good one, but no concrete decision was taken and no one raised the matter with him again, especially as everyone knew he would stay in only one of two places – the Kremlin or the nearby dacha. He hardly went to his other dacha at Semenovsky, and in November 1941 he turned it over to house war-wounded. The Supreme Commander-in-Chief's HQ was therefore Stalin's office in the Kremlin, or at the nearby dacha, or in the house on Kirov Street, or in the General Staff building.

Since Stalin held so many posts, and since no order of the Central Committee, Sovnarkom or Supreme Soviet was ever made without his approval, and since officials were constantly coming to consult him on every issue at every time of the day and night, no one was ever quite certain which particular body was 'operational' at any given moment. It might be the Politburo with coopted military men, or the State Defence Committee plus others, or the General Staff with some members of the Politburo. Stalin sometimes clarified the position by saying 'Note this as an order of the Defence Committee', or 'This should be written as a directive from the General Staff'. Sometimes Malenkov would write up the minutes of a discussion as orders of the Politburo. Virtually everything uttered by Stalin was final and decisive, regardless of the way the order was drafted. He apparently gave little regard to the question of his formal membership of this committee or that. This, however, created difficulties for the functionaries who had to decide as they went along which agency was to handle which job.

As a rule, no minutes or notes were made. The Stalin archives are full of documents containing reports, enquiries, orders and dispositions, but there is practically nothing on the General Staff's discussions of strategic questions. Once he had recovered from his initial shock, Stalin would simply summon two or three members of the General Staff and together they would decide operational issues. From the outset, the senior General Staff officers learned that when summoned they must come with their proposals and arguments fully prepared. This enhanced Stalin's rôle as supreme arbiter and high priest.

The members of Stalin's Staff knew that each member of the State Defence Committee was responsible for a given sector: ammunition, aircraft, transport, foreign affairs and so on. There was no such distribution of responsibilities in Stalin's Staff HQ, which ran the fronts on a day-to-day basis with the help of the General Staff, Air Force Headquarters Staff, and the agencies of the commissariat of defence. Instead of advisers serving Stalin's Staff, an institute of his representatives began to function 'spontaneously' within the armed forces. As a rule, Stalin did not detain the members of the Staff in Moscow and seemed to prefer it if they were away somewhere else. Thus, Zhukov,

Timoshenko, Voroshilov, Vasilievsky, Voronov and, at the beginning, Mekhlis, all of whom held crucially important jobs, made frequent visits to the troops.

Stalin expected them to report to him daily, either in writing or by telephone, and he would reprimand them, often crudely, if they were late in doing so. In his memoirs, Vasilievsky, with whom Stalin was on what might be called good terms, has cited part of one of Stalin's telegrams to him, dated 17 August 1943. The full text merits quotation:

> It is already 3.30 on 17 August and you have not yet deigned to report to the Staff on the results of the operations on 16 August and to give your assessment of the situation.
>
> I have for a long time obliged you, as a Staff plenipotentiary, to send special reports by the end of each day of operations. Almost every time you have forgotten your responsibility and have not sent reports.
>
> 16 August is the first day of an important operation on the Southwestern front where you are the Staff representative. And yet again it has pleased you to forget your duty to the Staff and you have sent no report.
>
> You cannot use the excuse that you have no time, as Marshal Zhukov is doing just as much at the front as you are, yet he sends us his report every day. The difference between you and Zhukov is that he is disciplined and knows his duty to the Staff. Whereas you lack discipline and often forget your duty to the Staff.
>
> I'm warning you for the last time that if you allow yourself to forget your duty to the Staff once more, you will be removed as head of the General Staff and will be sent to the front.[3]

One would be hard put to find a single marshal or senior officer who worked in the General Staff or visited the troops as a Staff representative or who commanded a front, who did not experience this sort of treatment from Stalin, often undeserved.

Similarly, if, after a visit from a Staff emissary, the situation at that part of the front did not improve, Stalin would draw the 'appropriate conclusions'. Thus, in February 1942 he sent Voroshilov to the Volkhov front. Voroshilov's reputation as an inferior military leader was already well established and, accomplishing nothing on this occasion either, he was embarrassed when Stalin proposed on the direct line that he become commander of the front. He began to refuse. This was too much for the Supremo and a month later, when Voroshilov had returned to Moscow, Stalin dictated a memorandum 'on the work of Comrade Voroshilov' that would end up as a Politburo decision taken on 1 April 1942. It is worth citing, even in abbreviated form:

> First. The war with Finland in 1939–1940 exposed great shortcomings and backwardness in the leadership of the defence commissariat. The Red Army lacked mortars and machine-guns, there was no exact inventory of aircraft and tanks, no proper winter clothing for the troops, or concentrated food products. Such important sections as artillery, military training, air force administration and so on were

in a state of neglect. All this led to the war being dragged out with unnecessary losses. As Commissar of Defence at the time, Comrade Voroshilov was compelled at the plenum at the end of March 1940 to admit to the inadequacy of his leadership of the commissariat that had been exposed. The Central Committee was obliged to remove him from the job.

Second. At the beginning of the war with Germany, Comrade Voroshilov was made commander-in-chief Northwestern front with the main task of defending Leningrad. As it later emerged, he was unable to handle the job and was unable to organize the defence of Leningrad. Comrade Voroshilov committed serious errors in the work he did in Leningrad: he issued orders that commanders of Home Guards battalions could be elected, an order rescinded by Staff Headquarters as one that would lead to disorganization and a weakening of discipline in the Red Army; he set up a Leningrad defence council but did not join it himself: this order was similarly rescinded by Staff Headquarters as incorrect and damaging, since the workers of Leningrad might have thought that Comrade Voroshilov did not join the defence council because he did not believe in defending Leningrad; he wasted time on workers' battalions armed with light weapons, such as shotguns, pikes, knives and so on, and neglected the artillery defences of the city ...

Third. At his own request, in February Comrade Voroshilov was sent as Staff representative to the Volkhov front to assist and he was there about one month. His stay there, however, did not produce the desired results. Wishing once more to give Comrade Voroshilov the chance to use his experience in frontline work, the Central Committee suggested to him that he take over the direct running of the front himself. But Comrade Voroshilov received this suggestion negatively and did not want to take on the responsibility, despite the fact that this front is now of crucial importance for the defence of Leningrad, and he excused himself by saying that the Volkhov front was a difficult one and he didn't want to fail in the job.

In view of the foregoing, the Central Committee:

First: recognizes that Comrade Voroshilov has not justified the job he was given to do at the front.

Second: is sending Comrade Voroshilov to do war work in the rear.[4]

By constantly referring to 'Comrade Voroshilov' in this mocking and sarcastic 'decree', Stalin was making it plain that the former 'first marshal' was a complete has-been. Despite the typically Stalinist style, this was nevertheless a sensible decision. But Voroshilov was lucky: he was not cashiered, like Marshal Kulik, and he would float to the surface again after Stalin's death, becoming head of state in 1953. Others faced harsher judgement. A defeat at the front or an unsuccessful report could bring immediate dismissal, arrest and the worst consequences. Let me give two or three examples.

On 22 February 1943, the 16th Army of the Western front began its offensive, striking at Bryansk from southwest of Sukhanichi and from the north. The enemy's defences were, however, firm and the offensive petered out. Based on a routine report from General Staff of 27 February, Stalin came to the conclusion that the army must be marking time. Without attempting to acquire further clarification and consulting no one, he dictated Staff Order No. 0045 dismissing Colonel General I. S. Konev as commander Western front for incompetence.[5] Konev at least had the chance to prove himself later in the war, whereas others were not so lucky. The commander of the Caucasian front, Kozlov, for instance, was ordered to arrest Major General Dashichev, commander of the 44th Army, for incompetence and to send him to Moscow at once.[6]

Never hesitant when it came to dealing with individual officers, Stalin constantly moved commanders from one position to another, usually for no accountable reason. Dismissed from one post and appointed to another in February 1943, Konev disappointed Stalin for some reason in June and was switched again.[7] Stalin seems to have thought that these 'lateral movements' improved leadership, and of course no one would think of contradicting him.

Stalin's lack of military knowledge soon became apparent to the officials of the General Staff, and they would make their own attempts to put his orders into more orthodox form. The military leaders regarded military incompetence in a politician as normal, but they could not express their thoughts about Stalin in this respect. After Zhukov had retired, he told the military historian N. G. Pavlenko that Stalin 'always somehow remained a civilian'.

Strategic planning was devised by Stalin in accordance with the ideas of Shaposhnikov, Zhukov and Vasilievsky. At first, he would just express his opinion of General Staff proposals. Later, however, when Shaposhnikov had already left the General Staff and had become director of the Voroshilov Military Academy, Stalin would invite him to meetings to hear proposals from the various sections. Shaposhnikov's method was to listen to the opinions of the front commanders, whether oral or written, and only then to approach the question of making a final plan of operation. Stalin was at first discouraged by so much cumbersome, 'long and routine work', as he put it. But Shaposhnikov, whose rôle as the teacher of Zhukov, Vasilievsky, Antonov and Stalin himself is still unrecognized, would patiently explain that it was the minimum necessity, saying that 'some operations needed only a few days to devise, while others would take months'. Stalin knew Shaposhnikov was right, but felt his lack of training all the more. However, he soon devised an appropriate line of conduct over operational planning which, while preserving his image as the war chief, allowed him to minimize the risk to his reputation. The archives show that he usually worked out his ideas on two levels. One was general, such as at the Staff meeting of January 1942 where he said: 'We mustn't allow the enemy to recover his breath, we must pursue him westwards.'[8] This expressed a wish reflecting the mood of the people, but lacking any precise strategic concept. It expressed the intent of a statesman, not a military leader. The other level on which he contributed was that of adjustment or refinement of a concrete plan, an idea or a timetable, but since here his remarks were usually summings-up or resumés, they tended to make their mark. The entire plan would have been worked out in detail by the General Staff, but Stalin's cosmetic touches to the final picture created the impression that the plan was entirely his.

Utterly insensitive to the countless tragedies caused by the war, Stalin was guided by the desire to inflict the greatest possible damage on the enemy without regard to the human cost for the Soviet people. The thousands and millions of human lives became for him cold, official statistics. Two appalling orders, dictated by him, illustrate this. The first, No. 0428, signed on 17 November 1941, ordered that:

1 All inhabited locations up to a distance of 40–60 kilometres in the rear of German troops and up to 20–30 kilometres on either side of the roads, are to be destroyed and burnt to ashes. This objective is to be accomplished by immediately putting into action the air force, artillery and mortar fire on a large scale, reconnaissance teams, ski-troops and partisan diversionaries armed with petrol-bombs.

2 Each regiment is to have a team of volunteers of 20–30 men to blow up and burn down inhabited locations. Those who excel themselves in the job of destroying settled locations are to be put forward for government awards.[9]

The fire-raisers got to work. Possibly this scorched-earth policy did create difficulties for the enemy, but for so many Soviet people their roof was the last fragile shelter where they might hope to survive the nightmare, to wait for their nearest and dearest to return and to save their children. Whether the decision was made in the light of military necessity or insane cruelty remains an open question, but in either case it was a typically Stalinist, callous act. General N. G. Lyashchenko described to me an episode from this frightful story.

At the end of 1941 I was commanding a regiment in a defensive position. There were two villages ahead of us, Bannovskoe and Prishib, as I recall. We got an order from division to burn down all villages within reach. We were in the dug-out where I was explaining how we were to carry out this order, when suddenly, breaking all regulations, the radio operator, a middle-aged sergeant, butted in.

'Comrade Major. That's my village! My wife and children and my sister and her children are all there. How can we burn them down? They'll all die!'

'You mind your own business, it's for us to sort out,' I told him.

I sent the sergeant out and conferred with the battalion commanders. I remember calling the order 'stupid', which nearly got me into hot water, since the order had come from Stalin. But I was saved from the security police by General R. Ya. Malinovsky and war council member I. I. Larin. As for the two villages, we captured them the next morning with the permission of divisional commander Zamortsev and we managed not to burn them down.

The second instruction, No. 170 007, was sent to the commander of the Kalinin front on 11 January 1942 and ordered the capture of Rzhev, a city of 54,000 people:

In the course of the 11th, and in no case later than the 12th of January, the town of Rzhev must be captured. Staff recommends for this purpose that all available artillery, mortars and aircraft be used to smash the entire city and that you should not be deterred from destroying it.

Confirm receipt of this order and inform when it has been executed. I. Stalin.[10]

Of course, it made sense during the retreat to destroy much that the people had built, such as bridges, railways and factories and similar strategically important objectives. But what good was a poor peasant's hut to the Germans?

CHAPTER 46

Dawn Over Stalingrad

Enough has been written about the great campaign of Stalingrad for me not to have to deal with it here in detail. Instead, I propose to highlight the rôle of the Supreme Commander-in-Chief in that crucial conflict.

At the beginning of June 1942, the enemy having broken through the Soviet defences to a great depth at the meeting point of the Bryansk and Southwestern fronts, the 21st and 40th Armies were encircled. Stalin sent Vasilievsky to the south in haste, but the reports he sent back were not encouraging. The Germans widened their breakthrough to some 300 kilometres in the course of the next week, and in a few days a strike force penetrated up to 150–170 kilometres, outflanking the main armies of the Southwestern front from the north. The Germans then struck again, this time in the direction of Kantemirovka. Surveying the threat on his map, Stalin was haunted by the catastrophic vision of the Southwestern front being surrounded, as in 1941, for a second time. By now, however, he had learnt something and, having assimilated the concrete strategic issues at stake, did not object to the proposal to withdraw the 9th, 28th, 37th and 38th Armies. Staff Headquarters gave the order urgently to prepare a defence line for Stalingrad.

Stalin now had the opportunity to judge his own lack of foresight. In May, following the Kharkov débâcle, Vasilievsky had proposed reinforcing the strategic reserves in the Southwestern and Southern sectors. Stalin had disagreed. He had been worried about Moscow. Now enormous numbers of troops had to be transferred urgently to face a new strategic crisis. The situation was made worse by the fact that many units were retreating in disorder, with the result that numerous divisions and units lost contact with their headquarters for days on end. Once again, German Junkers and Messerschmitts had the skies to themselves and could strafe at will the retreating troops in their thousands. At times it seemed the chaos and confusion of June 1941 was being replayed. Stalin sent cable after cable, ordering the front commanders to restore order among the retreating troops, to fight to the last man, not to retreat without the order to do so, and so on. Here are some examples:

> The enemy has broken through your front in small numbers. You have sufficient opportunity to smash him. Assemble the aircraft of both fronts and use them against the enemy. Mobilize the armoured trains and put them on the circular track around Stalingrad. Use smoke screens to disorient the enemy. Make contact with the enemy at night, not only by day. Use artillery and rocket fire to the full.
>
> Once again, by his incompetence and inefficiency. Lopatin has let down the Stalingrad front. Put in some effective supervision over him and organize a second line behind his army.
>
> Most important, don't panic, don't be afraid of this audacious enemy and keep your faith in our success.
>
> 23 August 1942.[11]

When he went to see Stalin in those July and August days of 1942 Chief of General Staff Vasilievsky felt like a lamb going to the slaughter. Stalin did not hide his aggravation, made impulsive decisions, sent successive cables with the same message. He would start switching his generals around again, he demanded to be connected with one headquarters after another, and he always gave the same order: fight to the death. Meanwhile the troops continued to retreat. On 28 July 1942, after a routine report from Vasilievsky, Stalin suddenly stopped his nervous pacing and launched into a new subject: 'They've forgotten Staff Order No. 270 of 16 August 1941. They've forgotten it! Write a new one on the same lines: "Retreating without permission is a crime that will be punished with all the rigour of wartime ..." '

'When do you want me to report with the new order?'

'Today. Come back as soon as it's ready.'[12]

That evening he signed the notorious Order No. 227 of the USSR Defence Commissariat, with many changes and amendments made by him in his own hand. This document, which remained carefully hidden in the military archives for many years, has recently become accessible and has been reproduced in various publications. I should like here to refer only to those parts of it which reflect Stalin's direct intervention, his phrasing and personal style:

> The enemy is throwing more and more fresh forces into the fight and, regardless of his losses, he is creeping forward and breaking into the depths of the Soviet Union, seizing new districts, laying waste to our towns and villages, raping, looting and murdering the population. Part of the Southern front forces followed the panic-mongers and left Rostov and Novocherkassk without serious resistance, covering their colours with disgrace.
>
> Some unwise people at the front console themselves by saying we can retreat still further to the east, as we have so much territory, so much land, so much population, that we have no shortage of grain, and they use this to justify their

shameful behaviour at the front. But all such talk is utterly false and untruthful and it only helps our enemies.

After the loss of the Ukraine, Belorussia, the Baltic, the Donbass and other regions, we have a lot less territory than we had. So it follows there must be far fewer people, less grain, less metal, less factories and mills. We have lost more than 70 million of the population, more than 12 million tons of grain and 10 million tons of metal a year. We have even lost our superiority over the Germans in human reserves and grain reserves. To retreat further would mean to destroy ourselves and with us our Motherland.

Not one more step backwards! That has to be our main slogan from now on.

We will no longer tolerate officers and commissars, political personnel, units and detachments abandoning their battle positions of their own free will. We will no longer tolerate officers, commissars and political personnel allowing a few panic-mongers to determine the position on the field of battle and to induce other fighters to retreat and open the front to the enemy. Panic-mongers and cowards must be destroyed on the spot.

a) the retreat mentality must be decisively eliminated.

b) army commanders who have allowed voluntary abandonment of positions must be removed and sent to Staff HQ for immediate trial by military tribunal.

c) one to three punitive battalions (of 800 men each) should be formed within the limits of the front to which middle-ranking and senior officers and political officers of corresponding rank are to be sent.[13]

He then reverted to an idea he had embodied in a telegram to all fronts in September 1941, namely, that each rifle division should form a detachment of reliable troops, of no more than divisional size, whose job was to arrest the flight of panic-ridden servicemen, not stopping short of the use of weapons.[14] Now the old idea acquired a new shape:

Three to five well-armed detachments (up to 200 men each) should be formed within an army and placed directly behind unreliable divisions and they must be made to shoot the panic-mongers and cowards on the spot in the event of panic and disorderly retreat. Depending on circumstance, from five to ten penal companies (of from 150 to 200 men each) should be formed within the army and posted to difficult spots so as to give them the chance to atone with their blood for the crimes they have committed before the Motherland.

This order is to be read to all companies, squadrons, batteries, crews and headquarters.[15]

Panic reigned in many units. The psychological training of servicemen had been neglected before the war, and of course the officers corps itself had been decimated by the purges. It is well known that, under stress, and when confidence has been lost, a negative emotional reaction to danger can escalate into uncontrolled behaviour. The herd instinct spreads and the capacity for rational thinking is sapped. Stalin tried to deal with this problem by the use of 'surveillance' units and penal companies, but he did nothing to raise the profile of commanders and political officers in these extreme conditions. Nor did he restrict himself to issuing threatening regulations. In 1942, as in 1941, great numbers of servicemen escaped from encirclement, either in entire groups or individually. Officers were at once despatched to special NKVD concentration camps. And since the position in July-August 1942 was that much more critical, Stalin went even further. Officers who had been in enemy-occupied territory for any length of time and had not served with the partisans, and who were now in the NKVD's special camps, should be given the chance 'to take up arms to prove their loyalty to the Motherland'. Special assault rifle battalions were to be formed of precisely 929 such officers for use in the most active parts of the front.[16]

Events meanwhile were mounting throughout the period August to November 1942, when they reached their culmination. Yet even when the fate of Stalingrad was hanging by a thread, Vasilievsky ordered a group of General Staffers, including A. A. Gryzlov, S. I. Teteshkin and N. I. Boikov, to devise a secret scenario for capturing the enemy forward attack group by a combined action from the north and south. A map exists showing Boikov's first outlines of the future famous operation. Stalin did not yet know of this. The year, which he had described as 'the year of destruction for the German occupier', looked like turning into another great catastrophe for the Soviet Union. For several days he did not leave his office, snatching fitful spells of sleep and always warning Poskrebyshev to wake him after two hours. Once, taking pity on his drastically overworked master, Poskrebyshev let him sleep for an extra half-hour. Stalin glanced at the clock and quietly cursed his assistant: 'A philanthropist, all of a sudden! Get Vasilievsky on the line. Quick! The bald philanthropist ...'

Vasilievsky, who had flown back from Stalingrad two days earlier, came on the phone. Stalin at once asked him whether the 1st Guards, 24th and 66th Armies had yet engaged the enemy and whether the long awaited ammunition had arrived. Vasilievsky reported the position as at the evening of 3 September: one of the German tank formations had broken through into the suburbs of Stalingrad. Stalin butted in angrily:

'What's the matter with them, don't they understand that if we surrender Stalingrad, the south of the country will be cut off from the centre and we will probably not be able to defend it? Don't they realize this is not only a catastrophe for Stalingrad? We would lose our main waterway and soon our oil, too!'

Vasilievsky replied calmly, but the tension was plain in his voice: 'We are putting everything that can fight into the places under threat. I think there is still a chance we won't lose the city.'

Stalin called Vasilievsky again a few minutes later. Vasilievsky could not be found. Bokov was on the line. Stalin at once ordered him to find Zhukov in Stalingrad and give him a message, which Stalin then dictated:

The situation in Stalingrad has got worse. The enemy is six miles from the city. Stalingrad could be captured today or tomorrow if the northern group does not give immediate assistance. Tell the commanders of the forces to the north and north-west of the city that they must attack the enemy and come to the aid of the people of Stalingrad. The delay is inexcusable. Delay is tantamount to a crime. Use all the aircraft to help Stalingrad. There are very few aircraft now left inside the city. 3.9.42[17]

Zhukov was soon compelled to report that forces from the front had been unable to break through into a corridor to combine with forces of the Southeast front inside the city. The German defence line had been substantially reinforced at the cost of newly arrived forces from the environs of Stalingrad. Further attacks by the same forces in their present grouping would be pointless and they were bound to suffer heavy losses. Stalin summoned Zhukov and Vasilievsky to Moscow.

There, over the maps and with their General Staff advisers, they resolved to adopt the tactics of wearing the enemy down by stubborn resistance and attrition, while simultaneously preparing for a major counterattack. They planned the main assaults to take place on those flanks of the German force that were being covered by the less threatening Romanian troops. This was the plan they took to Stalin on 13 September, and it was a plan that was destined to become a classic of the Second World War. It was like an awakening, and it was not Stalin, but his two military leaders, who inspired it. At first, Stalin was not especially impressed, remarking only that the main thing was to hold Stalingrad and not allow the Germans to advance any further towards Kamyshin. It seems that either he did not appreciate the audacity of the plan or thought it unworkable. All his attention was fixed on defending Stalingrad.

Meanwhile, in Stalingrad itself the Germans had broken into the city and for more than two months, day and night, the fighting went on at an unprecedented level of ferocity. Where the Germans had at first measured their advance from the southwest in terms of tens of kilometres, then in a few kilometres, in September they had to think in terms of hundreds of metres in a day, and by October they regarded an advance of 40 or 50 metres as a great success. By mid-October they had been brought to a halt. Stalin's Order No. 227 was now being fulfilled to the letter. Although the Germans had twenty-two divisions at their disposal in Stalingrad, plus as many formations of their allies, the Nazi war machine had stalled.

During November Stalin spent nearly every day thinking about the forth-coming three-front operation – Stalingrad, the Southwestern and the Don. The plan was given the provisional title 'Uranus', and Stalin insisted on its being kept strictly secret within a very narrow circle. Responsibility for coordinating the three fronts was placed on Vasilievsky. When the counterattack opened on 19 November, Stalin probably felt confident of victory, not because the Soviet side was so far superior in men and weapons, but because no previous Soviet operation had been prepared with such care and thoroughness. True, a week before it began, Stalin had some doubts, chiefly because Soviet air power was no more than equal to that of the enemy, and he always attributed enormous importance to air power. He was so concerned he was even prepared to postpone the operation and on 11 November cabled Zhukov to say that, if Yeremenko and Vatutin had inadequate aircraft, the operation would fail: 'Experience in this war has shown that one can win against the Germans only if one has air superiority.' If this could be not guaranteed, he went on, 'it would be better to put the operation off for a time.'[18] Relying on Zhukov as totally as he did for the carrying out of the operation, however, four days before it was due to open he again cabled to say that he, Zhukov, had full discretion as to when to launch the offensive.[19]

Zhukov used his judgement and on 19 November the combined force of the Southwestern and Don fronts went into action, followed the next day by the Stalingrad front. By 23 November the enemy's Stalingrad group was encircled. Stalin had always enjoyed geography and perusing atlases of the world. By now, he had learned how to read an army map, marked by Staff with red and blue and jagged lines, circled reserve districts and dotted lines showing tank movements. When on 23 November he saw a large red ring showing the Soviet forces lined up in a complete circle, he felt both exhilarated and nervous; exhilarated because his forces had done it at last, and in of all places the symbolically named Stalingrad. He did not yet know the number of German troops inside the noose – more than 330,000, as it turned out – but he knew that if the operation was brought to a successful conclusion, it would mark the turning point of the war. And he was nervous because he expected the German command to do everything in their power to extract the twenty-two divisions of the Wehrmacht from the trap. Soviet forces had once before completed an encirclement, at Demyansk, and failed to destroy the Germans inside it. Now, the strategic initiative was with the Soviet army, although it would take some time to subdue General von Paulus. On 24 December, Paulus addressed an order to his encircled forces, of which Stalin was given a translation. It read:

The Russians of late have been making unceasing efforts to enter talks with the army or its units. Their aim is quite plain: they want to break our will to resist by making promises in these surrender talks. We all know what threatens us if the army ceases to resist: certain death awaits most of us, either from an enemy bullet or starvation and suffering in shameful Siberian captivity. One thing is sure: whoever surrenders will never see his nearest and dearest again. We have only one way out: to fight to the last bullet, despite the growing cold and hunger. Therefore any attempt to hold talks should be repelled, left without reply and the bearers of the flag of truce sent packing under fire. Meanwhile, we will continue to hope earnestly for the deliverance that is already on its way to us.[20]

CHAPTER 47

The Commander and his Generals

During the war, Stalin had little time for reading anything other than despatches, coded telegrams, operational plans and diplomatic correspondence, yet the archives contain a memorandum to him from Poskrebyshev, enclosing a list of fifteen books on the art of military leadership. Those Stalin marked with a star include *Kutuzov* by S. Borisov, volume I of Napoleon's works, *The Science of Winning* by Suvorov, and *The Brains of the Army* by Shaposhnikov. Nor was it accidental that, at the beginning of the war, he ordered portraits of Suvorov and Kutuzov to be hung in his office.* Similarly, when he spoke briefly to the troops on Red Square on 7 November 1941, he declared: 'Let us be inspired in this war by the courageous images of our great forefathers – Alexander Nevsky, Dimitry Donskoy, Kuzma Minin, Dimitry Pozharsky, Alexander Suvorov, Mikhail Kutuzov! Let the victorious banner of the great Lenin shield you!'[21]

Stalin frequently resorted to the great war leaders of Russia's past, drawing from them faith in victory, and he created the Orders of Suvorov, Kutuzov, Bogdan Khmelnitsky, Alexander Nevsky, Nakhimov and Ushakov – all war heroes of old Russia – for rewarding his generals. Instinctively understanding the value of military tradition as a boost to national pride and honour, he ordered that pamphlets on these old war leaders be written for distribution at the front.

As we have already seen, the greatest influence on Stalin as a military leader was exerted by Shaposhnikov, Zhukov, Vasilievsky and Antonov, and it was through them that he learned the basic demands of tactics, in which he remained at the level of mediocrity, and of strategy, in which he did rather better. Of the four, all of whom were at one time either Chief of Staff or Deputy

---

* Generalissimo Count Alexander Suvorov was Russia's greatest soldier of the eighteenth century; Field Marshal Mikhail Kutuzov was responsible for Napoleon's defeat in Russia.

Supreme Commander-in-Chief, it is probably true to say that Shaposhnikov's contribution was the greatest. He did not have the good fortune to live to see the culmination of the great Soviet victories of 1943–45, since he died in March 1945, but his intellectual influence on the military leadership is beyond doubt.

As a marshal and professor, Shaposhnikov, who had been a colonel in the tsarist army, combined high military culture with an excellent education, much experience as a commander, theoretical depth and great personal charm. Not one to submit to the will of others, as Stalin got to know Shaposhnikov he felt his own lack of knowledge and logic more acutely. Shaposhnikov did not have an overbearing personality, expressing his will rather through his subtle, flexible and wide-ranging mind, and Stalin evidently found this irresistible. Everyone was aware of this and Zhukov wrote of the Supremo's great respect for Shaposhnikov: 'He always addressed him as Boris Mikhailovich, his name and patronymic, and never raised his voice when they spoke, even if he disagreed with him. Shaposhnikov was the only man Stalin permitted to smoke in his office.'[22]

This was a rare example indeed of Stalin's confidence in one of the old régime military experts, the rest of whom he had liquidated before the war. Shaposhnikov was one of the very few people to whom Stalin would actually turn without embarrassment for an explanation, advice and help. It was characteristic of Stalin to take notice of anyone in whom he recognized the presence of great intelligence. The Artillery chief, Marshal N. N. Voronov, recalled once being present when Shaposhnikov was reporting to Stalin. The Chief of Staff mentioned that, despite measures having been taken, no information had been forthcoming from two fronts. Stalin asked him: 'Have you punished these people who don't want to tell us what's happening on their fronts?' Shaposhnikov replied that he had reprimanded both commanders but, judging by his tone of voice, it seemed he equated a reprimand with the most extreme form of punishment. Stalin gave him a sullen smile and said, 'Every party cell dishes out reprimands. That's hardly punishment for a military man.' Shaposhnikov then reminded him of an old Russian army tradition, namely that if the Chief of Staff reprimanded a headquarters commander, the latter had there and then to hand in a request to be relieved of his command. Stalin looked at Shaposhnikov as if he were an incorrigible idealist, but said nothing. The former tsarist colonel's intelligence had disarmed Stalin, and it was this quality that helped him tactfully to teach Stalin strategic thinking, military skill and even tactics.

If Shaposhnikov helped Stalin to acquire the stern logic of armed conflict, the importance of lines of defence and attack, the rôle of strategic reserves during operations, then it was Zhukov who inspired Stalin as a man of strong will and uncompromising military leadership. General A. A. Yepishev, a senior political officer during the war and later head of the army's political administration, told me that Stalin had had the idea of placing high government officials at the front as early as the civil war, and that this was why he constantly sent such people to the front during the Second World War. Stalin regarded Zhukov as his chief representative because he trusted him to carry out his orders, however harsh they might be and come what may. Zhukov's immense contribution to the defeat of the Germans at Moscow, in the salvation of Leningrad, at Stalingrad and a host of other operations, is widely recognized. Characteristically, as the war progressed and Zhukov's popularity rose, so Stalin's attitude towards him grew more reserved, and in the final push for Berlin Stalin did not entrust the coordination of the three-front campaign to him, but kept it formally for himself, sending Zhukov to run the Belorussian front. He had no intention of sharing the glory of the victory with anyone else, certainly not as popular a war leader as Zhukov.

Stalin knew that Zhukov conceded nothing to him in toughness of character. He noticed this especially at the beginning of the war. For instance, in the first days of September 1941, the commander of the Leningrad front, Voroshilov, and War Council member Zhdanov requested Stalin's permission to prepare the warships of the Red Banner Baltic Fleet for scuttling, should the surrender of Leningrad become likely. Stalin gave his consent and by 8 September Voroshilov and Zhdanov had signed the appropriate dispositions. Then, just as the War Council was finalizing the order, Zhukov flew in from Moscow with full powers from Stalin. 'Here's my mandate,' he said, showing Voroshilov that he was the new commander-in-chief of the front. 'I forbid the blowing-up of the warships. There are forty full battle complements on them.'

Recalling this episode in 1950, Zhukov wrote: 'Why blow up the warships? Maybe they were going to be sunk, but if so, it should only be in battle, firing their guns. When the Germans were advancing along the coast, the sailors fired on them and they simply ran away. And so they would, from sixteen-inch guns! Imagine the power!'[23] When Stalin heard from Zhdanov that Zhukov had effectively rescinded one of his, Stalin's, orders, the Supremo did not comment: he could not but appreciate Zhukov's audacity and far-sightedness and he let it be known that it should be left to Zhukov to decide what to do. He knew that in a crisis Zhukov could be pitiless and uncompromising. This impressed him and was in harmony with his own approach. Zhukov was merciless towards panic-mongers and cowards and was capable of introducing the harshest measures, if circumstances demanded it. At a critical moment in September 1941, during the defence of Leningrad, he dictated Order No. 0064, announcing to all army and political officers and rank and file that anyone who abandoned his post without written permission would be shot immediately.[24]

Stalin often lost his temper with Zhukov, especially at the beginning of the war. In July 1941, when the situation in the Vyazma district was critical, Zhukov proposed mounting a counterattack in the district of Yelnya in order to prevent the Germans from moving into the rear of the Western front. Without waiting to hear him out, Stalin interjected: 'What counterattacks, why talk such rubbish? Our troops are not even capable of mounting a proper defence, and you're talking about counterattacks!'

Zhukov retorted: 'If you think that I, the chief of the General Staff, am only good for talking rubbish, I request you to relieve me of my post and send me to the front where I can be more useful than I am here.'

Mekhlis, who was present, protested to Zhukov: 'Who gave you the right to speak to Comrade Stalin in such a way?'

As a consequence of this conversation, Zhukov was appointed commander of the Reserve front, but, despite the efforts of Beria and Mekhlis to compromise him in Stalin's eyes, Stalin could not long do without this outstanding military man as his trouble-shooter. In early October 1941, when a series of clumsy moves by the Soviet Central Army group command led to a significant part of the Western and Reserve front troops being surrounded, Stalin sent Zhukov to deal with the disastrous situation. As Zhukov recalled, Stalin said to him: 'Look at the mess Konev has got us into. In three or four days the Germans can be in Moscow. The worst of it is, neither Konev nor Budenny knows where their troops are and what the enemy is up to. Konev must be punished. I'm sending a special commission headed by Molotov tomorrow.'

Using extraordinary powers, Zhukov managed to stabilize the position, and it was thanks to him that Konev was spared a military tribunal and rescued by being taken on as Zhukov's deputy on the Western front. Stalin soon discovered that it was not only by his self-assurance, decisiveness and firm hand that Zhukov was capable of bringing about change in the organization of military operations, but rather that his very presence at the front always somehow became known to the troops and lifted their fighting spirit. General L. F. Minyuk told me that when Golikov and Khrushchev lost control of their men on the Voronezh front at Belgorod, Zhukov 'virtually took over command and, amazingly, the troops could see he had a clear head. When it looked as if everything was lost and becoming desperate, he would be calm, collected, decisive and determined. He was not worried by danger; on the contrary it increased his resolve and he would become like a tightly coiled spring.'

Stalin did not have favourites. He simply relied on some people more than on others. Apart from Beria to some extent, he took little notice of what his entourage told him about individuals. It is well known, for instance, that after the war Beria and Abakumov fabricated a case against Zhukov. They even used his photograph albums, which contained snaps of the marshal with American, British and French military men and politicians. They bugged his phones, rifled his personal files and intercepted his mail. In an order signed by Stalin on 9 June 1946, there is a reference to a senior war leader having written to the leadership about 'facts concerning unworthy and harmful behaviour by Marshal Zhukov towards the government and the Supreme Commander-in-Chief'. Zhukov was said to have lost his modesty, 'ascribing to himself the merit of having accomplished the greatest of the major victories', and becoming the centre of a group of malcontents.[25] But Stalin was not devoid of common sense and stopped short of getting rid of the war leader who had covered himself in so much glory. No doubt Zhukov's arrest was planned. Stalin convened a special session, attended by Beria, Kaganovich and some other senior party officials, as well as a group of top military brass, and, on the basis of evidence from some arrested generals, Zhukov was accused of 'awarding himself the laurels of the chief victor'. Some of the generals, for instance, P. S. Rybalko, spoke up in Zhukov's defence. Stalin vacillated and then decided that, instead of arresting him, he would send Zhukov to some outlying post, at first to Odessa, and then the Urals. The final decision was Stalin's and no one else's.

It is sometimes said that Stalin was harsh, but fair. The case is cited of his treatment of his younger son, Vasili, whom he mercilessly removed from his post because he was not doing his job, but in fact because Vasili had discredited his father. Stalin fired his son both after and during the war. On 26 May 1943, Beria reported to Stalin that Vasili's drunkenness was causing trouble again. Vasili had by now become commanding officer of an air regiment. Furious, Stalin at once dictated the following order to Marshal of the Air Force Novikov:

1 V. I. Stalin is to be removed at once from the post of commanding officer of his air regiment and be given no other command post without my orders.
2 Both the regiment and its former commander, Colonel Stalin, are to be told that Colonel Stalin is being removed from his post as regimental commander for drunkenness and debauchery and because he is ruining and perverting the regiment.
3 You are to inform me that these orders have been carried out.[26]

After a symbolic dismissal, however, well-wishers reported that Colonel Stalin had 'come to his senses' and was ready to carry out his responsibilities as a commanding officer again. By the end of 1943 he was promoted to the command of an air division.

Stalin was invariably pitiless and implacable in his decisions over matters of personnel. Certainly, he was capable of changing his mind, but usually after the fact and without outside influence. As a rule, he would not explain his decisions. That way, he could create the impression that his views on appointees were determined by the needs of the job and the qualities of the candidate. He replaced all his military leaders at one time or another, often with good cause, but he also gave them the opportunity to show that their previous mistake had been accidental. Giving them this chance, however, did not mean he had forgotten the earlier fault. For instance, when the question arose of who should carry out the final annihilation of the enemy at Stalingrad, opinions were divided. Beria proposed Yeremenko, while Zhukov preferred Rokossovsky. As Zhukov recalled, Stalin listened to both sides and then summed up:

'I would assess Yeremenko below Rokossovsky. The troops aren't fond of Yeremenko. Rokossovsky has greater authority. Yeremenko did very badly as commander of the Bryansk front. He is boastful and bragging.'

'Yeremenko will be terribly hurt,' Zhukov commented.

'We're not high-school girls. We're Bolsheviks and we must put worthy leaders in charge.'[27]

Stalin knew Zhukov to be ruthless as a commander. When Zhukov was commanding offensive operations on the Western front in the summer of 1942, he gave an order of which he could not have been proud and would never refer to later. His report to Stalin on the results of the operation make clear what sort of order he had given:

In order to warn detachments against retreating and to combat cowardice and panic-mongering, the first line of every assault battalion was followed by a tank carrying officers specially picked by the army war councils. As a result of these measures, the troops of the 31st and 20th Armies successfully broke through the enemy's defences.

7 August 1942.[28]

Zhukov was put in charge of the 1st Belorussian front when it was preparing the assault on Berlin in April 1945, an operation which Stalin studied with intense concern and interest. He barely interfered with Zhukov's and Antonov's handling of the operation, but his days began and ended with reports of the progress of both the preparations and the offensive itself. Zhukov was reporting that the Germans had practically stopped fighting in the west but were putting up a desperate fight for every house in the east. Stalin's reply dated 17 April 1945 was characteristic:

I received your despatch with the German prisoner's information that they [were being told] not to yield to the Russians and to fight to the last man, even if the Americans are right behind them. Pay no attention to what the German prisoner is saying. Hitler is weaving a web in the Berlin district in order to create discord between Soviet troops and the Allies. We must break this web by capturing Berlin with Soviet forces. Cut the Germans down without mercy and you'll soon be in Berlin.[29]

As he followed events in Berlin, Stalin was especially interested in the question of Hitler's capture. His triumph would be complete if he could take the Nazi leader alive and have him tried by an international tribunal. But, although Zhukov was reporting fighting at the Reichstag and on the approaches to the Chancellery, the longed-for news did not come. Finally, on 2 May 1945, Zhukov sent a copy of the order issued by General Weidling, the head of the Berlin defence forces, stating that Hitler had committed suicide and asking for an immediate armistice.[30]

As the war had progressed and victory seemed more certain and post-war matters began to preoccupy Stalin, he had empowered others to sign operational instruments in his name, above all Antonov. When it came to the most historic act of the war, the ratification of the German surrender, he evidently did not hesitate to bestow the privilege on Zhukov.[31] General Antonov was deputed to send the message and, having dictated it, Stalin stood up and shook him firmly by the hand.

Yet he had cause to think Zhukov ungrateful, when, with Moscow's approval, the marshal gave a press conference in Berlin to Western journalists. He described in detail the preparation of the Berlin campaign, and talked about Allied cooperation, demobilization of the Red Army, Soviet treatment of war criminals, the superiority of the German over the Japanese soldier, but he uttered not a single word about Stalin. It was left to Ralph Parker, the correspondent of *The Times*, to 'rescue' Zhukov by asking him whether Stalin had played a day-to-day part in the operations. Zhukov replied tersely that 'Marshal Stalin led all sectors of the Soviet–German front on an active and daily basis, including the front I was on'.* To Stalin, it looked as if Zhukov was beginning to exhibit Napoleonic tendencies and he saw to it that the marshal was sent off to distant and unimportant jobs when the war was over.

One of the main links between Stalin and the front was Alexander Mikhailovich Vasilievsky, who was deputy chief of the General Staff's operational administration when the war began, becoming its chief and deputy Chief of Staff on 1 August 1941, and Chief of the General Staff and Deputy Commissar for Defence from June 1942 to February 1945. Vasilievsky commanded the 3rd Belorussian front and later served as Commander-in-Chief Soviet forces in the Far East.

His rôle in the General Staff reflected Stalin's original style of work in the highest military body, the Staff Headquarters. Most of Vasilievsky's time was spent as the Staff representative at the front, where he carried out Stalin's orders, rather than in Moscow dealing with General Staff matters. Whenever a particularly important operation was being prepared, or if a crisis occurred, Stalin as a matter of course sent either Zhukov or Vasilievsky to deal with it, or, as at Stalingrad, both of them together. In other words, Vasilievsky was an all-round military leader and commander who excelled both as a field commander and staff officer. Stalin saw that he was equally calm at critical moments in both defensive or offensive operations, and equally at home with strategic planning as Staff representative or front commander.

'Did your religious education do anything for you?' he once asked Vasilievsky. 'Do you ever think about it?'

Vasilievsky had not been expecting this question but quickly came up with an apt reply: 'No knowledge is entirely wasted. Some of it turned out to be useful in military life.'

Stalin looked at the marshal with interest – Minsk had just been liberated, so he was in a good mood – and added: 'The thing the priests can teach best is how to understand people.' And then he abruptly changed the subject.

Stalin could always rely on Vasilievsky getting what he wanted at the front without resorting to extreme measures. Vasilievsky rarely raised objections,

---

* Ralph Parker was *The Times*'s Moscow correspondent during the war, charged with fostering Anglo-Soviet understanding. At the end of the war, he settled in Moscow, where he eventually died. His story is told in Iverach McDonald, *History of the Times*, volume 5.

nor was he temperamental like Zhukov, but he was perfectly capable of quietly pursuing his line in argument with Stalin. With rare exceptions, on every day of the war, either face to face if he was in Moscow or by telephone when he was on his innumerable trips, Vasilievsky gave Stalin the benefit of his counsel, always patient and economical with words, as if he was thinking aloud.[32]

The activities of the General Staff during the second half of the war are very much associated with the name of Alexei Innokentievich Antonov. The majority of operational documents from the end of 1943 were signed either by Antonov and Stalin together, or by Antonov on Stalin's behalf. Soon after being brought into Stalin's presence as Chief of Staff, the observant Antonov noticed that the Supremo had some ritualistic habits. For instance, while listening to Antonov's report, often when Molotov, Malenkov and Beria were present, Stalin would interrupt him and ring for Poskrebyshev, who would appear bearing a glass of tea. Everyone would watch in silence as Stalin performed his ministrations: he would slowly squeeze the lemon into the tea, then go into the rest-room that was located behind his desk, open a cupboard that was concealed in the wall and bring out a bottle of Armenian brandy. He would pour one or two teaspoonfuls into the tea, put the bottle back in its storage place, then come back and sit down at the table and, stirring his tea, mutter: 'Carry on.'

Having served as Vasilievsky's deputy for many months, Antonov was perfectly aware, when he became Chief of Staff, that he was luckier than his predecessor in the job. The worst scenes of the war had already been played out in the first act. By the time he joined the Headquarters Staff it had acquired a modicum of order in its round-the-clock activity, and a degree of experience. But, being something of a pedant, in the best sense of the word, Antonov like no one before him brought something new to the General Staff's working practices. He established precise periods for the processing of information, proper times for reports to be submitted by intelligence, rear, front and reserve representatives. He drew clear lines of responsibility for his deputies, A. A. Gryzlov, N. A. Lomov and S. M. Shtemenko. In order to ensure that his procedures were irreversible, he set them out on three pages and presented them to Stalin. They included a norm for reporting to the Supreme Commander three times every twenty-four hours, and more often by telephone; summaries for Stalin; a procedure for preparing and ratifying order papers; and the creation of a system of contacts between the various organs of administration.

After giving one of his daily summaries, he suggested that Stalin might care to look over the procedures he had established at General Staff and Staff Headquarters, and give his approval. Stalin gazed at him in amazement, but then studied the document carefully and without a word wrote on it 'Agreed, I. Stalin.' He must have thought Antonov was no fool: not only had he got Stalin to regulate the work of others, but Stalin's own, as well. If hitherto Stalin had been able to summon anyone to report to him at any time that pleased him, he would now have to try to adhere to the procedure he himself had just approved. Antonov managed to define the main functions of the General Staff as, first, its work for the Supremo, giving him essential information for making decisions, and secondly, preparing orders and seeing to the operational management of the fronts in close collaboration with the defence commissariat.[33] He may have made as much of an impression on Stalin as Shaposhnikov, Zhukov and Vasilievsky, for Stalin loved order, the cataloguing and pigeon-holing of business, and here was a man whose natural talent lay in precisely this.

Antonov rose rather fast through the upper ranks. He arrived at the General Staff in 1942 as a lieutenant general, in April 1943 he was already a colonel general and reached full general in the same year. But he never made marshal, despite Stalin's favourable disposition towards him. Beria got in the way. Beria's position among the upper reaches of the military hierarchy was not very strong and he very much wanted to have his own people among the top brass. We now know that the senior officers always kept him at arm's length and did not trust him. For his part, he tried to recruit supporters among them and to their credit none succumbed. The fact that his arrest, trial and liquidation was carried out by the military is itself eloquent evidence of their attitude.

Beria was an odious person. People were afraid of him, and no one had any sympathy for him. But he needed support in the army. He could see Stalin ageing before his eyes, and already by the end of the war he may have had far-reaching plans for his own aggrandizement which, in a system where democracy was a fiction, it would be impossible to accomplish without the support of the army. Beria's efforts to establish a special relationship with Antonov came to nothing. The general behaved with cool correctness. Beria, true to form, then set out to compromise him. Although Stalin did not believe what Beria whispered to him about Antonov, he did not give the general the rank of marshal, which he had planned to do when victory was proclaimed. In 1946, moreover, Stalin demoted Antonov to the rank of deputy chief of the General Staff, and in 1948 dropped him even lower, to the position of first deputy commander of the Transcaucasian military district.

The war was over and Stalin ascended to glory, like Caesar, on the triumphal chariot. But whereas Julius Caesar had racked his brains to find ways of rewarding his loyal legionaries, Stalin gradually distanced those whose presence most reminded him of the contribution they had made to the victory. Antonov, whose signature appears more than anyone else's alongside that of the Supreme Commander-in-Chief in the last two years of the war, and the only general to earn the highest Order of Victory, was in the last analysis not fully appreciated by Stalin. The war was over, and for Stalin it was the result that counted. As for the cost of victory, he preferred to talk only about the Nazi atrocities. His own mistakes were never mentioned. To the long list of his epithets – great leader, wise teacher, unsurpassed guide, strategist of genius – one more was added, 'the greatest war leader'. For this reason, we must touch on his strategic thinking.

CHAPTER 48

The Thoughts of a Strategist

When famous Soviet war leaders wrote their memoirs, they only wrote what was permitted, and any negative comment about Stalin was regarded as slander. For some twenty years I worked in the Main Political Administration of the Soviet Army and Navy. This was during the period when the Administration's publishing department had to examine all memoirs in accordance with instructions from Suslov. I have talked with the people who scrutinized military memoirs in the 1950s, 1960s and later. Manuscripts would circulate among the top authorities and authors therefore soon learned what one was permitted to say. As a result, Soviet history retained its totally successful image, for neither Glavlit* nor the countless manuscript readers could afford to ignore the prescriptions of an ideological system committed to a single vision of the past.

I also know that not everything the generals wrote got into their published works. Similarly, and equally under outside pressure, some of them tried to find space for and a reason to make mention of influential people whose place in the war effort one would have needed more than a very powerful magnifying glass to locate. For instance, it took a great deal of patience and zeal to identify the station at which K. U. Chernenko had once alighted with gifts for the front, or the unit in which L. I. Brezhnev had served. Many otherwise respectable books were sullied by such compulsory references to Brezhnev's service. One would never have found mention, for instance, of a report of August 1942 by regimental political commissar Sinyansky to the effect that Brezhnev, among other political officers in the 18th Army, was 'incapable of bringing about the desired improvement in mood and behaviour among the political workers at

---

* Glavlit, or the Main Administration for the Protection of State Secrets in Print, to give it its full title, was the chief censoring agency responsible for reviewing all printed matter before publication. In the late 1980s, its rôle diminished to the point where it was only concerned with the protection of state secrets, ratherly narrowly understood. It was abolished in July 1990.

the front'. Brezhnev and the others were said to be 'a negligent, complacent, familiar, mutually backscratching bunch of boozers'.[34]

We were prisoners of false consciousness. People often had to choose between including everything that was 'required' in a book, or not having it published. And that was not all. It is a fact that most of the war leaders' memoirs were ghost-written by people who had little, if any, direct knowledge of the events they described. To be sure, they would incorporate interviews and materials provided by the memoirists, but in the end it was they, and not the authors, who wrote the books. The personal perception of the author was therefore often lost, however unintentionally. As I. Kh. Bagramyan put it, 'It depended to a large extent on who the colonel ended up with.'

In examining Stalin's strategic thinking, I have to say right away that he was superior to many of his advisers in a number of fields, while in others he never rose above amateur ability, one-sidedness, incompetence and cliché.

If by 'military leader' we mean someone whose talents include creative thinking, profound strategic insight, war experience and ability, intuition and will, then Stalin did not fit the bill. He was, however, a political leader, harsh, strong-willed, determined and power-hungry, who was compelled by historic circumstance to deal with military matters. As Supreme Commander-in-Chief, his strength lay in his absolute power. But it was not this alone that raised him above the other military leaders. Unlike them, he could see the profound dependence of the armed struggle on an entire spectrum of other, non-military factors: economic, social, technical, political, diplomatic, ideological and national. Better than the other members of the Headquarters Staff, he knew the country's real possibilities in terms of its agriculture and industry. His thinking was more global, and it was this that placed him above the others in the military leadership. The military facet was only one of many.

In the course of 1943–45, and with the help of his military advisers, Stalin the strategist learned a number of important truths about the operational art. He learned, for instance, that one could and should go over to defence not only when the enemy dictates it, but also, as in a number of operations in 1942, in one's own good time and, subsequently and with premeditation, for the purpose of preparing offensive operations. As we have seen, Stalin did not like defensive operations at all. Some of his worst memories were of such moments. He remembered 16 September 1942 when, just after dinner, Poskrebyshev entered silently and placed before him a special report from the General Staff Main Intelligence Department, signed by General Panfilov, about a radio intercept from Berlin. It said that 'Stalingrad has been taken by brilliant German forces. Russia has been cut into two parts, north and south, and will soon collapse in her death throes.'

Stalin read the terse message several times, stood for a while at the window, gazing vaguely south towards the distant scene of the disaster, and then told Poskrebyshev to connect him at once with the General Staff. A minute later, he dictated through General Bokov a telegram to Yeremenko and Khrushchev:

Report some sense about what is happening in Stalingrad. Is it true Stalingrad has been captured by the Germans? Give a straight and truthful answer. I await your immediate reply.

    16.9.42.[35]

For him only the goal mattered. He was never tormented by conscience or grief at the enormous losses. News that large numbers of divisions, or corps or armies had been destroyed would alarm him, but there is not a single document in Staff HQ archives showing his concern about the number of human lives lost. He was oblivious of the fundamental principle of the military art, namely, that the objective should be gained at minimal cost in human life. He believed that both victories and defeats inevitably reaped a bitter harvest, that it was an inescapable fact of modern warfare. Perhaps he thought this way because, as Supremo, he had an enormous number of armies at his disposal. By the end of the war, the armed forces deployed about 500 infantry divisions, not counting artillery, tanks and aircraft. This was twice as many as before the war. To be sure, the Germans had a greater number, but this was because Stalin resisted his advisers' repeated urging to break the formations down into smaller size and greater number. Given such vast military strength and a well-organized system of reserves, it seemed to Stalin quite unnecessary to make the attainment of strategic targets dependent on the scale of losses.

At the same time, he was attracted to new forms of strategic action, such as operations by the forces of combined fronts. This entailed the most complicated and massive complex of battles, framed by a single concept, and all coordinated as to aim, time and place. Some of these operations involved between 100 and 150 divisions or more, tens of thousands of guns, three to four thousand tanks, five to seven thousand aircraft. This colossal force would be set in motion in accordance with a scenario of strategic moves and calculations made by the General Staff and front headquarters staffs on the basis of countless factors and options, both our own and the enemy's. It was precisely during such combined operations that Stalin felt most like a military leader. Such massive scale meant not only the quantitative expression of the force employed. It also represented his own self-expression and self-assertion as a strategist.

After the battles of Moscow and Stalingrad, he constantly sought to couple the efforts of several fronts in ever newer combinations. Kursk, Belorussia, East Prussia, Vistula-Oder, Berlin and Manchuria all represented the objective course of the war, but they also corresponded to Stalin's predilection for the massive, overwhelmingly large-scale operation. The length of the front in such operations was often as much as 500–700 kilometres, with depths of up to 300–500 kilometres, and they could last as long as a month. As a rule, Stalin would be impatient for them to start, dissatisfied with their rate of progress, irritated by hitches. He would grasp the general concept of an offensive operation quickly, and occasionally made relevant suggestions which were aimed at increasing the force of the attack.

Very rarely, however, did he suggest alternatives to the main idea, which would have been conceived and born in the General Staff, the brains of the army. Stalin tended to emphasize the rôle of the air force, but then, after the summer of 1942 when tank armies began to come into being, he would constantly offer detailed advice on their targets and follow the mighty attacking formations as they carried out their tasks. While there is no evidence in the archives to suggest that Stalin's suggestions had a major effect on the planning, course, development and completion of strategic operations, it is true to say that by 1943–45 he was capable of assessing their relative values. If he showed any 'genius' at all, it was during this latter period of the war, when he gave his approval to the plans drawn up and submitted by Zhukov, Vasilievsky, Antonov and the front commanders.

On the other hand, he paid a great deal of attention to boosting the fighting spirit of the troops, usually by radical methods. The decision to hold the 7 November parade of 1941 on Red Square was such an idea, and similarly, in the summer of 1944 he suddenly proposed that a large mass of German prisoners of war be marched through the streets of Moscow.

'It'll raise the morale of the people and the army still further and speed up the defeat of the Fascists. What do you think?'

After a brief moment of silent confusion, Molotov, Beria, Voroshilov and Kalinin piped up together and began vying with each other to express their complete agreement.

'A wise move, Iosif Vissarionovich!'

'Only you could have thought of it!'

'A decision of genius!'

Within a week, on 13 July, Beria submitted for Stalin's approval a plan for this unusual operation in morale-boosting: 'In accordance with your proposals, Iosif Vissarionovich, on 17 July 55,000 prisoners of war will be paraded through the streets of Moscow. They will include eighteen generals and 1,200 officers. Twenty-six special trains will bring them to Moscow from the 1st, 2nd and 3rd Belorussian fronts. Generals Dmitriev, Milovsky, Gornostaev and security commissar Arkadiev already have the matter in hand. Security and escorting in Moscow will be handled by NKVD officials Vasiliev and Romanenko. The prisoners will all be concentrated at the Hippodrome and the NKVD motorized cycle area on the evening of 16 July. From the twenty-six trains we will have twenty-six columns. The route: Moscow Hippodrome, Leningrad Highway, Gorky Street, Mayakovsky Square and along the Sadovaya; then from Sadovaya-Triumfalnaya, to Karetnaya, Samotechnaya, Sukharevskaya, Spasskaya, Chernogryazskaya, Chkalov Street, Crimea Station, Smolensk Boulevard, along Barricade and Krasnaya Presnya Streets back to the Hippodrome. The procession will set off at 9 a.m. and be over by 4 p. m.'[36]

'Will you be able to keep the columns intact?' Stalin interrupted.

'Yes, Comrade Stalin.'

'What happens afterwards?'

'Early next morning, they'll set off from eleven departure points for camps in the east.'

Beria was ready to go on with his explanation of the plan, but Stalin did not want to hear any more. 'I give them an idea and they carry it out. Why can't you think of anything yourselves?' Stalin said, looking around at his entourage with derision. (As it happened, both the time and route were changed.)

As part of his concern to raise morale, particularly of the officers, Stalin was quite inventive in the matter of decorations. For instance, on 9 September 1943 he ordered that:

in the case of officers who have successfully carried out the forcing of a difficult river, such as the Desna,
1 army commanders should receive the Order of Suvorov, 1st Class,
2 corps, divisional or brigade commanders should receive the Order of Suvorov, 2nd Class,
3 regimental, engineering, sapper and pontoon battalion commanders should receive the Order of Suvorov, 3rd Class.
For forcing a river such as the Dnieper, or rivers of equal difficulty, unit and formation commanders are to be made Heroes of the Soviet Union.[37]

He was on the whole punctilious about awards. For instance, in 1949 he would not agree to Malenkov's suggestion that his 70th birthday be marked by conferring on him his second Gold Star Hero of the Soviet Union. He decided enough was enough after receiving the Order of Victory and he stopped the flow of decorations, realizing that a surfeit of such awards debased their value and could therefore undermine his own authority. The man who occupies the first place in an undemocratic state can give himself any award that takes his fancy, but it does not increase his authority – rather, the contrary. This was something Brezhnev and Chernenko did not understand. In all, Stalin had about as many decorations as, say, Mekhlis, and four or five times fewer than Brezhnev. He was similarly punctilious about the indiscriminate award of medals to others and would cancel decorations if he thought them undeserved. 'Medals are for fighters who distinguish themselves in battle with the German aggressors, and are not to be dished out to anyone who comes along,' he wrote to the commander-in-chief 1st Baltic front on 16 November 1943, when he was told that General Yeremenko had been awarding medals without the agreement of the War Council.[38]

In his memoirs, *The End of the Third Reich*, and in a number of other publications and speeches, Marshal V. I. Chuikov expressed the view that it would have been possible to capture Berlin in February 1945, rather than wait until May. Zhukov, A. Kh. Babadzhanyan and others rejected this notion, in print and elsewhere, and Chuikov wanted to publish a reply in the journal *Voenno-istoricheskii zhurnal* (Journal of Military History). Refused permission, he wrote to the party Central Committee, where it was decided something should be done to deal with the obstinate marshal. On 17 January 1966 the chief of the Main Political Administration, General A. A. Yepishev, convened a meeting of leading marshals, generals and specialists to 'talk sense' to Chuikov.[39] In his speech, Chuikov again insisted that 'in February, Soviet forces, having advanced 500 kilometres, stopped 60 kilometres short of Berlin ... Who was holding us back? The enemy or the leadership? We had more than enough troops to advance on Berlin. The two and half months breathing space we gave the enemy helped him prepare for the defence of Berlin.'

Chuikov's opponents, who included General Yepishev, Marshals Konev, Zakharov, Rokossovsky, Sokolovsky and Moskalenko, tried to convince him that the offensive thrust had petered out, that the rear had fallen behind, that the troops were tired, that fresh reserves and ammunition were needed. Possibly the majority was right, but I think this meeting should be seen differently: it took place at a time when the moratorium on criticism of Stalin had already begun. In examining the question of whether or not the assault on Berlin could have taken place earlier, the participants, as if by common agreement, made absolutely no connection between the decision of Staff HQ and Stalin. Even the fact that the question had been raised at all was condemned. In his summing up, Yepishev said that Chuikov's views on the matter were 'unscientific', and that one should not 'blacken our history, otherwise we shall having nothing on which to raise the young people'.

But to return to the war. Once Stalin was convinced victory was on the side of the Allies, he began to set aside thirty or forty minutes, usually at night, to watch newsreels from the front, and occasionally they would prompt him to take quite large-scale decisions. One such film, for instance, contained scenes of a half-burnt-out village near the front. where two members of the German-sponsored local police, who had either failed to hide or gave themselves up, had been caught. Stalin at once sent a directive, with a copy to Beria, to all front commanders, demanding strict compliance with the Staff order of 14 October 1942. That order had established the frontal zone from which the entire population without exception was to be evacuated to ensure that no enemy agents and spies remained. In his own hand, he had added: 'This is especially important. The front-line zone is to be inaccessible to spies and enemy agents. It is time to understand that inhabited places close to the rear make a convenient refuge for spies and espionage'.[40] There is nothing in the directive about removing Soviet citizens from danger or of taking care of them.

Throughout the war, Stalin kept Malenkov by his side. Malenkov carried out various of Stalin's orders in the apparatus of the defence commissariat and Central Committee, as well as supervising the aircraft industry. When aircraft production got on to a sure footing from September 1943 onwards, Stalin made Malenkov a Hero of Socialist Labour and chairman of a Sovnarkom committee for the reconstruction of the economy in the liberated areas. Stalin also decided to try out Kaganovich on war work. In July 1942 he sent him to the Caucasus as a member of the war council of the Northern Caucasus front.

Kaganovich, however, made no mark there. Like Malenkov, he felt like a civilian playing at war, being Stalin's 'eye' at front headquarters and in the political administration. And he was on the receiving end of Stalin's criticism when in mid-August 1942 the front left its defence lines without Staff agreement:

> What's the good of a defence ridge if it is not defended? And it seems you haven't managed to turn the situation around even where there is no panic and the troops are fighting quite well. Suvorov said: 'If I have scared the enemy, even if I haven't looked him in the eye, then I've already won half the battle: I bring my troops to the front to defeat a frightened enemy.'[41]

Among other things, Beria was employed by Stalin to assist in supplying the rear area of the front, to 'sift' camp inmates who had emerged from enemy encirclement, and to mobilize hundreds of thousands of prisoners on war-related work. He was also involved in the formation of a number of detachments and units. For instance, on 29 June 1941 he was charged by Staff HQ with forming fifteen divisions based on NKVD units.[42] In August 1942 and March 1943 he was in the Caucasus to assist in the defence of the region. It was from there that he sent Stalin a series of telegrams announcing that he was removing Chechens and Ingushes from army units as untrustworthy, giving his assessments of Budenny, Tyulenev and Sergatskov, reporting his decisions on various military appointments, some of them patently inappropriate. It was at Beria's suggestion that on 20 August 1943 Stalin cabled Shchadenko, the commander of the Caucasian front, ordering:

1 the removal of 3,767 Armenians, 2,721 Azerbaidzhanis and 740 members of Dagestani ethnic groups from the ranks of the 61st infantry division.
2 that the troops so removed be sent to reserve posts at the Western front, while the shortfall caused by these removals is to be covered by reserves from the front, using Russians, Ukrainians and Belorussians.[43]

An inveterate trouble-maker, during his tours of the front Beria tried to subvert Generals Tyulenev, Maslennikov, Sergatskov, I. E. Petrov and Shtemenko among others, all of whom cabled Stalin to ask for their staffs to be protected from Beria's mob. It seems likely that Beria succeeded only with Maslennikov, who worked directly under him for a while. Generals Pokrovsky and Platonov, who researched this matter in 1955, came to this conclusion in their 'Report on Beria's Criminal Activity During the Defence of the Caucasus in 1942–43'. They wrote:

To defend the eastern part of the Caucasian range, a Northern group of the Caucasian front was created on 8 August under the command, it would seem at Beria's insistence, of General Maslennikov, who had until then been the unfortunate commander of the Kalinin front. General Maslennikov, who undoubtedly had Beria's protection, frequently ignored orders from the front commander and hindered the regrouping of the troops by his actions.[44]

While it is possible that Maslennikov was not 'Beria's man', the correspondence between them in 1942 does suggest a special relationship. As commander of the 39th Army, Maslennikov went over the heads of the army chiefs to make direct requests to Beria, 'reminding you of your promise to give all possible assistance'.[45] When Maslennikov saw an article, entitled 'The Battle in the Caucasus', by two officers, Zavyalov and Kalyadin, in the August 1952 issue of the journal *Voennaya Mysl* ('Military Thought'), he wrote (24 November 1952) to the head of the General Staff War Studies Administration to express his disagreement with the assessment of Beria's rôle given in that article:

Describing on page 56 the measures of the Staff of the Supreme Commander-in-Chief of the USSR, the authors mention only in passing and extremely briefly the enormous creative work and fundamental political and organizational measures introduced by Comrade Lavrenti Pavlovich Beria, who brought about a profound breakthrough which altered the whole position, despite the extremely difficult circumstances that had come into being on the Caucasian fronts in August 1942.

The description given of Comrade L. P. Beria's activities does not provide an exhaustive account of all the measures which were carried out under the personal supervision of Comrade Lavrenti Pavlovich Beria.

L. P. Beria, who exercised the Stalinist style of leadership, was by his personal example a model of Bolshevik, state, military, party-political and economic leadership of the Transcaucasian front (August 1942 to January 1943) and put Comrade Stalin's orders into practice brilliantly.[46]

Deep down, Stalin no doubt despised Beria, but he could not manage without him. Beria was his inquisitor, his right-hand man and his spy. Beria, for instance, informed him that Berlin had for a long time been planning to carry out a terrorist act against the Soviet leader. According to some information received, he said, a special Messerschmitt Arado-332 was to drop a trained group of terrorists from Vlasov's Russian Army of Liberation, while other reports suggested that the Germans were going to leave a commando group behind as they retreated. Almost every month Beria told Stalin of new measures he had taken to increase his master's security. But Stalin needed Beria for a range of other duties. For instance, he needed to know why 140 out of 400 fighter planes, allocated for use on the Kalinin and Western fronts, had to be withdrawn from service after three or four days of action.[47] On the other hand, he did not like it when Beria poked his nose into the affairs of Staff HQ and the General Staff.

When Beria returned from his trips to the front and reported his views on the state of affairs, the bombardments, or the poor showing of some 'suspect' general or other, Stalin felt a certain vulnerability. He had not been near the front since October 1941, when he had gone to the Volokolamsk Highway to watch the anti-aircraft fire in the sky. Meanwhile, he had to listen to Beria and Malenkov describing their 'baptism by fire'. He therefore determined he would go to the front, too, even if only for the sake of posterity. And a very carefully prepared trip did indeed take place. Stalin spent some time on the Western and Kalinin fronts in August 1943 and thereafter felt his image as a war leader was safe.

On 1 August he left Kuntsevo by a special train consisting of an ancient locomotive and some broken-down carriages. Both the platform and the small train itself were camouflaged with branches. Stalin was accompanied by Beria, his special assistant, Rumyantsev, and bodyguards in plain clothes. Arriving at Gzhatsk, Stalin met the commander of the Western front, Sokolovsky, and Bulganin, who was a member of the war council. He heard their reports, wished them well, went to bed for the night and set off next day in the direction of Rzhev, on the Kalinin front, which was commanded by Yeremenko. Here he stayed in a simple peasant hut in the village of Khoroshevo, set off somewhat from the other huts. (The peasant woman who lived there had already been cleared out bag and baggage.) The little hut, with its ornamental cornice and memorial plaque, still stands to this day as a monument to Stalin's 'exploits' at the front. It is said that it was while he was staying here that he prepared the order for a gun salute to take place in honour of the recapture of Orel and Belgorod. But he showed no desire to go to the front to meet the troops or their officers. After the night in Khoroshevo, the procession made its uneventful way back to Moscow, where Stalin could be comfortable with the thought that now no one would be able to imagine that he had only seen the front on newsreels.

Perhaps there was no need for him to visit the front, in any case? After all, he never visited factories, yet he had brought the country through a quantum leap in industrial output. He had only once toured some villages, yet what a revolution he had produced in that sector. Why should the battlefield be an exception, when he could follow everything that went on, and indeed run it all, from his office in the Kremlin? The visit was required for 'history'. His biography had to include an account of the morale-boosting arrival of the Supremo among the fighting troops. He also regarded it as essential that the Allied leaders know of it. He wrote to Roosevelt on 8 August 1943:

> Having just returned from the front, I am only now able to reply to your letter of 16 July. I have no doubt that you are aware of our military situation and will therefore understand the delay. I have to make personal visits to the various sectors of the front more and more often and to subordinate everything else to the interests of the front.

And to Churchill he wrote the following day in the same vein, adding that the likely event of new assaults by the Germans made more frequent personal visits to the front all the more necessary.[48]

To be sure, these letters also served to explain why Stalin had to decline an invitation to meet the other two leaders at Scapa Flow in the Orkney Islands. But they were also meant to dispel any notion that he was running the war from his armchair. To his great satisfaction, in their joint reply on 19 August

1943, both Roosevelt and Churchill commented that they 'fully understood the weighty reasons that compel you to remain in close proximity to the battle fronts where your personal presence has so contributed to the victories'.[49]

CHAPTER 49

Stalin and the Allies

At the end of April and in early May 1945, Poskrebyshev was daily reporting to Stalin on meetings that were taking place between Soviet and Allied units. For Stalin – and not alone for him – the Alliance had represented a side of the war that had been full of expectation and disappointment, haggling, suspicion and distrust, then again hope and disillusion, and finally reasonably functional military collaboration. In the spring of 1945 it seemed the Alliance was firm and long-lasting. For the sake of the anti-Fascist coalition, Stalin had sacrificed Comintern, set ideological postulates far to one side, closed his eyes to the long-standing anti-Communist sentiments of Churchill and the Western democracies, and taken a purely pragmatic line.

As a rule he read only General Staff papers, reports from the front and memoranda from Staff HQ. Now, however, he began to look at other kinds of material. For instance, he read a report from S. R. Rudnik, chief of staff 58th Guards Infantry Division, to the effect that 'at 1530 hours on 25 April 1945, near the bridge at Torgau, a meeting took place between officers of the 173rd Guards Infantry Regiment and patrols from the American 1st Army, 5th Army Corps and 69th Infantry Division. Five men led by US army officer Robinson had crossed to the east bank of the River Elbe for talks.'[50]

Stalin might well wonder how men like this Rudnik would behave with Allied soldiers from another world. Would they fraternize or would there be friction? Only three weeks earlier he had received a cable, marked 'very important', from Abakumov who reported that, according to Smersh sources at the Soviet air force base at Poltava, which the Americans were using for shuttle purposes, Major General Kovalev had declared that 'we are not getting on with the Americans, and it could even come to an armed conflict'. Kovalev had taken precautionary measures. Stalin cursed loudly when he had read Abakumov's telegram. 'Where do we get such idiots? This Kovalev has even worked out a plan of attack.' He wrote a message to Air Force commander

Falaleev, in large letters right across the page, 'Request you pacify Comrade Kovalev and prohibit any further unauthorized actions on his part.'

On the other hand, he was also receiving reports that meetings with American and British forces were taking place in an atmosphere of enthusiasm. During a meeting between the commander of the 58th Infantry Division, General Rusakov, and the commander of the 69th US Infantry Division, General Reinhardt, toasts were raised, speeches were made and gifts exchanged. The chief of the 5th Guards Army political section, General Katkov, reported that the Americans had wanted stars, shoulderboards and buttons for souvenirs. The Soviet soldiers were apparently surprised to find it was hard to distinguish between a US general and their other ranks. 'They all wear the same uniform, whereas you can pick out one of our generals from a long way away.' Katkov also mentioned that the writer Konstantin Simonov was present at this meeting.[51]

Now was the time to move on from the long period of mutual distrust between the Soviet Union and the Western democracies. What had been impossible before the war had now been made possible by Hitler. By waging war on two fronts Hitler had inadvertently turned the USSR and the West into allies. Stalin might well now recall the visit of the British ambassador, Stafford Cripps, and his aides on 12 July 1941. Still in shock from the news he had received half an hour before that the Germans were on the Dnieper, Stalin had shaken hands mechanically with the British and gazed in detachment at the backs of Molotov and Cripps as they signed a treaty of mutual aid. A week later, the Soviet envoy in London, Ivan Maisky, and the Czechoslovak foreign minister, Jan Masaryk, had signed a similar agreement, and then, during that same July in London, there had been the agreement on mutual aid between the USSR and the Polish government in exile. At Polish insistence, the first clause stated that 'The Government of the USSR recognizes that the Soviet–German treaties of 1939 relating to territorial changes in Poland have no force.'[52] That day Stalin had met Roosevelt's personal envoy, Harry Hopkins, who said, 'Whoever fights against Hitler is on the right side in the conflict and we intend to help that side.'[53] Stalin asked briefly about technical help and expressed the hope that the President understood the Soviet position. The agreement on aid would be concluded some time later, but meanwhile Hopkins's visit had laid the basis for cooperation.

Still in July, Stalin had sent a special mission to London, headed by General F. I. Golikov. Stalin personally briefed the general, as did Shaposhnikov, Timoshenko and Mikoyan, on detailed matters. Golikov had two main aims: first, to awaken Britain's strategic interest in landing troops in Europe or the Arctic, and, secondly, to elicit more rapid technical help from the British. Soon after his return to Moscow and his half-hour report to Stalin, Golikov was despatched to the United States, where Stalin focussed his attention on the main issue, namely the delivery of a broad range of supplies in the shortest possible time.

Facing the threat of defeat, Stalin pushed ideological antagonism out of sight, as of secondary importance. Being a pragmatist, he easily overcame his ideological prejudices and decisively reached out to the Western powers. In practice, he had little choice, but in the event he played a prominent part in the anti-Nazi coalition. From the outset of the war, as he recovered his emotional balance, Stalin tried to secure the support of as many countries as possible, and he did everything possible to see that Japan and Turkey remained neutral towards the USSR. But it was of Great Britain and the USA that he had the highest expectations.

He set about getting the new cooperation on to a businesslike footing. Thus, in virtually his first message to Churchill, dated 18 July 1941, he declared: 'It seems to me that the military situation of the Soviet Union, like that of Great Britain, would be significantly improved if a front against Hitler were opened in the West (northern France) and the North (the Arctic).' And, as if to justify the Soviet annexations of 1939, he added, 'It would have been much better for the Germans if Soviet forces had had to bear the brunt of their attack not in Kishinev, Lvov, Brest, Belostok, Kaunas and Vyborg, but in Odessa, Kamenets-Podolsk and Leningrad.'[54]

Stalin persisted in all his messages to Churchill in urging the opening of a second front, and we know that as early as 26 July 1941 Churchill had stated that it was not yet possible. As the position grew critical in August, Stalin again sent a personal and impassioned message. Referring to the recent heavy defeats suffered by Soviet forces, he pleaded: 'How can we get out of this more than unpleasant situation?' And he gave the reply himself:

I think the only way out is this very year to create a second front, somewhere in the Balkans or in France, capable of drawing thirty to forty German divisions off the eastern front, and simultaneously to guarantee the Soviet Union 30,000 tons of aluminium by the beginning of October this year, and minimal aid of 400 aircraft and 500 (small or medium) tanks every month.

Without these two kinds of aid, the Soviet Union will either be defeated or so weakened that it will lose its capacity to help its allies for a long time to come.

I know that this message will cause Your Excellency distress. But what can I do? Experience has taught me to look reality in the face, however unpleasant it may be, and not to be afraid to speak the truth, however undesirable.[55]

If Stalin was able to acquire military aid from the Allies on a massive scale – either consistently ignored or underestimated by Soviet historians – he was less successful in his efforts to get them to open a second front. Until the middle of 1944 this question occupied centre-stage in his diplomatic efforts. True, as the wind of victory filled his sails, he became less insistent, and indeed the front in western Europe was only opened when it had become obvious that the Soviet Union was capable of destroying Nazi Germany on her own.

Stalin's persistence and the British position over the second front reached a point where it was felt the two leaders ought to meet in person. As a result,

Churchill went to Moscow in August 1942 and, in the presence of US ambassador Averell Harriman, tried to persuade Stalin of the impossibility of opening a front in western Europe or the Arctic at that time. Stalin had little choice but to accept the argument,[56] but he made it plain that he regarded the British position as a breach of faith.[57] Believing that the USSR was bearing the main brunt of Nazi aggression, Stalin felt he had the right to demand a special place in the alliance. This applied particularly to the Soviet Union's requests – which sounded more like demands – for aid. In the country's interests, Stalin behaved like a tough, uncompromising politician and incidentally won his partners' respect in the process. Roosevelt, Churchill and de Gaulle all regarded him as a clever and harsh dictator. He knew this and made no attempt to alter his image in their eyes.

In seeking to gain the maximum amount of aid, especially military aid, from the Allies, Stalin sought ways to overcome their ideological differences. As he sat talking with Churchill in the Kremlin deep into the night, he was aware that only a few blocks away was housed the Executive Committee of the Communist International, Comintern, the institution which identified the class enemy not only in Hitler, but also in the British prime minister. Stalin's decision to dismantle Comintern – by a Comintern decree, of course – came as no surprise to intelligent observers who remembered that, as recently as 1939, he had shown how ready he was to abandon an ideological principle in the interests of a particular goal. Nor did he take much care to camouflage his decision. Speaking on 6 November 1942 at a ceremony to celebrate the twenty-fifth anniversary of the October Revolution, he stressed the fact that ideological differences were no obstacle to military and political cooperation with the Allies.[58] He was saying in effect that class logic had no place in the struggle for survival.

Comintern's fate was sealed. In the spring of 1943 it dissolved itself, and on 28 May 1943, replying to a Reuters correspondent, Stalin said:

The dissolution of the Communist International is both appropriate and timely, for it will ease the organization of pressure by all peace-loving nations against the common foe, Hitlerism, and expose the lie of the Hitlerites that Moscow allegedly intends to interfere in the life of other states and to 'bolshevize' them.[59]

Another area to which Stalin applied his pragmatic approach was that of the Russian Orthodox Church, a body on which the former seminarist had hitherto not lavished much care. On the contrary, in 1925, on his initiative, the church had been prevented from electing a new patriarch. Its temporary head, or locum tenens, was Metropolitan Sergius. Stalin would not even allow the Local Church Council to convene, hence making it impossible to complete the membership of the Holy Synod, which ceased to function for a long period. Suddenly, on 4 September 1943, Stalin invited G. G. Karpov, chairman of the Council on Russian Orthodox Church Affairs, to come to his dacha. During their conversation, which included Malenkov and Beria, they discussed the rôle the church might play in the war effort. It should be noted that the church was already making large cash contributions for war needs and had handed over substantial treasures to the state fund, while priests did what they could to strengthen the people's faith in final victory over the invader.

Having listened to Karpov, Stalin decided there and then to receive the church leaders, and a few hours later Metropolitans Sergius, Alexei and Nikolai arrived, somewhat bemused by the unexpectedness of the occasion. During their long discussion, they agreed to convene the Church Council, to appoint a patriarch and open religious teaching institutions. As he warmed to his own generosity, Stalin also promised the church material help and various indulgences, giving Beria a meaningful glance as he said this. Stalin, the failed seminarist, must have felt deep satisfaction at this unimaginable opportunity to influence not merely the fate of the highest church dignitaries, but of the religion itself. And most of the promises he made were actually kept.

On the next day, 5 September, *Pravda* reported the meeting – the only one between the leadership of the country and the head of the church until 1988 – and announced that Metropolitan Sergius would convene the Council of Bishops to elect a new patriarch. 'The head of government, Comrade I. V. Stalin, was sympathetic to these proposals and stated that the government would not stand in the way.'

Stalin took this step for two reasons. First, because he recognized the patriotic value of the church and wanted to encourage it. The second reason was connected with the international situation. He was preparing for the summit conference in Teheran at the end of the year, and it was his intention to press again for the opening of a second front and also to seek an increase in aid. An important part in this, so he believed, could be played by the British Aid to Russia Fund, on which sat both Mrs Churchill and the Dean of Canterbury, Hewlett Johnson. Having received a number of messages from the Dean, Stalin decided it was time to make a public gesture to demonstrate his loyalty to the church. He believed the West would acknowledge this signal and that it would evoke the desired response. His main motive, therefore, was not to gratify his vanity as a failed seminarist, but was aimed purely pragmatically at relations with the Allies.

These relations reached their peak with the meetings of the Big Three, in Teheran (28 November–1 December 1943), Yalta (4–11 February 1945) and Potsdam (17 July–2 August 1945). The outcome of these meetings is well known. My intention here is only to touch on Stalin's attitudes to some of the issues discussed.

Stalin was a 'homebody'. While he was willing to meet the Allied leaders he was reluctant to travel either far or for long periods from the USSR. Churchill and Roosevelt suggested locations such as Cairo, Asmara, Baghdad, Basra and other points south. Churchill even thought Stalin would agree to meet in the desert where three tented encampments would be set up and where they would be able to talk in safety and seclusion. Stalin insisted on Teheran because he would, in his words, be able to continue 'the day-to-day running of the Staff' from there. After lengthy correspondence, Churchill and Roosevelt agreed. Naturally, Stalin had not revealed that he was somewhat afraid of flying. This would be his first flight ever, and his last. Never one to take risks, he saw no good reason why he should start now. He was at the peak of his glory and even the possibility of unpleasantness, however slight, troubled him. Two days before the flight, he cabled Roosevelt and Churchill in Cairo that he would be 'at your service' in Teheran on the evening of 28 November. An odd phrase, coming from him, but one that was no doubt meant to project the image of a gentleman.

This was Stalin's first international conference outside his own country, and he was careful to watch his partners closely. It was all new to him. Churchill was less interesting, as he had already met him and knew him to be an unusually clever and cunning politician. But there was something about Roosevelt, with his piercing eyes and the mark of fatigue and illness on him, that appealed at once. Perhaps it was his frankness. In their last conversation, on 1 December, Roosevelt said with evident forthrightness that he did not want to discuss Polish border questions in public at that moment, as he would most likely be putting himself forward as a presidential candidate the following year. There were 'six or seven million US citizens of Polish extraction', and being a 'practical man, he had no wish to lose their votes'. Stalin, who was not accustomed to such frank expressions of political self-interest, nevertheless admired this quality in Roosevelt.

The President was the youngest of the Big Three and in his opening address called the trio 'members of a new family'. Churchill added that they represented 'the greatest concentration of world power there had ever been in the history of mankind'. They then waited to hear Stalin's opening words. 'I think that history is indulging us,' he began abruptly. 'She has put very great powers in our hands and very great opportunities. I hope we will take all measures to see that this conference uses the strength and force entrusted to us by our peoples, properly and within a framework of cooperation. And now let's get down to work.'

The issue of the second front was at last agreed. At breakfast on 30 November, Roosevelt shook out his table napkin, turned to Stalin with a smile and said: 'Today Mr Churchill and I have taken the decision on the basis of proposals from our combined staffs: Operation Overlord will begin in May, together with a simultaneous landing in southern France.'

'I am satisfied with this decision,' Stalin replied as calmly as he could. 'But I also want to say to Mr Churchill and Mr Roosevelt that, at the moment the landings begin, our troops will be preparing a major assault on the Germans.' This news pleased the other leaders.

As at Yalta and Potsdam later, the Polish question preoccupied the Big Three at Teheran. At the last session, Churchill read a proposal, evidently agreed beforehand with Roosevelt, to the effect that 'the hearth of the Polish state and people must be located between the so-called Curzon Line and the River Oder with the inclusion into Poland of East Prussia and the province of Silesia.' Stalin replied: 'If the English will agree to transfer to us [the warm water ports of Koenigsberg and Memel], we will accept the formula proposed by Mr Churchill.'[60]

During the exchanges on the future of Poland which took place later at the Yalta Conference, only three months before the destruction of Hitler's Germany, Stalin presented the formula that he had worked out long before, namely that the Polish question was not only one of honour, but was also one of security:

It is a question of honour because the Russians have committed many sins against the Poles in the past, and the Soviet government wishes to make amends. And it is a question of security because Poland presents the gravest of strategic problems for the Soviet Union. Throughout history, Poland has served as a corridor for enemies coming to attack Russia. Why have these enemies found it so easy up to this time to pass through Poland? Mainly because Poland was weak. The Polish corridor could not be closed from outside solely by Russian force. It could only be reliably closed from inside by Poland's own efforts. That meant Poland had to be strong. That is why the Soviet Union is interested in the creation of a mighty, free and independent Poland. The Polish question is a question of life and death for the Soviet state.[61]

Stalin made it plain that he was more concerned about governments than borders. He immediately accepted the Curzon Line, with some adjustments in Poland's favour, but he would make no concession over the question of the Polish government, despite the fact that at the beginning of the war he had been willing to cooperate with it. On 18 August 1941 he had ordered Major General Vasilievsky to sign a military treaty between the Soviet High Command and the Polish High Command. It had been agreed that the Soviet side would bear all the costs of maintaining a Polish army on Soviet territory and open a Soviet military mission at the Polish High Command in London.[62] And now Churchill and Roosevelt were calling the legitimate government the 'Lublin government', as if it were no more than a provincial authority, whereas it was already based in Warsaw and was controlling the situation in the country.

In the last phase of the war, and after it, Stalin found himself inundated by issues of a diplomatic character. Of course he had the assistance of Molotov, A. Ya. Vyshinsky, S. I. Kavtaradze and I. M. Maisky, among others, but often he took decisions on his own. He was irritated when Churchill poked his nose into East European affairs: since Soviet forces were there, it was for the USSR to settle the question of the future of the region, so he believed.

Stalin again realized what a faithful executive Molotov was. For Molotov, an order from Stalin took precedence over any party statute. On 15 October 1945, Averell Harriman had almost 'assaulted' him, as he was to tell Stalin the following month. Stalin had been preparing for his first post-war vacation and had no wish to receive the US ambassador, who was pressing for an audience. He had told Molotov: 'You receive him yourself. I'm not going to. Tell them what they need to know.'

According to Molotov, Ambassador Harriman and First Secretary Page had come to see him, and their conversation had been recorded in his diary as follows:

Harriman: 'I have received a telegram from the President for the Generalissimo. I am instructed to deliver it personally and to discuss certain matters with Stalin personally.'

Molotov: 'Stalin has gone on holiday for about a month and a half. I will inform Stalin of the President's wish.'

Harriman: 'The President is aware that Stalin is on vacation, but hopes he will nevertheless agree to receive the ambassador. It is about the London Conference. I am prepared to go anywhere.'

Molotov: 'Generalissimo Stalin is not working at the moment, that is to say he is on holiday far from Moscow.'

Harriman: 'The President hopes that Stalin will receive the ambassador.'

Molotov: 'I will inform Stalin.'

Harriman: 'The President thinks the Generalissimo deserves a vacation.'

Molotov: 'We all think that Stalin should take a proper break.'

Harriman: 'During the sports parade, I noticed how fit Stalin looked.'

Molotov: 'Stalin is a very fit man.'

Harriman: 'In the newsreel of the sports parade, Generalissimo Stalin looked very hale and hearty.'

Molotov: 'We Soviet peoples are happy to see Stalin in a good mood.'

Harriman: 'I would like a copy of that film.'

Molotov:'Of course, you shall have one.'

Harriman: 'I have nothing more to add to explaining the purpose of my visit.'

Molotov: 'I will inform Stalin, who is taking a complete rest.'

Harriman: 'I don't have to say how important the matter is ...'

Molotov: 'That is understood.'

Harriman: 'I would like to go to Stalin as a friend ...'

Molotov: 'I will tell Stalin. But he is on holiday.'[63]

It may well have been this episode that Harriman was recalling when he wrote, in his memoirs, that 'Stalin remains for me the most inscrutable, enigmatic and contradictory person I have ever known.'[64] The notes of the conversation, taken by Molotov's assistant, V. Pavlov, fully preserve the two men's stubborn persistence. No important conference or appeal by the President could shake Molotov, for whom his master's will was paramount. And so he had carried out his instructions to the letter. There could be no question of flexibility. Molotov was of the Stalinist school. Yet when he had finished his interminable monologue, Stalin said: 'But what if Harriman really did have something important to tell me from the President?' Molotov and Beria exchanged glances. They were not sure if Stalin was joking or if he was sincerely regretting a missed opportunity.

Among the countless files that Poskrebyshev was depositing on his desk were a number requiring Stalin's attention; they dealt with the liberated countries, of which there were quite a few. The memory was still fresh of President Risto Ryuti's machinations in Helsinki. Signals had been coming in from Alexandra Kollontai, the Soviet ambassador in Stockholm, to the effect that the Finns were getting ready to leave the war, when suddenly on 26 June 1944, following a visit to Helsinki by Ribbentrop, Ryuti had declared that Finland would neither make peace, nor allow any armistice talks to take place with the USSR, without the agreement of the German empire.[65] Stalin reacted by ordering the immediate speed-up of offensive operations on the Karelian front. He had by now learnt that heavy blows made the enemy more tractable. The manoeuvre worked, even though the operation was less successful than expected. On 4 September 1944 the Finns accepted the Soviet conditions for ending the war and the armistice was signed on 19 September.

In August 1944 Stalin had received reports that Allied aircraft were landing in Soviet-occupied territory in growing numbers and he had admonished Voroshilov in Hungary, Susaikov in Romania and Shatilov in Warsaw for their 'dangerous good humour, unnecessary trustfulness and loss of vigilance which allowed hostile elements to use these landings to infiltrate Polish terrorists, saboteurs and agents of the Polish government in London'.[66]

On 18 October 1944 he had occasion to send a 'very important' cable to Marshal Tito, with a copy to Marshal Tolbukhin:

You have asked Marshal Tolbukhin to remove Bulgarian forces from Serbia and to leave them only in Macedonia. Moreover, you have informed Tolbukhin of the incorrect behaviour of Bulgarian troops over the division of booty seized from the Germans. On both these matters I regard it as necessary to inform you of the following:

1. Bulgarian troops are operating on Serbian territory under the general plan for giving Soviet troops substantial assistance, as agreed with you and at your request, as in your telegram number 337 of 12.10.44. As long as a major German group remains on Yugoslav territory, we are unable to remove Bulgarian troops from Serbia.

2. On the matter of booty. The law of war is such that whoever seizes booty, keeps it.[67]

To the commander of the 3rd Ukrainian front Stalin cabled on 4 April 1945 that he should trust the Austrian Socialist, Karl Renner – elected Chancellor that month – and that he should tell him that Soviet forces in Austria would assist in the establishment of a democratic régime there. 'Tell him that Soviet troops have crossed the Austrian border not in order to seize Austrian territory, but to chase the Nazi occupiers out.'[68]

On the day of victory in Europe, Beria brought Stalin a decree which he signed two days later. It was addressed to the commanders of the 1st and 2nd Belorussian fronts, the 1st, 2nd, 3rd and 4th Ukrainian fronts, and to the security chiefs:

To ensure the orderly reception and containment of former Soviet prisoners of war and Soviet citizens liberated by Allied forces on West German territory, and also for the handover of former prisoners of war and citizens of Allied countries liberated by the Red Army, the Supreme High Command orders:

that war councils are to create rear-zone camps to accommodate and contain former prisoners of war and Soviet citizens destined for repatriation, allocating 10,000 people to each camp. The requirement is: the 2nd Belorussian front – 15 camps; the 1st Belorussian front – 30; the 1st Ukrainian front – 30; the 4th Ukrainian – 5; the 2nd Ukrainian – 10; the 3rd Ukrainian – 10 camps. Some camps may be set up on Polish territory.

The checking of former Soviet prisoners of war and liberated citizens is to be carried out as follows: counter-intelligence organs of Smersh are to deal with former servicemen, while checking commissions of the NKVD, NKGB and 'Smersh', under the chairmanship of the NKVD, are to deal with citizens. Checking is not to take longer than one or two months.

The handover of former Allied prisoners of war and citizens to commissions of the Allied command is to be handled by the war councils and a representative of the Sovnarkom of the USSR.

11 May 1945. 2400 hours.[69]

A hundred camps? Stalin wondered how many Soviet prisoners of war had survived, how many there had been in all, but it was not something to think about in this hour of triumph. As he leafed through some of the papers he had signed, he paused on one that he had dictated towards the end of the war, on the subject of encounters between Soviet and Allied forces:

1 The senior officer ... is to make contact with the senior Allied officer and establish with him the dividing line. Nothing about our plans and battle aims is to be divulged to anyone.
2 No initiative is to be taken to organize friendly meetings. Allied forces are to be met in a friendly manner.[70]

He was already irritated by news of the flood of fraternizing, meetings and parties. Zhukov and Vyshinsky had flown out at Eisenhower's invitation to Frankfurt-am-Main, and now Zhukov had cabled back to ask Stalin's permission to decorate ten of Eisenhower's staff officers with the Red Banner and another ten with the Battle Merit medal.[71] First they want to decorate the Americans, he thought, and then they'll be wanting medals for themselves. They're already celebrating, but post-war affairs were far from settled. He was thinking of the forthcoming Potsdam Conference which would have to deal with difficult questions concerning the shape of the post-war world. Nor was the war itself yet over. Unlike his partners over the second front, Stalin would not drag his feet, but would fulfil the obligation he had given at Yalta to enter the war against Japan within two to three months after the war in Europe was over.[72] On 28 June he signed the order to prepare for the offensive. 'All preparations for the operations are to be carried out in the greatest secrecy. Army commanders are to be given their orders in person and orally and without any written directives.'[73]

10

THE CLIMAX OF THE CULT

'The harshest tyranny is that which acts
under the protection of legality and the banner of justice.'
– Montesquieu

CHAPTER 50

Victory at a Price

Stalin was aware that the authority he had enjoyed before the war within the country, and of course in Comintern, had now acquired world stature. The Western leaders, both in their personal meetings with him and their extensive correspondence, lauded the leader of the Soviet state and Supreme Commander-in-Chief of the Soviet armed forces. The new US president, Harry Truman, remarked in a letter to him that he had 'demonstrated the ability of a peace-loving people, with the highest degree of courage, to destroy the evil forces of barbarism, however strong they may be. On the occasion of our common victory we greet the people and army of the Soviet Union and their splendid leadership.'[1] Churchill sent a somewhat more effusive message, broadcast on the radio on 9 May by his wife, Clementine, calling for the friendship to continue in peacetime.[2] General de Gaulle, regarded by Stalin as pompous and proud, said in his victory telegram that Stalin 'had made of the USSR one of the main elements of struggle against the oppressor states, and it was precisely thanks to this that the victory could be won. Great Russia and you personally have earned the gratitude of the whole of Europe ...'[3] Similar greetings came from all the world leaders.

Compared to Churchill and the semi-paralysed Roosevelt, Stalin had been a stationary body during the war. Apart from his one and only flight to Teheran in 1943, his meeting with Churchill and Roosevelt in the Crimea in 1945, and his secret visit to the 'front' in August 1943, he limited himself to commuting between the Kremlin and the nearby dacha, and kept to his narrow circle of the Politburo, a few commissars and some military men. Soon, however, he would be making the last foreign trip of his life. At sixty-five, he was an exhausted man and was already planning a long rest in the sun as soon as the war with Japan was over. Yet through the US President's special adviser, Harry Hopkins, whom he met on 26 June, he proposed to the Allied leaders that they convene an early summit meeting in Berlin.

Truman and Churchill agreed to meet, setting the date at 15 July 1945, by which time Truman expected to know the result of an atom bomb test, about which Stalin knew nothing. (The Soviet Union was also carrying out experiments under Beria's supervision. In March Stalin had asked the chief of the political administration of the army, Colonel General F. I. Golikov, if physicists were being released from the army for work in D. V. Skobeltsyn's and other research institutes. Beria had already reported that a number of laboratories had been set up within the Gulag by the NKVD where political prisoners were working as scientists.) In Potsdam, when Truman informed Stalin of the successful test in New Mexico, Stalin displayed no outward sign of interest, as Gromyko, who was present, confirmed in his memoirs.[4] The Allies could not guess that Stalin would cable Beria in Moscow that very evening to speed up the work. But that would be on 24 July in Potsdam. Meanwhile Stalin prepared himself for the trip.

He turned down flat the idea that he should fly there in a Dakota. Citing the experts, Beria tried to convince him that it would be perfectly safe, but he was inflexible on this matter. He had a vivid and unpleasant memory of the flight to Teheran, when the plane had several times dropped into air pockets above the mountains. He had clung to his armrests with an expression of utter terror on his face and would not look at Voroshilov, sitting opposite, to see if he had noticed his master's condition. When he did, it seemed the marshal was suffering similar discomfort. It was therefore decided to go to Berlin by train. Beria mapped out a route, more northerly than usual, and laid on a special train, with armoured carriages, a special guard and special escort.

This trip, which was planned with greater care than many a military operation, is worth describing in some detail. Tens of thousands of people were involved in the operation. On 2 July, two weeks before the departure, Beria sent Stalin details of the arrangements he had made:

The NKVD of the USSR reports that preparations are complete for the reception and accommodation of the forthcoming conference. Sixty-two villas have been made ready (10,000 square metres plus a two-storey detached house for Comrade Stalin of 400 square metres: fifteen rooms, an open veranda, a mansard roof). The house is completely equipped. It has a communications centre. Stocks of game, poultry, delicacies, groceries and drink have been laid in. Three supplementary sources of supply have been established seven kilometres from Potsdam with livestock and poultry farms and vegetable stores; there are two bakeries at work. All the staff is from Moscow. Two special aerodromes have been prepared. Seven regiments of NKVD troops and 1,500 operational troops will provide security. This will take the form of three concentric circles. Chief of security at the house will be Lieutenant General Vlasik. Kruglov will be in charge of security at the conference.

A special train has been prepared. The route is 1,923 kilometres in length (1,095 in the USSR, 594 in Poland, 234 in Germany). Security along the route will be provided by 17,000 NKVD troops and 1,515 operational troops. Between six and fifteen men will be posted at every kilometre of track. Eight armoured trains with NKVD troops will be patrolling the track.

A two-storey house of eleven rooms has been made ready for Molotov. There are fifty-five villas, including eight detached houses, for the delegation.[5]

All this was a far cry indeed from Stalin's 'asceticism' of the 1920s. The older he got, the more he feared for his life. The nearer the trip approached, the more often he consulted Beria, sometimes several times a day – on the secrecy of the departure, on the thickness of the train's armour-plating, on the route through Poland.

In Potsdam, having exchanged greetings with Truman at midday on 17 July, Stalin said, 'Please forgive me for the delay of one day. I was held up by talks with the Chinese. I wanted to fly, but the doctors forbade it.' Truman replied, 'I quite understand. I'm glad to meet Generalissimo Stalin.'*

Stalin was late purely in order to accentuate his importance. It was not the only time he used this ploy, as William Hayter, a member of the British delegation, and later ambassador in Moscow, recalled.[6]

That evening the Big Three began to divide up the fruits of their victory, an easier matter than preserving their alliance, which each of them sensed was in its last days.

For two weeks, beginning on 17 July, the Big Three held thirteen meetings, while their foreign ministers met twelve times. During these sessions they settled the future of Germany, argued about the fate of the Eastern European countries, searched for a solution to the 'Polish question', divided up the German fleet, fixed the amount of reparations, agreed to put war criminals on trial, assessed how much longer the war with Japan would last, and discussed a host of other issues.

Being in Germany, Stalin might have been reminded of Ernst Thälmann, head of the German Communist Party before the war. At the end of 1939 Molotov had reported that the Soviet envoy in Berlin, Kobulov, had reported that Thälmann's wife, having heard about the treaty of friendship, had come to the embassy and asked for help in getting her husband out of a Nazi prison. According to Kobulov, she herself had no means of support and was literally starving. Kobulov told her he could do nothing. In tears, she had pleaded: 'Surely all his work for Communism counted for something?' Kobulov reported that she was asking for Soviet advice as to whether she should appeal to Goering. 'I told her that was her business. She left in a very distressed state.'[7]

Thälmann managed to get several letters out of prison to Moscow, asking for help, but Stalin would not accept them. He had no wish to ask Hitler for favours, though he could easily have helped Thälmann and others, considering that he had sent back a group of German anti-Fascists at Hitler's request. In May 1945, however, Beria reported that NKVD troops had found Rosa Thälmann,

---

* This new title had been conferred on Stalin only recently, on 27 June 1945.

having escaped from a concentration camp, hiding in the town of Fürstenberg, and also that Thälmann's daughter, Irma Fester, had been liberated by units of the Red Army from Brandenburg concentration camp. Rosa Thälmann said she had last seen her husband in the presence of the Gestapo on 27 February 1944 in Beuthen prison. He had told her he was being constantly tortured to make him recant his views.[8] Stalin told Poskrebyshev to arrange proper conditions and help for Thälmann's family.

Such cases were now emerging daily.* For instance, Serov reported that the 1st Polish Infantry Division had liberated the former prime minister of the Spanish Republic, Francisco Caballero, from Oranienburg concentration camp, that he was in an exhausted condition and wanted his family to know he was alive.[9] Kruglov reported that King Michael of Romania had helped his cousin, Major Hohenzollern, and the son of the German industrialist Krupp, Ober-Leutnant von Bolen und Holbach, to escape from captivity.[10] Stalin left such matters to Molotov and Beria: he had more important affairs to attend to.

The war, he felt, had made him into a military figure and as such from now on he was always to be seen in his marshal's uniform. Indeed, the uniform itself had been the object of much high-level thinking. Three dashing young officers, wearing uniforms covered in gold braid and gold-striped trousers, had been brought in by A. V. Khrulev, chief of the Red Army rear administration, and members of the Politburo, to parade before Stalin.

'What's all this?' Stalin asked.

'Three samples of the uniform for the Generalissimo of the Soviet Union,' Khrulev replied.

Stalin took one look and told them all to get the hell out of his office. Did they want him to look like the doorman of an expensive restaurant or a clown? On the other hand, Khrulev had done a good job for him on the design for the Victory Order. The first sketch Stalin had seen on 25 October 1943 had had silhouettes of himself and Lenin in the centre. He had not liked the idea of thousands of such medals in which he could only be identified by his big nose and moustache. He suggested instead the Kremlin wall and the Spasskaya tower on a pale blue background, in platinum and with a liberal use of diamonds.

As he listened to the translations of the speeches at Potsdam, he followed his usual practice of doodling with one of the coloured pencils or fountain pens that were supplied. Sometimes he wrote the same word over and over again, dozens of times, as if seeking to find its inner meaning: 'reparations', 'contributions', 'parts, shares of reparations'. Or, as Beaverbrook noticed, he drew an enormous number of wolves and filled in the background in red pencil.[11]

On 26 July it was announced that the Conservatives had lost the elections in Britain. Churchill was replaced by Clement Attlee. Stalin had said to Truman

---

*Despite my extensive searches in the archives, I have been unable to trace a single document relating to the fate of Raoul Wallenberg.

on 17 July that 'the English people would not forget the victor,'[12] and now he could not understand what had happened. The 'rotten democracies' seemed to be undermining themselves. This sort of leapfrog was impossible in the Soviet system. He would stay in power as long as his health permitted. Like the French 'Roi-Soleil', Stalin had long identified himself with the state. As chairman of the Council of People's Commissars he was accustomed to speak in the name of the people. The more majestic the state, the more imperious its ruler. The war had advanced the USSR to the highest rank, and for Stalin this meant he had also been raised to the highest peak. In the first months after the war, he began to approach the apogee of his world fame, his power and his sacred cult.

He saw the fruits of victory not only in the destruction of Fascism and the transformation of the USSR into one of the most influential states. He also felt the early tremors in the anti-Fascist alliance that would soon raze the edifice to its foundations. But even he could not have guessed how quickly it would happen. Only the most perceptive eye could have noticed that the allies at the table in the Cecilienhof were in reality both friends and enemies. Stalin was not taken in by Truman's remark, when they met, that he, Truman, wanted 'to be the friend of Generalissimo Stalin'. Stalin sensed this especially during the discussion on reparations. The Americans abandoned the position they had taken at Yalta and now sided with the British who were seeking a solution which was seriously disadvantageous to the USSR. A vast area of Soviet territory had been occupied and an enormous amount of industrial plant destroyed. The USA and Britain had not suffered in this way. Stalin stressed that the USSR, like Poland and Yugoslavia, had not only a political but also a moral claim to compensation for these losses. The USA and Britain were, however, deaf to Stalin's appeals. Only at the thirteenth and last session did Stalin finally give in and accept the unfavourable conditions on offer, having risked getting a great deal less. He took his revenge, however, in the decisions on the 'Polish question', notably on the Oder-Neisse Line being made the border. In effect he was pushing Poland westwards, thus creating a powerful Slavonic state on Germany's border.

The fact that the President and Prime Minister were keen to discuss Eastern Europe at length, while saying nothing about Western Europe, gave Stalin justified grounds for concern. When he raised the issue of the Fascist régime in Spain, he was met by incomprehension. The Western Allies expressed concern over the position in Bulgaria and Romania, but saw nothing wrong in giving help to one side in the Greek civil war that had flared up. At times Stalin felt he was talking not to allies but long-standing rivals who wanted a bigger piece of the pie they had all had a hand in baking. And he was not mistaken. As the problems of the war receded, politics took centre stage, and politics is an extremely hypocritical and merciless game. On the political stage, the positions occupied by the partners were too disparate to yield the sort of results that were gained at, for example, Yalta. Then, the war had posed a common danger, and common strategic aims had drawn the Allies together. As soon as these aims had been achieved, political interest came once more to the fore. However expert the interpreters at Potsdam, they could not get the leaders to speak the same political language, the language of allies.

In general, however, Stalin was satisfied with the results of the conference, as indeed were the British and Americans. It was still possible in the summer of 1945 to attain what only two years later would be quite impossible. The Big Three managed to agree on the demilitarization of Germany and on various other important issues. Truman insisted that the USSR state publicly its intention to declare war on Japan, which Stalin duly did.

On the eve of the Soviet campaign against Japan, Stalin ordered Vasilievsky, commander of Soviet forces in the Far East, not only to liberate the southern half of the island of Sakhalin and the Kurile Islands, but also to occupy half the island of Hokkaido to the north of a line between the towns of Kusiro and Rumoi, deploying two infantry divisions, one fighter and one bomber wing. When Soviet forces had reached the southern half of Sakhalin, on 23 August 1945 Stalin ordered the embarcation of the 87th Infantry Corps for a landing on Hokkaido.[13] This order had not yet been carried out when, on the 25th, southern Sakhalin was already liberated. Stalin paused: what would he gain by a landing? It would probably spoil his already deteriorating relations with the Allies. He cancelled the order for the landing on Hokkaido. The Far East chief of headquarters staff, General S. P. Ivanov, passed on his instructions: 'In order to avoid conflict and misunderstanding with our Allies, the launching of any ships or aircraft in the direction of Hokkaido is strictly forbidden.'[14] All this, however, was to take place several weeks hence.

At the closing session of the Potsdam Conference, held on the night of 1 August and attended by the heads of delegation, Stalin's last words were: 'I think we can regard the conference as a success.' Truman closed the conference by expressing the hope that their next meeting would take place soon. 'Please God,' Stalin responded.[15]

For the Soviet people, the victory over Fascism yielded bitter fruit, for it further consolidated Stalin in the infallible messianic rôle of arbiter of their fate. The victory turned him finally into a god. Having defended freedom against the Nazis, the Soviet people would have to wait decades before they became free of Stalinism. Like their forefathers after the defeat of Napoleon, they were hoping for improvements in their lives. The victory which had been won at the cost of millions of lives gave birth to vague hopes. People wanted to live without fear and without the goad. While once again they lauded Stalin, bowed down before him, exalted and glorified him, they believed that there would be no more terror, no more endless campaigns, no more constant shortages of the most basic necessities, which had become the bane of Soviet life.

Victory convinced Stalin, however, of the unshakeability of the Soviet state and its social institutions, the profound viability of the Soviet system and the correctness of his domestic and foreign policies. He soon made it plain that there were to be no changes in the internal life of the country. The people must work to reconstruct the devastated national economy on rules determined by him. His address to the voters in the elections to the Supreme Soviet on 10 February 1946 contained not a word about democracy, the will of the people or the participation of ordinary working people in the business of government. It contained nothing but the old formulations about the people being able to trust in the party to create the correct policy, and it virtually added a warning that everyone should vote.[16]

The bureaucratic machine began to work at full tilt, turning out one party regulation after another. If before the war the Stalinist system had just got into its stride, then after the war it not only recovered but gathered pace. The course Stalin adopted after the war was in effect that of total bureaucratism. Many agencies began issuing shoulderboards to their staff, the railways being among the first to do so. New bodies were created whose only true function was to see that orders were carried out. To ensure the collective farmers stayed put, their internal passports were taken away from them. Exile and deportation went on until the late 1940s, and Beria's organization was never idle.

Social scientists were finally turned into mindless commentators on the 'great' dogmas, while once again the debilitating and stupifying rituals of glorifying the Leader were relaunched. Once more it became extremely danger-ous to speak frankly even in intimate circles. Zhdanov's intellectual police killed freedom of thought. The reinforced bureaucratic régime soon began to bear the dangerous fruit of indifference and apathy and willingness only to obey orders. There was a spread of moral degradation which expressed itself as the split Soviet personality which said one thing while doing another. The party and state became shadows of each other. No one could have an opinion that was different from the official view. Despite the egalitarian slogans of socialism, a bureaucratic élite began to emerge.

Stalin used the victory consciously and resolutely to preserve the system. To strengthen his already limitless power, he regularly removed party secretaries, ministers, marshals or other officials, accusing them of a lack of party-mind-edness, of abusing their power, or ignoring superior orders, or neglecting the people's interests. In the eyes of the people Stalin was already the 'good tsar', and these acts only raised his authority higher. He became the saviour, the architect of the great victory, the peerless war leader, and this blind faith only further weakened a people long deprived of truth and justice. Yet the people also now felt that victory had vindicated socialism, and despite all the obstacles and hardships, the mendacity and criminality, the people preserved their faith in a better future.

In an unbelievably short time, the country's economic potential was res-urrected on the ruins of war. When at the end of 1945 Stalin was told the extent of the economic damage, he asked Voznesensky if it was not an exaggeration. The economist replied that if anything the figures were an underestimate and that it was too soon to give an accurate assessment. On 21 May, Stalin had told the senior military that the first troops to be demobilized would be anti-aircraft and cavalry personnel, while tank units and the fleet would not be affected. 40–60 per cent of infantry units were to be demobilized, but not the forces of the Far East, Trans-Baikal and Transcaucasian commands. Every demobilized serviceman was to be sold captured goods at low prices and given wages according to length of army service.[17] Stalin wondered how quickly the new labour force could be put to work getting the economy back on its feet.

The people were in a desperate condition. Reports were coming in from Beria and other interior ministry officials of starvation in the provinces.[18] In Chita province there were reports of people eating dead animals and the bark of fallen trees, and there was an account of a peasant woman and her sons murdering her small daughter and eating her dead body.[19] Beria hastily reassured his boss that 'a certain amount of flour has been set aside before the new harvest. They'll have to be patient.'

Voznesensky, who was a candidate member of the Politburo, had a deeper awareness than any full member of that body of the enormity of the task. Stalin had long had ambivalent feelings about him, recognizing that he was undoubtedly the ablest of the entourage, but finding his independence and his tendency to utter brusque judgements unacceptable. Nevertheless, at the February 1947 plenum of the Central Committee he surprised everyone by making Voznesensky a full member of the Politburo.

Voznesensky's summary, and a first report compiled by the Extraordinary State Commission on the damage caused by the Nazis, enumerated 1,710 towns and townships destroyed, 70,000 villages and hamlets burned to the ground – albeit many of them by Soviet hands – 32,000 factories blown up or rendered unusable, 65,000 kilometres of railway track destroyed, around 100,000 collective and state farms laid waste, along with thousands of machine and tractor stations. Twenty-five million people were homeless and were now sheltering in dugouts, barns or cellars. The direct cost of the invasion was assessed at about 700 billion roubles, at pre-war prices. In effect, the country had lost 30 per cent of its national wealth.[20] The people's standard of living was the lowest imaginable.

Stalin was already of the view that only by maintaining the people's mood in a state of permanent tension and mobilization, akin to civil war, could all these difficulties be overcome. A report by Khrushchev followed the same lines. On 31 December 1945 Khrushchev reported that Ukrainian nationalists in the west of the republic had become active in connection with the forthcoming elections to the Supreme Soviet of the USSR, and he requested reinforcements for the Carpathian and Lvov military districts, which Stalin duly approved.[21] Bulganin then submitted a request for the formation of assault battalions to deal with 'banditry' in Latvia, these forces to be paid for, incidentally, by local funds.[22] Merkulov and Kruglov were reporting 'strengthened activity by the anti-Soviet nationalist underground' in Lithuania, involving the abduction and murder of many Soviet officials in charge of the local elections.[23] The bloodletting in the Baltic region was destined to last several years. Besides such 'enemies', Stalin was convinced that many soldiers had returned from the front with revolutionary ideas.

It was clear from Voznesensky's report of January 1946 and others compiled by the military that Soviet losses could only be guessed approximately. Unlike the Germans, who kept precise data on all their actions, Soviet statistics, especially in the early stages of the war, had not been carefully recorded. According to Voznesensky, it would not be possible to establish the exact human cost for several months, but on such information as he had he suggested more than 15 million. The General Staff figure for the total number of dead and missing in battle was 7.5 million, and it was this figure that Stalin decided to accept in 1946, not wanting to speak of a higher cost in human life and thus dim his image as a war leader.

What then was the true cost? In his letter to Swedish prime minister T. Erlander in 1956, Khrushchev mentioned more than 20 million for the first time. What was the basis for this number, which has now become common currency? The only thing that is certain about Khrushchev's statement are the words 'more than'. The full account is being worked out only now.

My own calculations, based as they are on the statistics in military archives, including those on Soviet prisoners of war, the analysis of army lists and data on losses in major operations, and taking into account the work of researchers, such as I. Ya. Vyrodov, Yu. Ye. Vlasievich, A. Ya. Kvasha and B. V. Sokolov, lead me to a figure for the losses of service personnel, partisans, underground fighters and civilians in the order of 26 to 27 million, of whom something like 10 million fell on the field of battle or died in captivity. The worst casualties were among the first, in 1941, above all among the officer corps, when some 3 million men were taken prisoner. Losses in 1942 were only slightly lower.

The most nebulous and politically ambiguous category were those who had gone 'missing'. This included those who had fallen in battle but who were not included in the official lists or in information about losses, and those who were taken prisoner or who joined the partisans and were rounded up. Among these were a number who succumbed to the temptation of joining Vlasov's Russian Liberation Army or the German local police. They represented, however, only a tiny minority. The fate of the great majority of those who went missing was deeply tragic: either they died an unknown death in battle, or died in prisoner-of-war camps, or were trapped by the NKVD's endless 'checks' in the camps and remained there for many long years.

My estimate of the comparison between German and Soviet losses is 3.2 to 1 in the Germans' favour. Of course, one must not lose sight of the Germans' barbaric policy of systematically exterminating the civilian population, especially the Slavs, the Jews, the Gypsies and other ethnic groups. This was one reason for the astronomical Soviet figure. The main losses were in fact among the civilian population, but even leaving aside the catastrophic beginning of the war, Soviet military losses were somewhat higher than the Germans', and this was at least in part due to Stalin's insistent urging that goals were to be achieved 'regardless of the losses'. Sacrificial Stalinist socialism demanded sacrificial victory. This indisputable fact not only underlines the great patience and forbearing of the Soviet people, but also testifies to the fact that the Soviet people *allowed* Stalin to become the figure he did. The rôle of the masses as a factor in this process should not be underestimated.

Now that the war was won, Stalin could think about relaxing in the pure air of the Caucasus, and Beria set about making the arrangements, though the task was far less complicated than that of getting the boss to Potsdam. The security chief in Krasnodar reported to Merkulov that the anti-Soviet element in Sochi was under surveillance and would be arrested in due course. The woodland park between the rivers Golovinka and Psou was being combed. One hundred and eight-four security posts had been set up between the railway station and the dacha and the entire route was under guard. A power train was standing by.[24] Even in his own country, the 'father of the peoples' feared for his life.

Part of the journey was made by road. As always when he went on vacation, Stalin was accompanied by Vlasik, Poskrebyshev, Istomina, countless attendants, guards and other staff. It was indeed after this particular trip that he ordered the building of a motorway to Simferopol. As they drove through Orel, Kursk and other towns and villages, they stopped to talk to the locals. The self-sacrifice of the women and children who had survived unspeakable conditions was amazing. Everywhere there were towns in ruins, yet when they reached the south Stalin was informed that new summer villas for state officials were being built under the pressing orders of Beria's agencies.

Stalin soon had enough of rubbing shoulders with the masses, enough of the loyal hurrahs, the tears of joy from the women, the bold assurances of the men that, 'Things have gone well, Comrade Stalin!', and the amazed stares of the old men and children, asking if that really was Stalin. He knew moreover that it was better for his image to wave to the crowd from the Mausoleum, or smile at them from the cinema screen, that it was best to appear every day only in portraits, statues and busts. Now, instead, the people found themselves looking at a short man with a truncated torso and relatively long arms and legs, a distinct paunch, thinning hair, a pasty, pock-marked face and yellow teeth. In Kursk one woman was even bold enough to touch the sleeve of his tunic as if to see if this was the same man as the one she knew from his pictures. To his one-word questions they gave one-word exclamatory replies expressing amazement, ingrained worship and the expectation of a miracle. They did not expect him to speak, but were simply feasting their eyes on him, unable to believe that this was their Leader. He began to notice in the eyes of the crowds not only joy and ecstasy, but also a barely concealed disappointment that he was not much to look at. Aware that it is impossible for any earthly god not to disappoint on direct contact, Stalin decided he would not repeat this nonsensical practice, but would henceforth sustain the illusion of omnipresence by being majestically remote from the people. He must remain for the people the man who built socialism, who destroyed all their enemies, who defeated Fascism and who would soon call upon the people to return to the 'great construction of Communism'. This was the system he had built and that could not do without him. Those who expected changes would wait in vain. The system must be strengthened, the power of the state reinforced, all those he did not need must be got rid of. The great victory was the best proof of his having been right.

If this account seems too imagined or too fanciful, it is based on logical deduction from the evidence. Stalin's actions and decisions make it plain that he decided to change nothing of significance. People could and would be changed, but not the order that had raised him to the peak of power. He was convinced that the system he wanted to preserve was now, after the war, closer to that envisaged by the founders of scientific socialism. Everything was programmed, planned, prescribed, determined. Now, as he set about rebuilding the war-torn edifice of socialism, he would relaunch the slogan 'We must catch up and overtake!'

Stalin could reasonably judge that following the war the world would take a discernible move to the left. The anti-Fascist struggle had united the masses, revived democratic energy and pushed reaction into retreat. The heroic feats of the Soviet people aroused deep and genuine sympathy for the Soviet state. There were even White émigrés, as well as intellectuals and ordinary ex-Russians, who were eager to return. Stalin was especially interested in signals coming from the Georgian Mensheviks in Paris, many of whom he had known personally. As soon as the war was over, he sent the Georgian Central Committee's propaganda chief, P. A. Shariya, to Paris, and he read his report thoroughly when it was delivered to him by Beria and Merkulov.

Shariya reported that the Georgian émigrés had given him ancient manuscripts, gold and silver artefacts, rare coins and archaeological treasures for repatriation to Georgia. On Moscow's instructions, Shariya met Noah Zhordaniya, Yevgeni Gegechkori, Iosif Gobechiya and Spiridon Kediya – all names which must have reminded Stalin of his life as an underground revolutionary, as well as the harsh period when the Union republics were formed after the civil war. At the beginning of the meeting, Zhordaniya restated his view that there was no democracy, no freedom of speech and the press, no free elections and no private initiative in the USSR. However, he then stated – and these words were underlined by Stalin – that:

Stalin won the war. I regard him as the greatest of men. It would be idiotic to deny his greatness because of our political differences. History will have more to say about his greatness. It will disclose aspects of his activities that are still unknown to his contemporaries.[25]

How true! But since so many former political opponents were expressing a desire to return home, Stalin might well be forgiven for thinking that the victor is always right.

As the victory greatly enhanced the Soviet Union's position in the world and brought her friends and supporters, it seemed the country was getting its second breath. But the outbreak of the Cold War, signalled by Churchill's speech at Fulton, Missouri, on 5 March 1946, arrested this process. Internal problems also sharpened. In 1946 huge expanses of the country were hit by severe drought and the country remained gripped by shortages of the basic essentials. The Western Ukraine and the Baltic states were the scene of little-noticed but fierce clashes between government forces and opposition groups. Despite several personal orders from Stalin to 'speed up the destruction of the gangs', it was some years before this was accomplished. In the Western Ukraine sporadic clashes were taking place with armed groups as late as 1951.

The economic hardships added to the psychological tension as expectations of impending change and hope for a better life were again postponed to an indefinite future. In his election speech in the Bolshoi Theatre, Stalin called for yet greater sacrifice and patience. This also represented part of the price the people would have to pay for the great victory.

CHAPTER 51

A Shroud of Secrets

Only now have we begun to ask ourselves how a man as physically unattractive and politically repellent as Stalin was able to make an entire nation love him, and to turn the nation's tragedy into his personal triumph, and why millions of people outside the country adored him.

It is natural to want to separate the idea of Stalin from socialism and the people, and indeed many Soviet writers are now attempting to do so. I started out with a similar intention, but I came to the conclusion that it was impossible to achieve this without distorting the historical truth. How can the 1930s and 1940s be assessed as if the people and the party were in some way separate from the leader whom they worshipped? He succeeded in becoming the very symbol of socialism, when in fact the positive achievements of the Soviet people were accomplished despite rather than thanks to him. Having determined on force to solve the country's economic, social and ideological problems, Stalin knew it was vital to recruit public opinion, if he was to remain as the centre of the system. The party apparatus was the means he used to manipulate this end.

Former Central Committee secretary (and briefly foreign minister) D. T. Shepilov, told me that Stalin was in the habit of inviting important figures from the cultural or scientific establishment to come in for a chat, and that he often used the occasion to issue an ideological pronouncement. One evening, Shepilov was told to call a certain number which turned out to be Stalin's.

'Comrade Shepilov,' he heard, 'do you have a little time? Could you come and see me right away?'

Shepilov had barely managed to say 'Of course,' when Stalin hung up. Shepilov was still wondering where he was supposed to go when the phone rang again and he was told a car was on its way for him. He soon found himself being led by a silent escort through endless corridors in the Kremlin past sentries at every turn.

The conversation lasted more than an hour. Stalin opened with a vague comment about new times requiring new economics. The leaders of industry, he said, had a very low level of economic knowledge. What was needed very quickly was a good, popular textbook on the economics of socialism. Shepilov realized that he was being told to write it with the help of two leading economists. In an obviously prepared way Stalin then recited the recommendations the book should contain: the nationalization of the means of production must be increased, planning improved, the plan made an iron law, labour efficiency raised, and a number of other points in a similarly coercive vein.

Stalin had spoken. A very tight schedule was imposed. Shepilov and his colleagues were 'incarcerated' in a dacha outside Moscow. At the end of each week, Suslov would ring and ask how things were going and when it would be possible to read the manuscript. 'Comrade Stalin is waiting, don't forget!'

Maintaining a state of permanent tension in the public mind was one of Stalin's most tested methods. A state of potential 'civil war', or more accurately a permanent struggle with 'enemies of the people', 'spies', 'doubters', 'cosmopolitans', 'degenerates', 'wreckers', created an atmosphere in which his injunction to be vigilant fell on fertile soil. He sensed that, after the war, the people, especially the intelligentsia, were harbouring vague hopes for change. It was as if the war had partly liberated them. According to Shepilov, Stalin therefore commanded Zhdanov to 'deal a blow against works lacking ideological content. There has been a marked departure from class principles in creative literature. Check up on one or two magazines. Especially in Leningrad.'

The Central Committee duly issued instructions to the magazines *Zvezda* and *Leningrad*, and Zhdanov travelled to the former capital. There he declared that the question had been raised at the Central Committee by Stalin 'who is abreast of developments in the magazines, who proposed that we discuss the shortcomings in the leadership of these magazines, and who also took part in the debate and incidentally also provided the basis for the decision'. By naming the writers whose work he regarded as 'alien to Soviet literature', Stalin was setting out to return post-war society to a climate of suspicion and fear, and to reactivate the witch-hunt that had raged in the 1930s.

For him the idea of class struggle was a primary rule. Once the capitalists and old landowners had been destroyed, he found another 'class' to destroy, namely the kulaks. Then, having no enemies to face, he had devised a formula that would ensure their existence. Sitting in the Kremlin late into the night the week before the sinister February–March 1937 plenum, he searched for the definition or the argument that would make the condition of struggle within society a permanent feature. The endless variations and amendments in the draft of his speech show how exhaustively he worked on this. As we have seen, the result lay in the words:

The further we progress, the more success we have, the more embittered will the remnants of the destroyed exploiting classes become, the sooner will they take to severe forms of struggle, the more they will resort to the most desperate means, as the last acts of the condemned ... We shall smash our enemies in the future, as we do now and as we did in the past.[26]

Despite having secured the unquestioning obedience of the people, Stalin did not rest. In January 1948 he called in his Minister of the Interior, Kruglov, and ordered him to devise 'concrete measures' for constructing new, additional concentration camps and prisons for special purposes. Stalin had detected barely perceptible signs of discontent, of efforts to cross the line, as some writers fell silent in protest against the stranglehold of Stalinist rule. 'Submit draft decrees in February,' he told Kruglov. 'We need special conditions for holding Trotskyites, Mensheviks, SRs, anarchists and Whites.' 'It will be done, Comrade Stalin, it will be done,' Kruglov assured him.

Was Stalin, in 1948, really thinking about Trotskyites and Mensheviks, or were neo-Trotskyites and neo-Mensheviks now stalking his thoughts? Be that as it may, Kruglov acted promptly and in the middle of February submitted his draft decree, which called for the incarceration of 'Trotskyites, terrorists, Mensheviks, SRs, anarchists, nationalists and Whites' in dozens of new camps and prisons in Kolyma, Norilsk, in the Komi Autonomous Republic, Yelabug, Karaganda and elsewhere. 'Chekist methods' were to be used, moreover, on those condemned in order to uncover similar enemies still at large. Periods of isolation and other punishments were not to be reduced, and 'where necessary, the release of prisoners is to be delayed, in retrospective conformity to the law.'[27]

As with any absolute, class struggle as an absolute was a destructive concept which trampled on the best socialist values – social justice, humanism, freedom of the individual. Stalinist absolutism was a degeneration. Trotsky was right when he predicted that Stalin would lead to reactionary terror. Similarly, the Russian thinker Dmitri Merezhkovsky had written in 1921:

Whether the class struggle is good or bad, noble or despised, we, living people, who take part in this struggle, whether as hangmen or victims, know something about it that Marx never knew, and that none of the wise men of social democracy ever dreamed of. For them class struggle was nothing but an idea in their minds, while for us it is in our blood and bones; we shed our blood and break our bones because of it.[28]

Stalin did indeed do everything possible to turn the idea of class struggle into the dominant force in politics, the economy, ideology, culture and ordinary life. It was as if he could not rest if he could not hear and feel the convulsions of the victims of that idea. After the war, when the world took a marked turn to the left, it might have seemed that history had vindicated Stalin. Many believed that the iron plough of socialism was again about to start turning over the soil. People had not yet begun to think globally, nor acquired full awareness of the nuclear sword of Damocles hanging over their heads.

Stalin's first post-war speeches were all about restoring the economy, as always making heavy industry chief among his priorities, and about reviving agriculture, whose condition was extremely poor. The first year after the war saw a bad harvest. The cessation of grain imports from the USA, coupled with a low return in the European part of the country, created a critical situation. The abolition of ration cards was postponed until the autumn of 1947. There had also been bad harvests in 1943, but then the Americans had supplied the front, while the civilian population, as always, bore their suffering stoically. In April 1944, Beria showed Stalin an eight-page report on the situation in Chita, Kazakhstan. The commissar of the interior of Kazakhstan, Bogdanov, stated that the crop failure of 1943 had caused serious hardship: thousands of people had swollen bellies from starvation, and many were dying, especially the political exiles. Bogdanov's account included stories of suicide, of peasants eating dead animals and garbage, eating their cats and dogs, and even of peasants on a collective farm digging up a dead horse to divide among themselves for food.[29] Nevertheless, in that year 1,300 kilogrammes of grain per hectare were collected by the state. Neither the radio nor press mentioned the famine and among the piles of documents I have examined, there is not one that shows Stalin taking a constructive attitude to the appalling hardships faced by the country.

Stalin apparently did not keep a diary and he was careful about what he wrote down. Many documents were destroyed on his orders,[30] as on occasion were reports that his instructions to the NKVD had been carried out. On the other hand, many documents remained in Stalin's private archive. For instance, there is a copy of a paper, dated 1923 and headed 'Biographical Details on I. V. Stalin', located in the Commissariat of Nationalities. Its author and purpose are not indicated, but it seems likely that it was prepared under Stalin's guidance.

The file gives a detailed account of Stalin's 'revolutionary services' before October:

During the October days, I. V. Stalin was one of a team of five (a collective) whose task was to give political leadership in the uprising ... Like his pre-revolutionary work, Stalin's present revolutionary work is of enormous importance. Distinguished by his tireless energy, his exceptional and outstanding mind and his implacable will, Comrade Stalin is one of the main, unseen, truly steel springs of the revolution, which with invincible force are turning the Russian revolution into a worldwide October. An old follower of Lenin's, better than anyone else he has absorbed Lenin's methods and ideas on practical activity.

Thanks to this, he is at present brilliantly deputizing for Lenin in the sphere not only of party activity, but also of state construction.[31]

It is barely believable that such a document could have been written while Lenin was still alive. Who was the author? What had 'truly steel springs of the revolution' to do with 'biographical details'? Perhaps Stalin, realizing that Lenin was not going to be returning to the political helm, was getting ready to take over as early as 1923?

A. A. Yepishev, who was at one time deputy Minister of State Security, told me that Stalin kept a black oilskin exercise book in which he would make occasional notes, and that for some time Stalin kept letters from Zinoviev, Kamenev, Bukharin and even Trotsky. All efforts to discover either the note-book or these letters have failed, and Yepishev did not reveal his source. Only Beria, Poskrebyshev and Vlasik had direct access to Stalin, and only they can have known of these notes, but Poskrebyshev and Vlasik were compromised by Beria shortly before Stalin's death and were therefore distanced from him. In other words, at the time of Stalin's death, only Beria remained close to him, and when the physicians were finally brought to the comatose leader, after a twelve or fourteen-hour interval, Beria realized the game was up for him, too. Leaving Khrushchev, Malenkov and the other members of the Politburo at the dacha with the dying Stalin, Beria made a dash for the Kremlin where it is reasonable to assume he cleaned out the safe, removing the boss's personal notes and with them, one assumes, the black notebook.

Beria must have been aware that Stalin's attitude towards him had cooled markedly over the last year or eighteen months. For his part, Stalin must also have been aware of Beria's intentions. Maybe Stalin had left instructions or some sort of last will that the ever-willing entourage would be all too ready to carry out? Beria had good reason to hurry. Only he had permission to enter Stalin's office, and of course Stalin's guards were on duty, yet when the safe was opened officially, it was found to be empty, apart from its owner's party card and some insignificant papers. Having destroyed Stalin's notebook, if indeed it was there, Beria would have cleared the path to his own ascendancy. Perhaps the truth will never be known, but Yepishev was convinced that Beria cleaned out the safe before the others could get to it.

Stalin had the habit of filing certain documents of special interest to him, for example, Hitler's last will, in which the Führer spoke of ending his 'earthly life', as if he was expecting to go to a better place.[32] Or a letter addressed to Stalin on 27 October 1935 by the graduating class of the Institute of Red Professors, complaining that they were being evicted from their hostel, while 'class-hostile elements, such as Princess Bagration,* were being allowed to stay'.[33] Another file dealt with the dissolution of the Society of Ex-Political Prisoners and Exiles. Ya. Peters and P. Pospelov wrote that the 'Society consists mostly of SRs and Mensheviks who have close connections. Forty to fifty

---

* The Bagration family were Georgian nobility. The wife of Grand Duke Vladimir Kirillovich, one of the pretenders to the Russian imperial throne, is a Princess Bagration who left the Soviet Union in 1935.

members of the Society were arrested after the assassination of Kirov.' One of
the members was allegedly saying, 'they should defend the members who had
been arrested by the Soviet régime.'[34] Once Stalin saw this report, the fate of
the Society was sealed.

There was a letter from the friend of Stalin's daughter, A. Ya. Kapler, who
was serving ten years in prison, requesting in 1944 to be sent to the front.
There was a note from Beria containing information supplied by the Yugoslav
General Stefanović, about Stalin's son, Yakov, with whom he had spent time
in captivity; a report from Kruglov about the transfer of the Russian Foreign
Archive from Prague;[35] and many other letters addressed to Stalin which show
how diligently such aides as Zhdanov and Suslov worked to ensure that the
people at large were given only the absolute minimum of information about
their government.

One of the unsolved mysteries of the story, and one that is likely to remain
so, is the death of Stalin's wife. None of the well-known official or unofficial
explanations is fully convincing. In this connection, one document in the
archive is worth mentioning. Written in purple pencil on several pages from
a school exercise book and dated 22 October 1935, it is an appeal to Kalinin
for clemency from Alexandra Gavrilovna Korchagina, a prisoner in Solovki
concentration camp. It emerges from the letter that Korchagina, a party
member, had worked for five years as a domestic servant in Stalin's household.
She had been arrested when a prisoner, called Sinedobov, also a former member
of the Kremlin staff, testified that she had said Stalin had shot his wife.
Korchagina denies this rather unconvincingly in her letter, and cites the official
version, namely that her mistress died of a heart attack. She writes that Burkov,
Sinedobov (neither has initials), Korchagina's live-in companion, security
guard Ya. K. Glome and an unnamed secretary of a party cell all wondered
why this cause of death had not been mentioned in the press. It appeared that
many people were questioning the official explanation of a sudden illness,
especially, as Korchagina writes, because Stalin followed his wife back to the
Kremlin that night. These conversations must have reached Stalin and caused
him some alarm, for the decision to remove Korchagina must have been
intended to silence anyone else who might know something.

Korchagina writes that the investigator, one Kogan, had intimidated her
into confessing, after which she was deported without trial to Solovki. Attached
to her letter is the judgement, signed by NKVD officer Lutsky, to the effect that
Korchagina had been involved in 'counter-revolutionary terrorist groups in
the government library, the security staff of the Kremlin and elsewhere'. Kalinin
wrote on the file, 'Refused'.[36]

Another mystery remains over the fate of Stalin's elder son, Yakov. There is
a variety of evidence to suggest that a number of attempts were made to
organize his escape from German captivity, including the testimony of Dolores
Ibarruri referred to earlier. The Germans, however, mentioned Yakov less and
less and finally said nothing. Stalin was probably not completely reassured

until he received a report, dated 5 March 1945 and signed by Beria, which stated:

At the end of January this year, a group of Yugoslav officers were liberated from German camp by the First Belorussian front. Among them was Yugoslav Gendarmerie General Stefanović, who gave the following account:
'First Lieutenant Yakov Dzhugashvili and Captain Robert Blum, son of the former French premier, shared a cell in the camp at Lübeck. Stefanović called on Dzhugashvili fifteen times to offer material help, which the latter declined, being independent and proud. He refused to stand up for German officers and was put in solitary for it. Dzhugashvili said the rumours about him in the German press were false. He was convinced of a Soviet victory. He gave me his address in Moscow: 3 Granovsky Street, apartment 84.'[37]

When the military reported to Stalin soon after the war that the Czech government wanted to make a gift to the USSR of the Russian Foreign Archive in Prague, he gave orders for the reception and examination of the documents. On 3 January 1946 Kruglov reported that nine wagonloads of documents had been delivered to Moscow, including the archives of the civil war governments of Denikin and Petliura, as well as the personal papers of Generals Alexeyev and Brusilov, and of the politicians Savinkov, Milyukov, Chernov and many other pre-revolutionary figures who had left Russia during or soon after the civil war.[38] The work involved in reviewing all this material was carried out by specialists from the Academy of Sciences, including I. Nikitinsky, S. Bogoyavlensky, I. Mints and S. Sutotsky, but they were under the control of senior NKVD officials, who also reported directly to Stalin and who were responsible for the future of the archives. Some documents sat for a long time in Stalin's cupboards and safes.

Among these was a manuscript by A. A. Brusilov, a former general in the tsarist army who achieved fame in the First World War for his breakthrough on the Southwestern front. He served in the Red Army in 1920 as a cavalry inspector and in 1924 was put on special army duty. The manuscript, entitled 'My Reminiscences', he wrote while taking medical treatment at Carlsbad in 1925, and he died the following year. In a note attached to the manuscript, he wrote:

Everyone will understand that I could not write anything in the USSR. I leave these notebooks to the care of friends abroad and I ask them not to publish them until after I am dead. If people in Europe want to save their way of life, the family, their fatherland, let them know my mistake and not repeat it. Our political parties argued and fought until they destroyed Russia![39]

Stalin had to know everything. Even the returns for the 1939 census, giving the names of families of his top officials, had to be shown to him. Only he knew why he placed ticks in thick red against certain names:

Beria, Nina Teimuradovna, Georgian, scientist, son Sergei aged fourteen.

Kaganovich, Maria Markovna, daughter Maya and son Yuri.

Voroshilova, Yekaterina Davidovna.

Zhemchuzhina, Polina Semenovna; daughters Svetlana Vyacheslavovna, Rita Aronovna Zhemchuzhina.

Andreyeva – Dora Moiseyevna Khazan, daughter Natalya Andreyevna.

Seeing potential plots and enemies everywhere, Stalin ensured that there was always 'ammunition' in his arsenal to repel any attack. All his life he expected an attempt on his life, but it never came. Only too aware of their master's pathological fear, his immediate circle were themselves pathologically afraid of arousing any suspicion of themselves.

CHAPTER ■ 52 ■

A Spasm of Violence

Long before Stalin's seventieth birthday in 1949, Malenkov prompted the Politburo to consider a long list of measures designed to make it a worthy celebration. It was not only to be an occasion for perpetuating the leader in new monuments and by giving his name to ever more factories and constructions, but also for receiving reports from all sectors.

From these reports Stalin learned that nearly all the destroyed factories had been reconstructed and hundreds of new ones built. The economy was progressing at a rapid pace. Characteristically, Stalin had urged greater and greater effort in industry, to which the greater part of financial investment was committed and from which higher output was expected, though not higher quality. Neither agriculture nor consumer goods were of any consequence in Stalin's reckoning. Agriculture therefore declined. The collective farmers were offered no incentives, but were forced to pay increased taxes in kind and money on every living thing in the collective, including even the fruit trees; the size of the household plot was reduced. The peasants were a group without rights or the possibility to protest or to change anything. The entire harvest was paid for at derisory or symbolic rates. The young people were finding any excuse to leave the land, crowding the trade schools and becoming cheap labour on construction sites and timber workings. The collective farmers decided nothing for themselves, while the authorities decided everything, from the time to sow to who should be the next farm chairman.

During his anniversary year, on the other hand, Stalin introduced a measure that is still popular with elderly citizens who can recall it. He reduced prices on a range of consumer goods: 10 per cent off bread, flour, butter, meat and meat products and wool, 28 per cent off vodka, 20 per cent off toiletries and bicycles, 25 per cent off television sets and 30 per cent off clocks and watches. Prices in restaurants, tea-rooms and other public eating places were to be reduced correspondingly.[40]

The standard of living was low. The security organs were reporting that several regions, notably in the east, were again suffering from starvation, and people were poorly dressed. In Stalin's view, however, giving the people anything above the bare minimum would only corrupt them. Not that it was possible to give them any more, since the defences had to be reinforced and heavy industry strengthened. The country must be strong, so the people must tighten their belts. The population must expect the standard to drop year after year, and so it did. According to some indicators, the standard of living in the early 1950s was barely above the 1913 level, and even if this is not a wholly accurate assessment, it does not diminish the belief that the endless experiments carried out by the régime had yielded very little for the people.

At the same time, it must be acknowledged that the cultural level of the population had been raised, that friendly relations with other countries had been enhanced, that the people were assured of a certain degree of social security, with pensions, paid holidays, maintenance for the families of those lost in the war and for mothers of large families. All this, however, was at the level of the absolute minimum, reflecting the country's general poverty. Setting a course for the further development of heavy industry, while agriculture was fast declining, offered a bleak outlook indeed.

It is sometimes argued that then at least we had order, discipline, respect for the law, whereas now we have prostitution and drugs, as if these and other social evils did not exist under Stalin. The difference, however, is that all the facts were concealed as top-secret criminal statistics.

Delinquency was rife. The system for training workers was widely held to be a great achievement, yet Kruglov reported that in 1946 the security police had arrested 10,563 pupils who had escaped from Factory Training Schools, as well as trade and railway schools: 'Many crimes had been committed, including robbery and gangsterism. The living conditions in the schools are unsatisfactory, they are unsanitary and cold, and often without electric light.'[41]

Barracks-style discipline and coercion were more likely to cause than eradicate criminality, and it was not in Stalin's nature to believe that respect for the law, civilized relations and democratic principles would help combat crime. The absolute power of one and the unfreedom of the many, the reinforcement of the totalitarian bureaucracy and the vital need for civil action, the imposition of like-mindedness and the natural demand for creative thinking – all these contradictions, bred by Stalin's autocratic rule, laid the foundations for future crises. Whether or not he intended or realized the consequences that must follow, Stalin persistently applied the ideological, rather than the economic lever. As before, he now relied on 'socialist competition', while stifling the creative spirit, and resorting increasingly to the tried and tested methods of threats and imperative instructions.

All of his 'triumphs' were associated with violence. Even his socio-economic programmes were carried out in conditions of 'civil war', if on a local scale. It was not surprising that the peak of the Stalinist cult, coming as it did on his seventieth birthday, should coincide with the so-called 'Leningrad affair'.

A decree of 1946, directed against the Leningrad literary journals *Zvezda* and *Leningrad*, was issued by Stalin himself. As a result, a number of film and theatre people were blacklisted and theatre repertoires condemned. Stalin felt that in the field of literature and art attempts were being made, however tentatively, to go beyond the bounds set by the party, that is, by himself. This represented a threat to uniform thinking and hence to one-man rule. Stalin's intellectual world was based on unshakable postulates to which free thinking posed an intolerable threat. The satirical writer Mikhail Zoshchenko and the poet, Anna Akhmatova were attacked for their writings in the Leningrad journals and expelled from the Writers' Union. This gave the signal for an ideological purge to begin. Barely having recovered from the inhuman suffering it had faced during the war, Leningrad was now stigmatized as a heretical city. Stalin was showing the rest of the country that, if there was to be no let-up for the heroic city of Lenin, they could expect even less.

The Zhdanov archives contain a long letter, dated 4 September 1947, from Zoshchenko's wife, Vera, which she asks Poskrebyshev to pass on to Stalin, 'and if it's too tiring for him, please convey its contents to him'. The letter contains the sort of statutory obeisance typical of the time, but which makes bitter reading today: 'The greatest joy in my life has been the thought that you exist in this world, and my greatest wish is that you should go on living for as long as possible.' She goes on:

> I was literally shattered by the Central Committee's decree on the journals *Zvezda* and *Leningrad* ... How could this happen, when everyone so loved Zoshchenko? Gorky, Tikhonov, [Marietta] Shaginyan, A. A. Kuznetsov, Maisky, they all said they did. There was never a question of his running away from Leningrad ... He was working on his book on the partisans right through the winter of '44. There is no trace of slander or malevolence in his books.

While defending her husband and repudiating the accusations that had been made against him, the brave woman in her desperation disclosed that Zoshchenko was:

> highly neurotic ... and has strange obsessions. He was terribly afraid of going mad, like Gogol. He began to cure himself by self-analysis and had some success. His illness is what gave him the gift of satire, and that's his problem. But he is incapable of submitting to the will of others, he cannot act on someone else's orders.[42]

Stalin evidently read the letter, as it bears the mark of his red pencil, and he must have realized that the writer's wife was not the only one to reject his view of Zoshchenko. Yet, amazingly, beyond expulsion from the Writers' Union – a severe enough penalty in itself, since the Union provided a writer's access to print and hence his livelihood – he went no further than inflicting psychological terror on Zoshchenko and his family.

Two years after launching the ideological campaign in Leningrad, Stalin followed it up with a political and punitive onslaught which many people saw as the first act in a replay of the mass repressions of the 1930s. In the middle of February 1949 Malenkov was briefed by Stalin and despatched to Leningrad. The pretext for the mission was alleged malpractice during a party conference in the city. It was a typical situation: despite having received some votes against them, a number of provincial party leaders, P. S. Popkov, G. F. Badaev, Ya. F. Kapustin and P.G. Lazutin, were declared by the conference chairman, A. Ya. Tikhonov, to have been elected unanimously. One of the electoral committee members had thereupon written an anonymous letter to the Central Committee, prompting a harsh response from Stalin, himself a past master at fixing ballots, for example in 1934 at the Seventeenth Party Congress. He told Malenkov that 'there have been too many danger signals about the Leningrad leadership for us not to react.' Malenkov was to 'go there and take a good look at what's going on. Comrade Beria has further information.' Malenkov left by train that very night.

The 'signals' coming from Leningrad alleged that, with the connivance of Central Committee secretary A. A. Kuznetsov, the local party boss was not taking notice of the central party authorities. The facts were that in January 1948 a wholesale trade market had been set up in Leningrad without the permission of the centre. At a joint session of the regional party bureau and city party committee, Malenkov, diligent pupil of Stalin that he was, strung together one 'error' after another into a skein of accusations. The assembly sat in depressed silence as Malenkov, who was becoming more incensed, fired off the charges. He described the wholesale market as an anti-party, group-minded initiative in opposition to the local organization of the Central Committee. Worse was to come. Following the line that had been laid down in Moscow, Malenkov quoted unfortunate utterances by P. S. Popkov, a local leader, and made the accusation that they represented an attempt to create a Communist Party of Russia with far-reaching aims. Everyone in the hall realized that Malenkov's speech augured great misfortune.

They did not, however, know that their former secretary, Kuznetsov, who had recently been made a secretary of the Central Committee, had already been removed from that post a week before. Naturally, the entire local leadership lost their jobs after Malenkov's speech, but that was only the beginning. A 'case' was rapidly fabricated against each suspected official and arrests followed. 'Spies' were identified, e. g. Kapustin, and 'degenerates', e. g. Popkov, and 'inspirers of an anti-party line', e. g. Kuznetsov.

In March 1949, N. A. Voznesensky, another Leningrad Communist, was removed from the Politburo. A primary organizer of the wartime economy, an academician and a man of outspoken, direct character, he had come to seem too dangerous to Stalin, and with Beria's help a huge and utterly groundless case was fabricated against him by Kruglov, Abakumov and Goglidze. Interrogations got under way with the sole purpose of extracting a confession that anti-party, anti-state activity had taken place. Having launched this major provocation, Malenkov could rub his hands with satisfaction: Stalin's wishes had been carried out, he had done a thorough job. Like his close friend, Beria, Malenkov had no love for either Voznesensky or Kuznetsov. The witch-hunt was on and everyone expected the worst, especially as former Leningrad officials were being picked up in other republics where they had been transferred to other jobs.

Why did Stalin carry out this criminal action? Why on the eve of his seventieth birthday? Why was he following up the ideological campaign of August 1946 with a more terrifying, punitive one two and a half years later? Only he knew the real answer to these questions, but on the basis of the documents we may deduce the following.

Stalin could not forgive independent, free thinking. Both Voznesensky and Kuznetsov had glorified him, orally and in writing, but the fact that they showed more independence than others put Stalin on permanent guard against them. For a time, he ignored the calumnies made by Malenkov and Beria, and indeed he even made flattering public references to the two Leningraders, and they in turn might have thought themselves possible successors, given the leader's advancing age. This was not acceptable to the Stalinist camarilla in Moscow, however. In one secret report to Stalin after another, they pointed out that before the war Voznesensky had not discovered any 'enemies' in Gosplan and may even have been shielding them, while Beria complained that, when he had been in charge of the chemical and metallurgical industries as chairman of Gosplan, Voznesensky had patently lowered the output norms for those branches, while he, Beria, had raised them for the timber industry.

For the time being, Stalin had paid no heed to all this. He was however displeased with a speech Voznesensky made at the Politburo, advancing a number of convincing arguments against the imposition of new taxes on the collective farmers. Nor was he pleased when Kuznetsov, who was responsible for Central Committee cadres, expressed his intention to take tighter control of the Ministry of Internal Affairs and State Security. Stalin also got to hear about Kuznetsov's expressed view that the investigation of the Kirov case had not revealed the true inspirers of the crime.

For Stalin the chief quality of any official, however valuable and essential, was reliability and loyalty to him personally. He was by now not merely dubious about the obstinate Leningraders, he saw them as potential enemies. According to S. I. Semin, who was a departmental manager in Gosplan, Voznesensky put remarkable energy and careful preparation into planning the national economy. Despite the severely administrative character of the economic system, Voznesensky tried wherever possible to bring the workers into the process of planning and management and also of setting the aims of each enterprise. He never took days off or holidays. Up to the present, he was probably the greatest economist in the Soviet leadership after Bukharin.

Even though before their arrest Voznesensky and some of the other

Leningraders sent Stalin a note declaring their total innocence, the leader scarcely wavered. At first, it is true, he wanted to tranfer Voznesensky to be head of the Marx-Engels-Lenin Institute, but he changed his mind, deciding instead to let the whole Leningrad crew drink the bitter cup together. The trial, which took place in September 1950 at Officers' House on Liteiny Boulevard in Leningrad, was conducted in accordance with Stalin's orders. Nearly two hundred people were implicated, including N. A. Voznesensky, A. A. Kuznetsov, P. S. Popkov, Ya. F. Kapustin, M. I. Rodionov, all of whom perished, a fate shared a little later by G. F. Badaev, I. S. Kharitonov, P. I. Kabatkin, P. I. Levin, M. V. Basov, A. D. Verbitsky, N. V. Solovyov, A. I. Burlin, V. I. Ivanov, M. N. Nikitin, V. P. Galkin, M. I. Safonov, P. A. Chursin and A. T. Bondarenko.[43]

The court heard no repentant speeches from Voznesensky or Kuznetsov, the latter declaring: 'I was a Bolshevik and remain one; whatever sentence I am given, history will vindicate us.' In April 1954 the Supreme Court of the USSR, under A. A. Volin, overturned the case, citing the following evidence from September 1950:

The accused pleaded guilty to having formed an anti-Soviet group in 1938, carrying out diversionary activity in the party aimed at undermining the Central Committee organization in Leningrad and turning it into a base for operations against the party and its Central Committee . . . To this end, they tried to arouse local discontent with Central Committee measures, they spread slanderous allegations and uttered traitorous plots . . . They also sold off state property . . . As the documents show, all the accused fully confessed to these charges at the preliminary investigation and in court.[44]

The means by which these confessions were extracted was revealed on 29 January 1954 by Turko, while he was still serving his sentence:

I committed no crimes and did not regard myself as guilty, nor do I now. I gave my evidence after being systematically beaten because I denied my guilt. Investigator Putintsev began beating me systematically at the interrogations . . . he beat me about the head, in the face and the legs. Once he beat me so severely that blood came out of my ears. After these beatings he sent me to solitary confinement, threatened to kill my wife and children and give me twenty years of camp if I did not confess. As a result, I signed whatever he wanted me to.[45]

In this paroxysm of violence, Stalin got rid of three Bolsheviks with family ties: the Voznesensky brothers, Nikolai, the Politburo member, and Alexander, the Rector of Leningrad University, and their sister, Maria, a party worker. The blatant absurdity of the case was revealed by the fact that Maria was charged with having shared the views of the Workers' Opposition in the 1920s. It is also noteworthy that the grounds for rehabilitation in 1954 were equally ludicrous, namely, that 'there is no proof that Voznesenskaya shared the views of the Workers' Opposition'.[46] And what if there had been such evidence? Such was Stalinist justice.

They were all shot in Leningrad, except possibly Nikolai Voznesensky himself who, according to Semin, may have been kept in prison for a further three months following sentence. Then in December, on someone's orders, he was taken to Moscow by truck, wearing only light clothes. Either he died of cold on the way, or he was shot.

The Leningrad massacre was followed by waves of further violence against not only those who had known the condemned men, but security personnel as well. The habit of coercion and violence was deeply ingrained in Stalin, encouraged as he was by the passivity of the doomed and the timidity of the party and the population. The spasm of violence which accompanied this escalation of his personal glory is not easily explained. The country had quickly licked its war wounds. The internal situation appeared to be secure. No one was making oppositional speeches. The national solidarity around the political leadership, embodied in Stalin, was real. International relations seemed stable. The party's ideological influence was undivided. Yet, with all this, Stalin resorted again to violence and coercion, turning his attention now to a particular region, now to a particular social group or agency. Having survived at the summit of power for a quarter of a century by means of coercion, he was unable to do without it. Only this can explain the special attention he paid to the security organs and the Ministry of Internal Affairs.

Beria, Kruglov, Serov, Abakumov and other officials of these agencies reported to Stalin regularly on the situation in the Gulag, which apart from its punitive and isolating functions, was also an important source of cheap labour. On one occasion, Malenkov managed to persuade Stalin into performing a 'humanitarian' act. He showed his boss a report from the head of the Gulag, Dobrynin, which stated that in 1949 there were 503,375 women in camps and exile colonies. Malenkov suggested they should consider releasing women with children under the age of seven, since the cost of maintaining children in the camps was running at 166 million rubles a year. After careful scrutiny of the figures, Stalin agreed, and went further by decreeing that such mothers should henceforth be employed on forced labour in their home towns. Any women who had been sentenced for counter-revolutionary activity, however, were to be excluded from this category.[47]

In September 1951 a delegation of Englishwomen – a rare enough occurrence in those days – asked if they might visit a women's camp. Naturally their hosts were thrown into confusion. They called a department at the Ministry of Internal Affairs which of course could not help. They then applied to the deputy Minister of State Security, Serov, but he too lacked the proper authority. They contacted Kruglov, with the same results. Eventually they got to Suslov who in turn approached Malenkov and only he, being a member of the Politburo, and only after consulting Stalin, could place his stamp of approval on the application. The camp was of course carefully got ready, cleaned and spruced up and everyone was told what to do. The 70 per cent of the camp population who looked in worst condition were sent to work outside the camp, while those seen by the Englishwomen were mostly ordinary Soviet citizens who happened to be there temporarily, and were not typical camp inmates. The delegation even wrote a comment in a Visitor's Book that was hastily produced: 'We were greatly impressed by the directness with which people approached us. It is clean everywhere. We think this is a valuable experiment and that it will be successful.'[48]

Of all the state institutions, Stalin devoted most of his time and attention to the punitive organs, which were in effect out of control by the state and under his personal supervision. Only during the war, perhaps, did he give more time to the army than to the NKVD, and at all times since the late 1930s he devoted more attention to the NKVD than to the party bodies.

What was the cost of the Stalinist régime? How many victims did it create? How many people perished by the will of the tyrant and his machine of terror? I doubt if we will ever know the precise number. The most complete figures may be provided by the commission for further study of materials connected with the repressions of the 1930s, 1940s and 1950s, which has been set up by the Supreme Soviet of the USSR. Numerous estimates have already been made by specialists. My own interim figures are based on what I have gleaned from the archives. Collectivization in 1929–33 cost 8.5 to 9 million peasant lives. In 1937–38 the number of citizens arrested was between 4.5 and 5.5 million. Between those two great waves, however, the NKVD was not idle and about another million people were arrested. After the war, especially in the late 1940s, the number of camps was markedly increased, along with the number of inmates and deportees who amounted to 5.5 to 6.5 million. It might be rightly argued that these figures included ordinary criminals, but, according to Beria's own data, up to Stalin's death between 25 and 30 per cent of people sentenced for 'counter-revolutionary activity' were in the camps.[49] Thus, between 1929 and 1953 we can say that Stalin's victims amounted to between 19.52 and 22 million, and this of course does not include the war losses. Of this total, not less than one-third were sentenced to death or died in camp and exile. My figures may err on the conservative side, but they are based on what I have found, and I am the first to agree that there is much I have not been able to ascertain.

After the war, the social and political system was not merely preserved, it acquired a number of new and sinister features of a bureaucratic, police character. Stalin was able to combine the uncombinable, by every available means maintaining the enthusiasm and zeal of the Soviet people in their belief that the bright uplands were just over the horizon, while at the same time threatening them with individual and mass terror. And yet the people loved him. It is noteworthy that, just before Voznesensky was arrested, he wrote the last chapters of his book *The Political Economy of Communism*, in which even he, one of the most sophisticated men in the leadership, could write that, led by Stalin, society was approaching a bright future. Ironically, Voznesensky was charged, among other things, for 'compiling and publishing politically harmful works'.[50]

CHAPTER ■ 53 ■

The Ageing Leader

Stalin's seventieth birthday was approaching. He knew that from the Politburo down, everyone was hectically making arrangements. He called in Malenkov and said, 'Don't even think of presenting me with another Star!'

'But, Comrade Stalin,' Malenkov protested, 'for a jubilee like this, the people won't understand ...'

'Leave the people out of this. I've no intention of arguing about it. Don't insist! Got it?'

'Of course, Comrade Stalin, it's just that the members of the Politburo ...'

Stalin cut him off, making it plain that the subject was closed, and ordered him instead to show him the scenario for the celebration which was to take place in the Bolshoi Theatre.

Mention of the 'Star' had not been accidental. After the Victory Parade and reception in honour of the front commanders in June 1945, a group of marshals had suggested to Molotov and Malenkov that they should mark the 'leader's extraordinary contribution' by conferring on him the country's highest award, the title of Hero of the Soviet Union. They referred to the fact that for his sixtieth birthday Stalin had been awarded the title of Hero of Socialist Labour, and that during the war he had received three decorations, the Victory Order No. 3 – numbers 1 and 2 having gone to Zhukov and Tolbukhin – the Suvorov 1st Class, and the Red Banner, which he was given 'for service in the Red Army'.

Over the next day and a half, Molotov and Malenkov had debated the matter with their colleagues and on 26 June two decrees were issued by the Supreme Soviet ordering that the title of Hero of the Soviet Union and a second Victory Order be conferred on Marshal of the Soviet Union I. V. Stalin. The same day, the title of Generalissimo of the Soviet Union was created and on the 27th it was conferred on Stalin. This was probably the only occasion when they disobeyed their leader. That morning before breakfast, Stalin unfolded his copy of *Pravda* as usual and flew into a rage. They had not consulted him! They had not asked him! As soon as he arrived at the Kremlin he summoned Molotov, Malenkov, Beria, Kalinin and Zhdanov and gave them a severe dressing-down. Kalinin, whose office was nominally responsible, and Malenkov, who had failed to restrain the loyal impulse of his comrades, were the most terrified. Molotov, Beria and Zhdanov knew that Stalin's anger was fake.

Stalin was elevated to so high a degree of glory that decorations intended for ordinary mortals, who were eager to receive them, meant nothing to him, or rather they mattered in that they put him on the same level as others who received them. Possessing supreme power, the leader who loaded himself down with medals and orders only demeaned himself.

Beria, who knew better than most what his master wanted to hear, wrote in his article 'The Great Inspirer and Organizer of Communism's Victories': 'Our leader's genius combines simplicity, modesty, exceptional personal attraction, implacability towards the enemies of Communism, and sensitivity and fatherly concern for people. He has the utmost inherent clarity of thought, calm greatness of character, scorn and impatience for any sort of fuss and outward effect.'[51] The wretched, naive Kalinin, who had never raised an objection to anything or anyone, had simply thought he was fulfilling his ritualistic duty and had not realized that medals which others could receive were not to be conferred on Stalin.

'Say what you like,' Stalin had said conclusively, 'I will not accept the decoration. Do you hear me, I will not!'

The comrades tried another two or three times to persuade him, even recruiting Poskrebyshev and Vlasik in their cause. But in vain. Then, one evening at the dacha, nearly five years later, Stalin suddenly brought up the subject of his old decorations, notably the two Hero stars and two Victory orders which were still appearing on his portraits and photographs. Finally, on the eve of the May Day celebrations of 1950, Shvernik managed to hand Stalin the medals he had been awarded in 1945, plus an Order of Lenin for his seventieth birthday of 1949.

'You're indulging an old man,' Stalin muttered. 'It won't do anything for my health.'

Behind these words lay yet a new fear that assailed him on the eve of his birthday. He had been getting up to leave for the dacha one evening, and as he rose from his desk to put on his coat, he had a dizzy spell. Orange circles swam before his eyes, but he recovered quickly. Poskrebyshev gripped him firmly by the arm with both hands and asked in some alarm, 'Let me call the doctors, Comrade Stalin. You shouldn't go out right away. You need a doctor.' Stalin told him not to fuss.

The dizziness soon passed. Stalin waited a little while and drank some tea. He felt pressure at the back of his neck but would not have the doctors called in. True, he did not trust them, but he trusted Beria, who was in charge of the 4th Main Administration of the Ministry of Health, even less. He did not want it to get around that he had been unwell. He would soon be at the dacha where he would drink an infusion, recommended long ago by Poskrebyshev. It had always helped, and so it would now.

The Politburo resolved to celebrate Stalin's birthday with a splash. Shvernik was appointed to handle the festivities. He soon received a memorandum, signed by P. Ponomarenko, V. Abakumov, N. Parfenov, A. Gromyko and V. Grigoryan, which gave the cost of the celebrations as around 6.5 million rubles. Shvernik eventually signed a requisition for 5,623,255 rubles in respect of the reception and servicing of delegations and for organizing an exhibition of Stalin's birthday presents.[52]

The organizers also prepared a surprise in the form of the Stalin Prize, the cost of which was calculated at 7 rubles 64 kopeks per medal, while the total quantity of metal for one million medals was worked out at 24 tons of bronze and 6 tons of nickel. There was also to be an international Stalin Peace Prize.[53] Thirteen versions of the medal were submitted for Stalin's approval by the artists N. I. Moskalenko, A. I. Kuznetsov and I. I. Dubasov.[54] Everything was set for the presentation of this most prestigious decoration, when at the last moment Stalin dug his heels in, despite having given his preliminary approval of the idea.

Having looked over all the designs and read all the draft decrees (while his comrades-in-arms were waiting in hopes of being the first to receive the new prize), Stalin suddenly declared: 'I will only approve the decree on the international prize.' After a pause he added: 'And orders of this kind are only to be given posthumously.' Immediately a din went up, but Stalin raised his hand and calmly told the gathering: 'There is a time for everything.' Perhaps he felt that, as the whole country was already plastered with every kind of image of him, from vast monuments to the names of towns and villages, something should be left for when he was dead, and what better than a prize in his name?

On the great day, Stalin rose at his usual time of eleven in the morning, feeling quite normal. The episode of the previous evening had been insignificant. But there was a heavy day ahead of him. After a celebration with the Politburo, there would be an entire evening of endless eulogies and speeches in his honour. Everyone would be competing to find new and more grandiloquent epithets. *Pravda* had devoted the whole of December to printing articles and accounts of the preparations that were in hand throughout the country. The wave of glorification rose higher with each day. Reports were coming in from all the republics and regions, while accounts of no less enthusiastic celebrations were even coming from the Gulag, where there were expectations of an amnesty. It was not, however, the prisoners themselves who were sending reports, but Interior Ministry officials representing those in their 'care'.

Nearly an hour before the ceremony was due to start, the carefully selected and screened audience had filled the Bolshoi Theatre. Half an hour later Stalin entered the room set aside for the Presidium (as the Politburo was now called) where he exchanged greetings with such luminaries of the Communist world as Palmiro Togliatti, Mao Tse-tung, Walter Ulbricht, Dolores Ibarruri and Matthias Rakosi, among others.

When the Presidium went out on to the stage, the audience could not contain themselves. The day before, Stalin had altered Malenkov's seating plan, which had placed him in the centre, but he compromised over his usual custom of sitting 'modestly' in the second row at all such meetings and put himself well to the right of the chairman, placing Mao on his right and Khrushchev on his left.

The speeches began after a short introductory statement by Shvernik, which was interrupted by 'stormy applause' every time he mentioned Stalin. Apart from Mao, who described Stalin as 'great', speaker after speaker called Stalin 'genius', 'thinker and leader of genius', 'teacher of genius', 'war leader of genius', while representatives of the republics, the Communist parties, youth and cultural organizations, chorussed the 'love of the peoples' in undiluted form. By the end of the evening, everyone was exhausted. Photographs of the occasion show Beria, Voroshilov, Molotov and Malenkov looking distinctly worn-out from all the standing up and sitting down.

Paeans and poems of glorification poured out, and even those of such talented and decent men as Alexander Tvardovsky must have been sincerely meant, representing as they did an expression of the universal, blind adulation of the chief idol. As they praised the leader, the people entered into a kind of religious ecstasy. Stalin embodied socialism. Believing in the leader, we believed also in the ideals he supposedly personified.

Next day, as he was going through the congratulatory telegrams from foreign leaders, Stalin suddenly turned to Poskrebyshev and asked: 'And who gave you the idea of writing about citrus fruits?' Poskrebyshev replied, 'It was Suslov and Malenkov. They read it in the propaganda department, and Suslov himself looked at it.' The subject of this exchange was an article by Poskrebyshev in that day's issue of *Pravda*, entitled 'Beloved Father and Great Teacher'. The author had written that Stalin not only helped the Michurin school of geneticists to smash that of Weissmann and Morgan, but had also shown how advanced scientific methods could be applied in practice. 'Comrade Stalin, who has been involved for many years in the cultivation and study of citrus culture on the Black Sea coast, has shown himself to be a scientific innovator. Other examples include the introduction of eucalyptus trees on the Black Sea coast and melons in the Moscow region.'

For the whole of December, the newspapers were full of such loyal and devoted anniversary articles. The humiliation of a great nation was in full swing, and of course seemed perfectly natural to Stalin. As early as 1931 the German social democrat and long-standing opponent of Bolshevism, Karl Kautsky, had asked, 'What is there left for Stalin to do to arrive at Bonapartism? You might say the affair will not reach its essence until he crowns himself tsar.'[55] The totalitarian bureaucratic state needed at least a first consul, if not an emperor; the bureaucratic system itself, behind the formal façade of democracy, could not exist without a political figure of the despotic type.

Stalin began to decline more rapidly after his seventieth birthday. His blood pressure was continually high, but he did not want doctors, he did not trust them. He still listened half-heartedly to Academician Vinogradov, but gradually Beria convinced him that 'the old man was suspect' and tried to foist other doctors on to him. Stalin, however, would have no one new. When he heard that Vinogradov had been arrested, he cursed ominously but did nothing about it. He now finally stopped smoking, but continued his unhealthy life-style in all other respects, rising late and working into the night. Despite the hypertension, he kept up the habit of the steam bath that he had acquired in Siberia, and after dinner he took small sips of aromatic Georgian wine and avoided medicines. On Poskrebyshev's advice, he might occasionally take some pills and before dinner he would drink a glass of boiled water to which he would add a few drops of iodine. Trustful of no one, he would not entrust himself to doctors.

He was simply afraid of death, as he had always been afraid of attempts on his life and of plots and sabotage. He was afraid that his evil acts would become known after his death. He was afraid for the fate of his brainchild and did not want it to be changed into something different. And indeed, after he had gone, his world and his cult did not survive for long.

The ageing tyrant was perpetually afraid. His daughter wrote that as he approached the end he felt empty, 'He had forgotten all human attachments, he was tortured by fear which in the last years of his life became a genuine persecution mania, and in the end his strong nerves gave way. But the mania was not a sick fantasy: he knew and understood that he was hated, and he knew why.'[56] His old belief in Georgian longevity was shaken by a series of dizzy spells which knocked him off balance.

Earlier he had hardly given a thought to his children. There had simply been no time. He barely knew them. When Yakov died, with him died the irritation Stalin had felt at the mere mention of his name. He could not have a calm conversation with Vasili, who, he felt sure, was only kept in his job because of his name and the highly placed 'friends' who constantly hovered around him. Svetlana meanwhile did as she pleased. After she left another husband, Stalin arranged an apartment for her and then washed his hands of her. She would occasionally visit him at the dacha and listen to his grumbling or ask for money, whereupon Stalin would give her a wad of notes out of his deputy's salary.

CHAPTER 54

Icy Winds

On the night of 6 March 1946, just as Stalin was preparing to leave for the dacha, Poskrebyshev hurried in and handed him a cipher from the Washington embassy reporting a speech made by Churchill at Fulton, Missouri, in the presence of President Truman, a native of that state. Despite the considerable respect Stalin had for Churchill's encyclopedic knowledge, he had never trusted him, but even he was surprised by the harsh tone the former prime minister had used. While expressing his admiration for 'the heroic Russian people and my war comrade Marshal Stalin', Churchill went on to warn of a 'Red threat' hanging over the Western democracies. 'From Stettin in the Baltic to Trieste in the Adriatic, an iron curtain has descended across the Continent.'

This was true. Soon after the war, Stalin had taken energetic measures to reduce all contact with the West and the rest of the world. A curtain, whether of iron or ideology, had decidedly come down, and henceforth for many years the Soviet people could know about the West only what officials, of Suslov's ilk, thought they should know. The huge chasm of information that lay between the two worlds impoverished Soviet intellectual life and deprived the Soviet Union of contact with world culture.

Stalin pushed the report away and stared with unblinking eyes through the window into the dark March night. Churchill's speech was both a signal and a challenge. Stalin telephoned Molotov, who was at his post – as a rule Politburo members waited until they were sure Stalin had left before themselves going home. Molotov arrived and the two architects of foreign policy talked for a good hour. They did not know that Churchill's speech had been preceded by a long cable to Washington from George Kennan, the US chargé d'affaires in Moscow, giving a biassed account of Stalin's February speech. Kennan had reported that the Soviet leaders regarded a Third World War as 'inevitable'.[57]

Stalin was in a difficult position. The USA had become immeasurably stronger than the USSR. Besides possessing the atom bomb, America's industrial potential had grown 50 per cent in the course of the war. This contrasted sharply with the position in the USSR, where thousands of centres of population lay in ruins, where the famine of 1946 was imminent, where virtually the entire western part of the country was engulfed in partisan warfare which threatened to spread to the surrounding territory. This aspect of modern Soviet history has yet to receive its due attention. After the expulsion of German forces from the Western Ukraine and the Baltic region, armed detachments carried on the fight against the Soviet régime. On several occasions, Stalin ordered Beria to finish off the 'outlaws in the shortest possible time', but he could not imagine that it would continue for a full five years after the end of the war, most vigorously in the western Ukraine.

On 12 April 1946, Interior Minister Kruglov sent a long account of events during March. It mentioned that in the western regions of the Ukraine 8,360 partisans had been either killed or captured, along with eight mortars, twenty machine-guns, 712 sub-machine-guns, 2,002 rifles, 600 pistols, 1,766 grenades, four printing presses and thirty-three typewriters. Also captured were a number of local leaders of the Ukrainian Nationalist Formation, while some 200 troops of the Interior and Security Ministries, as well as of the Red Army, had been killed. In Lithuania, 145 partisans had been killed and 1,500 captured. Forty-four machine-guns, 289 rifles, 122 pistols, 182 grenades and twelve duplicating machines had been seized, with the loss of 215 government troops. The report further recounted that armed clashes had taken place in Belorussia, Latvia and Estonia.[58] Stalin told Beria and Kruglov that he was most dissatisfied with the ineffectiveness of the regular forces.

Faced with multiple problems at home, the USSR was also totally isolated in the United Nations, although there at least it had the power of veto in the Security Council. Stalin felt that a difficult and unequal confrontation had begun, but he had no thought of yielding. He would turn the country into a fortress. In his view, the anti-Communist Truman Doctrine made it impossible for the USSR to accept the Marshall Plan. While the USSR was desperate for economic aid, and could have benefited under the Marshall Plan, it could have done so only at the cost of accepting virtual US control over the Soviet economy. Through Molotov, at the Paris conference of 27 June–2 July 1947, Stalin said no.

Stalin's understanding of the Marshall Plan had not been mistaken. Truman later wrote frankly in his memoirs that 'Marshall's idea was to liberate Europe from the threat of enslavement which was being prepared for it by Russian Communism.'[59] The long Cold War had begun. The only way out, Stalin believed, lay in terminating the American monopoly on the atom bomb. At the cost of enormous effort, by 1952 the USSR had doubled its pre-war output of steel, coal and cement, and sharply increased production of oil and electricity. Stalin never tired of asserting that the absolute priority of heavy industry was a 'constant law' of socialism. The redoubled efforts of heavy industry and science created the preconditions for a quantum leap in the nuclear sphere. As we have mentioned above, Stalin entrusted the work of this secret enterprise to Beria and he demanded weekly progress reports from him.

Soviet experience in this field had a solid background. Before the war the ideas of A. F. Ioffe, I. V. Kurchatov, G. N. Flerov, L. D. Landau and I. E. Tamm had made possible the construction of the first uranium reactor. The work had been halted and it was not until 1942 that it started again under Kurchatov's supervision. Stalin pressed hard for results and urged that no expense be spared. Kruglov, M. Pervukhin and Kurchatov reported to Stalin in October 1946 that, on the instructions of the Special Committee of the Council of Ministers, Kurchatov and Kikoin had checked special sites and taken measures to step up the rate of construction by taking on up to 37,000 workers.[60]

At the same time, Kruglov and A. Zavenyagin reported to Stalin and Beria that the work would be speeded up by employing experts who were then serving ten-year sentences, among them S. A. Voznesensky, N. V. Timofeyev-Resovsky, S. R. Tsarapkin, Ya. M. Fishman, B. V. Kiryan, I. F. Popov, A. S. Tkachev, A. A. Goryunov and I. Ya. Bashilov.[61]

In December 1946 Soviet scientists achieved their first chain reaction and commissioned their first nuclear reactor the following year, making it possible for Molotov to announce in November 1947 that the secret of the atom bomb was out. The first Soviet atomic bomb was tested in the summer of 1949, followed in 1953 by its first hydrogen bomb. Apart from the economy, Stalin now devoted his major energy to defence matters, and a substantial section of the Gulag was committed to this purpose. Ministers customarily now initiated their tasks with an approach to Beria.

For instance, an application dated July 1946 to build a camp within a camp in Siberia to house 1,000 prisoners engaged on scientific research.[62] Or, still more cynically, a request from the minister in charge of fuel industry construction, A. Zademidko, for permission in March 1947 to relocate 5,000 prisoners from Siberian concentration camps, plus an allocation of 30,000 metres of tarpaulin for tents and 50 tons of barbed wire.[63] Such were the moral depths to which the Stalinist system had sunk, that scientists, already languishing in camps, must be kept in tents and behind barbed wire while working on the most advanced and important defence interests of the state.

Forty or so years after these events, I managed to find Zademidko and to show him the document bearing his signature – a common enough phenomenon of the period. I asked him how he felt now about his note. He replied: 'That's how things were ... We were building socialism with the help of a vast army of prisoners. Now of course I think it was savage.' He paused and then recounted an example of the 'technology' of force used in construction.

Once, late at night, I was summoned with my deputy to see Beria. His eyes glittering menacingly behind his pince-nez, he asked quietly, referring to a special construction: 'Why aren't you reporting that the workshop has been finished?'

I replied: 'They haven't finished installing the equipment.'

'*Who* hasn't finished?' and, without waiting for my reply, he snapped at an assistant: 'Call the manager of the plant.'

Three or four minutes later a distant voice came on the line from the Donbass. Beria at once barked into the phone: 'Hello, this is Beria. Why hasn't the job been done on time? Installation is to be completed by eight o'clock in the morning! Good night!' One can imagine what sort of good night that plant manager had! Beria then told his assistant to get hold of the head of administration, to whom he said, 'I've just ordered so-and-so (Zademidko couldn't recall the name) to finish the work by eight in the morning. If he doesn't, put him in your cellar. Good-bye!'

My deputy and I of course knew about Beria's working methods, but hearing him give his quiet, terse instructions made our flesh creep. That's how things were done in those days ...

Despite the low productivity of forced labour, Stalin believed that the widespread use of prisoners on defence projects was not only a cheap way of increasing Soviet military potential, but also a tried and tested way of 're-educating' hundreds of thousands of 'enemies' and 'traitors'.

Whatever we may think of Stalin, by his pitiless determination and at enormous cost to the Soviet people he did accomplish the impossible leap forward: the American nuclear monopoly was broken and the foundation stone of strategic parity was laid. Stalin was prepared to use any means, including the international labour and Communist movements and the emerging peace movement, if it gained ground for the Soviet Union in its competitive struggle with the transatlantic colossus. After prolonged discussion with Molotov and Zhdanov, he decided on a move that was bound to be seen by the West in an extremely negative light. He resolved to establish an agency to coordinate the activities of the Communist Parties. In Europe and the US this step was interpreted as Stalin's official acceptance of the challenge of Cold War.

He had been persuaded to dissolve Comintern right at the beginning of the war, but had had the tactical good sense to see that such a move would have been interpreted as weakness, and had therefore delayed and chosen a good moment to do so, namely the spring of 1943, hoping the Allies would thus be encouraged to open the second front. He knew perfectly well that Comintern was a purely Soviet agency and his personal mouthpiece, but its dissolution, he had calculated, would bring him more advantages than disadvantages. Now, suddenly, he was set on creating a new international Communist centre. What was he thinking?

When Comintern had been established in 1919, its leaders – notably Lenin, Trotsky and Zinoviev – believed in an imminent world revolution. But when the tidal wave of revolution had receded, the foundations of the old world had been shown to be intact. It was clear that Comintern's rôle would be both limited and subordinate to the country where its headquarters were located, namely the Soviet Union. The fact that it was directed by one centre seriously undermined the Communist movement and permitted its critics and enemies to make the easy and justified charge that it was 'the hand of Moscow'. Now, however, given the emergence of a bi-polar, two-camp world, Stalin reasoned that collaboration between the Communist Parties was once again on the agenda, though not in the old style or form of organization.

On 22–27 September 1947, the Polish Communists, encouraged by Stalin, organized a meeting of nine European Communist parties in the Polish town of Szklarska Poreba. On the eve of the meeting, Zhdanov, who had been deputed by Stalin to represent the Soviet Communist Party, sent a coded telegram to Moscow outlining the preliminary results of a working party:

> It was proposed to start with informational reports from all the participating Communist parties. Then to work out an agenda. We will suggest 1) the international situation, the speech to be made by us, 2) coordinating the parties' activities. The outcome should be a coordinating centre with its residence in Warsaw. I think special stress should be laid on voluntary principles in this matter. I await your instructions.'[64]

Stalin gave his approval. As a result of the Szklarska meeting, and four years after the dissolution of Comintern, the Information Bureau of the Communist and Labour Parties came into being as Informburo, or Cominform in Western parlance. According to Zhdanov, the most active and positive participants were the Yugoslavs. For content, purposefulness and constructive approach, Zhdanov ranked as the best reports those of the Yugoslav Eduard Kardelj and the Czech Rudolf Slansky.[65] Within a year he would describe Kardelj as an imperialist spy, in November 1949 Cominform would denounce the Yugoslav Communists as murderers and spies, and in 1951 Slansky would be tried and executed as the leader of a Zionist plot to overthrow the Czech state.

Zhdanov's speech on the international situation contained the thesis that would become virtually the cornerstone of Soviet propaganda, namely the division of the world into two opposing camps, in effect the response to the Truman Doctrine. The Marshall Plan was described as 'a programme for the enslavement of Europe'. Zhdanov was especially scathing in his references to the social democratic parties, reflecting Stalin's lifelong hatred and the distrust which was responsible for weakening not only progressive forces in the West, but also the developing movement for peaceful East–West relations.

The next meeting was planned to take place in Belgrade, but events made this impossible. The peoples of Yugoslavia had made a major contribution to the defeat of Fascism, and the first Soviet treaty of friendship, mutual aid and post-war collaboration agreed with a new socialist country was that signed with Tito when he visited Moscow in April 1945. Stalin met him several times and they got on well together. It was agreed that the Soviet Union would give the Yugoslav army military technology and armaments for twelve rifle and two air divisions.[66] The two countries seemed to have got off to a great start. A large contingent of Soviet military experts worked in Yugoslavia, while in the USSR thousands of Yugoslav military personnel were undergoing training. Then, suddenly it all went wrong.

A series of issues were debated without consulting Stalin first: for instance, a Bulgarian–Yugoslav treaty of friendship, the despatch of a Yugoslav air regiment to Albania, and Bulgarian leader Dimitrov's statement at a press conference to the effect that a federation of European socialist states was a possibility. Stalin was furious. The almighty dictator at home, he also believed himself to be the supreme arbiter over the lives of his allies.

A meeting of Soviet, Bulgarian and Yugoslav delegations took place on Stalin's suggestion in Moscow on 10 February 1949. Headed by Stalin, Dimitrov and Kardelj, the Soviet side included Molotov, Malenkov, Zhdanov and Suslov, while the Bulgarians included T. Kostov and V. Kolarov, and the Yugoslavs were represented by Milovan Djilas and V. Bokarić.

Stalin expressed his dissatisfaction in a plainly irritated manner, castigating the Yugoslavs and Bulgarians for 'following a particular foreign-policy line'. The Yugoslavs and Bulgarians were in the course of protesting that there were no grounds for such imprecations and that the recriminations were of a personal nature, when Stalin suddenly declared the need for the creation of a federation of Bulgaria and Yugoslavia. Accustomed to his utterances being taken as orders, Stalin now sensed a degree of resistance. Both Kardelj and Dimitrov, while not repudiating in principle the idea of federation, argued that the time was not ripe for such a move. Kardelj, moreover, said he could not give a definitive answer until the political leadership of his country had expressed a view. This was the first serious resistance Stalin had experienced in years, and it was coming moreover from Communists. He was not prepared for it. The rush of blind fury required an outlet.

Djilas later recalled, in his well-known memoirs, that Stalin jumped on Dimitrov and Kardelj for keeping their affairs from Moscow, and for doing so, moreover, on principle. 'We got away after three or four days. They took us at dawn to Vnukovo airport and shoved us into the plane without ceremony.'[67] The meeting could hardly have been called a dialogue. Stalin had behaved as if his visitors were party leaders from one of his own republics. Sanctions followed quickly. The Soviet military advisers were recalled from Yugoslavia and a sharp letter, signed by Stalin and Molotov, was sent to the leaders in Belgrade. Tito replied with a measured response, rejecting the charges of unfriendly actions and Trotskyism, and adding: 'However much we all love the USSR as the land of socialism, none of us can love any less our own countries which are also building socialism.'

Stalin's reply was sent in May in the form of a twenty-five-page letter. Instead of a cool, collected response, which might have been expected, given Stalin's usual style, Yepishev recalled that Stalin's reaction was both crude and impulsive and that he gave it without pausing to analyse the reality of the situation. Beria's people had concocted a host of 'facts' which demonstrated the 'deviation' and 'treachery' of Tito and the entire Yugoslav leadership. Stalin did not yet realize that he had suffered his first post-war defeat.

He decided to bring Cominform into the conflict. Two notes were sent from

Moscow to Belgrade, inviting the Yugoslavs to send a delegation to a Cominform meeting in Bucharest. The Yugoslavs replied with a firm but polite refusal on the grounds that this represented interference in their internal affairs. They expressed the desire, however, to normalize relations. Stalin decided to hold the meeting without the 'accused', but the split was already a fait accompli. Earlier, on 15 June 1948, Stalin had read Zhdanov's report for the Bucharest meeting, entitled 'On the Position of the Communist Party of Yugoslavia', a text already seen by Malenkov and Suslov. All three of them were sent by Stalin to Bucharest with a text bearing corrections in Stalin's own hand. Zhdanov's speech included such statements as:

Tito, Kardelj, Djilas and Ranković are entirely to blame for the present situation. They get their methods from the arsenal of Trotskyism. Their policy in town and country is wrong. Such a shameful, purely Turkish-style terrorist régime is intolerable in a Communist party ... Such a régime must be got rid of. The Communist Party of Yugoslavia will have the honour of carrying out this honourable task.[68]

Stalin felt confident that, as Khrushchev put it at the Twentieth Congress, he need only wag his little finger and Tito would be no more. His confidence, moreover, was reinforced by everything Zhdanov wrote in his reports from Bucharest. The other leaders – Chervenkov, Togliatti, Duclos, Rakosi, Gheorghiu-Dej – had 'all without exception taken up an irreconcilable position with regard to the Yugoslavs'.[69] Parading itself as the champion of proletarian internationalism, a great power was exerting its muscle in order to intimidate a smaller neighbour and thus to assuage the ruffled feelings of the enraged dictator. Stalin did not hesitate to renounce the treaty of friendship, recall the Soviet ambassador and cut economic ties. The conflict culminated in November 1949 in Budapest with the Cominform resolution entitled 'The Yugoslav Communist Party is in the Power of Murderers and Spies'. Suslov had worked on the text of the resolution and it contained every imaginable charge. The Yugoslav leaders were compared to the Nazis and were accused among other things of spying, making an alliance with imperialism and fostering kulak regeneration.

The few years left to Stalin after the war were as turbulent as any in his life after the October Revolution, while his concerns now stretched well beyond Soviet borders. In the socialist countries, described by Zhdanov as now forming a 'camp', the problems mounted. Instead of leaving each country to develop socialism in its own way and in accordance with its own national traditions, historical experience and current situation, Stalin insisted they adopt the same model, the same bureaucratic and dogmatic patterns in their political structures, as the Soviet Union, doing no small damage to the general cause in the process.

There are grounds for thinking that before his death he was having doubts about the 'united centre'. The defeat he had suffered at the hands of the

Yugoslavs made him look again at his dogmatic methods. This much is demonstrated by his declining interest in Cominform. Following the Yugoslav débâcle, Cominform met only once or twice and then quietly and unnoticed ceased to exist. The attempt to transplant command methods in the international Communist movement had manifestly failed.

Only two events could Stalin regard as brightening those gloomy years, namely, the creation of the Chinese People's Republic and the growth of a powerful international peace movement. The late 1940s and early 1950s were an anxious period, and it seemed at times as if the world leaders had lost their common sense. Even the Pope declared that any Catholic who supported the Communists would be excommunicated. The witch-hunt was widespread. It was hard to believe that in only a matter of two or three years after their great victory, the Allies would be facing another war, this time against each other. The Soviet perception was that America could not accept the rise of another colossus, and even that plans were being made in the Pentagon for the nuclear bombardment of the USSR. In these circumstances, Stalin pursued a cautious policy, developing his military might, while avoiding any provocation of his former ally. While he did not go as far as Mao in declaring that nuclear force was a 'paper tiger', he repeatedly made it plain that the decisive rôle in a future war would be played by the masses.

There was, it is true, a brief moment when it seemed possible that the threat might recede. On 1 February 1949 the European chief of International News Service, Kingsbury Smith, sent the following cable to Stalin from Paris: 'White House official representative Charles Ross today announced that President Truman would be happy to have the opportunity to meet with you in Washington. Would you, Your Excellency, be prepared to go to Washington for this purpose? If not, where would you be willing to meet with the President?' Next day, Stalin replied:

> I am grateful to President Truman for his invitation to Washington. A trip to Washington has long been my desire, which I mentioned to President Roosevelt in Yalta and to President Truman in Potsdam. Unfortunately, I am at present unable to fulfil my desire to travel any significant distance, especially by ship or air, as the physicians strictly forbid it.[70]

Instead of Washington, Stalin suggested the meeting take place in Moscow, Leningrad, Kaliningrad, Odessa, Yalta, Poland or Czechoslovakia, knowing that Truman would refuse. There was nothing for them to discuss. Truman believed that America had more chance of making the USSR say what he wanted to hear, but it seems he, too, came to the conclusion that such hopes were groundless. Stalin had no thought of giving in to the other's dictates.

Then, suddenly, in a world grown used to the stamp of soldiers' boots and the rattling of sabres, the first feeble voices were heard to call for reason. In 1948 pacifists from both 'camps' gathered in the Polish city of Wroclaw, to be followed by the All-World Peace Congress in Paris.

At first Stalin regarded this 'intellectual trend' with typical scepticism, but gradually it dawned on him that it was rife with possibilities. Given America's nuclear advantage and the corresponding disadvantage of the socialist camp, it was essential to make maximum use of world public opinion against those who sought to resolve the fundamental confrontation by nuclear means. Official Soviet propaganda therefore supported the idea of peaceful coexistence, and Stalin, together with Molotov, personally selected the Soviet representatives to the World Peace Congress when it opened in the Paris Salle Pleyel in April 1949.

In the dangerous confrontation between the two worlds, Stalin received enormous support in the form of the Chinese revolution, which fundamentally altered the correlation of forces. The twenty-year struggle of the Chinese people for their social and national liberation culminated in the triumphant proclamation of the Chinese People's Republic on 1 October 1949.

Stalin had watched events in China closely. When he heard that the new US ambassador to Peking had declared complete support for Chiang Kai-shek, he realized that, if the US gained predominant influence in China, the position for the USSR would become more difficult. At first, he did not understand precisely the nature of the conflict between Mao Tse-tung and Chiang Kai-shek, and he even once declared that a rising of millions of starving peasants had nothing in common with a socialist or democratic movement. When he heard in October 1945 that Chiang and Mao were holding talks in Chunking on China's internal affairs, he felt the Chinese Communists were behaving more realistically and progressively.[71]

In his time Stalin wrote a good deal about China, and his collected works contain a dozen or so pieces about the Chinese revolution, some of them politically very primitive. For instance, he wrote that 'the revolutionizing of the East will give a decisive push to sharpening the revolutionary crisis in the West. Attacked from both sides, as well as in the rear and the front, imperialism will be forced to see that it is doomed to perish.'[72] Characteristically, he frequently adopted a didactic tone when writing towards the Chinese: 'The Communists of China must pay attention to work in the army, they really must study military matters, they must take part in the future revolutionary régime in China ...'[73]

It is noteworthy that Stalin's position on the Chinese question had been vigorously attacked by Trotsky. In the draft of his speech to the Eighth Plenum of the Comintern Executive Committee in May 1927, Trotsky had written: 'Stalin's theses can survive only so long as the party is deprived of the opportunity to hear them criticized, but the party press under Bukharin, instead of publishing genuine views, ascribes its own thinking to us ... Stalin's theses, which are false to the core, are pronounced virtually inviolable.'[74] Trotsky himself was not right about everything, but he had spotted the cracks in Stalin's understanding of Eastern affairs, while the other Bolsheviks had tried to paper them over with revolutionary rhetoric of 'universal' significance.

After the war, Stalin gave a great deal of assistance to the Chinese revolution. Arms and equipment of all kinds were delivered to the People's Liberation Army, and by the second half of 1947 the winds of victory were filling its sails and Chiang was forced to flee with his remnant to Taiwan. Given persistent US hostility, Mao was bound to opt for friendship with the Soviet Union, and after the Chinese revolution relations developed rapidly in numerous spheres, culminating in Mao's invitation to Moscow to join in the celebration of Stalin's seventieth birthday.

Stalin awaited the Chinese leader's arrival with no small measure of uncertainty. Despite having written about China, he knew nothing about China's history or culture and had little notion of the Chinese national psychology or indeed of Mao himself. He met Mao several times after the Chinese leader's arrival in Moscow on 16 December 1949. Since most of their conversations were not recorded, the memoirs of the Soviet Sinologist N. T. Fedorenko, who served as interpreter, and of Andrei Gromyko, who was present, are of particular value.[75]

The situation must also have been somewhat unusual for Mao, who had never been outside China, had not participated in the work of Comintern and whose links with other Communist parties were minimal. The two men sitting opposite each other at the conference table also thought differently, had different scales of values, represented different civilizations. Even their Marxism gave them little in common, since Mao was fond of mixing his with Confucianism, while Stalin generally confined himself to quoting his own works. They were, however, both pragmatists.

While Stalin watched his guest with curiosity and carefully concealed mistrust, Mao would suddenly shift from talking about current problems and regale his host with parables from the mysterious and magical world of Chinese folklore. He told Stalin the tale of Yui-gun who moved the mountains. In ancient times, he said, there lived in the north of China an old man of the mountains by the name of Yui-gun, or 'foolish old man'. The road from his house to the south was blocked by two high mountains and Yui-gun decided to remove them with the help of his sons and using hoes. Another old man, by the name of Dzhi-sou, meaning 'wise old man', saw them and, laughing, told them, 'That's foolish, how do you think you're going to dig up two such high mountains?' Yui-gun replied, 'I will die but my children will remain, they will die and my grandchildren will remain, and so the generations will follow each other in an endless succession. These mountains are indeed high, but they will not grow any higher; they will be less by whatever amount we dig away, so why should we not be able to remove them altogether?' And Yui-gun worked every day digging away at the mountains. This moved God who sent his saints to earth and they carried away the mountains.[76]

The story was intended to illustrate the fact that China was weighed down by the twin mountains of imperialism and feudalism, which the Communist Party of China had undertaken to remove, God being represented by the

Chinese people who had been moved to help. Stalin and Mao agreed that more must be done than merely remove these mountains. According to Fedorenko, the conversations were long and unhurried, the two leaders taking leisurely mouthfuls of the excellent food, sipping the dry wine and chatting about international, economic, ideological and military affairs. In the course of these evening meals they also discussed the treaty of friendship, union and mutual assistance that was being drawn up. According to Gromyko, however, the two leaders managed only a sporadic exchange and his impression was that they had little to say to each other.

Stalin had not trusted Mao for a long time, influenced no doubt by reports that Mao was hostile to Chinese Communists who had been trained by Moscow, and also by the fact that Mao had done nothing when Moscow and Stalingrad were under threat during the war. Gradually, however, Stalin's attitude to the Chinese altered, as Peking became more plainly anti-American. The Korean War undoubtedly strengthened Stalin's confidence in Mao, thus setting Sino-Soviet relations on a positive footing as a whole. No doubt Stalin's successors, and Mao himself, could have done a great deal more to preserve the good relations of the 1950s, and one reason for the deterioration was certainly Mao's negative response to Khrushchev's denunciation of Stalin in 1956.

The Cold War was felt not only in the West but in the East, also. The deployment of American and Soviet troops in Korea soon after the war predetermined the creation of different political structures in the two parts of the peninsula, north and south. After elections in South Korea on 10 May 1948, legislative and executive bodies were created, and on 25 August of the same year elections took place in North Korea. Two states came into being, thus artificially dividing the Korean nation in two. Soviet troops withdrew from the North to be followed by the withdrawal of US troops from the South. Each side believed that in each case the government was supported by a majority of the population. Unfortunately, it seems clear that the conflict arose because each side wanted to extend its authority over the entire peninsula.

From indirect sources, I have been able to establish that Stalin took an extremely cautious view of events in Korea and from the outset made every attempt to avoid direct confrontation between the USSR and the USA. Mao was more decisive. During their meetings from November 1949 to February 1950, they frequently discussed Korea. Stalin's view was that the Americans had departed so far from the Potsdam agreement over Korea that it would be difficult to create a unitary state painlessly. He was as sceptical of the American idea of trusteeship over Korea as he was of the idea of 'free' elections. After all, there was a significantly bigger population in the South, where the American forces were based. The 38th parallel had been fixed without any political basis, but merely as a line of demarcation between Soviet and American troops.

Once thirty Chinese divisions were on the move, however, the situation on the peninsula changed markedly. Chinese and North Korean forces not only drove US troops out of the territory north of the 38th parallel, but also succeeded in advancing 100 kilometres further south. As US morale sank, Stalin realized that the most dangerous moment had arrived, that is, when the Americans might resort to the extreme measure of nuclear attack. US General MacArthur was calling for the bombing of Manchuria and Truman hinted that the use of nuclear force was not excluded. The threat of a Third World War never seemed closer, but neither Stalin nor Mao wanted to confront the Americans with the possibility of defeat. Talks began against a background of constant battle. The Americans ruled in the air, while the Chinese had control on the ground. Stalin acknowledged that the only way out of the stalemate was by some form of compromise. Agreement was reached, however, only in July 1953, six months after his death.

Whether Stalin absorbed the lessons of the Korean War is hard to say. One thing is certain, however, and that is that in the modern world, conflict is almost bound to end in stalemate. This was shown in Korea, in Vietnam and in Afghanistan. The Korean War demonstrated that America was not omnipotent and it also led Stalin, after the 'cold shower' the Yugoslavs had given him, to revert to his customary cautiousness.

11

THE RELICS OF STALINISM

'Caesar did not feel like celebrating his
triumph over the miseries of his country.'
– Plutarch

CHAPTER 55

A Historical Anomaly

Stalin frequently thought of having his *Short Biography* replaced by a monumental study. A number of indications suggest this, including his orders for the archives to be 'surveyed', his occasional remarks to Zhdanov and Poskrebyshev, his frequent requests to G. F. Alexandrov, M. B. Mitin and P. N. Pospelov, the compilers of his official biographies, for enlightenment on matters of party historiography and the 'rôle of Lenin's pupils'. He was often reminded now of the past, returning more and more to the turn of the century, to the post-October struggle, to the names of the people whose lives he had destroyed. Sometimes he was reminded of the past by relatives of his former comrades. On occasion, after making a routine report, Beria would show him a list of personal letters from the relatives of executed or exiled 'enemies of the people'. Stalin as a rule would scan the list and hand it back without a word. Beria would give his master an understanding glance, gather up his papers and leave.

Sometimes he would ask Beria for information about a particular petitioner. For instance, there was a letter from one Jadwiga Iosifovna, a relative of Felix Dzerzhinsky, the founder of the Cheka, who was enquiring about her mother, Jadwiga Genrikhovna Dzerzhinskaya, who had been sentenced by the Special Court and had been languishing for years in the camps of Karaganda. The daughter wrote that her mother was 'very ill, with tuberculosis, scurvy and brucellosis. She is in a very bad way.'[1] A similar case was that of Radek's daughter, Sofia, who wrote to Stalin that a year after her father had been sentenced on 30 January 1937, she and her mother were exiled to Astrakhan for five years. 'In Astrakhan my mother was re-arrested and given eight years in the Temnikov camps [in the North] where she died.' In November 1941 Sofia was exiled from Astrakhan to Kazakhstan. Her exile ended in June 1942. She went on: 'I'm also a human being; if I'm the daughter of an enemy of the people, does it mean I'm also an enemy? I was seventeen when my father was sentenced in 1937 and since then I have been branded an enemy. I have an education but there is nothing I can put my knowledge to in Chelkar. I still have no internal passport. The Chelkar NKVD chief, Comrade Ivanov, doesn't answer my enquiries. Help me atone for my father's guilt!'[2] Stalin left it to Beria to deal with such matters as he saw fit.

In less than three decades he had raised the country to the status of a great power, and yet so many people were still discontented. The Interior Minister had reported in April 1949 that there were 180,000 inmates in special camps and he asked for permission to increase the capacity of such camps by 70,000 to a quarter of a million.[3] These were special category prisoners, and yet Beria kept on telling him that it was not possible to satisfy all the demands from the ministries for labour from the special camps.

How did Marxist-Leninist ideology fit into this picture? However remote they may have been from twentieth-century concerns, many of their dogmas were taken on trust from the very outset by the Soviet régime. In the 1920s it was often said 'the working class cannot make mistakes', or 'the party cannot make mistakes', but both did.

Many such mistakes were pointed out early on. In November 1917, in his paper *Novaya Zhizn* (New Life), Gorky published an article entitled 'For the Attention of the Workers', in which he wrote:

Having forced the proletariat to agree to the destruction of freedom of the press, Lenin and his henchmen have made it legal for the enemies of democracy to shut the mouths of others, threatening to inflict starvation and pogroms on anyone who does not agree with Lenin's and Trotsky's despotism; these 'leaders' are justifying a despotism of authority of the kind all the best elements of the country have fought against so bitterly for so long.[4]

Regrettably, such warnings against 'the despotism of authority' were not heeded, then or later. Stalin contributed nothing to the theory of Marxism. He relied uncritically on Marxist ideas, many of them half a century out of date, and few people raised objections of principle. Supported by the party and sticking to the letter of the doctrine, Stalin crushed anyone who dared to depart from it. While claiming to be 'confirming' socialism, he turned the precepts of Marx, Engels and Lenin into dogma and then used that dogma to enhance his own position as autocrat. We may therefore speak of Stalinism as having grown in the soil of Marxism, and been nourished by twisting its arguments, but it does not follow that Marxism was responsible for Stalinism. As an intellectual system of philosophical, economic and political views of society, nature and thought, Marxism cannot be blamed for the way it has been interpreted. Marxism is neither a book of kitchen recipes nor a plan of action, though that is precisely how Stalin understood it. His rigid, mechanistic, primitive rendering of Marxism, already plainly in evidence in the late 1920s, was a harbinger of the misfortunes to come, misfortunes that he would emblazon on the banner of Marxism as great victories of socialism.

The tendency to canonize everything the early Marxist thinkers had said, however, and to make it a basis for Soviet propaganda, had been well established long before the rise of Stalin. Stalin inherited and developed this tradition. While we have no intention of justifying Stalin and Stalinism, much has appeared in print recently that attempts to tie all the deformations, the mistakes and crimes to one man only. Had this been the case, we would long have been free of Stalinism.

Stalinism was one way – one extremely negative way – of realizing the ideas contained in Marxist doctrine. The age-old desire to achieve freedom, happiness, equality and justice was expressed in Marxism in a very appealing manner. But well before the revolution, Lenin attacked other Marxists who interpreted the doctrine in their own way as heretics and revisionists, with the result that any 'unauthorized' view became stigmatized as 'hostile'. Russian Marxism thus acquired the character of a political doctrine that sought not to adapt itself to changing conditions, but to adapt conditions to fit its postulates. Much too late in the day, Lenin tried to put the party into reverse, to make the Bolsheviks of the early 1920s take a practical view of the situation that had arisen in the overwhelmingly peasant country they were ruling. They were not up to the task and the dogmatic tendency was left to flourish.

Stalinism exploited to the full the Russian revolutionaries' love of radicalism, their readiness to sacrifice everything – history, culture and human beings – in the name of an idea. The deification of an ossified ideal turned into indifference towards the needs of real people in real time. Russian radicalism donned the mantle of revolutionary romanticism and rejected bourgeois notions of happiness along with bourgeois culture. Stalin above all proclaimed the view that everything was permitted for the sake of the idea. No one ever objected that this was a profoundly anti-human idea in itself and a social crime against the people. The main thing was to 'overtake', 'overthrow', 'destroy', 'crush', 'break', 'unmask' and 'nail down'. This revolutionary radicalism, which nourished Stalin, manifestly created a new pseudo-culture in which his ideas came to occupy pride of place.

There is another aspect of the intellectual conflict, both preceding and following the October Revolution, that should not be overlooked. Lenin attacked the Mensheviks as politically impotent, but their criticism throws light on the phenomenon of Stalinism, and they persistently spoke up against the dogmatic Bolshevism that was dehumanizing and undermining Marxism from within.

The Mensheviks in exile – Martov, Abramovich, Dan, Nicolaevsky, Dallin, Schwartz – tried for a long time to conduct a battle on two fronts; that is, they defended the ideals of the revolution in Russia, while simultaneously criticizing its degeneration. Up to 1965 in New York they still had their newspaper, *Sotsialisticheskii Vestnik* ('Socialist Messenger'), on which the most influential leaders were Fedor Dan, who leaned more and more towards the USSR and who died in 1947, and the more staunchly anti-Soviet Rafail Abramovich who died in 1963.

After Lenin died the Mensheviks directed their fire against the anti-democratic methods of Stalin, pointing out, among other things, his departures from Lenin's positions. For instance, while welcoming the New Economic Policy in 1921, some Mensheviks also advocated a new line in politics that would prevent the emergence of a Bonapartist trend in the party.[5] They observed that a narrow group of people exercized power in the name of the Bolshevik Party, while the growing rôle of one man at its head threatened degeneration. According to Abramovich, only a state that allowed pluralism could be the guarantor of democracy. The Mensheviks foresaw two negative possibilities in the development of the USSR, either counter-revolution or false revolution, and they correctly perceived that Stalin opted for the second alternative. The essence of Stalinism, they asserted, lay in his rejection of the traditions of social democracy.

After the revolution, however, the Mensheviks were not a united political or ideological force. Their influence fell steadily. In due course, Dan split with the majority, founded his own journal, *Novyi Mir* ('New World') in 1939, and during the war propagated the idea that, after the defeat of Fascism, the Soviet Union would return to genuine socialism. In his major work, *The Origins of Bolshevism*, written shortly before he died, he asserted that Stalin had failed to combine socialism and democracy, but he also claimed that socialism did not begin and end with Stalin, and that socialism was capable of bringing freedom to the people.[6]

The countless 'oppositions', 'fractions' and 'deviations' that erupted after the October Revolution, however inconsistent some of their ideas, at least had the merit that they offered alternatives, and undoubtedly it was the abolition of this revolutionary pluralism that deprived the society of the possibility of historic renewal. Such Menshevik Internationalists as Martov, Ermansky and Astrov were not enemies of the revolution, and the same is true of the Left Socialist Revolutionaries who formed their party in late 1917. It was precisely in the denial of any other point of view that the seeds of future dogmatism and monolithic rule were to be found. Numerous ideas on democracy, the New Economic Policy, the peasantry, trade, state and party structures were not applied because the party majority stuck to what was laid down as the orthodox line. Views of reality were all forced into a black and white dichotomy. And yet at the beginning there was revolutionary pluralism, as when the Bolsheviks and Left SRs agreed to form a coalition in December 1917.

True, there was insufficient socialist pluralism in practical policy, and what there was was soon destroyed without mercy. Stalin was the right man for this job but, as we have seen, there was no real struggle to resist or to shift the political process in a different direction. Bukharin voiced a number of appealing ideas, though he was forced later to recant. This is not, however, to suggest that Stalin and Stalinism were somehow 'pre-determined' to emerge.

On the contrary, what is here suggested is that Stalinism emerged in conditions when ideas, formed by Marx in the middle of the nineteenth century in the absence of other revolutionary alternatives, were being made into dogmas and absolutes. The abolition of socialist pluralism launched the monopoly on both social truth and political power. Making allies and constructive critics into enemies led to the replacement of the revolutionary democracy by totalitarian bureaucracy.

While the party was not in power this approach threatened no great harm, but once it became the ruling party under Lenin, the application of dogma had its destructive effect. Stalin went further by perverting socialist principles, by promoting a one-dimensional view of the world, and by sanctioning the use of the most radical means to achieve defined aims which themselves became deformed in the process.

The consolidation of Stalinism as a phenomenon went through several stages. The first was the 'deafness' of Lenin's comrades to his 'Testament'. It was probably then that Stalin first sensed that the Olympus of power was not beyond his reach. The second stage was the period 1925 to 1929, when the stabilization of the capitalist world coincided with the emergence of the bureaucratic structure in the USSR and the expulsion of Trotsky. A further level was collectivization and the end of the moderate line in the Central Committee. It was at this stage that Stalinism, with the use of mass coercion, finally gained the upper hand over alternative paths of development. At the next stage, leading to the Seventeenth Congress, Stalin was preparing for his 'coronation' as the sole leader. Thereafter Stalinism merely hardened in its casing of orthodoxy.

Stalinism was not merely a mental or social disease, it was the negation of human values. It became an earthly religion of sorts, demanding that the people have faith in it alone. Starting in the early 1930s, it is impossible to find any trace of public disagreement with the Stalinist dogmas, and as early as 1927 the party adopted the Code of Laws in which the first chapter contained the notorious Article 58* and its eighteen 'amendments'.[7] No one would question the idea that a state must defend its interests, but when an unofficial view is defined as 'anti-Soviet propaganda or agitation' and is punished in the most severe manner, then loyalty to the ideology of Stalinism in word and deed became the only way to adapt and survive, and even that did not always help, if the axe was already poised.

A vast chasm opened up between genuine social activity and its imitation. Henceforth, activity became wholly organized: what toasts were to be proposed at Komsomol or trade-union meetings, what 'initiatives' were to be taken, what election speech to make and to what audience, whose portraits and how many were to be paraded in demonstrations, how many 'volunteers' should

---

* A law against spreading anti-Soviet propaganda that was widely interpreted to include any spoken, written or even hinted criticism of the system.

be sent to local sites for 'shock work', to whom reports should be sent and on what – everything was fixed and decided from above. People gradually got used to someone else doing all their thinking for them. They were required only 'to approve', 'to applaud', 'to support'.

In addition to every party, state or organizational decision having to be approved by him, Stalin was even approached to invent slogans for writers. On 2 January 1936, A. S. Shcherbakov, then first secretary of the Moscow Party Committee and secretary of the Writers' Union, wrote to Stalin:

> In the interests of the cause I must disturb you by asking for help and advice. Quite good new works have been written by Korneichuk, Svetlov, Levin, Yanovsky, Leonov, Avdeyenko. Some of the 'silent' old masters, such as Faiko, Tikhonov, Babel and Olesha have also begun to say something. New names have appeared: Orlov, Kron, Tvardovsky. On the whole, however, the lag in literature has not been liquidated. Criticism doesn't help. One writer (Vinogradov) was talking about suicide after being crudely attacked. And the critic in question (Yermilov) said in reply: 'If people like that poison themselves, no one will be sorry.' That's the position in literature. What it needs right now is a militant, concrete slogan to mobilize the writers. Help us, Comrade Stalin, to find such a slogan.[8]

Having from the mid-1930s shifted his main attention away from the Central Committee to the NKVD and the army, when the war was over Stalin was especially lavish with the medals and orders he bestowed on the senior officers of these services. Beria, who was made a Marshal of the Soviet Union in 1945, received many other high military honours, and on 7 July 1945 Stalin approved Beria's application to the Council of Ministers to promote seven police and security chiefs to the rank of colonel general: V. S. Abakumov, S. N. Kruglov, I. A. Serov, B. Z. Kobulov, V. V. Chernyshev, S. A. Goglidze and K. A. Pavlov.[9] Active generals at the front never received such signs of 'mass' love from the chairman of the defence committee.

It was an unwritten law of the dictatorship that tension must be maintained at all times among the top officials of the apparatus. Stalin believed that authority must inspire not only respect, but also fear, and he introduced unofficial rules of conduct even into the circle of his closest comrades-in-arms. For instance, they knew they must never assemble in groups of two, three or more without his permission, whether at home, at their villas or in their offices. The only exceptions to this rule were Beria and Malenkov, who often drove out together to Stalin's villa in the same car. If the others met each other at all, it was at Stalin's house and at his invitation.

As a system of government Stalinism relied mainly on reports received from organizations, chiefly the police and security agencies. After the war, for instance, Stalin became interested in the Academy of Sciences. Beria reported that its president was said to be frequently ill, that his research was not of a high standard and that the work of other academicians also merited looking into. Stalin requested information and brief descriptions of other scientists and the files were soon on his desk. Needless to say, they were not compiled in the Academy administration or party committee, but in an office of State Security. One such document included the following notes:

Academician Vavilov, S. I. – physicist, is at the peak of his ability. Brother of N. I. Vavilov, the geneticist who was arrested in 1940 for sabotage in agriculture, sentenced to fifteen years and died in Saratov prison.

Academician Lysenko, T. D. – non-party, director of genetics institute. President of Academy of Agricultural Science, twice Stalin Prize winner. Academician Lysenko does not enjoy respect, including that of the President [of the Academy], Komarov. Everyone blames him for N. I. Vavilov's arrest.[10]

Stalinism took the primacy of the state over society to absurd limits. It was a system that depended on a vast and powerful bureaucracy at all levels and in all spheres of activity, and within this environment of political absolutism, the leader's decisions were increasingly divorced from economic reality. Stalinism was above all the separation of thought and action, theory and practice, the splitting of the mind, making it possible for people to say one thing and do another. The deepest corruption of the Stalinist system was in removing man as such from the centre of society's goals, and in replacing him with the state as a machine which magnified one man only. Man was replaced by the faceless apparatus, a fact observed by, among others, the former Communist Victor Serge, who wrote in 1937 that 'in the Stalinist state man counts for nothing.'[11]

CHAPTER 56

Mummified Dogmas

Dogmatism was one of the most important pillars of Stalinism. It was an attribute that was capable of gradually leading the study of society, and in due course society itself, into an intellectual and psychological blind alley. A past master of dogmatic thinking, Stalin knew how to deaden Marxist propositions and mummify them into deformed clichés.

Typical of the tyrant, Stalin chose eclectically which of Marx's propositions were to be mummified; he himself determined what could and what could not be published of the works of the founders of Marxism. The archives contain many requests for permission to publish this letter of Lenin or that fragment of a manuscript by Marx or Engels. In June 1939, for instance, M. B. Mitin, the director of the Marx-Engels-Lenin Institute, asked for Stalin's permission to publish two letters from Lenin to Inessa Armand in the next issue of *Bolshevik*. These letters expressed Lenin's hostile reponse to the formation of the Provisional Government in Petrograd, following the overthrow of the tsar in 1917. Stalin wrote 'No objection'. But the Institute did not always obtain permission so easily. In July 1940, Zhdanov, Mitin and Pospelov were doubtful about an article by Engels, 'On the Foreign Policy of Russian Tsarism', and submitted it for Stalin's opinion. Stalin read the piece and made the following marginal notes: 'aggressive vileness is not a monopoly of the Russian tsars', 'he exaggerates the rôle of foreign policy in Russia', 'in attacking tsarist foreign policy, [Engels] resolved to deprive it of any trust in the eyes of European public opinion'. He concluded: 'Considering all this, is it worth publishing Engels's article in our militant organ, *Bolshevik*, whether as a leading article in all respects, or as a profoundly instructive article, for to publish it in *Bolshevik* would mean giving it unspoken recommendation. I think it is not worth it.'[12]

The true encyclopedia of dogmatism, the miscellany of mummies, half-truths and anti-truths, was the notorious *History of the Party. Short Course*, which came out in more than three hundred editions and some 43 million copies, and became as much required reading for adult Soviet citizens as the Koran is for observant Muslims. A group of historians, including Knorin (who was soon arrested), Pospelov and Yaroslavsky undertook to write the *Short Course* in accordance with a Politburo instruction of 16 April 1937. The book was based on Stalin's own breakdown of party history into periods and his definition of its central feature as 'the Bolshevik struggle against anti-Bolshevik factions'.[13] The chapters were regularly sent to Stalin, as were several mock-ups of the book. He twisted virtually every chapter to conform with his basic notion of the history of the party as an internal struggle. At its head stood the true comrade-in-arms and heir of Lenin's cause, Stalin. Judging from the quantity and nature of his marginal comments, Stalin must have devoted a great deal of time to his 'history', knowing that it would become an important mechanism for ensuring his enduring influence over the minds of the millions.

Similar ideological fodder, as dogmatic and anti-historical as the *Short Course*, led to spiritual pauperization and intellectual primitivism. Stalin was preparing the soil for rearing a broad stratum of people who thought in elementary terms, people who would provide a constant supply of careerists, informers, time-servers and mindless functionaries for his system. It was precisely this stratum that staffed the bureaucratic apparatus, the punitive organs and offices at all levels. Malenkov's archives show that thousands and thousands of people, elected automatically at the plenums, passed through his hands for work in the party, in the organs of the Interior Ministry and the administration of other ministries. The criteria for intellectual and theoretical maturity were an absence of compromising comment from the security organs and knowledge of Stalin's 'reference book'. Occasionally candidates for jobs were summoned to Moscow to be interviewed by Malenkov, who would recline in his large armchair and puff out his cheeks pompously, as he fired off such posers as, 'Which deviation is the most dangerous?' or 'When and where did Comrade Stalin say, "The cadres determine everything"?'

The intellectual energy in the *Short Course* was sufficient for more than a decade. Before the war it dominated the public mind not only because the propagandists made good use of it, but also because millions of people, as we have already said, seemed to find in it a predigested and accessible outline of an entire epoch. Most people were not aware that the picture it painted was distorted beyond real recognition. The whole system of political education instilled dogmatic thinking throughout society. The most ardent exponent of the Stalinist line in this sphere was Zhdanov.

Stalin had taken note of Zhdanov very early on. The young party secretary of Nizhni Novgorod province (renamed Gorky in 1932) was the strapping type of Communist organizer becoming typical of the time. A candidate member of the Central Committee in 1925, in 1929, at the age of thirty-three, he was invited by Stalin to the Kremlin, where he made the right impression. Stalin questioned him about the situation in Nizhni, the mood of the population there and how they had reacted to the expulsion of Trotsky from the party.

At the next opportunity, which turned out to be a party conference in the Sormovo district of his province, Zhdanov made a speech in which he called on members to remain on guard against the continuing danger of Trotskyists who still lurked in the party.[14] At the Sixteenth Party Congress, which took place the following year, he was made a full member of the Central Committee and thereafter his career was meteoric. He was put in charge of the Leningrad party organization after the murder of Kirov and simultaneously made a Central Committee secretary. In February 1935 he became a candidate member and in 1939 a full member of the Politburo. He was on close personal terms with Stalin and they even became related when his son, Yuri, married Stalin's daughter, Svetlana, though the marriage did not last. Stalin was also pleased with Zhdanov's performance as a member of the Leningrad war council, and in 1944 made him a colonel general, a rank attained by very few in the political branch at that time.

At the end of the war, Stalin as it were tested Zhdanov on the diplomatic front when he deputed him to negotiate a peace treaty with the Finns. On 18 January 1945, Zhdanov informed Stalin and Molotov by 'super-express' telegram that he had that day had a one-to-one conversation with Field Marshal Mannerheim lasting two hours:

Mannerheim said that, after many years of hostility, the time has come for a radical change in relations between our two states. Defence lines against the USSR are useless, he said, if there are not good relations. He said he had not wanted war in 1939, nor in 1941–44, and had not expected a satisfactory outcome even before it had begun. He expressed agreement for collaboration over coastal defences, but would defend the interior of the country himself. He asked if there were standard treaties and I replied that the one with Czechoslovakia might be taken as one such. I await instructions.[15]

It was not Stalin, but Molotov who replied rather tersely:

You have gone too far. A pact with Mannerheim of the sort we have with Czechoslovakia is music of the future. We have to re-establish diplomatic relations first. Don't frighten Mannerheim with radical proposals. Just clarify his position.

Next day Zhdanov reported again to Stalin that he had seen Mannerheim:

I told him a pact of the sort we have with Czechoslovakia was 'music of the future', to follow the re-establishment of diplomatic relations. Mannerheim said he understood: Finland was under surveillance as a country and could not have relations of a different kind with the USSR as yet. He was obviously disappointed.[16]

As was his custom, Stalin had tested Zhdanov and his own judgement of people. Sometimes he went on testing his aides for a long time, sometimes all their lives, but he never forgave a major error. Zhdanov always justified Stalin's confidence in him, although it is also true that, had he not died suddenly in 1948 at the age of fifty-two, he too might well have been swallowed up in the Leningrad massacre that he himself unleashed. His son, Yuri, claims that Stalin was cooling towards his father, just as he was cooling towards Voznesensky, Kuznetsov and later on towards Molotov as well. Stalin's attitude towards Zhdanov, however, can only be judged by circumstantial evidence.

During his time in the Central Committee, Zhdanov showed himself to be a harsh and pitiless custodian of ideology and culture. Dogmatism was inculcated not merely by means of deifying the 'creative genius of the leader', but also by installing an entire system of prohibitions in the mind: what may not be shown on the cinema screen, what theatre producers must not stage, what writers should or should not write, musicians play and philosophers and historians debate. The taboos were countless. Cultural life after the war became numb again, before being given the chance to thaw out after the nightmare of 1937–38.

In these conditions, the social sciences could only vegetate. The primitive commentaries of the day both killed the soul of scholarship and severely limited the sphere of its influence. As we have seen, since the late 1930s, it was possible only to comment on what Stalin had said. From fledgling social scientists to full academicians, everyone's 'research' was related to the same theme: the rôle of I. V. Stalin in the development of economics; the significance of I. V. Stalin's *Economic Problems of Socialism in the USSR* for the development of philosophy; I. V. Stalin on the theory of state and law; I. V. Stalin's decisive contribution to the development of military science. A cursory survey of libraries has revealed over five hundred books and articles on these and analogous themes written between 1945 and 1953. Scientific thought was in the grip of leaden, primitive dogmas, and all real talent and creative endeavour atrophied.

The natural and technical sciences suffered no less. The development of genetics lagged by decades and cybernetics was banned, because new ideas and new fields of learning were approached from crudely, if not utterly ignorant standpoints. The hunt for 'cosmopolitans', for the most part a code word for Jews (see below), condemned the sciences to still greater isolation from the international world of learning. Articles like 'Cosmopolitanism in the Service of Imperialist Reaction', published in the government newspaper, *Izvestiya*, on 18 April 1950, killed off any desire Soviet scientists may have had to make contact with foreign research establishments. Mention of a Soviet scientist in a foreign scientific journal, or an invitation to an international congress, could be disastrous.

Attempts to transfer Stalin's formulations mechanically to the development of biology was tantamount to killing off Soviet efforts in that field, and had it continued for another five years or so, the science as a whole would have gone right off the rails. In these circumstances, it was the likes of T. D. Lysenko who seized on Stalin's dictum, 'We need immediate practical results in science', and who therefore floated to the top. As far as Stalin was concerned, the sciences were so much alchemy, a magical and mysterious world somehow connected with the achievement of the new. It seemed to him that the main thing about science was how to organize it. He believed scientific work could even be done in the Gulag, if properly organized, and indeed results showed him to be not altogether wrong. Those he regarded as dangerous and who would not run on his dogmatic rails were either destroyed without mercy or sent to join the vast camp population, among them some of the country's finest scientific minds.

Scientists whose lives were spared were put to work in camp and prison laboratories – *sharashkas* – under the supervision of the 4th special section of the Ministry of the Interior. In this area Stalin adopted a purely pragmatic approach, the world outlook or political views of those serving sentences being no longer of any consequence. Quick results were what mattered, and when they were achieved, Stalin could even show a little kindness, sometimes reducing a sentence or even releasing a prisoner. Beria's agency kept Stalin constantly informed of the work of the scientists in the prisons and camps. On 18 May 1946, for instance, Kruglov reported that:

a group of prisoner-scientists, including Professor K. I. Stakhovich, Professor A. Yu. Vinblat and Engineer G. K. Teifel, have been working for a long time on building a turbo-prop engine of our own. Basing their work on the results of their theoretical research, the group is proposing to build the TRD-7B engine. I request you examine the Council of Ministers' draft decree.[17]

And on 8 February 1951 Kruglov reported that:

in 1947 prisoner-specialist A. S. Abramson (sentenced to ten years) proposed a new and original system for an economic automobile carburettor. Tests on a ZIS-150 produced a fuel saving of 10.9%. It is proposed that A. S. Abramson, mechanical engineer M. G. Ardzhevanidze and engine-builder G. N. Tsvetkov have their sentences reduced by two years.

I request your decision.[18]

Stalin gave his consent.

In high schools students were tested first and foremost for their ability to summarize Stalin's works. I remember being kept back by the teacher when I was attending the Orel tank school. He was a lieutenant colonel, no longer a young man, and was much liked by the class for his good nature. When we were alone he handed me my work, which was a summary of the sources, and said to me in a quiet and fatherly voice: 'It's a good summary. I could see right away you hadn't just copied it down but had given it some thought. But my advice is, summarize the Stalinist works more fully. Understand, more *fully*! And another thing. In front of the name Iosif Vissarionovich don't write "Com." Write "Comrade" in full. Got it?' That night one of my roommates told me they'd all had similar conversations with the teacher of party history. The exams were coming up and there were rumours that in a neighbouring school 'they had paid attention' to the sort of 'political immaturity' I had shown in my summaries.

CHAPTER 57

Absolute Bureaucracy

All states need an administration. Bureaucracy, in the sense in which we apply it to the Stalinist system, arises where the civil administration is divorced from the economic functioning of the state and where the system lacks democratic methods of self-regulation. In the early days of the Soviet régime it looked as if the executors of Bolshevik policy were not going to pose a great threat in this regard. Soon after the October Revolution, Lenin, reflecting on the new apparatus, said, 'In the interests of the people, it should not possess any sort of bureaucratism.'[19] Yet even then it was plain that the apparatus harboured a more serious danger than was anticipated. We know that in difficult moments Lenin could be very harsh towards the bureaucracy. In January 1919, he said, 'A bureaucratic attitude to the work, or inability to help the starving workers, will be severely punished, to the point of shooting.'[20]

The apparatus grew in the process of consolidating the Soviet régime, especially during the period of War Communism from 1918 to 1921. War Communism envisaged total control of production, distribution and consumption, and it was a system that called for the employment of many, many people. New elements of state structure came into being, new intermediate, coordinating, connecting links, and so on. The system was growing at an alarming rate under Lenin, absorbing a considerable amount of energy and resources to ensure its own proper functioning. If Stalin was an expert at anything in those early years, it was in the field of organization. Head of two commissariats and a long-standing member of the Central Committee, councils, commissions and committees, he quickly became aware of the strengths and weaknesses, as well as the possibilities, of the administrative and party organizations.

Having been appointed General Secretary, Stalin ordered the apparatus to work out a system for classifying jobs in the commissariats which in time developed into the notorious nomenklatura. On his orders, for instance, in

February 1923 the chief administrator of the Commissariat for Nationalities, Brezanovsky, prepared a paper entitled 'The Disposition of Posts According to Grades in the Administrative Structure of the People's Commissariat for Nationalities'. Departmental heads were defined in four groups: national problems, administrative-economic services, political-scientific-educational work, and literary-scientific publishing. Party workers were graded as most qualified, highly qualified, middle and low qualified; two or three jobs were listed as accessible to non-party people. The system of grading, which Stalin approved, subdivided the growing organization according to precise ranks (similar to the grades used in the old tsarist civil service invented by Peter the Great), thus cutting through the already weak links connecting the commissariat with the real problems of the nationalities and ethnic groups.[21] In effect, then, once he became General Secretary, Stalin set about building a vast, all-embracing army of functionaries.

As an expert in bureaucracy, Stalin quickly acquired one of the main tricks of the bureaucrat's trade, that of inaccessibility. A 1922 plenum had established the days and times when the General Secretary was to receive enquiries, but Stalin soon abandoned this practice, and as early as 1924 there were complaints, for instance, to Yenukidze, that 'it's impossible to get through to Comrade Stalin'.[22]

In his last letters, Lenin launched an attack on the growing bureaucracy, seeing danger not merely in its proliferation – he referred to plagues of 'clerical locusts' and 'bureaucratic rats' – but mainly in the way it was taking the place of popular participation. He believed that the way to limit the power of the bureaucracy was to bring in more workers and peasants. Now, of course, we know that this, too, would have been an inadequate measure, since everyone in the Soviet bureaucracy of today is 'flesh of the people's flesh' and no one is taking refuge there because of their social origin, as used to be said after the revolution. Lenin also placed his faith in the party purge as a way of getting rid of those members who 'not only are incapable of combatting red tape and bribery, but prevent others from fighting it'.[23] His main solution was to raise the culture of the society as a whole. The people must not depend on the apparatus, but vice versa. He wrote bitterly: 'Look how many laws we've written! So why are we having no success in this battle? Because propaganda isn't enough, and we can only win if the masses themselves help.'[24]

In the second half of the 1920s, two alternative concepts arose. One was personified by Bukharin, who advocated relatively moderate rates of development, both in industrialization and cooperative production; the other was to bank on an unprecedented leap forward in industry and agriculture. The latter alternative found its fullest expression in Stalin. It would have been impossible to accomplish such a leap by relying solely on economic methods. Administrative coercion was therefore necessary and this led inexorably to the proliferation and entrenchment of a broad bureaucratic stratum. Since the task was going to be accomplished mainly at the expense of the peasantry, coercion was virtually predetermined. Perhaps certain administrative measures were a necessity at a certain stage, but repression was not one of them. Stalin, however, knew that Lenin had written: 'It would be the greatest mistake to think that the NEP has put an end to terror. We will return to terror and to economic terror.'[25]

Having got rid of his opponents, Stalin opted for the coercive alternative, and the creation of the bureaucratic system followed automatically. Reliance on non-economic compulsion created an 'estate' which did not depend on the quantity or quality of production, but to a great extent on political arrangements. The bureaucracy automatically gave first place to political and ideological means of exerting force on the masses, and it put economic levers somewhere in second or third place. The socialist state quickly lost what vestiges of democracy it had possessed.

From the outset, many Bolshevik leaders were in favour of dictatorship without democracy. In 1922 Trotsky wrote that 'If the Russian revolution ... had tied itself down with the fetters of bourgeois democratism, it would long ago have been lying on the highway with its throat cut.' He did not even mention socialist democracy, for he believed that it would only come when the revolution had spread to other countries. The Bolsheviks, who were permeated with the idea of the dictatorship of the proletariat – perhaps because they saw no other path to power – and who paraded their radicalism as the hallmark of revolutionary-mindedness, had the clear intention of solving Russia's problems by violent means.

Most people, even today, see bureaucracy as red tape, paper-pushing and obstructiveness. That was the way many revolutionaries of the time saw it. Speaking on 28 May 1926 at the Third All-Union conference of town and village correspondents, Trotsky defined bureaucratism in the relatively narrow terms of servility, time-serving, conservatism and so on.[26] While these were and are features of the condition, this definition obscured its chief characteristic, namely, that of displacing democratic forces by the all-powerful organization. In September 1927 at a Comintern Executive Committee session, Trotsky, to his credit, more accurately predicted that 'the bureaucratic régime will lead irreversibly to one-man rule.'[27]

Not everyone saw that this would happen, and those who did were not heard. A few minutes after Trotsky made this prophetic statement, Bukharin attacked with, 'We should ask Trotsky why he does not stand to attention before the party, like a soldier?' To which Trotsky replied, 'You have the party by the throat.'[28] Bukharin did not yet realize that the dictator's hand was beginning to squeeze mercilessly not only the throat of the party, but also that of the people, and indeed his own, too.

The essence of the Stalinist form of bureaucracy was its totality. This process was expressed by the unwritten laws which began to govern all state, party and judicial organs and public organizations. The bureaucracy as it were synthesized them all into a unitary, coagulated, all-pervading, clinging, invulnerable entity, each element in the system, each functionary performing only what was prescribed, permitted and ordered. In such a system it was the power of instructions, directives and orders that ruled, that carried the threat of punishment, condemnation and ostracism, and that encouraged zealous executives and vigilant functionaries. The end product had the appearance of a collective administration.

Total bureaucracy was independent of economic expediency. It worshipped at the shrine of the omnipotent apparat. Whatever the problem or shortcoming, the solution was to create a new agency, a new organization, with the result that, despite the flow of instructions to curtail the administrative apparatus, it grew all the faster, for an administrative system cannot be combatted with administrative methods. Only economic, social and political means could have rid society of the bureaucracy, especially as it was so multi-faceted, with its endless titles, degrees, ranks and offices rising to the mysterious heights of the top echelons, where it was – and remains – impossible to find a 'responsible' official.

This bureaucratic system, emerging gradually as it did, inculcated a corresponding mentality in society as a whole. People became part of it, even used to it, and in time many came to associate its very style of doing things as one of the 'advantages' of socialism. This subject raises difficulties. It would be wrong to deny that much has been achieved in the social and cultural life of the country: employment, social security (albeit on a very low level), universal education of quite a high calibre, bringing the rudiments of culture to the broad masses, free (if poor quality) medical treatment, low prices for basic foodstuffs, extraordinarily low rents for (uncomfortable) state-owned apartments, children's summer camps, kindergartens and crèches at nominal charges, and various other social amenities. The trend towards gradual but perceptible improvement inspired the people.

Not that these 'successes' should be attributed to Stalin's leadership. The unstinting, arduous labour of the Soviet people was bound to yield some fruit. There was no obvious widespread corruption or moral decay among the leadership groups which came into prominence after Stalin's death. The general atmosphere indeed created the impression of a society enjoying moral good health and public well-being.

The total bureaucratic order seemed to suit the masses, as well, and for a number of reasons. Several generations had grown up under Stalin. They knew no other form of socialism, just as they had no true picture of the world on the other side of the ideological curtain. Most people sincerely believed that workers in capitalist countries lived in poverty, they were told ceaselessly that the morals of the West were ferocious and that the Soviet Union was superior to the 'free world' in virtually every respect. This was a firm belief and it was both created and sustained by a mighty propaganda machine.

In its way, total bureaucracy may well have been suited to a people raised in a spirit of unfreedom, lies and secrecy, since it prescribed, determined and organized everything. To a certain extent, it also guaranteed a fair share of goods. Similarly, total bureaucracy suited the executives and their bosses, for it facilitated the formation of an egalitarian and simplistic outlook.

It is often said nowadays that under Stalin there was order, certainty about tomorrow, unconditional fulfilment of the plan, a slow but sure rise in the standard of living. People too readily overlook the fact that under Stalin there was also the ever-present fear of punishment and arrest and that these were sufficient to sustain economic production and the functioning of the state institutions. Perhaps if – God forbid – the threat of Stalinist-style sanctions were held over the workers' and managers' heads today, they too would meet their planned targets. Human dignity, blind obedience and an atmosphere of terror, however, have been shown to be too high a price to pay for economic advance.

The most monstrous feature of the Stalinist bureaucracy was the omnipotent apparatus of the punitive organs which until the Twentieth Congress were in effect subordinate to one man. It was not merely a matter of the violence and coercion these bodies applied, but their penetration into every pore and cell of the state, whether political, economic, cultural or ideological. 'Revolutionary expediency' had been the rationalization of terror under Lenin, but, as we have seen, Stalin, too, was never short of explanations.

It is a sad fact of Soviet history that the Bolsheviks so often resorted to violent means. At times there may have been good cause, but in time it became a habit, a normal, legitimate fact. Lenin himself called for terror on several occasions. On 20 June 1918, V. Volodarsky, a member of the Petrograd party committee and Commissar for Press, Propaganda and Agitation, was assassinated by an SR. A week later Lenin sent the following letter to Zinoviev and other members of the Petrograd Central Committee:

> We have heard just today that the workers of [Petrograd] wanted to respond to the murder of Volodarsky with mass terror and that you (not you personally, but the Central Committee or Petrograd Committee) have held them back.
>
> I protest most strongly!
>
> We are compromising ourselves: even in the resolutions of our Soviet of Deputies we threaten the use of mass terror, but when it comes down to it, we put a brake on a fully justified revolutionary initiative of the masses
>
> This is im-poss-ible!
>
> The terrorists will take us for milksops. We are in a state of extreme war. We have to encourage energy and the massive presence of terror against the terrorists, especially in [Petrograd] which sets a decisive example.[29]

Such instructions were not rare. Bloodshed on a massive scale seemed a natural consequence of civil war. Lenin wrote to Trotsky in Sviyazhsk, probably in late 1918: 'Thank you, the convalescence is going wonderfully well. I'm confident that the crushing of the Kazan Czechs and White Guards, as well as the kulak bloodsuckers who are supporting them, will be carried out with exemplary lack of mercy. With passionate greetings.'[30]

'Exemplary lack of mercy' would in time virtually become the hallmark of revolutionary-mindedness. What Lenin permitted in a time of 'extreme war', when everything hung by a thread, later came to be viewed as the 'revolutionary norm', and Stalin's violence against the general population became an everyday affair. While Russia lacked democratic traditions, her experience of police affairs was well developed, though what Stalin created bore little resemblance to the amateurish efforts of tsarism in this respect.

At the turn of the century, the exile population of Siberia was one third of a million, of whom political exiles made up only about one per cent, plus about 11,000 doing hard labour,[31] and anything up to half of all exiles were on the run at any one time. The police system under tsarism was not especially harsh. To leave the country, for instance, one had only to write to the governor of the province and pay a small charge. In 1900, some 200,000 Russians spent several months abroad. It was hardly surprising, therefore, that the chief enemies of tsarism were to be found abroad. Many of them knew the weaknesses of the tsarist police department and after the revolution created a new structure that went much further in establishing a harsh régime and harsh new rules to ensure the loyalty of the citizen to the Soviet state.

Raised on Lenin's teachings that the 'correct' path was known only to the Bolsheviks, and imbued with his injunctions on party discipline, the Communist Party came to power with little democratic tradition of its own, and its leaders immediately inherited the police practice of the tsarist system. It was therefore hardly surprising that soon after October 1917 they would begin using repression against the opponents of the new order, thus simultaneously threatening freedom and clearing the path for a future Caesar. The Politburo minutes for 9 March 1922 contain a note from Kalinin's correspondence, in which Unshlikht reports on the struggle against banditry. The Politburo accepted Unshlikht's proposal that 'The GPU be given the right a) to execute summarily persons found guilty of armed robbery, criminals, recidivists in possession of a weapon, b) to exile to Archangel and imprison clandestine Anarchists and Left SRs.'[32]

The Stalinist bureaucracy continued this kind of practice, making it an everyday feature of Soviet life. A feeling of mutual distrust permeated the whole of society. Reports poured in of 'nests of anti-Soviets', whether among technicians in Moscow, or university students or even fifteen-year-old schoolchildren in Krasnodar.[33]

The security organs increasingly took over functions that ought to have been the responsibility of other more appropriate bodies. For instance, during the war Lenin's remains had been taken for safekeeping to Tyumen in western Siberia, and responsibility for replacing them in the Mausoleum was in the hands of Beria's people. In September 1945 he informed Stalin that the Mausoleum was ready to admit visitors, and he suggested it be reopened for this purpose on Sunday 16 September.[34]

As we have seen, prisoners were used to satisfy the demands for extra labour coming from all the ministries. The Soviet prisoner population made its contribution to building roads and bridges, mining coal and uranium, felling timber, building nuclear reactors, apartment blocks, great hydroelectric schemes. I will never forget visiting the Kuibyshev power station with a group of Komsomols in 1952. We were amazed by the scale of the project. From the upper platforms one could see hundreds of grey-clad figures swarming and scurrying over the site. As we were passing one such group, a tall thin lad leaned over and, in a voice meant to be heard by the guards standing nearby, said: 'Tell them outside how we are working on a great construction of the Stalin epoch!' Some time later, I came across a book called *Great Constructions of the Stalin Epoch* and the intended irony came home to me.

I grew up in the village of Agul, Irbei district, in the south of Krasnoyarsk region. In the distance one could see the majestic snows of the Sayan mountains and their spurs jutting out towards the Yenisei, the Kana and the Agala. This was the genuine, drowsy taiga, the land of the Kerzhaks, indigenous Siberians who had migrated from the western territories of Russia a century or two earlier. In 1937 or 1938 some soldiers turned up in our little village, followed by columns of prisoners. They started cordoning off zones, and in some six months camps were established in Agul and a number of neighbouring settlements. Barbed wire appeared and high fences behind which one could just make out the huts, the armed sentries on watch-towers and the guard dogs.

The locals soon began seeing long columns of exhausted people constantly arriving on foot from the railhead sixty miles away. It seemed the camps must be infinitely expandable. Later they understood what was happening. Long ditches started appearing beyond the outskirts of the settlements, and the corpses of dead prisoners would be taken on carts or sleighs, covered with tarpaulins, and buried there at night. Many died from the sheer hardship. Many were shot out in the taiga. Boris Frantsevich Kreshchuk, who was living then in Agul and whose father, a blacksmith, and elder brother had been shot, told me of the time he and some other boys were out looking for pine nuts when they suddenly heard the crack of gunfire nearby, 'just like the sound of a large canvas being ripped apart'. They ran to the place and from behind some bushes watched as the firing squad threw some twenty executed prisoners into a ditch. 'I remember one of them was clinging to the grass, obviously he wasn't dead. We ran away.'

My mother was the head of a primary school (for children aged seven to fourteen). The authorities allowed two prisoners to come and help put her library in order, repair bindings and so on. Life was very hard for us, especially after they arrested and executed my father and exiled us to Agul. As we were already living in the Maritime region, there was nowhere further east to send us, so they sent us west, to Agul. There were no teachers in the place, so the authorities allowed my mother to teach. She had graduated from university after the revolution. When there was no one else around, my mother used to have long conversations with one of the prisoners, whose name I cannot recall. Once, he took a bit of rag from inside his shirt and quickly unwrapped a photograph and showed it to my mother. We were in the long, low room that served as the library, and I was standing on tiptoe and looking over my mother's shoulder. The small photograph was mounted on board and there was some foreign writing below. The prisoner spoke in a low whisper: 'We were in emigration then. In Switzerland. That's Lenin, that's me next to him with my wife, and those two were German Communists.'

I couldn't help wondering how someone so shabby and emaciated could have known Lenin personally. He was brought under escort to the school on two further occasions and then he vanished. Either he died or he was shot in the forest, like the others. Those childhood impressions have never left me.

Still a relatively young woman, my mother died soon after the war, leaving me, my sister and my brother very much uninformed. We buried her in the village cemetery not far from the place where the prisoners were shot. The ditches had already settled down to ground level, unmarked, forgotten places that had witnessed the appalling tragedy of a people. I doubt if many survived those camps. Two of my own uncles, simple peasants who had said something incautiously, never returned.

It may be said that this book is my way of avenging the wrongs done to my family. But I would deny it. When Stalin died I was a young tank commander. I thought the sky would fall in. I understood nothing when my family were taken away, and even later did not link that tragedy with Stalin. They told me my father had died. My mother had wept in secret. Not until July 1952 did I discover that I myself was a marked man. We had just had our celebration dinner on graduating from officer school and were collecting our simple cardboard suitcases, prior to dispersing to our units, when one of my friends (whom I will not name) took me aside and said:

'Swear you'll never tell anyone what I'm going to tell you.'

'Of course,' I said, utterly bemused.

'I've been "looking after" you for three years, reporting what you said, you know, keeping an eye on you in general. Forgive me, but I had no choice.'

'What are you saying?' I couldn't grasp it.

'As you've graduated, and with honours, it means nothing bad happened. Anyway, the best of luck. Don't think badly of me. But, remember, that may not be the end of it ...'

This digression into my personal background serves as a reminder that it is senseless to try to take revenge on history. What was done cannot be undone. It must, however, become known and remembered.

How much did Stalin and his cronies in the Kremlin know of what was happening in Agul and the thousands of other places in their far-flung Gulag? The answer is, a great deal. The archives are full of letters describing the agony, begging for help, asking Stalin to look into things, to intervene, to review dispassionately this or that case. One came from an inmate of Section 14 of NKVD Camp No. 283 and Coal Mine No. 26:

> The prisoners' situation is hard. The medieval Inquisition would be paradise by comparison. Former soldiers and partisans are cooped up with collaborators and Polizei.* No one knows how long their sentence is, which is no easier than being shot. We are beaten up regularly. Our clothes are louse-infested rags. The food is disgusting, often they dish up mice. They chop the cabbage up in a fodder-machine, so there is often horse dung in it. The prisoners get beaten up by the escorts. They are picked from among the most savage people. This letter contains not one word of a lie, but to sign it would mean instant penal servitude.[35]

Stalin passed the letter on to Malenkov, who scribbled on it 'For Comrades Beria and Chernyshev', while Beria merely signed his name on it. The circle was complete. The bureaucracy was wrapped in a mantle of lawlessness. The rare occasions when someone in a high position raised a feeble protest are all the more amazing when they turn up in the archives. Molotov's papers contain a letter to Stalin and Molotov from the Minister of Justice, N. Rychkov, written in May 1947:

> In accordance with USSR government instructions and Order No. 058 of 20 March 1940 of the Commissariat of Justice and Procuracy of the USSR, persons acquitted in cases of counter-revolution are not subject to immediate release, but are returned to their place of detention and may be released only upon receipt of a report from the Ministry of Internal Affairs to the effect that there are no obstacles from their point of view. This arrangement means that liberated persons continue to remain in prison for months.
>
> For example, on 5 April 1946, the military collegium of the Supreme Court of the USSR, acting on a protest by the Procurator General of the USSR, overturned a sentence by the military tribunal of the Taman rifle division, according to which Citizeness Litvinenko was charged with treason and condemned to be shot (the sentence being commuted to ten years in the camps by a tribunal of the Maritime army). The military collegium of the Supreme Court terminated the case on grounds of lack of evidence. This verdict was sent to the Siberian camp where the prisoner was being held. There the document was sent for ratification by the 1st special department of the Ministry of Internal Affairs, who sent it on to the Tauride military district. The case has been dragging on for months.
>
> There are many such cases. This undermines the authority of the court. I request that Order No. 058 of 20 March 1940 be rescinded.[36]

How Stalin reacted is not known. Molotov sent the letter on to Interior Ministry officials in May 1947, but it would be a long time before the insanely cruel regulations were altered. Stalin and the system he fashioned taught the

---

* i.e. local nationals recruited as police by the Germans during the war.

people to be patient, to be silent and to submit. On the whole, people did not think too much about these things, nor did they know very much about the nightmare hidden behind the screens of the Stalinist system.

If his physical death came to Stalin sooner than expected, his political demise was long delayed. His historical death is unlikely, since the people will never forget what was done in his name.

CHAPTER 58

Earthly Gods are Mortal

Although he was now ageing and sick, Stalin was nevertheless still active in seeking out and dealing with real or imagined enemies. A few months before the Nineteenth Congress of October 1952, he had taken steps to stage the long-planned trial of the Jewish Anti-Fascist Committee. In May-June, the military collegium of the Supreme Court of the USSR examined the case of a group of Jewish intellectuals who had previously been connected with the work of the Jewish Anti-Fascist Committee. This body had been created by the Soviet government at the beginning of 1942 and had done much during the war to mobilize world, in particular US, public opinion in the common cause against Nazism. Soon after the war, however, the witch-hunt began.

As early as November 1946, Mikhail Suslov (who was to become the dominant force in ideological control until his death in 1982) had sent Stalin a note on the Committee's 'harmful' activity. Security Minister Abakumov forcibly extracted detailed confessions about the Committee's 'espionage activities' from I. I. Goldshtein and Z. G. Grinberg. All this was reported to Stalin. Blatantly anti-Semitic articles began appearing in the press and the Committee was closed down by a Politburo decree of 20 November 1948. Malenkov and Beria carried on from there.

Arrests soon followed. The most significant figure among them was that of Solomon Abramovich Lozovsky, an Old Bolshevik and former deputy Foreign Minister who had worked during the war as head of Sovinformburo and who had had frequent meetings with Stalin. Also arrested were an entire group of scientists, poets, physicians, editors, translators, theatre figures – 110 people in all. On 13 January 1949, Malenkov, in the presence of M. F. Shkiryatov, summoned Lozovsky and tried to make him confess to criminal plans. In particular, he wanted Lozovsky to admit that he had helped the chairman of the Committee, the actor Solomon Mikhoels, and the journalist, Sh. Epshtein, and the poet I. S. Feffer, to write a letter to Stalin, proposing that the Crimea be turned into the 'Jewish Socialist Republic'. Two weeks later Lozovsky was arrested.

Stalin was informed as soon as they had all 'confessed' (B. A. Shmelyovich did not sign a confession, not that this saved him from execution), and without further ado, he ordered a trial, indicating as usual the sentences he wanted handed down.

Between May and July 1952, fourteen people were tried in a closed court presided over by A. A. Cheptsov. Only one defendant, Academician Lina Shtern, escaped with a prison sentence. The rest were shot.[37.] While the anti-Semitic purpose of the court was blatant enough, Stalin's object in 'exposing internal enemies' was to paralyse the will of the already long-silenced intelligentsia in general.

Such was the 'intellectual' background to his last party congress. The bureaucratic dictatorship had reached its peak of anti-human behaviour, and now Stalin crowned it with his 'historic congress', which in reality represented the most profound social and intellectual crisis of the system.

In the course of August and September 1952, Malenkov reported to Stalin several times on the preparations being made for the congress, showing him outlines of the speeches of the members of the Politburo and so on. Stalin, however, was more preoccupied with what he himself was going to say. Suslov and a whole team of assistants had produced a number of versions, but Stalin himself added the final touches to the one he eventually chose.

A few days before it was due to begin, Stalin stipulated that the congress should open at 7 p.m., thus imposing on the highest party forum the pattern of his own way of life. The congress presidium was not very large, but, as an innovation, all the members were bunched together at the left-hand end of the table, while Stalin sat in total isolation to the right with no one next to or behind him. The constant mention of his name brought forth standing ovations and chanting, and the mood of exaltation rose to hysteria. Stalin gazed at the spectacle and in the interval got up and left. He appeared at the congress only at the opening and closing sessions. Perhaps his health was responsible, but it is more likely that he was bored with meetings at which there was no conflict and where everything had been decided in advance. Not that he would have tolerated any other kind. Party congresses merely provided the 'democratic' trappings of his one-man rule. As for the population at large, the congress meant nothing by comparison with the question in everyone's mind: namely, would Stalin make a speech?

Until the last day of the congress the delegates did not know if Stalin would speak. In the closing session, when they saw him rise from the presidium and tread slowly along the carpeted walkway to the podium, they all rose to give him yet another ovation. He was not dressed as a marshal, but was wearing his usual 'party' uniform, with only one Hero star on his chest. He was playing the 'modest leader' part with his usual relish. His speech was short, possibly exceeded in length by the applause that continually interrupted it, and was utterly devoid of anything new, merely rehearsing the old stereotypes about the decline of the capitalist world and the bankruptcy of the socialist parties. At this, his last congress, Stalin did no more than reaffirm the stale old Communist positions that were so plainly lagging behind the changes taking place in the world.

Some of the more perceptive delegates to whom I have spoken sensed that Stalin was thinking about his legacy, and this is borne out by the long speech he made at the plenum that was elected at the congress. Malevolently and in an accusing tone, he expressed doubt that his comrades would follow the agreed course, and wondered whether they would not capitulate before the country's domestic difficulties, as well as the imperialists' threats. Would they show the courage and firmness needed to withstand the new tests?

Stalin had also apparently been preparing the ground to remove a number of his longest-serving comrades-in-arms, people who might well act as suitable scapegoats after the Nineteenth Congress was over. In November 1952, at Beria's insistent prompting and heavy hints of involvement in the 'Doctors' Plot', Stalin finally got rid of Poskrebyshev. Although he was becoming daily more suspicious of Beria, Stalin let him have his way. If Beria said Poskrebyshev needed looking into, so be it. The Leningrad leadership, and their friends in Moscow and elsewhere, had also recently been 'looked into' in connection with the Jewish Anti-Fascist Committee.

At the end of his life, Stalin trusted no one. First the long-serving, loyal Poskrebyshev, and then Lieutenant General Nikolai Sidorovich Vlasik, who was arrested on 16 December 1952. Vlasik was interrogated by Beria personally, as well as by Kobulov and Vlodzimirsky. As head of the security department of the Ministry of State Security, Vlasik was accused of 'indulging the poisoner-doctors', of knowing the 'spy' V. A. Stenberg and of abusing his position by 'appropriating state produce'. These were of course merely the pretexts for his arrest. He revealed the real reason later. From Krasnoyarsk, where he was in exile, he wrote in May 1955 to Voroshilov, as chairman of the Supreme Soviet. Quaintly referring to Stalin throughout as 'the Head of government', Vlasik described a conversation that had taken place between him and Stalin, when they were on holiday in the south after the war:

The Head of government expressed his dissatisfaction with Beria, saying that the work of the state security organs did not justify the protection they got. He said he had given orders to remove Beria from the job of running the MGB. He asked me what I thought of Merkulov and Kobulov, and later of Goglidze and Tsanave. I told him what I knew. When I later found out that my conversation with the Head of government had definitely become known to them, I was staggered.

Beria had obviously been alarmed by Stalin's attitude to him, but how did he know what his boss and Vlasik had said about him when they were alone? Had Stalin relayed their conversation, or did Beria have some means of bugging the leader himself?

Vlasik went on to say that, once he had been summoned by Beria for interrogation, 'I knew I could expect nothing but death, as I was sure they had deceived the Head of government.' The purpose of the exercise was apparently to make him incriminate Poskrebyshev. When he refused, they told him he would die like a dog in prison. He was given the full treatment, and, as he wrote to Voroshilov:

> given my age and state of health, I could not take it. I became confused, I was in a state of total shock and lost all self-control and common sense. Shackled by handcuffs that bit right through to the bone, I was not even in a condition to read what they had written down as my answers, and I signed the compromising document while they cursed and shouted threats ... they took the handcuffs off then and promised to let me go and sleep, but this did not happen, as they went on torturing me in my cell.[38]

The holiday in Sochi had not restored Stalin's energy and the dizzy spells were still occurring. Listlessly, he sifted through the papers Malenkov's secretariat prepared, looked at the newspapers and journals and the foreign books and articles that were translated for him. He phoned Malenkov and told him not to send him any more papers. Accompanied by a dozen bodyguards, he went to the Bolshoi Theatre to see *Swan Lake*. The theatre manager, A. T. Rybin, who was also the security chief, was waiting at the box. On other occasions Stalin would have invited Molotov or Zhdanov to go with him, but now he sat forlornly in a corner and watched the ballet. Feeling vaguely ill at ease and alarmed by the sense of growing weakness, he got up and left before the end.

On 28 February 1953, he rose later than usual, feeling somewhat better. He read reports from Korea, the interrogation reports on the Jewish doctors, M. S. Vovsi, Ya. G. Etinger, B. B. Kogan, M. B. Kogan and A. M. Grinshtein. He took a short walk. Late that evening, as arranged, Malenkov, Beria, Khrushchev and Bulganin arrived at the dacha. As usual, they discussed a wide range of topics. Bulganin gave an account of the war in Korea, confirming Stalin's view that the situation had reached a stalemate. He decided he would tell Molotov next day to advise the Chinese and North Koreans to 'try to get the best deal they could in talks', but in any event to try to bring the armed conflict to a halt.

Beria spoke for a long time. Knowing that Stalin was losing faith in him, he decided that today he must make a special effort:

Ryumin has produced incontrovertible evidence that this entire fraternity of Vovsi, Kogan, Feldman, Etinger, Yegorov, Vasilenko, Shereshevsky and the others have been surreptitiously shortening the lives of the leadership for a long time. Zhdanov, Dimitrov, Shcherbakov – we're making up a precise list of their victims at the moment – they were all got rid of by this gang. For instance, Zhdanov's electro-cardiogram was simply falsified. They hid the fact that he'd had a heart attack and let him go on working and going about his business and this soon laid him low. But the main point is that the whole thing was the work of the agency of the

Jewish bourgeois-nationalist organization, the 'Joint'.* The threads run deep and are linked to party and military officials. Most of the accused have confessed.

The case of the doctors had begun when Professor V. N. Vinogradov made his last call on Stalin in 1952 and, finding him in poor condition, advised him to do as little work as possible henceforth. Stalin was furious and Vinogradov was never called on again. Indeed, he was soon arrested. Stalin's dissatisfaction with his physicians was played on by State Security investigator Ryumin, who saw it as a way to advance his own career. Sensing the way Stalin was thinking, and playing on the turn in world events, which shifted Soviet Middle East policy against the new state of Israel, the security organs prepared a huge case about a widespread 'doctors' plot' of a blatantly anti-Semitic nature. There would undoubtedly have been a trial and the whole affair could easily have ended up in another large-scale bloodbath. Only Stalin's sudden death averted the likely course of events.

During the last evening of his life, Stalin inquired several times about progress on the case, and specifically about Vinogradov. Beria told him that, 'apart from his other unfavourable qualities, the professor has a very long tongue. He has told one of the doctors in his clinic that Comrade Stalin has already had several dangerous hypertonic episodes.'

'Right,' Stalin said, 'what do you propose to do now? Have the doctors confessed? Tell Ignatiev that if he doesn't get full confessions out of them, we'll reduce his height by a head.'

'They'll confess. With the help of Timashuk and other patriots, we'll complete the investigation and come to you for permission to arrange a public trial.'

'Arrange it,' Stalin muttered, and then turned to other matters.

They sat up till 4 a.m. on the morning of 1 March. By the end of the nocturnal conversation, Stalin was visibly irritated with the company. Only Bulganin escaped his angry reproach. They were all waiting for the host to get up, so that they could go home to bed. The host, however, was harping on the theme that there were people in the leadership who thought they could get by on their past merits. 'They are mistaken.' This sounded ominous. They all knew something sinister was brewing. Perhaps the old man meant to kick them all out of the Politburo so that he could blame all his past crimes on them? But this angry outburst was to be his last. Breaking off in mid-sentence, he suddenly got up and went to his room. The others silently dispersed and went home, Malenkov and Beria travelling in the same car.

As Rybin described events to me, it was midday on 1 March before the domestic staff began to get worried. Stalin had not appeared, nor called anyone. And no one could go into his room unless summoned. The concern grew, and then at 6.30 p.m. the light went on in his room. Everyone sighed with relief and waited for the bell to ring. Stalin had not eaten, or looked at the mail or

---

* The American Jewish Joint Distribution Committee.

any papers. It was all most irregular. Rybin, who did not conceal his personal sympathy for his old boss, went on to say that there was no bell. Eight o'clock came, then 9.30, but still the silence continued in Stalin's room. Something approaching panic began to set in. The staff started arguing about whether someone should go in and look, as the uneasy feeling grew that something was seriously wrong. Duty officers, M. Starostin and V. Tukov, and the maid, M. Butusova, decided that Starostin should investigate, and at 11 p.m. he went in, taking the day's mail with him in case he needed an excuse.

Starostin had to pass through a succession of rooms to get to Stalin's, turning on the lights as he went. When he switched on the light in the small dining room, he froze. There on the floor, wearing an undershirt and pyjama bottoms, lay Stalin. He just managed to raise his hand to beckon Starostin, but could not speak. His eyes expressed horror and fear and were full of pleading. There was a copy of *Pravda* on the floor and an open bottle of mineral water on the table. He must have been lying there a long time, as the light had not been turned on. Starostin called out and the other servants came running in great agitation. They lifted Stalin on to the divan. He tried several times to say something, but only incoherent noises emerged. The stroke had paralysed his power of speech and in due course he lost consciousness.

According to Rybin, the security staff immediately began calling Ignatiev at the Ministry of State Security. He advised them to call Beria and Malenkov. Beria was nowhere to be found, and Malenkov could not bring himself to do anything without Beria. Nor, according to the rules, could physicians be summoned without Beria's permission. Finally Beria was run to earth in a government villa in the company of one of his latest women, and at 3 a.m. he and Malenkov arrived. Beria had plainly been drinking. Malenkov, tucking his new shoes under his arm in case they squeaked, went into Stalin's room in his socks and found his master breathing his last gasps. Beria would not call the doctors and instead turned on the servants: 'Why did you panic? Can't you see Comrade Stalin is sound asleep? All of you get out and leave our leader in peace. I shall deal with you in due course!'

Malenkov gave Beria some half-hearted support. According to Rybin, there seemed to be no intention at all of getting medical help for Stalin, who must have had the stroke some six to eight hours before. Everyone appeared to be following a scenario that best suited Beria. Having got rid of the staff, after forbidding them to telephone anyone, the leaders dispersed noisily. It was not until 9 a.m. that Beria, Malenkov and Khrushchev returned, followed soon by the other members of the Politburo and the doctors.

Great bustle now ensued. Svetlana Alliluyeva recalled that the doctors applied leeches to the back of Stalin's head and neck, took cardiograms, X-rayed his lungs and subjected him to a constant series of injections. Despite all their efforts, everyone was perfectly aware that the end was near. Beria went over to the doctors and, speaking loud enough for everyone to hear, asked them if they could guarantee Stalin's life. 'You understand that you are responsible for Comrade Stalin's health? I am warning you.' The doctors who had looked after Stalin for many years were now of course in prison and awaiting trial, while those who were now vainly struggling to save him were new and unfamiliar. Pale with mortal fear, the professors and doctors and nurses whispered anxiously to each other as they went about their vain tasks, knowing that there would be a far worse ordeal to face when it was all over.

Beria did not hide his look of triumph. All the other members of the Politburo, including Malenkov, were afraid of this monster. The death of one tyrant promised a new orgy of bloodletting by his successor. Exhausted by all his exertions, and now sure that Stalin had crossed the dividing line between life and death, Beria dashed away to the Kremlin for some hours, leaving the other leaders at Stalin's deathbed. I have already outlined the version of Beria, as first deputy chairman of the Council of Ministers, now forcing the great political game that he had long planned. His hasty departure for the Kremlin was possibly connected with his effort to remove from Stalin's safe documents which might contain instructions about how to deal with him, a last will that might not be so easy to contest, made while Stalin was in full control of his faculties.

He returned to the dacha in a mood of self-confidence and proceeded to dictate to his crestfallen colleagues that they must prepare a government statement to the effect that Stalin was ill and also publish a bulletin on the state of his health. The statement, which was read out on the radio and appeared in the newspapers, reported, in part, that:

in the small hours of 2 March, Comrade Stalin, who was at home in Moscow [in fact, he was outside Moscow at the dacha], suffered a brain haemorrhage which has affected areas of the brain that are essential to life. Comrade Stalin has lost consciousness. His right arm and leg are paralysed. He has lost the power of speech. The functioning of the heart and lungs has been seriously impaired. Treatment of Comrade Stalin is being carried out under the constant observation of the Central Committee of the CPSU and the Soviet government. Comrade Stalin's serious illness will mean his more or less long-term inability to participate in government affairs.

Two further bulletins were issued, at 2 a.m. and 4 a.m. on 5 March. The medical luminaries – A. F. Tretyakov, I. I. Kuperin, P. E. Lukomsky, N. V. Konovalov, A. L. Myasnikov, E. M. Tareev, I. N. Filomonov, I. S. Glazunov and others, all of them Russian to a man, as Beria had made sure after the case of the Kremlin doctors that no Jews attend Stalin – could not hide the fact that, despite Beria's threats, the end was at hand. They declared that there had been 'sharp disruption of circulation in the coronary arteries and fundamental changes in the rear coronary wall', a 'serious collapse', and that 'the situation continues to remain critical'. They were not aware that earlier disturbances of brain function had caused numerous cavities, or cysts, in the brain tissue, especially in the lobes. Such changes, modern specialists have suggested, would have been responsible for effects in the psychological sphere, making an impact on Stalin's despotic character and exacerbating his tyrannical tendencies.[39] My impression, however, is that Stalin was not a suitable case for psychiatric interest. His 'sickness' was social; it was that of Caesarism and tyranny. Moreover, it was not only the leader who was sick, but the whole society.

Meanwhile the last act of the drama was being played out. Stalin's son, Vasili, kept coming in and shouting in a drunken voice, 'They've killed my father, the bastards!' Svetlana was standing frozen next to the bed, while the members of the Politburo, in a state of exhaustion from lack of sleep and the fear of an unknown future, were slumped in armchairs. Voroshilov, Kaganovich, Khrushchev and some others were weeping openly. Beria approached Stalin several times and said in a loud voice: 'Comrade Stalin, all the members of the Politburo are here, say something to us!' Beria was behaving like the crown prince of a vast empire with the power of life or death over all its citizens. For him, Stalin was already the past.

The moment came at 9.50 a.m. on 5 March 1953. Before the other leaders lay their master, their idol, judge, boss and benefactor and, be it said, their potential hangman. On her knees, her head on his chest and wailing like a peasant, was V. V. Istomina, Stalin's housekeeper who for some twenty years had looked after him, accompanied him on all his trips to the south and even on two of the three international wartime conferences.

The members of the Politburo quickly recovered from the shock of Stalin's death, pulled themselves together and jostled to leave. There were things to be done, arrangements to be made for the funeral and so on. As they sped back to Moscow in their long black limousines, some of them wondered if Stalin had left a will and whether Beria was now in charge.

Shepilov recalled:

I was then working as editor-in-chief of *Pravda*. The country waited in silence for news from Moscow. At five in the morning, the phone rang and Suslov was on the line: 'Come at once to the little corner.' This was the nickname for Stalin's study in the Kremlin. 'Comrade Stalin is dead.' I put down the phone. When I got to the Kremlin, the funeral was being discussed. I was struck by the behaviour of the members of the Politburo. They were sitting at the long table and Stalin's chair at the head of it was empty. Beria and Malenkov faced each other across the table next to the empty chair. They were both obviously in an excited state, constantly interrupting their colleagues and speaking more often than the others. Beria simply blossomed. Khrushchev said very little, clearly still in a state of shock. I was particularly struck by the fact that Molotov was silent, aloof, his expression more stony than ever, and throughout the entire rather pointless meeting, which lasted one and a half hours, said absolutely nothing.

A meeting took place next day between the party Central Committee, the Council of Ministers and the Presidium of the Supreme Soviet of the USSR. It had proved impossible to find any instructions from Stalin about what to do in the event of his death. Since Stalin's stroke, only Beria had been in the study, once, after which he had ordered the room to be sealed. The question of succession had to be resolved. Malenkov chaired the meeting, but the decisions had already been taken beforehand by an inner group.

It was decided that one of Stalin's posts, that of chairman of the Council of Ministers, should go to Malenkov, who had been the leader's favourite for the last two or three years. His first deputies were to be Beria, Molotov, Bulganin and Kaganovich. The Ministries of Security and Interior were combined, with Beria in charge of the newly enlarged Interior Ministry. It seemed clear that Beria not only intended to maintain the situation as it had been under Stalin, but also to enhance the rôle of his ministry in the making of internal and foreign policy. Molotov was made Foreign Minister and Bulganin Defence Minister. Shvernik was moved to the trade unions, while his place as chairman of the Supreme Soviet was given to Voroshilov.

Important changes were also made in the party leadership. The inner circle which had met the night before the session, less than twelve hours after Stalin's death, supported a proposal by Molotov that the Presidium of the Central Committee (or Politburo) be sharply reduced in number. At the end of his life, Stalin seems to have been preparing gradually to rid himself of his long-term comrades – Beria, Voroshilov, Kaganovich, Mikoyan, Molotov, Khrushchev and perhaps some others. He must have sensed that there was very little time. His solution (accepted by the others unanimously, of course), had been to enlarge the Presidium to twenty-five, with eleven non-voting members, and the secretariat to ten. The intention was plainly to 'dilute' the old guard among the new functionaries. It is extremely likely that, had he not had the stroke, he would have found ways to frame Molotov, Mikoyan and Beria, in order both to remove them from the leadership and to offload the guilt for much that might mar his own historical image. The old guard had known what was afoot, however, and so now, soon after his death, they removed the new appointees from the leadership.

The joint session ratified the inner circle's proposal to reduce the size of the Presidium to ten, plus four non-voting members. Only three of the new faces remained, namely N. A. Bulganin, M. Z. Saburov and M. G. Pervukhin. (Among those who were removed, after only five months in the job, was Leonid Brezhnev, who now became deputy head of the Main Political Administration of the Soviet Army and Navy.) In a somewhat vague formula, it was resolved that Khrushchev 'should concentrate on work in the party Central Committee and should therefore be relieved of his duties as first secretary of the Moscow party committee'.

As for the population, most people did not take note of these subtle changes, although they were perfectly aware that the new figures were but shadows of the former leader. Hungry for any fragment of news, the people took it as perfectly natural that Stalin's body should lie next to Lenin's, until the completion of a Pantheon, to which the remains of them both, 'along with those of the outstanding figures of the Communist Party and Soviet state buried in the Kremlin wall,' were supposed one day to be transferred.

The ancient custom of embalming and mummifying, against which Krupskaya had so vehemently protested in her day and on which Stalin had so insisted, also seemed perfectly natural. The centre of Moscow was packed with mourning crowds, in some places so dense that there were a number of fatalities.

During the funeral, thirty-gun salutes were fired in the capitals of all the Union republics and elsewhere, after which the body was carried into the Mausoleum, which was closed for a further eight months, while the embalming process went on. Few indeed would then have predicted that on the night of 31 October 1961 Stalin's mummy would be removed for burial by the Kremlin wall.

Throughout his rule, Stalin had defended the institutions he had created, but he clearly overestimated their stability. Literally within hours of his death his heirs would start ignoring his precepts. Gradually, the eulogizers of the 'greatest of great geniuses' changed their tone. It was as if almost unnoticed the blindfold began to slip. In less than a month the case against the doctors was dropped and Ryumin was shot in the time-honoured way. In only a short while, the emboldened new leaders performed a 'palace operation' and got rid of Beria. A year later the Supreme Court under A. A. Cheptsov terminated the 'Leningrad affair' as 'having been falsified by the former Minister of State Security of the USSR and his accomplices'. The three Voznesenskys, along with dozens of other victims, were posthumously rehabilitated.[40] In the following year, *Pravda* announced that, at an open session of the military collegium in Leningrad, those guilty of fabricating the Leningrad Affair (V. S. Abakumov, A. G. Leonov, V. I. Komarov and M. T. Likhachev) had been sentenced to death, while others were given prison sentences of varied lengths. The chief culprits were, of course, already dead by then.

CHAPTER 59

Defeat by History

Khrushchev was on the podium at the Twentieth Party Congress. In a state of shock, the nearly 1500 delegates sat transfixed in total silence, interrupting only occasionally with cries of outraged indignation. They seemed to see a ghost standing at the shoulder of the speaker. The more Khrushchev revealed, the clearer the image of the ghost. It was a moment of rare historic significance. Only hours before the speech, no one could have predicted that the stagnant and deformed party would be capable of performing this genuinely civic feat.

We know now that soon after Stalin's death the leadership began to loosen the bonds of Stalinism, and that these steps were hastened after the arrest and execution of Beria, an act which made it possible to look deeper into the dark recesses of the Stalinist past, although of course many of the leaders knew very well what had been going on. Once the date for the congress had been fixed, Khrushchev suddenly proposed at a meeting of the Presidium the setting up of a commission to look into the abuses of the Stalin period. It was not, as he would later claim, 'the call of heart and conscience' that prompted him, so much as the mounting torrent of letters, pouring into the Central Committee, government offices and other state bodies from those who had spent long years behind the barbed wire of the Gulag, and their relatives, voicing their protest and hope, and their faith that justice would now be restored.

On the basis of these letters, Khrushchev set about preparing several broadly-based memoranda which would reveal that the 'Leningrad affair' and various other cases under review had been fabricated. It became clear that in the next year or two an enormous number of prisoners would be completing their terms of imprisonment and exile. It was equally clear that they would need to be allowed to return home, together with their pain, their perplexity and their demand that the real guilty ones be punished. With Stalin and Beria gone, which of the new leaders would dare to allow these people to go on rotting in the camps?

The party faced a difficult choice. Even the proposal to create the commission met stiff resistance from Molotov, Kaganovich and Voroshilov, but the balance was tilted towards Khrushchev by Bulganin, Mikoyan, Saburov, Pervukhin and the still wavering Malenkov. The commission was set up. It was headed by the long-serving editor of *Pravda* and director of the Marx-Engels-Lenin Institute, P. N. Pospelov. Khrushchev set about gaining access for the commission to the papers of the Ministry of State Security and its successor in 1953, the KGB (Committee of State Security). Pospelov worked on this project as industriously as he had a few years earlier on Stalin's *Short Biography*. When he reported to Khrushchev on the eve of the congress, the First Secretary finally realized that this document would either crack open the concrete casing of lies and legends about Stalin, or serve as the oration at his own funeral.

Several times he returned to Pospelov's report and asked the other members of the Presidium what should be done. How should the commission's findings be conveyed to the congress? Who should do it? Should it be Pospelov himself? The resistance from Molotov, Voroshilov and Kaganovich was long and hard and at times fierce. No minutes were taken, but from Khrushchev's memoirs it emerged that the opponents of the report had some strong arguments. They asked, for instance, who was forcing them to wash their dirty linen in public? Wouldn't it be best to correct the excesses on the quiet? Did Khrushchev realize what consequences might result from publishing the report? And, finally, had not all the members of the Presidium themselves been party to these events in varying degrees?

Khrushchev, however, won the argument and on 13 February 1956 the Central Committee agreed that the report should be read at a closed session of the congress. Khrushchev felt new doubts, but when he remembered the letters from the Gulag he reassured himself that the crimes of the Stalin era could be kept hidden no longer. Sooner or later the facts would come out. Better seize the initiative and tell the party the awful truth. He had no intention, however, of telling the people at large.

As the congress was moving uneventfully towards its predictable close, Bulganin, who was presiding, announced there would be a closed session and called on Khrushchev to speak. It was his finest hour. An orthodox Stalinist in his day, a loyal and diligent executor of the leader's every order, suddenly he showed the historic and civic courage and indeed the ability to shed long-held prejudices.

Concentrating his speech – entitled 'On the Personality Cult and its Consequences' – on the 1930s, the terror and the methods used by Stalin's henchmen to gain confessions, Khrushchev touched on Lenin's Letter to the Congress, of which many delegates had never heard before. And while he stuck to the Stalinist position on Trotsky and Bukharin, he nevertheless uttered the heretical idea that even under Lenin the struggle against opposition had not been conducted on exclusively ideological lines, implying, though not expressing, the fact that Lenin too had used terror against his political enemies.

The main burden and impact of the speech, however, was concerned with the lawlessness of the Stalin era, the repression and massacre of innocent people. The delegates froze as Khrushchev described the way cases were fabricated against so-called 'enemies of the people'. In a matter of three or four hours, he achieved the impossible: he uncrowned Stalin and exposed him as an incompetent leader who 'knew the country and agriculture only from the movies', and who during the war 'worked out military operations on a globe', and so on.

The speech achieved a number of aims. First, it exposed Stalin's leadership qualities as a fantasy. Secondly, it established that the blame for all the crimes lay on Stalin. It created an eruption in public consciousness; it was the boldest, most unexpected attack on Caesarism, lawlessness and totalitarianism. But Khrushchev was a man of his time. There can be no argument about his contribution to the decisive exposure of the cult, and for that alone he has earned his place in history. His speech, however, prepared as it had been by the old-style Stalinist theoretician, was not probing, it skated over the surface of the facts, barely touching on the origins of Stalinism, and it did not even recognize that socialism had been distorted, let alone attempt to find the causes of the distortion. Khrushchev expressed the hope that the discussion of the personality cult would remain within party circles and not get into the press, 'not expose our sores to our enemies', and that this alone would suffice to liquidate the Stalinist perversions.

Paradoxically, to want to keep the discussion from the people and from world opinion was typical Stalinist thinking on Khrushchev's part. The inconsistency and the half-spoken re-emerged in the official statement of the Central Committee of 30 June 1956 'On Overcoming the Personality Cult and its Consequences'. This document, which bore little resemblance to Khrushchev's speech, was nonetheless a clearer expression of compromise with the Stalinists. It spoke of 'serious mistakes' having been committed only 'during the later years of Stalin's life', and of the dictator's 'occasionally' resorting to unworthy methods. And it asserted that it would be wrong to seek the source of the cult in the nature of the Soviet social order.[41]

It would seem as if, having defeated the ghost at the congress, Khrushchev was alarmed by his victory and tried to limit its effect by keeping the truth from the people. However, the speech was leaked through the delegations of the foreign parties and soon appeared in the pages of the Western press. By contrast, in the USSR the pretence that it had not happened would be maintained until the spring of 1989, when it was finally published in *Izvestiya TsK KPSS* ('Central Committee News'), demonstrating, if demonstration were needed, that Stalinism is not dead yet, but has merely changed its shape. The party, moreover, has yet to produce its own proper analysis of the phenomenon.

Khrushchev made his second assault on Stalin at the Twenty-Second Party Congress in 1961, publicly squeezing the throat of the Stalinist way of thinking

and acting, but not finishing it off. There followed a twenty-five-year moratorium during which Brezhnev, who could not quite bring himself to rehabilitate Stalin fully, was advised by Suslov and others to opt for the creation of
gaps or empty spaces in Soviet history. It was as if Stalin had never existed,
nor Stalinism, nor the millions of tortured and executed victims, nor the Gulag,
nor, of course, the countless figures who had played a prominent part during
the pre-Stalinist phase of Soviet and party history.

Most of the history books of that period were simplified beyond belief and, if
Stalin was mentioned at all, it was as merely one among many other leaders,
and one moreover who had merely 'committed some mistakes'. For that matter,
the Twentieth Congress itself disappeared behind the smokescreen for many
years. None of this is surprising: Stalin had died but the system survived and
the new people who came along merely continued to operate it.

Khrushchev's successors managed without great difficulty to paste over the
cracks breached by his two daring attacks. The speech had nevertheless done
its work, and the non-Soviet Communist Parties embarked on the long and
painful process of reassessing their history, their values, their programmes and
views, some of them following the reformist line, others attacking it.

Khrushchev can hardly have expected that the drama of the Twentieth
Congress would be played out on the world stage, that it would engender an
extended contest between different notions of socialism. On the one hand,
there was the orthodox, harsh, bureaucratic, forceful, uncompromising, one-
dimensional notion, capable of justifying even criminal methods in the name
of the great idea. On the other, the democratic, humanitarian, multi-faceted
notion, derived from the belief that the great idea must rest on clean, humane
methods and on the basis of historic compromises and the coexistence of
different systems and ideologies. Khrushchev himself did not of course hold
these views as such, but it is true to say that he at least opened the door of the
socialist world to the ideas which today we call 'new thinking'. He lifted the
veil of infallibility from the tyrant, and Stalin turned out to be an unsurpassed
master at combining the great idea with the grotesque.

In my attempt to paint a political portrait of Stalin, I have been acutely aware
that much of what happened in the Soviet Union did so because freedom had
been disregarded, scorned, neglected. One of the main aims of the October
Revolution had been freedom, and yet its victory did not free the people.
Freedom can exist only in conditions of real democracy. Without democracy,
only the shadow of freedom can be present, only ideological slavery, ritual
myths and clichés. The new ideology assumed that freedom could derive only
from society. Social freedom, however, can only emerge in partnership with
spiritual freedom.

In this book I frequently refer to conscience. People like Stalin regard conscience as a chimera. One cannot speak of the conscience of a dictator; he
simply did not have one. The people who did his dirty deeds for him, however,

knew full well what they were doing. In such people conscience had 'gone cold'. In consequence, the people allowed their own consciences to be driven into a reservation, thus giving the grand inquisitor the opportunity to carry on with his dark deeds.

The Soviet people have not entirely lost their belief in high ideals. They have shown themselves to be capable of repentance, rebirth and renewal, and this has had much to do with the liberation of their consciences from the shackles of shameful unfreedom. They have freed themselves, certainly, but it is too soon to beat the drum. In Russian and Soviet history there have been many brave attempts at making a new start, but too many of them ended with the defeat of the reformers. Perhaps it is premature now to say that the process of renewal is irreversible. Stalinism is after all not yet dead politically. Crises and their solutions have not only a progressive, but also a conservative logic. One can only pray that one's worst fears will not turn out to be prophetic. But our history gives one pause.

Chronology

(Dates according to New Style or Western Calendar)

1879

7 November   Trotsky born in Yanovka, near Yelizavetgrad (Kirovgrad) in the Ukraine.

21 December   Stalin born in Gori, Georgia.

1888–93   S. attends church school in Gori.

1894   S. enters theological seminary in Tiflis.
Coronation of Nicholas II.

1898

March   Russian Social Democratic Labour Party (RSDLP) formed in Minsk.

1899   S. expelled from seminary.

1900   Lenin and Martov start their newspaper *Iskra* ('The Spark').

1901   S. elected member of Tiflis Social Democratic Committee.

1902   S. arrested for first time.
Trotsky meets Lenin in London.

1903   S. marries Yekaterina Svanidze.
S. transported to Eastern Siberia.
RSDLP splits at its Second Congress in London into Bolsheviks, led by Lenin, and Mensheviks, led by group including Martov and Trotsky.

1904   S. escapes from Siberia, returns to Tiflis and becomes Bolshevik, adopts alias Koba.

S.'s son Yakov born.

1904–06	Russo–Japanese War and 1905 revolution.
1905	Tsar concedes political reform, including a legislative assembly, the State Duma. S. attends Bolshevik conference in Tammerfors, Finland, meets Lenin for first time.
1906	S. attends Fourth Party Congress in Stockholm. S. in Caucasian combat unit, takes part in bank robberies for Bolshevik funds.
1907	S. attends London Congress, his first trip abroad. Yekaterina Svanidze dies of tuberculosis.
1907–09	S. member of Baku Bolshevik Committee.
1909	S. exiled to Solvychegodsk, Northern Vologda. Escapes after four months, returns to Baku.
1910	Trotsky establishes his independent newspaper *Pravda*.
1912	S. arrested during visit to St Petersburg, deported to Western Siberia, escapes after two months and returns to capital. S. visits Lenin in Cracow and proceeds to Vienna, where he meets Bukharin and Trotsky and writes essay on national question. Adopts alias Stalin. S. coopted *in absentia* on to Bolshevik Central Committee at Twelfth Party Conference in Prague. Lenin appropriates the name of Trotsky's newspaper, which has remained the organ of the Bolshevik Central Committee until the present day.
1913	S. arrested in St Petersburg, exiled for four years to Turukhansk.
1914	First World War breaks out.
1917 March November	Tsar abdicates. Bolsheviks seize power. Council of People's Commissars (Bolshevik government) formed, with Stalin as Commissar of Nationalities and Trotsky as Commissar of Foreign Affairs.

| December | Soviet–German armistice. |

1918

January	Constituent Assembly dispersed by Bolsheviks after one session.
	Red Army founded.
February	Chicherin replaces Trotsky as Foreign Commissar.
March	Brest-Litovsk peace treaty signed with Germany.
April	Civil war begins in Russia.
July	Constitution of Russian Soviet Federated Socialist Republic (RSFSR).
	Tsar and family executed in Ekaterinburg.
	'War Communism' adopted.
	Allied Intervention begins.
August	Attempt on Lenin's life by Socialist Revolutionary, Fanny Kaplan.
November	Allied–German armistice.

1919

| March | Communist International (Comintern) founded in Moscow. |

1920

April	Poles invade Soviet Ukraine.
July	Anglo–Soviet trade treaty.
October	Armistice with Poland.
November	Civil war ends with defeat and evacuation of White armies in Crimea.

1921

March	Kronstadt uprising.
	Tenth Party Congress adopts Lenin's New Economic Policy and bans party factions.
	Independent state of Georgia under Menshevik government overthrown by Bolsheviks.

1922

February	Cheka renamed GPU.
April	S. elected General Secretary of the party.
May	Lenin's first stroke.
December	Lenin's second stroke.
	Formation of Union of Soviet Socialist Republics.

1923

| March | Lenin's third stroke. |

| April | Twelfth Party Congress. |

1924

January	Lenin dies.
	Constitution of USSR becomes law.
May	Thirteenth Party Congress.
	Diplomatic recognition from Austria, Britain, China, Denmark, France, Greece, Italy, Norway and Sweden.

1925

| December | Fourteenth Party Congress. |

1926

| July | Zinoviev expelled from Politburo and leadership of Comintern. |
| October | Trotsky and Kamenev expelled from Politburo. |

1927

| November | Trotsky and Zinoviev expelled from party. |
| December | Fifteenth Party Congress. |

1928

| January | Trotsky banished to Alma-Ata, Kazakhstan. |

1929

January	Trotsky expelled from USSR.
April	First Five-Year Plan adopted by Sixteenth Party Conference.
November	Bukharin expelled from Politburo.
December	S. proclaims end of the NEP and start of collectivization.

1930

March	Collectivization suspended.
April–June	Sixteenth Party Congress.
December	Trials of various groups accused of sabotage and wrecking in the agricultural sector.

1931

| March | Trial of Mensheviks for wrecking. |
| | Rewriting of history begins under S.'s guidance. |

1932

| November | S.'s wife, Nadezhda Alliluyeva, commits suicide. |
| December | Internal passports, or identity cards, issued to urban |

population. Collective farmers denied the right to leave the village.

1933
January
November

Hitler becomes Chancellor of Germany.
Diplomatic and trade relations established between USSR and USA.

1934
January
September
December

Seventeenth Party Congress, the 'Congress of Victors'.
USSR joins League of Nations.
Sergei Kirov assassinated in Leningrad.

1935
May

USSR signs military treaties with France and Czechoslovakia.

1936

Trial and execution of Zinoviev, Kamenev and fourteen others.
Trial of seventeen, including Radek and Pyatakov; thirteen executed.
Execution of Red Army leadership.

1937–39

The great purge, with mass arrests, executions and long sentences to prison and forced labour in concentration camps.

1938
March
July

December

Trial and execution of Bukharin, Rykov and sixteen others.
Armed clashes with Japanese at Lake Khasan on the Mongolian–Chinese border.
Beria replaces Yezhov as People's Commissar for Internal Affairs (NKVD).

1939
April

May

August

September

Talks begin between USSR, Britain and France for a military alliance against Hitler.
USSR also seeks to improve relations with Nazi Germany.
Litvinov replaced by Molotov as Commissar for Foreign Affairs.
Further armed clashes with Japanese at Khalkhin Gol on Mongolian border.
Soviet–German Non-Aggression Pact signed in Kremlin with secret protocol on division of Poland and spheres of interest.
Germany invades Poland.

	USSR invades Poland.
	Soviet–German Treaty on Borders and Friendship signed.
November	USSR annexes Western Ukraine and Western Belorussia in accordance with Border Treaty.
	Soviet–Finnish Winter War.
December	USSR expelled from League of Nations.

1940
February	Soviet–German trade agreement.
March	Soviet–Finnish peace treaty.
April	Massacre of Polish officer POWs by NKVD at Katyn, Smolensk.
June	USSR regains Bessarabia (Moldavia) and annexes Northern Bukovina.
August	USSR annexes Lithuania, Latvia and Estonia.
	Trotsky assassinated in Mexico by NKVD.

1941
April	Soviet–Yugoslav Treaty of Friendship and Non-Aggression signed.
	Soviet–Japanese Neutrality Pact.
6 May	S. becomes Chairman of Council of People's Commissars.
21 June	Germany invades USSR.
3 July	S. makes radio appeal to Soviet people to save the fatherland.
November	USA begins Lend-Lease for USSR.
	Germans reach suburbs of Moscow.
December	Japanese open Pacific War with attack on Pearl Harbor.
	Germany declares war on USA.

1942
January	Wannsee Conference. Hitler adopts 'final solution' to 'Jewish question'.
August	German army reaches the Caucasus.
December	Creation of Russian Army of Liberation under General Vlasov in German POW camps.

1943
January	S. becomes Marshal of the Soviet Union.
February	German troops surrender at Stalingrad.
May	S. dissolves Comintern.
	People's Commissars renamed ministers.
July	Ranks and shoulder boards created, and the title 'officer' replaces that of 'commander', current since creation of Red Army.
September	S. permits election of new Patriarch of Russian Orthodox Church.

| November | Teheran conference with Stalin, Roosevelt and Churchill. S.'s one and only trip by air. |

1944

March	USSR re-establishes diplomatic relations with Italy.
June	Second front established in Europe by Allied invasion of Normandy.
August	Warsaw Uprising against Germans.
	Red Army enters Bucharest.
September	Red Army enters Sofia.
October	Red Army enters Belgrade.

1945

February	Yalta conference with Stalin, Roosevelt and Churchill.
April	Red Army enters Vienna.
2 May	Red Army conquers Berlin.
8 May	Germany accepts unconditional surrender.
July–August	Potsdam conference with Stalin, Truman and Churchill, succeeded by Attlee.
6 August	US drops atomic bomb on Hiroshima.
8 August	USSR declares war on Japan.
9 August	US drops atomic bomb on Nagasaki.
	USSR opens offensive in Manchuria.
2 September	Japan signs unconditional surrender.
24 October	United Nations founded.

1946

March	Churchill's 'iron curtain' speech at Fulton, Missouri.
August	General Vlasov and others executed in Moscow.
	Zhdanov launches ideological campaign against Western cultural influence.
November	Jewish Anti-Fascist Committee put under suspicion.

1947

| September | Foundation of Cominform in Poland. Zhdanov proclaims the doctrine of the two camps. |

1948

January	Chairman of Jewish Anti-Fascist Committee, actor Solomon Mikhoels, assassinated by secret police in Minsk.
	Marshall Plan for aid to Europe.
April–June	Berlin blockade and airlift.
May	Jewish State of Israel proclaimed.
June	Cominform expels Yugoslav Communist Party.
	Czechoslovak People's Republic proclaimed.

August	Zhdanov dies suddenly.
	'Leningrad affair'.
November	Jewish Anti-Fascist Committee closed down and its members arrested.

1949

January	Council for Mutual Economic Assistance between socialist countries (Comecon) set up.
	Campaign launched against Jewish intelligentsia, labelled 'rootless cosmopolitans'.
April	NATO formed.
May	Israel admitted to United Nations.
	USSR begins anti-Zionist propaganda.
September	USSR tests atomic bomb.
October	Chinese People's Republic proclaimed.

1950

February	Sino–Soviet treaty of friendship.
	Political trials in socialist countries.
June	Korean War begins.

1951

November	Slansky trial and anti-Zionist purge of Czech Communist Party.

1952

May–July	Trial and execution of Jewish Anti-Fascist Committee.
October	Nineteenth Party Congress. Politburo renamed Presidium, General Secretary renamed First Secretary.
November	US tests first hydrogen bomb.

1953

January	'Doctors' Plot'.
5 March	Death of Stalin.
June	Workers' revolt in East Berlin suppressed.
July	Arrest of Beria.
August	Armistice signed in Korea.
	USSR tests hydrogen bomb.
September	Khrushchev elected First Secretary.

1955

May	Warsaw Pact signed.

1956

February	Twentieth Party Congress, Khrushchev makes 'secret speeches' denouncing Stalin.

April	Dissolution of Cominform.
June	Anti-Soviet riots in Poznan, Poland.
October	Hungarian national uprising suppressed by Soviet tanks.

1957

July	'Anti-party' group expelled from Presidium.

1958

October	Boris Pasternak awarded Nobel Prize for Literature for *Doctor Zhivago*. Persecution of Pasternak begins in USSR.
December	Andrei Sakharov urges test ban on hydrogen bomb.

1961

October	Twenty-Second Party Congress. Khrushchev intensifies de-Stalinization. Stalin's mummy removed from Mausoleum.

Notes

Abbreviations of names of archives cited:

Arkhiv IKKI – Archives of the Executive Committee of the Communist International

AVP SSSR – Soviet Foreign Policy Archives (i.e. Foreign Ministry)

TsAMO SSSR – Central Archives of the Soviet Ministry of Defence

TsGAOR – Central State Archives of the October Revolution

TsGASA – Central State Archives of the Soviet Army

TsPA IML – Central Party Archives at the Institute of Marxism-Leninism.

FOREWORD

1 Trotsky, L. *Stalin*, Benson, Vermont, 1947, p. 7.
2 TsGASA, f. 918, op. 3, d. 80, l. 591.
3 Jaurès, Jean, *Sotsialisticheskaya istoriya frantsuzskoy revolyutsii*, Moscow, 1983, vol. 6, p. 446.
4 Plutarch, *Sochineniya*, Moscow, 1983, p. 429.

1: THE GLOW OF OCTOBER

Ch. 1: A Portrait

1 Stalin, I. V. *Sochineniya*, 13 vols., Moscow, 1946–48, vol. 13, p. 113.
2 TsPA IML, f. 558, op. 1, d. 5978, 5080.
3 Narym Memorial Museum of Bolshevik Political Exiles, f. 998.
4 Sverdlova, K. T. *Ya. M. Sverdlov*, Moscow, 1960, p. 199.
5 Lenin, V. I. *Polnoe sobranie sochinenii* (hereafter *PSS*), 55 vols., Moscow, 1960–65, vol. 48, p. 169.
6 Ordzhonikidze, G. K. *Put' Bol'shevika*. Moscow, 1956, pp. 128–129.
7 TsPA IML, f. 17, op. 2, d. 577, l. 18–25.
8 TsGAOR, f. 9401, op. 2, d. 2000, l. 304.
9 TsPA IML, f. 558, op. 1, d. 4358, l. 1.
10 Cited in Trotsky, L. *Stalin*, op. cit. p. 148.
11 Stalin, op. cit. vol. 6, pp. 52–54.
12 Lenin, *Biograficheskaya khronika*. vol. 3, p. 147.
13 TsPA IML, f. 2, op. 1, d. 23851, l. 1.

14   Lenin, op. cit. pp. 456–457.
15   Stalin, op. cit. vol. 13, p. 121.

Ch. 2: February: the Prologue

16   Florinsky, M. *The End of the Russian Empire*, New Haven, 1931, p. 228.
17   Alekseyev, S. A. ed.: *Fevral'skaya revolyutsiya*. Preface and notes by A. I.
     Usagin, Moscow–Leningrad, 1926, p. 153.
18   Shulgin, V. V. *Dni*, Belgrade, 1925, p. 108.
19   Arkhiv IKKI, f. 555, op. 1, d. 2802, l. 1–2.
20   Alekseyev, op. cit. p. 153.
21   Ibid. p. 131.
22   Lenin, *PSS*, vol. 31, p. 156.
23   Kerensky, A. F. *The Crucifixion of Liberty*, London, 1934, p. 146.
24   Alekseyev, op. cit. pp. 336–337.
25   Stalin, I. V. *Kratkaya biografiya*, Moscow, 1951, p. 57.
26   Trotsky, L. D. *Fevral'skaya revolyutsiya*. Berlin, 1931, pp. 321–322, 325.

Ch. 3: The Supporting Players

27   *Pravda*, 15 March 1917.
28   Stalin, *Sochineniya*, vol. 3, p. 8.
29   Ibid. vol. 6, p. 333.
30   Sukhanov, N. *The Russian Revolution 1917*, Oxford, 1955, p. 230.
31   Sukhanov, N. N. *Zapiski o revolyutsii*, 7 vols, Berlin, Petrograd, Moscow,
     1922. vol. 7, p. 44.
32   *Protokoly VII konferentsii RSDRP(b)*, Moscow, 1980, p. 80.
33   Stalin, *Sochineniya*, vol. 3, p. 55.

Ch. 4: Uprising

34   *Velikaya Oktyabr'skaya sotsialisticheskaya revolyutsiya*. Entstiklopediya.
     Moscow, 1987, p. 109.
35   Lenin, *PSS*, vol. 34, p. 25.
36   Ibid. vol. 49, p. 445.
37   Lenin, *Biograficheskaya khronika*, vol. 4, p. 282.
38   TsPA IML, f. 4, op. 3, d. 813.
39   Lenin, *PSS*, vol. 34, p. 392.
40   Ryabinsky, K., *Revolyutsiya 1917 goda. Khronika sobytii*. Moscow–Leningrad,
     1926, vol. 5, p. 172.
41   Lenin, *PSS*, vol. 34, pp. 435, 436.
42   *Rabochaya Gazeta*, TsPA IML, f. 325, op. 1, d. 11, l. 11.
43   Lenin, *PSS*, vol. 35, p. 102.
44   Stalin, *Sochineniya*, vol. 3, p. 389.
45   TsGAOR, f. 130, op. 1, d. 1, l. 20.
46   Trotsky, L. D. *Stalinskaya shkola fal'sifikatsii*. Berlin, 1932, p. 26.

47 Trotsky, L. D. *Moya zhizn'*, 2 vols., Berlin, 1932, vol. 2, p. 60.
48 Stalin, *Stat'i i rechi 1921–1927*, Moscow–Leningrad, 1928, pp. 104–105.

Ch. 5: Saved by Chance

49 Lenin, *PSS*, vol. 35, p. 250.
50 Trotsky, L. D. *Sochineniya*, vol. 17, 'Sovetskaya respublika i kapitalisticheskii mir', part 1, Moscow–Leningrad, 1926, pp. 103, 106.
51 Lenin, *PSS*, vol. 35, pp. 369–370, 490.
52 Ibid, vol. 36, p. 30.
53 *Sed'moi s'ezd RKP. Stenograficheskii otchet.* Moscow, 1923, pp. 32–50.

Ch. 6: Civil War

54 Lenin, *PSS*, vol. 39, p. 343.
55 TsPA IML, f. 2, op. 1, d. 6157.
56 TsGASA, f. 1, op. 2, d. III, l. 84.
57 TsPA IML, f. 2, op. 1, d. 6235.
58 Stalin, *Sochineniya*, vol. 4, p. 118.
59 *Leninskii sbornik*, Moscow, 1970, vol. 37, p. 139.
60 TsGASA, f. 10. op. 1, d. 123, l. 29–30.
61 *Leninskii sbornik*, vol. 37, p. 136.
62 TsGASA, f. 100, op. 9, d. 34, l. 26–27.
63 TsPA IML, f. 2, op. 1, d. 6324, l. 1–2.
64 Lenin, *PSS*, vol. 36, p. 463.
65 Ibid. vol. 42, p. 47.
66 TsPA IML, f. 588, op. 1, d. 486.
67 *Leninskii sbornik*, vol. 37, p. 139.
68 TsPA IML, f. 2, op. 1, d. 10 022.
69 Stalin, *Sochineniya*, vol. 4, p. 210.
70 TsGASA, f. 33988, op. 2, d. 289, l. 19–20; Lenin, *PSS*, vol. 51, p. 428.
71 Lenin, *PSS*, vol. 51, p. 206–207.
72 Ibid. p. 208.
73 *Direktivy komandovaniya frontov Krasnoy Armii, 1917–1922 gg.* Moscow, 1972, vol. 2, p. 720.
74 Ibid. p. 410.
75 Ibid. vol. 3, p. 244.
76 Ibid. vol. 3, p. 244.
77 Stalin, *Sochineniya*, vol. 4, p. 261.
78 Trotsky, *Moya zhizn'*, vol. 2, p. 41.
79 TsGASA, f. 33 987, op. 3, d. 46, l. 413.
80 Lenin, *PSS*, vol. 45, p. 357.
81 TsGASA, f. 104, op. 4, d. 484, l. 11.
82 TsGASA, f. 104, op. 4, d. 484, l. 11.
83 Lenin, *PSS*, vol. 41, p. 321.

2: THE LEADER'S WARNINGS

Ch. 7: Comrades in Arms

1 *Izvestiya*, 23 January 1924. Cited in *U velikoy mogily*, Moscow, 1924, p. 63.
2 TsPA IML, f. 2, op. 1, d. 23 315.
3 *XII s'ezd Rossiiskoy Kommunisticheskoy Partii (bol'shevikov). Stenograficheskii otchet.* Moscow, 1923, pp. 60–61.
4 Ibid. p. 61.
5 *Leninskii sbornik*, vol. 37, p. 106.
6 Trotsky, *Moya zhizn'*, vol. 2, pp. 213–214.
7 Lenin, *PSS*, vol. 45, p. 345.
8 Lunacharsky, A. *Revolyutsionnye siluety*, Moscow, 1923, p. 31. Also in English as *Revolutionary Silhouettes*, trans. Michael Glenny, London, 1967.
9 *XIV s'ezd Vsesoyuznoy kommunisticheskoy partii (bol'shevikov). Stenograficheskii otchet.* Moscow–Leningrad, 1926, pp. 453–454.
10 Ibid. pp. 274–275.
11 Stalin, *Sochineniya*, vol. 7, pp. 380, 382.
12 *Sbornik Feliks Dzerzhinskii*, Moscow, 1931, pp. 141, 186.
13 *Krasnaya Zvezda*, 31 October 1930.
14 Stalin, *Sochineniya*, vol. 7, p. 251.
15 TsPA IML, f. 17, op. 2, d. 1.
16 Manfred, A. A. *Velikaya frantsuzskaya revolyutsiya*, Moscow, 1983, p. 328.

Ch. 8: The General Secretary

17 *XI s'ezd Rossiiskoy kommunisticheskoy partii (bol'shevikov). Stenograficheskii otchet*, Moscow, 1922, pp. 47, 49, 51, 52.
18 Ibid. pp. 69–70.
19 TsPA IML, f. 17, op. 2, d. 29.
20 TsPA IML, f. 17, op. 2, d. 78, l. 1–2.
21 TsPA IML, f. 17, op. 2, d. 78, l. 1–9.
22 Lenin, *PSS*, vol. 45, p. 188.
23 Ibid. p. 211.
24 TsPA IML, f. 4, op. 1, d. 142, l. 126; Lenin, *Biograficheskaya khronika*, vol. 12, p. 388.
25 Adam Ulam, *Stalin. The Man and his Era*, New York, 1973, pp. 213–214, cites the Trotsky Archive (Harvard University), T 755.
26 Lenin, *PSS*. vol. 45, p. 357.
27 Ibid. p. 358.
28 Ibid. vol. 54, p. 329.
29 Ibid. pp. 674–675.
30 Ibid. pp. 329–330.
31 Ibid. p. 330.

Ch. 9: Letter to the Congress

32 Gramsci, A. *Izbrannye proizvedeniya v 3 tomakh*, Moscow, 1959, vol. 3, p. 185.
33 Lenin, *PSS*, vol. 45, p. 20.
34 Ibid. p. 308.
35 Bukharin, N. I. *Izbrannye proizvedeniya*, Moscow, 1988, pp. 120–121.
36 Lenin, op. cit. p. 710.
37 Ibid. p. 174.
38 Ibid. pp. 343–344.
39 Ibid. pp. 344–345.
40 Ibid. p. 345.
41 Ibid. p. 345.
42 *XI s'ezd RKP(b). Protokoly i stenograficheskie otchety s'ezdov i konferentsii KPSS.* Moscow, 1969, p. 262.
43 Lenin, op. cit. p. 710.
44 Ibid. p. 474.
45 Ibid. p. 344–346.
46 Ibid. p. 247.
47 Ibid. p. 346.
48 Lunacharsky, A. *Revolyutsionnye siluety*, op. cit. p. 26.
49 Lenin, op. cit. p. 387.
50 TsPA IML, f. 17, op. 2, d. 88.
51 *XII s'ezd RKP(b)*. Moscow, 1969, pp. 80–81.

Ch. 10: Stalin or Trotsky?

52 *XII s'ezd RKP(b)*. op. cit. pp. 50–53.
53 *IX s'ezd RKP(b)*. Moscow, 1920, p. 81.
54 Trotsky, *Moya zhizn'*, vol. 2, pp. 218, 226.
55 Cited in *U velikoy mogily*, Moscow, 1924, pp. 27, 63.
56 Ibid. p. 248.

Ch. 11: The Roots of the Tragedy

57 Lenin, *PSS*, vol. 45, pp. 594–595.
58 Ibid. p. 594.
59 Ibid. p. 110.
60 Stalin, I. *Sochineniya*, vol. 10. pp. 175–176.
61 TsPA IML, f. 558, op. 1, d. 86, l. 15; Stalin, *Sochineniya*, vol. 7, p. 387.
62 Radek, K. *Itogi XII s'ezda RKP.* Moscow, 1923, p. 25.
63 Berdyaev, N. *Samoznanie. Opyt filosofskoy autobiografii.* Paris, YMCA, 1949, p. 251.

3: CHOICE AND STRUGGLE

Ch. 12: Building Socialism

1   Napoleon, *Izbrannye proizvedeniya*, Moscow, 1941, p. 62.
2   *KPSS v rezolyutsiyakh*. Part 1, 7th edn., Moscow, 1953, p. 511.
3   TsPA IML, f. 558, op. 1, d. 4870.
4   TsPA IML, f. 17, op. 2, d. 112.
5   Trotsky, L. D. *Uroki Oktyabrya*, Moscow, 1925, p. 49.
6   Trotsky, L. D. *Permanentnaya revolyutsiya*, Berlin, 1930, p. 16.
7   Lenin, *PSS*, vol. 45, p. 309.
8   Ibid. p. 309.
9   *Bol'shevik*, No. 8, 1925, p. 7.
10   TsPA IML, f. 2, op. 2, d. 103.
11   TsPA IML, f. 17, op. 2, d. 109, l. 12.
12   TsPA IML, f. 558, op. 1, d. 1.
13   Stalin, *Sochineniya*, vol. 6, p. 237.
14   Ibid. p. 357.
15   *XIV konferentsiya RKP(b)*, Moscow–Leningrad, 1925, pp. 248, 253.
16   TsPA IML, f. 558, op. 1, d. 2816, l. 3–5.
17   Stalin, *Sochineniya*, vol. 7, pp. 365, 383.
18   Ibid. p. 390.
19   Ibid. pp. 390–391.

Ch. 13: Leninism for the Masses

20   Stalin, *Sochineniya*, vol. 1, p. 299.
21   Ibid. vol. 7, p. 375.
22   Ibid. vol. 9, pp. 315, 321.
23   Ibid. vol. 8, pp. 95, 96, 98.
24   TsPA IML, f. 17, op. 2, d. 154, l. 54.
25   TsPA IML, f. 17, op. 2, d. 154, l. 54.
26   TsPA IML, f. 17, op. 2, d. 154, l. 67.

Ch. 14: Intellectual Disarray

27   Trotsky, L. D. *Literatura i revolyutsiya*, Moscow–Leningrad, 1924, p. 26.
28   *Bol'shevik*, Nos. 7–8, 1926, pp. 107–108.
29   *Bol'shevik*, No. 9, 1928, p. 6.
30   *O partiinoy i sovetskoy pechati*. Moscow, 1954, p. 347.
31   Stalin, *Sochineniya*. vol. 11, pp. 327–328.
32   Ibid. vol. 13, pp. 23, 27.
33   *O partiinoy i sovetskoy pechati*. pp. 346–347.
34   Korolenko, V. *Pis'ma k Lunacharskomu*, Paris, 1922, pp. 61–62.
35   *Dom Iskusstv*, Petrograd, 1920, No. 1, p. 65.
36   Bogdanov, A. *O proletarskoy kul'ture*, Moscow–Leningrad, 1925, p. 12.
37   Trotsky, L. D. *Literatura i revolyutsiya*, Moscow, 1924, p. 13.

38   *Pravda*, 26 October, 1926.

Ch. 15: 'Enemy Number One' Defeated

39   *XV konferentsiya Vsesoyuznoy kommunisticheskoy partii (bol'shevikov).*
      Stenograficheskii otchet. Moscow–Leningrad, 1927, pp. 535, 536.
40   TsPA IML. f. 3, op. 1, d. 2827.
41   Trotsky, *My Life*, New York, 1930 and 1960, p. 538.
42   Stalin, *Sochineniya*, vol. 10, p. 193.
43   Ibid. pp. 204, 205.
44   Ibid. p. 191.
45   Ibid. p. 173.
46   *Bol'shevik*, No. 16, 1925, p. 68.
47   Stalin, *Sochineniya*, vol. 10, p. 175–177.
48   Essad Bey, *Stalin*, Riga, 1932, p. 234.
49   *Sotsialisticheskii vestnik*, Berlin, April 1931, No 8 (245), p. 8.
50   Trotsky, *Moya zhizn'*, op. cit. pp. 539–540.
51   Ibid. p. 556.
52   Trotsky, L. D. *Chto i kak proizoshlo. Shest' statei dlya mirovoy burzhuaznoy pechati.* Paris, 1929, p. 9.
53   Ibid. p. 60.

Ch. 16: The Leader's Private Life

54   Lenin, *PSS*, vol. 54, p. 518.
55   TsPA IML, f. 558, op. 1, d. 2908.
56   *Memorias de Dolores Ibarruri*, Barcelona, 1985, pp. 530–535.
57   TsGAOR, f. 9401, op. 1, d. 2181.
58   Berdyaev, N. *Ekzistentsial'naya dialektika bozhestvennogo i chelovechestvennogo.* Paris, 1952, p. 132.

4: DICTATORSHIP OR DICTATOR?

Ch. 17: The Fate of the Peasantry

1   TsPA IML, f. 558, op. 1, d. 3112.
2   *Sobranie Zakonov i Rasporyazhenii Raboche–Krestyanskogo pravitel'stva*, Moscow, 1925, p. 313.
3   Lenin, *PSS*, vol. 45, p. 372.
4   Ibid. p. 236.
5   Stalin, *Sochineniya*, vol. 10, p. 311.
6   *XV s'ezd VKP(b). Stenograficheskii otchet.* Moscow–Leningrad, 1928, p. 976.
7   Ibid. pp. 1057, 1091.
8   Ibid. p. 1308.
9   *Planovoe khozyaistvo*, 1927, No. 7, p. 11.
10   Stalin, op. cit. vol. 11, pp. 2, 4, 6, 7.
11   Ibid. vol. 12, p. 166.

12 Churchill, W. *History of the Second World War*, London, 1951, vol. 4, pp. 447–448.

13 Stalin, *Voprosy Leninizma*, p. 344.

14 Stalin, *Sochineniya*, vol. 12, p. 149.

15 *Bol'shevik*, 1940, No. 1, p. 2.

16 Stalin, *Voprosy Leninizma*, p. 195.

17 Stalin, *Sochineniya*, vol. 13, p. 392.

18 Ibid. p. 245.

19 *Istoriya SSSR s drevneishikh vremen do nashikh dnei*. Moscow, 1966, vol. 9, pt. 1, pp. 189–190.

Ch. 18: The Drama of Bukharin

20 Stalin, *Sochineniya*, vol. 12, p. 1.

21 Bukharin, N. *Ataka, sbornik statei*. Moscow, 1924, pp. 98, 99.

22 Bukharin, *Izbrannye proizvedeniya*. Moscow, 1988, p. 133.

23 *Bol'shevik*, No. 5, 1925, pp. 6, 8, 14.

24 Bukharin, op. cit. p. 137.

25 Ibid. p. 121.

26 Cohen, S. *Bukharin and the Bolshevik Revolution: A Political Biography, 1888–1938*. London, 1974, p. 325.

27 Stalin, *Sochineniya*. vol. 12, p. 69.

28 Ibid. pp. 70, 79.

29 Ibid. p. 132.

30 *Itogi noyabr'skogo plenuma TsK (VKP(b)*. Leningrad, 1929, p. 193.

31 *Sotsialisticheskii vestnik*, Berlin, April 1931, No. 8 (245).

Ch. 19: Dictatorship and Democracy

32 Lenin, *PSS*, vol. 45, p. 441.

33 Stalin, *Sochineniya*, vol. 13, pp. 207, 208.

34 Ibid. p. 210.

35 *XVI s'ezd VKP(b)*. Moscow–Leningrad, 1930, p. 38.

36 TsGAOR, f. 9492, op. 2, d. 6, l. 78–81.

37 TsGAOR, f. 7523, op. 67, d. 1, l. 5.

38 Stalin, *Sochineniya*. vol. 13, pp. 107, 111, 114, 119–120.

39 *Arkhiv Verkhovnogo suda SSSR*, f. 75, op. 35, d. 319, l. 26.

40 TsGASA, f. 33 987, op. 3, d. 773, l. 102.

41 TsPA IML, f. 558, op. 1, d. 5088.

42 *Pravda*, 7 April 1931.

Ch. 20: The Congress of Victors

43 *Pravda*, 5 August 1933.

44 *XVII s'ezd VKP(b)*, Moscow–Leningrad, 1934, p. 255.

45 Ibid. p. 18.

46 Ibid. p. 28.
47 Ibid. p. 253.
48 Ibid. p. 125.
49 Ibid. p. 211.
50 Ibid. p. 250.
51 Ibid. pp. 493, 496, 497.
52 Ibid. p. 521.
53 TsGASA, f. 918/33 987, op. 3, d. 155, l. 88.
54 *XVII s'zed*, p. 235.

Ch. 21: Stalin and Kirov

55 *XVII s'ezd*, p. 115.
56 Stalin, *Sochineniya*, vol. 13, p. 19.
57 TsPA IML, f. 558, op. 1, d. 5228, l. 1.
58 TsPA IML, f. 558, op. 1, d. 5228, l. 2.
59 Arkhiv Genshtaba, op. 16, stack 17, shelf 9.
60 *XVII s'ezd KPSS. Stenograficheskii otchet*. Moscow, 1962. vol. 2, p. 403.
61 Cited in Pompeyev, Yu. *Khochetsya zhit' i zhit'. Dokumental'naya povest' o S. M. Kirove*. Moscow, 1987, p. 8.
62 Ibid. p. 18.
63 TsPA IML, f. 558, op. 1, d. 3334.
64 *Pravda*, 3 December 1934.
65 *Sbornik materialov po istorii sotsialisticheskogo ugolovnogo zakonodatel'stva*. Moscow, 1938, p. 314.
66 Arkhiv Verkhovnogo suda SSSR, f. 75, op. 35, d. 319.
67 Stalin, I. V. *Beseda s angliiskim pisatelem G. Uell'som*, Moscow, 1935, pp. 13, 14, 16.
68 TsPA IML, f. 558, op. 1, d. 3179.

5: THE LEADER'S MANTLE

Ch. 22: A Commanding Personality

1   *KPSS v rezolyutsiyakh i resheniyakh*, 8th edn. Moscow, 1970, vol. 2, p. 90.
2   TsPA IML, f. 17, op. 2, d. 633.
3   *KPSS v rezolyutsiyakh* (1970), p. 220.
4   TsPA IML, f. 558, op. 2, d. 2915.
5   *Bol'shevik*, No. 9, 1937, p. 9.
6   Stalin, *Kratkaya biografiya*, 1948, p. 163.
7   TsPA IML, f. 17, op. 120, d. 313.
8   Suetonius, *Zhizn' dvenadtsati tsezarei*, Moscow, 1987, p. 135.
9   TsPA IML, f. 3, op. 1, d. 3399.
10 Stalin, *Sochineniya*, vol. 13, p. 92.

Ch. 23: Stalin's Mind

11 Yaroslavsky, Ye. *O tovarishche Staline*. Moscow, 1942, p. 149.
12 TsPA IML, f. 558, op. 1, d. 2510.
13 TsPA IML, f. 558, op. 3, d. 461, l. 9–21.
14 TsPA IML, f. 3, op. 1, d. 4674, l. 1–3.
15 TsPA IML, f. 558, op. 2, d. 5374, l. 1–3.
16 TsPA IML, f. 558, op. 1, d. 5374.
17 TsGASA, f. 33 987, op. 3, d. 273, l. 36.
18 TsPA IML, f. 558, op. 1, d. 2898.
19 Churchill, *History of the Second World War*, op. cit. vol. 4, p. 443.
20 Stalin, *Sochineniya*, vol. 12, pp. 53–54.
21 TsPA IML, f. 17, op. 120, d. 24, l. 1–3.
22 Stalin, *Sochineniya*, vol. 11, pp. 239–240, 241.
23 TsPA IML, f. 558, op. 2, d. 4074, l. 35.
24 Zhukov, G. K. *Vospominaniya i razmyshleniya*, 5th edn. Moscow, 1963, vol. 2, p. 95.
25 Vasilievsky, A. M. *Delo vsei zhizni*. 3rd edn. Moscow, 1978, p. 501.
26 Churchill, W. op. cit. p. 434.
27 *K pyatidesyatiletiyu so dnya rozhdeniya I. V. Stalina*. Moscow, 1940, pp. 268–274.
28 TsPA IML, f. 17, op. 2, d. 612, l. 26.
29 TsGAOR, f. 9401, op. 2, d. 149, l. 108.

Ch. 24: Caesarism

30 Feuchtwanger, L. *Moskva 1937. Otchet o poezdke dlya moikh druzei*. Trans. from German. Moscow, 1937, pp. 58–59.
31 Ibid. p. 64.
32 Ibid. pp. 59–60.
33 Berdyaev, N. *Sud'ba Rossii*, Moscow, 1918, p. 58.
34 TsPA IML, f. 325, op. 1, d. 365, l. 79.
35 TsPA IML, f. 17, op. 2, d. 612, l. 12.
36 Ibid. l. 28.
37 Stakhanov, A. *Rasskaz o moei zhizni*. Moscow, 1938, p. 149.
38 TsPA IML, f. 558, op. 1, d. 2218.
39 TsPA IML, f. 17, op. 2, d. 612.
40 *Pravda*, 21 October 1937.

Ch. 25: In the Shadow of the Leader

41 Lenin, *PSS*, vol. 4, p. 392.
42 TsPA IML, f. 17, op. 2, d. 612.
43 *XXII s'ezd KPSS. Stenograficheskii otchet*. Moscow, 1962, vol. 2, p. 404.
44 TsGAOR, f. 9401, op. 2, d. 203, l. 366.
45 TsPA IML, f. 558, op. 1, d. 2897.
46 TsPA IML, f. 17, op. 2, d. 612, l. 32.

47   Ibid.
48   Ibid. l. 32.
49   Ibid. l. 24–35.
50   *Leninskii sbornik*, vol. 37, pp. 138–139.
51   TsPA IML, op. cit. l. 83.
52   *XXII s'ezd KPSS*, vol. 2, p. 403.
53   TsGASA, f. 33 987, op. 3, d. 1048, l. 251–258.
54   Arkhiv Genshtaba, op. 165, stack 17, shelf 9, d. 60, 63, 78.
55   TsGASA, f. 33 987, op. 3, d. 1045, l. 176.

Ch. 26: Trotsky's Ghost

56   Stalin, *Sochineniya*, vol. 13, p. 111.
57   Trotsky, L. D. *Sochineniya*, vol 15, 'Khozyastvennoe stroitel'stvo Sovetskoy respubliki.' Moscow–Leningrad, 1927, pp. 41–51.
58   Stalin, *Sochineniya*, vol. 6, p. 331.
59   TsPA IML, f. 17, op. 2, d. 612.
60   Lunacharsky, A. V. *Revolutionary Silhouettes*, London, 1967, p. 66.
61   Deutscher, I. *The Prophet Outcast: Trotsky 1929–1940*. London, 1963, p. 26.
62   Trotsky, L. D. *Sochineniya*, op. cit. vol. 8, 'Politicheskie siluety'.
63   Ibid, vol. 17, 'Sovetskaya respublika i kapitalisticheskii mir'. Part 1, p. 144.
64   Ibid. vol. 21, 'Kul'tura perekhodnogo perioda'. pp. 93–94.
65   TsPA IML, f. 17, op. 2, d. 612, d. 577, l. 633.
66   Trotzki, L. *Stalins Verbrechen*. Zürich, 1937, pp. 366–367.
67   Trotsky, L. *History of the Russian Revolution*, London, 1934, p. 344.

Ch. 27: A Popular Victor

68   *Narodnoe khozyastvo SSSR za 70 let. Yubileinyi staisticheskii ezhegodnik.* Moscow, 1987, p. 32.
69   Ibid. p. 37.
70   Ibid. p. 39.
71   *Pravda*, 6 March 1937.
72   Stakhanov, A. *Rasskaz o moei zhizni*. Moscow, 1938, p. 50.
73   TsPA IML, f. 17, op. 2, d. 612.
74   Feuchtwanger, op. cit. p. 60.
75   TsGASA, f. 918/33 987, op. 3, d. 301, l. 26–27.
76   TsPA IML, f. 558, op. 1, d. 2915.
77   *K shestidesyatiletiyu so dnya rozhdeniya I.V. Stalina*, Moscow, 1939, p. 177.
78   TsPA IML, f. 538, op. 3, d. 86, l. 16.
79   *Izvestiya TsK KPSS*, No. 3, 1988, p. 138.

6: THE EPICENTRE OF THE TRAGEDY

Ch. 28: Enemies of the People

1   *Pravda*, 13 January 1936.
2   *O Konstitutsii SSSR*, pp. 16–17.
3   Orlov, A. *Protsessy*. New York, 1973, p. 135.
4   *Izvestiya TsK KPSS*, No. 7, 1989, p. 70.
5   Ibid. No. 8, p. 89.
6   Stalin, *Sochineniya*, vol. 13, p. 212.
7   *Kanal imeni Stalina* (Belomoro-Baltiiskii kanal imeni Stalina. Istoriya stroitel'stva pod red. M. Gor'kogo, L. Averbakha, S. Firina). Moscow, 1934, p. 12.
8   TsPA IML, f. 17, op. 2, d. 612, l. 1–3.
9   Ibid. l. 6.
10 TsGASA, f. 33 987, op. 3, d. 1075, l. 37–42.
11 TsPA IML, f. 17, op. 2, d. 612, l. 8–16.
12 Ibid. l. 57.
13 Ibid.
14 Ibid. l. 8.
15 Ibid. l. 9–11.
16 Ibid. vyp. III.
17 TsPA IML, f. 17, op. 2, d. 577, l. 5–15.
18 Ibid. l. 5–20.
19 Ibid. l. 10–25.
20 TsPA IML, f. 77, op. 1, d. 439, l. 118.
21 TsPA IML, f. 77, op. 1, d. 644, l. 42–89.

Ch. 29: Political Farce

22 *Protsess anti-sovetskogo trotskistskogo tsentra*. Moscow, 1937, pp. 42–45.
23 Trotsky, L. *The Revolution Betrayed*. New York, 1937, p. 216.
24 *Arkhiv voennoy kollegii Verkhovnogo suda SSSR*, f. 75, op. 35, d. 319, l. 10–35.
25 Ibid. f. 74, op. 35, d. 315, l. 61.
26 *Pravda*, 12 March 1938.
27 *Pravda*, 5 March 1938.
28 TsGASA, f. 33 987, op. 3, d. 891, l. 25–31; see A. L. 'Bukharina', *Nezabyvaemoe*. Moscow, 1989, p. 319.
29 *Pravda*, 13 March 1938.
30 Feuchtwanger, op. cit, p. 98.
31 *Pravda*, 13 March 1938.
32 'Clarification' for NKVD, TsPA IML, f. 17, op. 2, d. 612, l. 7.
33 *Pravda*, 13 March 1938.
34 *Pravda*, 8 March 1938.
35 *Pravda*, 27 January 1937.

Ch. 30: The Cadres on Trial

36 TsPA IML, f. 558, op. 1, d. 3175, l. 2–10.
37 TsGASA, f. 31 983, op. 3, d. 152, l. 150.
38 TsPA IML, f. 17, op. 2, d. 627.
39 TsGAOR, f. 9401, op. 2, d. 199, l. 197.
40 Ibid. l. 366.
41 TsGAOR, f. 9401, op. 2, d. 269, t. 1, l. 57–65.
42 *XXII s'ezd KPSS. Stenograficheskii otchet,* vol. 3, p. 199.
43 TsPA IML, f. 17, op. 2, d. 624.
44 TsPA IML, f. 17, op. 2, d. 630.
45 Arkhiv voennoy kollegii Verkhovnogo suda SSSR, f. 74, op. 35, d. 315, l. 51.
45a Ibid. l. 50.
46 TsPA IML, f. 17, op. 2, d. 639, l. 24–29.
47 Ibid. l. 24–32.
48 TsPA IML, f. 17, op. 2, d. 640, l. 20–45.
49 TsPA IML, f. 17, op. 2, d. 639, l. 20–35.
50 Ibid.
51 TsPA IML, f. 17, op. 2, d. 633, l. 2–26.
52 TsGAOR, f. 9401, op. 1, d. 2181.
53 TsPA IML, f. 17, op. 2, d. 577.

Ch. 31: The Tukhachevsky 'Plot'

54 TsGASA, f. 33 987, op. 3, d. 1036, l. 270–274.
55 TsPA IML, f. 17, op. 2, d. 615.
56 Cited in Ivanov, V. *Marshal Tukhachevskii.* Moscow, 1985, p. 128.
57 TsGASA, f. 614, op. 2, d. 18, l. 7.
58 TsGASA, f. 33 987, op. 3, d. 400, l. 137–139.
59 Viktorov manuscript in author's possession.
60 *Bol'shevik,* No. 12, 1937.
61 TsAMO, f. 5, op. 176 703, d. 21, l. 64, 68.
62 TsGASA, f. 33 987, op. 3, d. 1075, l. 19–26.
63 TsGASA, f. 33 987, op. 3, d. 1046, l. 207–208.
64 TsGASA, f. 33 987, op. 3, d. 1048, l. 37.
65 TsPA IML, f. 17, op. 2, d. 640.
66 TsGASA, f. 33 987, op. 3, d. 1140, l. 18–22.
67 TsGASA, f. 25 880, op. 4, d. 1, l. 2–3.
68 TsGASA, f. 33 987, op. 3, d. 993, l. 164, 179, 180, 217.
69 TsGASA, f. 33 987, op. 3, d. 1048, l. 23–25.

Ch. 32: The Stalinist Monster

70 TsPA IML, f. 17, op. 2, d. 612 (vyp. 3).
71 TsGAOR, f. 9401, op. 1, d. 2180, l. 247.

Ch. 33: Guilt Without Forgiveness

72 TsPA IML, f. 17, op. 2, d. 577, l. 57.
73 Arkhiv voennoy kollegii Verkhovkogo suda SSSR, f. 74, op. 35, d. 315, l. 46.
74 TsGASA, f. 33 987, op. 3, d. 1075, l. 57–63.
75 *Izvestiya TsK KPSS*, No. 3, 1988, pp. 141–142.
76 Ibid. pp. 141–142.
77 TsAMO, f. 32, op. 701 323, d. 38, l. 14–16.
78 Ibid.

7: ON THE THRESHOLD OF WAR

Ch. 34: Political Manoeuvring

1 *XVIII s'ezd Vsesoyuznoy Kommunisticheskoy partii (bol'shevikov). Stenografichaeskii otchet.* Moscow, 1939, p. 18.
2 Ibid. p. 26.
3 Ibid. p. 2.
4 *Dokumenty i materialy kanuna vtoroy mirovoy voiny,* 1937–39. 2 vols. Moscow, 1981, vol. 2, p. 47.
5 TsPA IML, f. 17, op. 2, d. 109, l. 32–33.
6 TsGASA, f. 33 987, op. 3, d. 1235, l. 9.
7 AVP SSSR, f. 06, op. 1, p. 19, d. 206, l. 551.
8 AVP SSSR, f. 06, op. 1, p. 1, d. 5, l. 554.
9 AVP SSSR, f. 082, op. 22, p. 93, d. 7, l. 798.
10 *SSSR v bor'be protiv fashistskoy agressii,* 1933–1945, Moscow, 1976, p. 66.
11 TsAMO SSSR, f. 5, op. 176 703, d. 7, l. 431.
12 *SSSR v bor'be...* p. 74.
13 TsGASA, f. 33 987, op. 3, d. 1235, l. 57–59, 86.
14 AVP SSSR, f. 06, op. 16, p. 27, d. 1, l. 766.
15 AVP SSSR, f. 06, op. 1a, p. 26, d. 1, l. 1176–1177.
16 TsGASA, f. 33 987, op. 3, d. 1235, l. 66–72.
17 *Dokumenty i materialy...* vol. 2, pp. 10, 11.
18 *SSSR v bor'be...* pp. 78–79.
19 AVP SSSR, f. 06, op. 1b, p. 27, d. 5, l. 22–32.
20 TsGASA, f. 33 987, op. 3, d. 1235, l. 73.
21 *XVII s'ezd VKP(b). Stenografichsekii otchet.* Moscow, 1934, p. 11.
22 Geiden, K. (Heyden, C.) *Istoriya germanskogo fashizma.* Moscow–Leningrad, 1935, p. 60.
23 *XVII s'ezd.* 1934, p. 12.
24 AVP SSSR, f. 011, op. 4, p. 27, d. 61, l. 1218.
25 AVP SSSR, f. 011, op. 4, p. 27, d. 59, l. 178–180.
26 AVP SSSR, f. 0745, op. 15, p. 38, d. 8, l. 126–128.
27 AVP SSSR, f. 0745, op. 19, p. 45, d. 4, l. 122–125.
28 AVP SSSR, f. 0745, op. 19, p. 45, d. 9, l. 129–132.

29   *Akten zur deutschen auswärtigen Politik 1918–1945.* Baden-Baden, 1956, vol. 7, p. 131.

Ch. 35: A Dramatic Turn of Events

30   AVP SSSR, f. 0745, op. 15, p. 38, d. 8, l. 149.
31   Zhilin, P. A. *O voine i voennoy istorii.* Moscow, 1984, p. 145.
32   *Pravda,* 27 August 1939.
33   *Documents diplomatiques français, 1932–39.* 2e serie, vol. 18, p. 243.
34   AVP SSSR, f. 059, op. 1, p. 300, d. 2077, l. 233–234.
35   TsGASA, f. 33 987, op. 3, d. 1237, l. 379, 381.
36   *Dokumenty i materialy... 1937–1939,* vol. 2, pp. 85–86.
37   *Pravda,* 18 September 1939.
37a TsAMO, f. 5, op. 362 360, d. 175 704, l. 90.
38   TsAMO, f. 5, op. 391, d. 175 704, l. 96.
39   TsGASA, f. 33 987, op. 3, d. 1237, l. 436–437.
40   TsGAOR, f. 9401, op. 2, d. 105, t. III, l. 19–22.
41   TsGAOR, f. 9401, op. 2, d. 105, t. III, l. 205.
42   TsGAOR, f. 5325, op. 1, d. 244, l. 2.
43   TsGAOR, f. 5325, op. 1, d. 244, l. 9.
44   TsGASA, f. 33 988, op. 3, d. 373, l. 130.
45   TsGASA, f. 33 988, op. 3, d. 373, l. 113.
46   TsGASA, f. 33 987, op. 3, d. 1236, l. 376–380.
47   TsGASA, f. 33 987, op. 3, d. 1366, l. 60–62.
48   TsGASA, f. 33 987, op. 3, d. 1366, l. 27–29.
49   TsGASA, f. 33 987, op. 3, d. 1235, l.99.
50   *Izvestiya,* 3 December 1939.
51   *Izvestiya,* 16 December 1939.
52   TsAMO, f. 8, op. 1, d. 23, l. 34.
53   TsAMO, f. 15, op. 11 600, d. 160, l. 96.
54   TsAMO, f. 132, op. 264 211, d. 73, l. 67–110.
55   Ibid.

Ch. 36: Stalin and the Army

56   *Voenno-istoricheskii zhurnal,* 1987, No. 9, p. 50.
57   TsAMO, f. 37 837, op. 10, d. 142, l. 93.
58   *Voennye kadry Sovetskogo gosudarstva, 1941–1945.* Moscow, 1963, p. 12.
59   TsGASA, f. 33 987, op. 3, d. 993, l. 3, l.
60   TsAMO, f. 5, op. 176 703, d. 21, l. 16.
61   Arkhiv Verkhovnogo suda SSSR. f. 75, op. 35, d. 319.
62   TsGASA, f. 33 987, op. 3, d. 1305, l. 175, 192.
63   TsAMO, f. 32, op. 11 309, d. 4, l. 153.
64   TsGASA, f. 4, op. 18, d. 77, l. 56.
65   TsGASA, f. 4, op. 18, d. 76, l. 20.
66   TsGASA, f. 4, op. 18, d. 79, l. 9–10.

67 TsGASA, f. 365, op. 1, d. 18, l. 6.
68 TsAMO, f. 32, op. 11 309, d. 3, l. 85–91.
69 *Voenno-istoricheskii zhurnal*, No. 9, 1987, p. 49.

Ch. 37: The Defence Arsenal

70 TsGASA, f. 33 987, op. 3, d. 1302, l. 3.
71 Zhilin, P. A. *O voine i voennoy istorii*, Moscow, 1984, p. 185.
72 Ustinov, D. F. *Vo imya pobedy*. Moscow, 1988, p. 223.
73 Nekrich, A. M. *22 Iyunya 1941*. Moscow, 1965, p. 73.
74 TsAMO, f. 15a, op. 2154, d. 4, l. 224–233.
75 TsAMO, f. 75 284, op. 1, d. 119, l. 18.
76 Voznesensky, N. A. *Voennaya ekonomika SSSR v period Otechestvennoy voiny*. Moscow, 1948, p. 78.
77 TsAMO, f. 15a, op. 2154, d. 4, l. 224–233.
78 TsPA IML, f. 17, op. 2, d. 653.
79 *Pravda*, 22 February 1941.

Ch. 38: The Murder of the Exile

80 Trotsky, *Dnevniki i pis'ma*. pp. 160–162.
81 Siqueiros, D. A. *Menya nazyvali likhim polkovnikom*. Moscow, 1986, p. 220.
82 Trotsky, op. cit. pp. 164–166.

Ch. 39: Secret Diplomacy

83 *The Public Papers of Franklin D. Roosevelt*, 1939, pp. 201–205.
84 *Vneshnyaya politika SSSR. Sbornik dokumentov*, vol 4. Moscow, 1946, p. 417.
85 *Istoriya vneshnei politiki SSSR 1917–1945*. Moscow, 1980, vol 1, pp. 371–372.
86 *Voenno-istoricheskii zhurnal*, No. 9, 1987, p. 49.
87 TsGASA, f. 3987, op. 3, d. 1175, l. 33–34.
88 TsGASA, f. 32 871, op. 1, d. 72, l. 216.
89 AVP SSSR, f. 06, op. 1a, p. 26, d. 1, l. 1179.
90 Leonhardt, W. *Der Schock des Hitler-Stalin Paktes*. Freiburg, 1986, pp. 66–68, 79–84.
91 AVP SSSR, f. 011, op. 4, p. 25, d. 11, l. 1462–1463.
92 TsAMO, f. 500, op. 12 458a, d. 34, l. 17.
93 TsAMO, f. 500, op. 12 462, d. 7, l. 1–6.
94 *Voenno-istoricheskii zhurnal*, No. 9, 1987, p. 54.
95 Churchill, W. *History of the Second World War*, vol. 3, p. 493.
96 Sandalov, L. M. *Perezhitoe*. Moscow, 1961, p. 75.

Ch. 40: Fatal Omissions

97 TsAMO, f. 32, op. 11 302, d. 6, l. 522–523.
98 TsAMO, f. 32, op. 11 302, d. 6, l. 526–561.
99 *Izvestiya*, 28 September 1939.
100 *Pravda*, 1 November 1939.
101 *Pravda*, 2 September 1939.
102 TsGASA, f. 25 871, op. 2, d. 285, l. 8–9.
103 A conversation with A. A. Yepishev recorded in Vlasik's unpublished memoirs and seen by the author.
104 TsGASA, f. 9, op. 39, d. 72, l. 44, 133, 536.
105 TsAMO, f. 16a, op. 2951, d. 239, l. 10–14.
106 As recorded by Shtemenko and Vasilievsky in TsAMO.
107 TsAMO, f. 16a, op. 2951, d. 239, l. 84–90.
108 TsAMO, f. 16a, op. 2951, d. 239, l. 245–279.
109 TsAMO, f. 16, op. 2951, d. 239.
110 TsAMO, f. 16a, op. 2951, d. 242, l. 238.
111 Zhukov, G. K. *Vospominaniya i razmyshleniya*. Moscow, 1969, p. 233.
112 TsAMO, f. 32, op. 11 306, d. 5, l. 140–146.
113 TsGASA, f. 33 988, op. 4, d. 36, l. 56.
114 TsAMO, f. 32, op. 11 309, d. 3, l. 85–90.
115 TsAMO, f. 127, op. 12 195, d. 16, l. 199–204.
116 TsAMO, f. 127, op. 12 915, d. 16, l. 308–314.
117 TsAMO, f. 208, op. 2513, d. 70a, l. 424–427.
118 TsAMO, f. 15, op. 725 588, d. 36, l. 214–242.
119 TsAMO, f. 208, op. 2513, d. 71, l. 34.
120 Zhukov, op. cit. p. 233.

8: A CATASTROPHIC BEGINNING

Ch. 41: A Paralysing Shock

1 TsAMO, f. 32, op. 11 309, d. 101, l. 23, 35, 37.
2 TsAMO, f. 16, op. 2951, d. 239.
3 TsAMO, f. 16, op. 2951, d. 243, l. 123–130.
4 In *Politicheskoe Obrazovanie*, No. 9 , 1988, pp. 69–75.
5 TsAMO, f. 132a, op. 2642, d. 41, l. 1–2.
6 TsAMO, f. 15, op. 881 474, d. 12, l. 246–253.
7 TsAMO, f. 48a, op. 1554, d. 90, l. 260–262.
8 TsAMO, f. 32, op. 1071, d. 1, l. 6–8.
9 TsAMO, f. 208, op. 2513, d. 71, l. 203–204.
10 TsAMO, f. 15, op. 725 588, d. 36, l. 239.
11 Kumanev, V. 'Iz vospominanii o voennykh godakh', *Politicheskoe Obrazovanie*, No. 9, 1988, p. 75 omits the obscenity which is on the original tape as heard by the author.
12 TsAMO, f. 132a, op. 2642, d. 28, l. 1.

13 Memoirs of General D. I. Ryabishev, TsAMO, f. 15, op. 881 474, d. 12, l. 175–190.
14 TsAMO, f. 48-A, op. 1554, d. 9, l. 47.
15 TsAMO, f. 48-A, op. 1554, d. 9, l. 25.
16 *Politicheskoe obrazovanie*, 1988, No. 9, p. 75.
17 TsAMO, f. 32, op. 701 323, d. 38, l. 53.
18 *Pravda*, 3 July 1941.

Ch. 42: A Cruel Time

19 TsAMO, f. 3, op. 11 556, d. 1, l. 1744.
20 TsAMO, f. 8, op. 11 627, d. 954, l. 65.
21 TsAMO, f. 8, op. 1855, d. 7, l. 27.
22 TsAMO, f. 32, op. 11 309, d. 70, 65–71.
23 TsAMO, f. 3, op. 11 556, d. 2, l. 252.
24 TsAMO, f. 48A, op. 1554, d. 91, l. 40–42.
25 TsAMO, f. 32, op. 11 309, d. 70, l. 65–71.
26 TsAMO, f. 33, op. 725 588, d. 36, l. 10.
27 TsAMO, f. 33, op. 725 588, d. 36, l. 308–310.
28 TsAMO, f. 208, op. 2513, d. 71, l. 131, 221.
29 TsAMO, f. 33, op. 11 454, d. 179, l. 144–145.
30 TsGAOR, f. 9401, op. 2, d. 68, t. V, l. 231–232.
31 TsAMO, f. 33, op. 11 454, d. 179, l. 320–321.
32 TsAMO, f. 3, op. 11 556, d. 9, l. 324.

Ch. 43: Disasters and Hopes

33 TsAMO, f. 96-A, op. 2011, d. 5, l. 21–24.
34 TsAMO, f. 132-A, op. 2642, d. 30, l. 12–13.
35 TsAMO, f. 3, op. 11 556, d. 1, l. 315.
36 TsAMO, f. 298, op. 2526, d. 5a, l, 443–448.
37 TsAMO, f. 32, op. 11 306, d. 36, l. 82–84.
38 TsAMO, f. 96-A, op. 2011, d. 5, l. 28–30.
39 TsAMO, f. 96-A, op. 2011, d. 5, l. 96–99.
40 TsAMO, f. 48-A, op. 1554, d. 9, l. 470.
41 TsAMO, f. 229, op. 161, d. 103, l. 93.
42 TsAMO, f. 8, op. 11 627, d. 954, l. 61.
43 TsAMO, f. 7, op. 11 250, d. 29, l. 37–38.
44 TsAMO, f. 48-A, op. 1133, d. 7, l. 139–140.
45 TsAMO, f. 48-A, op. 1554, d. 9, l. 431.
46 TsAMO, f. 219, op. 679, d. 3, l. 17–21.
47 *Voenno-istoricheskii zhurnal*, No. 9, 1987, p. 50.
48 Zhukov, G. K. *Vospominaniya i razmyshleniya*. Moscow, 1983, vol. 2, p. 257.
49 TsAMO, f. 3, op. 11 556, d. 8, l. 212–214.
50 TsAMO, f. 48-A, op. 1910, d. 11, l. 16–19.
51 TsAMO, f. 96-A, op. 2011, d. 5, l. 141–143.

52 TsAMO, f. 32, op. 11 306, d. 24, l. 7.
53 Stalin, I. V. *O Velikoy Otechestvennoy voine Sovetskogo Soyuza*. Moscow, 1950, p. 35.

Ch. 44: Captivity and General Vlasov

54 *Encyclopaedia Britannica*. London, 1973, vol. 18, p. 563.
55 TsAMO, f. 8, op. 11 627, d. 954, l. 62.
56 TsAMO, f. 32, op. 11 309, d. 70, l. 155.
57 TsAMO, f. 3, op. 11 556, d. 9, l. 16.
58 TsAMO, f. 32, op. 11 306, d. 24, l. 8.
59 Gerns, Ditte, *Hitlers Wehrmacht in der Sovjetunion*. Frankfurt am Main, 1985, p. 41.
60 TsPA IML, f. 77, op. 3, d. 135, l. 1–2.
61 TsAMO, f. 33, op. 11 454, d. 179, l. 1–2.
62 TsAMO, f. 38, op. 11 389, d. 2, l. 164–166.
63 TsAMO, f. 132-A, op. 2642, d. 42, l. 18–22.
64 TsAMO, f. 48-A, op. 1640, d. 26, l. 296.
65 TsAMO, f. 32-A, op. 11 309, d. 163, l. 15–45.
66 TsAMO, f. 3, op. 11 556, d. 7, l. 201.
67 TsAMO, f. 32, op. 11 306, d. 195, l. 249–253.
68 TsGAOR, f. 9401, op. 2, d. 142, t. III, l. 102–103.
69 TsGAOR, f. 9401, op. 2, d. 68, t. V, l. 102.
70 TsGAOR, f. 9401, op. 1, d. 2010, l. 67–69.
71 TsGAOR, f. 109, op. 1, d. 2010, l. 67–69.
72 In *Politicheskoe obrazovanie*, 1989, No. 4, pp. 58–63.
73 TsGAOR, f. 9401, op. 2, d. 64, t. 1, l. 1.
74 TsGAOR, f. 9401, op. 2, d. 64, t. 1, l. 158
75 TsPA IML, f. 58, op. 2, d. 966, l. 5.
76 Hoffmann, J. *Die Geschichte der Wlassow Armee*. Rombach, 1986, p. 3.
77 TsGAOR, f. 9401, op. 2, d. 64, t. 1, l. 9–12.

9: THE SUPREME COMMANDER

Ch. 45: Headquarters

1 TsAMO, f. 132-A, op. 2642, d. 30, l. 24.
2 Zhukov, G. K. *Vospominaniya i razmyshleniya*. Moscow, 1983, vol. 2, p. 97.
3 TsAMO, f. 3, op. 11 556, d. 13, l. 247–248.
4 TsAMO, f. 132, op. 2642, d. 233, l. 285–286.
5 TsAMO, f. 3, op. 11 556, d. 14, l. 18.
6 TsAMO, f. 3, op. 11 556, d. 6, l. 47.
7 TsAMO, f. 3, op. 11 556, d. 14, l. 62.
8 TsAMO, f. 132-A, op. 2642, d. 41, l. 75–81.
9 TsAMO, f. 3, op. 11 556, d. 5, l. 51.
10 TsAMO, f. 3, op. 11 556, d. 6, l. 20.

Ch. 46: Dawn Over Stalingrad

11   TsAMO, f. 3, op. 11 556, d. 9, l. 316.
12   TsAMO, f. 3, op. 11 556, d. 9, l. 128–129.
13   Ibid.
14   TsAMO, f. 3, op. 11 556, d. 2, l. 175.
15   TsAMO, f. 3, op. 11 556, d. 9, l. 128–129.
16   TsAMO, f. 3, op. 11 556, d. 13, l. 7, 8.
17   TsAMO, f. 3, op. 11 556, d. 10, l. 9.
18   TsAMO, f. 3, op. 11 556, d. 10, l. 336.
19   TsAMO, f. 3, op. 11 556, d. 10, l. 339.
20   TsAMO, f. 32, op. 11 309, d. 159, l. 87.

Ch. 47: The Commander and his Generals

21   Stalin, op. cit. p. 71–72.
22   Zhukov, op. cit, vol. 2, p. 99.
23   *Marshal Zhukov. Kakim my ego pomnim.* Moscow, 1988, p. 81.
24   TsAMO, f. 249, op. 1544, d. 112, l. 144.
25   TsAMO, f. 48, op. 7, d. 2.
26   TsAMO, f. 132, op. 264, d. 230, l. 15.
27   *Marshal Zhukov. Kakim my ego pomnim,* p. 245.
28   TsAMO, f. 8, op. 11 627, d. 988, l. 81.
29   TsAMO, f. 3, op. 11 556, d. 18, l. 103.
30   TsAMO, f. 48-A, op. 3412, d. 63, l. 46–47.
31   TsAMO, f. 132-A, op. 2642, d. 39, l. 115.
32   Vasilievsky, A. M. *Delo vsei zhizni.* Moscow, 1983, p. 470.
33   Gaglov, I.I. *General Antonov.* Moscow, 1978, p. 87.

Ch. 48: The Thoughts of a Strategist

34   TsAMO, f. 32, op. 11 302, d. 62, l. 546.
35   TsAMO, f. 3, op. 11 556, d. 10, l. 27.
36   TsGAOR, f. 9401, op. 2, d. 265, t. II, l. 340–347.
37   TsAMO, f. 132-A, op. 2642, d. 41, l. 271–272.
38   TsAMO, f. 3, op. 11 556, d. 14, l. 82–84.
39   The account of this meeting is to be found in the current archives of the army's Political Section, where the author worked and where he made detailed notes of the occasion.
40   TsAMO, f. 3, op. 11 556, d. 10, l. 324.
41   TsAMO, f. 132-A, op. 2642, d. 32, l. 145–147.
42   TsAMO, f. 3, op. 11 556, d. 5, l. 6.
43   TsAMO, f. 3, op. 11 556, d. 9, l. 313.
44   TsAMO, f. 15, op. 178 612, d. 86, l. 132, 140.
45   TsAMO, f. 15, op. 178, 612, d. 86, l. 345–347.
46   TsAMO, f. 15, op. 178 612, d. 86, l. 198.
47   TsAMO, f. 3, op. 11 556, d. 9, l. 165–166.

48 *Tegeranskaya konferentsiya rukovoditelei trekh soyuznykh derzhav. Sb. dokumentov.* Moscow, 1978, vol. 2, pp. 52, 53.
49 Ibid. p. 54.

Ch. 49: Stalin and the Allies

50 TsAMO, f. 1178, op. 1, d. 38, l. 93.
51 TsAMO, f. 236, op. 2675, d. 170, d. 108–311.
52 *Vneshnyaya politika SSSR. Sbornik documentov.* Moscow, 1947, vol. 5, p. 40.
53 Ibid. p. 54.
54 *Perepiska Predsedatelya Soveta Ministrov SSSR s Prezidentami SShA and Premier-Ministrami Velikobritanii (1941–1945 gg.).* Moscow, 1976, vol. 1, p. 19.
55 Ibid. p. 29.
56 *The Diaries of Sir Alexander Cadogan, 1938–1945.* New York, 1971, p. 471.
57 *Perepiska Predsedatelya Soveta Ministrov SSSR.* p. 74.
58 Stalin, *O Velikoy Otechestvennoy voine.* Moscow, 1950, p. 132.
59 *Pravda,* 30 May 1943.
60 *Tegeranskaya konferentsiya rukovoditelei trekh soyuznukh derzhav. Sbornik dokumentov.* vol. 2, p. 167.
61 *Tegeran. Yalta. Potsdam. Sbornik documentov.* Moscow, 1970, p. 22.
62 TsAMO, f. 32, op. 11 309, d. 101, l. 338–341.
63 TsGAOR, f. 9401, op. 2, d. 172, t. II, l. 247–248.
64 Harriman, W. Averell and Elie Abel, *Special Envoy to Churchill and Stalin, 1941–1946,* New York, 1976, p. 536.
65 Lundin, C. L. *Finland in the Second World War.* Bloomington, 1957, p. 216.
66 TsAMO, f. 3, op. 11 556, d. 18, l. 74.
67 TsAMO, f. 3, op. 11 556, d. 16, l. 183.
68 TsAMO, f. 3, op. 11 556, d. 18, l. 93.
69 TsAMO, f. 3, op. 11 556, d. 18, l. 142–144.
70 TsAMO, f. 3, op. 11 556, d. 18, l. 110.
71 TsAMO, f. 48-A, op. 3412, d. 63, l. 187–188.
72 *Krymskaya konferentsiya rukovoditelei trekh soyuznykh derzhav. Sbornik dokumentov.* Moscow, 1979, p. 273.
73 TsAMO, f. 3, op. 11 556, d. 18, l. 177–190.

10: THE CLIMAX OF THE CULT

Ch. 50: Victory at a Price

1 *Vneshnyaya politika SSSR.* Moscow, 1947, vol. 5, p. 598.
2 Ibid. p. 597.
3 Ibid. pp. 602–603.
4 Gromyko, Andrei, *Memories.* Edited and translated by Harold Shukman, London, 1989, p. 108.
5 TsGAOR, f. 9401, op. 2, d. 97, t. VI, l. 124–130.
6 Hayter, W. *Meeting at Potsdam.* London, 1975, p. 136.
7 TsGAA, f. 33987, op. 3, d. 1241, l. 61.

8 TsGAOR, f. 9401, op. 2, d. 96, t. V, l. 4.
9 TsGAOR, f. 9401, op. 2, d. 95, t. IV, l. 323.
10 TsGAOR, f. 9401, op. 2, d. 135, t. II, l. 277.
11 W. Averell Harriman and Elie Abel, op. cit. p. 92.
12 *Berlinskaya (Potsdamskaya) konferentsiya rukovoditelei trekh soyuznykh derzhav – SSSR, SShA i Velikobritanii (17 iyulii-2 avgusta 1945 g.) Sbornik dokumentov.* Moscow, 1980, pp. 42–43.
13 TsAMO, f. 66, op. 178499, d. 9, l. 34–37.
14 TsAMO, f. 66, op. 178499, d. 9, l. 61.
15 *Berlinskaya konferentsiya*, pp. 299–300.
16 *KPSS v rezolyutsiyakh i resheniyakh...* 9th edition, vol. 8, pp. 7–16.
17 TsAMO, f. 132, op. 2642, d. 15, l. 1–9.
18 TsGAOR, f. 9401, op. 2, d. 96, t. V, l. 147.
19 TsGAOR, f. 9401, op. 2, d. 103, t. III, l. 149–60.
20 Voznesensky, N. A. *Izbrannye proizvedeniya*, Moscow, 1979, p. 584.
21 TsAMO, f. 132, op. 104, d. 16, l. 22.
22 TsAMO, f. 132, op. 2, d. 54, l. 97.
23 TsGAOR, f. 9401, op. 2, d. 134, t. I, l. 1–7.
24 TsGAOR, f. 9401, op. 2, d. 2223, l. 235–238.
25 TsGAOR, f. 9401, op. 2, d. 97, l. 139–142.

Ch. 51: A Shroud of Secrets

26 TsPA IML, f. 17, op. 2, d. 612 (vyp. 3) l. 8, 10.
27 TsGAOR, f. 9401, op. 2, d. 199, l. 197.
28 Merezhkovsky, D. *Tsarstvo Antikhrista.* Munich, 1921, p. 16.
29 TsGAOR, f. 9401, op. 2, d. 64, t. 1, l. 270–277.
30 TsGAOR, f. 9401, op. 2, d. 199, l. 1.
31 TsGAOR, f. 1318, op. 3, d. 8, l. 85.
32 TsGAOR, f. 9401, op. 2, d. 134, t. I, l. 143–151.
33 TsGAOR, f. 3316, op. 2, d. 1682, l. 3–7.
34 TsGAOR, f. 3316, op. 2, d. 1613, l. 3–18.
35 TsGAOR, f. 9401, op. 2, d. 134, t. I, l. 1–2.
36 TsGAOR, f. 3316, op. 2, d. 2016, l. 1–10.
37 TsGAOR, f. 9401, op. 2, d. 93, l. 276–278.
38 TsGAOR, f. 9401, op. 2, d. 134, t. I, l. 1–2.
39 TsGAOR, f. 9401, op. 2, d. 201, l. 79–81.

Ch. 52: A Spasm of Violence

40 *Pravda*, 1 March 1949.
41 TsGAOR, f. 9401, op. 2, d. 172, t. I, l. 85–92.
42 TsPA IML, f. 71, op. 3, d. 121, l. 122–132.
43 TsGAOR, f. 7523, op. 107, d. 261, l. 12.
44 TsGAOR, f. 7523, op. 107, d. 261, l. 13–15.
45 Ibid. l. 13.

46 Ibid. l. 28.
47 TsGAOR, f. 9401, op. 2, d. 255, t. I, l. 118–119.
48 TsGAOR, f. 9401, op. 2, d. 319, 192–198.
49 TsGAOR, f. 9401, op. 2, d. 269, 199, l. 57–77, 366.
50 Ibid. l. 30.

Ch. 53: The Ageing Leader

51 *Bol'shevik*, December 1949, p. 34.
52 TsGAOR, f. 7523, op. 65, d. 739, l. 1, 9, 12.
53 TsGAOR, f. 7523, op. 63, d. 218a, l. 9.
54 TsGAOR, f. 7523, op. 65, d. 2186, l. 1–15.
55 Kautsky, K. 'Sozialdemokratie und Bolschewismus' in *Die Gesellschaft*, No. 8, 1931, vol. 1, p. 101.
56 Alliluyeva, S. *Tol'ko odin god*. New York, 1968, pp. 109–110.

Ch. 54: Icy Winds

57 Kennan, G. *Memoirs (1925–1950)*. New York, 1969, pp. 583–598.
58 TsGAOR, f. 9401, op. 2, d. 135, t. II, l. 287–296.
59 Truman, H. *Mémoires*, vol. 2 'L'appel des decisions'. Paris, 1955, p. 112.
60 TsGAOR, f. 9401, op. 2, d. 151, t. VIII, l. 99–112.
61 TsGAOR, f. 9401, op. 2, d. 176, t. II, l. 235–254.
62 TsGAOR, f. 9401, op. 2, d. 149, t. VI, l. 35.
63 TsGAOR, f. 9401, op. 2, d. 176, t. II, l. 360.
64 TsPA IML, f. 77, op. 5, d. 54, l. 14–15.
65 TsPA IML, f. 77, op. 3, d. 92, l. 47, 55.
66 *Belgradskaya operatsiya*, Moscow, 1964, p. 85.
67 Djilas, M. *Razgovory so Stalinym*. New York, 1962, pp. 169–176.
68 TsPA IML, f. 77, op. 3, d. 105, l. 1–8.
69 TsPA IML, f. 77, op. 3, d. 106, l. 5–7, 17–19.
70 *Pravda*, 3 February 1949.
71 TsGAOR, f. 9401, op. 2, d. 2223, l. 291.
72 Stalin, I. *Sochineniya*, vol. 7, p. 231.
73 Ibid, vol. 8, pp. 363, 364, 376.
74 TsPA IML, f. 325, op. 1, d. 155, l. 3a.
75 *Pravda*, 25 October 1988: see Gromyko, A. *Memories*, (Trans. H. Shukman), London, 1989, and additional material in *Memoirs*, New York, 1990, pp. 248–53.
76 Mao Tse-tung, *Izbrannye proizvedeniya*, Moscow, 1953, vol. 4, p. 580.

11: THE RELICS OF STALINISM

Ch. 55: A Historical Anomaly

1 TsGAOR, f. 9401, op. 1, d. 2180, l. 120–121.
2 TsGAOR, f. 9401, op. 1, d. 2180, l. 50–51.
3 TsGAOR, f. 9401, op. 2, d. 269, t. I, l. 169–170.
4 *Novaya Zhizn'*, November 1917.
5 *Sotsialisticheskii vestnik*, 25 April 1925.
6 Dan, F. I. *The Origins of Bolshevism*, New York, 1964, p. 400–440.
7 *Ugolovnyi kodeks (kodeksy RSFSR)*, Moscow, 1938, pp. 26–32.
8 TsPA IML, f. 88, op. 1, d. 474, l. 4.
9 TsGAOR, f. 9401, op. 2, d. 97, t. VI, l. 276.
10 TsGAOR, f. 9401, op. 2, d. 97, t. VI, l. 283–292.
11 Serge, V. *Destin d'une revolution. URSS 1917–1936.* Paris, 1937, p. 323.

Ch. 56: Mummified Dogmas

12 TsPA IML, f. 558, op. 1, d. 906, l. 44–52.
13 TsPA IML, f. 558, op. 1, d. 3212, l. 27.
14 TsPA IML, f. 77, op. 1, d. 268, l. 5–10.
15 TsPA IML, f. 77, op. 3, d. 54, l. 1–4.
16 Ibid.
17 TsGAOR, f. 9401, op. 2, d. 136, t. III, l. 205.
18 TsGAOR, f. 9401, op. 2, d. 302, t. I, l. 29–31

Ch. 57: Absolute Bureaucracy

19 Lenin, *PSS*, vol. 35, p. 113.
20 Ibid, vol. 50, p. 238.
21 TsGAOR, f. 58, op. 1, d. 9, l. 3–4.
22 TsGAOR, f. 567, op. 1, d. 89, l. 29.
23 Lenin, *PSS*, vol. 44, p. 171.
24 Ibid.
25 Ibid, p. 428.
26 Trotsky, *Sochineniya*, vol. 12, pp. 261, 267.
27 TsPA IML, f. 505, op. 1, d. 65, l. 10.
28 TsPA IML, f. 505, op. 1, d. 65, l. 21.
29 Lenin, *PSS*, vol. 50, p. 106.
40 TsPA IML, f. 325, op. 1, d. 403, l. 87a.
31 Wood, A. 'Siberia before 1917'. In Shukman, H. *The Blackwell Encyclopedia of the Russian Revolution.* Oxford, 1988, p. 258; Pipes, R. *Russia under the Old Regime*, Cambridge, MA., 1981, p. 417.
32 TsGAOR, f. 7523, op. 65, d. 230. l. 12.
33 TsGAOR, f. 9401, op. 2, d. 2223, i. 338–357.
34 TsGAOR, f. 9401, op. 2, d. 98, t. VII, l. 380.
35 TsGAOR, f. 9401, op. 1, d. 2180, l. 533–534.

36   TsGAOR, f. 9401, op. 2, d. 172, t. I, l. 325–326.

Ch. 58: Earthly Gods are Mortal

37   *Izvestiya TsK KPSS*, No.12, 1989, pp. 34–40.
38   TsGAOR, f. 9401, op. 2, d. 176, t. II, l. 235–254.
39   Rapoport, Ya. L. *Na rubezhe dvukh epokh. Delo vrachei 1953 goda.* Moscow, 1988, pp. 208–209.
40   TsGAOR, f. 7523, op. 107, d. 261, l. 28–34.

Ch. 59: Defeat by History

41   *KPSS v rezolyutsiyakh i resheniyakh s'ezdov, konferentsii i plenumov TsK (1898–1971).* 8th edn. Moscow, 1971, vol. 7, pp. 203, 205, 209, 210.

Index